Capital Markets

To Margaret, Ashley, and Sheun

Currency codes and currency quotes: ISO currency codes and bid and ask quotes for April 22, 1999

Country and its currency	ISO symbol	Bid/ask
Australian dollar	AUD	0.6469/74
Argentine peso	ARS	0.99961/63
Brazilian real	BRL	1.670/75
British pound	GBP	1.6127/37
Canadian dollar	CAD	1.4777/87
Chilean peso	CLP	477.50/80
Chinese yuan	CNY	8.2787
Dutch guilder	NLG	2.0590/99
Euro	EUR	1.0698/703
French franc	FRF	6.1287/1316
German mark	DEM	1.8274/82
Hong Kong dollar	HKD	7.7478/88
Indonesian rupiah	IDR	8600/8700
Irish punt	IEP	1.3584/90
Japanese yen	JPY	117.72/82
Mexican nuevo peso	MXN	9.480/500
New Zealand dollar	NZD	0.5443/50
Philippine peso	PHP	38.000/300
Singapore dollar	SGD	1.7010/20
South African rand	ZAR	6.0750/850
Spanish peseta	ESP	155.46/53
Swiss franc	CHF	1.4963/68
United States dollar	USD	

Source: Quotes were obtained from the Reuters web site at http://quotes.reuters.com/.

Capital Markets

A Global Perspective

Thomas H. McInish

BLACKWELL
Business

The right of Thomas H. McInish to be identified as the author of this work has been asserted in accordance with the Copyright, Designs and Patents Act 1988.

First published 2000

2 4 6 8 10 9 7 5 3 1

Blackwell Publishers Inc.
350 Main Street
Malden, Massachusetts 02148
USA

Blackwell Publishers Ltd
108 Cowley Road
Oxford OX4 1JF
UK

Library of Congress Cataloging-in-Publication Data has been applied for.

ISBN 0-631-21159-4 (hardback) ISBN 0-631-21160-8 (paperback)

British Library Cataloguing in Publication Data
A CIP catalogue record for this book is available from the British Library.

Typeset in 10 on 12pt Ehrhardt
by Best-set Typesetter Ltd., Hong Kong
Printed in Great Britain by TJ International, Padstow, Cornwall

This book is printed on acid-free paper.

Contents

Figures

Tables

Preface

This book is written for market professionals and advanced students who seek a knowledge of capital markets. Two central propositions have guided the writing. Successful finance professionals need an understanding of each of the four major types of financial products – equities, debt, foreign exchange, and derivatives. Modern portfolio theory and financial engineering are blurring the line between product types, so knowledge of just one product type is no longer adequate. Hence, the book endeavors to integrate across product types. Next, a text should take into account the fact that capital now flows more easily from country to country, that managers now commonly move from country to country as their careers progress, and that individuals from a given country may go to university in a different country, and, after graduation, work in many other countries. Hence, the book also endeavors to give a global perspective.

These twin goals of integrating across product types and providing a global perspective have practical implications. I have attempted to develop definitions that are applicable to all product types rather than having the same term mean one thing for one product type and something else for another product type. For example, the definition of an exchange needs to take into account the fact that both equities and derivatives are traded on exchanges. This effort proved to be more difficult than originally anticipated, and in several cases the best I could achieve was to say that a particular word means either this or that. Nevertheless, the exercise was very worthwhile, and readers are encouraged to engage in similar efforts of their own. In addition, the global perspective required that definitions and descriptions also be applicable around the world. For example, just describing the operations of US stock exchanges is not sufficient, because stock exchanges in many other countries are considerably different.

The global perspective also led me to focus on explaining broad principles and the variety of ways that markets operate, rather than institutional details of particular markets. These specific institutional details must be left to more specialized sources. Nevertheless, I am from the USA and have worked and invested in US markets for many years, so bias toward the use of US examples has not been completely eliminated.

Having decided to write this book, I realized that my central area of research lent itself to this project. My research and teaching focus primarily on market microstructure, the study of the way financial markets are organized and how that organization affects prices, risk, liquidity, and other variables of interest. When I began my work in this area in the early 1980s, only a few academics were working on microstructure issues. Now hundreds of academics claim microstructure as their primary area of interest. This growth has resulted from three factors. The first is the growing worldwide emphasis on capital markets and stock exchanges. Today stock exchanges have become crucial to the economic health of many countries in which these institutions did not even exist a few years ago. This is especially true in Eastern Europe and China. Adding to the importance of capital markets has been the sale of many large firms by governments. These privatizations have dramatically increased the size of capital markets in many countries. A second trend has been the increasing availability of data, especially transaction data that comprises every trade and quote on a market. This new level of detail has made it possible to explore issues such as the effects of specific stock exchange rules that could not be examined as effectively before. The third factor has been the increased availability and reduced cost of the computers that are needed to analyze huge transaction databases.

In order to enhance the global perspective of the book, I traveled extensively, visiting exchanges, universities, brokerage firms, banks, and other businesses in many countries, including Australia, Canada, China (PRC), Denmark, England, Estonia, Finland, France, Germany, Greece, Hong Kong, Indonesia, Japan, the Netherlands, New Zealand, Norway, the Philippines, Poland, Portugal, Russia, Singapore, Sweden, Switzerland, Taiwan, Thailand, Turkey, and the USA.

The book begins with an introduction to the four product types and to capital markets in general. The next chapter discusses the trading of equities and fixed-income securities after their initial sale and the markets in which derivatives are created. Then three important topics – namely, transaction costs, clearing and settlement, and regulation – are considered in successive chapters. At least one chapter is devoted to each of the four product types – equities, debt, foreign exchange, and derivatives. Issues related to debt, foreign exchange, and derivatives, such as the term structure of interest rates, purchasing power parity, and hedging, are dealt with in separate chapters.

The author's web address is http://www. people.memphis.edu/~tmcinish/. In addition to information about Tom McInish, the site provides updates for *Capital Markets: A Global Perspective*.

Acknowledgments

The author acknowledges the help of the following individuals in the preparation of this book:

Michael Aitken, Peter Alonzi, Jean van Altena, Asli Ascioglu, Joseph P. Bauman, Frank E. Baxter, Graham Beale, Billy F. Beaver, Golbert L. Beebower, Peter Bennet, J. H. A. Berger, Jim Berry, Stanley B. Block, John E. Boddie, Martin U. Bosshard, Alan D. Bosworth, John R. Brien, Hans J. K. Brouwer, Scott Brusso, Pierce Bunting, Michael E. Cahill, Yang Chaojun, Olivia Cheung, Peter Chia, Paul M. Y. Chow, Kee Ho Chung, Teng Leong Chye, Donald Clarkson, Jerome J. Cornille, C. Joyce Courtney, Vincent De Santis, Rudolf F. de Soet, Jin Dehuan, Jack Demsey, David Ding, Ulf. L. Doornbos, Thomas Enright, A. D. Erskine, O. C. Ferrell, Stephen P. Ferris, Robert A. Ferstenberg, Giulia F. Fitzpatrick, Lawrence Fok Kwong Man, Nancy Foote, Marc A. Foreman, Charles Forman, Dan W. French, Alex Frino, Warren H. Funt, Dean Furbush, Jim Gallagher, David Gaynes, William V. Wehrlein, James A. Gray, Gary Grear, Marc Gresack, W. Van Harlow III, Fredrick H. deB. Harris, William A. Herman, Richard Hinz, Takato Hiraki, Peter W. Y. Ho, Fred J. Hodges, Helen Hogarth, Loo-Lim Kin Hong, Holly T. Horrigan, Lee Yew Huat, Wang Huizhong, Nik Salina Nik Idris, Ajaz H. Jafri, Elvis Jarnecic, Ong Seng Jin, Frank J. Jones, Phil Jorgenson, David M. Kemme, Chee Kah Khuin, Martin Kinsky, Douglas O. Kitchen, Ben M. Th. Kok, Andres D. Kolinsky, Eugene Krupinski, Ronald J. Kudla, Lynn Kugele, William H. Lawson Jr., C. F. Lee, Charles M. C. Lee, Wong Sang Lee, Pranee Leksrisakul Antsong Lin, Richard R. Lindsey, Larry J. Lockwood, James Lodas, Richard Loke, Helmut Mader, Andrew H. Madoff, Kris Mahabir, Ike Mathur, Susan McArthur, Michael McCorry, Sheelagh McCracken, Gina McFadden, Tan Ji Mian, R. Scott Morris, Tennence J. Mulry, Tan Soo Nan, Philip V. Newcomb, Brian T. O'Day, Karen Oon, Donald J. Puglisi, Timothy F. Quinn, Daryl L. Rabert, Margaret R. Rappaport, David M. Reeb, S. Ghon Rhee, Giovanna Righini, Ivers W. Riley, H. W. N. Rogers, Remko J. Rood, David D. Ross, David J. Rothenberg, Chaipat Sahasakul, Erwin M. Saniga, Pina De Santis, I. H. Schuilwerve, Julia Ho Seow, Paul Shang, John C. Shaw III, Yutaka Shimomoto, Rajendra K. Srivastava, Stephen J. Staszak, Stefan Stenzel, Hans R. Stoll, Pataravasee Suvarnsorn, Peter Swan, Peggy Swanson, Gabriela Swiader, Clifford C. H. Tan, Jeffrey S. H. Tan, Masaru Tanaka,

ACKNOWLEDGMENTS

Tan Tze Teng, Dawn Thomas, Peter Thomas, John Thornton, Roland Tibell, Sie Ting Lau, Yap Yon Ting, Seha Tinic, Yiuman Tse, Eytan Udovich, R. G. C. van den Brink, Tjemme van der Meer, Jan H. Van der Weij, Bonnie G. Van Ness, Robert A. Van Ness, C. Michael Viviano, John T. Wall, Michael Waller-Bridge, Leonard E. Ward, Ronald D. Watson, Ronald Weichert, Martin Wheatley, Karith Wilkes, John J. Williams, Kok Kar Wing, Terry S. Wlater, Robert A. Wood, Andrew A. Yemma, Jun Zhang.

The author and publishers gratefully acknowledge permission to reproduce an excerpt from "How to stay in the money, internationally," *Financial Executive*, May/June 1994, © 1994 by Financial Executives Institute, 10 Madison Avenue, P.O. Box 1938, Morristown, NJ 07962-1938.

xiv

CHAPTER ONE

Financial Markets and Their Products

■ Key terms ■

Agency theory theory that deals with the problems that arise from carrying out projects through others rather than directly.

Barter the exchange of goods or services directly for other goods and services without the use of money.

Best efforts an underwriting in which the investment banker does not purchase securities from the issuer without a firm order from an investor.

Bond a security issued by firms and governments evidencing debt that requires that the issuer make one or more payments to the owner.

Book building underwriting a method of underwriting in which the underwriter collects information from investors about potential demand before setting a price.

Business risk risk due to the firm's type of business.

Capital all assets used in production.

Capital market the market for financial instruments with an initial life of one year or more.

Capital market instruments financial instruments with an initial life of one year or more.

Capital structure the mix of the various types of equity and debt that the firm uses.

Cash coins or currency.

Coins metal objects produced by the government or its authorized representative that are used as money.

Common stock a security evidencing ownership of residual claims on the earnings and assets of the firm after the firm has paid its other commitments.

Consumption the use of goods and services for fulfilling individuals' needs and not for production.

Cost of capital all payments made to obtain funds.

Counterpurchases a variation of countertrade in which the goods to be exchanged are not exactly identified in advance, and the actual exchanges are separated in time.

Countertrade   the exchange of goods for goods in international trade so that no money changes hands between the buyer and the seller.

Currency   a paper product produced by the government or its authorized representative that is used as money.

Deposits   liabilities of financial institutions that are generally accepted as a medium of exchange and are therefore classified as money.

Depreciation   the value of products that are used up in the production process.

Derivative   a contract that specifies the conditions under which each party transfers assets, at least some of which are uncertain in amount, to the other during the life of the contract.

Direct investments   expenditures on all items intended to be used in production.

Downtick   see **Minus tick**.

Equities   securities representing capital contributed to the firm for which there is no legal obligation to repay.

Financial instruments   (1) instruments evidencing a transfer of funds among individuals and organizations for the purpose of allowing those receiving the funds to make investments, (2) derivative instruments, and (3) money.

Financial investment   ownership of an economic position in a financial instrument.

Financial market   a set of institutional arrangements that facilitate the transfer of funds from financial investors to direct investors and among financial investors.

Financial risk   the risk of bankruptcy if the firm is not able to make required principle and interest payments.

Firm underwriting   an underwriting in which an investment banker commits to buy an issue and resell it to the public.

Fixed-income securities   securities promising to pay specified amounts to investors at specified dates.

Fixed price underwriting   an underwriting method in which the underwriter fixes the price early in the offering process.

Foreign exchange   nondomestic currencies.

Foreign exchange market   the market in which currencies are traded.

Forward contracts   nonstandardized contracts in which one party acquires the right to receive and the other the obligation to deliver a specified amount and type of an asset at a specified future date at a price stated in the contract; in some cases there is no delivery of assets, but, instead, one party pays the other the liquidating value of the contract.

Futures   standardized contracts in which one party acquires the right to receive and the other the obligation to deliver a specified amount and type of an asset at a specified future date at a price stated in the contract; in some cases there is no delivery of assets, but, instead, one party pays the other the liquidating value of the contract.

Going public   selling common stock to the public for the first time.

Goods   tangible products.

Gross national product   the monetary value of all the goods and services produced during the year.

Hard currency   a major currency that is freely and readily exchangeable for another currency.

Indifference curve   the graph of all the points representing combinations of the consumption of two items that have equal utility.

Initial public offering   the sale of common stock to the public for the first time; abbreviated IPO.

Investment   the use of resources to facilitate future production rather than for current consumption. Investments can be made either directly or indirectly through financial markets. See **Direct investments** and **Financial investments**.

Investment banking   the activity of helping with the initial sale of securities.

Investor   any individual or organization entering into a direct or financial investment.

Law of diminishing marginal utility   as more and more units of any item are owned or consumed, a point is reached beyond which the addition to total utility of additional units declines.

Marginal utility   the addition to total utility from the addition of one additional item of consumption.

Market microstructure   the study of the way financial markets are organized and how this organization affects prices, risk, trading costs, and other market characteristics.

Minus tick   a price lower than the last price.

Money   anything used as a medium of exchange.

Money market   the market for financial instruments with an initial life of less than one year.

Money market instrument   a debt obligation with an initial maturity date of less than one year.

National income   gross national product less depreciation.

Nonsatiation   the assumption that more wealth is preferred to less.

Offset arrangement   a variation of countertrade in which the goods to be exchanged are identified in advance, but the actual exchanges are separated in time.

Option   a contract with a stated life in which one party acquires, in return for a fee, the right to receive something if it is advantageous to do so.

Plus tick   a price higher than the last price (also called an uptick).

Preferred stock   a security evidencing ownership of a claim to earnings, and perhaps also assets superior to those of the common stockholders, but one that comes after all other obligations of the firm.

Primary market   the market in which a security is sold to the public for the first time.

Production   the use of land, labor, and goods and services to produce other goods and services.

Prospectus   part of a US registration statement that is required to be given to investors in a public offering of securities.

Real investments   another name for direct investments.

Registration statement   a document describing a proposed offering of securities filed with the US Securities and Exchange Commission (USSEC).

Reserve requirements   governmental regulations that require banks to maintain a certain proportion of their deposits at a central bank or in coins and currency.

3

Right a short-term warrant that is distributed to the holders of a firm's common stock as a dividend and entitles the owner to purchase an asset, typically the common stock of the firm distributing the right, at a price that is less than its current market price.

Road show a procedure in which the underwriter goes from city to city making presentations about the company and the offering.

Savings deferred consumption.

Secondary market trades in a security after the initial sale to the public.

Security all financial instruments issued by firms or governments to raise capital.

Selling group brokerage firms that are recruited to help market a new issue.

Services intangible products.

Short sale against the box a short sale of assets actually owned.

Short selling the process whereby an investor borrows a security and then sells it, with a subsequent repurchase and return to the lender.

Swap a contract evidenced by a single document in which two parties agree to exchange one or more periodic payments based on the value or change in value of something specified in the contract.

Syndicate co-managers the term for each firm when more than one firm acts as a manager for an offering.

Syndicate manager the firm that originates the deal for a new issue and is in direct contact with the issuer.

Transactions costs the costs of transferring funds from financial investors to direct investors and of transferring financial assets among investors.

Travelers' checks negotiable instruments issued by financial institutions that are signed by the purchaser at the time of purchase and signed again at the time they are used.

Underwriting group members of an underwriting syndicate who participate in the risks and rewards of selling a new issue.

Underwriting spread the difference between the amount paid to the issuer and the sales price.

Uptick see **Plus tick**.

Utility the ability of an item to provide an individual with satisfaction.

Warrant a security issued by a firm that gives the holder the right to acquire stock in the issuing firm or sometimes in another firm at a stated price for a specified period.

Zero-minus tick a price that is the same as the last price but lower than the last different price.

Zero-plus tick a price that is the same as the last price but higher than the last different price.

IN THIS CHAPTER, the primary goal is to introduce the four major types of financial products: equities, fixed-income securities, derivatives, and money. Specifically, we describe

- the types of financial instruments constituting each of these product types
- the way each of these product types is created

We also provide background on the environment within which investment decisions are made by

- describing the goals of individuals and firms
- describing potential conflicts between investors and firm managers
- explaining the relationship among production, consumption and savings, and savings and investment
- describing the role of capital in the economy, the sources of capital, and the cost of capital
- explaining the role of financial markets in the economy

1. INTRODUCTION

World product and financial markets are becoming integrated. **Financial markets** are the set of institutional arrangements that facilitate the transfer of funds among investors.[1] On November 17, 1998, Daimler-Benz AG and Chrysler Corporation merged to form a new company called DaimlerChrysler. The merger is the largest between two enterprises in industrial history. Two individuals who serve as co-chairmen and co-chief executive officers head the new company. They are Jürgen E. Schrempp, former chairman of Daimler-Benz, and Robert J. Eaton, former chairman and chief executive officer of Chrysler Corporation. While DaimlerChrysler is domiciled in Germany, the firm has dual operational headquarters, one in Stuttgart and the other in Auburn Hills, Michigan. Both co-chairmen have offices and staff in each location. At the time of the merger, the distribution of share ownership was: Europe, 44 percent; USA, 44 percent; and the rest of the world, 12 percent.[2] Daimler-Benz shares are traded in both the USA and Germany, as well as in a number of other countries throughout the world.

Turning to another example, Pharmacia & Upjohn Inc. is a large pharmaceutical company with more than 30,000 employees primarily in Europe and the USA. The company's best-known products are the incontinence treatment Detrol and the baldness treatment Rogaine. In 1998 the firm relocated its headquarters from London to New Jersey in the USA because most of the firm's growth is coming from the US market.

These two examples illustrate a major premise of this book: namely, that financial executives must develop a global perspective. It is now much more common for an executive to grow up in one country, go to university in several different countries, and then work in a number of countries during a career – hence the need for a global perspective. Several aspects of this book contribute to developing this global perspective:

1 *We integrate across the product types of equities, fixed-income securities, derivatives, and foreign exchange* One or more chapters deal with each of these product types. **Foreign exchange markets**, the markets in which the currency of one country is traded for the currency of another country, are particularly neglected in traditional finance courses. But whether one is a portfolio manager, a banker, or a financial officer for an operating firm, it is becoming impossible to ignore the impact of foreign exchange markets on one's business. Both real and portfolio investors are becoming global in operations.

2 *We focus on trading, especially in the first part of the book* Equities, fixed-income securities, derivatives, and foreign exchange are all traded on markets throughout the world. There are only so many ways of trading, but it is important for investors and managers to understand how these markets work and to gain an appreciation of their similarities and differences. Markets for all types of financial instruments are becoming 24-hour-a-day markets. The shares of DaimlerChrysler issued in the merger of Daimler and Chrysler are intended to be global shares traded throughout the world. Hence, it is no longer sufficient to understand how trading takes place in just one place. We are interested in all aspects of trading, including how trades are executed and paid for, the costs of trading, and how trading is regulated. These issues are the concern of a relatively new area of finance, called **market microstructure**, which deals with the way financial markets are organized and how this organization affects prices, risk, trading costs, and other market characteristics.

3 *We do not eschew institutional details, but we strive to insure that the institutional details we cover are of sufficient gravity to be of interest to an international audience rather than just an audience in one country* We do not want to be international just for the sake of being international, but because an international focus helps us to sort out the more important from the less important. While particular examples will often come from one country, hopefully, they have international relevance. While preparing this text, I have traveled extensively in Asia, Australia, and Europe and taught short courses in Asia and Europe. Nevertheless, my primary industry and teaching experience has been in the USA, so it is natural that I am more familiar with how things are done there.

This chapter's main goal is to describe the four major types of financial products used in modern economies: equities, fixed-income securities, derivatives, and money. We explore the types of financial instruments constituting each of these product types and discuss how each of them comes into existence. We also review the role of financial markets in the economy; much of this material is in the appendixes.

Financial markets enhance people's standard of living in several ways. One is to make it easier to transfer funds between savers and investors. (A discussion of production, consumption, savings and investment, and capital is provided in appendix 1-A1.) Financial markets greatly increase these fund transfers and also reduce their cost. As a result, financial markets increase the amount of capital used in the economy, thereby raising economic output. The principal way that funds are transferred is through the use of equities and fixed-income securities. Financial markets also increase production by allowing producers and investors to transfer risk among themselves, primarily through the use of derivatives. Producers who hold inventories may incur substantial losses if the prices of these inventories change. Financial markets provide a low-cost way for those facing these risks to transfer them to other parties at an advantageous cost. Innovative new derivatives are also being developed to help transfer risk associated with losses from floods, hurricanes, and other natural disasters.[3] A third way that financial markets improve living standards is by facilitating the creation and exchange of money. By reducing the cost of trade, money greatly increases the level of production that can be attained. **Barter**, the exchange of one good or service directly for another without the use of money, is undoubtedly the oldest form of trade. But barter is inefficient. Box 1.1 provides a discussion of the gains from trade and an example of a modern barter transaction.

In order to understand financial markets, we need to understand the behavior of the participants in these markets. Individuals carry out all economic activities, whether alone or in groups. In financial economics, we assume that individuals seek to maximize their satisfac-

---

BOX 1.1
Is barter dead?

In international trade, barter, which is called "countertrade," is very much alive. According to its assistant treasurer, Brian Fluck, AT&T arranged a sale of switching equipment to Sevtelecom, the local telephone company for Murmansk, Russia. Due to exchange restrictions, only one-half of the purchase price could be paid with hard currency, a currency than can be easily and freely exchanged for another, especially one of the major currencies. For the remainder, AT&T agreed to accept apatite concentrate, a rock phosphate that is an ingredient in fertilizer, for which it had no direct use. (Countertraders typically provide only goods that they are not able to sell easily themselves.) AT&T then contracted with a German trading firm, Helm A. G., to sell the apatite. After subtracting Helm's fee, some of the proceeds were paid to the apatite manufacturer, and the remainder were paid to AT&T. Fluck indicated that AT&T receives and evaluates many offers for countertrade. Variations of countertrade such as offset arrangements and counterpurchases are also considered. In an offset arrangement the goods to be exchanged are identified in advance, but the actual exchanges are separated in time. In counterpurchases the goods to be exchanged are not identified exactly in advance, and the actual exchanges are separated in time.[a]

In voluntary exchange both parties to the exchange gain utility. This can be explained in economic terminology. Marginal utility is the addition to total utility from the addition of one additional item of consumption, leisure, or the like. In economics, the law of diminishing marginal utility describes the fact that as more and more units of any item are owned or consumed, a point is reached beyond which the addition to total utility of additional units declines. Hence, there is typically a limit on how much of any single commodity an individual wants to own. Further, as the marginal utility of any item declines, there is an increasing likelihood that its marginal utility will fall below that of additional units of other items. In this case, the individual will gain in utility by swapping items with low marginal utility for items with higher marginal utility.

It should be evident from this discussion why both parties can gain from trade. It is because both are trading items which have lower marginal utility to them, but which have high marginal utility to the other party. Consider two individuals trapped on separate deserted islands within sight of each other. One has a natural spring providing an unlimited supply of water, but no fruit trees. Here the marginal utility of water is probably zero, because there is a limit to how much can be consumed, used for bathing and cooking, and the like. But the marginal utility of fruit is very high. The second islander has fruit trees whose production is many times what can be consumed, but the island has no water. In this case the marginal utility of fruit is very low, and the marginal utility of water is very high. Obviously, both islanders can benefit from exchanging water and fruit.

[a] *Financial Executive* 1994.

tion or **utility** (readers needing to review a standard utility treatment are referred to appendix 1–A2). A related goal is the maximization of wealth. We assume that more wealth is preferred to less (**nonsatiation**). In other words, more wealth provides greater utility. Hence, individuals also desire to maximize their wealth.

Individuals join together with others to form entities that participate in the production process. One common type of entity is a government, which presumably operates to promote the welfare of society as a whole. Another type of organization is a firm, which is organized by individuals to promote their own welfare. In financial economics, the goal of the firm is, by assumption, to maximize the wealth of the firm's shareholders. This does not mean that other potential goals are not recognized, but simply that all other relevant goals must contribute to the overall goal of shareholder wealth maximization.

When firms and individuals act to maximize their utility and wealth, actions that are in their own self-interest combine together to produce a result that is in the interest of the society as a whole. The famous English economist Adam Smith articulated this concept that the pursuit of individual interest leads to the best outcome for society as a whole. Smith described the mechanism that converts private interest to public welfare as the "invisible hand." Box 1.2 provides an excerpt from Smith's most famous book, typically referred to by the short title *Wealth of Nations*, published in 1776. Smith's views underlie, often implicitly, many statements by individuals who favor the market system as a method of organizing production. Box 1.3 provides my personal view about why it is important that decision-makers in a modern economy understand these fundamental principles.

BOX 1.2
A quotation from Adam Smith

Every individual who employs his capital in the support of domestic industry, necessarily endeavors so to direct that industry, that its produce may be of the greatest possible value.

The produce of industry is what it adds to the subject or materials upon which it is employed. In proportion as the value of this produce is great or small, so will likewise be the profits of the employer. But it is only for the sake of profit that any man employs a capital in the support of industry; and he will always, therefore, endeavor to employ it in the support of that industry of which the produce is likely to be of the greatest value, or to exchange for the greatest quantity either of money or of other goods.

But the annual revenue of every society is always precisely equal to the exchangeable value of the whole annual produce of its industry, or rather is precisely the same thing with that exchangeable value. As every individual, therefore, endeavors as much as he can both to employ his capital in the support of domestic industry, and so to direct that industry that its produce may be of the greatest value; every individual necessarily labors to render the annual revenue of the society as great as he can. He generally, indeed, neither intends to promote the public interest, nor knows how much he is promoting it. By preferring the support of domestic to that of foreign industry, he intends only his own security; and by directing that industry in such a manner as its produce may be of the greatest value, he intends only his own gain, and he is in this, as in many other cases, led by an *invisible hand* to promote an end which was no part of his intention. Nor is it always the worse for the society that it was not part of it. By pursuing his own interest he frequently promotes that of the society more effectually than when he really intends to promote it.

Source: Smith 1789, bk IV, ch. 2; italics added.

BOX 1.3
Personal reflections on Russia

I added the box on Adam Smith because of my experiences teaching in Russia. In general, Russian managers are technically proficient. But it will take many years to develop a modern economy. Russia lacks the entire basic infrastructure including banking and business education. Capitalism is not just a set of institutional arrangements. It is a way of thinking about the world. And most people know that changing one's way of thinking is very difficult. That is why we tend to make the same mistakes not just once and twice, but three and four times and more.

In light of the openness created by glasnost and the subsequent opening of capital markets, the Russians, especially younger Russians, are eager to meet non-Russians and learn about the way we do business. (They are also eager to learn English, so that they can understand MTV.) Learning the how is relatively easy. It is learning and believing the why of market economies that is tough. And even if the majority believes, there will still be many in positions of power who do not understand. Anyone who has tried to fundamentally change an organization knows that it is often easier to start from scratch. This applies very much to Russia.

Economic development of the world is not a win/lose proposition. Instead, development brings opportunities for everyone. St. Petersburg is a fabulous city. The art treasures of the Hermitage are beyond description, including rooms of Rubens and Rembrandt, wonderfully painted ceilings, and a huge collection of tables with beautiful stone tops, to name just a few. But how can one go there without a developed tourist industry?

A potential conflict between corporate officials and shareholders may be evident. As noted, financial economists assume that individuals maximize their own utility but that corporate officials maximize shareholder wealth. Strategies that are in the self-interest of corporate officials and of stockholders may not be the same. There is a substantial literature in financial economics called **agency theory** that deals with the problems that arise from the necessity of carrying out projects through others, rather than directly. Agency problems arise not only between principals and agents such as stockholders and managers, but also between principals such as stockholders and bondholders, potential stockholders, and current stockholders (Barnea et al. 1985; Copeland and Weston). Box 1.4 provides additional discussion of agency problems.

2. TYPES OF FINANCIAL INVESTMENTS

We have already indicated that this book deals with four product types: equities, fixed-income securities, derivatives, and foreign exchange. Each of these product types can be further divided into various types of financial instruments, as follows:

A. **Equities**
   a.   Common stock
   b.   Preferred stock
   c.   Warrants

BOX 1.4
Agency problems

If agency problems between managers and stockholders are important, as they often are, it may be wise for the firm to attempt to better align stockholders' and firm officials' interests through the use of suitable compensation packages. Such arrangements might include bonus arrangements tied to firm performance or opportunities to acquire ownership interests in the firm based on current values. If the managers are successful and increase the value of the firm, then they are able to make a profit by purchasing the shares at the contracted price and reselling them at the higher market price.

Compensation arrangements can also be used to address unethical and illegal behavior such as embezzlement. Many corporate officials are tempted by bribes, for example. And the higher the level of the official, the greater the size that these potential bribes are likely to be. Presumably, most individuals want to behave ethically and to act in the best interests of their employer. But a suitable compensation arrangement can help reduce the differences in rewards for ethical and unethical behavior and help minimize the risk that managers will succumb to temptation.

Another way of addressing agency problems is by the appropriate selection of the **capital structure** of the firm. Capital structure refers to the mix of the various types of equity and debt that the firm uses to raise funds. Capital structure varies from one firm to another. Often firms in the same industry have similar capital structures because they face similar risks. Risk due to the firm's business is called **business risk**. Sales of the firm's products can be strong or weak. Expenses can increase for many reasons, including weather and strikes. Firms also face **financial risk**, the risk of bankruptcy if the firm is not able to make required principle and interest payments. Firms that face high operating risk may try to have a capital structure with low financial risk, while firms with low operating risk may create a capital structure with more financial risk.

The particular capital structure of the firm can influence the way managers make decisions about which investments to undertake and which to avoid. Hence, firms need to have a capital structure that is appropriate given the particular agency problems that are likely to be encountered. The ways in which capital structure affects managers' decisions are addressed by the literature on corporate finance. Convertible bonds and warrants can be used to solve agency problems.[a]

Capital structure also differs across countries. In some countries, such as Germany and Japan, the major investors in a firm may own both common stock and debt. This is another possible way of solving agency problems. If stockholders and bondholders are the same, then maximizing the wealth of stockholders is equivalent to maximizing the wealth of both stockholders and bondholders and to maximizing the value of the firm.

[a] See Green 1984 for information about this topic.

B. **Fixed-income securities**
    a.   Some preferred stock
    b.   Debt obligations
        i.   Bonds
        ii. Money market instruments
C. **Derivatives**
    a.   Options
    b.   Futures
    c.   Forwards

    d. Swaps
    e. Warrants
D. Money
    a. Currency and coins
    b. Deposits

The list shows the categories within each of these product types that we will consider in this chapter. Before beginning, it may be useful to indicate what we mean by financial instruments. **Financial instruments** are (1) instruments evidencing a transfer of funds among individuals and organizations for the purpose of allowing those receiving the funds to make investments or increase consumption, (2) derivative instruments typically created for the purpose of transferring risk, and (3) money.

Some financial instruments are securities, and others are not. A **security** is a financial instrument used by a firm or government to raise capital.[4] **Capital** is any asset used in production. Calling equities "securities" is not just semantics, but indicates that they differ from other types of financial instruments, especially derivatives and foreign exchange, which we do not typically classify as securities.[5]

2.1. EQUITIES

Equities are **securities** representing capital contributed to the firm for which there is no legal obligation to repay. Once they have fully paid the purchase price of their shares, investors can lose only the amount of their investment and cannot be called upon to put up additional funds. This limited liability is a major advance in modern finance that has resulted in a significant increase in the ability of firms to raise capital. The advantage of this system from the point of view of investors can be seen in the case of the insurance firm Lloyds of London, which is organized as a series of partnerships. Major losses due to hurricanes and other insured risks resulted in calls on the partners, called "names," for millions of British pounds (GBP) in additional capital, resulting in the bankruptcy of many names. Many of the names in the USA sought court protection from the requirement to contribute additional capital.

Equities include all types of stock issued by the firm. Shares of **common stock** represent ownership interests in a firm. The owners of stock are called "stockholders" or "shareholders." Common stock represents ownership of the residual claim on the earnings and assets of the firm after the firm has paid its other commitments. The shareholders are the owners of the firm. They run the firm through an elected board of directors. Of course, the shareholders are not the only investors in the firm. Many firms borrow money, becoming debtors, and those lending the money become creditors of the firm. But the creditors make their decisions on how much to lend the firm and what rate of interest to charge with full knowledge that operating decisions are in the hands of the board of directors and the firm's officers and managers.

Another equity security is **preferred stock**, which has a claim to earnings and, typically, also assets that is superior to or ahead of that of the common stock, but that comes after all other obligations of the firm. Many issues of preferred stock have a fixed dividend payment that is specified in the firm's documents such as the corporate charter or by-laws. This specified dividend payment does not generally represent a legally enforceable claim against the firm, but firms are often required to give certain privileges to preferred stockholders if the specified dividends are not met. These privileges may include the right to receive any back dividends owed before the common stockholders can receive any dividends and the right to elect some or all of the members of the board of directors. Because many preferred stock issues have the right to receive fixed dividend payments and no more, preferred stock is often regarded as being a fixed-income security.

A **warrant** is a security issued by a firm that gives the holder the right to acquire stock in the issuing firm, or sometimes in another firm, at a stated price for a specified period. Warrants are often issued in combination with other securities such as common stock or bonds. Traditionally, warrants have been considered as equities, and the funds raised from the sale of warrants are part of the firm's capital.

A **right** is a short-term warrant that is distributed to the holders of a firm's common stock as a dividend. Each right entitles the owner to purchase an asset, typically the common stock of the firm distributing the right, at a price that is less than the current market price of the firm's common stock. The goal is to have the stockholders exercise the right so that the firm can increase its equity. Rights offerings are a popular way of raising equity in many countries, including Japan and the United Kingdom. They were also popular in the USA at one time, but their use has declined substantially in recent years.

2.2. FIXED-INCOME SECURITIES

Fixed-income securities are securities that promise to make payments of specified amounts to investors at specified dates. We have already seen that preferred stock is often a fixed-income security. But most fixed-income securities are debt instruments. A **bond** is a security which is evidence of debt issued by firms and governmental bodies, including nations and their subdivisions and international organizations such as the World Bank (the International Bank for Reconstruction and Development), that requires that the issuer make one or more payments to the owner. A **money market instrument** is a debt obligation with an initial maturity date of less than one year. **Capital market instruments** have lives of one year or more.[6] Money market instruments are traded in the **money market**, in contrast to the market for bonds, equities, and warrants, which are traded in the **capital market**.

2.3. DERIVATIVES

A **derivative** is a contract that specifies the conditions under which each party transfers assets, including cash, to the other during the life of the contract. While the derivative contract specifies how the amounts to be transferred are to be determined, at least some of the amounts are intended to be uncertain.[7] The contract may involve cash payments or the transfer of real or financial assets. The types of items that may be transferred or that may be the basis for calculating cash payments are highly varied and include (1) commodities such as precious metals (silver, gold, platinum), agricultural products (corn, soybeans, live cattle, pork bellies), and industrial commodities (gasoline, heating oil, lumber); (2) equities and equity indexes; (3) currencies; (4) debt instruments; (5) other derivatives; and (6) price indexes or other type of pricing arrangements such as the movement over time of the US Consumer Price Index, freight rates, or insurance claims. This definition encompasses the six types of derivatives examined in this text: options, futures, forwards, swaps, warrants, and rights. While warrants are considered equities, they also have the characteristics of derivatives.

An **option** is a contract with a stated life in which one party acquires, in return for a fee, the right to receive something if it is advantageous to do so. Some option contracts provide for the payment of the cash value of the difference between an asset's price and a stated price. Other options allow the purchase of a real asset such as corn at a predetermined price, the purchase of a financial asset such as common stock at a predetermined price, the sale of a real asset at a predetermined price, or the sale of a financial asset at a predetermined price.

Futures are standardized contracts in which one party acquires the right to receive and the other the obligation to deliver a specified amount and type of an asset at a specified future date at a price stated in the contract. Some futures contracts call for one party to pay the liquidating value of the contract to the other party rather than for the delivery of an asset in exchange for cash. Nonstandardized contracts similar to futures contracts, except that the terms are individually negotiated on a bilateral basis, are called **forward contracts**.

A **swap** is a contract evidenced by a single document in which two parties agree to exchange one or more periodic payments based on the value or change in value of something specified in the contract. The payments that are exchanged can be based on any number of items, including interest rates and exchange rates. Depending on the terms of the swap, one party's payments can be fixed while the other's fluctuate, or both parties' payments may fluctuate. The terms for many types of swaps have become standard so that the market price can be determined from usual information vendors.

Warrants were defined previously. A warrant is equity because the funds received from the sale of a warrant do not have a definite repayment obligation. But because the value of a warrant comes from the potential for the future exchange of assets the value of which is uncertain, a warrant is also a derivative as defined here.

2.4. MONEY AND FOREIGN EXCHANGE

Money is anything used as a medium of exchange. In modern economies there are three principal types of money. Coins are metal objects produced by the government or its authorized representative that are used as money. Currency is a paper product produced by the government or its authorized representative that is used as money. And deposits are liabilities of financial institutions that are generally accepted as a medium of exchange and are therefore classified as money.[8] The trading of money of one country for that of another is called the **foreign exchange market**, and the money itself is **foreign exchange**. In this book we are concerned primarily with these foreign exchange or forex markets, rather than with a country's domestic money supply.[9] The International Organization for Standardization has established standard codes for each currency, and we use the designations throughout this book.[10]

3. THE CREATION OF FINANCIAL INSTRUMENTS

This section provides an introduction to the ways in which financial instruments come into existence. From an overall perspective, all financial assets are in zero net supply. For each asset there are two equal and opposite economic positions. Every share of stock and fixed-income security has a private or governmental issuer and an owner. When firms issue their stock, its supply is expanded. Firms also frequently buy back their stock, decreasing its supply. Firms and governments are constantly issuing and retiring debt. Every derivative has contractual parties with opposite positions. The supply can be expanded or contracted by agreement among the parties. Governments issue currency by printing it and using it to make purchases of services, real assets, and financial assets. Currency can be retired when the government accepts it as payment for obligations. Deposits are liabilities of financial institutions, but assets of those owning the deposits. Printing more currency and using it to make purchases can expand the amount of currency. When individuals and organizations pay money to the government for services or taxes, the amount of currency declines.

3.1. THE CREATION OF EQUITIES AND FIXED-INCOME SECURITIES

There are four primary ways that equities, fixed-income securities, and warrants come into existence: private placements, public offerings, auctions, and short selling. The first three of these represent the ways that firms and governments first sell their securities. The institutional arrangements for the initial sale of securities (equities, fixed-income securities, and warrants) are called the **primary market**. In primary market transactions the proceeds of the sale go from the purchaser to the issuer, possibly through an intermediary. This is how firms and governments raise funds. All trades of these securities following the initial sale are considered **secondary market** transactions.

Investment banking is the activity of helping with the initial sale of securities. The types of firms that engage in investment banking differ from country to country. In the USA brokerage firms are investment bankers. The US Banking Act of 1933 (commonly called the Glass–Steagall Act) prohibits commercial banks from acting as investment bankers or as brokers or dealers in securities transactions. Following World War II, Japan adopted many aspects of US regulations. In most countries investment banking is one of the activities carried on by commercial banks. In the United Kingdom merchant banks carry out investment banking. These firms may provide assistance with both private placements and public offerings. Investment banking and merchant banking firms often perform other services, such as trading of securities, that are dealt with in other places in this book. While there have been differences in the types of businesses carried on by investment banks and merchant banks in the past, today these two terms essentially represent different terminology for the same type of firm.

There is a growing trend toward raising new capital through cross-border issues of debt and equity. Both first-time offerings and offerings of additional securities for debt and equity already being traded are included. "Targeted registered offerings" are exempt from US laws concerning withholding taxes and information reporting. It is not necessary to reveal the identity of the beneficial owners of these securities. To qualify, the offering must be made simultaneously with a domestic US offering; the registered owner must be an offshore financial institution; interest and dividends must be paid to that institution; the issuer must certify that it has no knowledge that a US taxpayer is the beneficial owner; and the issuer and registered owner must follow USSEC certification requirements. Several studies have shown that these offerings lower the cost of capital.[11] In 1994 Daimler-Benz raised the equivalent of about 2 billion USD in a global equity offering, part of which was sold to US investors. To qualify for offering securities in the USA and listing these securities on the New York Stock Exchange (NYSE), the company issued financial statements conforming to US Generally Accepted Accounting Principles (USGAAP).[12]

3.2. Private Placements

One way of raising capital by the sale of securities is through a private placement in which the securities are sold directly to an investor, often a wealthy individual or a financial institution. Pension funds, insurance companies, and banks commonly purchase securities in private placements. The sale can often be arranged quickly, and the terms can be tailored to the specific needs of the investor and the issuer. The negotiation of individualized terms may be important to investors, especially those purchasing fixed-income securities. The most important issuers of private placements are mid-sized firms, large firms with complex transactions, and large firms that want to avoid public disclosure. Issues in the private placement market require more monitoring than would be feasible for a publicly issued security, but less than would be available from most banks. Private placements tend to have more restrictive covenants than public offerings. Negative covenants prohibit or restrict certain actions such as dividends or specify that certain financial ratios will be maintained at an indicated level. Affirmative covenants require certain actions such as that financial reports be made available regularly. Many private placements include the pledge of collateral. While covenants in private placements are more restrictive than those in public offerings, they are also frequently renegotiated. Carey et al. (1993) provide an extensive discussion of the private placement market.

3.3. Public Offerings

Many securities are sold through a public offering. In an **initial public offering** (IPO) a firm offers common stock to the public for the first time. This process is called **going public**. In a public offering the terms are standardized, and the issue is sold to a large number of investors. The issuer may sell directly to the public or may use the services of an investment banker. In most cases the investment banker buys the issue from the issuer and resells it to the public so that the investment banker bears market risk between the time of purchase and resale.[13] This procedure is called a **firm underwriting**. Except for very small issues, firm underwritings typically involve a selling syndicate organized by the lead underwriter or underwriters. The syndicate shares the risk involved in the underwriting. The **syndicate manager** is the firm that originates the deal and is in direct contact with the issuer. If more than one manager is involved, the firms are referred to as **syndicate co-managers**. The managers may invite other firms to join an **underwriting group** to share in the risks and rewards. In some cases additional firms are invited to join a **selling group**, which helps sell the issue. The difference between the price paid by the underwriters to the issuer and the price at which the issue is sold to the public is called the **underwriting spread**. The underwriting spread is shared between the co-managers, the underwriting group, and the selling group.

Firms that need to raise relatively small amounts of money commonly have difficulty finding an investment banker willing to take them public, especially with a firm underwriting. Many of these firms attempt to raise funds by having investment bankers sell their shares on a **best efforts** basis. This type of offering reduces the risk for the investment banker. In a best efforts offering the firm specifies a price for its shares and the minimum and maximum number of shares that it is willing to sell. Then the firm attempts either to sell the shares directly to the public or to enlist investment bankers to sell its shares. The offer continues at least until the maximum number of shares are sold, the minimum number of shares are sold and the issuer feels that sufficient time has passed, or the issuer has not sold the minimum number of shares within any prescribed time limits. Sherman (1992) argues that the possibility that a best efforts offering can fail is an advantage for small issuers, because investors who may have better insight into the likely success of the proposed business provide valuable information to the issuer.

In fact, both underwritten and best efforts offerings can fail. Best efforts offerings fail when investors do not subscribe to the minimum number of shares that the issuer requires for the offer not to be withdrawn. Since the offering price is set early in the process, unfavorable developments can cause investors to believe that the issue is overpriced. Also, best efforts offerings require more time to sell, which also allows more time for unfavorable events to occur. Underwritten IPOs fail when the issue is withdrawn prior to purchase by the underwriter. Dunbar (1998) reports that both best efforts and underwritten offerings fail at about the same rate. Successful best efforts offerings tend to have smaller sizes, lower prices, and underwriters with lesser reputations. Successful underwritten offerings tend to have larger sizes, higher prices, and underwriters with higher reputations.

A new trend is for issuers to attempt to sell shares directly to the public through offerings on the Internet. A number of sites have been developed on which these firms can advertise their offerings.[14] The Internet provides a low-cost way for companies to reach investors directly. But the absence of underwriters means that investors must assess the merits of an issue on their own, perhaps without even having seen company management. In June 1997 the Australian Stock Exchange announced plans to set up a market on the Internet for small- and medium-sized firms to raise capital. The site would allow these firms to post information about their needs in the hopes of attracting capital. Venture capitalists can also post information concerning the types of investments they desire to make (*Asian Wall Street Journal* 1997). William Hambrecht has formed a firm to take companies public over the Internet. The firm plans to offer shares using a Dutch auction, in which investors indicate a price and the number of shares they are willing to buy at that price. When the shares are sold, the underwriter ranks the bids by price. For each bid price, the number of shares sought at that price and higher are cumulated. The offering price is the highest price for which all of the shares can be sold (Bransten and Wingfield 1999).

Regardless of the type of offering, there may be stringent regulatory requirements that the issuer must meet prior to initiating the offering. In the USA most issuers are required to file a **registration statement** describing the offerings with the Securities and Exchange

Commission (USSEC). A **prospectus** is the part of a registration statement typically given to investors. Further, the issuer may face extensive post-offering requirements such as the US requirements concerning the dissemination of annual and quarterly reports. Internet offerings raise many regulatory issues: Is a US firm that sells shares to a citizen of Indonesia through the Internet subject to Indonesian rules concerning new issues?

IPOs tend to be underpriced, producing short-run price gains for those who buy them at the initial offering price (Rock 1986). Examining studies for 25 countries, Loughran, Ritter, and Rydqvist (1994) conclude that "the phenomenon of short-run underpricing of IPOs exists in every country with a stock market." Barry and Jennings (1993) demonstrate that almost all of this underpricing is corrected on the first post-offering trade, so that only investors purchasing the IPO from the underwriter benefit. A number of reasons have been proposed for underpricing, including:

1 **Informational differences between informed and uninformed investors.** On this view there are two groups of investors, informed and uninformed, both of which are necessary for a successful IPO. Informed investors acquire information about the future prospects on an issue through research or application of specialized knowledge. They buy only those issues on which the information is favorable. Uninformed investors buy some of every issue. For uninformed investors to break even, their losses on overpriced issues must equal their profits on underpriced issues. Since informed investors are also making money on underpriced IPOs, the aggregate profits for the informed and uninformed investors on underpriced IPOs must be greater than the losses of informed investors on overpriced IPOs. Hence, IPOs must be underpriced on average.

2 **Minimization of lawsuits.** Tinic (1988) compares the level of underpricing before and after the adoption of US laws providing for recovery of damages by investors if the offering documents are misleading. As predicted by the lawsuit avoidance hypothesis, Tinic finds greater underpricing after the adoption of US regulations. Hensler (1996) argues that if the risk of a firm is low and, consequently, the probability of a lawsuit is low, there may be overpricing of the IPO. More risky firms would tend to underprice their IPOs. On the other hand, Loughran, Ritter, and Rydqvist (1994) conclude that lawsuit avoidance is not a major cause of underpricing in the USA.

3 **Information asymmetry between the issuer and underwriter.** Baron (1982) postulates that underpricing results from the fact that investment bankers know less about an issuer than the issuer itself and, therefore, tend to underestimate the equilibrium value. This information asymmetry hypothesis is not supported by the findings of Muscarella and Vetsuypens (1989), who report that investment bankers underprice their own offerings.

4 **High-quality issuers to facilitate subsequent offerings.** Evidence supporting this hypothesis comes from Loughran, Ritter, and Rydqvist (1994) and Uhlir (1989), who demonstrate that high-risk IPOs are underpriced more than low-risk ones.

5 **Effect on underwriter share price.** Nanda and Yun (1997) show that underwriters that substantially overprice new IPOs experience a decline in their own firm's stock value, which they attribute to a loss of reputation. On the other hand, underwriters that moderately underprice issues experience positive returns on their own firm's stock.

In a few cases IPO prices are not voluntary.[15] In Korea and Malaysia, the government has determined offering prices. More typically, the offering prices are determined voluntarily. Contracts that are voluntary can be described by two characteristics, the first of which is the amount of information that is collected before setting the offering price. Historically, a **fixed price underwriting** has been used in the UK and its former colonies (India and Singapore). In this approach the price is set early in the process, and investors are given a period of time, typically from two weeks to two months, to subscribe to the issue. This method is used in the USA for best efforts underwritings. The alternative is the **book building underwriting** prevalent in the USA for larger issues.[16] In this method considerable information is collected from potential buyers, and the underwriter attempts to build interest (though formal offers and orders are not permitted). Part of the process of collecting this information is a **road show**, so named because the underwriter goes from city to city making presentations about the company and the offering. The second characteristic that can be used to categorize IPO contracts is whether discrimination is allowed in price and/or quantity allocations. In practice, price discrimination has been rare, but there have been instances in Portugal, Singapore, and Japan. On a worldwide basis the use of procedures that allow the underwriter to selectively allocate IPO shares is common and is used in both best efforts and book building in the USA. Large customers may be preferred to small, or vice versa. Large customers generate other business, and the underwriter may seek to keep them happy by allocating them more IPO shares. On the other hand, the underwriter may seek to develop a larger shareholder base by limiting large purchases. Mello and Parsons (1998) present a framework in which underwriters increase IPO proceeds by carefully balancing the sale of shares to large and small investors. Large investors provide monitoring, which benefits small investors and increases the price these small investors are willing to pay. Hence, it can make sense to favor large investors, but care must be taken to insure that larger investors pay a competitive price.

Maximization of proceeds is not always the goal in IPOs. In many privatizations of government firms, one important goal is to insure that the investors, many of whom have never owned stocks before, earn good returns. An IPO may be priced below its true value to attract more investors. Underpriced shares may be used to reward employees or politicians.

3.4. Auctions

Auctions are also used as a way to issue securities, especially fixed-income securities. US government debt, the debt of US states and their subdivisions, and some issues of utility companies are sold by auction. Other governments such as that of Singapore also use auctions to sell debt. In Chile IPOs are sold by brokers using a special stock exchange auction session. These auction sessions were a popular way for state enterprises involved in privatizations to sell their shares to the public. Since there are no underwriters, there is no underwriting spread. Instead, brokers charge commissions to the parties. French companies tend to use a system in which those seeking to purchase an IPO indicate a price and quantity. Subsequently an offering price is determined, and applications below that price are rejected. In the 1990s in Japan 50 percent or more of the shares of each issue were offered by auction, and the remaining shares were sold at a price based on the auction price. For a description of the Japanese system see Pettway and Kaneko 1996.

3.5. SHORT SELLING

Through a process called **short selling**, investors can create equities and fixed-income securities. Consider two investors, A and B, who initially have no ownership positions in the stock of, say, International Business Machines, along with a third investor, C, who owns 100 shares of IBM. B's broker enters into a contract with C in which B borrows C's 100 shares of IBM. B agrees to return C's shares whenever C requires and promises to reimburse C for any dividends that are paid on IBM while the shares are borrowed. B also pays C a fee as an inducement for entering into the contract. B then sells 100 shares of IBM to A on the floor of the NYSE. B's broker delivers C's shares to A's broker in return for the sales proceeds. The sales proceeds are typically given to C or C's broker as collateral. If IBM's price increases, additional collateral may be needed. Depending on the results of the negotiating process, C may retain any interest earned on the funds deposited as collateral or may share the interest with B or B's broker. In this situation A is in exactly the same position as would arise from a normal purchase of IBM, while B is in an opposite position which is similar to that of the issuing firm. When the short position is closed out, B purchases shares on the floor of the NYSE and returns the shares to C in return for the collateral. If the repurchase price plus commissions and dividends is less than the previous sales price, B has a profit. Otherwise B has a loss.[17]

On the NYSE most short sales can be executed only on a plus tick or a zero-plus tick. A **plus tick** (or **uptick**) is a price higher than the last price, and a **minus tick** (or **downtick**) is a price lower than the last price. A **zero-plus tick** is a price that is the same as the last price but higher than the last different price. Similarly, a **zero-minus tick** is a price that is the same as the last price but lower than the last different price. Hence, the uptick rule on the NYSE effectively means that a stock can only be sold short at a price higher than the last different price. This rule is designed to prevent short selling in a market that has only declining prices.[18]

One objective of short sellers may be to profit from a decline in the price of the assets sold short. In this case the investor attempts to sell the shares and repurchase them subsequently at a lower price. Some short sales may be motivated by other considerations, such as tax avoidance. In a **short sale against the box** the seller actually owns shares but instead of selling these shares sells short. This procedure may allow the seller to postpone tax on the profits on the original shares. Short selling is used by dealers, specialists, block traders, and other market professionals to facilitate trading if they do not hold the inventory needed to accommodate a buyer.

Short selling benefits financial markets if it moves prices to equilibrium values more quickly than would be the case without short selling. In fact, without short selling investors who do not own a stock cannot easily take advantage of a view that a stock is overpriced. Despite these potential benefits, short selling is generally not popular with company management. Short sellers necessarily have a negative view of the prospects for the firm and sometimes even spread rumors about adverse developments. Short selling tends to depress stock prices initially, though the evidence shows that in general short selling does not materially affect prices. In fact, short selling adds liquidity by selling in up markets and buying in down, although there is evidence that short sellers do not earn abnormal returns (see Woolridge and Dickinson 1994).

In the USA in the past short selling has been associated with various types of stock price manipulation. In some cases syndicates have been formed that would sell large amounts of a firm's stock short and then buy back later when public selling drove the price even lower. This strategy can backfire. There are instances in which a single individual would simultaneously purchase shares and lend these shares to short sellers. Eventually the individual would own more than 100 percent of the firm's stock. Then the lender would request the return of the securities. It would be impossible for the short sellers to return the securities except by purchasing them from the lender, since the lender owns all the real shares. The owner/lender could demand a high price from the short sellers, forcing them to incur large losses. These types of incidents have lead some countries to prohibit short selling entirely, and others to prohibit certain types of investors such as individuals from selling short. (A number of these incidents are discussed in Walker 1991.)

Options, futures, and swaps are created whenever agreement can be reached between two parties. These agreements can be reached through telephone calls, computer negotiations, or on exchanges. There is no fixed supply of derivatives. Rather, the market can expand and contract, depending on the needs of the parties to the contracts. These derivatives are not created to raise capital for firms or governments, but instead are created as part of the risk management or investment strategies of the parties.

Most warrants are created initially through sale to investors in the same way as equities and fixed-income securities. Warrants may be created as speculative or risk management tools for investors; but, unlike options, futures, and swaps, warrants are often created to raise capital for firms. Rights, as we indicated previously, are issued as stock dividends to existing stockholders. The goal of rights issues is to raise capital for the firm.

3.6. THE CREATION OF MONEY

We also deal with the trading of currencies in this book.[19] Governments mint coins and print currency, creating money, and banks create deposits, which also creates money. As noted, barter is a very inefficient way to conduct trade. It is far easier to use a medium of exchange, money. The use of money especially facilitates multiparty trade. Two additional roles of money are described in box 1.5. Historically, the most common forms of money have been physical items such as gold and silver. These precious metals are still traded on a worldwide basis. In modern economies money comprises not only coins made of various metals, but also paper currency and deposits in various types of financial institutions. Paper currency is typically issued by the government or by a bank or other financial institution authorized by the government. The government authorizes the use of currency to pay debts, taxes, and other obligations. In addition, the government may use money to buy goods and services.

Financial institutions also create money as part of their normal operations. Banks accept demand deposits from their customers, who then use checks to transfer these funds to others. Demand deposits are deposits that can be withdrawn on demand. While demand deposits typically are considered money, other types of deposits that are readily transferable may also be considered money. Even travelers' checks can be considered money. **Travelers' checks** are negotiable instruments issued by financial institutions that are signed by the purchaser at the time of purchase and signed again at the time they are used.

BOX 1.5
The roles of money

In the main body of the text, we describe money in terms of its principle use as a medium of exchange. But money is also typically viewed as having other roles. One is as a unit of account. Money is useful in that, given a standard measure of value, each item in an economy can be valued in terms of that standard. Then the prices at which everyone is willing to buy and sell can be stated in terms of units of money. This facilitates comparisons, especially in multiproduct trade. It is difficult to imagine the profession of accounting without the use of money. Otherwise statements of account would be little more than lists of disparate products.

Money is also a store of value, in that it can be held as a financial asset just like any other asset. The advantage money offers in this usage over other assets is that money can be converted into other assets directly without first trading them for money. Both real and financial assets can be ranked according to the ease and costliness of quickly exchanging them for money, which we call "liquidity." Of course, money itself is the asset with the greatest liquidity.

Here we use the term "cash" to mean coins or currency, but in some contexts it may have a different meaning. A reporter interviewed several financial analysts about the large amounts of cash held by several US corporations. In commenting on the response of one of the analysts, the reporter stated, "Like most analysts, she uses the term 'cash' to include bank deposits and any marketable securities with a maturity of one year of less" (Anders 1994).

Suppose for simplicity that there is only one bank and that the bank's customers never ask for cash but always redeposit the checks they receive in their own account at this bank. Further, suppose that individuals do not hold cash but also deposit any cash that they receive in their bank account. Then the bank can lend money to its customers simply by crediting the amount of the loan to the customer's account. Since the bank never has to pay out any cash, there is no limit on the amount of money that the bank can create. For this reason, the government typically regulates the creation of money by banks.

One form of regulation is to require that banks transfer a portion of their deposits to a central bank. This has the same effect as requiring that the bank hold a certain portion of its deposits in cash. These restrictions are called **reserve requirements**. If there are no reserve requirements, then the bank can create an unlimited amount of money by lending to its clients. But suppose there is a reserve requirement that the bank hold cash equal to 20 percent of its deposits. To see how this works, consider that 100 units of currency are initially deposited in a bank. With a 20 percent reserve requirement, the bank can lend 80, so that it holds 20 in reserves. When the borrowers redeposit the 80 loan in the bank, the bank can lend another 64 (80 percent of 80), keeping 16 as reserves. The bank's overall liabilities are the 180 of deposits, and its assets are the 36 of reserves and the 144 of loans. Again, when the 64 is redeposited, the process continues. In general the maximum amount of demand deposits will be the reciprocal of the reserve requirement, and the maximum amount of lending will equal the maximum amount of demand deposits less the amount of reserve requirement. In this case the original 100 of money created by the government can lead to the creation of 400 of additional money by the banking system. Ultimately, the maximum amount of demand deposits that the bank can have is 500, and the bank will hold 100 in currency and 400 in loans.

If we relax the assumption that there is only one bank, we obtain the same outcome. But in this case it would be important for banks to be able to trade their assets among themselves in response to shifts in the liabilities (deposits) of each bank. Governments typically do not control the creation of money by the banking system through cash reserve requirements, but instead by requiring deposits with a central bank. The government can expand the supply of money by paying for its purchases with checks drawn on the central bank. When these are deposited by the recipients in their own bank, the bank's reserves against which it can lend are increased in exactly the same way that a deposit of cash would increase reserves in our previous example. Governments can also increase the money supply by purchasing financial assets.

In this book we are not concerned primarily with the process of money creation. Instead, we are interested in the markets for trading the money of one country for that of another – i.e., in the foreign exchange markets. These markets are quite similar to the secondary markets in which equities and fixed-income securities are traded. We are also concerned with money, because investments in various countries are denominated in different currencies.

3.7. THE ROLE OF FINANCIAL INSTITUTIONS

There are many different types of financial institutions involved in the creation and trading of financial instruments. All these institutions facilitate the operations of the economy, increase efficiency, and lower the cost of funds. Commercial banks and investment banks participate in the initial issuing of stocks and bonds. Commercial banks and governments create money. Institutional arrangements, including organized exchanges and foreign exchange markets, facilitate the transfer of these financial instruments after their initial creation. Insurance companies, mutual funds, and banks aid in the transfer of funds from those with excess to those with greater opportunities for profitable investment. All these secondary market activities facilitate the initial sale of securities by allowing investors to sell their investment if a need arises for funds. Financial institutions perform a number of activities that facilitate investment, including the assessment and monitoring of firm risk.

4. SUMMARY

Four major types of financial products traded are examined: equities, fixed-income securities, derivatives, and money. Equities are securities representing capital contributed to the firm for which there is no legal obligation to repay. The principal types of equities are common stock, which has a claim on all the earnings and assets of the firm remaining after others have been paid, and preferred stock, which typically has a claim to specified payments from the firm. Warrants are a type of equity, which give the right to purchase additional stock at a specified price under specified terms. Equity owners cannot usually force the firm to make specific payments through the courts.

Fixed-income securities are principally debt instruments. Bonds are debt obligations issued by firms and governments that require specific payments by the issuers. Money market instruments are debt obligations that have initial maturities of less than one year. These claims can be enforced in courts. Many preferred stock issues also have a claim to a fixed payment stream.

Derivative instruments are financial instruments that confer rights and obligations based on an underlying interest. Derivatives differ from stocks and fixed-income securities in that owners of derivatives are sometimes required to make payments of securities or cash to fulfill their obligations arising from their derivative contracts.

The fourth type of financial product is money, which comprises coins and currency and certain deposits with financial institutions. The chief role of money is as a medium of exchange to facilitate trade.

Governments and firms issue equities and fixed-income securities at specific times in large quantities to raise funds. The parties to the derivative contract create derivatives (excluding warrants) as the need to transfer risk arises. Money is created by governments through the minting of coins and the printing of paper currency and by the banking system through the creation of deposits that can serve as a medium of exchange.

We have seen that the most basic goal of individuals is to maximize their utility – i.e., their satisfaction. The maximization of utility translates into the financial goal of maximizing wealth. For a firm this means maximizing the wealth of its owners. Production is the way that wealth is created in the economy. Individuals can directly consume the production for a given year, or they can divert some of the production for use in producing other goods and services. This diversion of production from immediate consumption to use in facilitating additional production is called saving or direct investment. Savings and direct investment are just two names for the same thing.

Direct investment is the use of resources to produce other goods and services. But not everyone who wishes to defer consumption wants to invest directly. Instead, some prefer to give their funds to others to invest. Financial markets are institutional arrangements designed to facilitate the transfer of resources from those who have more to those who have less than they wish to consume.

Financial markets and instruments contribute to the enhancement of wealth. They increase the use of capital in the economy, and they lower the cost of transferring capital from those with a surplus to those with a shortage. Another financial product, money, increases wealth by reducing the need for trade using the inefficient method of barter.

Questions

1 How accurate is the assumption that investors seek to maximize their wealth as a description of the world?
2 How do financial markets increase the wealth of an economy?
3 How can an executive compensation package be tailored to reinforce ethical behavior?
4 What is the difference between financial investment and direct investment?
5 How does the cost of capital affect the wealth of an economy?
6 List the four major types of financial instruments?
7 Is there a limit on the amount of money that a banking system can create?
8 Which are more important in economic development – attitudes or institutions?

9   What are some of the ways that barter is carried on today in international trade?
10 Is money a financial instrument?
11 What might prompt the choice of a best efforts offering rather than a firm underwriting by an investment banker? an issuer?
12 Describe a bond that could be classified as a derivative.
13 What are the characteristics of common stock that prevent it from being classified as a derivative?
14 If managers attempt to maximize their own wealth, is it true that, to prevent embezzlement, managers' compensation must be greater than the gains from embezzlement?
15 Explain how individuals' pursuit of self-interest can be good for an economy.

APPENDIX 1

Production, consumption, savings and investment, and capital

In this appendix, we define and review the roles of production, consumption, savings and investment, and capital. Understanding of the roles of each of these is necessary to appreciate the role of financial markets in the economy.

1. Production

Before individuals can consume or invest, they must produce. **Production** is the use of land, labor, and goods and services to produce other goods and services. The monetary value of all the goods and services produced during the year is the Gross National Product (GNP). Some production is used simply to replace assets used up in the production process. The value of products used up in the production process is called **depreciation**. If depreciation is subtracted from GNP, the remainder is National Income. People can accomplish the production of goods and services individually or through businesses, governments, universities, and many other types of organizations. To produce these services, individuals and organizations must hire labor and acquire land, buildings and equipment, raw materials, supplies, and similar items. Table A1.1 shows the percentage of employment devoted to agriculture, industry, and services in ten nations for 1960, 1970, 1980, 1990, and 1996. In the last half of the twentieth century developed nations have been shifting resources dramatically away from agricultural production. And, to a lesser extent, resources have also been shifted away from industry. Over this period the percentage of employment devoted to services increased from 58.1 percent in 1960 to 74.3 percent in 1996 in the USA and from 41.9 percent to 61.8 percent in Japan. There is no indication that this trend is abating.

Consider the collection of products produced in the economy this year or, alternatively, the monetary value of these products. For simplicity, we concentrate on individuals and ignore governments, firms, and exports/imports. This is a reasonable approach, because governments and firms are simply entities through which individuals operate. Of course, all the production during the year belongs to individuals either directly or indirectly through governments and firms. It is this collection of goods and services that is available for individuals to use during the year. We can denote the production in the economy during the year by Y.

Individuals must decide how to use this production. One possibility is to consume the assets. Consumption is the use of goods and services to fulfill individuals' immediate needs and not for investment. If the goods and services are not immediately consumed, they are saved, since we define savings as deferred consumption. Economists often present the following equation:

$$Y = C + S$$

where Y is income (i.e., the collection of goods and services available for disposition during the year), C is consumption, and S is savings. It may be helpful to note that Y, C, and S can be thought of as actual goods and services (i.e., 100 trucks, 80 of which are consumed by being used for personal transportation, and 20 of which are used in production) or as the monetary value of these goods and services. Sometimes it is easier to understand economic concepts by thinking about real products rather than by thinking in monetary units.

2. Consumption

As noted, **consumption** fulfills individuals' immediate needs. Sometimes the distinction between consumption and investment is not easy to make. Educational expenditures often are made to increase the quality of life and thus have a consumption element. But education also increases individuals' ability to produce goods and services and therefore can be, and often is, considered to be production.

Individuals must consume to survive. Individuals consume a variety of products. The types of items consumed and the quantity consumed vary widely from country to country. Consider statistics obtained from the US Department of Commerce for the year 1992. Denmark leads in per capita consumption of pork, the US in per capita consumption of poultry, and Argentina in per capita consumption of beef (including veal). Hong Kong ranks tenth in per capita consumption of pork and third in per capita consumption of poultry, but does not rank among the top ten in per capita consumption of beef.

Consumption also differs from individual to individual even within the same country. In the USA, for example, the proportion of total expenditures devoted to health care in 1991 was 2.1 percent for individuals under 25 years old and 11.5 percent for individuals over 65 years of age. On the other hand, the share of expenditures devoted to personal insurance and pensions was 11.3 percent for those aged 45–54, 5.4 percent for those under 25, and only 3.6 percent for those over 65 years old.

3. Savings and investment

Savings are deferred consumption. The savings decision is important, because those assets that are not consumed, and only those assets, are available for use in producing additional goods and services in the future. We define **direct investment** as the use of resources to facilitate production rather than for current consumption. Since savings is deferred consumption, and direct investment comprises products produced but not consumed, savings and investment are just two different ways of looking at the same thing. Hence, S = I, where I is direct investment (i.e., the 20 trucks in our earlier example). Without savings there can be no direct investment and, therefore, no capital, where capital is defined as all resources such as land, labor, raw materials, and buildings used in production. The usual distinction between land and capital made by economists has no relevance for our purposes.

The terminology typically used in finance courses, in finance publications that one finds on most newsstands, and by financial economists differs from that used in economics texts in several ways. First, financial economists do not typically refer to savings. Instead, since real investment equal savings, financial economists prefer to call both sides of the S = I equality investment. Next, financial economists expand the definition of investments to include financial investments. **Financial investments** represent ownership of an economic position in a financial instrument. We describe a wide variety of financial investments such as stocks and bonds in some detail in this chapter. Because S and I represent the portion of Y that is not consumed immediately, but is used in production, these are real or direct investments. Financial investments are claims on these direct investments and their outputs. Hence, **investments** comprise both real and financial investments.

4. The role of capital

Assets used in production are called **capital**. Capital plays an important role in production. Capital includes plant and equipment, inventory (including cash transaction balances) and the like. Further,

Table 1A1.1 Percentage of employment in agriculture, industry, and services for the years 1960, 1970, 1980, 1990, and 1996 for ten nations[a]

Year	USA	Canada	Australia	Japan	France	Germany	Italy	Netherlands	Sweden	United Kingdom
Agriculture										
1960	8.5	13.3	—	29.5	23.2	14.0	32.5	9.8	15.5	4.7
1970	4.5	7.6	8.0	16.9	13.5	8.6	20.1	6.2	8.2	3.2
1980	3.6	5.4	6.5	10.1	8.7	5.6	14.2	5.0	5.6	2.6
1990	2.9	4.2	5.6	6.9	5.6	3.5	8.9	4.7	4.0	2.1
1996	2.8	4.1	5.1	5.3	4.6	—	6.9	4.0	3.3	2.0
Industry										
1960	33.4	32.0	—	28.5	37.5	45.9	34.2	39.5	40.4	46.1
1970	33.1	29.8	35.0	35.7	38.4	47.6	39.8	38.0	38.0	43.2
1980	29.3	27.4	28.9	35.1	35.0	43.2	38.1	30.5	31.5	36.2
1990	25.1	23.7	23.7	33.9	29.1	38.9	32.5	25.8	28.2	30.3
1996	22.9	21.7	21.7	32.9	25.0	—	32.3	22.3	25.1	26.9
Services										
1960	58.1	54.7	—	41.9	39.3	40.1	33.4	50.7	44.1	49.2
1970	62.3	62.6	57.0	47.4	48.0	43.7	40.1	55.8	53.9	53.6
1980	67.1	67.2	64.5	54.8	56.3	51.3	47.7	64.5	62.9	61.2
1990	72.0	72.1	70.7	59.2	65.3	57.6	58.6	69.5	67.9	69.6
1996	74.3	74.2	73.3	61.8	70.4	—	60.8	73.7	71.6	71.2

[a] Agriculture includes forestry and hunting and fishing. Industry includes manufacturing, mining, and construction. Services include transportation, communication, public utilities, trade, finance, public administration, private household services, and miscellaneous services.
Source: US Department of Labor, 1998.

since workers typically require compensation within a short time, the cost of this labor is also part of the capital required for production. Land (including not only the land itself but minerals found in or on the land such as oil and coal) is also part of the capital required for production. While land and labor are sometimes considered as making separate contributions to the production process, here we are concerned with the mechanism that allows the employment of labor and land in production rather than in consumption (such as in the form of leisure). Suppose that the workers in a factory make a product for which they receive wages. These wages can be consumed immediately. Investors have supplied the products consumed by the workers in exchange for the products produced by the workers. Until the factory's output is consumed, it is part of the production process and represents an investment or capital.

The provision of capital for use in production is called "investing," the capital itself is called an "investment," and those providing the capital are called "investors." In general, the greater the amount of capital, the greater the amount of output of goods and services once the productive facilities have been completed.

4.1. Sources of capital

Investors supply capital through both direct investment and financial investment. Expenditures on all goods and services used in production, including plant and equipment, legal fees, labor, and rent, are direct investments. Direct investments are also sometimes called "real investments." Purchases of financial assets are "financial investments." In general, the term "investments" encompasses both direct and financial investments. But the focus of this book is on financial investments, which are referred to simply as "investments." Direct investments are typically considered in texts dealing with financial management, and the study of financial aspects of direct investments is called "capital budgeting."

4.2. Financing production

Many individuals make direct investments, perhaps combining them with those of their friends and family. Historically, almost all business funds were raised in this way. And even today this is an important source of business funding. Individuals or small groups own many retail stores, medical offices, legal practices, accounting firms, as well as manufacturing facilities. Most of the businesses that rely on a small group of individuals for funds are small, but some are very large.

In modern economies money or currency is needed to make purchases of goods and services that can, in turn, be used to make additional goods and services. As the size of enterprises has increased over the last several hundred years, in many instances the required funds have grown beyond the resources available to an individual or small group. On the other hand, there are many individuals who do not wish to make direct investments. Many individuals and organizations have money that they do not wish to spend for current consumption. But even people who have unmet current needs may decide to postpone consumption so that they will have assets available for consumption in the future. They may want to have funds available for their retirement, to leave an estate to their heirs, and to have resources for emergencies and unexpected contingencies. Thus, individuals and organizations wishing to make direct investments may be able to obtain funds from organizations that do not wish to make direct investments. The deferred consumption from all these sources provides the resources for investment.

Deferred consumption also results from the nature of the transaction process. Income and expenditures both typically occur at discrete points in time. There is a period of time between the receipt of income and its expenditure, when funds might be available for investment. In some cases, such as purchases of food, expenditures are small and frequent, and the deferral of current consumption is short. In other cases, purchases are relatively large and infrequent, and the delay of consumption is often lengthy. For individuals, typical large and infrequent purchases include automobiles, houses, and university education.

A source of funding for investments can also arise within the production sector for a variety of reasons, including the mismatch of revenues and expenditures. In addition to short-term mismatches, firms may accumulate funds for larger-scale projects such as the purchase of plant and equipment.

4.3. Cost of capital

Producers must pay financial investors in order to obtain funds with which to make investments. These payments are called the **cost of capital**. The cost of capital, then, comprises all payments made to obtain funds. Naturally, it is advantageous for producers to be able to obtain these funds at as low a cost as possible. Part of the cost of capital arises due to the payments to the suppliers of the capital. Another part, called "transaction costs," is the cost of arranging for the raising of new funds and also for the subsequent transfer of ownership among financial investors. Transaction costs include under-writer fees, commissions, legal fees, and all other expenses associated with these transfers. Transaction costs are costs of production. If transaction costs can be reduced, goods and services can be produced more cheaply. These cost savings then allow producers to charge less for their products. Financial markets are the primary tools used to reduce the cost of capital.

Of course, even if transaction costs were zero, the cost of capital would still be positive as long as producers have projects than yield returns greater than their costs before taking into account the cost of capital. Typically, there are many projects that producers could undertake profitably if the cost of capital were just a little lower. Therefore, if more capital becomes available, if interest rates fall suf-ficiently, producers can absorb it. The amount that producers can afford to pay to obtain capital depends on the value of the products that can be produced with the capital. While producers will pay as little as they can to obtain capital, they can afford to pay as much as the value of the marginal prod-ucts produced with the added capital. If there is competition for capital, then producers will actually have to pay as much as they can afford.

Just as the producers desire a low cost of capital, financial investors would like to receive as much as possible for their funds. If there is competition among financial investors, then, this competition will insure that the cost of capital for producers is as little as possible for various levels of capital supply.

APPENDIX 2

Individual behavior

As we noted in the text, individuals carry out all economic activity either alone or in groups. Hence, it is important to state in the beginning how we believe that these individuals and other entities behave. We begin by introducing the term "utility," which is used by economists to describe the ability of an item to provide people with satisfaction. The utility that a particular item provides is, of course, subjective and varies from individual to individual. In financial economics, it is assumed that the goal of individuals is to maximize their utility. This is the assumption that we use in this book. A related goal is the maximization of wealth. We assume that more wealth is preferred to less (nonsatiation). In other words, more wealth provides greater utility. Hence, individuals also desire to maximize their wealth.

Resources are scarce. To acquire more of one item necessitates giving up others. On a graph with the amount of one item consumed on the vertical axis (Good A) and the amount of a second item on the horizontal axis (Good B), an indifference curve is the plot of all the points representing combi-nations of the consumption of the two items that have the same utility (see figure A2.1). Of course, no two indifference curves can overlap. There is a family of indifference curves that represent higher levels of utility as one moves upward and to the right.

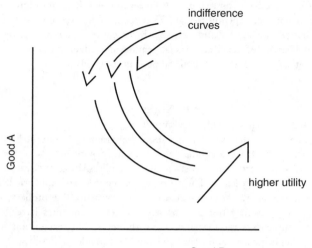

Figure 1A2.1 Illustration of a family of indifference curves.

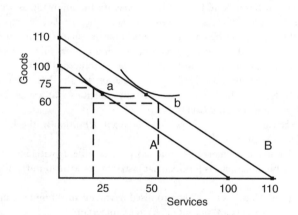

Figure 1A2.2 Budget lines with tangent indifference curves.

Because of the wide diversity of items produced and consumed in the economy, it is customary to classify these products into goods, which are tangible products, and services, which are intangible products. Goods include food, clothing, housing, automobiles, and similar items. Services include medical care, government, and education. Cabs, airlines, bus companies, and others provide transportation services. Specialized financial services are also widely used. Banks, credit unions, insurance companies, brokerage firms, foreign exchange dealers, credit card companies, pawnshops, and many other businesses may provide financial services.

Suppose that you can spend 100 percent of your income on consumption of goods, 100 percent on consumption of services, or any combination of the two. Figure A2.2 shows a budget line intersecting both the vertical and horizontal axes at 100. This budget line shows the various combinations of an individual's budget that can be spent on either goods or services or various combinations of goods and services A, good B, or combinations of goods A and B. In other words, all the points on the line represent the same level of spending, but different proportions of expenditures on goods and services. Like indifference curves, no two budget lines can cross. If an indifference curve is tangent to this budget line at point a, expenditures are 75 percent of income on goods and 25 percent on services. A second budget line representing a higher income level intersects the vertical and horizontal axes at about 110. If an indifference curve is tangent to this budget line at point b, about 60 percent of income is spent on services, and only about 50 percent on goods.

■ Notes ■

1   See appendix 1-A1 for a more explicit definition.

2   Following the merger, the shares of Daimler-Benz were removed from the S&P 500, and the percentage of ownership of US shareholders fell to about 25 percent.

3   The ways in which property can be lost are almost endless. Fire, hurricanes, floods, and other natural disasters cause many losses. The property may be stolen or embezzled. The property may be destroyed in a riot or war or confiscated by a government. The property may be taxed at a high rate. The property may become obsolete. Modern economies have developed ways for investors to limit these risks and to share them with others. The recognition of firms as separate legal entities through incorporation laws and the like provide investors with a way of limiting their risk. Insurance can be purchased to minimize the losses from many types of events. The use of derivatives to help manage risks resulting from natural disasters is just beginning, but has the potential to become a major tool in the management of these risks.

4   In the USA the securities acts of 1933 and 1934 classify the following as securities: investment contracts, bonds, calls, certificates of deposit for securities, collateral trust, certificates, puts, stocks, transferable shares, voting trust certificates, treasury shares, certificates of interest in any profit-sharing agreement, debentures, notes, options, and pre-organization subscriptions. Notes with a maturity of less than nine months are exempt. Commercial loan transactions are also not subject to the acts. Securities are subject to regulation by the US Securities and Exchange Commission (USSEC). In the USA futures are not securities, but are subject to regulation by the Commodity Futures Trading Commission.

5   The definition used in this book differs from the legal definition in the USA, where puts and calls are classified as securities.

6   Some prefer to define money markets as markets for instruments with an initial maturity of one year or less, and capital markets as for financial instruments with an initial life of more than one year.

7   A bond is not typically a derivative. The promised payments on a bond are uncertain due to risk of default, but the payments are not intended to be uncertain.

8   For a discussion of the US experience with money see http://www.frbchi.org/pubs-speech/publications/BOOKLETS/money_matters/money_matters.html.

9   It may be apparent that there is no exact agreement on classifications of particular instruments into the four product types used here or on the definition of terms related to the products. Using our definition, a warrant is a derivative, a security, and an equity. This differs from many discussions, which view a warrant as an equity and a security, but often do not include warrants in discussions of derivatives. Both equities and fixed-income securities can have option features that blur the distinction between product categories. There are many issues of bonds and preferred stock outstanding that allow conversion of the issue into other securities, most commonly the common stock of the issuer. These provisions allow the issuer to obtain funds at a lower initial rate, preserving the firm's cash for other uses.

10   See ISO 4217 Codes for the representation of currencies and funds. The International Organization for Standardization web address is http://www.iso.ch/.

11   In 1985 US firms raised a total of 89 million USDs by issuing new seasoned equity outside the USA. By 1992 this amount had increased to more than 3,500 USD. For additional details see

Chaplinsky and Ramchand 1995; Marr, Trimble, and Varma 1991; or Radebaugh, Gebhardt, and Gray 1995.

12 The US shares were issued in the form of depository receipts.

13 Information on leading investment bankers for various types of financial instruments can be found at http://www.emwl.com/index.html.

14 Examples of these sites include (1) Hoover, Inc. (http://www.hoovers.com/), which provides links to news, stock quotes, and other products, including more than 13,500 brief company descriptions and financial statements for free and more than 3,400 company profiles via online subscription; the profiles cover US and non-US public and nonpublic companies; the firm also offers information concerning IPOs at http://www.ipocentral.com/. (2) Direct IPOs (http://www.directipo.com/), a consulting and publishing service which helps technology companies raise capital through the Internet. (3) Nikko Investor relations company provides information of Internet IPOs in Japan at http://www.nikkoir.co.jp/sinki-e/sinki-e.htm.

15 The way IPOs are handled differs from country to country. The procedures in a particular country may change, but for our purposes we are only interested in particular practices that have existed from time to time. Hence, changes in the practices in a particular country since press time are not a major concern here.

16 Benveniste and Busaba (1997) show that both methods can be optimal, depending on the characteristics of the issuing firm.

17 If shares sold short represent 1 percent of the firm's shares, some investors own claims that are identical to 101 percent of IBM (the 100 percent issued by the firm and the 1 percent created by the short seller). But other investors are short 1 percent of the outstanding shares, so that from their point of view investors hold exactly 100 percent of the firm's stock.

18 Suppose one is considering whether a short sale can be made at 50. If the previous price sequence, beginning with the oldest price, is 49.875, 49.875, 50, then a trade at 50 would be on a zero–plus tick and would be permissible. If the previous price sequence, beginning with the oldest price, is 50.125, 50.125, 50, then a trade at 50 would be on a zero–minus tick and would not be permissible.

19 It seems more natural to talk about trading currencies, even though it is actually deposits that are typically traded.

■ References ■

Anders, George 1994: HMOs pile up billions in cash, try to decide what to do with it. *Wall Street Journal*, December 21, A1.

Asian Wall Street Journal 1997: Australian Stock Exchange plans Internet market for smaller firms. June 12, p. 22.

Barnea, Amir, Haugen, Robert A. and Senbet, Lemma W. 1985: *Agency Problems and Financial Contracting*. Englewood Cliffs, NJ: Prentice-Hall. (Provides additional information concerning agency problems.)

Baron, D. P. 1982: A model of the demand for investment banking advice and distribution services for new issues. *Journal of Finance* 37, 955–76.

Barry, Christopher B. and Jennings, Robert H. 1993: The opening price performance of initial public offerings of common stock. *Financial Management* 22, 54–63.

Benveniste, Lawrence M. and Busaba, Walid Y. 1997: Bookbuilding vs. fixed price: an analysis of competing strategies for marketing IPOs. *Journal of Financial and Quantitative Analysis* 32, 383–403.

Bransten, Lisa and Wingfield, Nick 1999: New company aims to shift IPO playing field. *Wall Street Journal*, February 8, p. C1, C16.

Carey, Mark, Prowse, Stephen, Rea, John and Udell, Gregory 1993: The economics of private placements: a new look. *Financial Markets, Institutions & Instruments* 2, 1–67.

Chaplinsky, Susan and Ramchand, Latha 1995: The rationale for global equity offerings. Working paper, University of Virginia.

Copeland, Thomas E. and Weston, J. Fred 1988: *Financial Theory and Corporate Policy*, 3rd edn. New York: Addison-Wesley. (Provides additional information on agency problems.)

Dunbar, Craig G. 1998: The choice between firm-commitment and best-efforts offering methods in IPOs: the effect of unsuccessful offers. *Journal of Financial Intermediation* 7, 60–90.

Financial Executive 1994: How to stay in the money internationally. 10 (May/June), 16–22.

Green, Richard C. 1984: Investment incentives, debt, and warrants. *Journal of Financial Economics* 13, 115–36.

Hensler, Douglas A. 1996: The over/underpricing of initial public offerings. *Review of Quantitative Finance and Accounting* 6, 233–43.

Loughran, Tim, Ritter, Jay R. and Rydqvist, Kristian 1994: Initial public offerings: international insights. *Pacific Basin Finance Journal* 2, 165–99.

Marr, M. Wayne, Trimble, John L. and Varma, Raj 1991: On the integration of international capital markets: evidence from Euroequity offerings. *Financial Management* 20, 11–21.

Mello, Antonio S. and Parsons, John E. 1998: Going public and the ownership structure of the firm. *Journal of Financial Economics* 49, 79–109.

Muscarella, Chris J. and Vetsuypens, Michael 1989: A simple test of Baron's model of IPO underpricing. *Journal of Financial Economics* 24, 125–35.

Nanda, Vikram, and Yun, Youngkeol 1997: Reputation and financial intermediation: an empirical investigation of the impact of IPO mispricing on underwriter market value. *Journal of Financial Intermediation* 6, 39–63.

Pettway, Richard H. and Kaneko, Takashi 1996: The effects of removing price limits and introducing auctions upon short-term IPO returns: the case of Japanese IPOs. *Pacific-Basin Finance Journal* 4, 241–58.

Radebaugh, Lee H., Gebhardt, Gunther and Gray, Sidney J. 1995: Foreign stock exchange listings: a case study of Daimler-Benz. *Journal of International Financial Management and Accounting* 6, 158–92.

Rock, Kevin 1986: Why new issues are underpriced. *Journal of Financial Economics* 15, 187–212.

Sherman, Ann Guenther 1992: The pricing of best efforts new issues. *Journal of Finance* 47, 781–90.

Smith, Adam 1789: *An Inquiry into the Nature and Causes of the Wealth of Nations*. Repr. Chicago: University of Chicago Press, 1976.

Tinic, Seha 1988: Anatomy of initial public offerings of common stock. *Journal of Finance* 43, 789–822.

Uhlir, H. 1989: Going public in the F.R.G. In Guimarares et al. (eds), *A Reappraisal of the Efficiency of Financial Markets*, Berlin: Springer-Verlag.

US Department of Labor 1998: *Handbook of Labor Statistics*. Washington: USDL.

Walker, Joseph A. 1991: *Selling Short*. New York: Wiley.

Woolridge, J. Randall and Dickinson, Amy 1994: Short selling and common stock prices. *Financial Analysts Journal* 50, 20–8.

Secondary Markets

■ **Key terms** ■

Ask   the price at which a market participant is willing to sell.

Basis point   a pricing unit used for bonds, in which one basis point equals 0.01 percent and 100 basis points equals 1 percent of the face value of the bond.

Batch trading   a method of trading on exchanges in which orders are accumulated until trading is opened, when these orders are executed simultaneously.

Beta   a measure of the change in a security's return in relation to the change in the return on the market; in the regression of the return on a security with the return on the market, beta is the coefficient of the return on the market.

Bid   the price that a market participant is willing to pay to buy.

Block trade   a large trade. The actual size that constitutes a block differs from market to market and also, perhaps, from instrument to instrument.

Broker   a person or firm executing orders for the account and risk of another.

Buy side   all investors.

Call market   the same as **Batch trading**.

Churning   the fraudulent practice of inducing customers to trade for the purpose of generating commissions.

Circuit breaker   exchange rules that/require trading halts when market indexes have changed by prescribed amounts.

Day traders   traders who buy and sell financial assets within the same day.

Dealer   a person or firm engaged in the business of buying and selling financial investments for its own account.

Depth   the size of a financial investment that can be traded at a given price.

Discretionary account   an account for which the authority to trade in the account has been formally turned over to the broker.

Electronic communication network a privately owned organization that facilitates trading among institutions without the use of the facilities of an exchange (see also **Proprietary trading system**).

Equilibrium the number of shares investors seek to buy matches the number of shares investors want to sell at a given price, so that there is no pressure for a change in price.

Equilibrium (Walrasian) a single price such that there are no unsatisfied buyers at that price or higher and no unsatisfied sellers at that price or lower.

Exchange an organization whose members trade financial assets in a given location such as a trading floor or a computer.

Floor broker members of the exchange who do not work for a particular brokerage firm but handle orders for other members who are busy.

Frontrunning the use by a broker-dealer of a customer's information for the firm's own profit or that of its employees.

Holding period return $(P_t - P_{t-1})/P_t$, where P_t is the price of a security in period t.

Immediacy the speedy execution of orders of a given size at a reasonable cost.

Index arbitrage a form of program trading in which both securities and derivatives are traded.

Information leakage the revelation of information in the process of executing an order.

Informed trader someone buying and selling financial instruments who is acting on information concerning the value of the security.

Inside information any information about a security issuer obtained through a position of trust.

Letter stock stock issued in the USA that is not registered with the USSEC.

Limit order an order for the purchase or sale of a financial asset that is to be executed at a specified price or better.

Limit order book a set of limit orders.

Liquidity the ability to buy or sell an asset readily without substantial impact on its price and at a low cost.

Liquidity traders another name for uninformed traders.

Listed approved for regular trading on an exchange.

Make-a-market always willing to buy and sell at a price close to the current market price.

Markdown the difference between the amount a dealer receives for an asset and the amount the dealer pays a customer.

Market order an order for the purchase or sale of a financial asset that is to be executed immediately at the best possible price.

Marketability in this text, a synonym for liquidity.

Marketable limit order a limit order with a specified price that allows the immediate execution of the order.

Markup the difference between the amount a dealer paid for an asset and the amount the dealer charges a customer.

Member an institution or firm that owns a seat that enters the right to trade on an exchange.

Microstructure   the study of the way financial markets are organized and regulated and the effect of these on transactions costs, liquidity, risk, and other market characteristics.

Noise traders   uninformed traders.

Nonsynchronous trading   a reference to the fact that assets do not all trade at the same time.

Odd lot   less than the usual unit of trading.

Offer   an ask quote.

Open outcry   calling out bid and offer prices and quantities to a crowd of traders often with the aid of hand signals.

Order   an instruction to a broker-dealer concerning the purchase or sale of a financial investment.

Order-driven   investors trade against orders that have been previously placed by other traders.

Over-the-counter   trading that does not occur on an exchange.

Pit   the location, which may be a staired depression, on the floor of futures exchanges where trading takes place.

Position traders   owners of financial assets for periods of days, weeks, months, or even years.

Post   the location on the floor of an exchange where particular stocks are traded.

Precedence rules   rules that determine which characteristics of the orders are most important.

Price discovery   the process whereby a market determines the equilibrium price of a financial instrument.

Price limit   a price range established by an exchange usually for a day outside which trading is not permitted.

Price risk   risk of loss due to a change in the price of an asset.

Program trading   the trading of a large group of different financial instruments at the same time.

Proprietary trading system   a privately owned organization that facilitates trading among institutions without the use of the facilities of an exchange (see also **Electronic crossing network**).

Quotation or **Quote**   a bid and ask together.

Quote-driven   dealers post quotes against which orders can be executed.

Reinsurance   insurance purchased by one insurance company from another to protect against risk of loss from claims by its policyholders.

Resiliency   the speed with which prices return to their initial level after they change in response to a large trade by uninformed traders.

Round lot   the usual unit of trading.

Scalpers   buying and selling quickly to take advantage of minimal fluctuations in prices.

Scienter   the intent to deceive, manipulate, or defraud.

Seat   a membership on an exchange.

Sell side   all intermediaries involved in helping investors make and trade financial investments.

Specialist   a member of a stock exchange that is a designated market-maker.

Spread   the difference between the bid and the ask.

Stop order   an order to purchase or sell a financial asset that becomes a market order if there is a trade at a specified price or worse.

Thick   assets that are traded frequently.

Thin   assets that are traded infrequently.

Tick   the minimum unit of price change permitted in a financial market by rule or custom.

Trading halt   a suspension of trading due to market conditions that prevent determination of a fair price or orderly trading.

Trading profit   a gain earned by a dealer due to a favorable price change on an inventory position.

Transparency   the dissemination of price, quantity, and other information about trading.

Uninformed traders   buyers and sellers, who are not acting on information, sometimes called **Noise** or **Liquidity traders**.

Upstairs market   the market for block trades on the NYSE.

IN THIS CHAPTER we explore various ways of trading. This chapter focuses on the secondary markets for trading equities, fixed-income securities, and currencies and the similar market in which many derivatives are created. First, we describe the participants in these financial markets and the reasons why financial markets exist. Specifically, we

- describe the various roles that investors and market professionals can play in secondary markets
- explain how secondary markets create value
- describe the characteristics of secondary markets

Next, we explain how secondary markets operate, including

- the types of orders that can be placed and rules concerning their execution
- exchange and over-the-counter trading
- call and continuous markets

---

1. INTRODUCTION

During the last fifteen years, there has been an explosion of interest in the area of financial economics known as market microstructure. We define **microstructure** as the study of the way markets are organized and the effect of this organization on prices, transactions costs, liquidity, risk, and other market characteristics. In this book we restrict our attention to financial markets. By financial markets we mean the markets in which equities, fixed-income securities, derivatives, and currencies are created and subsequently traded. There are a surprising number of ways to trade financial assets. The same types of assets are traded in many different ways, and different ways of trading are found even within the same country. Also, regulations may not be the same for different financial assets within the same country and for the same financial asset in different countries. These differences in ways of trading and regulation affect the costs of trading, the ease of trading, and the risk faced by investors.

The growth of interest in microstructure has been fueled by several trends. One is the increasing availability of transaction data – every trade and quote on a financial market. Another is the reduction in the cost of computer processing and storage, making the analysis of large data sets more feasible. And a third is the growth of worldwide interest in using financial markets, especially stock markets, to raise capital.

A financial market is a set of institutional arrangements designed to facilitate the transfer of ownership of financial instruments from one financial investor to another. This chapter describes the characteristics of secondary markets in which equities, fixed-income securities, derivatives, and currencies are traded. A secondary market is the market for trading of equities, fixed income-securities, warrants, and currencies after the initial creation and sale of these assets to investors. Derivatives originate in markets that share many characteristics of these secondary markets. From now on in this chapter, when we refer to secondary markets, we include the markets in which derivatives are created.

Section 2 describes why financial markets exist and who participates in these markets. Topics covered include the economic role of markets, market participants, and the characteristics that are used to evaluate markets. Section 3 explores the how of markets – the way trading is actually conducted. The trading venue section describes various types of secondary markets, and the next section explains the most common types of market orders. Then we turn to several topics related to the way trading is done. A summary wraps up the chapter.

2. WHY FINANCIAL MARKETS EXIST AND WHO PARTICIPATES IN THESE MARKETS

2.1. ECONOMIC FUNCTIONS OF SECONDARY MARKETS

Secondary markets reduce the cost of capital by providing liquidity, price discovery, and risk transfer capability. For this reason corporations and individuals are willing to pay substantial amounts to create these markets. Examination of the real resources devoted to financial markets just in the USA alone illustrates this point. In 1996 there were 406,000 individuals employed as sales representatives in the securities and financial services field.[1] Of course there are also many other types of workers in the financial sector.[2] Further, many individuals work for US state and federal regulatory agencies such as the Securities and Exchange Commission (USSEC) and the Commodity Futures Trading Commission (USCFTC). Obviously the fact that investors are willing to pay for such a large amount of resources indicates that these markets are of great value. But investors also view these resources as costs that need to be minimized.

Liquidity is the ability to buy or sell an asset readily, at low cost and without substantial impact on its price. Some prefer the term **marketability** instead of liquidity. In this book we use the terms "liquidity" and "marketability" interchangeably. Liquidity reduces the cost of capital because investors value liquidity. Liquidity gives them the option of selling their investment if they need funds unexpectedly or if their assessment of the invest-ment changes. Consequently, investors are willing to accept a lower return on more liquid investments. Assets that are actively traded are **thick**, and those that are inactively traded are **thin**. **Nonsynchronous trading** (or **thin trading**) refers to the fact that assets do not all trade at the same time, so that the trades are not contemporaneous in time. The most recent trade for a security does not reflect information that has come to the market since the time of that trade. Hence, the thicker a stock, the more recent the information that is likely to be reflected in its price at any randomly selected time. See box 2.1 for a discussion of thin trading and an illustration of some of the reasons why it is important.

BOX 2.1
Thin trading

Thick securities trade more often than thin securities, but, regardless of how often securi-ties trade, none trades at every instant. Our ability to see that securities do not trade at the same time depends to some extent on how we record trade times. If we recorded the time of security trades in nanoseconds, we would see that very few actually occur at the same time. Thin, or nonsynchronous, trading is an issue when comparing prices of securities or when comparing returns, which, of course, are computed from prices. As an example, the **holding period return** is $(P_t - P_{t-1})/P_t$, where P_t is the price of a security in period t. Because they actually occur at different times, the prices and returns for trades of different securities may reflect different information. The fact that not all the trades reflect the most recent infor-mation can lead to problems such as:

1. Suppose we want to study how a particular type of news affects security prices. Following a news event, it takes time for the news to become fully reflected in prices. Hence, our ability to ascertain how the news affects different securities is hampered to some extent by the fact that each price occurs at a different time, so that the information is reflected more fully in some prices than in others.
2. Mutual funds are organizations that own a portfolio of securities. Most mutual funds sell shares in their fund and repurchase shares from stockholders based on the closing prices, which represent the last trade price of the day, of the stocks in their portfolio. The thinner the security, the less the end-of-the-day price reflects the most recent information. Hence, to some extent the mutual fund's stockholders are buying and selling at prices that reflect out-of-date information.
3. In the regression of the returns on a security against the returns on the market (rep-resented by a market index such as the S&P 500), **beta** is the coefficient of the return on the market index. Beta is a popular measure of how a security's price moves in relation to the market. It is well known that if a security is thinner than the index, the estimate of beta is biased downward. This result occurs because, when the index values are moving, the security's prices do not appear to move. The secu-rity's price probably would have changed if there had been a trade, but we do not observe the change. If a security is thicker than the index, the estimate of beta is biased upward. There have been numerous efforts to adjust betas for this thin trading bias. McInish and Wood (1986) provide a review and an assessment of these techniques.
4. Some derivatives markets trade financial instruments whose prices are based on the prices of equities traded on stock exchanges. The value of the derivative cannot be measured exactly, because some of the equity prices are stale. The thinner the equi-ties, the more difficult it is to price the derivative.

Another important benefit of secondary markets is that they provide information concerning the value of assets that is useful to individuals, businesses, and governments in decision making and planning. The signals concerning asset values, interest rates, exchange rates, and the prices of other financial products are important in helping investors make decisions about the allocation of capital among potential investments. The process by which financial markets arrive at prices for assets is called price discovery. **Price discovery** is the identification of the equilibrium or market-clearing price. **Equilibrium**, of course, means that the number of units of an asset that investors seek to buy matches the number of units that investors want to sell, so that there is no pressure for a change in price. Economists often describe markets in which there is an auctioneer who finds a market-clearing price for which there is no excess demand or supply. This type of equilibrium for which there is a single market-clearing price is referred to as **Walrasian equilibrium**. All buyers and sellers who are willing to trade at the established price are accommodated in a Walrasian market. All sellers who are not accommodated seek a higher price for their assets, and all buyers who are not accommodated seek to pay a lower price. Since these bids and asks are away from the equilibrium price, they cannot be executed at this time. Attainment of an equilibrium price is facilitated if all buyers and sellers are small and meet in a central location, at a particular time, and fully reveal the number of shares they seek to buy and sell at each price.

The **bid** is the price that buyers are willing to pay for an asset, and the **ask**, or **offer**, is the price that sellers demand for an asset. In equilibrium, the ask must be greater than the bid. Otherwise trading would take place until either the demand or the supply were exhausted. If the ask and the bid are equal, trading will take place at that price. If the bid temporarily exceeds the ask, the trading price will have to be determined according to the rules of the particular market where the order is placed. The difference between the ask and the bid is called the **spread**. The spread can be viewed as a cost of trading.

In a Walrasian market there is no spread. The existence of a bid–ask spread is evidence of Walrasian disequilibrium, in that there is not a single market-clearing price. The spread reflects the need to pay for liquidity. In markets with a positive spread, a non-Walrasian equilibrium can be established as long as the trades at the ask and the trades at the bid are such that there is no pressure for the bid and the ask to change. If a particular individual is assigned to provide market liquidity, generally, a non-Walrasian equilibrium requires that purchases at their bids are exactly matched by sales at their asks over a reasonable time period.

Knowledge of equilibrium prices of commodities of all kinds (such as grains, livestock, industrial materials, and precious metals) and of financial instruments (stocks, bonds, and other financial products) provides valuable information for use in contracting and planning. By providing a way for producers and investors to transfer risk among them, financial markets allow these market participants to avoid unwanted risk and thereby reduce production costs. The remainder of this section explores liquidity and price discovery in greater detail. The risk transfer aspects of financial markets are explored more fully in later chapters.

2.1.1. Liquidity

The chief way in which secondary markets reduce the cost of capital is by providing liquidity. Liquidity has a number of dimensions, including width, depth, immediacy, and

Table 2.1 Discounts on purchase price of restricted common stock classified by size of transaction and sales of issuer, January 1, 1966, to June 30, 1969 (publicly held companies only)

Discount Sales of issuer (in '000 USD)	50.1% or more		40.1% to 50.0%		30.1% to 40.0%		20.1% to 30.0%		10.1% to 20.0%		0.1% to 10.0%		total	
	No.	USD size	No.	USD size	No.	USD size	No.	USD size	No.	USD size	No.	USD size	No.	USD size
Less than 100	11	2,895	7	2,554	17	19,642	16	12,197	6	12,267	9	12,566	66	62,122
100–999	7	474	2	1,221	0	—	1	500	1	1,019	2	3,878	13	7,091
1,000–4,999	8	4,606	13	8,171	12	10,675	15	9,866	10	9,352	3	2,295	61	44,964
5,000–19,999	6	1,620	4	1,147	13	25,986	25	27,238	24	21,441	47	12,750	119	90,183
20,000–99,999	3	606	3	4,373	6	11,499	8	11,818	18	22,232	17	36,482	55	87,009
100,000 or more	2	1,805	0	—	2	2,050	3	7,904	10	24,959	7	10,833	24	47,551
Total	37	12,005	29	17,466	50	69,853	68	69,523	69	91,270	85	78,804	338	338,920

Source: Discounts involved in purchases of common stock, in U.S. 92nd Congress, 1st Session, *House Institutional Investor Study Report of the Securities and Exchange Commission* (Washington, DC: US Government Printing Office, (Mar. 10, 1971), 5:2444–56 (Document No. 92-64, Part 5).

resiliency (Harris 1990). Width refers to a specific type of cost of transacting, the spread. (A detailed discussion of transactions costs, including the spread, is provided in chapter 3.) More liquid investments have lower execution costs. **Depth** is the size (i.e., number of shares, number of contracts) of a financial investment that can be traded at a given price. **Immediacy** measures the speed with which orders of a given size can be executed at a particular cost. The more quickly a transaction can be executed without additional cost, the better. **Resiliency** measures the speed with which prices return to their initial level after they change in response to a large trade by uninformed traders.

Unless further specified, in this book general references to liquidity should be taken to mean the willingness of market participants to fill orders quickly at a reasonable cost. If this willingness is greater, the liquidity of the market is greater. Liquidity has value. To assess its value, we examine letter stock. Companies in the USA sometimes issue or sell letter stock in connection with mergers or to raise money quickly in private placements. **Letter stock** is stock issued in the USA that is not registered with the USSEC. Under US law, this lack of registration means that the stock cannot be sold freely as long as the restriction lasts. Hence, letter stock is identical in all respects to publicly traded stock of the same corporation except that it is not registered and therefore has lower liquidity. The duration of the restrictions on trading varies from one situation to another, but usually lasts for 2–3 years. Thus, differences in the prices of letter and nonletter stock indicate the value of liquidity.[3] Since the value of the letter stock is less than that of comparable registered stock, the letter stock is said to sell at a discount. (For additional discussion of marketability discounts see Pratt 1981.) The size of the discount indicates the value of liquidity.

In 1970 the USSEC conducted a study of the discounts on letter stock sales. Excerpts from the study are presented in table 2.1. These data are from the most comprehensive study of its type. While the data are old, there is no reason to believe that the insights gained would be different if the study were replicated today. The exhibit shows the range of percentage discounts from open market prices categorized by the size of the issuing firm in terms of USD sales. Seventeen percent (11 out of 66) of the smallest firms in the sample reported discounts of more than 50 percent, whereas only 8 percent of the largest firms reported discounts as large as 50 percent. Assuming that the discounts for the over 50 percent category are 60 percent on average, and using the approximate midpoint for each of the other categories (i.e., 5 percent for 0.1 percent to 10.0 percent, etc.), the average discount is 25 percent if each observation is equally weighted. In another study, Silber (1991) found that even credit-worthy companies offered discounts of more than 30 percent to sell restricted securities. In one case a discount of 84 percent was needed to sell the shares.

One factor that is important in determining the liquidity of an asset is the size of the market for the asset. (For an alternative view see Crabbe and Turner 1995.) If there are many potential buyers and sellers for the same asset, the market is generally more liquid. The number of potential buyers and sellers is greatly affected by the homogeneity of the asset. Assets that are homogeneous are alike. Real estate is an example of an asset with low homogeneity. Each lot, building, or plant is essentially unique. Since each piece of real estate has a unique location, it also has a unique value. Hence, real estate has low liquidity. Large price discounts must be given to sell it quickly, and transaction costs are often 5 percent or more. Investors require a higher rate of return on illiquid assets such as real estate.

Most collectibles also have low liquidity. The primary reason is again that each item is unique. It is difficult to attract a large number of buyers or sellers for a given item. By contrast, most financial investments are relatively liquid. Typically, there are numerous assets of the same type. Each share of Disney stock is like every other share. Each Thai bhat (TBH) is like every other. This homogeneity allows for the development of liquid markets.

Of course, a distinction needs to be made between pure investments and investments that also combine elements of consumption. The latter might include residential real estate and art. To the extent that individuals derive pleasure from owning these particular types of assets, the required return may be lower than it is for similar investments with similar risk characteristics but without any consumption benefits.

While the liquidity differences are not as great from one publicly traded investment to another, these liquidity differences do affect value. Consider two assets that are identical except that the cost of liquidity for one is 1 percent of asset value higher. Amihud and Mendelson (1988) report that the asset with the higher cost of liquidity requires an additional monthly return of 0.21 percent. While this may seem high, the authors note that trading costs are incurred repeatedly throughout the life of an asset. Therefore, the current value of the asset reflects not just a one-time transaction cost but the present value of all future transaction costs.

Consider an investment yielding a perpetuity of 12 USD per year and whose required rate of return is 24 percent per year. The value of the investment is the capitalized value of the cash flow at the required rate of return, USD 12/0.24 = USD 50. The return earned by investors must be sufficient to cover not only their required return but also their transaction costs. Therefore, we can view transaction costs as affecting the required return (an alternative approach would be to reduce cash flows by the amount of transaction costs). Thus, our assumed required return of 24 percent reflects the current level of transaction costs for this investment.

An increase in liquidity can lower transaction costs by decreasing the bid–ask spread. Suppose that the quote on our investment is 49.50–50.50, a spread of 1 point, or 2 percent, of the investment's value $(1/((49.50 + 50.50)/2))$. If the spread could be reduced to 0.50 so that the new quote was 49.75 bid and 50.25 ask, the new percentage spread would be 1 percent. This is a reduction in the spread of 1 percent of asset value. The reduced spread comes about through an increase in liquidity. As noted, Amihud and Mendelson estimate that a reduction in the spread of 1 percent of the value of the asset will lower the required return by 0.21 percent per month, or 2.52 percent per year. Hence, the increased liquidity will lower the required return from 24 percent to 21.48 percent. The decrease in the required rate of return will, in turn, increase the value of the investment to USD 12/21.48 = USD 55.86. In other words, the value of the investment has increased by 11.7 percent (USD 55.86/USD 50) due to the increase in liquidity.

Longstaff (1995) uses a very interesting options approach to establish upper bounds on the value of liquidity and presents evidence that actual discounts approximate these levels. Potential percentage discounts are presented in table 2.2. Even restrictions on marketability of a day can result in discounts of up to 1.268 percent for volatile stocks. Regulators who close markets even for short times need to recognize that these restrictions on trading can result in meaningful declines in asset values. And the discount for restrictions on marketability of 5 years can exceed 65 percent for volatile stocks.

Table 2.2 Upper bounds for percentage discounts for lack of marketability[a]

Marketability restriction period	σ = 0.10	σ = 0.20	σ = 0.30
1 day	0.421	0.844	1.268
5 days	0.944	1.894	2.852
10 days	1.337	2.688	4.052
20 days	1.894	3.817	5.768
30 days	2.324	4.691	7.100
60 days	3.299	6.683	10.153
90 days	4.052	8.232	12.542
180 days	5.768	11.793	18.082
1 year	8.232	16.984	26.276
2 years	11.793	24.643	38.605
5 years	19.128	40.979	65.772

[a] The standard deviations, σ, correspond to the range typically observed for equity securities.
Source: Longstaff 1995, p. 1772. Reprinted by permission of the *Journal of Finance*.

2.1.2. Price discovery

Price discovery is one of the central functions of secondary markets. Price discovery is the process whereby market participants attempt to find an equilibrium price. There are numerous methods used throughout the world. The relative ability of various market mechanisms to discover equilibrium prices has not received a great deal of study by either academics or security industry professionals. As a result, little is known about the relative performance of various trading systems.

In addition to providing the actual prices at which trading takes place, price discovery also provides information that is useful in making economic decisions. Each month the Bureau of Economic Analysis of the US Department of Commerce publishes an index of leading economic indicators. One of the eleven components of the index is the change in stock prices. Derivatives trading provides information concerning expected future prices of a myriad types of commodities, currencies, precious metals, and interest rates. Businesses can use these to determine whether to expand production and to aid in entering into pricing commitments with their customers. Long-term interest rates implicitly carry information about expected future short-term interest rates. Both governments and businesses use these indicators in their planning.

2.2. MARKET PARTICIPANTS

The owners of financial investments are often referred to as the "buy side." The buy side designation does not depend on whether a particular individual or institution is buying or selling in a secondary market transaction. Instead, the **buy side** comprises all investors, regardless of whether they are buyers or sellers at a particular time. This terminology arises from the idea that investments are sold and not bought. In other words, investors do not spontaneously call a broker to trade securities. Instead, brokers initiate transactions by calling potential clients. This, of course, is not nearly as accurate a description as it once was, given the increasing sophistication of individual and institutional investors. But the terminology persists.

Transactions among buy side individuals and institutions usually require the services of intermediaries. Intermediaries involved in helping investors buy or sell financial investments are collectively called the **sell side**. The sell side earns revenue from the transactions of the buy side and also from advising the buy side concerning investment strategies. Sometimes the role of the sell side is that of a broker. The **broker** is the client's agent. In fact, in the USA the terms "broker" and "agent" mean the same thing. A broker is not a party to the transaction and does not assume risk due to fluctuations in the price of the investment. **Price risk**, risk of loss due to a change in the price of an asset, is entirely that of the client. Of course, the broker might face liability if the order is not executed according to the instructions of the client. The broker might (1) buy the wrong stock, (2) buy a larger or smaller quantity than instructed, (3) fail to execute the order entirely, or (4) delay excessively in executing the order. For their services, brokers typically charge a commission, which must generally be disclosed.

In some cases sell side intermediaries act as dealers rather than as brokers. A **dealer** is a person or firm engaged in the business of buying and selling financial investments to make a profit. How can those operating a business be distinguished from investors who are simply trading securities? Evidence that can be used to differentiate a dealer from an investor includes whether the individual or firm solicits business or effects transactions for others.

Dealers do not charge commissions. Instead, dealers make money from the markup or markdown on their merchandise. A **markup** is the difference between what the dealer paid for the financial instruments and what the customer pays the dealer. This difference is the dealer's fee for executing the trade. Thus, a dealer may buy 1,000 shares of stock at USD 11 from a client. Subsequently, the dealer may sell the stock for USD $11\frac{1}{8}$ to another client or to another dealer, making a profit of USD 125 on 100 shares. But the dealer bears the risk that the stock will decline in value before it can be sold. If the investment does decline in value, the dealer may lose money. Of course, if the dealer is to stay in business, the profits on the winning transactions must more than compensate for the losses on the losing transactions. A **markdown** is the difference between the amount the dealer pays a client for an asset and the amount the dealer receives upon selling the asset. To recap, when a dealer sells to a client, the price may include a fee called a "markup," and when a dealer sells to a client, the price may be less a fee called a "markdown." The markup/markdown may be shown separately from the asset price, or in some cases it may be combined with the asset price, making it impossible to tell what fees the broker actually charged.

In some cases dealers hold small amounts of each investment for short time periods, which can often be as little as a few minutes or less. This would be typical of small stock transactions in the USA. Some dealers may be willing to take large positions to facilitate a client's transaction. The inventory position is worked off over as short a period of time as possible, consistent with not disturbing the market price too much. The dealer has price risk and risk of loss due to a change in the value of an investment, as long as this inventory is held.

In judging the reasonableness of a markup, reference should be made to the current market value of the investment rather than to historical values. If the dealer paid USD 8 for the investment, but the current market price is USD 11, the economic markup would be figured from USD 11. The gain from USD 8 to USD 11 would be **trading profit**, not markup.

Another way of classifying individuals and institutions that are buying and selling securities is by the amount of information that they have. An **informed trader** is acting on information concerning the value of the security. We need to distinguish an informed trader from one trading on inside information. **Inside information** is any information about a security issuer obtained through a position of trust. This is the type of information that would be possessed by senior employees, directors, and large shareholders of a firm. In many countries it is illegal to trade based on inside information. But inside information is not the only source of informed trading. Information useful in trading is often developed through superior analysis. A firm trading commodities might develop a superior way of forecasting weather conditions that affect crops. Or a bond trader might develop a model for valuing more accurately a particular type of instrument. Both these types of information might be useful in trading.

Buyers and sellers who are not acting on information are called **uninformed traders** or **liquidity traders**. An individual investor may decide to sell some shares of stock in order to raise funds to buy a car or a house. Investors may use part of their salary to purchase stocks and bonds each month. A financial institution may buy or sell securities in response to inflows and outflows of funds from its customers.

Financial market participants can also be classified according to the length of time their positions are held. **Scalpers** attempt to buy and sell quickly to take advantage of minimal fluctuations in prices. **Day traders** buy and sell or sell and buy within the same day and rarely hold positions from one trading day to the next. **Position traders** hold positions for days, weeks, months, or even years. Position traders are more common in equity and fixed-income markets. On the other hand, scalpers and day traders are more common in futures and derivatives markets due to their relatively low transaction costs.

2.3. CHARACTERISTICS OF MARKETS

In order to serve their economic purpose, it is generally believed that financial markets should be efficient, fair, and orderly. Efficiency is closely related to the cost of transacting. Fairness and orderliness are discussed in this section. Transaction costs are discussed in a later chapter.

2.3.1. Fairness

Financial markets are built on trust. Deals for large sums are consummated verbally, so reliability and honesty of all participants is essential. A fair market is free from fraud and manipulation. In a fair market there are mechanisms for promoting market integrity and for promoting fidelity between the sell side and the buy side. The Financial Executives Institute is a professional organization with more than 13,000 senior-level financial managers from 7,000 companies in the USA and Canada. In a survey of a subset of the membership, the institute asked these executives to rank their level of concern about 14 economic issues, including recessions, interest rates, and inflation. Three of the areas of greatest concern were insider trading, securities market fraud and abuse, and honesty and ethics of stockbrokers (NYSE 1990).

Probably one of the most widespread violations of market trust is frontrunning. **Frontrunning** is the use by a broker-dealer of a customer's information for the firm's own profit or that of its employees or other clients. Information might be contained in the order itself (Goldberg 1979). Suppose that an institution places an order to buy 100,000 shares of an illiquid stock for which the average daily volume is, say, 20,000 shares. This order might be expected to increase the price of the stock, at least temporarily. After learning of the customer's order, the broker-dealer might execute an order in this stock for their own account and execute the customer's order only thereafter. Thus, the broker-dealer would gain from any change in price due to the order. The customer, on the other hand, would probably lose, since it is probable that the cost of the customer's shares would be greater.

It should be made clear that frontrunning is different from information leakage. **Information leakage** is the revelation of information in the process of executing an order. If a broker-dealer is attempting to assemble a large block of stock for a client, it is often necessary to talk to a number of potential sellers. Some of these might use the knowledge gained in the search process in executing their own trades.[4] It can be argued that information leakage is good, in that it facilitates price discovery. On the other hand, investors placing orders in markets with substantial information leakage would naturally view this as a disadvantage.

The discussion of information leakage leads naturally to the topic of transparency. **Transparency** is concerned with what information about trading is disseminated, when it is disseminated, and who receives the information. In general, exchange markets throughout the world have considerably more transparency than markets for bonds and currencies. The market operated by the US National Association of Security Dealers (NASD) called NASDAQ (which stands for the NASD Automated Quotation system) also has considerable transparency, because it disseminates a great deal of information to participants and investors in real time. The issue of transparency can be broken down into dissemination of pre-trade and post-trade information (IOSC 1992).

Consider post-trade information first. Some make a distinction between post-trade disclosure and reporting. If the goal of transparency is to prevent manipulation and fraud, it may be sufficient that transaction prices and quantities are reported to exchange officials and/or government officials without further public dissemination, especially on a real-time basis. Others argue that when publication of real-time price and volume data is not mandatory, investors are less able to monitor the quality of trade executions. By comparing their own prices with those of others, investors can better ascertain whether their broker obtained a good price. Differences exist from one market center to another concerning what information is considered proprietary. The Toronto Stock Exchange and the Australian Stock Exchange release the identification number of the broker on each side of every transaction. These exchanges believe that this information is useful to the investment community, and that its release does not harm brokers. In Toronto brokers consider an appearance on the list of major buyers or sellers of a stock to be a good form of advertising. But the NYSE considers this information to be confidential.

Delay in reporting trade executions may aid in the execution of block trades by increasing the willingness of a dealer to take the other side of a trade. Suppose that an institution seeking to sell a block of stock approaches an exchange dealer. If the dealer buys the block for his or her own account, subsequently the stock must be sold. If others in the market know of the dealer's position, they may sell, driving the price down, before the dealer has a chance to sell. Having sold first, these traders can then buy the dealer's stock at an even lower price and make a profit at the dealer's expense. On the NYSE the trade would be reported within a few minutes, but when the London Stock Exchange (LSE) operated as a dealer market, dealers were permitted to delay reporting large block trades for 90 minutes or longer.

Turning to pre-trade issues, institutions are quite naturally concerned with information leakage that can damage the quality of their execution. Another area of concern is the dissemination of information to all market participants prior to the resumption of trading following trading halts. These halts may have occurred due to temporary imbalances in supply and demand or due to the markets having been closed. Investors who do not have an adequate feel for the prices that are likely to prevail when trading resumes have difficulty placing strategic orders. Thus, issues connected with the dissemination of advisory quotes and related information prior to periodic trading is of major concern to investors.

Another way in which brokers violate their clients' trust is **churning**, the fraudulent practice of inducing customers to trade for the purpose of generating commissions. In the USA brokers found to have churned an account can be fined, or even expelled from the industry, and sometimes customers can recover the commissions and perhaps even their trading losses. To churn an account, a broker must have control, but the account need not be **discretionary**, in which the authority to trade in the account is formally turned over to the broker. Instead, the broker may exercise effective control through superior knowledge, intimidation, and the like. Also, there must be an element of **scienter**, the intent to deceive, manipulate, or defraud. Negligence alone is not sufficient.

2.3.2. Orderly markets

The concept of orderly markets can have different meanings. One aspect of orderly markets is the continuity of prices from trade to trade. It is probably undesirable to have trade prices fluctuate widely from trade to trade due to temporary imbalances in supply and demand. Exchanges address this concern in a variety of ways, including the imposition of stabilization duties on certain members (specialists on the NYSE) or the prohibition of price movements outside a specified range (Tokyo, Chicago Board of Trade).

Volatility is also of concern to investors. But care must be taken in discussing volatility. Volatility may simply reflect the changing asset values in response to world events. But while volatility reflecting the discovery of appropriate asset prices is desirable, it is possible that the operating rules of a financial center could increase volatility either on a trade-to-trade basis or over longer periods. This type of volatility would be undesirable. Also, governments might induce unnecessary and undesirable volatility through erratic economic policies. To provide historical perspective, table 2.3 reports the 25 largest and smallest monthly percentage returns on the NYSE index during the period 1802 through the crash of October 1987. The table clearly shows that even portfolios comprising whole markets can have significant price movements on both the upside and the downside. Given the choice between two investments with the same expected long-run return, but with different intermediate volatility, most investors would prefer the investment with the lower volatility. Hence, the level of volatility, especially of the market as a whole, can affect the return that investors demand and, thereby,

Table 2.3 The 25 largest positive and negative returns, 1802–October 1987

Smallest percentage return		Largest percentage return	
September 1931	−28.79	April 1933	37.68
October 1857	−24.37	August 1932	36.19
March 1938	−23.46	July 1932	32.68
May 1940	−22.02	June 1938	23.49
October 1987	−21.64	May 1933	21.10
May 1861	−20.29	March 1858	17.59
May 1932	−20.21	December 1857	17.24
October 1929	−19.56	October 1974	16.80
April 1932	−17.87	September 1939	15.95
July 1893	−17.81	January 1863	15.72
June 1930	−15.66	October 1862	15.43
September 185	−14.31	April 1938	14.36
October 1907	−14.00	July 1837	14.10
January 1842	−13.84	May 1898	13.80
September 193	−13.45	June 1931	13.75
December 1931	−13.34	May 1843	13.64
May 1931	−13.27	April 1834	13.53
February 1933	−13.19	January 1975	13.48
December 1860	−13.08	August 1891	13.40
October 1932	−12.89	June 1933	13.38
September 193	−12.32	January 1934	12.96
November 1929	−12.04	January 1987	12.82
March 1939	−11.86	December 1873	12.81
July 1914	−11.70	October 1879	12.79
November 1855	−11.64	October 1885	12.60

Source: Schwert 1990.

the cost of capital. Therefore, it is desirable to establish policies that do not interfere with price discovery yet at the same time do not induce unnecessary volatility.

3. HOW MARKETS OPERATE

In this section we deal with how trading takes place in various locations or venues. We also describe issues associated with trading, such as the types of orders that can be placed, the units of trading, how large trades are transacted, and other issues related to trading.

3.1. TRADING VENUES

Trading can be conducted on exchanges or off exchanges in the over-the-counter market. Exchange trading is largely confined to stocks, futures contracts, and options. Both stock

BOX 2.2
A legal view of exchanges

In the text we provide definitions based on ways of operating and economic functions. Here we discuss the legal definition of an exchange in the USA. Under the US Securities and Exchange Act of 1934, an exchange is "any organization, association, or group of persons, whether incorporated or unincorporated, which constitutes, maintains, or provides a market place or facilities for bringing together purchasers and sellers of securities or for otherwise performing with respect to securities the functions commonly performed by a stock exchange as that term is generally understood, and includes the market place and the market facilities maintained by such exchange." The Exchange Act requires that exchanges register with the Securities and Exchange Commission (USSEC) unless the USSEC grants an exemption. According to Domowitz (1994) "even very recent decisions have deferred to [US]SEC interpretations of what the phrase 'generally understood' is supposed to mean." In other words, an exchange is whatever the USSEC generally understands an exchange to be. Note that the Exchange Act does not apply to futures. Futures exchanges are regulated by the US Commodity Futures Trading Commission established under the Commodity Futures Trading Commission Act of 1974. (For additional information see Domowitz 1996.)

and options are traded over-the-counter. Most bonds and currencies and many stocks are traded over-the-counter. Further, in recent years, nontraditional trading forums called proprietary trading systems (PTSs) have developed. While PTSs are technically over-the-counter, they compete with traditional forms of over-the-counter trading. This section explores each of these ways of trading.[5]

An **exchange** is an organization whose members trade financial assets in a given location such as a trading floor or a computer. Box 2.2 contrasts our definition with the legal definition in the USA. Typically, only members can trade with each other on an exchange. Nonmembers must arrange transactions through members. The terminology associated with exchanges often comes from decades ago, when operations were much different than today. A membership on an exchange is called a **seat**, even though members of leading exchanges with floor trading systems rarely have an opportunity to sit down. In a carry-over from the days when trading was done in coffeehouses, messengers on the floor of the London Stock Exchange were called "waiters." There is typically a market for exchange seats, and members owning seats may sell their seats to qualified owners. Some exchanges limit ownership to individuals, and some have only corporate members. Occasionally, an exchange will offer new seats for sale directly. The value of an exchange seat is determined by supply and demand and depends on factors such as the number of seats, the volume of trading on the exchange, and the commission structure. The average price for a seat on the New York Stock Exchange in 1997 was 1,750,000 USD.

Most exchanges now have web sites that provide much information, often including a glossary of terms, details of how the exchange operates, and the types of financial instruments traded on the exchange. Box 2.3 provides the web address of a number of these sites.

Secondary market trading that does not occur on an exchange is called **over-the-counter** trading. With the increasing sophistication of off-exchange, computer-based markets, it is becoming harder and harder to distinguish many types of exchange trading from over-the-counter trading.

BOX 2.3
Web sites for exchanges and related organizations

Many exchanges have web sites. The site for the International Federation of Stock Exchanges, http://www.fibv.com/, provides links for many exchanges. Nanyang Technological University also provides links to many exchanges at its web site: http://www.ntu.edu.sg/library/sxsm-az.htm. The site at http://www.qualisteam.com/eng/act.shtml and the site at http://www.nyse.com/public/intview/4b/4bix.htm provide additional links.

The web addresses of selected individual exchanges are as follows:

Australian Stock Exchange: http://www.asx.com.au/
Bolsa de Valores de São Paulo: http://www.bovespa.com.br/indexi.htm
Bolsa Mexicana de Valores: http://www.bmv.com.mx/
Chicago Board of Trade: http://www.cbot.com/index2.html
Chicago Mercantile Exchange: http://www.cme.com/
Hong Kong Stock Exchange: http://www.sehk.com.hk/english/default.htm
Johannesburg Stock Exchange: http://www.jse.co.za/
London International Financial Futures and Options Exchange: http://www.liffe.com/
London Stock Exchange: http://www.londonstockex.co.uk/
New York Stock Exchange: http://www.nyse.com/
Stock Exchange of Singapore: http://www.ses.com.sg/
Tokyo Stock Exchange: http://www.tse.or.jp/eindex.html
Toronto Stock Exchange: http://www.tse.com/

Many of these sites have a glossary of terms. See, e.g., the New York Stock Exchange, the London International Financial Futures and Options Exchange, the Tokyo Stock Exchange, and the Toronto Stock Exchange.

3.1.1. Floor-based and screen-based exchanges

In the past, all exchanges were floor-based, each having a trading floor where members gathered to trade. The world's major exchanges, including the New York Stock Exchange, the Tokyo Stock Exchange, the Chicago Board of Trade, and many others, still operate in this way. The Pacific Stock Exchange in the USA has two trading floors, one in San Francisco, another in Los Angeles. With the growing power and sophistication of computers has come the advent of screen-based exchanges. Computer-based exchanges do not have a trading floor. Instead, the members submit their orders to a central computer, which automatically executes trades according to the rules of the exchange. Computer exchanges have the potential to reduce transaction costs by reducing the number of people involved in executing trades. Errors in the execution process may be reduced through reduction in the number of individuals handling an order. Computer exchanges may also alter the level of transparency, since observers who are typically part of the crowd on a floor-based exchange are absent from computer-based exchanges. Further, information that may have been difficult to capture on a floor-based exchange can be saved by the computer.

The first exchange to adopt computer-based trading was the Toronto Stock Exchange, which developed its Computer Assisted Trading System (CATS) in the late 1960s. Initially, only thin stocks were traded on CATS, but in 1997 the exchange leadership finally overcame opposition, and the Toronto Stock Exchange closed its trading floor. Following the lead of the Toronto Stock Exchange, most new exchanges that have been established have been computer-based. The Australian Stock Exchange, which was formed through the merger of a number of stock exchanges in Australia, has been computer-based since its inception. Eurex, which was formed from the merger of Deutsche Terminbourse and SOFFEX in 1998, operates a screen-based futures exchange. Moreover, many exchanges have closed their trading floors and switched to screen-based trading. These include the London Stock Exchange, MATIF, the Stock Exchange of Singapore, the Kuala Lumpur Stock Exchange, the Paris Stock Exchange, and the Vancouver Stock Exchange. The Sydney Futures Exchange (SFE press release, October 23, 1998) and LIFFE (*Wall Street Journal*, September 15, 1998) have announced forthcoming switches of their security market design from floor-based to screen-based trading. The CBOT (*Financial Times*, June 6, 1998) is studying the possibility of switching from floor-based to computer-based trading.

Many exchanges have stringent requirements that must be satisfied before a security can be traded on the exchange. **Listed** means that an instrument has been approved for regular trading on an exchange. A number of exchanges have more than one class of listings. On the Tokyo Stock Exchange the 150 most active stocks are classified in the First Section and are traded on the stock-trading floor. The remaining Japanese domestic stocks, along with nondomestic stocks, are traded on a computer using the Computer-assisted Order Routing and Execution System (CORES). Of the 1,800 companies with securities listed on the Vancouver Stock Exchange, about 300 more mature companies are classified as Senior Board companies that receive additional services from the exchange. But more than 80 percent are classified as Venture shares. Many of these are small start-up companies. Some exchanges, such as the Oporto Stock Exchange in Portugal, permit the trading of unlisted securities.

Today many major companies list their shares on multiple exchanges. Royal Dutch Shell is traded primarily on the London Stock Exchange, but it is also traded in Belgium, France, and Germany. Bank depository receipts representing the shares of Royal Dutch Shell are traded on a number of exchanges in the USA. At the beginning of 1999 the shares of more than 50 non-Japanese companies were traded on the Tokyo Stock Exchange, though this is down substantially from the 125 companies traded in 1991.[6] In the mid-1990s the Tokyo Stock Exchange eased listing requirements in an effort to attract foreign firms, but these efforts have yet to bear fruit. The NYSE actively seeks listings of non-US firms, and at the beginning of 1999 about 500 non-US firms were trading on the NYSE. Werner and Kleidon (1996) examine stocks cross-listed in New York and London and conclude that intraday patterns for these stocks follow those in the market in which the market is being traded rather than the home market. They also conclude that the order flow is segmented, so that traders prefer to trade in a nearby market. A study of trading in the shares of a major Malaysian conglomerate on the Stock Exchange of Singapore and the Kuala Lumpur Stock Exchange concludes that both exchanges contribute to the process whereby the equilibrium price is discovered (Ding et al. 1999). Non-US stocks listed on US exchanges have positive returns on the listing day, which is interpreted to mean that these listings increase the market value of the listing firm (Jayaraman, Shastri, and Tandon 1993). Moreover, the returns are the largest for firms listed on the NYSE or NASDAQ and for those using a depository receipt program to raise new equity (Miller 1999). On the other hand, the evidence that US firms benefit from listing on non-US exchanges is less persuasive. Positive returns are reported on the day the application is accepted, but negative returns are reported on the day trading begins (Lau, Diltz, and Apilado 1994).

3.1.2. Ownership of exchanges

Ownership of exchanges is usually vested in the members. The NYSE is typical. On May 17, 1792, 24 New York stockbrokers and merchants involved in buying and selling securities signed an agreement pledging to avoid "public auction," to collect a minimum commission on all transactions, and "to give preference to each other" in their dealings. At first, trading was outdoors, so that this agreement has subsequently come to be known as the "Buttonwood Agreement" after a tree located near the trading site. In inclement weather, trading was conducted in a nearby coffeehouse. The NYSE is still owned by its members, each of whom owns a seat.

Like other organizations, exchanges exist to serve their owners. Most exchanges are owned and controlled by investment bankers and dealers, the so-called sell side. Exchange rules and operating procedures are written by the exchange and often favor the interests of members over those of investors trading on the exchange. While this is no different than for other organizations, many investors do not realize that an exchange's ownership may affect the way trading is done. Over time there is a tendency for the rules of an exchange to become outdated. But these rules are often difficult to change because many members of the exchange benefit from the existing rules. Specific members who would be harmed by changes can often be identified, and the extent of the economic harm can be readily quantified. The identity of members who would benefit financially from changes is likely to be less certain. Moreover, there is an incentive to ignore benefits that would accrue to nonmembers. This is illustrated by the difficulty that the Toronto Stock Exchange faced in fully implementing its pioneering work in computerizing exchanges. Due to pressure from those handling trades on the floor, initially only thin issues were traded on CATS. It took exchange officials until 1997 to overcome resistance and switch fully from floor trading to screen-based trading.

There is increasing pressure to allow institutions to have direct access to exchanges. Large buy side institutions often believe that they have the expertise to trade without the need for a member to act as an intermediary. In fact, 17 institutions were not only members of, but actually owned, the DTB futures exchange in Germany until its merger in 1998. These institutions included commercial banks, savings banks, cooperative banks, regional banks, and private banks. Another unusual ownership arrangement is the Swedish Futures and Options Market, OM Stockholm, which is owned by OM Gruppen AB, a company listed on the Stockholm Stock Exchange. The Australian Stock Exchange members voted to restructure the ASX from a mutual company to a regular for-profit company. The government approved this change in ownership structure, and trading began in ASX shares in 1998. The ASX actually lists its own shares. Following the precedent of exchanges in Australia, Britain, Sweden, and Germany, in December 1998 the USSEC voted to allow US exchanges to operate as for-profit corporations.

3.1.3. Price limits and trading halts on exchanges

Almost all exchanges have provisions for stopping trading under some circumstances. These can be broadly classified as price limits and trading halts. **Price limits** prohibit trading at prices outside prescribed levels usually during a trading day. The Taiwan Stock Exchange prohibits trading at prices that are more than ±7 percent from the previous day's close. The Tokyo Stock Exchange prohibits trading at prices that differ from the previous day's close by a fixed yen amount rather than a percentage. Futures exchanges also often prohibit trading outside a prescribed range based on the previous day's trading prices. These limits too are usually in fixed monetary amounts rather than in percentages. The magnitude of the range typically varies from contract to contract and in general depends on the volatility of the underlying interest.

Trading halts stop trading completely for some period, after which time trading is resumed, although often subject to additional halts. Exchanges usually have a mechanism for halting trading if market conditions prevent the fair determination of prices or an orderly market. Trading may be halted pending unusual news announcements about a firm or if there is an unusual imbalance between the quantity of shares demanded and supplied. The Tokyo Stock Exchange enforces daily price limits on listed stocks based on the previous day's closing prices.

Following the market crash of October 1987, the NYSE implemented rules designed to close the market temporarily following large price declines. These rules, called **circuit breakers**, allow time for traders to make decisions off the exchange floor and, hopefully, provide liquidity. The circuit breakers halt trading for specified times, depending on the severity of the price decline. The point values for each level of circuit breaker are reset quarterly. Effective October 1, 1998, the following circuit breakers (rule 80B) were in effect:

1 *An 800-point drop in the Dow Jones Industrial Average (DJIA).* Trading is halted for 1 hour if the decline occurs before 2 p.m. and for 30 minutes if it occurs after 2 p.m. but before 2:30 p.m.
2 *An 1,600-point drop in the DJIA.* Trading is halted for 2 hours if the decline occurs before 1 p.m., for 1 hour if it occurs after 1 p.m. but before 2 p.m., and for the remainder of the day if it occurs after 2 p.m.
3 *An 2,350-point drop in the DJIA.* Trading is halted for the remainder of the day.

Program trading involves the trading of a basket of securities concurrently. On the NYSE the term is defined more specifically as trading strategies involving the purchase or sale of 15 or more stocks having a total market value of 1 million USD or more. **Index arbitrage** is a form of program trading in which the purchase or sale of a basket of stocks is accompanied by a corresponding trade in a derivative, such as a futures contract, to take advantage of prices differences in the equities and derivatives markets. Following moves of 50 points in the DJIA from the previous day's close, program trades in stocks comprising the S&P 500 are subject to a tick test. In down markets sell orders may be executed only on a plus or zero-plus tick; in up markets buy orders may be executed only on a minus or zero-minus tick.

The Chicago Mercantile Exchange (CME) coordinates circuit breakers with the NYSE on derivative products based on equities. Trading in these derivative products is halted when NYSE trading is halted. Contracts begin trading when a specified number of stocks have resumed trading on the NYSE. The CME also implements short 10-minute trading halts when prices decline by 2.5 percent and 5 percent.

3.1.4. Internet exchanges

There are more than 50 private markets in the USA, and as a result, in December 1998 the USSEC adopted rules governing private electronic trading systems.[7] These systems may choose to be regulated as broker–dealers or as exchanges. Those regulated as broker–dealers will face increasingly stringent requirements as their trading volume increases. Historically, institutional traders have used computer-based systems, but this is changing as individual investors "flock to the Internet to trade stocks. As a result, the Internet will become an increasingly important market. Several exchanges are planning Internet-based systems" (Wall Street Journal 1998). About 4 percent of US stock trading and 20 percent of all trading in NASDAQ stocks occurs on alternate trading systems. One USSEC official predicted that those levels might triple during the next three years.

In 1997 Texas Beef Group submitted an application to the Commodity Futures Trading Commission, the US futures regulatory body, to establish a new exchange. The exchange would trade live cattle derivatives initially. If the application is approved, the CFTC expects a number of similar applications to trade a wide variety of contracts. Texas Beef proposes to purchase **reinsurance** to provide additional clearing and settlement protection. One of the principal difficulties that Texas Beef faces in gaining approval for its proposal is the problem of security on the Internet (Morse 1997).[8]

3.1.5. Traditional over-the-counter trading

Over-the-counter trading may be informal. In the USA many stocks and almost all bonds are traded over-the-counter. Essentially all currency trading is over-the-counter. There is also a large volume of trading in derivatives over-the-counter. In the USA almost all securities firms must belong to the National Association of Security Dealers (NASD), a self-regulatory organization for the securities industry established by the US government. NASD organizes an electronic over-the-counter market, primarily in equities, called NASDAQ. The OTC Bulletin Board® is a regulated quotation service for market makers that displays real-time quotes, last-sale prices, and volume information in over-the-counter (OTC) equity securities.[9] The Bulletin Board is separate from NASDAQ, but the quotes are available over NASDAQ terminals. Market makers apply for permission to quote a firm on the Bulletin Board. All trades in US and Canadian issues and ADRs must be reported within 90 seconds, and all other trades may be reported the first business day following the trade (t + 1).

In the USA there are also other ways in which over-the-counter dealers communicate. Bond traders advertise in places such as the *Bond Buyer*, a publication devoted to the dissemination of bond quotes. The National Quotation Bureau (NQB) provides a weekly service for brokers commonly called the Pink Sheets® that lists market makers and quotes. An electronic version is distributed over data terminals once a day. These publications provide brokers with a way to identify dealers who make markets or have trading interests in particular securities.[10]

3.1.6. Proprietary trading systems

As a result of institutional interest in dealing with each other more directly and in avoiding established exchange and over-the-counter markets, a number of profit-making entities have established trading systems which they have marketed to institutions as alternatives to exchange trading. Since these businesses are privately owned, they are called "proprietary trading systems." A **proprietary trading system** (PTS) or **electronic communication network** (ECN) is a privately owned organization that facilitates trading among institutions without the use of the facilities of an exchange. PTSs, including POSIT and Instinet in the USA and Tradepoint in London, have been growing and taking market share away from the exchanges. The multinational information services company, Reuters Holdings, PLC, owns Instinet. Investment Technologies Group, Inc., which is owned by the US broker-dealer Jefferies & Co. in a joint venture with BARRA, a leading US investment advisor, operates POSIT. Tradepoint was incorporated in England and Wales in 1991. In 1992 the company became a publicly held firm through an offering of 2.1 million units comprising one share of common stock and 1 warrant. The leading underwriter was Canaccord Capital Corporation in Vancouver, British Columbia. The units were listed on the Vancouver Stock Exchange. Reuters Dealing 2000 and the Electronic Broking Service (EBS) are examples of PTSs for dealing in foreign exchange.[11]

3.2. ORDERS

To buy or sell in secondary markets, financial investors must give the broker–dealer an order. An **order** is an instruction to a broker–dealer concerning the purchase or sale of a financial investment. Many different types of orders are permitted in various markets. Also, it is often possible to restrict orders in various ways (box 2.4 presents a number of additional order

---

BOX 2.4
Illustrative types of orders and order designations

Additional orders types

Difference order   sell one asset and buy another at a stated difference in price.

Scale order   specifies the total amount to be bought or sold at indicated variations.

Stop limit order to buy or stop limit to sell   becomes a limit order when the stock trades at a specified price or above (order to buy) or at a specified price or below (order to sell).

Swap order   an order to sell one stock and buy another.

Designations

All or none   execute the entire order or none of the order.

At the close   an order to be executed at or as near as possible to the close.

Fill or kill   execute the order immediately in its entirety or not at all.

Immediate or cancel   execute as much of the order as possible immediately and cancel the remainder.

Good today   the order expires at the close of the day's trading.

Good until canceled   continue to try to execute the order until instructed otherwise.

Not held   an indication that a broker is permitted to use judgment in executing an order, such as in deciding whether to execute an order immediately or to wait for a better price.

Participate but do not initiate   execute the order when sellers or buyers appear in the market, but do not initiate the selling or buying.

types and designations). Despite the wide variety of order types that are available, an investor could survive knowing only three basic types of orders. Each of these is considered, in turn.

3.2.1. Market orders

A **market order** is an order to be executed immediately at the best possible price. Thus, the investor selects the quantity to be transacted, but the price is not known until the transaction is completed. Investors placing market orders are said to be demanders of immediacy. Recall that immediacy is the speed with which orders of a given size can be executed at a particular cost.

In some markets, it is possible to transact between the posted bids and asks. On the NYSE buy and sell orders placed by nonmembers can meet and transact between the posted quotes. On the NYSE the location where a particular security is traded is called the **post**, and **members** of the exchange who are gathered at the post are called the **crowd**. When a public limit order arrives, carried by a floor broker, the specialist or a member of the crowd may make a better offer than the best posted quote. On the floor of a stock exchange dealers may quote wide quotes until they learn the intentions of the trader and then offer better terms to certain customers. But on screen-based computer exchanges, such as those in Singapore and Paris, it is not possible to trade between the posted quotes.

3.2.2. Limit orders

A **limit order** is an order to be executed at a specified price or better. What constitutes "or better" depends on whether the order placer is buying or selling. When buying, a better price is a lower price, but when selling, a better price is a higher price. Both investors placing limit orders and dealers making markets (described below) are suppliers of immediacy. A **limit order book** is a set of limit orders. Originally, the orders were likely to be kept in a book, but today the limit order book is typically a computer or simply a stack of orders. Once more, the terminology has carried over from previous days.

A trader placing a limit order to buy is establishing a bid, and a trader placing a limit order to sell is establishing an ask or offer. A **quotation** or **quote** is a bid and ask together. The **spread** is the difference between the bid and the ask.

In USA equity market dealers or specialists supply liquidity by continuously posting bids and asks. On the exchanges, nonmembers can also supply liquidity by placing limit orders. The NYSE also has more than 900 floor brokers, members of the exchange who do not work for a particular brokerage firm, but, instead, handle orders for other members who may be too busy. **Floor brokers** actively participate in one-third of transactions. By contrast, on screen-based exchanges other traders supply the liquidity. On the SES all orders are limit orders. But those orders that are away from the market and cannot be executed immediately supply liquidity. By contrast, limit orders that are marketable – i.e., which can be executed immediately against a counterparty order already in the computer – demand liquidity. Suppose that a market participant places a limit order to buy 5,000 shares of an SES stock at 27 USD when the best ask is 26.50 USD for 2,000 shares, and the best bid is 26.00 USD. There would be an immediate trade of 2,000 shares at 26.50 USD. Then, the remaining buy limit order would be displayed as a new bid at 26.50 USD for 3,000 shares. In other words, even though there might be stock for sale at 27 USD, the buy limit order would not be permitted to walk up the limit order book automatically. Instead, to avoid potential errors, traders must enter an order at the higher price following the execution of the first part of the order.

There are at least three ways that investors can use limit orders. One of the most common ways of using limit orders is to capture part of the bid–ask spread. Suppose that the limit order book contains bids for 2,000 shares at $52\frac{1}{8}$ and offers of 2,500 shares at $53\frac{1}{8}$. An investor could place a limit order to buy at $52\frac{1}{8}$ and join the queue at that price. When a counterpart order (either a market order to sell or a limit order to sell with a limit price of $52\frac{1}{8}$ or lower) is sent to the market, that order would be executed against one of the orders on the limit order book at $52\frac{1}{8}$. In this case the investor placing the limit order becomes a supplier of immediacy.

A second way to use limit orders is to gain protection concerning execution price. Suppose that a stock is quoted 52.125 bid for 2,000 and 52.25 ask for 2,500. On the New York Stock Exchange a market order to buy 2,500 shares at 52.25 would probably be executed at 52.25. In fact, even a larger order, say for 3,000 shares, might be executed at 52.25. But the execution price of 52.25 is not assured, and it is especially problematic for the 500-share excess of this market order over the quantity shown in the book. Further, someone else could take the 52.25 offering before this order arrives. In these two cases, it is impossible to tell what price a trader would pay for the portion of the order that is not executed at 52.25. An investor might seek to gain some protection by placing the order as a limit order for 2,500 at 52.25. In this case any unfilled portion of the order at 52.25 would become a bid for that number of shares at $52\frac{1}{4}$. The limit buy could be placed at a price above the current ask. In this case the designation "or better" might be added to prevent the broker from thinking that the order price was a mistake.

To illustrate a third way of using limit orders, the example in the previous paragraph will be continued. Suppose that an investor is interested in selling only if a specified price, say 53, can be obtained sometime during the next few days. Given a quote of 52.125–52.25, the best price currently available for selling shares is 52.125. In this case, the investor can place an order to sell at 53 limit good until canceled. Then, the order will be executed if market conditions ever allow. If market conditions do not allow the limit order to be executed, it can be canceled.

3.2.3. Stop orders

A **stop order** is an order that becomes a market order if there is a trade at a specified price or worse. For a sell order a worse price is a lower price. For a buy order a higher price is a worse price. Stop orders to sell are often referred to as "stop loss orders." A stop order to buy (sell) would be entered by someone who believes that a trade at a specified price or higher (lower) indicates that the price is likely to increase (decrease) quickly.

Since it may not be possible to execute limit orders and stop orders right away, these orders also carry an instruction indicating how long the order is to be valid. In Paris, the date that the limit order expires is specified. In the USA the two most common time limits are "good today" and "good until canceled." An order that is good today expires at the end of the day's trading session if it has not been executed by that time. As of 1999, the Stock Exchange of Singapore permits only "good today" limit orders. Each morning the exchange simply opens for business with no outstanding orders carried over from the previous day.

A good-until-canceled order actually expires semiannually in the USA. Further, investors with outstanding limit orders are typically reminded periodically by their broker.

3.2.4. Precedence

On many occasions it is necessary to decide which orders to execute first. **Precedence** rules determine which characteristics of the orders are most important. Three common precedence rules are price, time, and size. Price is virtually always the most important precedence rule. Orders at better prices have priority over other orders. Time is often the second most important precedence rule. For orders at the same price, orders that are placed earliest typically have priority. Most computer-based trading systems follow strict price and time precedence rules. On the Paris CAC investors placing limit orders can designate that a portion of the order will not be displayed to the market – i.e., it will be hidden. The portion of the limit order that is hidden loses its time priority and is at the end of the limit order queue at its limit order price. But on the ASX the undisclosed portion of an order does not lose its priority.

In some cases the size of an order also determines its priority. On the NYSE the oldest order in the limit order queue at a given price has priority. Thereafter, size also plays a part in determining priority. All orders at a given price that are of sufficient size to fill any remaining portion of an order are executed using time priority, beginning with the oldest. If no limit orders on the book are large enough to fill the remaining portion of the market order, then larger orders have priority and are executed before smaller orders. This may result in some older but smaller orders being skipped over and not executed. The reason that the NYSE follows these rules rather than following strict price/time precedence rules is to minimize the number of transactions needed to execute an order.

On the NYSE, for orders at a given price, public orders have priority over those of members of the exchange known as specialists. But in a violation of time priority, traders on the NYSE floor can participate pro rata with the limit order book once there has been a trade at a given price. Suppose that a trader arrives on the floor with a market order to sell 100 shares and is quoted a price of $50-50\frac{1}{8}$ from the limit order book with 10,000 shares on the bid side. The order is then executed at 50. Next, suppose that a second market order to sell 1,200 shares arrives on the floor and is once again quoted a price of $50-50\frac{1}{8}$. Also, suppose that there are five other traders on the exchange floor that are interested in buying. Since the stock has already traded at 50 USD, these floor traders can participate pro rata with the book. Hence, in this case the orders on the book will receive 200 shares, and the five floor traders will each receive 200 shares. This allocation is calculated by dividing the 1,200 shares in the sell by one plus the number of floor traders.

3.3. TICK SIZE

A **tick** is the minimum unit of price change permitted in a financial market by rule or by custom. In the USA, stock exchanges generally use 1/8 of 1 USD for all stocks with a price of more than 3 USD and 1/16 of 1 USD for shares selling below 3 USD. For bonds, trading would typically be in 1/32 of 100 basis points, or, in other words, 3.125 basis points. A **basis point** is 0.01 percent of the face value of a bond, so 100 basis points is 1 percent. Minimum tick size, on the Tokyo Stock Exchange: up to 2,000 yen, 1 yen; up to 3,000 yen, 5 yen; up to 30,000 yen, 10 yen; up to 50,000 yen, 50 yen; up to 100,000 yen, 100 yen; up to 1,000,000 yen, 1,000 yen; more than 1,000,000 yen, 10,000 yen.

The minimum tick size used on an exchange is more important than it might seem at first. The minimum tick size determines the minimum bid–ask spread, which is a major factor in the cost of buying and selling investments. If the minimum tick size is small, investors may be discouraged from placing limit orders, because others can step in front of their limit order by making only a slight improvement in the quote. On the other hand, the larger the tick size, the more significant a change in equilibrium price must be to result in a new quote.

3.4. ROUND LOTS AND ODD LOTS

A **round lot** is the usual unit of trading, and an **odd lot** is less than the usual unit of trading. The usual unit of trading varies from instrument to instrument and also from market to market. For the international swaps market, the standard unit of trading is generally 25 million USD. On the ASX there are no round and odd lots, and trades can be for any number of shares. In the USA, stocks almost always trade in round lots of 100 shares, whereas in Japan the customary unit of trading is 1,000 shares. In the USA, bonds are typically thought of as having a face value of 1,000 USD, but trade in round lots of 100,000 USD, 1,000,000 USD, or more, depending on the type of instrument.

3.5. BLOCK TRADES

A **block trade** is a relatively large trade. Exactly what size constitutes a block may differ from market to market and instrument to instrument. On the NYSE 10,000 shares is frequently used as the criterion for a block. Many blocks of this size are handled routinely on the NYSE floor. The author accompanied a floor trader who made numerous trades of 10,000 shares in the pharmaceutical firm Merc during a short time. In fact, in recent years blocks of this size or greater have constituted more than 50 percent of NYSE volume, though less than 5 percent of the number of orders. In many cases blocks can be handled using the normal trading procedures. But beyond some point special procedures may be needed. On the NYSE the order goes to a broker in the so-called **upstairs market**. Here many of the normal exchange rules do not apply. The broker can actively solicit a counter-party, act as both a broker and a dealer in the same transaction, charge a commission on all shares traded, and can, potentially, earn a profit in unwinding any position acquired in the process of facilitating the transactions. In effect, the block trader is arranging both sides of a transaction.

When the deal is agreed to, the trade must be crossed on the floor. This presents a problem in that there may already be limit orders on the books that will interfere with the cross. Suppose that a stock is quoted 50 bid and $50\frac{1}{8}$ ask on the NYSE floor, but that a block trader has arranged a trade of 1 million shares at 49.50. Then all the limit orders to buy at prices of 49.625–50 would have price priority, and the block dealer would be required to fill these orders. Limit orders on the book to buy at 49.50 would have time priority. If there is substantial demand at 49.5, this could interfere with the block trader's ability to cross the stock. Since the block dealer would receive a markdown or commission only from one side of the trade for shares crossed with the book, the dealer is naturally reluctant to trade with the book. In the USA one potential solution is to cross the shares on a regional exchange. Since the limit order book is not integrated across exchanges, the likelihood that a regional exchange's book would interfere with a block trade is typically less than that for the NYSE book. Or large orders can be given precedence, as on the NYSE. Another solution is for the cross to be made in a jurisdiction with more favorable rules. Dealers in Paris may cross their blocks in London. Many exchanges have special rules for handling block trades. In Singapore brokers can cross trades on the exchange that exceed specified sizes without consideration of limit orders on the book. These married deals may trade at prices higher than the best ask or lower than the best bid without the necessity of executing these orders.

Holthausen, Leftwich, and Myers (1987) report that on the NYSE for seller-initiated block trades, buyers receive temporary price concessions that are larger for larger-sized blocks. For buyer-initiated trades, a premium, which is larger the larger the block size, is offered to sellers, and this premium is permanent. Choe, McInish, and Wood (1995) report that there is a dearth of block trades early in the trading day relative to later in the day.

3.6. Methods of Trading

There are basically two ways of conducting secondary market trading. Continuous trading allows parties to transact whenever they agree on a price. This section will consider three types of continuous trading systems: dealer markets, consolidated limit order markets, and open outcry markets. Then, a system of noncontinuous trading referred to as "batch" or "call" markets will be described in the next section. These methods are not mutually exclusive. In fact, the New York Stock Exchange, the Tokyo Stock Exchange, and the Australian Stock Exchange, among others, begin each day with a call market and then operate both a dealer market and a consolidated limit order market concurrently for the remainder of the trading day.

Another way of dichotomizing markets is by whether they are quote-driven or order-driven. NASDAQ is a **quote-driven** market, in which market makers post the ask price at which investors can buy shares and the bid price at which investors can sell shares. The Tokyo Stock Exchange is an **order-driven** market, in which investors buy and sell at the ask and bid established by previously placed limit orders. The NYSE and Amex are hybrid markets, in which both designated market makers and limit-order traders establish prices.

3.6.1. Continuous trading in dealer markets

In a continuous trading system trades take place during trading hours whenever two counterparties reach an agreement. By contrast, a periodic market may be open and accepting orders, but trading takes place only at times set by the market.

Almost all bond and foreign exchange trading and significant derivative and equities trading are done in continuous dealer markets. In these markets dealers often **make-a-market** in financial instruments. Make-a-market means that the dealer is always willing to buy and sell at a price close to the current market price. Recall that the price at which the dealer is willing to buy is called the "bid," and the price at which the dealer is willing to sell is called the "ask." On the New York Stock Exchange the dealers who make markets are called **specialists**. Of course, the specialists are members of the exchange, since one of the central features of exchanges is the restriction of trading to members. Members who perform similar functions are found on many exchanges, including the Amsterdam Stock Exchange. In the USA the majority of over-the-counter trading in stocks is conducted on NASDAQ, which links broker-dealers and allows approved dealers to display markets that they are making electronically. The identity of each market maker is given on a computer screen along with their bid and ask (each market maker must post a two-sided market) and the number of shares for which the quotation is good. Thus, the NASDAQ system greatly facilitates the identification of dealers who are making a market in a particular over-the-counter stock. Some orders can be executed automatically through a Small Order Execution System (SOES), but larger-sized orders must be handled over the telephone or through other communications links.

3.6.2. *Continuous trading with limit order books*

Some continuous markets function without designated dealers. These markets use consolidated limit order books in which investors, using brokers as intermediaries, can place limit orders. Other investors can place market orders or marketable limit orders that are then executed against limit orders already on the limit order book. A **marketable limit order** is a limit order with a specified price that allows the immediate execution of the order. Members can also act as market makers by posting limit orders. Virtually all screen-based exchanges, including those in Paris, Singapore, Toronto, and Vancouver, operate in this way. As mentioned previously, allowing orders to walk up the limit order book could create significant problems if an erroneous price were entered inadvertently. Hence, on most screen-based exchanges marketable limit orders are not allowed to walk up or down the limit order book. In other words, suppose that in Singapore 600 shares are being offered at 11.50 and 500 shares are being offered at 11.60. An investor placing a marketable limit order to buy 1,000 shares at 11.60 will receive an immediate execution of 600 shares. The remaining 400 shares will be converted to a limit order at 11.50. The investor can immediately change the limit order price to 11.60 and receive an execution. Of course, given this rule, the trader would realize that only 600 shares were available at 11.50 and would select an execution strategy accordingly. The purpose of this type of rule is to prevent a keystroke error by the data entry clerk from executing against multiple quotes. A different approach is used in Tokyo, where a limit order that exceeds the best posted price can execute against the next best price after a 5-minute wait (and assuming that daily price limits have not been exceeded) during which a warning quote is flashed.

Suppose that the limit order book for a screen-based exchange looks as shown in table 2.4, panel A. This is a typical example, in that many screen-based trading systems display the five best prices along with their associated sizes on both sides of the market. If a broker enters a market order to sell 2,200 shares in the exchange's computer system 2,000 shares would be automatically executed at 291. We assume that our exchange follows the same rule in effect in Paris, where limit orders could be hidden in whole or in part with the understanding that the hidden portion of the limit order is at the back of the queue at that price.

Table 2.4 Hypothetical limit order display on a screen-based exchange

Panel A: Before execution of limit order (assuming no hidden limit orders)

Bids		Offers	
Price in FFR	*Number of shares*	*Price in FFR*	*Number of shares*
291	2,000	292	3,000
290	1,400	293	3,200
288	2,100	295	3,700
287	2,800	298	4,100
285	3,200	300	4,200

Panel B: Afterwards, assuming execution of a market order to sell 2,200 shares, no hidden limit orders, and no new order entry

290	1,400	291	200
288	2,100	292	3,000
287	2,800	293	3,200
285	3,200	295	3,700
284	2,100	298	4,100

If 200 or more shares are hidden these shares would not be reflected on the screen, but the marketable limit order would receive an immediate execution for 2,000 shares plus the number of hidden shares. Assuming no new order had been entered and that there are no hidden limit orders, the limit order book would look like panel B, following the execution of the 2,000 shares.

3.6.3. *Continuous trading with open outcry*

Many futures exchanges, including those in the USA, Singapore, and Australia, use a system of trading referred to as **open outcry**. In this method of trading members of the exchange stand in a location of the floor called a **pit**. In Chicago the pits are staired depressions in the floor so that traders can stand on different levels and see each other. Members desiring to trade must shout out their intentions and are required to trade with the first counterparty that catches their eye. This methods works well for actively traded contracts such as those on US Treasury bills, where there may be scores of traders in the pit at a given time. Naturally, with so many people in the pit and so much shouting, traders cannot hear each other. Hence, the exchanges have adopted a system of hand signals that can be used to communicate buy and sell intentions and prices. When the number of members wishing to trade a particular contract is low, the open outcry becomes, in effect, a dealer market with a limit order book.

3.6.4. *Periodic trading using call or batch trading*

One method of trading on exchanges is by a periodic **call** or **batch**. This is a method of trading in which orders are accumulated until trading is opened, when these orders are executed simultaneously. The time interval can be fixed or variable. Some investors place market orders, and some place limit orders. In some trading systems an exchange official will attempt to open the market at a price that will result in the largest volume or trade size. Of course, it is unlikely that the number of shares sought for purchase will exactly equal the number of shares which investors desire to sell. One possibility is that a dealer such as the specialist on the NYSE will have the responsibility of absorbing the excess demand or supply so that all market orders and all limit orders at the trade price or better will be executed. If there is no designated dealer, then a rule must be used to allocate executions to the heavy side (i.e., the side with the preponderance of orders). Executions could be allocated on a pro rata basis or based on time of order entry or size of order. Market orders could be given precedence over limit orders.

Call systems are especially common for stock exchanges. The NYSE opens trading in each stock each day with a batch trade for orders accumulated from the previous close until the batch trade is completed. The Tel Aviv Stock Exchange operates a continuous market for thick stocks and a call once each day for thin stocks.[12]

3.7. How Technology Affects Trading

Technology can have important effects on both the way trading is conducted and the outcomes from trading. Historical evidence is provided in box 2.5. Screen-based trading systems, such as the exchanges in Frankfurt, London, Paris, Singapore, Toronto, Vancouver, and on Tradepoint and Instinet, allow traders to submit limit orders that are displayed to interested traders. On these exchanges and trading systems, the best available ask and the best available bid, along with the aggregate number of shares offered and bid for, are displayed to the market. But additional quote levels and the sizes available at those levels are also shown. The Paris CAC shows the five best bids and asks with their associated size, while the Stock Exchange of Singapore displays all quote levels in the computer with their associated sizes. By contrast, as of 1994, the NYSE system permits the display of only one quote

---

BOX 2.5
The effect of the telegraph on exchange rates in New Orleans and New York

Many identical financial assets trade in multiple, geographically dispersed locations. Communications technology, especially in the past, limited the ability of participants in one market to learn the trading prices in another. In the 1840s exporters of cotton in the southern USA drew numerous 60-day bills of exchange on London merchants. These were purchased by dealers and sold to importers in the northern states who needed to make remittances to London for imports. The principal cities where these bills were exchanged were New Orleans and New York. In July 1848 telegraph communications were initiated between these two cities. Garbade and Silber (1978) calculated the absolute difference between the rates in New Orleans and the rates in New York. For the period prior to the introduction of the telegraph, the difference between New Orleans and New York prices averaged 0.057 USD. After the introduction of the telegraph, the difference fell to 0.034 USD. This difference was both economically and statistically significant. The fact that the difference did not fall to zero is probably due to the presence of transaction costs that were high enough to make additional arbitrage unprofitable. (For additional information see Garbade and Silber 1978.)

price (and its size) on the bid and ask side. Given the limitations of the NYSE system, what should the specialist display? Suppose that there is a bid at 50 USD for 10,000 shares and another bid at 50.125 USD for 100 shares. The investor placing the 100-share limit order and others interested in trading in small lots would probably prefer that the quotes reflect the higher bid. But institutional traders who wish to trade only in larger sizes might prefer to have the 10,000-share limit order displayed. The specialist might try to accommodate both groups by displaying the 100-share order, by temporarily "flashing" the 10,000-share order. In other words, the 100-share order would be displayed most of the time, but occasionally the 10,000-share order would be displayed for a few seconds. Some specialists follow this practice. The question of what to display has led to the problem called hidden limit orders (see box 2.6).

Technology is also affecting the provision of trading services to the public. Gomez Advisors tracks and provides links to more than a score of Internet brokerage firms.[13] At times the rapid growth of Internet brokers has lead to bottlenecks or customers who have had difficulty reaching web sites to conduct their trading. Nevertheless, a survey of more than 600 investors found that more than 80 percent believed that most investors in the USA would be investing online within the next five years.

4. SUMMARY

This chapter describes the participants in secondary markets and explains the reasons for the existence of these markets. We are specifically concerned with the secondary markets for trading equities, fixed-income securities, and currencies, and the related markets in which many derivatives are created.

Broadly speaking, there are two categories of participants in secondary markets: the buy side and the sell side. The sell side includes brokerage firms, exchanges, and others involved in the transfer of financial assets among owners. The buy side is individuals and firms investing their own funds and financial institutions that are investing on behalf of these individuals and firms. On the sell side, brokers act as agents for customers, while dealers buy and sell for their own account and thus are a party to the transaction. On the buy side, transactions that are based on information are called "informed," and those that are motivated by the need for liquidity are "uninformed." We use the terms "uninformed traders," "liquidity traders," and "noise traders" interchangeably to refer to traders acting on liquidity needs and not on the basis of information.[14]

Market participants can also be characterized according to how long they hold their positions. Scalpers attempt to profit quickly from minimal price fluctuations in price. Day traders typically do not hold positions overnight. Position traders hold their positions for days or even years.

Financial markets increase the value of financial assets in several ways. They provide investors with liquidity, the ability to sell the asset if their financial circumstances change. Secondary markets provide price discovery and information concerning the equilibrium prices of assets. This information is useful for investors interested in buying and selling the assets. Firms investing capital can use these signals in making their capital budgeting decisions. Financial markets also allow producers and investors to transfer risk among themselves to better accommodate their risk preferences.

BOX 2.6
Undisplayed limit orders on the NYSE

Screen-based trading systems, such as the exchanges in Frankfurt, London, Paris, Singapore, Toronto, Vancouver, and on Tradepoint and Instinet, allow traders to submit limit orders that are displayed to interested traders. On these exchanges and trading systems, not only are the best bid and ask displayed with their associated sizes, but a montage of the next levels of bids and asks with their associated sizes are also displayed.

By contrast, the NYSE system permits the display of only one quote each (and its size) on the bid and ask side. Given the limitations of the NYSE system, what should the specialist display? Suppose that there is a bid at 50 USD for 10,000 shares and another bid at 50.125 USD for 100 shares. The investor placing the 100-share limit order and others interested in trading in small lots would probably prefer that the quotes reflect the higher bid. But institutional traders who wish to trade only in larger sizes might prefer to have the 10,000-limit order displayed. The specialist might try to accommodate both groups by displaying the 100-share order, but temporarily "flashing" the 10,000-share order. This practice is followed for some stocks.

McInish and Wood (1995) define a hidden limit order as a limit order submitted to the NYSE that betters an existing displayed quote but that the specialist fails to display. These authors examine data for 144 randomly selected NYSE firms from November 1990 to January 1991. Of 253,982 limit orders in the sample, 48,072 were submitted at prices that bettered existing displayed quotes. The remaining limit orders were either at the displayed quotes and thus already displayed or could not have been displayed because they were at prices inferior to the displayed quotes. In 46% of the cases where a limit order is submitted which betters an existing NYSE quote, the specialist fails to update the quote to reflect the new limit order.

McInish and Wood argue that while the existence of hidden limit orders may be beneficial to exchange members on the floor, especially the designated market maker, it harms smaller traders and the regional exchanges. Hidden limit orders

1. impede strategic decisions on order placement,
2. result in trade troughs on both the NYSE and regional exchanges,
3. result in publicly submitted market orders receiving inferior prices,
4. hamper the monitoring of order executions,
5. reduce the probability of a limit order being executed,
6. result in a delay in reporting limit order executions,
7. interfere with the ability of the regional exchanges to execute public orders,
8. artificially improve NYSE performance relative to the regional exchanges using a common benchmark, executions between the displayed quotes,
9. inaccurately portray some closing quotes which are used by investors after the market close,
10. impose a fiduciary responsibility on the part of money managers to execute trades on the NYSE, since the possibility exists to obtain better executions than if an order were executed at the displayed quotes off the exchange floor.

The practice of hiding limit orders may be a violation of USSEC regulations that state: "Every exchange shall, at all times such exchange is open for trading, collect, process and make available to quotation vendors the highest bid and the lowest offer communicated on the floor of that exchange . . . by any responsible broker or dealer."

Source: McInish and Wood 1995. This copyrighted material is reprinted with permission from the *Journal of Portfolio Management*, Spring 1995 (a publication of Institutional Investor, 488 Madison Avenue, New York, NY 10022).

To serve their economic purpose, secondary markets must be perceived as being fair to participants. One practice that is inherently unfair is frontrunning, the practice of brokers and dealers buying or selling ahead of their customers. Another issue closely related to fairness is transparency, which is concerned with what and how rapidly information is disseminated to market participants. In general, fair markets provide rapid and widespread access to information.

We also describe how trading is conducted in secondary markets. There are three common types of orders. The market order is an order to be executed immediately at the best possible price. A limit order is an order to be executed at a specified price or better. And a stop order is an order that becomes a market order if a trade takes place at a specified price.

Secondary market trading takes place on an exchange, an organization whose members trade financial assets in a given location, or off an exchange, called "over-the-counter trading." In many market centers trading takes place continuously. Dealers are market professionals who facilitate the trading process by buying and selling for their own account. This trading can be conducted by one (the NYSE) or more dealers (NASDAQ), by open outcry (the CBOT), or using computer-based limit order systems (Paris, Frankfurt, Singapore, and Toronto). Some exchanges accumulate orders that are subsequently matched in a single batch trade (NYSE and Tel Aviv).

Questions

1 Can computer-based trading systems offer price improvement?
2 How can letter stock be used to measure the value of liquidity?
3 Explain why fairness is important to the functioning of financial markets.
4 What are the three most common forms of precedence?
5 Name at least two benefits that an economy receives from having viable secondary markets.
6 Explain four dimensions of liquidity.
7 Why do exchanges exist? Who benefits from exchanges?
8 Suppose that one is comparing investments in two firms that are identical except that one is closely held and the other trades publicly. Do these firms have the same value? Explain.
9 Transparency involves a tradeoff between the interests of parties to a transaction in keeping details secret and the interests of nonparties in gaining information from these details? Which is more important and why?
10 List at least three desirable characteristics of a secondary market and explain how achieving one of these might conflict with achieving another.
11 From an economic and legal point of view, is NASDAQ a stock exchange?
12 How could the ownership structure of an exchange affect its ability to serve customers, the government, listed companies, and other stakeholders?

■ **Notes** ■

1 Table 645, Statistical Abstract of the US.
2 Stoll (1993) reports that in the USA alone the revenue for securities firms from their commissions and trading gains amounted to 14.5 billion USD, and 430,000 people were employed in US securities in 1989.

3   It is also worth noting that in order to be comparable, the trades in both the letter stock and the publicly traded stock should be for minority interest, since positions large enough to give corporate control would have higher value.

4   Frontrunning was important in the collapse of Baring Brothers, which cost creditors and shareholders more than 1 billion USD. There are many ways to frontrun a client order. According to Fay (1997, p. 136), Nicholas Leeson, the rogue trader responsible for the collapse of Barings, was frontrunning: "there cannot be any argument about it." When Leeson received an order to be executed in Singapore, he would first buy in Osaka for his own account. Leeson called this "working the information curve." Leeson managed to convince Barings that because he placed his order in a different market he was not breaking SIMEX rules.

5   For a site providing links to a variety of information about Japanese financial markets see http://www.asiadragons.com/japan/finance/stock_market/japan_link.shtml.

6   For information on the Tokyo Stock Exchange see http://www.tse.or.jp/ee/ee01.html.

7   On December 10, 1998, The Island ECN, Inc. announced plans to apply to the USSEC for permission to become a self-regulated stock exchange. Source: http://www.isld.com/.

8   For additional information see http://www.futurecom.org.

9   The OTC Bulletin Board's web address is http://www.otcbb.com/aboutOTCBB/about.stm.

10   The web address for the National Quotation Bureau is http://ww.nbq.com.

11   Additional information concerning these proprietary trading systems can be obtained from the following web sites: Instinet, http://www.instinet.com/; POSIT, http://www.itginc.com/; Tradepoint, http://www.tradepoint.co.uk/; Reuters Dealing, http://www.reuters.com/products/tran001.htm; the Electronic Broking Service, http://www.ebsp.com/chrono.html; Island ECN, http://www.isld.com/; and Bloomberg Tradebook, http://www.bloomberg.com/products/trdbk.html.

12   For additional information see http://www.tase.co.il/.

13   The Gomez Advisors web address is http://www.quote.com/specials/gomez/whoweare.htm. For additional information on Internet brokerage see Spinner 1998.

14   The classification is based on whether a trader actually has information. In other words, these traders may think that they have information, but, if, in fact, they do not, they are noise traders.

■ **References** ■

Amihud, Yakov and Mendelson, Haim 1988: Liquidity, volatility, and exchange automation. *Journal of Accounting, Auditing and Finance* 3, 369–95.

Choe, Hyuk, McInish, Thomas H. and Wood, Robert A. 1995: Block versus nonblock trading patterns. *Review of Quantitative Finance and Accounting* 5, 355–63.

Crabbe, Leland E. and Turner, Christopher M. 1995: Does the liquidity of a debt issue increase with its size? Evidence from the corporate bond and medium-term note market. *Journal of Finance* 50, 1719–34.

Ding, David K., Harris, Frederick H. deB, Lau, Sie Ting and McInish, Thomas H. forthcoming: An investigation of trading in Malaysia and Singapore: price discovery in informationally-linked markets. *Journal of Multinational Financial Management.*

Domowitz, Ian 1996: An exchange is a many-splendored thing: the classification and regulation of automated trading systems. In Andrew Lo (ed.), *The Industrial Organization and Regulation of the Securities Industry*, National Bureau of Economic Research Conference Report. Chicago: University of Chicago Press.

Fay, Stephen 1997: *The Collapse of Barings*. New York: Norton.

Garbade, Kenneth D. and Silber, William L. 1978: Technology, communication and the performance of financial markets, 1840–1975. *Journal of Finance* 33, 819–32.

Goldberg, Stuart C. 1979: Securities law (part I): recognizing fraudulent broker-dealer practices. *Trial* 15, 42–68.

Harris, Lawrence E. 1990: *Liquidity, Trading Rules, and Electronic Trading Systems*, Monograph 1990–4. New York: New York University Salomon Center.

Holthausen, Robert W., Leftwich, Richard W. and Myers, David 1987: The effect of large block transactions on security prices. *Journal of Financial Economics* 19, 237–67.

International Organization of Securities Commissions (IOSC) 1992: *Transparency on Secondary Markets*. Milan: International Organization of Securities Commissions, Dec.

Jayaraman, N., Shastri, Kuldip and Tandon, K. 1993: The impact of international cross listings on risk and return: the evidence from American Depository Receipts. *Journal of Banking and Finance* 17, 91–103.

Lau, Sie Ting, Diltz, J. David and Apilado, Vincent P. 1994: Valuation effects of international stock exchange listings. *Journal of Banking and Finance* 18, 743–55.

Longstaff, Francis A. 1995: How much can marketability affect security values? *Journal of Finance* 50, 1767–74.

McInish, Thomas H. and Wood, Robert A. 1986: Adjusting for beta bias: an assessment of alternate techniques. *Journal of Finance* 41, 277–86.

——1995: Midden limit orders on the NYSE. *Journal of Portfolio Management* 21, 19–26.

Miller, Darius P. 1999: The market reaction to international cross-listings: evidence from depositary receipts *Journal of Financial Economics* 51, 103–23.

Morse, Laurie 1997: Internet exchange challenges Chicago. *Derivatives Strategy* 2, 42.

New York Stock Exchange (NYSE) 1990: *Market Volatility and Investor Confidence*. New York: NYSE.

Pratt, Shannon P. 1981: *Valuing a Business*. Homewood, IL: Dow Jones-Irwin.

Schwert, G. William 1990: Stock market volatility. *Financial Analysts Journal* 46, 23–34.

Silber, William L. 1991: Discounts on restricted stock: the impact of illiquidity on stock prices. *Financial Analysts Journal* 47, 60–4.

Spinner, Karen 1998: Challenging the status quo. *Supplement to Wall Street and Technology*, Nov., 10–13.

Stoll, Hans R. 1993: Equity trading costs in-the-large. *Journal of Portfolio Management* 19, 41–50.

Wall Street and Technology Magazine. (Recommended for insights on how technology affects financial markets.)

Wall Street Journal 1998: Private electronic trading systems face new controls, competition in SEC system. Dec. 3, p. C14.

Werner, Ingrid M. and Kleidon, Allan W. 1996: U.K. and U.S. trading of British cross-listed stocks: an intraday analysis of market integration. *Review of Financial Studies* 9, 619–64.

CHAPTER THREE

Transaction Costs

■ Key terms ■

Adverse information costs   the costs incurred or anticipated by a dealer as a result of trading with counterparties who are motivated by the possession of superior insight into the appropriate equilibrium price of the asset.

Best execution   the use of reasonable diligence to ascertain the best market for a security so that the resultant price to the customer is as favorable as possible under prevailing market conditions.

Bid–ask bounce   the movement of stock prices between the bid and the ask.

Commission   a direct charge that broker-dealers make for executing orders when acting as agents.

Dealer spread   the quoted spread of a particular dealer.

Direct costs   same as **Explicit costs**.

Directed   a client or investment manager designates that the order be given to a specific firm for execution.

Effective half-spread   the effective spread divided by 2.

Effective spread   the trade price minus the quote midpoint.

Execution costs   explicit and implicit costs that are actually incurred from executing a trade.

Explicit costs   costs of executing a trading strategy that typically can be identified and paid for directly, such as commissions, taxes, and transfer fees.

Gaming   actions that improve one's performance on an evaluation, but that are contrary to its spirit.

Implementation shortfall   a way of evaluating execution costs that involves comparing hypothetical trades with actual trades.

Implicit transaction costs   costs of executing a transaction that are not itemized and paid for directly, such as the bid–ask spread, market impact costs, market-timing costs, and opportunity costs.

Indirect transaction costs   same as **Implicit transaction costs**.

Information costs   the costs of acquiring any type of information used in investment decisions.

Inventory holding costs   the costs incurred or anticipated by a dealer as a result of inventory positions acquired in the process of market making.

Market impact   the change in market price resulting from the execution of an order.

Market spread   the difference between the best ask and the best bid quoted in the market.

Market-timing costs   the cost incurred when the stock's price moves in response to factors unrelated to the particular transaction before the transaction can be executed.

Markup/markdown   a direct charge that broker-dealers make for executing orders as principal.

Opportunity costs   the lost profit from trades that are missed or not executed due to changes in market conditions before the execution can be completed.

Order processing costs   costs associated with the actual mechanics of providing a dealer market, such as paperwork costs and transfer taxes.

Price improvement   in a dealer market, a trade price that is better than the posted price.

Principal   a broker-dealer who is a party to the transaction with the client rather than an agent.

Quoted half-spread   one-half of the ask minus the bid.

Realized spreads   the spreads a dealer actually receives, as opposed to those that are quoted.

Soft dollars   in the USA, a rebate provided by brokerage firms to investment managers for use in purchasing anything that materially aids in investment management.

Spread   the difference between the ask and the bid.

Tick size   the minimum price variation permitted in a market.

Trader   an employee of a firm who has the responsibility for executing buy and sell orders.

Transaction costs   all the costs associated with a transaction, including the costs of failing to execute the trade.

THIS CHAPTER is divided into two main parts. In the first part we

- examine the nature and importance of transaction costs
- discuss components of transaction costs, including commissions, information costs, and the bid–ask spread

Then, in the second part, we deal with the measurement and quantification of transaction costs, including the following topics:

- problems and issues in quantifying transaction costs
- findings of previous studies
- ways of defining the bid–ask spread
- factors that determine the size of the spread
- how exchange tick rules affect the size of the spread
- ways of inferring the size of the spread and applications of these techniques

1. INTRODUCTION

Increasingly, investors realize that the cost of buying and selling their investments is an important determinant of how much money they make (or lose). In the first part of this chapter, we describe explicit and implicit transaction costs. Explicit costs include commissions and information costs. Implicit costs, also called "execution costs," include several costs, such as the difference between the price at the time the decision is made to execute the trade and the price actually paid and the bid–ask spread. The second part of this chapter deals in greater detail with the measurement quantification of transactions costs, especially the difficulties in quantifying implicit costs. We present the results of previous studies that attempt to quantify the level of transactions costs for equity portfolios.

One of the most important implicit costs is the bid–ask spread. We present several alternative definitions of the spread, discuss in some detail what factors determine the size of the spread, and explain how exchange tick-size rules sometimes increase the size of the spread. We also describe two ways of estimating the realized spread and how these techniques can be applied to actual situations.

2. TYPES OF TRANSACTION COSTS

Broadly defined, **transaction costs** are all the costs associated with the management of investments, including the time involved in making investment decisions. (For additional information see Schwartz and Whitcomb 1988.) Transaction costs can be classified as direct and indirect, or, alternatively, as explicit or implicit. **Direct** or **explicit costs** are itemized separately, and investors pay for these just like any other expenses. The most common explicit cost is a **commission** or **markup/markdown**. Recall that markdown is the difference between the amount a dealer receives for an asset and the amount the customer receives, while a markup is the difference between the amount a dealer pays for an asset and the amount the dealer receives from a customer. Other explicit costs include the costs of acquiring information, taxes, and transfer fees. Explicit costs are set administratively or negotiated. Because they can be measured easily, we do not focus much attention on explicit transaction costs in this chapter, with one exception. We do consider **information costs**, the costs involved in the acquisition and search for information for use in making investments. We also classify the value of an investor's time spent in making investment decisions as an explicit cost, even though these costs are not typically quantified. Some investments require more of an investor's attention, and these costs are real even if they are paid for with the investor's effort, rather than in cash.

We also consider four **implicit transaction costs** or **execution costs**. The bid–ask **spread** is the cost involved in providing immediacy. **Market impact** is the cost resulting from any change in market price due to the execution of an order. **Market-timing costs** are incurred when the stock's price moves in response to factors unrelated to the particular transaction before the transaction can be executed. Rushing a trade to reduce market-timing costs may only result in higher market impact costs. Market-timing costs are a cost of executing a trade. If the trader fails to execute a desired trade, an **opportunity cost** is incurred, which is the loss in profits from trades that are missed or not executed due to changes in market conditions before the execution can be completed. Sometimes, if the market moves before an order can be completed, then the remainder of the order must be abandoned.

When an institutional investment manager makes a decision to buy or sell, the order is typically given to the firm's **trader** for execution. Also, when a brokerage firm's retail or institutional salesperson receives an order, that order is transmitted to the brokerage firm's trader (traders work at a trading desk) for execution. Hence, in this usage a trader is an employee of a firm charged with the task of executing a buy or sell order. Box 3.1 discusses attributes of a good trader. Execution costs are the costs of actually buying and selling investments. Execution costs include commissions, market impact costs, market-timing costs, and information costs, but, depending on whose definition one uses, may not include opportunity costs, because no trade is executed.

The measurement of transaction costs has relevance for portfolio managers for a variety of reasons. Transaction costs have a direct impact on portfolio performance. Also, it is sometimes easier to reduce costs, say, by reducing portfolio turnover, than to increase the portfolio's returns to pay for higher trading costs. In the USA the Employee Retirement Income Security Act (ERISA) of 1974 stimulated an interest in monitoring and assessing the cost of asset management (Kehrer 1991, pp. 259–71). ERISA requires that plan assets must be used for the exclusive benefit of the plan and its participants, and that fiduciaries' actions must be consistent with professional money management practices. Because transactions

---

BOX 3.1
What makes a good trader?

The following are a question and an answer from Gilbert Beebower, executive vice-president of SEI corporation, a leading US provider of accounting and related services to investment and pension managers.

Question: You have probably looked at more data evaluating trading prowess than anyone in the world. What, in your opinion, distinguishes a great trader from a good trader? Have you noted any common mistakes that could be avoided?

Beebower: Trading is necessarily an integral part of the investment process. The ability to demonstrate exceptional skill as a trader depends to a large extent on how much trading flexibility the demands of the portfolio manager permit. Demands for immediacy are likely to be costly, albeit less costly, for the expert trader. A "great" trader is one who makes an effort to be a part of the investment decision-making process, thus bringing his understanding of market liquidity and trading opportunities to bear before, during, and after investment decisions are made. A "good" trader satisfies the portfolio manager only after the decision has been made.

A common mistake that lesser traders often make is to second-guess the portfolio manager as to when the trade should be executed on the basis of predicting where the price will be tomorrow or days later, not on the basis of current liquidity. If a trader can predict where prices will be tomorrow or some days later, he should be in charge of the investment process.

Source: Wagner, *The Complete Guide to Securities Transactions*, copyright © 1989. Reprinted by permission of John Wiley & Sons, Inc.

costs can greatly affect investment performance, those administering pension assets in the USA have been forced to take an active interest in assessing transactions costs. Interest in measuring and assessing transaction costs has spread to other managers as well.

The relative importance of brokerage commissions and indirect costs have implications for the strategies that portfolio managers use to minimize execution costs. In evaluating the quality of execution services provided by brokerage firms, it must be kept in mind that, despite their importance, transaction costs are not the only concern of brokerage firm clients. Another, probably more important concern is **best execution**, according to the National Association of Security Dealers:

> In any transaction for or with a customer, a member . . . shall use reasonable diligence to ascertain the best inter-dealer market for the subject security and buy or sell in such market so that the resultant price to the customer is as favorable as possible under prevailing market conditions.[1]

But best execution does not necessarily imply best price. In deciding whether best execution has been achieved, other factors must be considered, including speed and the security involved. In comparing the execution costs of one firm with another, an inferior execution is an additional cost that must be taken into account (Macey and O'Hara 1996).

Transaction costs, especially implicit costs, are often difficult to measure. One firm that monitors transaction costs is Plexus Group, Inc., which analyzes trading costs and strategies for over 125 clients, who manage over 1.5 trillion USD in assets. Clients include domestic managers, global managers, sponsors, brokers, and exchanges.[2] Wagner and Banks (1992, p. 9) identify four factors that increase transaction costs:

- "Speed: Faster trades may demand more supply than is readily available.
- Size: Similarly, size of trade can overwhelm the marker's ability to accommodate the transaction.
- Momentum: It will be more expensive to buy a stock in a crowd of buyers than in a crowd of sellers.
- Liquidity: Thin or dull markets extract higher transaction costs than markets that are robust and vibrant."

Table 3.1 provides information concerning the relative size of transaction costs. Note that the cost of executing the average small cap order is more than four times as high as that of the large cap order.

2.1. Direct Transaction Costs

Direct transaction costs are less than implicit costs, but nevertheless account for an important part of the cost of trading. Aitken and Swan (1997) analyze the effect of a reduction in taxes on securities transactions from 0.3 percent to 0.15 percent. These authors report an increase in share prices of 1.73 percent, reflecting the imputed present value of tax savings. Average volume rose 21 percent, which resulted in a reduction of 18 percent in bid–ask spreads.

73

Table 3.1 Explicit and implicit trading costs, November 1997

	Overall	Average cost (%)	
		Large cap (market cap over 1 billion USD)	Small cap (market cap less than 1 billion USD)
Commission	0.15	0.12	0.22
Impact	0.23	0.20	0.33
Total *Brokerage* Cost: Use These Numbers When Evaluating Brokers	0.38	0.32	0.55
Delay	0.60	0.53	1.72
Total *Execution* Cost: Use These Numbers When Evaluating Completed Trades	0.98	0.85	2.27
Missed Trades (Foregone Price Movement On 10% Of Trades Not Completed)	0.18	0.16	2.22
Total *Implementation* Cost: Use These Numbers When Planning Trading Strategy	1.16	1.01	4.49

2.1.1. Commissions

Commissions are an important cost of owning securities. As a percentage of the value of the asset, commissions on options are typically higher than for other financial assets. Commissions on equities have the second-highest transaction costs. Commissions and markups/markdowns on fixed-income securities are probably more varied than on other types of financial instruments. Commissions and markups/markdowns on actively traded securities such as US Treasury bills are low, but commissions on the bonds of smaller issuers can be high. The markups/markdowns and commissions on currencies and futures are generally lower than those on other financial instruments.

We turn now to the consideration of several issues related to commissions. The first is whether commissions should be fixed as they are on some exchanges or negotiated as they are on other exchanges. The Stock Exchange of Singapore (SES) is a typical example of an exchange that has fixed commissions. SES commissions are described in box 3.2. There is a growing trend toward permitting the negotiation of commission rates between brokers and customers. Fixed commission rates were abolished in the USA by the USSEC on May 1, 1975. There was considerable controversy concerning the proposal to abolish fixed rates prior to the implementation of this rule. Many in the brokerage industry argued that the elimination of fixed commissions would lead to the ruin of a number of firms. But, in fact,

---

BOX 3.2
Commission rates on the Stock Exchange of Singapore

The Stock Exchange of Singapore (SES) is typical of exchanges that have fixed commissions. The commission rates in effect in 1994 were 1 percent for the first 250,000 SGD of contract value; 0.9 percent on the next 250,000 SGD of contract value; 0.8 percent on the next 250,000 SGD of contract value; and 0.7 percent on the next 250,000 SGD of contract value. Commissions on the SES are negotiable on the amounts of contract value exceeding 1,000,000 SGD subject to a minimum commission rate of 0.50 percent. For shares, rights, and other securities the commission rate is 0.005 SGD if the price is less than 0.50 SGD and 0.01 SGD if the price is from 0.50 SGD to 0.99 SGD. In addition, there are contract, stamp, and clearing fees, which collectively amount to about 0.10 percent of the contract value.

---

the brokerage industry has prospered and has since enjoyed record profits. In fact, Blom and Lewellen (1983) report that the commissions paid by individuals with low trading volumes actually increased, while high–volume traders enjoyed commission reductions. Traditional brokerage firms such as Merrill Lynch have continued to offer a variety of services, including recommendations concerning the merits of particular investments. But other firms, such as Charles Schwab, have been established primarily to offer execution services. These firms are known as "discount brokers." Discount brokers can employ less skilled, and therefore less highly paid, personnel to take buy and sell orders. As a consequence, these firms charge lower commissions. Saunders and Smirlock (1987) show that financial markets expected banks entering the discount brokerage business to provide substantial competition to traditional brokers.[3] Box 3.3 describes a study of investors who use discount and full service brokers.

Mutual funds pay their management companies fees to advise the fund on its investments. This fee can amount to 1 percent of the value of the assets under management. In addition, the mutual fund pays brokerage firms commissions for buying and selling investments. Brokerage firms typically rebate some of these commissions to the investment manager. These rebates are called **soft dollars**. Beginning in 1986 the USSEC allowed brokerage firms to provide the investment manager with "anything that materially aids the manager in the performance of his investment duties." In the USA it is estimated that 25 percent of annual institutional brokerage commissions are directed to brokerage firms that will provide soft dollars. **Directed** means that a client or investment manager designates that an order be given to a specific firm for execution. Soft dollars are available only on agency trades.

The practice of allowing brokerage firms to provide soft dollars to management companies has been controversial, because of the obvious agency problem involved. The mutual fund pays the brokerage fee, but the management firm receives the rebated services. Management companies argue that the rebate provides additional resources that are used to improve the investment process. Others think that the mutual fund is paying twice for the same service – once when the fund pays the management fee and again when it pays brokerage commissions. It seems self-evident that a brokerage firm could charge lower commissions if it did not have the expense of soft dollars.

> ## BOX 3.3
> ### Usage of discount versus full-service brokers
>
> On May 1, 1975, fixed minimum brokerage commissions on security transactions were abolished in the USA. One result was the establishment of "discount" brokerage firms that offer fewer services, but at a lower commission rate, than traditional "full service" brokerage firms. McInish, Ramaswami, and Srivastava (1991) investigate investors' choices between full service and discount brokers. Their results are based on a financial diary panel comprising 980 members of upscale households (income over 25,000 USD) from the continental United States who use discount brokers, full service brokers, or both. Less than 11 percent of the sample used discount brokers exclusively, while about 78 percent used full service brokers exclusively.
>
> Results indicate that investors who use both discount and full service brokers have a greater number of stock and bond purchases and a smaller dollar amount of stock sales, controlling for critical variables such as income, wealth, and the size of stock and bond portfolios. The results also indicate that investors who use discount brokers exclusively tend to (1) sell stocks more often, (2) have relatively more education, (3) be older, (4) have lower income and net worth, (5) have a greater desire for aggressive capital accumulation, and (6) rate savings for retirement lower.
>
> Interestingly, investors who are buying stock deal relatively more with full service firms, while individuals who are selling stock deal relatively more with discount brokers. Since they typically only sell stock that they already own (e.g., they do not usually sell short), but can buy any stock, investors may need less advice concerning sales than purchases. Also, full service firms do not give much investment advice concerning which stocks to sell. This evidence is consistent with the view that stock purchases are more likely to be initiated by the broker, while stock sales are relatively more likely to be customer-initiated.
>
> Choice of type of broker is also related to investment objective. Those using both full service brokers and discount brokers are relatively more interested in saving for retirement and relatively less interested in either aggressive or speculative capital accumulation. The investment objectives that are more closely associated with individual circumstances (such as investing for family education and for travel/entertainment) are not useful in discriminating between investors who choose different types of brokerage firms. Instead, objectives that might be more closely associated with investment horizon are important discriminators. Customers of full service firms might be viewed as having longer investment horizons than customers of discount brokerage firms.
>
> *Source*: McInish, Ramaswami, and Srivastava, 1991.

2.1.2. Information costs

In his article on the economics of information, Stigler (1961) argued that the more one searched, the less would be the returns for that search. Paroush and Peles (1978) were the first to develop a model for the optimal search process across different product types. These authors derived several interesting propositions: (1) the optimal amount of search is an increasing function of excess expected return; (2) investors should spend search dollars where they can get the greatest uncertainty reduction for the same outlay; and (3) the incidence of ownership of high information cost investments should increase with wealth. Because a large part of information costs are fixed costs, the more money one has to invest, the lower the cost per unit of investment. This is one reason why wealthy investors are more likely to own the high information cost investments. A related proposition is that investment types with less information costs are likely to be more widely held.

Using data collected from a survey of wealthy investors, Srivastava, McInish and Price (1984) provide evidence supporting the propositions of Paroush and Peles. These authors show that higher perceived information costs are associated with excess returns and a greater range of returns. They also show that product types that require the advice of a lawyer, an accountant, or a financial advisor have higher perceived information costs. Commodity funds are an example of a product type with high information costs. These were held by only 5.7 percent of investors with a net worth of 401,000–500,000 USD, but by 17.2 percent of investors with a net worth of over 1 million USD. On the other hand, growth common stocks, a product type with low perceived information costs, were owned by 97.1 percent of investors with a net worth of 401,000–500,000 USD and by 98.5 percent of investors with a net worth of over 1 million USD. The ownership of similar types of assets goes together. Investors who become knowledgeable about residential rental property are more likely to purchase commercial rental property. Investors who learn about government bonds are more likely to purchase corporate bonds. This allows investors to make better use of their investment in acquiring knowledge. Also, the professionals an investor gets to know in making investments reinforce this concentration. Once an investor uses an investment type that requires use of a lawyer, that investor is more likely to invest in other products that also require the use of a lawyer.

2.1.3. Taxes

Taxes, transfer fees, and the like can have a substantial impact on the cost of trading. If costs are high, the amount of trading may be significantly reduced, damaging the liquidity of the market. The harm may be mitigated if investors can direct their trades to alternative market centers.

2.2. IMPLICIT TRANSACTION COSTS

Implicit transaction costs typically amount to several times direct costs or even more. Barclay, Kandel, and Marx (1998) examined the effect of changes in bid–ask spreads on prices and trading volumes. They found that higher spreads significantly reduce trading volume, but do not have an effect on prices.

2.2.1. Bid–ask spreads

We have seen that the bid–ask spread represents a significant cost to investors. The spread is a cost of immediacy. It makes sense that investors who do not need immediacy should not pay for it. Instead, those investors can supply immediacy by placing limit orders rather than market orders. Box 3.4 describes a patient-trading program initiated by RJR Investment Management. This program is estimated to have saved RJR 144,000–548,000 USD on a portfolio of 40 million USD.

We have previously defined the bid–ask spread as the ask quotation minus the bid quotation. The spread exists because suppliers of immediacy must be compensated. In many

> ## BOX 3.4
> ### Patient trading
>
> In 1988, RJR Investment Management established a self-managed 40 million USD small capitalization investment fund, which was to own 250 stocks selected from the Russell 2000 index. (Additional information is provided in Bodurtha and Quinn 1989.) The cost of acquiring these shares over a period of 1–5 days was projected to be 2.5 percent of the portfolio's value, and costs of as much as 3.5 percent of the portfolio's value would not have been surprising. A plan was developed to reduce trading costs by implementing a patient trading strategy. Each morning the stocks in the target list of 250 were evaluated to identify those that were under-performing the Russell 2000 index. Limit orders designated "good today" were submitted to purchase these issues. At the end of the day the remaining buy list was submitted to an electronic proprietary trading system. According to the firm, "we would trade only if we could buy stocks at 'our' prices, and we were virtually indifferent whether we bought ten stocks, eighty stocks, or no stocks on a given day." After 75 percent of the total shares sought had been acquired, RJR adopted a more aggressive strategy. At the end of 2 weeks, the remaining shares needed to complete the program were purchased using market orders.
>
> RJR used the Perold (1988) implementation shortfall approach to evaluate the cost of acquiring the portfolio. Following this methodology, RJR compared the performance of two portfolios. The first comprised the stocks actually acquired at their actual acquisition prices and times. The second comprised a hypothetical portfolio using prices that would have been paid if the stocks had been purchased immediately. The difference between the two is the gain or loss as a result of the trading decisions. Naturally, the performance of the paper portfolio reflects general market movements during the implementation period. In order to put the actual portfolio on an even footing, its performance was adjusted by assuming that initially the entire 40,000,000 USD was invested in the Russell 2000. Then, as stocks were actually purchased, the funds were assumed to come from selling the Russell 2000 portfolio. RJR considered actually using such a hedge, but decided that in this case hedging was unnecessary, since the program was being funded through sales of large capitalization stocks.
>
> The results of the implementation shortfall analysis showed that the actual portfolio under-performed the paper portfolio by 2.13 percent. Comparing the actual cost with the expected cost of 2.50 percent to 3.50 percent, the patient program saved 0.36 percent to 1.37 percent, and a substantial part of the overall transaction costs.

markets, dealers who must cover their costs supply this immediacy. But what are these costs? The earliest investigations of spreads focused on **order processing costs**. These include the costs of the dealer's time, paperwork costs, and transfer taxes and other expenses incurred by the dealer in providing immediacy. In the process of making a market, the dealer may have money invested in the asset, incurring opportunity costs. Another cost of providing immediacy is **inventory holding costs**.[4] Moreover, the dealer may lose money on the inventory because of price changes. Both of these are a source of inventory costs in providing immediacy.

More recently, a third cost incurred by dealers who provide immediacy has received attention: namely, **adverse information costs**. Some investors are likely to be better informed than the dealer. When these informed investors buy from the dealer, subsequently, prices are likely to rise. And when informed investors sell to the dealer, subsequently, prices are likely to decline. Therefore, in dealing with informed investors the dealer is often buying just before price decreases and selling just before price increases. For examples of

Table 3.2 Representative bid, ask, and percentage spread for 11 currencies for January 26, 1995

Currency	bid	ask	% spread
European Currency Unit	1.2496	1.2506	0.08
Hong Kong dollar (HKD)	7.7308	7.7318	0.01
Danish krone (DKK)	5.9734	5.9895	0.26
Japanese yen (JPY)	99.25	99.30	0.05
German mark (DEM)	1.5144	1.5149	0.03
French franc (FFR)	5.2430	5.2480	0.01
British pound (GBP)	0.6277	0.6281	0.06
Canadian dollar (CAD)	1.4145	1.4150	0.04
Irish punt (IEP)	0.6342	0.6350	0.11
Australian dollar (AUD)	1.3048	1.3057	0.07
Spanish peseta (ESP)	131.60	131.75	0.11

asymmetric information models see Copeland and Galai 1983 and Glosten and Milgrom 1985.

Bid–ask spreads are a feature of trading when dealers are providers of immediacy. All the product types that we consider in this book – equities, fixed-income securities, derivatives, and currencies – have bid–ask spreads. Table 3.2 shows the bid and ask quotations for the currencies of ten countries and for the European Currency Unit on January 26, 1995, along with the percentage bid–ask spread. Bessembinder (1994) provides a discussion of bid–ask spreads in currency markets. These are quotations for transaction sizes of 1 million USD or more. Even though the spreads are relatively low, one might be able to get better quotes by shopping with other dealers. And on occasion one might be able to trade between the quotes. Trading between the quotes is called **price improvement**.

Amihud and Mendelson (1986) develop a model in which they predict that "higher-spread assets yield higher expected returns and that there is a clientele effect whereby investors with longer holding periods select assets with higher spreads." Atkins and Dyl (1994) test whether higher bid–ask spreads are associated with greater holding periods as proxied by the turnover ratio for a firm's stock. For NASDAQ stocks they find that a 1 percent difference in spread is associated with a 1.34-year difference in investors' average holding periods, and that the relationship is mildly nonlinear. There is more nonlinearity in the NYSE sample, where an increase in spread from 0.2 percent to 1 percent is associated with a $1\frac{1}{3}$-year increase in holding period, but an increase in spread from 4 percent to 5 percent leads to only a $\frac{2}{3}$-year increase in holding periods.

In many cases prices are quoted for financial products on a net basis. In other words, the price paid is the price indicated, and there is no explicit markup/markdown. Currencies are often quoted in this way worldwide. Bond and stock prices may also be quoted on a net basis in many financial centers. Investors should not assume that just because a net price is quoted, the broker is not charging a markup/markdown. In fact, in some cases the markup/markdown may be substantial.

Sometimes exchange tick-size rules can increase the size of the spread. **Tick size** is the minimum price variation permitted in a market. On the SES stocks selling for more than 25 SGD have traditionally been quoted in whole-dollar prices, such as 25 SGD, 26 SGD, and 27 SGD, or in half-dollar prices, such as 25.50 SGD, 26.50 SGD, and 27.50 SGD. Hence, in this case the minimum price variation is 0.50 SGD. The minimum tick size is important for several reasons.

The minimum tick size determines the minimum market spread. The size of the spread is important in determining trading costs. If the minimum tick size is larger than the spread warranted by the spread determinants identified by McInish and Wood (1992), then the market spread and, consequently, trading costs are increased. On the other hand, if the minimum tick size is too small, investors can step to the front of the limit order book by placing orders at better prices that are not economically different from those already on the book. This could make time priority meaningless and discourage liquidity suppliers from keeping quotes on the limit order book and thereby reduce liquidity.

Suppose that the equilibrium price for a stock on the SES is 25.50 when the minimum tick size is 0.50. Then market participants can submit orders to buy and orders to sell at that price, and trading can occur. But if information arrives that changes the equilibrium price to, say, 25.75, with a minimum tick size of 0.50, the price must be either 25.50 or 26.00, and there is no way to reflect the desired equilibrium of 25.75 in the market price. On an exchange with market makers, market participants with larger orders could conceivably agree to trade, say, 5,000 shares at 25.50 and 5,000 at 26.00, so that the average price is 25.75. Such trades are typically difficult to arrange in dealer markets and are not possible in anonymous electronic markets such as the SES. Trading is restricted to those willing to trade away from the equilibrium price, which, on balance, should reduce the volume of trading. For these reasons, the issue of the appropriate tick size has received considerable attention in the USA. In US equity markets, the minimum tick size is typically 0.125 USD. The USSEC Division of Market Regulation (1994) concluded that the minimum price variation of US 0.125 USD "can cause artificially wide spreads and hinder quote competition by preventing offers to buy or sell at prices inside the prevailing quote" (p. 18).

Harris (1991) developed and estimated a model of stock-price clustering to predict the effects of a reduction in the minimum tick size. He concluded that in the USA, if exchange rules permitted, traders would frequently use odd sixteenths to trade low-priced stocks, lowering transaction costs.[5] Subsequently, using a different model, Harris (1994) shows that smaller minimum price variations would significantly reduce bid–ask spreads.[6] This model predicted a reduction in bid–ask spreads of 36 percent. In June 1997 the NYSE, NASDAQ, and other US stock exchanges began quoting and trading stocks in minimum price increments of one-sixteenth of 1 USD.

As on other exchanges, the minimum tick size on the SES is set arbitrarily by the exchange. The importance of tick size can be seen by examining a reduction in tick size implemented by the SES on July 19, 1994, when the minimum tick size for stocks trading at 25 SGD or more was reduced from 0.50 SGD to 0.10 SGD. Lau and McInish (1995) investigate this reduction in tick size. As shown in table 3.3, the mean spread declined for each of the three firms. In the pre-reduction period, eleven of the twelve quotes had a spread of 0.50 SGD, but in the post-reduction period eleven of the fifteen quotes were below 0.50 SGD.

Table 3.3 Statistics for stocks affected by the reduction in tick size on the SES

		Spread			Size		
		BS	CT	SPH	BS	CT	SPH
B	July 12	1.00	0.50	0.50	33,000	39,700	164,000
E	July 13	0.50	0.50	0.50	21,000	150,100	67,000
F	July 14	0.50	0.50	0.50	26,000	20,950	63,000
O	July 15	0.50	0.50	0.50	17,000	4,350	350,000
R							
E	Mean	0.625	0.50	0.50	24,250	53,775	161,000
A	July 18	0.70	0.40	0.20	23,000	350	6,000
F	July 19	0.50	0.10	0.90	6,000	8,650	6,000
T	July 20	0.20	0.20	0.10	36,000	13,250	41,000
E	July 21	0.20	0.10	0.20	2,000	12,550	9,000
R	July 22	0.10	0.10	0.20	2,000	11,300	15,000
	Mean	0.24	0.18	0.32	13,800	9,220	15,400
t-statistic		−1.53*	−5.71**	−1.76*	−0.98	−1.61*	−4.66**

The firms affected by the reduction in tick size are Singapore Press Holdings Limited (SPH), Bukit Sembawang Estates Ltd. (BS), and Creative Technology Ltd. (CT). CT is a Singapore-based firm that is also actively traded on the NASDAQ. The spread, computed for the best bid and ask, and SIZE, the sum of the shares available at the best offer and the best bid, are presented. For each firm, the spreads are ranked from lowest to highest, and a t-test of the difference in the mean ranks for the before and after sample is provided.
* Significant at the 0.095 level.
** Significant at the 0.056 level.
Source: Lau and McInish 1995. Reprinted with kind permission from Elsevier Science – NL, Sara Burgerhartstraat 25, 1055 KV Amsterdam, the Netherlands.

Table 3.3 also presents information on the sum of the number of shares sought at the best bid and offered for sale at the best ask, which is labeled "Size" in the table. The values of size decline dramatically after the tick reduction. This is predicted from normal supply/demand considerations. At a lower ask price, investors are willing to offer less for sale, and at a higher bid price, investors are willing to purchase fewer shares.

Assuming that spreads do not change because of order flow, the spread can be earned in two trades, one to acquire the initial position and the second to liquidate this position. One-half of the difference in the average spread in the pre- and post-reduction periods is $(0.83 − 0.25)/2 = 0.29$ SGD. The three stocks in the sample traded an average of 80,333 shares daily in the post-reduction period, so a reduction in the spread costs of 0.29 SGD would result in a savings of 70,693 SGD ($0.29 \times 3 \times 80,333$) to market participants requiring more immediate execution. Lau and McInish (1995) concluded that this reduction in market spread is economically significant.

McCorry and McInish (1997) examined the tick size reduction on December 4, 1996, on the Australian Stock Exchange (ASX). The ASX reduced the minimum tick size for 332 stocks trading at less than $0.50 and for more than $10.00. Stocks trading in the price range from $0.50 up to $10.00 were not affected, providing a natural control group. We find that spreads and liquidity were both reduced following the tick size reduction, providing evidence of a tradeoff between these two variables. There was no statistically significant change in the volume of trading in ASX stocks either on the exchange or in off-exchange trading. The stocks most constrained by the pre-reduction tick size experienced the largest declines in spreads. Niemeyer and Sandas (1996) examined tick sizes on the Stockholm Stock Exchange and reported that larger tick sizes are associated with larger bid–ask spreads and larger depth. Contrary to others, these authors also reported that larger tick sizes are associated with lower trading volume.

2.2.2. Market impact costs

The execution of an order has the potential to move the market price. Here we are talking about more than the change from the bid to the ask. Market impact involves moving the bid and/or ask either temporarily or permanently. Suppose that a market has sellers willing to sell 5,000 shares at 50 and 5,500 shares at 50.10. An order to buy more than 5,000 shares will exhaust the supply at 50, and if immediate execution is required, will necessitate executing part of the order at 50.10. Hence, this order will have market impact. Market impact is a cost associated with implementing an investment decision. Typically, the larger the size of the order, the greater the market impact. For example, in an early study, Wood, McInish and Ord (1985) showed that on the NYSE a price change (either up or down) of $\frac{1}{8}$ is associated with an average trade size of 1,300 shares, but a price change of $\frac{1}{4}$ is associated with an average trade size of more than 1,400 for a price increase and more than 1,700 shares for a price decrease.

3. QUANTIFYING EXECUTION COSTS

Explicit transaction costs can be observed and can usually be measured easily. Execution costs (implicit transactions costs), the difference between the transaction price and the "true" price of the security in the absence of a trade, are not easily measured. Although the execution price is known, the prevailing price in the absence of a trade is not observable, and therein lies the difficulty in measuring indirect execution costs. The practical alternative is to use some benchmark price as a proxy for the true price. Benchmarks can be based on pre-trade, post-trade, or average prices. (For a discussion of these issues see Collins and Fabozzi 1991.)

3.1. ISSUES IN QUANTIFYING EXECUTION COSTS

One issue that must be dealt with, whether using pre-trade or post trade performance measures, is **gaming**, the execution of a trade using knowledge of events that have already occurred to enhance the evaluation of one's performance. Pre-trade measures, which use prices occurring at the time of the decision to trade, rather than at the actual time of the trade, are the closest approximation to a true execution cost measure. The problem with pre-trade measures is that they are subject to gaming, because the trader knows the benchmark before executing the trade. If the current market price is better than the benchmark, the trader can execute the trade quickly and show favorable performance. If the comparison with the benchmark is unfavorable, the trader can delay execution or perhaps even choose not to execute the trade.

While it is easy to see how a pre-trade measure can be gamed, it is not as easy to recognize potential types of gaming that can occur with post-trade measures. Post-trade measures use prices occurring after the execution of the trade. Post-trade measures avoid most gaming problems, although sometimes they can be gamed in the sense that, say, a closing price could be manipulated up or down a tick with a very small transaction. Post-trade measures have the drawback of possibly being influenced by the trade itself. A good post-trade benchmark should be based on a trade occurring after the influence of the trade has dissipated. Unfortunately, this interval is neither fixed nor known; if it extends too far after the trade, the measure becomes contaminated by other variables influencing the market price and ceases to be a measure of indirect execution cost.

Some claim that the use of an average of prices over some period around the trade decision provides a better measure of execution costs. Typically, these measures are computed as the average of the high and low price for the day or as a volume-weighted average price. Unfortunately, average measures are also subject to gaming. It may be easy for the trader to guess whether the high for the day has probably already occurred. Average measures may also induce a trader to spread a trade out over the trading day to guarantee performance closely matching the benchmark.

One of the broadest ways of measuring trading costs is the approach of Perold (1988). The method involves comparing the performance of two portfolios. The first is a "paper" portfolio that assumes that decisions to invest are implemented immediately at the average of the bid and ask price. The second is the performance of the portfolio actually purchased. The difference between the performance of the two portfolios is the **implementation shortfall**. If direct costs such as commissions are included, then the difference in performance is a measure of all trading costs. If some investments are not actually made because the market moves away before the decision to invest can be implemented, then comparison of these two portfolios reveals the opportunity cost. The method also captures all the other types of execution costs. A difficulty is that the implementation shortfall method requires the continuous "management" of the paper portfolio, regardless of how much it diverges from the actual portfolio. The paper portfolio must also be managed in conformity with any restrictions that limit the portfolio's investments.

3.2. PREVIOUS STUDIES OF TRANSACTION COSTS

We examine four studies of transaction costs in some detail.[7] The main results of these studies are summarized in table 3.4. We begin with the study of Beebower and Priest (1980), who used a post-trade measure based on the closing price of the stock on the day of the trade (and on following days adjusted by market return). These authors found that commissions represent 0.49 percent of the transactions amount (sample 1) for purchases and

Table 3.4 Mean and standard deviation (in parentheses) of execution costs reported in four studies

	All trades	Purchases	Sales
	Commissions – % of transactions amount		
Beebower and Priest – sample 1		0.49	0.74
Beebower and Priest – sample 2		0.47	0.63
Berkowitz, Logue, and Noser		0.18	0.18
	Indirect execution costs – % of transactions amount		
Beebower and Priest – sample 1		−0.12	0.15
Beebower and Priest – sample 2		−0.22	−0.14
Berkowitz, Logue, and Noser	0.055	0.009	0.101
Block, French, and McInish – C_q	0.1084	0.0930	0.1243
Block, French, and McInish – C_p	0.1135	0.0946	0.1330
Hasbrouck and Schwartz	0.148		
	Commissions – USD per share		
Block, French, and McInish – mean commission	0.0644	0.0644	0.0644
	Indirect execution costs – USD per share		
Block, French, and McInish – C_q	0.0358 (0.1661)	0.0315 (0.1526)	0.0402 (0.1792)
Block, French, and McInish – C_p	0.0373 (0.1734)	0.0324 (0.1602)	0.0423 (0.1862)

Source: Block, French, and McInish 1994, p. 170. Reprinted by permission Kluwer Academic Publishers.

0.74 percent of the transactions amount for sales. Indirect transactions costs were found to be −0.12 percent (sample 1) and −0.22 percent (sample 2) of trade value for buys and 0.15 percent (sample 1) and −0.14 percent (sample 2) for sells. A negative cost means that the trade was executed at a price more favorable than the benchmark. Thus, buy orders incurred indirect execution costs that were on average 12 cents lower per 100 dollars of stock purchased than the benchmark.

Negative average execution costs appear suspicious. Beebower and Priest's results may be biased because they used the closing price for the day as their post-trade measure (see Berkowitz, Logue, and Noser 1988). Stock prices tend to rise on average during the last few

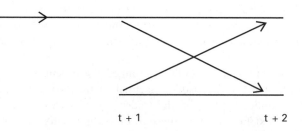

t   t + 1   t + 2

Figure 3.1 Bid–ask bounce. Assume that trades occur only at the beginning of a period and that the only possible prices are the ask (A) and bid (B). Then, there are eight possible sequences of prices over a three-period interval: namely, A, B, B; A, B, A; A, A, B; A, A, A; B, A, A; B, A, B; B, B, A; B, B, B. Graphically, the potential price sequences beginning with an initial ask price can be illustrated thus.
Source: Roll 1984. Reprinted by permission of the *Journal of Finance*.

trading minutes, so the closing price is probably an upwardly biased estimate of what the true benchmark should be (Wood, McInish, and Ord 1985). This tends to make execution costs for buys look lower than those for sells.[8]

Berkowitz, Logue and Noser (1988) reported commissions of 0.18 percent of the transaction amount. These researchers measured indirect execution costs using an average-price benchmark, defining execution cost as the difference between the trade price and the volume-weighted average price during the day. They concluded that execution costs represent about 0.009 percent for buys and 0.101 percent for sells, for an overall average of 0.055 percent. But the volume-weighted daily price is subject to gaming by the trader, because the jump in volume during the closing minutes of trading will weight the price more heavily toward end-of-the-day transactions, and this will bias the results to show lower costs for buying than for selling. (Upward bias of closing prices is addressed by McInish and Wood (1990, 1991).)

Taking a different approach, Hasbrouck and Schwartz (1988) reasoned that execution costs due to **bid–ask bounce** (the movement of stock prices between the bid and the ask), market impact, and the like temporarily push trading prices away from their true value (bid–ask bounce is illustrated in figure 3.1). Hence, comparison of volatility over different periods can be used to investigate the impact of transaction costs. These authors calculated the ratio of the variance of 12-hour returns to 24 times the variance of half-hour returns. Because these intervals cover the same calendar period, we know that the actual volatility is the same over these two measurement intervals. Therefore, the value of the ratio should be 1.0. Any temporary deviations provide a measure of execution costs. Using this methodology, these authors reported average execution costs of 0.148 percent of the transactions amount for NYSE-listed stocks (compared with 0.055 percent for Berkowitz, Logue and Noser). The comparable costs reported by Hasbrouck and Schwartz for American Stock Exchange and more liquid NASDAQ stocks were 0.123 and 0.438 percent, respectively. If the assumption that the entire difference in the variance ratios is due to transaction costs does not hold, the Hasbrouck and Schwartz measure will have overestimated execution costs. Stabilization activities of the specialist, the presence of limit orders, or the sequential arrival of information causing price adjustment delays might also affect short-term price volatility.

Block, French, and McInish (1994) examined the execution costs incurred by traders for NationsBank, a major US bank. Essential to measuring the potential effect of the trader is a clear understanding of the trader's role in executing an order. The traders in this study worked for the trust division of NationsBank. The bank has a number of portfolio managers who specialize in industry groupings and collectively manage equity portfolios for various plan sponsors. Once the portfolio manager makes a decision to trade, the manager communicates the instructions to a trader in the equity trading division. The order is immediately time stamped (for example, a request to buy 2,000 shares of Digital Equipment may come in at 9:21 a.m. on June 25). The trader is responsible for the trade and can immediately execute the order at the last quoted price or attempt to search for a better price. With the latter course, the trader brings all the buy–sell positions available in the market for the security up on a computer screen and searches for the best potential opportunity. The trader then quickly calls four or five brokers and attempts to fill the order at less than the existing ask price. Since the typical trader knows the behavior of 50–100 brokers with whom the trader deals on a wide array of stocks, the trader knows whom to call first and where to press hardest for execution. The trader maintains a close watch on market factors such as overhanging blocks, new stock buy-back programs, rumors, and stocks or groups that are most in demand or under the greatest pressure. (For additional discussion see Dannen 1984.) The strategies used by the traders were not known, so it was not possible to ascertain whether orders were broken up for execution (as suggested by Algert (1991)).

Of course, the trader may fail to execute a purchase below the original asking price and may even be forced to go above it as a result of the difficulty of the trade or the delay in executing the order during the search process. While the trader is trying to save 0.5 percent in execution costs, the stock price may go up 2.5 percent.

The role of the trading desk is also complicated by constraints that may be placed on the traders. These limitations may be either subjective or objective. When the transactions ordered by the portfolio managers are motivated by information rather than liquidity, there is likely to be strong pressure for immediate execution. Also, there may be actual dollar constraints on the commissions that can be paid to execute a trade, which may force the trader to give the order ticket to a discount broker. Some plan sponsors may direct the order to specific brokerage firms. Nevertheless, in the environment that existed at the time of the Block, French, and McInish study, the trading desk of NationsBank had substantial flexibility in executing trades.

Block, French, and McInish (1994) empirically investigated the trading costs incurred by NationsBank's traders using a random sample of their trades. These authors used two benchmark pre-trade prices – the average of the bid and ask quote immediately before the order (C_p) and the last trade price before the order (C_q). Each measure was computed as follows:

C = EP-B, for buy orders, and
C = B-EP, for sell orders,

Table 3.5 Summary statistics for institutional trades

	All trades	Purchases	Sales
Sample size	717	365	352
Shares per trade			
Mean	11,788	11,024	12,579
Minimum	100	100	100
Maximum	144,400	110,000	144,440
Execution prices			
Mean	36.472	36.379	36.569
Minimum	4.000	4.000	5.500
Maximum	140.375	117.250	140.375
Mean prices per share (in USD)			
Current bid	36.367	36.245	36.493
Current ask	36.598	36.476	36.725
Current quote average	36.482	36.360	36.609
Prior trade price	36.484	36.362	36.611

Source: Block, French, and McInish 1994, p. 169. Reprinted by permission Kluwer Academic Publishers.

where

C = the measure of execution cost,
EP = either the average bid–ask quote or the last trade price, respectively, and
B = the benchmark for measuring execution costs.

In this case the use of a pre-trade measure was justified, because the traders were not aware that their performance was going to be studied.

As shown in table 3.5, for the sample used by Block, French, and McInish (1994), the mean number of shares per trade was 11,024 for purchases and 12,579 for sales, giving an overall average of 11,788. The mean execution price, current bid, current ask, current quote, average price, and prior trade price were all in the 36–7 USD range. As shown in table 3.4, the mean brokerage commission are 0.0644 USD per share for all trades, and the mean of indirect execution costs was 0.0358 USD per share based on C_q. Estimated indirect execution costs were similar for the C_q and C_p measures. Thus commissions accounted for about 65 percent of transaction costs, and indirect execution costs accounted for about 35 percent. Information about indirect execution costs as a percentage of the transaction amount was also provided. Indirect execution costs were 0.1084 percent of the transaction amount for this sample. This result is about midway between the 0.055 percent reported by Berkowitz, Logue, and Noser (1988) and the 0.148 percent reported by Hasbrouck and Schwartz (1988).

3.3. Alternate Ways of Defining the Bid–Ask Spread

Because of the importance of spreads as a transaction cost, a number of ways of measuring spreads have been developed. A number of these focus on the half-spread. If an investor buys at the ask and then sells at the bid, the entire spread has been incurred as a cost. But since there are two transactions, the cost per transaction is the half-spread. Of course, the **quoted half-spread** is simply one-half of the ask minus the bid. The **effective half-spread** is the trade price minus the quote midpoint (the ask plus the bid) divided by 2. (For studies of trading costs that use the effective half-spread see Lee (1993) and Petersen and Fialkowski 1994.)

If quotes change as a result of trades, either because of the information contained in the trade or because of inventory considerations, then a distinction should be made between dealer spreads and market spreads. The dealer spread can be greater than the market spread, but the market spread cannot be greater than the dealer spread. Suppose that there are two dealers, each with a spread of USD 0.50. One might give a quote of 10.00–10.50, whereas the other could give a quote of 10.25–10.75. While both dealers have a spread of 0.50, from the point of view of investors, the market spread is 0.25, which is obtained by subtracting the best bid of 10.25 from the best ask of 10.50. Thus, the **dealer spread** is the quoted spread of a dealer, whereas the **market spread** is the difference between the best ask and the best bid quoted in the market. The effective spread is calculated from actual transactions. Hence, it reflects both the quoted market spread, market impact, and any undisplayed limit orders.

3.4. THE DETERMINANTS OF SPREADS

3.4.1. Overview of previous findings

There have been numerous attempts to explain the existence and size of bid–ask spreads, especially in US equity markets. These studies provide evidence that there are at least four categories of determinants of spreads: activity, risk, information, and competition.

Activity   Activity is closely related to economies of scale. The earliest papers focused on the costs of those providing immediacy. Market makers incur costs in buying and selling. These include the time involved, costs of paperwork and transfer taxes, and interest costs from holding inventory. With increased activity, the fixed portion of these costs can be spread over more trades and/or shares, and hence the per share execution costs are lower. Thus, market makers achieve economies of scale. Working in the opposite direction, inventory control models emphasize that the purchases and sales of market makers can move them away from their desired inventory position. Naturally, larger transactions move the dealer further away from the desired position and therefore lead to increased costs. The evidence shows that economies of scale predominate, and that there is an inverse relationship between spreads and trading volume.

Risk   Market makers also face risk from the effect of possible price changes on their inventory. Of course, these price movements can be either favorable or unfavorable. Individuals typically seek to avoid risk of loss even if the expected outcome is zero over a long horizon. If the expected outcome is zero, some investors may have gains, while others have losses. If the economy is good, most investors will have gains, but if the economy is bad, most will have losses. Market makers must be compensated for bearing these risks. Consistent with this view, the evidence shows that there is a direct relationship between the level of risk and spreads.

Information   More recently researchers have focused on the effect of information on spreads. Some investors' trades simply reflect their need for money. They may sell financial assets to cover living expenses or purchase financial assets to invest funds. Investors who merely want to change the assets held in their portfolio initiate many purchases and sales of financial assets. These trades are informationless, because they are not motivated by any special information. These traders are also referred to as "uninformed traders," "noise traders," or "liquidity traders."

Others trade because they have superior knowledge of the true equilibrium value of a financial asset. They may obtain this information from superior analysis or insight or from inside information. Market makers are vulnerable to being "picked off" by investors with superior information. In other words, market makers face the prospect of incurring financial losses in trades with informed traders. These losses must be offset by greater revenue from the informationless or uninformed traders. The evidence shows that there is a direct relationship between spreads and the amount of information coming to the market.

Competition   The final determinant of the spread is competition. Studies have shown that in the over-the-counter market the spread is inversely related to the number of market makers. Likewise, the level of the spread on the NYSE is inversely related to the number of other markets on which the stock is traded.

3.4.2. The study of McInish and Wood

McInish and Wood (1992) investigated whether the differences in the spread from stock to stock and from interval to interval of the trading day can be explained by the factors discussed in the previous section. They used data for a large sample of NYSE stocks during the first six months of 1989. Taking the mean of the spread for these stocks for each minute during the trading day gave the reverse J-shaped pattern depicted in figure 3.2. Spreads are high at the beginning of the day, decline until the late afternoon, and then increase until the close. McInish and Wood did not attempt to explain the pattern of the spreads, but they did attempt to ascertain whether they could identify variables that account for the differences in spreads among different stocks and for different days. For their analysis, each trading day during the first six months of 1989 was segmented into one 31-minute interval and twelve 30-minute intervals (9:30 a.m. to 10:00 a.m., etc.). Spreads and variables thought to influence the size of the spread were calculated for each firm for each interval.

Activity: economies of scale   The costs of providing a service may have a fixed and a variable component, so that at least over some range, a larger number of transactions can result in a lower unit cost per transaction. McInish and Wood used the number of trades and the number of shares per trade to investigate whether economies of scale affect the bid–ask spread.

Risk: loss due to price fluctuations   Dealers who hold long inventory incur losses if the price declines, while those with short inventory lose when prices increase. This risk can be

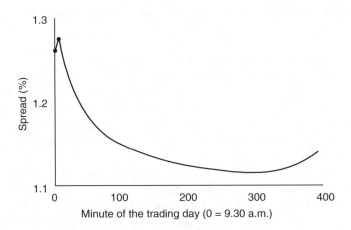

Figure 3.2 Mean bid–ask spreads for each minute of the trading day. First, a time-series of second-by-second percentage bid–ask spreads is created for each stock. The time-series begins with the initial quotation each trading day. For a given stock for every second during which a quotation is outstanding a percentage bid–ask spread is calculated as (ask − bid)/((ask + bid)/2). The process is repeated for each stock. Then, for each trading second of the calendar year, all of the percentage bid–ask spreads are averaged to create a second-by-second time series of "market" percentage bid–ask spreads. The percentage bid–ask spreads are then averaged within each trading minute to create a time series of minute-by-minute bid–ask spreads.
Source: Wood, McInish, and Ord 1985. Reprinted by permission of the *Journal of Finance*.

measured by the variability of the stock price, which can then be compared across stock. We call this risk "stock risk" in table 3.6. If inventory holding costs are an important determinant of spreads, assets whose prices fluctuate more should have higher spreads. Further, for a given asset, periods during which asset prices fluctuate more should also have higher spreads. This risk can be measured by how much the variability of prices in a particular interval differs from its usual level. We call this risk "interval risk" in table 3.6.

Risk: loss due to trading with informed traders Individuals with whom dealers trade may be better informed about the true value of the asset. Informed traders prefer to trade in larger sizes. Naturally, informed traders attempt to disguise their trades by placing smaller orders. On balance, this effort at disguise will probably not be entirely successful, so that measuring the extent to which trades in a particular asset during a particular period are of unusual size can capture this adverse information risk. We call this risk "adverse information risk" in table 3.6. Note that to the extent that a stock typically has large trades, it will have smaller transaction costs due to economies of scale, but unusually large trades may reflect informed trading and thus be associated with higher spreads. Of course, a 200-share trade may be large for one stock, while a 10,000-share trade may not be unusually large for another stock.

Competition It is likely that, *ceteris paribus*, competition results in lower spreads. In the USA many stocks listed and traded primarily on the NYSE are also traded on a number of

Table 3.6 Results for the regression of percentage spreads against activity, risk, information, competition and control variables

Independent variables	Coefficients	t-statistic
Intercept	0.0158	849.12*
Number of trades	−0.0005	−226.96*
Number of shares per trade	−0.0002	−82.28*
Stock risk	0.0668	320.45*
Interval risk	0.0004	137.23*
Adverse information risk	0.0005	80.98*
Competition	−0.0002	−24.66*
Price	−0.0018	−673.17*
Regression Results		
Interval 1	0.00065	49.12*
Interval 2	0.00042	32.35*
Interval 3	0.00030	23.46*
Interval 4	0.00021	16.09*
Interval 5	0.00016	11.97*
Interval 6	0.00009	6.58*
Interval 7	0.00001	0.05
Interval 8	−0.00005	−3.71*
Interval 9	−0.00038	−2.88*
Interval 11	0.00011	8.65*
Interval 12	0.00025	18.98*
Interval 13	0.00041	32.19*
Monday	0.00004	4.61*
Tuesday	0.00001	1.78
Thursday	0.00003	4.31*
Friday	0.00005	6.13*
R-Square	0.4652	N = 871,954
F-Statistic	32,983	

Each trading day during the first six months of 1989 was segmented into one 31-minute interval and twelve 30-minute intervals (9:30 a.m. to 10:00 a.m., etc.). Then, for each security i for each interval t, the mean of the time-weighted percentage bid–ask spread was regressed against the following variables: the number of trades, the number of shares per trade, stock risk as measured by the variability of the price (for each stock i, the risk is the same for all t), interval risk as measured by abnormal variability of price, asymmetric information as measured by the extent to which the trade was unusual, and level of competition. Dummy variables are included to capture time-of-day and day-of-the-week effects. To reduce the potential impact of unusually large observations, McInish and Wood used the square root of number of trades, number of shares per trade, the measure of competition, and price, rather than the untransformed values of those variables.
*Significant at the 0.01 level.
Source: McInish and Wood, 1992. Reprinted by permission of the *Journal of Finance*.

regional exchanges (the Pacific, Boston, Cincinnati, Chicago, Pacific, and Philadelphia exchanges) and on NASDAQ. Due to a USSEC rule prohibiting listing of shares on two exchanges in the same city, no issues are traded simultaneously on the NYSE and the American Stock Exchange, both of which are located in New York. McInish and Wood used the ratio of the sum of regional and NASDAQ trading to the sum of NYSE, regional, and NASDAQ trading as a measure of competition.

Price It is also desirable to take asset prices into account when investigating spreads. Many previous researchers have shown that there is a nonlinear relationship between spread and price. Suppose that two firms are identical in every respect except that one has 1,000,000 shares outstanding with a market price of 20 USD and the other has 2,000,000 shares outstanding with a market price of 10 USD. Would the absolute spread of the first stock be twice as large as that of the second stock? In fact, empirical evidence shows that the spread for the higher-priced stock would probably be less than twice as large as the spread for the lower-priced stock. The reason for this nonlinear relationship is not understood.

The results of estimating this regression are presented in table 3.6. Number of trades and number of shares per trade are inversely related to spread, and the relationship is statistically significant. As predicted, both firm risk and interval risk are directly and statistically significantly related to spread. Asymmetric information is positively and significantly related to spread size. As shown by the significance of the coefficient of competition, more competition results in smaller spreads. The significance of the coefficient of spread shows that higher-priced stocks have a lower percentage spread even when the other characteristics of the stock, such as trading volume, are the same.

There are dummy variables for each of the intervals 1–9 and 11–13. The tenth interval is omitted due to the requirements of linear regression. The coefficients of the nondummy explanatory variables capture the average relationship between these variables and BAS. The dummy variables indicate whether the relationship is the same over the trading day. The results in table 3.6 show that the size of the t-statistics is generally larger at the beginning and end of the trading day, and that these relationships are statistically significant. This evidence indicates that the relationship between spread and its determinants is not the same over the trading day.

There are also four dummy variables that equal 1 if the observation occurs on a Monday, Tuesday, Thursday, or Friday, respectively, and 0 otherwise. While the coefficients of these variables are statistically significant, they are much smaller than the other significant t-statistics. Because of the very large sample size, the t-statistics are statistically significant, but these day-of-the-week differences are not economically significant.

3.5. ESTIMATING BID–ASK SPREADS

Sometimes the bid–ask spread cannot be observed. On derivatives exchanges where there is no designated market maker, some traders may quote a bid and others an ask or offer, but no individual trader is obligated to quote a two-sided market. Even for stock exchanges where two-sided quotations are common, financial publications and data sources often report only closing prices, rather than bids and asks. In fact, bids and asks may not be

Table 3.7 Possible sequences of three trade prices when trades must be at either the bid or ask

Time when trade occurs	t – 1	t	t + 1
Trade price is at:	Bid	Bid	Bid
	Bid	Bid	Ask
	Bid	Ask	Bid
	Bid	Ask	Ask
	Ask	Ask	Ask
	Ask	Ask	Bid
	Ask	Bid	Ask
	Ask	Bid	Bid

Table 3.8 Restatement of data in table 3.7

Time when trade occurs	t	t + 1
Sequence designation	0	0
	0	+s
	+s	−s
	+s	0
	0	0
	0	−s
	−s	+s
	−s	0

Sequences of pairs of trades are denoted as: bid–bid, 0; ask–ask, 0; bid–ask, +s; and ask–bid, −s.

available for historical data, because these data may not be archived. Nevertheless, because the bid–ask spread is an important cost of executing an order, we might be interested in whether it is possible to estimate the spread.

3.5.1. The Roll estimation procedure

Roll (1984) uses a simple order processing cost model to develop a way of estimating the **realized spread**, the difference between the price paid by suppliers of immediacy and the price received. The Roll model is based on the idea that bid–ask bounce results in negative serial dependence in observed price changes (Niederhoffer and Osborne 1966). Suppose that we consider three points in time: t − 1, t, and t + 1. We assume that prices change only due to bid–ask bounce and not due to information. Then, if a trade occurs in period t − 1, the possible sequences of trade prices are shown in table 3.7. Now denote two trades in a row as 0, a trade at the bid followed by a trade at the ask as +s (plus the spread), and a trade at the ask followed by a trade at the bid as −s. Then, table 3.7 can be converted into table 3.8. Recognizing that the mean for t in table 3.8 is 0 and that all of the outcomes are equally likely, the covariance of t with t + 1, c, is

$$c = 0.25s^2 \qquad\qquad 3.1$$

Hence, the spread can be calculated by rearranging equation 3.1 to give:

$$s = 2\sqrt{c} \qquad\qquad 3.2$$

The principal problem with the Roll measure is that equation 3.2 cannot be solved if the covariance is positive.

3.5.2. Applications of the Roll procedure

The Roll approach is useful in quantifying spreads. Batch or call trading can be the principal way of trading in a market. This was the case in Paris for many years. Moreover, a call market can be combined with continuous trading, as on the New York Stock Exchange and the Australian Stock Exchange. In either case, since trades in the call market are all at a single price, there is no observed bid–ask spread. If the batch market is perfectly efficient, then all transactions take place midway between what would be the bid and the ask in a dealer market, and there is no bid–ask spread. But if there is an imbalance of supply or demand, even in the absence of information, prices may be pushed up or down until suppliers of immediacy are attracted to the call. Hence, even in a call market, traders may incur an implicit cost for immediacy.

Over the period 1970–87 on the Frankfurt Stock Exchange, large stocks were traded continuously in a dealer market and also were traded in call auctions at the opening, at noon, and at the close. Small stocks were traded only in the noon call auction. Haller and Stoll (1989) use Roll's procedure to estimate bid–ask spreads for both batch trades and for the continuous trades. The Roll procedure is applied to four return series: (1) auction prices at noon for large stocks; (2) auction prices at the opening, at noon, and at the close for large stocks; (3) prices in the continuous market for large stocks; and (4) auction prices at noon for small stocks. We noted that one problem with the Roll estimator is that the calculated serial correlation must be negative, but actual covariances are sometimes positive. Haller and Stoll deal with this problem by omitting any covariance that is positive.

In 1987 the implied spread for the noon auction was 0.6050 percent for large stocks and 0.7583 percent for small stocks. Thus, the spread was higher for small stocks. Spreads in 1987 were higher than in any other year in the 1970–87 period, probably reflecting the market crash in October 1987. The average spread for the noon auction market over the 1970–87 period was 0.0009 percent for large stocks and 0.2801 percent for small stocks. In some years the estimated spreads for the large stocks in the noon auction were actually negative, implying no spread costs or even gains from the spread. Negative estimated realized spreads are difficult to interpret. Negative estimated spreads were not found for the noon auction market for any year for the small stocks.

For February 1987 the estimated spread was 0.0983 percent based on the opening, noon, and closing auction prices and −0.0557 percent based on the prices from continuous trading. Thus, the estimated spreads were actually higher in the auction market than in the dealer market. In commenting on the characteristics of spreads in dealer and auction markets, Haller and Stoll concluded that "the implied spread based on dealer prices is not different from the implied spread based on auction prices."

3.5.3. Extension of the Roll procedure

We have seen that spreads arise due to order processing costs, inventory holding costs, and asymmetric information costs. The Roll procedure for estimating bid–ask spreads assumes that spreads arise simply from order processing costs. Stoll (1989) shows that the inventory holding cost model predicts that the serial covariance of changes in the bid (or in the ask) is negative, whereas the other two models predict that it will be zero. The quoted spread is observable, but the realized spread will be less than the quoted spread if dealers move their quotes in response to transactions. If it is possible to observe whether a transaction occurs at the bid or the ask, then the realized spread can be estimated directly. Otherwise, Stoll shows that the realized spread is

$$2(\pi - \delta)S = 2\pi S - 2\delta S \qquad\qquad 3.3$$

The quoted spread is S. Consider three transaction prices in succession. A reversal occurs under two conditions: namely (1) if the second price is higher than the first, but the third price is lower than the second; or (2) if the second price is lower than the first, but the third price is higher than the second. The probability of a price reversal is π, and the probability of a price continuation is $(1 - \pi)$. The size of the continuation is δS, and the size of the reversal is $(1 - \delta)S$. The first term on the right-hand side of equation 3.3 shows that if a bid or ask price is equally likely, so that $\pi = 0.5$, the dealer earns the spread on each round trip. A round trip is a buy and then a sale or a sale and then a buy, which together are two transactions, hence, the 2 in the equation. We know from empirical evidence that a trade at the ask is more likely to follow a trade at the ask, and a trade at the bid is more likely to follow a trade at the bid, so that π actually is less than 0.5. The second term on the right-hand side of equation 3.3 shows that to the extent that reversals are not the full amount of the spread, the dealer's profit will be lower. Stoll presents a method of estimating the realized spread using inputs from a regression of covariance of transaction returns on spreads and a regression of the covariance of quotation returns on spreads.

Stoll develops a procedure for decomposing the realized spread into adverse information, holding cost, and order processing components. Letting S denote the spread, Stoll estimates each of these components empirically and reports that the proportion of the spread accounted for by each component is: adverse information cost, 0.43S; holding cost, 0.10S; and order processing cost, 0.47S. These results may shed some light on the recent interest in the USA of liquidity-motivated trades in trying to trade with each other rather than through the central market. If there were only liquidity traders, the spread would be substantially smaller, perhaps by 50 percent or more.

4. SUMMARY

In this chapter, we describe two types of transaction costs: explicit costs and implicit costs. Explicit costs include commissions, taxes, and the like, and information costs, the costs associated with acquiring information for use in making the investment decision. In some market centers commission rates are fixed, but in others commissions are negotiable. In the USA, many brokerage firms give investment managers credits or rebates, called "soft dollars," that can be used to purchase any items useful in managing investments.

Implicit transaction costs include market-timing costs, the loss due to a change in price as a result of factors other than a particular order, and opportunity costs resulting from losses due to failure to execute a transaction. Implicit costs also include market impact costs, which arise when executing an order causes an unfavorable change in the price of a financial instrument.

Another type of implicit cost is the bid–ask spread. The bid–ask spread compensates providers of immediacy. We identify three components of the spread. Order processing costs constitute the direct costs of paperwork, labor, and the like involved in market making. Inventory holding costs are the costs associated with carrying inventory, including interest incurred and gains or losses due to price changes. Adverse information costs are the costs associated with dealing with individuals who have greater knowledge of the likely course of prices. The size of the spread is related to four primary factors: activity, risk, information, and competition.

Sometimes exchange rules can make spreads artificially high. A tick is the minimum monetary value allowed in quoting and trading financial assets. The minimum tick size determines the minimum spread. If the minimum spread is larger than justified, based on the underlying economic considerations, then spreads are artificially wide.

One way of identifying execution costs is the implementation shortfall approach, in which an imaginary portfolio is acquired at the midpoint of the bid and the ask at the time the decision to trade is made. The results of this imaginary portfolio are then compared with those of the actual portfolio.

Ways of estimating realized spreads have also been developed. One of the first, developed by Roll, uses the serial correlation in transaction price series. This technique can be useful not only for dealer markets, but also for call markets and derivatives markets. Stoll has developed a method for estimating the components of the spread.

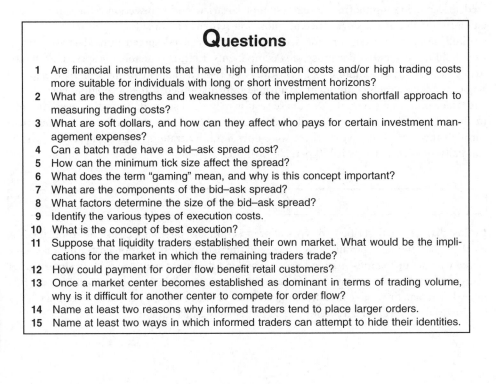

Questions

1 Are financial instruments that have high information costs and/or high trading costs more suitable for individuals with long or short investment horizons?
2 What are the strengths and weaknesses of the implementation shortfall approach to measuring trading costs?
3 What are soft dollars, and how can they affect who pays for certain investment management expenses?
4 Can a batch trade have a bid–ask spread cost?
5 How can the minimum tick size affect the spread?
6 What does the term "gaming" mean, and why is this concept important?
7 What are the components of the bid–ask spread?
8 What factors determine the size of the bid–ask spread?
9 Identify the various types of execution costs.
10 What is the concept of best execution?
11 Suppose that liquidity traders established their own market. What would be the implications for the market in which the remaining traders trade?
12 How could payment for order flow benefit retail customers?
13 Once a market center becomes established as dominant in terms of trading volume, why is it difficult for another center to compete for order flow?
14 Name at least two reasons why informed traders tend to place larger orders.
15 Name at least two ways in which informed traders can attempt to hide their identities.

■ Notes ■

1 *NASD Rules of Fair Practice, NASD Manual* (CCH), art. III, sec. 1, 2151.03.
2 The web site for Plexus Group is http://www.plexusgroup.com/.
3 Many discount brokers in the USA have web sites; e.g., see AccuTrade, http://www.accutrade.com/; American Express Financial Direct, http://www.americanexpress.com/direct/; Bull and Bear Securities: http://www.bullbear.com/; Charles Schwab, http://www.schwab.com/; Fidelity Brokerage Services, http://www.fidelity.com/.
  Swick and Henrich (1998) list more than 100 web sites for discount brokers in the USA.
4 An example of the inventory holding cost model is provided by Ho and Stoll (1981) who propose that after a dealer purchase bid prices are lowered to discourage additional sales and ask prices are also lower to encourage purchases from the dealer. Thus, the new bid and ask prices must reflect prices that make the dealer indifferent between a transaction at the bid and a transaction at the ask.
5 Odd sixteenths are 1/16, 3/16, 5/16, and 7/16. Even sixteenths, such as 2/16 = 1/8, are already used.
6 Ball (1988), Cho and Frees (1988), Gottlieb and Kalay (1985), and Hausman, Lo, and MacKinlay (1992) examine the implications that stocks can trade only at discrete prices for estimations of stock-return variances and other market statistics.
7 Previous studies on transaction costs include work by Demsetz (1968), Kraus and Stoll (1972), Radcliffe (1973), Cuneo and Wagner (1975), Trippi and Nora (1976), Condon (1981), Loeb (1983), Beebower (1988), Perold (1988), Schwartz and Whitcomb (1988), Birinyi (1989), and Stoll (1993a, 1993b).
8 Berkowitz, Logue, and Noser (1988) report that Beebower later refined his measure and found execution costs to be about 0.08 percent of the transaction amount. Also, Beebower and Kamath (1985) seem to have data showing execution costs to be at least equal to commissions.

■ References ■

Aitken, Michael J. and Swan, Peter L. 1997: The impact of a transaction tax on investors: the case of Australia's stamp duty reduction. Working paper, University of Sydney.

Algert, Peter 1991: Estimates of nonlinearity in the response of stock prices to order imbalance. Working paper, University of California, Davis.

Amihud, Yakov and Mendelson, Haim 1986: Asset pricing and the bid–ask spread. *Journal of Financial Economics* 17, 221–49.

Atkins, Allen B. and Dyl, Edward A. 1991: Transactions costs and average holding periods for common stocks. *Journal of Finance* 52, 309–25.

Ball, Clifford A. 1988: Estimation bias induced by discrete security prices. *Journal of Finance* 43, 841–65.

Barclay, Michael J., Kandel, Eugene and Marx, Leslie M. 1998: The effects of transaction costs on stock prices and trading volume. *Journal of Financial Intermediation* 7, 130–50.

—— 1989: Evaluating transactions cost. In Wayne H. Wagner (ed.), *The Complete Guide to Securities Transactions* (New York: Wiley), 137–50.

Beebower, Gilbert and Kamath, Vasant 1985: *Institutional Trading-Cost Study*. Oaks, PA: SEI Corporation.

Beebower, Gilbert and Priest, William 1980: The tricks of the trade: how much does trading really cost? *Journal of Portfolio Management* 6, 36–42.

Berkowitz, Stephen, Logue, Dennis and Noser, Eugene Jr. 1988: The total cost of transaction on the NYSE. *Journal of Finance* 43, 97–110.

97

Bessembinder, Hendrik 1994: Bid–ask spreads in the interbank foreign exchange markets. *Journal of Financial Economics* 35, 317–48.

Birinyi, Laszio 1989: Transactions costs: a trader's perspective. Greenwich, CT: Birinyi Associates, Inc.

Block, Stanley B., French, Dan W. and McInish, Thomas H. 1994: NYSE execution costs: a case study of a leading bank. *Journal of Financial Services Research* 8, 163–75.

Blum, G. A. and Lewellen, W. G. 1983: Negotiated brokerage commissions and the individual investor. *Journal of Financial and Quantitative Analysis* 18, 331–43.

Bodurtha, Stephen G. and Quinn, Thomas E. 1989: *The Patient Program Trade: a case study in measuring and lowering portfolio trading costs.* New York: Kidder, Peabody and Company.

Cho, D. Chinhyung and Frees, Edward W. 1988: Estimating the volatility of discrete stock prices. *Journal of Finance* 43, 451–66.

Collins, Bruce M. and Fabozzi, Frank J. 1991: A methodology for measuring transaction costs. *Financial Analysts Journal* 47, 27–36.

Condon, Kathleen 1981: Measuring equity transaction costs. *Financial Analysts Journal* 37, 57–60.

Copeland, Thomas E. and Galai, Daniel 1983: Information effects on the bid–ask spread. *Journal of Finance* 38, 1457–69.

Cuneo, Larry and Wagner, Wayne 1975: Reducing the cost of stock trading. *Financial Analysts Journal* 31, 35–44.

Dannen, Frederick 1984: Can the trading desk boost performance? *Institutional Investor* 18, 275–8.

Demsetz, Harold 1968: The cost of transacting. *Quarterly Journal of Economics* 82, 33–53.

Glosten, Lawrence and Milgrom, Paul 1985: Bid, ask and transaction prices in a specialist market with heterogeneously informed traders. *Journal of Financial Economics* 14, 71–100.

Gottlieb, Gary and Kalay, Avner 1985: Implications of the discreteness of observed stock prices. *Journal of Finance* 40, 135–53.

Haller, Andreas and Stoll, Hans R. 1989: Market structure and transactions costs: implied spreads in the German stock market. *Journal of Banking and Finance* 13, 697–708.

Harris, Lawrence 1991: Stock price clustering and discreteness. *Review of Financial Studies* 4, 389–415.

——— 1994: Minimum price variations, discrete bid–ask spreads, and quotation sizes. *Review of Financial Studies* 7, 149–78.

Hasbrouck, Joel and Schwartz, Robert 1988: Liquidity and execution costs in equity markets. *Journal of Portfolio Management* 14, 10–17.

Hausman, Jerry A, Lo, Andrew W. and MacKinlay, A. Craig 1992: An ordered probit analysis of transaction stock prices. *Journal of Financial Economics* 31, 319–80.

Ho, Thomas and Stoll, Hans R. 1981: Optimal dealer pricing under transactions and return uncertainty. *Journal of Financial Economics* 9, 47–73.

Kehrer, Daniel 1991: *The Pension Plan Investor.* Chicago: Probus.

Kraus, Alan and Stoll, Hans 1972: Price impacts of block trades on the New York Stock Exchange. *Journal of Finance* 27, 569–88.

Lau, Sie Ting and McInish, Thomas H 1995: Reducing tick size on the Stock Exchange of Singapore. *Pacific Basin Finance Journal* 3, 485–96.

Lee, Charles 1993: Market integration and price execution for NYSE-listed securities. *Journal of Finance* 48, 1009–38.

Loeb, Thomas 1983: Trading cost: the critical link between investment information and results. *Financial Analysts Journal* 39, 39–44.

Macey, Jonathan R. and O'Hara, Maureen 1996: The law and economics of best execution. Working paper, Cornell University, Ithaca, NY.

McCorry, Michael S. and McInish, Thomas H. 1997: Reducing tick size on the Australian Stock Exchange. Working paper, University of Memphis, Memphis, TN.

McInish, Thomas H., Ramaswami, S. N. and Srivastava, Rajendra 1991: Investors' choice of full service versus discount brokerage accounts. *Review of Business and Economic Research* 26, 11–21.

McInish, Thomas H. and Wood, Robert A. 1990: An analysis of transactions data for the Toronto Stock Exchange: return patterns and end-of-the-day effect. *Journal of Banking and Finance* 14, 441–58.

—— 1991: Hourly returns, volume, trade size and number of trades. *Journal of Financial Research* 14, 303–15.

—— 1992: An analysis of intraday patterns in bid/ask spreads for NYSE stocks. *Journal of Finance* 47, 753–64.

Niemeyer, Jonas and Sandas, Patrick 1996: Tick size, market liquidity and trading volume: evidence from the Stockholm Stock Exchange. Working paper, Stockholm School of Economics, Stockholm.

Paroush, Jacob and Peles, Yoram C. 1978: Search for information and portfolio selection. *Journal of Banking and Finance* 2, 163–77.

Perold, Andre F. 1988: The implementation shortfall: paper vs. reality. *Journal of Portfolio Management* 3, 4–9.

Petersen, Mitchell A. and Fialkowski, David 1994: Posted versus effective spreads: good prices or bad quotes? *Journal of Financial Economics* 35, 267–92.

Radcliffe, Robert 1973: Liquidity costs and block trading. *Financial Analysts Journal* 29, 73–8.

Roll, Richard 1984: A simple implicit measure of the effective bid–ask spread in an efficient market. *Journal of Finance* 39, 1127–39.

Saunders, A. and Smirlock, M. 1987: Intra- and interindustry effects of bank securities market activities: the case of discount brokerage. *Journal of Financial and Quantitative Analysis* 22, 467–82.

Schwartz, Robert and Whitcomb, David K. 1988: *Transaction Costs and Institutional Investor Trading Strategies*, Monograph Series in Finance and Economics 1988-2/3. New York: New York University, Stern School of Business.

Srivastava, Rajendra K., McInish, Thomas H. and Price, Linda L. 1984: Information costs and portfolio selection. *Journal of Banking and Finance* 8, 417–29.

Stigler, George J. 1961: The economics of information. *Journal of Political Economy* 69, 213–25.

Stoll, Hans R. 1989: Inferring the components of the bid–ask spread: theory and empirical tests. *Journal of Finance* 44, 115–34.

—— 1993a: *Equity Trading Costs*. Charlottesville, VA: Institute of Chartered Financial Analysts.

—— 1993b: Equity trading costs in-the-large. *Journal of Portfolio Management* 19, 41–50.

Swick, Marie and Henrich, Jean 1998: *The 1998 Discount Broker Survey: a guide to commissions and services* 20, 13–23.

Trippi, Robert and Nora, Yoris 1976: An analysis of price impacts of large block transactions on the New York Stock Exchange. *Journal of Economics and Business* 28, 88–95.

United States Securities and Exchange Commission, Division of Market Regulation 1994: *Market 2000: An Examination of Current Equity Market Development* Washington: USSEC.

Wagner, Wayne H. and Banks, Michael 1992: Increasing portfolio effectiveness via transaction cost management. *Journal of Portfolio Management* 19, 6–11.

Wood, Robert A., McInish Thomas H. and Ord, Keith J. 1985: An investigation of transactions data for NYSE stocks. *Journal of Finance* 40, 723–39.

CHAPTER FOUR

Clearing and Settlement

■ Key terms ■

Bearer   securities that are negotiable upon delivery, and physical (or book-entry) possession is all that is required to effect ownership changes.

Broker call rate   a money market rate that brokers pay to borrow funds by pledging eligible securities as collateral.

Cash   the settlement of a securities transaction on the same day.

Central depository   an entity that accepts deposits of securities and that accounts for transfers of these securities among participants.

Clearing   the process of determining accountability for the exchange of funds and financial assets among the parties to a financial transaction.

Clearinghouse   an organization that handles clearing and also typically some aspects of the settlement process.

Clearing member   a member of a clearinghouse.

Collateral sharing   arrangements in which the collateral held by one clearinghouse could be used by another in the event of the default of a clearing member.

Credit risk   the risk that a transaction will not settle for full value, either when due or at any time thereafter.

Cross margining   the use of netting of gains and losses on related positions held with different clearinghouses.

Dealing location   the location of a party to a trade.

Debit balance   the amount owed the broker.

Declaration date   the day on which the board of directors declares a dividend.

Default   the actual occurrence of a failure to settle for full value when due for economic reasons.

Delivery versus payment   the principle that both parties to a settlement should exchange assets at the same time.

Dematerialized   ownership records are in electronic book-entry form only.

Ex-dividend   the day on and after which a purchaser of stock is not entitled to the dividend.

Failed transaction   a counterparty does not settle an obligation for full value when due, but instead settles on some later date.

Global custodian   a firm that specializes in ensuring that its clients' trades settle, that their securities are properly registered, and that their ownership rights are safeguarded.

Good order   securities that have the required signatures and accompanying documents, so that they meet the requirements for legal transfer.

Herstatt risk   cross-currency settlement risk.

Hypothecation agreement   an agreement that permits the broker to pledge a customer's securities as collateral for a loan.

Immobilized   physical certificates evidencing ownership continue to exist, but these certificates are stored in a central vault to eliminate physical movements of the certificates in transfers of ownership.

Initial margin   the margin or equity that is required on settlement day.

Liquidity risk   risk that a counterparty will settle for full value, but at a date beyond the established settlement date.

Maintenance margin   the minimum equity that an account must have.

Margin   for individuals, for equities and fixed-income securities, margin is a downpayment that constitutes the equity in an account. For institutions and individuals, for derivatives margin is a performance guarantee. For institutions dealing with clearinghouses and the like, margin is a performance guarantee.

Margin call   a request that the percentage of equity in an account be increased.

Master agreement   an agreement that individual transactions between counterparties are part of a single contractual relationship.

Netting   the offsetting of obligations by trading partners.

Novation   the satisfaction and discharge of one contract by the substitution of a new contract.

Operational risk   the risk that there will be a breakdown in some aspect of the hardware, software, communications, or others physical aspects of the clearing and settlement process.

Principal risk   risk that after the settlement has been completed by one counterparty, another counterparty will default.

Record date   the day on which one must own stock to be entitled to receive the dividend.

Registered   the identity of the owner is recorded on the books of the registrar.

Registrar   keeps the record of ownership for a firm and checks that when transfers of ownership are made, the number of shares received by the new owner is the same as the number of shares taken from the former owner.

Regular way   in the USA, the settlement of a securities transaction within three business days.

Replacement cost risk   risk due to changes in the value of financial assets between the time of the trade and the default.

Risk monitoring and control   the use of sophisticated systems to keep track of and limit the exposure of participants.

Rolling settlement   a system in which settlement occurs on all business days.

Settlement   the fulfillment by each party of their obligation, typically by the transfer of funds or title to financial instruments. In a physical delivery system the instruments themselves may be transferred later.

Settlement date   the day on which settlement takes place.

Settlement location   the location of the country that issued the currency involved.

Special miscellaneous account   a record of rights to withdraw funds from an under-margined account.

Systemic risk   the risk that the failure of one counterparty to meet its obligations when due will result in the inability of other counterparties to meet their obligations when due, resulting in a collapse of the entire financial system.

Trade comparison   the process of confirming and matching the terms of a securities transaction, including such items as the identity of the counterparties and the financial asset, the price and quantity, whether there are special terms, and the like.

Transfer agent   a firm that makes sure that documents requesting the transfer of share ownership are in satisfactory order.

Undermargined   an account that is restricted because it meets the maintenance margin requirement, but not the initial margin requirement.

Value date   another term for **Settlement date**.

THIS CHAPTER
- describes the clearing and settlement process
- identifies the clearing and settlement risks faced by institutions

Then, having identified the risks, procedural and institutional ways of dealing with these risks are explored. Specifically, we describe:

- three procedural or operational methods used to deal with clearing and settlement risks, namely: netting, delivery versus payment, and margin
- three institutions that have been developed to deal with clearing and settlement risks, namely: clearinghouses, central depositories, global custodians, and telecommunications networks

1. INTRODUCTION

Clearing and settlement problems resulted in the collapse of Barings Bank and the loss of more than 1 billion USD of creditor and stockholder money. While this topic is often neglected, it is difficult to deny its importance, especially for international investors.

Investors and broker-dealers are increasingly trading different product types. An individual investor might buy equities or currencies and sell options on these assets. Institutional investors now regularly invest in a variety of financial assets throughout the world. Although not glamorous, clearing and settlement are essential parts of every financial transaction. Clearing and settlement practices and issues have been the focus of increased interest since the Group of Thirty[1] made nine recommendations concerning clearing and settlement of securities transactions (see box 4.1). Clearing and settlement practices often

---

BOX 4.1
Group of Thirty recommendations on clearance and settlement of securities transactions

1 *Trade comparison on T + 1* All comparisons of trades between direct market participants (brokers, dealers, other exchange members) should be accomplished by T + 1.

2 *Trade comparisons for indirect participants* All indirect participants (institutions and other nonbroker-dealers) should be members of a system that achieves positive affirmation of trade details.

3 *Central depository* Each country should have an effective and fully developed central securities depository, organized and managed to encourage the broadest possible industry participation.

4 *Netting* Each country should study its market and participation to determine whether a trade-netting system would be beneficial in terms of reducing risk and promoting efficiency.

5 *Delivery versus payment* Delivery versus payment should be employed as the method for settling all securities transactions.

6 *Same day funds* Payments associated with the settlement of securities transactions and the servicing of securities portfolios should be consistent across all instruments and markets by adopting the "same-day" funds convention.

7 *T + 3 rolling settlement* All markets should adopt a rolling settlement system. Final settlement should occur on T + 3.

8 *Securities lending* Securities lending and borrowing should be encouraged as a method of expediting the settlement of securities transactions. Existing regulatory and taxation barriers that inhibit the practice of lending securities should be removed.

9 *Use of ISO standards 7775 and 6166* Each country should adopt the standard for securities messages developed by the International Organization for Standardization (ISO 7775). In particular, countries should adopt the ISIN numbering system for securities issues as defined in the ISO standard 6166, at least for cross-border transactions.

Source: Group of Thirty 1992. Reprinted by permission.

differ both among equities, fixed-income securities, derivatives, and currencies, and even within each of these product types. Clearing and settlement practices also differ from country to country. Hence, there is an increasing need to understand the clearing and settlement process.

Clearing is the process of determining accountability for the exchange of funds and financial assets among the parties to a financial transaction. Trades are the most common form of transaction, but transactions may also involve the loaning of funds and securities, the posting of margin, and other types of transactions. Clearing involves reporting details of the trade to counterparties, clients, exchanges, regulatory bodies, and others. It also involves matching or comparing the details of the trade with clients and counterparties to make certain that all parties agree. Any errors identified must be corrected by getting one of the parties to acknowledge an error or canceling the trade. **Settlement** is the fulfillment by each party of its obligation, typically by the transfer of funds or financial instruments.[2] Parkinson et al. (1992) provide an overview of clearing and settlement in the USA, while the Bank for International Settlements (1992) describes cross-border security settlement.

Clearing and settlement entail many risks.[3] While some risks are more important than others, an understanding of the various types of risk gives investors and securities industry professionals an appreciation of the obstacles and challenges faced in continuing to integrate across product types and across countries.

2. TYPES OF RISK

2.1. CREDIT RISK

Credit risk is the risk that a transaction will not settle for full value, either when due or any time thereafter.[4] The actual occurrence of a failure to settle for full value when due for economic reasons is **default**. Since there is usually a positive probability of default by any counterparty, all counterparties face credit risk. If a counterparty defaults, the nondefaulting party may not receive securities or funds needed for a subsequent transaction. For example, if there is a default on a foreign exchange transaction, the nondefaulting party does not receive the currency that might be needed to settle a time-sensitive business transaction. Upon default, the counterparties face two additional types of risk: replacement cost risk and principal risk.

2.1.1. Replacement cost risk

Replacement cost risk arises due to changes in the value of financial assets between the time of the trade and the default. If the nondefaulting counterparty has a gain, the gain may not be realized in full, or possibly not at all. Replacement cost risk is an increasing function of both (1) the time between the trade and its settlement and (2) the volatility of the assets being traded. Near the time of the trade, the replacement cost is generally low, because the value of the asset is likely to be close to its trade price. But as time passes, the chances that the asset will change in value increase. Most types of financial assets are occasionally subject to major changes in value over a short time. For example on October 22, 1987, many equities throughout the world lost 20 percent or more of their value.[5]

2.1.2. Principal risk

The second type of credit risk, principal risk, is the most important type of credit risk. **Principal risk** is the risk that after the settlement has been completed by one counterparty, another counterparty will default. Principal risk is greater than replacement cost risk, because the entire value of the transaction may be lost. A seller may deliver financial assets and not receive payment, or a buyer may pay and not receive financial assets. Whether the financial assets or funds can be recovered may depend on the types of assets involved, the location of the counterparties, the location of the assets, and even the location of parties that are not direct participants to the transaction.

2.2. LIQUIDITY RISK

Both parties in the clearing and settlement process also face **liquidity risk**, the risk that a counterparty will settle an obligation for full value not when due, but on some unspecified later date. This event is a **failed transaction**, rather than a default, though at the time of the event it may be difficult to decide whether a default or failed transaction is involved. For the seller, the failure to receive payment promptly may require borrowing funds to settle transactions with other parties. On the other hand, the buyer does not receive the securities, which causes a problem if the securities have been resold. To complete delivery on this second sale, the securities will have to be borrowed. Otherwise, a second failed transaction will occur. The costs associated with these failed transactions depend on the level of interest rates and the liquidity of the markets. If interest rates are high, the cost of replacing funds not delivered on their due date may be high. In thick markets it may be easy to borrow securities, but the cost of borrowing securities in thin markets may be great.[6] Also, the failure to settle may lead to a loss of confidence and an unwillingness to complete other transactions with the failing institution. Then, the costs associated with liquidity risk are multiplied.

There are many liquidity pressures in the clearing and settlement process that could result in an institution encountering a failed transaction. The timing of payments during the day differs across types of assets. Institutions that have obligations to pay out funds before they will be received later in the day must have adequate credit and overdraft resources to meet these payment demands. In October 1987, a single member of the Chicago Mercantile Exchange received a request (i.e., a margin call – described in more detail below) for the immediate deposit, during the trading day, of over 200 million USD to prevent the liquidation of its position. Institutions may also need to receive securities before they can be delivered to the next party. If the securities are received late in the day, it may not be possible to arrange further deliveries that day.

2.3. OPERATIONAL RISK

Operational risk is the risk that there will be a breakdown in some aspect of the hardware, software, communications, or others physical aspects of the clearing and settlement process. Such breakdowns could occur due to fires, storms, earthquakes, power outages, epidemics, and similar events. The most widely cited event of this type is the problem encountered by the Bank of New York when it began operations of a new internal clearing system for US government securities in November 1985. The software had not been adequately tested and failed to operate properly. The bank could not process and resend securities sent to it by the US Federal Reserve (the US central bank). Payments were charged against the bank's account at the Federal Reserve, but no payments were credited, because it could not send securities to other participants. The Federal Reserve ultimately extended more than 20 billion USD in overnight credit to the bank. In December 1996 there was a major problem on the Hong Kong Stock Exchange at the opening, which resulted in the dissemination of a large number of incorrect prices for the previous day's close. Many stocks appeared to have fallen by half, and others had more than doubled in price. It took exchange officials until noon to manually correct all the erroneous prices' (*Wall Street Journal* 1996).

2.4. SYSTEMIC RISK

The Group of Thirty defines **systemic risk** as the risk that the failure of one counterparty to meet its obligations when due will result in the inability of other counterparties to meet their obligations when due. Given this definition, systemic risk is frequently encountered, since the failure of a party to deliver securities needed for onward delivery is common. (For additional information on systemic risk see OECD 1991.)

Systemic risk is often defined to be the risk that defaults and failed transactions will be so large that they cannot be managed and contained by the established systems. As a result, the entire financial system is destabilized. Many characteristics of the settlement system appear to offer potential vulnerability. The size of financial transactions is typically large compared with participants' capital and payments, and receipts are not perfectly synchronized, resulting in very large, but short-lived, financial exposure. Further, information is limited, especially concerning the risk exposure that counterparties face in their unsettled transactions. Hence, it is difficult for organizations to protect themselves from this indirect exposure. An initial default or failed transaction will cause institutions to curtail their lending and slow their own settlements, putting downward pressure on prices and resulting in further defaults. This could lead to a vicious cycle of default begetting default.

The failure of the medium-sized German bank Bankhaus Herstatt in 1974 and its default on its foreign exchange contracts put tremendous pressure on the payments system. This cross-currency settlement risk has become known as **Herstatt risk**. Herstatt risk has a natural international dimension, and the amounts involved in foreign exchange contracts are typically very large. Further, because of the varying times of the business day around the world, often there is effectively no overlap in the timing of payments of the two legs of a foreign exchange contract. Bankhaus Herstatt defaulted after the settlement of the DEM leg of foreign exchange trades, but before the settlement of the USD leg. Because counterparties expecting to receive payments did not receive their payments, general confidence in the soundness of the system was shaken. Some banks in New York refused to make payments on their own or their customers' accounts until the situation was clarified. The value of gross fund transfers fell from the daily rate of 60 billion USD to about 36 billion USD daily for three days following the failure, and the process of restarting the system proved difficult.

2.5. Errors Risk

In executing a transaction, the trade may be for the wrong security or for the wrong amount, the firm may buy instead of selling or vice versa, the wrong type of order may be used in executing the trade (e.g., a market order instead of a limit order), and so forth. The firm faces the prospect of correcting the transaction when prices may have moved. An error in processing an order for execution on the New York Stock Exchange illustrates this type of risk. Near the end of the trading day a large order for 20 million shares of the stock of a particular firm reached the floor, causing an increase in the price of both the target stock and other related stocks. After some 20 minutes, the brokerage firm executing the order announced that its order was in error, and that the order was for 20 million USD, not 20 million shares. What at first had seemed like a large order turned out to be only a small order. This error affected both the firm placing the erroneous order and others who traded or were prevented from trading due to the price changes resulting from the error. Box 4.2 presents an example of an error involving two Hong Kong banks.

BOX 4.2
Depositing a check today, Madam? $491 million? No trouble at all

Hong Kong – This town has no shortage of billionaires. Maybe that's why a woman barely raised eyebrows when she walked into a bank here on June 12 and deposited a personal check for HK$3.8 billion (US$491 million) into her husband's account.

The check – surprise – was not good. But it made it past the teller and into the bank's computer system before anyone noticed a problem. The bank that accepted the check, Hongkong & Shanghai Banking Corp., is the biggest financial institution in Hong Kong. The issuing bank, Hongkong Bank subsidiary Hang Seng Bank Ltd., went into deficit overnight for billions of dollars. Hong Kong regulators have launched an inquiry into the affair.

"I'm amazed that nobody spotted it," says Marc Faber, a fund manager. "Everybody should rush to their bank and try the same trick. If the check goes through, just cash it and run away. If you're caught, just say "Sorry, I put on five zeros too many."

Hongkong Bank says the teller at its Aberdeen Center branch who handled the check made some inquiries, but the branch manager allowed the settlement process to begin. Hongkong Bank debited Hang Seng Bank for the cheque. But Hang Seng Bank didn't have enough cash on hand that evening, so it borrowed at least HK$2 billion from Hongkong Bank overnight and was charged interest of more than HK$640,000.

Hongkong Bank blames the foul up on human frailty. "It was an honest error by a very junior employee," says Paul Selway-Swift, an executive director at the bank.

Internal guidelines have since been strengthened, the bank says. Hongkong Bank and Hang Seng Bank are negotiating over who will pay the interest charge.

Hongkong Bank says neither the mystery check writer, nor her husband (the banks decline to name the duo), had any access to the cash, and so far, they aren't facing criminal charges. But the wife might be liable for a service fee of HK$70 – and about HK$1.77 million interest on the overdraft. Hang Seng bank wouldn't say if it would press to collect the overdraft charges.

Source: Guyot and Stein 1995, p. 1. Reprinted by permission of the *Asian Wall Street Journal*, © 1995 Dow Jones & Company, Inc. All Rights Reserved Worldwide.

2.6. OTHER RISKS

Clients of brokerage firms, clearinghouses, exchanges, central depositories, and other entities involved in the clearing and settlement process face the risk that one of these organizations will fail. Investors and financial institutions could then face the loss of their investments. Moreover, the laws governing how losses will be apportioned if a failure occurs are typically not clear. Multiple jurisdictions may have conflicting laws, rules, and interests. The collapse of Baring Brothers, one of the oldest British merchant banks, due to losses from unauthorized trading, illustrates these concerns. Baring accounts in Singapore did not distinguish between bank proprietary accounts and customer accounts, so customer accounts were potentially available to satisfy bank losses. If the legal authorities had not protected customer funds, these funds could have been lost. There is no guarantee that officials in other countries will be equally protective of customer money, especially if this means that local institutions would be subsidizing noncitizens. Moreover, in the Baring case the possibility that the futures exchange would be bankrupted was definitely nonzero.

---

3. PROCEDURAL WAYS OF DEALING WITH CLEARING AND SETTLEMENT RISK

In this section we deal with three ways of conducting business that help mitigate clearing and settlement risk: namely, netting, delivery versus payment, and margin.

3.1. NETTING

Netting is the offsetting of obligations by trading partners. Netting can be applied to cash payments or to securities transfers. Because the sizes of mutual obligations are often dramatically reduced, netting can reduce costs, credit, and liquidity risks substantially. In some jurisdictions, the administrator of a failed financial institution can choose to perform those contracts that are profitable for the failing institution and repudiate those contracts that are not profitable for it. From the counterparties' viewpoint, its profitable contracts with the failing institution are not being honored, and its unprofitable contracts are being enforced. Counterparties to the unprofitable contracts of the failing institution might be low in the queue for receiving payment and, consequently, face higher risk of partial or complete loss of principal. A legally enforceable netting agreement helps limit exposure. If all the obligations to a failing counterparty produce a loss in aggregate, this amount is owed to the failing institution. But this amount would have been owed even if the institution had not failed. If all the obligations to a counterparty produce a gain in aggregate, this gain may not be received if the assets of the failing institution are insufficient to pay all its creditors. Without a netting agreement, the counterparty to the failing institution would have lost not only the gain on its profitable agreements, but might also have been liable to pay any losses on its unprofitable agreements with the failing institution. (Alton (1992), Glass (1994), and Hendricks (1994) examine issues related to netting.)

108

3.1.1. Bilateral netting

Bilateral netting agreements are common. **Novation** is the satisfaction and discharge of one contract by the substitution of a new contract. In the area of foreign exchange, "netting-by-novation" contracts allow for the discharge of individual forward commitments at the time of their confirmation and their replacement by new obligations that are part of a single agreement. Running balances are maintained for each future value date. According to the Bank for International Settlements (1990, p. 11), "in some markets participants may be able to achieve a reduction of more than 50% in total payments to be made in all currencies, both in terms of value and volume." The agreement may provide that in the event of default the net exposure is the net present value of the running balance.

Another bilateral mechanism for netting is the master agreement. An example is the master agreement of the International Swap Dealers Association. A **master agreement** provides that individual transactions between counterparties are part of a single contractual relationship. This allows the netting of obligations upon bankruptcy and the netting of payments due on a specific date. In contrast to novation, the individual transactions retain their separate terms, rates, and maturities, so they can be implemented individually.

Netting can be achieved bilaterally between two trading partners or multilaterally among a group of trading partners. A simple bilateral example may be worthwhile. Suppose that one morning Firm A sells 21,000 shares of Firm Z's common stock to Firm B for 2.1 million USD. Then, later in the day, Firm B sells 20,000 shares of Firm Z's common stock to Firm A for 2 million USD. If Firms A and B have a netting agreement, then on the settlement day only the net amounts of shares and cash would be exchanged. In this case, Firm B would pay Firm A 0.1 million USD, and Firm A would provide Firm B with 1,000 shares of Firm Z's common stock. Thus, the replacement cost risk has been eliminated for Firm B and has been reduced to 1,000 shares for Firm A. The credit risk is eliminated for Firm A and is reduced from 2.1 million USD to 0.1 USD for Firm B.

3.1.2. Multilateral netting

Multilateral netting arrangements are common. Payment orders between banks such as those for checks are typically netted so that only the net amount needs to be transferred. Sometimes a central party is substituted for the individual parties, so that once the contract is confirmed and accepted by the central counterparty, it becomes an obligation of that counterparty. Participants who have a net debit position make payments to the central counterparty, while those in net credit positions receive payments.

The way default is handled can vary greatly. Sometimes the positions of the defaulting party are unwound and the settlement process is redone as if the defaulting party were not involved. This type of procedure can lead to defaults of other participants, because they may have been counting on the funds or securities provided by the defaulting party to make their own settlements. On the other hand, the central counterparty may guarantee performance and then allocate the loss among the participants using a formula such as volume of transactions or volume of transactions with the counterparty. Note that in the former case, a participant may be exposed to losses caused by the failure of a participant with whom they did little or no business. The novation or substitution of a central counterparty for the original individual contracts is similar to novation encountered in bilateral netting.

Table 4.1 Illustration of benefits of netting

Gross flows	DEM	USD
Bank A	−2 million (a)	+1 million (a)
Bank B	+2 million (a)	−1 million (a)
	−4 million (b)	+2 million (b)
	+2 million (c)	−1 million (c)
Bank C	+4 million (b)	−2 million (b)
	−2 million (c)	+1 million (c)
Gross outflow	+8 million	+4 million
Net outflow		
Bank A	0	+1 million
Bank B	0	0
Bank C	+2	0
New outflow	+2 million	+1 million
Risk reduction = positive outflows avoided		
Bank A	0	0
Bank B	4 million	2 million
Bank C	2 million	1 million
Total risk reduction	6 million (75%)	3 million (75%)

In this example a positive number is an inflow and a negative number is an outflow. A reduction in outflows is a reduction in credit risk (both replacement cost risk and principal risk) and in liquidity risk. Note that in this case, if the netting arrangements are final and not subject to revocation, the risk of bank B is totally eliminated. Also, even though banks A and C did not trade with each other, nevertheless, they are exchanging payments. This aspect of netting schemes may increase the difficulty of limiting exposure to particular parties.

Netting can also reduce risk multilaterally. Suppose that one day we have the following transactions: (a) Bank A sells 2 million DEM to Bank B for 1 million USD, (b) Bank B sells 4 million DEM to Bank C for 2 million USD, (c) Bank C sells Bank B 2 million DEM for 1 million USD. Then, as shown in table 4.1, netting can reduce credit and liquidity risk substantially. Note that here, if the netting arrangements are final and not subject to revocation, the risk of Bank B is totally eliminated. Also, though Banks A and C did not trade with each other, they are exchanging payments. If a default occurs there is exposure to parties with whom one has not dealt directly.

3.2. SETTLEMENT DAY AND DELIVERY VERSUS PAYMENT

We have already mentioned that parties to a trade face replacement cost risk prior to sttlement. As a result, there are continuing efforts worldwide and in all types of markets to reduce the time between the consummation of a trade and its settlement. Once settlement day arrives, the focus changes to minimization of principal risk. A key to this risk reduction is delivery versus payment, the principle that both settling parties should exchange assets at the same time. The Bank for International Settlements (1992) provides a discussion of delivery versus payment systems.

3.2.1. Settlement day – securities

Settlement times differ by type of financial instrument and by country. For cash transactions, settlement is typically either in same-day funds or in next-day funds. The Group of Thirty has recommended the use of same-day funds for payments involving financial instruments. Exchange-traded derivatives, including options and futures, typically settle the next day (for exchange-traded futures in the USA before the next day opening), although occasionally same-day settlement may be required. The Group of Thirty recommended that securities settlement be on T + 3 where T is the trade day. This is the practice currently followed in the USA and Japan. For purchases on Mondays, if there is no holiday, payment would be due Thursday. Since Saturday and Sunday are not working days in the USA, a trade on Friday would be settled on Wednesday. This type of settlement is the **regular way** in the USA. Many securities markets also have arrangements for alternate settlements.[7] In the USA, for example, trades can be arranged for **cash** settlement, in which payments are made and the financial instrument is delivered on the day of the transaction. Since cash transactions typically cost the initiator more, they are seldom used.

Rolling settlement refers to a system in which settlement occurs on all business days. Because of the Group of Thirty recommendations, many exchanges that have not historically used a rolling settlement are beginning to do so. One is the London Stock Exchange. Historically, transactions on the London Stock Exchange were divided into trading accounts that were normally of 2 weeks' duration. All trades during one trading account were settled on the account day, usually the second Monday after the end of the account. Transactions on the Milan Stock Exchange were settled on the final day of each calendar month and referred to the previous trading interval that runs from mid-month to mid-month.

If both funds and securities are in electronic form (this type of registration is described later), both can be exchanged between brokerage firms and final customers on settlement day. But in some markets, such as the USA and India, there is still considerable use of physical certificates. Hence, while the seller may deliver the certificate to their brokerage firm on settlement day, there will be a delay in the purchaser receiving the certificate because it must first be sent to the buyer's brokerage firm. The brokerage firm arranges for the transfer of title and the issuance of a new certificate, and only then can the certificate be given to the buyer.

Suppose that the seller delivers the certificate to the seller's brokerage firm on the third business day following the transaction. Then the seller's firm must send the certificate to the buying firm. These transfers are typically handled through the banking system or a clearinghouse. If the banking system is used, the certificate, along with a draft, might be sent to the buying firm's bank. When the draft is accepted and paid, the stock certificate is released. The buying firm then sends the certificate to the **transfer agent**, a firm, often a bank, responsible for checking the transfer documents to make sure that they are in **good order**, meaning that they meet the requirements for legal transfer and for issuing a new certificate. The transfer agent must make sure that the new certificate is for the same number of shares as the old certificate. The transfer agent records the transaction and sends both the old and new certificates to the registrar. The **registrar**, also often a bank, is responsible for checking that the number of shares transferred to the new owner equals the number of shares supplied by the old owner. In other words, the registrar is responsible for checking the work of the transfer agent. In 1971 the NYSE began allowing one bank to serve as both transfer agent and registrar. In some jurisdictions, the firm itself can maintain these records. Then, the transfer agent sends the stock certificate directly to the customer or to the customer's broker to be sent on to the customer.

Differences between trade dates and settlement dates may cause problems in connection with dividends. The **settlement date** is the date on which funds and title to securities are transferred. The date on which corporations meet to declare a dividend is called the **declaration date**. The day on which an investor must own the stock to be entitled to the dividend is called the **record date**. The **ex-dividend** date is the day on, and after which, a purchaser of stock is not entitled to the dividend. Suppose that a market center settles on $T + 3$. Denote the record date as R. Consider a trade on $R - 3$. In this case $T = R - 3$ so that settlement is on $T + 3 = R$. Since the settlement day is the record day, the purchaser would receive the dividend. On the other hand, a trade on $R - 2$ would settle on $R + 1$ and would not receive the dividend. Hence, the ex-dividend date is two business days prior to the record date. On the ex-dividend date, if the price of shares of stock were unchanged due to market factors, the price would fall by the amount of the dividend. Suppose that a firm declared a dividend payable on November 19 to holders of record on Tuesday, November 10. Assuming no holidays, the ex-dividend date is Friday, November 6.

3.2.2. Settlement day – derivatives

Because of their higher level of risk, settlement times for derivatives have historically been short. In the USA, futures contracts are settled before the beginning of trading on the next business day, and options are settled on the next business day. These short settlement times are feasible, because the ownership records of derivatives are electronic and not in physical form.

3.2.3. Settlement day – currencies

For European currencies and the JPY traded against the USD, the settlement day is 2 business days after the transaction. The 2-day period is intended to give the parties sufficient time to process the trade. For Canadian dollar (CAD) and Mexican new peso (MXN) trades against the USD, the settlement day is the next business day. A **dealing location** is the location of a party to a trade, and a **settlement location** is the location of the country that issued the currency involved. Settlement payments take place in the country whose currency is involved. In other words, in a trade of DEM against USD, the payment of DEM would be in Germany, and the payment of USD would be in the USA. Thus, the settlement location depends on the currencies involved, not on the location of the parties to the trade.

For currencies that settle in 2 business days, if the first business day following a trade is a holiday in one settlement location, but not in the other, then which **value date** (another term for settlement date) applies? Typically, in the absence of special arrangements, the value date of the noncalling or dealer bank applies. That is to say, if Bank A calls Bank B to initiate a trade, then, the value date of Bank B applies. Note that in this instance the issue of holidays is relative to the dealing locations, since the purpose of the settlement period is to allow the parties sufficient time to process the trades.

The delivery-versus-payment principle mandates that both sides of the transaction settle on the same day. If the appropriate settlement day is a holiday in either settlement location or in either dealing location, the settlement is postponed to the next business day. Suppose that US and British banks consummate a USD/GBP trade on Friday. Banks in London and New York are closed on Saturdays and Sundays, so a trade on Friday ordinarily settles on the following Tuesday. If the following Tuesday is a holiday in either the USA or the UK, settlement is postponed until Wednesday. Further, suppose that a USD/GBP trade consummated by a Singapore bank and a Japanese bank is due to settle on Wednesday, but Wednesday is a holiday in either the USA or the UK. Then, if Thursday is not a holiday, settlement will be postponed until that day. Note that in this instance, the value date is affected by holidays in the settlement location rather than in the dealing location.

An exception to the delivery-versus-payment principle is made for Middle Eastern currencies because Islamic banks are closed on Friday but open on Saturday and Sunday. A trade on a Wednesday of non–Middle Eastern currency against a Middle Eastern currency would normally settle on Friday. But since Middle Eastern banks are closed, the delivery of the Middle Eastern currency cannot take place. Instead, only the non–Middle Eastern currency is delivered on Friday, and the Middle Eastern currency is delivered on Saturday.

3.3. MARGIN

3.3.1. Margin overview

The term **margin** can have different meanings, depending on the circumstances. For individual investors, margin on equities and fixed-income securities is a down payment that constitutes the equity in an account, with the remainder of the purchase price borrowed from the broker. For derivatives, margin is a performance guarantee. Brokers must often deposit margin with exchanges or clearinghouses to guarantee performance on contracts. Sometimes brokers post margin with clearinghouses to provide a fund that can be used if a clearing member defaults. These margin deposits are not down payments but performance guarantees. Although rules vary, government or sovereign debt, cash, bank guarantees and lines of credit, and equities often can serve to fulfill these obligations. Figure 4.1 shows the percentage of clearinghouses and guarantee funds that accept each of these types of margin.

Individuals also must post margin with their brokers. This margin may be redeposited with an exchange or a clearinghouse. Practices vary. In some cases the brokerage firm is required to deposit the gross amount, so the entire margin of its customers is redeposited. In other cases, only the net margin requirements of customers must be redeposited (so the brokerage firm is allowed to offset long and short customer positions before posting its margin). Margins for derivatives are considered performance guarantees. Exchanges establish margin requirements based on the volatility of the underlying assets. Margin can usually be posted in either cash or acceptable securities such as US Treasury bills in the USA. For securities, margin is a down payment on the cost of the securities, with the brokerage firm,

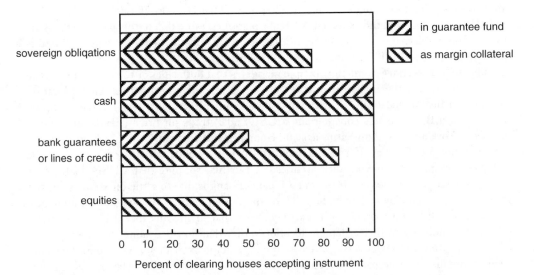

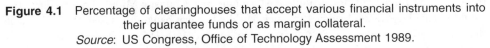

Figure 4.1 Percentage of clearinghouses that accept various financial instruments into their guarantee funds or as margin collateral.
Source: US Congress, Office of Technology Assessment 1989.

a bank, a finance company, or some other institution providing the remainder of the purchase price as a loan. The USA has a formalized system of providing margin loans through brokerage firms. The system is elaborate, but we will briefly describe its main features.

3.3.2. Equity and fixed-income margins for individuals

The rules for buying equities and fixed-income securities on credit are probably as complicated in the USA as anywhere.[8] Therefore, a brief discussion of margin requirements in the USA may help in understanding some of the issues arising in connection with trading on margin. In the USA margin requirements are set by the US Federal Reserve System, exchanges on which a security is traded (including NASDAQ), and individual brokerage firms. These regulations are arranged in a hierarchy, so that the lower-level organization can impose regulations as strict or stricter, but not less strict, than the requirements, imposed at a higher level. Hence, a brokerage firm can impose requirements more strict than or equal to those of the exchange on which a particular security is traded. An exchange, in turn, can impose requirements equal to or stricter than those of the Federal Reserve. Margin rules are so complicated that special individuals known as "margin clerks" calculate the actual requirements. This discussion can provide only a general overview of margin rules.

Purchases on margin are limited to approved securities. In general, approved securities include all stocks traded at a price of 3 USD or higher on a stock exchange or on the NASDAQ National Market System. For equities and fixed-income securities, margin is a down payment, which constitutes the equity in an account, with the remaining **debit balance** constituting the amount owed to the broker. The customer signs a **hypothecation agreement** that permits the broker to pledge the customer's shares as collateral on a loan. Brokerage firms obtain funds for their clients by using the customers' collateral for loans.[9] The broker pays interest on the firm's borrowing at the **broker call rate** on stock exchange collateral, a money market rate. The broker charges the customer on the debit balance. The exact interest rate charged varies from firm to firm but is typically based on the amount of the debit balance, and usually the higher the debit balance, the lower the rate. The customer's rate is a number of percentage points, say 1.5 or 2, that is added to the rate paid by the broker, so that if the broker pays 5 percent, then the customer would pay 6.5 percent (5 + 1.5) or 7 percent (5 + 2). Interest is typically charged on a daily basis but posted monthly.

On settlement day the customer must pay a down payment that constitutes the **initial margin**. Whenever the account equity exceeds the initial margin requirement, the customer can withdraw the excess from the account. The brokerage firm endeavors to insure that the assets in an account are worth more than the debit balance, so that there is positive equity. If the account equity falls below a **maintenance margin** requirement, then the customer is asked to put more margin into the account. The request for more margin is a **margin call**. The required margin or equity can be achieved by depositing cash or marginable securities, or by selling securities in the account. If a cash deposit of 1,000 USD is required, the value of marginable securities that must be deposited is greater than 1,000. Using marginable securities to meet a margin call is the same as borrowing against these securities, and loans must be for no more than the value of the securities less the initial margin requirement. The most difficult way to meet a margin call is by selling securities, because the value of the securities that have to be sold is large relative to the amount of cash that would have to be deposited. This results from the fact that the sale of securities reduces not only the debit balance, but also the collateral.[10]

If an account's equity falls below the initial margin requirement (such an account is called **undermargined**), but remains above the maintenance requirement, money or securities cannot be withdrawn except under special circumstances. These cases involve instances in which (1) an account has had more than the initial margin requirement at some time during its life; (2) there have been deposits of cash, including dividends, into an undermargined account; and perhaps even (3) when there have been sales of stock in an account. To illustrate why there may be a need to allow withdrawals from an undermargined account, suppose that an investor buys securities and deposits just enough funds to meet the initial margin requirement. If the value of the securities increases, the investor can withdraw funds from the account as long as the account still meets the initial margin requirement. Now think about what happens if the funds are not withdrawn and the value of the securities declines, so that the account is undermargined. The investor will no longer be able to withdraw funds that could have been withdrawn earlier. At one time brokerage firms actually transferred money from one account to another to preserve customers' ability to withdraw funds. This practice was obviously wasteful and has now been replaced with a special procedure.

These special rules involve the creation of a **Special Miscellaneous Account** (which is really more of a record of rights to withdraw funds than an account), which is used to keep track of the right to withdraw funds from an undermargined account. (Table 4.2 provides an illustration of the working of the Special Miscellaneous Account.) If an investor can withdraw funds from an account, but chooses not to do so, the right to withdraw these funds is tracked in the Special Miscellaneous Account. These funds can then be withdrawn

Table 4.2 Illustration of working of Special Miscellaneous Account

1 time t = 0
the investor begins with 10,000 USD of cash:

Cash	10,000 USD

2 t + 1
In period t + 1 the investor purchases 20,000 USD worth of stock, making a down payment of 10,000 USD, which leaves the account in the following position:

Cash	0
Value of stock	20,000
Debit balance	10,000
Margin or equity	10,000
Equity (%)	50.0

3 t + 2
In period t + 2 assume that the value of the stock increase to 30,000 USD, which leaves the account in this position:

Cash	0
Value of stock	30,000
Debit balance	10,000
Margin or equity	20,000
Equity (%)	66.7

Given the increased stock value, the investor can choose to either do nothing or to withdraw up to 5,000 USD from the account. We illustrate the position of the account for each of these choices:

	(a) Do nothing	(b) Withdraw 5,000 USD
Cash	0	5,000
Value of stock	30,000	30,000
Debit balance	10,000	15,000
Margin or equity	20,000	15,000
Equity (%)	66.7	50.0

4 t + 3
In period t + 3 assume that the value of the stock falls to 20,000 USD, which leaves the account in the following position, depending on whether funds were withdrawn at t + 2.

	(a) Nothing done at t + 2	(b) 5,000 USD withdrawn at t + 2
Cash	0	5,000
Value of stock	20,000	20,000
Debit balance	10,000	15,000
Margin or equity	10,000	5,000
Equity (%)	50.0	25.0

The problem that the Special Miscellaneous Account addresses is this. If the account on the left cannot withdraw 5,000 USD because it just meets the initial margin requirement, then investors would be likely to always withdraw funds when they could do so, since this would be the only way to protect the right to withdraw. The Special Miscellaneous Account keeps track of rights to withdraw so that a withdrawal is permitted for the account on the left to put it in the same position as the account on the right. Note that following a withdrawal, both accounts would just meet the Federal Reserve maintenance margin requirement, so it is likely that they would both receive a margin call.

at a later time, so long as the withdrawal does not reduce the margin to a level below the maintenance margin requirement. Individual brokers may limit withdrawals to a lesser amount. Similar reasoning applies whether funds could have been withdrawn due to appreciation of securities in the account, the receipt of dividends, or the deposit of cash or securities into the account. These deposits would be discouraged if they could not be subsequently withdrawn, even though there had been no change in the value of the account.

4. INSTITUTIONS FOR DEALING WITH CLEARING AND SETTLEMENT

A number of institutional arrangements have been developed to deal with clearing and settlement. The most prominent of these are clearinghouses, central depositories, and communications networks.

4.1. CLEARINGHOUSES

A **clearinghouse** is an organization that handles clearing and also typically some aspects of the settlement process.[11] Some clearinghouses provide trade comparison services. **Trade comparison** is the process of confirming and matching the terms of a securities transaction, including such items as the identity of the counterparties and the financial asset, the price and quantity, whether there are special terms, and the like. In some cases the trade comparison is performed by an exchange, in others by the parties themselves. Clearinghouses may also perform multilateral netting.[12] Exchange Clearing House, created by a group of European banks, and Multinet in the USA operate netting systems.[13]

Multilateral netting can be achieved in several ways. In some markets, participants enter into individual transactions. Then, if specified conditions are met, the clearinghouse is substituted as the counterparty for both the buyer and the seller. In others, the clearinghouse guarantees performance once the transaction has been accepted. In some systems the clearinghouse calculates a multilateral net position for each participant vis-à-vis other participants, but does not become a counterparty to the transaction and provides no guarantee.

Clearinghouses can use a number of methods for reducing risk due to the default of a participant. A **clearing member** is a direct participant in a clearinghouse. Direct participation in the system may be limited to those with only the best financial positions. Others who want to use the services of the clearinghouse must deal through the clearing members. While high membership standards serve to reduce risk from counterparty default, care must be taken that "the methods and criteria used to limit participation should be as objective as possible and not based on a desire to maintain the competitive advantages of some market players" (IOSCO 1992, p. 21). The International Organization of Securities Commissions (IOSCO) recommends that preference be given to another risk reduction strategy, risk monitoring and control. By **risk monitoring and control** we mean the use of sophisticated systems to keep track of and limit the exposure of participants. An example of risk monitoring and control is the Theoretical Intermarket Margin System (TIMS) developed by the Options Clearing Corporation (see box 4.3).

BOX 4.3
The Options Clearing Corporation's Theoretical Intermarket Margin System

The Theoretical Intermarket Margin System (TIMS) is a sophisticated system for measuring the monetary risk inherent in portfolios containing options, futures, and options on futures positions. TIMS allows clearing institutions to measure, monitor, and manage the level of risk exposure of their members' portfolios. TIMS can calculate risk exposure at different account levels and for different account types. In addition, TIMS uses advanced portfolio theory to margin all positions relating to the same underlying product and combines the risk of closely related products into integrated portfolios. This portfolio aspect of TIMS is important for the recognition of hedges used by market participants in increasingly interrelated markets. TIMS uses advanced pricing models to project the liquidation value of each portfolio given changes in the price of each underlying product. These models generate a set of theoretical values based on various factors, including current prices, historical prices, and market volatility. Based on flexible criteria established by a clearinghouse, statistically significant hedges receive appropriate margin offsets. TIMS is also used to predict a member's potential intraday risk under varying sets of assumptions regarding market behavior.

Source: By kind permission of the Options Clearing Corporation, n.d.

The clearinghouse must take steps to ensure that its assets are sufficient to meet any potential defaults. In October 1987 the Hong Kong Futures Guarantee Corporation, which guarantees trades on the Hong Kong Futures Exchange, had to be rescued.[14] The clearinghouse may seek outside protection through insurance of bank letters of credit, which the clearinghouse can draw on in times of stress. Loss-sharing arrangements may provide for contributions of the clearinghouse's members to a common fund.

Clearinghouses typically use collateral to limit risk. In some systems the clearinghouse requires that high-quality assets that can be sold readily secure extensions of credit. In others a margining system is used. We have already discussed how margin is used to reduce settlement risk. Clearinghouses typically require clearing members to post collateral or margin. Participants in financial markets often have positions for various types of products that may be cleared by separate clearinghouses. **Cross margining** allows the use of netting of gains and losses on related positions held with different clearinghouses. Cross margining is relatively new, but some clearinghouses are taking steps to develop mechanisms to allow it. Options on stock index futures are traded on the Options Clearing Corporation (OCC), while the futures contracts are traded on futures exchanges. The OCC and the futures exchanges have concluded agreements providing for cross margining of the futures and options positions. Clearinghouses are also beginning to develop **collateral sharing** arrangements in which the collateral held by one clearinghouse can be used by another in the event of the default of a clearing member. Such arrangements could provide benefits if the defaulting party's positions have gains in one market that could be used to offset losses in the other. Cross margining might also allow for the posting of less collateral if the combined positions at the two clearinghouses were lower in risk than the separate risks. In periods of market stress, there is a risk that the collateral posted will be insufficient, especially in periods of market stress, when the value of collateral may decline markedly.

We noted above that some clearinghouses such as the Options Clearing Corporation collect and hold money from their clearing members to be used in the event of the default of a member. Bank letters of credit may also be required, but there is substantial risk that in the event of default an institution will not be able to draw on its credit line.

Another device is to limit the amount of credit that is extended to each party in the clearing and settlement process. A given participant may be limited to a pre-specified net debit position. If that position is exceeded, then no further debit trades can be processed until additional collateral is provided. This approach has a number of limitations. It can result in failed transactions, which may present a serious problem to counterparties who were expecting securities, funds, or foreign exchange to complete their own trades. Clearinghouses usually try to process transactions in the order that will result in the fewest failed transactions. Often there are several cycles in the clearing process, and some clearing organizations operate both day and night. If a transaction cannot be processed in the first cycle during a day, then the participants have a chance to submit additional securities or collateral to facilitate settlement on the next round.

In 1968 the US firm J. P. Morgan established Euroclear[15] as a central depository to provide settlement and custody services for Eurobonds. Euroclear now clears Eurobonds, international equities, domestic government debt securities, and domestic equities. J. P. Morgan still operates Euroclear, but ownership has been transferred to more than 100 of its participants. Centrale de Livraison de Valeurs Mobilières (Cedel[16]) was founded in 1970 in Luxembourg and is owned by more than 100 banks and brokers. Both Cedel and Euroclear have more than 2,000 clearing members and have established links to scores of central securities depositories, banks, and brokers. Neither interposes itself as a counterparty to a trade and therefore does not guarantee that the settlement obligations of either party will be met. The Cedel web site describes the settlement process.

We have been discussing the risk faced by institutions whose business is dealing in financial markets. It might be worthwhile to consider briefly the risks faced by the customers of these firms. The primary risk faced by individuals is that their brokerage firm might collapse. Guarantee funds of exchanges and clearinghouses are typically designed to protect other members, not clients of members. Both the customers and the counterparties of a bankrupt firm may have claims on its assets. It is not always clear which parties will have priority. In the USA, individual brokerage accounts are protected against a broker's default by the Security Investors Protection Corporation within limits (500,000 USD per customer, 100,000 USD for cash).

4.2. CENTRAL DEPOSITORIES

A **central depository** is an entity that accepts deposits of securities and that accounts for transfers of these securities among participants.[17] The Japanese Securities Depository Center (JASDEC) serves as the depository for Japanese stocks, and as of October 1998, 3,255 Japanese companies had consented to have JASDEC handle their stock certificates.[18] In some countries there are multiple depositories dealing with different types of securities or particular groups of institutions and brokerage firms.[19] If they continue to exist, physical certificates evidencing ownership are **immobilized** and stored in a central vault to eliminate physical movements of the certificates in transfers of ownership. Certificates are delivered to the central depository; a book-entry account is created, and the participant's account is credited; and the certificate of ownership is transferred to the name of the central depository. The process is reversed if shares are withdrawn from the central depository. The ownership records are **dematerialized** if the certificates cease to exist, so all ownership records are in electronic form. Equities have been dematerialized in Israel, and treasury bills and other government debt has been dematerialized in the USA. Treasury securities and most derivatives are dematerialized in the USA. A central depository reduces costs and risks of transfers. Eliminating the printing of new certificates and the physical movement of certificates each time there is a change in ownership reduces costs. Risk of loss due to forgery and losses of certificates is also eliminated. However, in 1995 thieves accessed the accounts of three investment funds at the depository of the Czech Republic and stole more than 15 million USD of securities (Sesit 1997).

Clearing and settlement in India used to illustrated the worse aspects of a physical settlement system. In some cases transfer of a physical certificate could require scores of signatures. Registrars rejected 10–15 percent of certificates for various problems. Security was lax. One Indian bank stored certificates in a trailer parked in an alley (Karp 1997; Karp and Sharma 1997; Sesit 1997). In 1997 the Securities and Exchange Board of India[20] ordered institutional investors to use the country's electronic share depository, and the process of immobilization certificates began.

In Singapore, accounts at the Central Depository are in the names of individuals, so an individual can easily deal with more than one brokerage firm. When shares are bought, the brokerage firm simply has the Central Depository credit these shares to the customer's account. When the shares are sold, the brokerage firm has the customer's account debited for the shares. There is no need for the same brokerage firm to be used in buying and selling the shares. By contrast, US brokerage firms have vigorously opposed the establishment of individual accounts in the USA. Instead, these brokerage firms advocate having one or more central depositories with only institutional accounts allowed. The individual brokerage firms would then maintain their own customer accounts. Restrictions on individual accounts at the central depository make the use of one brokerage firm for buying and another for selling more difficult, which, of course, is the brokers' aim.

In most markets certificates exist in both registered and bearer form. **Registered** means that the identity of the owner is recorded on the books of the registrar. **Bearer** securities are negotiable upon delivery, and physical (or book-entry) possession is all that is required to effect ownership changes. The security requirements for bearer certificates are much higher than for registered certificates, and some central depositories do not accept bearer certificates.

4.3. GLOBAL CUSTODIANS

Global custodians are financial institutions that ensure that clients' financial transactions are settled properly and registered correctly.[21] They also protect the ownership rights of their clients, including protection in such matters as dividends, stock splits, and voting. Investors may also rely on custodians to know which brokers can be trusted. While developed markets have well-understood rules, the laws in countries with emerging markets may not even recognize private ownership. In 1997 one custodian refused to do custodial work in Russia unless the client signed a statement acknowledging the risks. In another case an investor believed that it owned 300 million USD of stock in a Russian firm, but discovered on the day of the annual meeting that its name had been erased from the company's registration records.

4.4. COMMUNICATIONS NETWORKS

The importance of communications is underscored by McPartland, Taylor, and Pozdena (1989), who state that "even in the derivatives markets, where there are fewer obstacles to the development of a 24-hour system, a switch to round-the-clock trading would still bring that market up against a powerful stumbling block: the lack of a 24-hour-a-day payment system offering finality of settlement." The most important communications network is the Society for Worldwide Interbank Financial Telecommunications (SWIFT). Another important network is the Clearing House Interbank Payments System (CHIPS) in the USA. We describe each of these in turn.

4.4.1. SWIFT

SWIFT supports the financial data communications and processing needs of 4,625 financial institutions in 126 countries (as of 1994). SWIFT is owned by its user banks, with shares allocated principally on the basis of usage.[22] These shareholder banks are known as "members." Other financial service organizations connected to SWIFT are called "participants" and are not allowed to own shares or vote on the governing board or other matters. SWIFT users exchange more than 2 million messages a day through SWIFT's interconnected operating centers located in Brussels, Amsterdam, and Culpeper, Virginia, USA. These centers operate 24 hours a day, 7 days a week.

SWIFT has been at the forefront of establishing message standards. Standardized message formats facilitate clear, precise, understandable communications, helping to eliminate language barriers and misunderstandings and to reduce costs. The need for re-keying is minimized, allowing transfers of data from one computer application to another. Figure 4.2 shows ten SWIFT message categories. The breakdown of SWIFT message volume by type is: payments, 72.6 percent; forex and money market, 13.6 percent; securities, 6.5 percent; trade finance, 6.4 percent; and other, 0.9 percent. Securities messages have the highest rate of growth.

SWIFT pioneered the use of computer and telecommunications technology for automated cross-border payments. More than 1 million messages a day concern these payments, divided about equally between customer transfers and interbank transfers. Consumers want ease of use; corporations want payment certainty and accounting reference information. Both want low costs. About 30 percent of the interbank payments sent through SWIFT cover payments of customer transfers, payments for checks, documentary collections and letters of credit, and the bank's own (nostro) account transfers. The remainder are in settlement of various types of contracts, including foreign exchange, money market, and securities trades.

Hallmarks of the SWIFT system are speed, reliability, and security. SWIFT insures reliability and security by checking the identity of the sender, the format of the message,

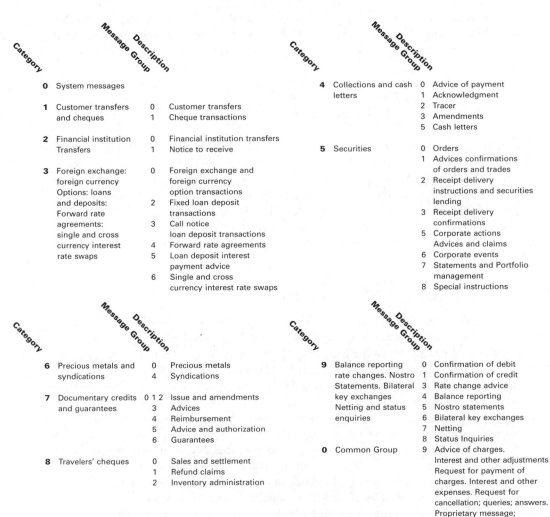

Figure 4.2 SWIFT message types.
Source: Society for Worldwide Interbank Financial Telecommunications.

acknowledging the message's acceptance by the system only if it conforms, encrypting the message during transit and storage, and guaranteeing delivery of the message.

SWIFT connected institutions using the network's securities markets facilities, including

1 Banks – institutions engaged in providing payment and custodian services, especially in their role of global, subregional, or domestic custodians.

2 Securities broker-dealers – institutions engaged in underwriting and/or dealing in securities and recognized by at least one regulatory agency or exchange.

3 Recognized exchanges – institutions with established rules and controlled by their members that provide exchange facilities, maintain a public list of securities, and are recognized by at least one regulatory agency.

4 Central depositories and clearing institutions – central systems for handling securities or equivalent book entries and/or transnational system for centralized handling of securities.

5 Trust and fiduciary service companies – institutions authorized to provide fiduciary services and cash accounts.

6 Subsidiary providers of custody and nominee services – wholly owned subsidiaries of SWIFT member banks.

7 Registrars and transfer agents – institutions maintaining the register of legal ownership of securities issues, authorized by a regulatory agency.

8 Investment management institutions – institutions that engage in the provision of investment management services authorized by a regulatory agency.

4.4.2. CHIPS

The Clearing House Interbank Payments System (CHIPS) is the international payments arm of the New York Clearing House Association, the USA's first and largest bank clearinghouse established in 1853.[23] Banks use CHIPS to transfer and settle USD transactions. CHIPS is an online, real-time electronic payment system that transfers and settles transactions in USD. All transactions are delivered in real time to a hot contingency center that gives CHIPS the capability of relocating its operations within 5 minutes in the event of a disaster. CHIPS handles 95 percent of all USD payments moving between countries around the world. On a typical day substantially more than 1 trillion USD in payments clears through CHIPS. The number of transactions is about 200,000 daily. Box 4.4 describes a typical CHIPS transaction.

5. SUMMARY

When a trade has been consummated, the parties to the trade exchange cash and other financial assets. Clearing is the determination of which financial assets must be delivered, when the deliveries should occur, and who is to make the deliveries. An important part of the clearing process is the identification of any error in connection with the trade. Settlement is the carrying out of each party's obligations under the terms of the trade. Clearing and settlement involve risk:

1 Credit risk, failure to settle due to economic reasons, is either replacement cost risk or principal risk.
   (a) Replacement cost risk arises from changes in asset values between the trade date and settlement date.
   (b) Principal risk, the most important credit risk, is the risk that a firm's counterparty will default (e.g., will fail to complete its part of the transaction) after the firm has delivered cash or securities, putting the entire principal at risk.

123

BOX 4.4
CHIPS: How funds are transferred

Consider the following: An importer in Lisbon, Portugal, asked its bank to send 5 million USD to a distributor in Mexico City, Mexico, in payment for a shipment. The payment process involves the following steps:

1 Lisbon Bank A transmits instructions to its correspondent, New York Bank B, which verifies the transmission.
2 A terminal operator at Bank B enters the relevant information for the funds transfer into Bank B's CHIPS interface computer, with the identifying documentation.
3 The central CHIPS computer at the clearinghouse, based on Bank B's information, edits and authenticates the message, stores the transaction, and causes a "store" acknowledgment message to be transmitted back to Bank B
4 Subsequently, Bank B approves the stored transaction and releases it to CHIPS, which screens the payment against risk controls. CHIPS then sends a "receive" message to Bank C, automatically debits Bank B, and credits Bank C.
5 Bank C notifies its Mexico City office by automated telecommunications message to pay the clothing exporter.

The clearinghouse nets this transaction with all other transactions between the two banks and further nets the positions of each of these banks with all other transactions in real time, so that each participant on CHIPS has a single net position (which will be a debit or a credit). At the end of the day, the clearinghouse sends a report to each participant showing its net position. Settlement of funds is made daily, using Fedwire, the public sector wire transfer system in the USA, to access reserve or clearing accounts on the books of the Federal Reserve Bank of New York (FRBNY). A CHIPS account at the FRBNY receives funds from settling participants with a debit position. These funds are used to pay participants in a net credit position. The settlement account is brought to zero balance and closed daily. CHIPS payments executed throughout the day are irrevocable and are paid through settlement at the end of the day.

Source: Based on information taken from CHIPS, n.d., pp. 5–6.

2 Liquidity risk is the risk that a counterparty will settle for full value, but at a date beyond the established settlement date. Default is the realization of credit risk, and a failed transaction is the realization of liquidity risk.
3 Operational risk arises from the possibility that there will be a failure in the hardware, software, communications, or others physical aspects of the clearing and settlement process.
4 Systemic risk is the possibility that the failure of one financial institution will result in the failure of additional firms, causing still more failures.
5 Errors risk arises from the possibility that there will be an error in executing a trade, such as buying when a sell was intended.

Risk can be reduced by netting, offsetting payments between parties, by consummating both sides of a transaction at the same time, called "delivery versus payment," and by requiring firms and individuals to post margin to guarantee performance of their obligations.

Several types of institutions have also been developed to reduce the risks and costs of clearing and settlement. Clearinghouses concentrate on many aspects of the clearing and settlement process, such as trade matching and netting. Central depositories own immobilized (securities for which there is a physical record of ownership) or dematerialized (securities for which the record of ownership is in electronic form) securities. Then, transfers of ownership can be made by debiting and crediting accounts at the central depository. Global custodians are financial institutions that ensure that clients' financial transactions are settled properly and registered correctly. Communication networks also facilitate clearing and settlement. The best known is the Society for Worldwide Interbank Financial Telecommunications, SWIFT, which operates a worldwide network on a 24-hour-a-day, 7-day-a-week basis. Participants use SWIFT to send details concerning transactions and orders for the transfer of cash and securities.

Questions

1   What is the difference between clearing and settlement?
2   Which has the most risk, clearing or settlement?
3   How many types of clearing and settlement risk can you name?
4   How can netting reduce clearing and settlement risk?
5   Why is it not possible to achieve perfect delivery-versus-payment?
6   What is the function of a clearinghouse?
7   What is the function of a central depository?
8   Who might lose if a central depository went bankrupt?
9   What is the difference between immobilization and dematerialization?
10   How do communications networks facilitate clearing and settlement?

■ Notes ■

1   The Group of Thirty, established in 1978, is a private, nonpartisan, nonprofit organization that aims to deepen understanding of international economic and financial issues. Foundations, banks, nonbank corporations, central banks, and individuals support the group. Current or former group members include Mr. Andrew D. Crockett, General Manager, Bank for International Settlements; M. Jacques de Larosière, President, European Bank for Reconstruction and Development; Mr. Paul A. Volcker, Chairman and Chief Executive Officer, James D. Wolfensohn, Inc. and former chairman of the US Federal Reserve Board.

2   The clearing and settlement process on the Tokyo Stock Exchange is described at http://www.tse.or.jp/eb/ebc.html. MBS Clearing Corporation provides clearing services for mortgage-backed securities to financial institutions in the USA; its web address is http://www.mbscc.com/pmbscc1.htm.

3   The first three types of risk discussed below are defined in Bank for International Settlements 1990, commonly known as the Lamfalussy Report.

4   The Committee on Payment and Settlement Systems of IOSCO addresses issues concerning the operation of securities settlement systems and their allocation of risk. Among other docu-

ments, the committee has prepared a Disclosure Framework for Securities Settlement Systems. Additional information is available at the committee's web site: http://www.bis.org/publ/cpss20.htm.

5　Jackwert and Rubinstein (1996) discuss the difficulties in analyzing return distributions caused by extreme outliers. If returns were distributed lognormal, the crash of October 1987 would be a -27 standard deviation event with a probability of 10^{-160}. The crash of October 1989 was a -5 standard deviation event that should occur once every 14,756 years.

6　Recall that a thick market is a market with frequent trading and a thin market is a market with infrequent trading. All assets have a degree of thinness, in that they do not trade continuously.

7　Bonte-Friedheim (1996) reports that the governor of the central bank of Kenya asked Michael Power, head of Baring Asset Management, for suggestions on how to make Kenya more attractive to foreign investors. Power suggested speeding up the settlement system, so that investors would not have to wait as long as 6 weeks to be paid when they sold stock.

8　For a discussion of margin on the Tokyo Stock Exchange see http://www.tse.or.jp/eb/eb09.html. An excellent discussion of margin trading and clearing and settlement on LIFFE is provided at http://www.esi.co.uk/public/liffe/publintr.html#A9.

9　In the USA the brokerage firm cannot pledge a customer's stock for more than the debit balance. In other words, a broker cannot use one customer's stock to secure another customer's loan.

10　In the USA the initial margin requirement currently is 50 percent for equities, but the requirement for bonds is typically lower. The US Federal Reserve maintenance margin requirement is 25 percent.

11　Established in 1976, National Securities Clearing Corporation is the largest provider of clearing and settlement services in the USA. The firm settles almost all equity and bond transactions. The NYSE, Amex, and NASD own NSCC. The web site for NSCC is: http://www.nscc.com/. For additional information on clearinghouses see: Australia: Austraclear, www.austraclear.com.au; Germany: Deutsche Börse Clearing AG, www.exchange.de; Japan: Bank of Japan, www.boj.or.jp; Latvia: Bank of Latvia, www.bank.lv; Lebanon: MIDCLEAR, www.bdl.gov.lb; United Kingdom: Bank of England, www.bankofengland.co.uk; Crest, www.crestco.co.uk.

12　As pointed out at http://www.numa.com/derivs/ref/c-risk/cr-hk.htm, clearing arrangements vary widely. In some cases the clearing entity is an integral part of the exchange (such as the Osaka Stock Exchange) or a subsidiary of the exchange (as is the case for the CBOT), or it may be a completely separate institution (e.g., the London Clearing Corporation which clears trades for LIFFE).

13　Exchange Clearing House (ECHO) is the first global foreign exchange clearinghouse providing multilateral foreign exchange contract netting and settlement service for participating banks in all major centers around the world. The ECHO web site is http://www.exchangeclearinghouse.co.uk/.

14　For additional discussion of this topic see http://www.numa.com/derivs/ref/c-risk/cr-hk.htm.

15　The Euroclear System in Brussels operated by J. P. Morgan is the largest clearance and settlement system for internationally traded securities. Edwards (1994) provides an interesting discussion of how J. P. Morgan profits from running Euroclear.

16　Cedel Bank was established in 1970 to reduce the costs and risks of settling transactions in the Euromarkets. Cedel Bank provides delivery-versus-payment settlement for more than 110,000 different internationally traded securities. Every business day about 35,000 transactions valued at 60 billion USD are cleared and settled. See Cedel bank's web site for additional information: http://www.cedelgroup.com/english/f_moz/_products.htm.

17　The Canadian Depository for Securities Limited, established in 1970, is Canada's national provider of depository, clearing, and settlement services. Its web site is http://www.sedar.com/sedar/about_cds.htm.

18　For additional information see http://www.iijnet.or.jp/jasdec/english/index.html.

19 One US depository is the Depository Trust Company, whose web address is http://www.dtc.org/in/.

20 For additional information see the Board's web site: http://www.sebi.com/.

21 Examples of global custodians include Brown Brothers Harriman & Co., http://www.bbh.com/general/brochure.htm; Lloyds Bank Securities Services, http://www.custody.lloyds-bank.co.uk/index.html; and Standard Chartered Equitor (Singapore), http://www.globewatch.com/eq/index.html.

22 SWIFT currently supplies secure messaging globally on a 24-hour basis to more than 6,000 financial institutions in 177 countries. The average daily value of payments messages is more than 2 trillion USD. SWIFT's web address is http://www.swift.com/.

23 The New York Clearing House, the oldest clearinghouse in the USA, was founded to simplify the exchange of checks and improve the efficiency of the payments system. Since its founding, the NYCH has never failed to settle. NYCH processes 1.462 trillion USD on an average day. For additional information see http://www.theclearinghouse.org/chfacts.html. For information concerning the Australian clearing system see http://www.apca.com.au/clearing.htm.

■ References ■

Alton, Gilbert R. 1992: Implications of netting arrangements for bank risk in foreign exchange transactions. *Federal Reserve Bank of St. Louis Review* 74, 3–16.

Bank for International Settlements 1990: *Report of the Committee on Interbank Netting Schemes of the Central Banks of the Group of Ten Countries*. Basel. Known as the Lamfalussy Report.

——1992: *Delivery versus Payment in Securities Settlements Systems*. Basel.

——1995: *Cross-border Securities Settlements*. Basel.

Bonte-Friedheim, Robert 1996: Managers flock to tiny stock warkets that aren't hot yet. *Wall Street Journal*, Nov. 13, p. A8.

Clearing House Interbank Payments System (CHIPS) 19.

Edwards, Ben 1994: Euroclear: Morgan's magic circle. *Euromoney*, Aug. 35–8.

Glass, Garrett R. 1994: A primer on netting. *Journal of Commercial Bank Lending* 77, 18–25.

Group of Thirty 1992: *Clearance and Settlement Systems Status Report*. Washington, DC Autumn.

Guyot, Erik and Stein, Peter 1995: Depositing a check today, Madam? $491 million? No trouble at all. *Asian Wall Street Journal*, June 29, p. 1.

Hendricks, Darryll 1994: Netting agreements and the credit exposures of OTC derivatives portfolios. *Federal Reserve Bank of New York Economic Policy Review* 19, 7–18.

International Organization of Securities Commissions (IOSCO) 1992: *Clearing and Settlement in Emerging Markets: a blueprint*. Montreal.

Jackwert, Jens Carsten and Rubinstein, Mark 1996: Recovering probability distributions from option prices. *Journal of Finance* 51, 1611–31.

Karp, Jonathan 1997: India: settlement problems, while still a nightmare are showing definite signs of improvement. *Wall Street Journal*, June 26, p. R14.

Karp, Jonathan and Sharma, Sumit 1997: Paper chase ends as Indian stocks go electronic. *Wall Street Journal*, Oct. 17, p. A14.

McPartland, John, Taylor, Kim and Pozdena, Randall 1989: Extended hour trading. Summary in US Congress, Office of Technology Assessment, *Study of International Clearing and Settlement*, vol. 1 (PB91 127 54B), 184.

Options Clearing Corporation n.d.: *Theoretical Intermarket Margin System*. Chicago.

Organization for Economic Co-operation and Development 1991: *Systemic Risk in Securities Markets*. Paris.

Parkinson, Patrick, Gilbert, Adam, Gollob, Emily, Hargraves, Lauren, Mead, Richard, Stehm, Jeff and Taylor, Mary Ann 1992: *Clearance and Settlement in US Securities Markets* (Washington DC:

Board of Governors of the Federal Reserve System). (Provides an excellent discussion of clearing and settlement in the USA.)

Sesit, Micaher R. 1997: Unsettled: custodial services are taken for granted in most developed countries, not in emerging markets. *Wall Street Journal*, June 26, p. R6.

US Congress, Office of Technology Assessment 1989: *Study of International Clearing and Settlement*, vol. I, VI (PB91 127 54B), 184.

Wall Street Journal 1996: Hong Kong snafu tests investors' nerve. Dec. 13, pp. CI, C14.

Regulation

■ **Key terms** ■

Absolute priority rule   each senior class of creditors receives full payment before any junior class or equity holders receive any payments.

Automatic stay   the filing of a bankruptcy petition automatically prevents creditors from enforcing their claims.

Bankruptcy   a legal process in which an organization is either liquidated or financially restructured, often requiring writing off debt and equity claims.

Best execution   the requirement that a broker execute a trade in such a way that the client receives the best terms.

Blue sky laws   state laws in the USA regulating the sale of securities within the state.

Central bank   an organization that performs functions typically including creating money, serving as a lender of last resort, and acting as the government's fiscal agent.

Cramdown   a bankruptcy plan that is forced on one or more groups of creditors.

Credit union   a financial institution created by and owned and controlled by its members, the individuals who use its services.

Debtor-in-possession   the case in which the existing board of directors is permitted to retain control of the assets of a firm after the filing of a bankruptcy petition.

Defined benefit plans   a type of pension benefit in which the payment of a specific sum is guarantee.

Defined contribution plans   a type of pension plan in which the contributions, rather than the benefits, are specified.

Information efficiency   everyone has the same beliefs and information, so prices reflect that information.

Insurance company   a firm that enters into contracts to bear risk of clients in return for premiums.

Keiretsu   a group of Japanese companies characterized by significant cross-ownership, cross-trading, and coordinated management.

Lender of last resort   the supplier of funds to banks, and sometimes other types of financial institutions, during times of liquidity crises. This role is typically performed by the central bank, since it can create money and is never in danger of running out of domestic funds.

Money laundering   the processing of criminal funds in order to disguise their illegal origin.

Mutual recognition   nondomestic firms enjoy the same operating rights within their own jurisdiction that they would have in their home countries.

Open economy   an economy permitting the free flow of financial and human capital without distinction between domestic and nondomestic firms.

Pareto efficiency   the *status quo* cannot be changed without making someone worse off.

Premium   the payment received by an insurance company for bearing risk. (Note that there are a number of other definitions of this term in finance.)

Prudent man rule   a US rule which states that in making investments a trustee must act as others would act in making investments for themselves. The rule has been extended by ERISA to require that trustees act as others knowledgeable about making investments would act.

Reciprocity   nondomestic firms enjoy rights of access to local markets if the firm's home country grants similar rights to local firms.

Regulatory capture   the process whereby current and former industry members come to dominate the boards and staffs of regulatory bodies.

Run   the simultaneous withdrawal of deposits by the customers of a bank or other depository institution.

Trust indenture   a formal agreement between the issuer of bonds and the bondholder.

Universal banking   a system in which banks own or control a major portion of the shares in firms and participate actively in corporate governance.

Virtue ethics   the view that ethical behavior must be the goal of individuals and organizations, rather than a constraint on their actions.

Today most countries regulate financial markets and products. **IN THIS CHAPTER** we

- explain three reasons for regulation
- describe alternative approaches to regulation
- discuss how economic systems affect regulation

Then we review the scope of regulation dealing with

- financial markets
- financial institutions
- nondomestic investors
- multinational institutions

In the second part of this chapter we address ethical concerns by

- explaining why ethical behavior is important in the finance profession
- examining alternative views of ethics
- briefly exploring the Code of Ethics and Standards of Professional Conduct of the Association for Investment Management and Research

---

1. INTRODUCTION

Regulation of financial markets is a relatively new phenomenon, having begun primarily in the first half of the twentieth century. Governments seek to prevent the failure of one institution from spreading and causing the failure of the entire financial system, to protect consumers of financial products and investors, and to influence the financial system to help achieve societal objectives. Regulation is the means to achieving these objectives. Regulation includes both self-regulation, through professional organizations, and government regulation. Regulation may mandate or prohibit particular actions, or it can simply require that information be provided.

Most regulations are developed and adopted by individual countries and govern activities within that country. But there is a growing trend toward coordination of regulation internationally. The Basil Committee is developing common policies for the regulation of banks, and the International Organization of Securities Commissions is developing regulations for securities markets.

Ethical behavior is important for the finance professional. The relationship between the finance professional and their clients is based on trust. Without trust there can be no business relationship. Handling other people's money gives rise to many opportunities to put individual and company interests ahead of client interests. Therefore, it is important that finance professionals make ethical behavior a goal of their professional life. The Association for Investment Management and Research has developed a Code of Ethics and Standards of Professional Conduct that represent minimum standards for members of the association.

---

2. REGULATION

2.1. REASONS FOR REGULATION

2.1.1. Preventing systemic risk

One reason why regulation is needed is that the abuses and failures of one organization can affect others with whom the organization does business. The failures of one firm can also affect similarly situated firms in the same industry. Imprudent lending by one bank might cause it to fail. This, in turn, could cause depositors to lose faith in the banking system and to simultaneously withdraw their deposits. Such a **run** could cause the collapse of the entire banking system. There were many bank runs in the USA until the creation of the system of government insurance of deposits. The possibility that problems of one institution can spill over and cause problems for other organizations is called systemic risk.

Systemic risk is also present in the securities markets. Margin calls[1] can lead to selling, which, in turn, leads to further margin calls and then further selling. Such a cycle could lead to the collapse of the investment banking community. In the 1980s the Hunts, a wealthy Texas oil family, faced millions of USDs of margin calls on their derivative contracts. The US Federal Reserve, the US central bank, which is described more fully later in this chapter, feared that failure to meet these margin calls would result in the bankruptcy of the brokerage firm holding the Hunts' account, precipitating a systemic crisis. To avoid this possibility, the US Federal Reserve arranged a loan for the family in exchange for asset pledges and other financial stipulations, one of which was that the family sell its silver holdings.

2.1.2. Protecting consumers and investors

Another important objective of regulation is to protect investors and consumers of financial products. The importance of investor protection increases when the proportion of investors in the economy grows, since this typically means that there are more unsophisticated investors who may be taken advantage of by unscrupulous financial professionals. Investors may need protection against insider trading and unfair use of corporate assets. The government may seek to require all vendors of certain products to provide the same information in the same format, so that consumers of these products can make a more informed judgment. The government may bar financial institutions from discriminating against certain consumers on the basis of race or other characteristics.

2.1.3. Achieving societal objectives

The government may seek to promote societal objectives that would not be feasible for individual organizations. A decision may be made to support certain segments of the economy, such as housing, by providing regulatory incentives for lending to these favored areas. Since criminals typically use the banking system to transact some of their business, governments have imposed regulations on money laundering in an effort to hinder illegal activities. In the USA, banks are required to report currency transactions of 10,000 USD or more. Switzerland eliminated anonymous bank accounts in 1992, so that it could better police illegal activities. In Malaysia the government favored the local Malay population by requiring that a certain proportion of new stock issues be set aside for them.

2.2. ALTERNATIVE APPROACHES TO REGULATION

2.2.1. Self-regulation versus governmental regulation

Historically, financial markets have been largely self-regulated, and a large measure of self-regulation continues. Self-regulation can have advantages over governmental regulation. Industry participants are likely to be more knowledgeable than governmental officials concerning the details of the operation of their businesses. Industry professionals also have self-interest in promoting fair dealing, at least among themselves. Self-regulation can also help to develop an ethical climate in which industry professionals go further than the rules required to obtain equitable outcomes. As Justice Douglas of the US Supreme Court observed, self-regulation "has the potential for establishing and enforcing ethical standards beyond those that the law can establish."

Governmental regulation, on the other hand, may take broad-based societal issues (such as lowering transaction costs) into account more fully. Governments typically can command more stringent penalties, including criminal sanctions. Governments may also have more resources to devote to regulation. A difficulty with governmental regulation is **regulatory capture**, in which industry members, because of their more intense interest and greater expertise, co-opt the governmental regulatory process. Current and former industry members may come to dominate the boards and staffs of regulatory agencies, causing them to promulgate regulations that favor the industry rather than its customers.

In the USA, governmental regulation of the banking industry increased significantly with the creation of the US Federal Reserve System in 1913. Debate as to the relative roles of self-regulation and governmental regulation is ongoing. Considering the role of regulation in establishing policies concerning banks' dealing in financial derivatives, Paul Volker, says:

> Plainly, the authors believe that the amount of capital needed to support derivatives exposure is a matter of judgment for individual institutions, depending on their appetite for risk and their ability to measure and manage it. (From the foreword to Global Derivatives Study Group 1993)

Stock exchanges have always had rules. But until the worldwide market crash of 1929 there was little governmental regulation. The crash prompted the USA to pass several pieces of legislation, such as the Securities Act of 1933 and the Securities Exchange Act of 1934. In many cases this legislation continued to emphasize self-regulation, but within a statutory framework. The Securities and Exchange Commission[2] was empowered to issue regulations governing the issuance and trading of securities and to enforce those regulations. But enforcement is also carried out through a number of self-regulatory organizations (SROs), including the stock exchanges themselves.

Many governments throughout the world have concluded that self-regulation alone cannot satisfy all regulatory needs, particularly in the area of market fraud. In the UK the Wilson Committee Report in 1980 concluded that self-regulation was preferable to other forms of regulation. But the UK moved more firmly to embrace self-regulation within a statutory framework in the securities markets with the passage of the UK Financial Services Act in 1986. In the UK the government is creating new laws to merge formerly independent regulatory bodies into the Financial Services Authority (FAS) (formerly called the Securities Industries Board). On June 1, 1998, the Bank of England Act 1998 came into force, transferring responsibility for banking supervision from the Bank of England to the FSA. More than 23,000 firms conduct investment business in the UK. The FSA recognizes four types of entities that regulate these firms: (1) self-regulating organizations, which regulate investment fund managers, firms involved in the investment business, and firms that market and advise the public on investments; (2) recognized professional bodies, which regulate members whose main activity is the practice of their profession (accountant, solicitor, etc.) but who have some minor involvement in investment business; (3) recognized investment exchanges, which are organized markets; and (4) recognized clearinghouses, which deal with the settlement of transactions.[3]

2.2.2. Disclosure versus merit regulation

In merit regulation the government requires certain actions in the public interest or prohibits certain actions that are deemed contrary to the public interest. The sale of specific financial products may be banned. The makeup of the board of directors may be specified. Specific securities may be reviewed and rejected for sale because they are too risky.

Disclosure regulation focuses on insuring that market participants fully disclose information, so that investors can make knowledgeable decisions. In the USA the USSEC does not try to decide how much investors should pay for shares. Instead, it tries to make sure that companies disclose sufficient financial information on which investors can base their decisions. Detailed rules are provided concerning the nature of the information that must be disclosed, and substantial penalties are imposed for violation of these rules. Disclosure is intended to prevent various types of problems, including conflicts of interest between a controlling owner and minority owners and between managers and owners. Sometimes controlling shareholders have sweetheart contracts with firms they are taking public in an initial public offering (IPO). These contracts may allow the controlling shareholder to charge above-market rates for services rendered to the firm or to make purchases from the firm at below-market rates. If investors buying shares in the IPO know in advance that a controlling shareholder has such a sweetheart contract, they can take this contract into account in valuing the firm. Hence, the value of the contracts to the controlling shareholder will be offset by a lower share price, so that the controlling shareholder does not benefit at the expense of the new investors.

George Benston (1973) argues that disclosure rules are superfluous, because markets will demand sufficient disclosure to insure fair pricing. If firms do not provide sufficient information, investors will refuse to buy the shares or will buy them only at a discount. This gives an incentive for those selling the shares to provide more information. But if the selling shareholders are themselves minority shareholders without sufficient information, as would probably be the case in a universal banking country, as described in the next section, they may not have any information to provide. In this type of market shares can sell at prices that vary significantly from their full-information price.

2.3. ECONOMIC SYSTEMS

The way in which an economy provides for risk sharing and corporate governance decision making has an important influence on the regulation of its economic institutions. There are two primary economic mechanisms used to share risk and make corporate governance decisions: stock markets and main banks. Stock markets allow investors to pool their funds, each buying shares according to their wealth and risk tolerance. The number of investors is relatively large, and these investors typically select some or all of the governing boards of the firms in which they hold shares. Information must be disseminated widely and in a sufficiently simple form to permit understanding by numerous individuals.

Universal banking is a system in which banks own or control a major portion of the shares in firms and participate actively in corporate governance. In addition to owning equity, banks are the primary underwriters of new equity offerings and also offer brokerage services. (Van Hulle (1996) provides discussion and figures showing the ownership structures of a number of European holding groups.) In Germany banks often own both the debt and the equity of a firm, which gives them a great deal of control over the firm. In addition, German banks typically have the right to vote the shares of others that are left with the bank. Based on data for 1974, Gorton and Schmid (1996) report that large concentrated shareholdings by banks improved firm performance. And banks were special, in that large holdings by other entities did not affect performance. But based on data for 1985 these authors no longer find that banks' holdings affect firm performance. They attributed this decreased influence of banks to the fact that securities markets had become more developed, decreasing firms' reliance on banks. Kester (1994) also reports a positive role for banks, which can monitor management to help insure efficient operations, mediate disputes among stakeholders, and even promote new business opportunities among related firms.

In Japan many companies are organized into groups called **keiretsu**. Keiretsu are characterized by cross holdings of equity among group members. In Japan perhaps two-thirds of corporate equity is held by other corporations. Since each keiretsu firm owns an interest in the other members of the group, control is vested in the current management rather than with the outside stockholders. The keiretsu may include a bank that functions as the main bank of most or all of the members of the group. The main bank often lends funds to group members, and these loans are typically rolled over at maturity. Further, the main bank provides flexibility, in that compensating balances and interest and principal payments can be deferred in times of adversity. Stockholders usually receive a fixed dividend payment, which rarely changes, and non-keiretsu stockholders usually have negligible influence on management.

In the main bank and universal bank system, public information needs may be low, since the banks can obtain information directly from the corporations in which they hold shares, in the same way that they would when making loans to these same corporations. Bank officials may be directors of the firms. Liquidity is less important, because the banks are long-term or even permanent investors in the enterprises in which they hold shares.

2.4. REGULATION OF FINANCIAL MARKETS

Governments may also prohibit or require certain types of activities. In the USA the USSEC has prohibited the stock exchanges from enforcing fixed commissions. Hence, each brokerage firm is free to set its own commission schedule, and commissions are negotiable. Insider trading, price manipulation, and other practices may be prohibited. Dale (1996) and Herring and Litan (1995) provide discussions of financial market regulation.

2.4.1. Bankruptcy

Bankruptcy is an important type of regulation of financial activity. **Bankruptcy** is a legal process through which organizations restructure their finances. There are at least two important dimensions of bankruptcy law that differ from country to country. One is whether the goal of bankruptcy is to liquidate the firm or to promote the possibility that the firm will remain a going concern. A closely related issue concerns who controls an insolvent firm. In the UK historically about three-quarters of all reorganizations have been liquidations, and about 22 percent have been receiverships. In liquidation, a liquidator is appointed to sell enough of the firm's assets to repay creditors. The liquidator may sell the entire firm or parts of the firm, but the liquidation must proceed expeditiously. Alternatively, a creditor with a type of claim known as a "floating charge" can unilaterally appoint a receiver for the firm. The appointment of a receiver typically does not require the permission of a court. When a receiver is appointed, control of the firm passes to the receiver, and the board of directors steps down. The goal of the receiver is to liquidate the firm for the benefit of the appointing creditor, and the receiver has little or no duty of care to other stakeholders, including stockholders, employees, the government, and other creditors. The receivership law does not provide for an **automatic stay**, in which other creditors are prevented from pursuing their claims in court. The ability of the receiver to operate the firm as a going concern pending liquidation may be hampered by the fact that creditors with claims against specific assets, called "fixed charges," can repossess those assets even if they are vital to the operation of the business.

In contrast to the UK, in the USA debtors usually have a much more important role in cases of corporate insolvency. There are two main bankruptcy provisions: Chapter 7 and Chapter 11. Under Chapter 7 the court appoints a trustee to oversee the liquidation of the firm. The firm is closed down, and the assets are sold under the supervision of the trustee. Under Chapter 11, the directors of the firm remain in control of the firm, which remains in operation. This is referred to as **debtor-in-possession**. In about one-half of the cases the existing management remains in control, and in most of the other cases new management is appointed. The filling of a bankruptcy petition causes an **automatical stay**: i.e., a suspension of any actions that creditors might take to enforce their claims. Further, those who have supplied equipment and buildings to the firm through leases are not likely to be able to reclaim their property until the reorganization plan is approved.

The **absolute priority rule** states that each senior class of creditors receives full payment before any junior class or equity holders receive any payments. As noted by Beranek, Boehmer, and Smith (1996) the absolute priority rule is not a part of US bankruptcy law, and deviations are common in the USA. (For a more theoretical discussion of the absolute priority rule see Longhofer 1977.) For an initial period, management has the exclusive right to present a plan to the court. Each class of creditors receiving less than it is entitled to receive appoints a representative to a creditors' committee to negotiate a plan with management. To be approved, a plan must receive the assent of each impaired class by majority vote in terms of numbers and by a two-thirds vote in terms of USD value of claims. If one or more impaired classes reject the plan, it fails. If all impaired classes reject the plan, the negotiations must continue or the firm must be liquidated. If one impaired class accepts the plan, the court may still order implementation of the plan, which is forced on the dissenting creditors. This is called a **cramdown**.

Bankruptcy law affects the operations of both solvent and insolvent firms. The effect on insolvent firms may be obvious. But the financing arrangements, investment decisions, and other aspects of the operations of solvent firms may be affected by bankruptcy practices that will become applicable if the firm becomes insolvent. Creditors and equity investors must factor these laws into their projections when they enter into investments.

Franks, Nyborg, and Torous (1996) propose three criteria for judging the efficiency of a bankruptcy code:

Does it preserve promising enterprises while liquidating uneconomic ones?
Does it allow the firm to be reorganized or liquidated at minimum cost?
Does it permit innovations in debt contracts to improve the insolvency process?

Another question that might be added to this list is: Does it treat nonequity and noncreditor stakeholders such as employees, customers, and governments fairly?

Most developed countries have well-established bankruptcy procedures. Kaiser (1996) provides a compansion of the bankruptcy laws in the USA, the UK, France, and Germany. On the other hand, many countries, especially those with relatively young capital markets, do not have well-developed bankruptcy laws. Lack of these laws is detrimental in a number of ways. Enterprises that are inefficient may be able to continue operating even when they are insolvent, because they cannot be forced to liquidate if their debts are not paid. In China large unprofitable state-owned enterprises are supported by the banking system. When state-owned Guangdong International Trust & Investment Co. was allowed to go bankrupt, creditors faced a number of issues. Some of the firm's holdings were quickly transferred to other state-owned firms, without any details of whether and to what extent the firm received payments. There was also concern over the disposition of assets, such as a nuclear power plant, that the government would be unlikely to allow to be transferred in to private hands (Smith 1999). In 1997 in Malaysia there were similar concerns about the transfer of assets from bankrupt firms to their parents on favorable terms, to the detriment of public stockholders.

2.4.2. Regulation of securities markets in the USA

We are interested in describing the various sorts of regulation faced by financial markets and financial institutions. Because the USA has a relatively comprehensive set of regulatory organizations, we briefly describe these. Later in the chapter we describe the regulation of US financial institutions. Similar financial services and regulatory needs are found around the world. Tan (1991) discusses government regulation and self-regulation in an international context.

Some of the first regulations for financial markets in the USA concerned the appropriate behavior of trustees who invested money for others. Traditionally, in English law, trustees were limited in their investments to an English Court of Chancery list of government securities. In the USA a case was brought against the trustees of a trust established for the benefit of Harvard College. The trust document had directed the trustees to "loan the same upon ample and sufficient security, or to invest the same in sage and productive stock, either in the public funds, bank shares of other stock, according to their best judgment and discretion." The trustees invested in several banks and insurance companies and in two manufacturing companies. Two trust remaindermen sued the trustees, seeking to recover the decline in value of the insurance and manufacturing stocks as not suitable trust investments. In 1830 in *Harvard College* v. *Amory* the court rejected the English rule, saying that the available US government securities were "exceedingly limited compared with the amount of trust funds to be invested" throughout the USA. Further, since mortgages, real estate, and all types of investments fluctuate in value, the judge concluded: "Do what you will, the capital is at hazard." The judge then announced what has come to be known as the **prudent man rule**, namely:

> All that can be required of a trustee to invest, is, that he shall conduce himself faithfully and exercise a sound discretion. He is to observe how men of prudence, discretion and intelligence manage their own affairs, not in regard to speculation, but in regard to the permanent

disposition of their funds, considering the probably income, as well as the probable safety of the capital invested.

The prudent man rule was not widely adopted in the USA at first. Instead, state legislatures adopted legal lists of securities that were suitable for trust investments. These legal lists typically comprised various debt instruments, and common stocks were taboo. Most trust investments in the USA were subject to these legal lists until the 1940s. With the collapse in bond value in the depression of the 1930s, there was substantial dissatisfaction with the legal list approach, and the prudent man rule came to predominate. (Longstreth (1986) provides a comprehensive discussion of the prudent man rule.)

Securities markets were not regulated by the US or state governments until 1911. The impetus for state regulation was begun by J. N. Dolly, the banking commissioner for the State of Kansas. Dolly argued that regulation was needed to prevent individuals from being lured into unprofitable investments by unscrupulous investment bankers. Legislation was passed requiring the approval of the banking commissioner before any security could be sold in the state. After the passage of the Kansas legislation, similar laws were passed in most other US states. State laws regulating the sale of securities are called **blue sky laws**. Some states simply mandated better disclosure, but most attempted to judge the merits of issues before granting approval. While the stated motive for this legislation was the protection of investors, Macey and Miller (1991) argue that the real motive was to protect banks, which offered relatively low interest rates, from competition and higher-yielding securities. State bank regulators, small bankers, farmers, and small businessmen supported the push for regulation. The farmers and small businessmen were interested in insuring the availability of credit and in keeping its cost low. Large banks, investment bankers, and large issuers of securities opposed the legislation. Eventually many issues such as those listed on stock exchanges were exempted from regulation in most states. Beginning in 1933 the US government began to regulate securities markets, but state regulation continued alongside federal regulation.[4]

The principal US federal regulator is the Securities and Exchange Commission (USSEC). The USSEC is an independent, nonpartisan, regulatory agency with responsibility for administering US securities laws. The USSEC is responsible for administering a number of US securities laws designed to protect investors by insuring that securities markets operate fairly. The USSEC attempts to see that investors have access to all material information concerning publicly traded securities. The USSEC regulates firms engaged in the purchase or sale of securities, individuals who provide investment advice, and investment companies. One of the most significant pieces of legislation enforced by the USSEC is the Securities Act of 1933, which

1 requires that investors be given all significant information concerning securities that are offered for public sale,
2 prohibits fraud and misrepresentation in the sale of securities.

Another is the Securities Exchange Act of 1934, which also requires disclosure of information concerning securities, especially those traded publicly on exchanges or over-the-counter, outlaws fraudulent practices such as insider trading, and establishes regulations for market participants including margin rules.

The USSEC enforces several other significant laws. The Investment Company Act of 1940 provides for the regulation of investment companies. The Investment Adviser Act of 1940 requires that individuals or firms that are compensated for advising others about securities investment register and conform to standards promulgated under the act. Under the Public Utility Holding Company Act of 1935, holding companies involved in the electric utility business or in the retail distribution of natural or manufactured gas are subject to regulation. The Trust Indenture Act of 1939 requires that, in addition to being registered with the USSEC, all debt securities offered for public sale must have a **trust indenture**, a formal agreement between the issuer of bonds and the bondholder, that conforms to the requirements of the act.

Five commissioners, one of whom is designated as chairman, govern the USSEC. The President of the United States, with the advice and consent of the US Senate, appoints all commission members for a 5-year term. The Division of Corporation Finance insures that registered companies meet disclosure requirements. The Division of Market Regulation oversees securities markets and market participants such as brokerage firms, self-regulatory organizations, transfer agents, and clearinghouses. The Division of Investment Management administers the Investment Company Act of 1940, the Investment Adviser Act of 1940, and the Public Utility Holding Company Act of 1935. The Division of Enforcement investigates potential violations of US securities laws, and the Office of Compliance Inspections and Examinations conducts all inspections of those regulated by the SEC.

A number of self-regulatory organizations (SROs) also have an obligation to monitor the financial markets. Each stock exchange is a SRO. This entails an obligation to ensure that trading on the exchange conforms to applicable rules and laws such as prohibitions against insider trading. These obligations are the basis of the complaints of the exchanges that competition from electronic crossing networks is unfair because these firms do not have to provide these types of public goods. An example of regulatory-type activities of an exchange is the Stock Watch of the NYSE, which is a computerized system for monitoring unusual trading activity, to help prevent price manipulation and insider trading. Box 5.1 describes this system in greater detail.

2.4.3. Regulation of derivatives markets in the USA

The Commodity Futures Trading Commission (CFTC), was created by the US in 1974 as an independent agency to regulate commodity futures and option markets. The agency fights against manipulation, abusive trade practices, and fraud. The CFTC reviews new futures contracts to insure that there is a sufficient market and that the contract conforms to existing commercial practices. The CFTC conducts market surveillance and can order an exchange to take specific actions concerning any futures contract being traded. Futures exchanges may not change or add rules without CFTC approval. Any individual or firm handling customer funds must register with the National Futures Association (NFA),[5] a self-regulatory organization approved by the CFTC. All registrants are required to complete ethics training. The CFTC requires the disclosure of market risks and monitors supervisory systems, internal controls, and sales practices.

A board comprising five commissioners appointed by the President of the United States for 5-year terms governs the CFTC. A commissioner is the chief administrative officer within the CFTC. The CFTC operates through five divisions. Duties of the Division of

---

BOX 5.1
Market surveillance

Stock Watch is a key NYSE tool for protecting the integrity of the market in NYSE-listed securities. It is a computerized system that automatically flags unusual volume or price changes in any listed stock, helping the Exchange guard against manipulation and insider trading.

Most large volume or price changes can be explained by company news, trends in the industry, or national economic factors. However, where no legitimate explanation is evident, the NYSE launches an investigation. The investigation begins by contacting the company to find out if there are any pending announcements. At the same time, surveillance personnel draw on an electronic audit trail to reconstruct the details of every trade that takes place. Rebuilding the "time of execution" enables NYSE investigators to see if any member firm(s) stand out in the trading.

The next step is to contact the firm(s) and obtain the names of the customers involved in the trade. These names are automatically matched against the names of officers, directors, and other corporate and noncorporate insiders to detect any possible connection or illicit flow of information. This task is performed using the Automated Search and Match (ASAM), which contains the names of 800,000 executives, lawyers, bankers, and accountants, plus public profile data on officers and directors of approximately 80,000 public corporations and 30,000 corporate subsidiaries. Customer and trading information is also analyzed for geographical concentrations and compared with names and chronological events provided by NYSE-listed companies and member firms.

If, after an investigation is completed, the NYSE uncovers suspicious trading practices by its members or their employees, it can take disciplinary action. For those outside the NYSE's jurisdiction, it can turn the information over to the Securities and Exchange Commission (SEC) for further consideration.

Regulation

The NYSE protects customer accounts by monitoring the financial and operational integrity of its member firms. To insure that the member firms have sufficient operating capital, the NYSE performs an annual audit, as well as several other examinations throughout the year. In addition, member firms must file a monthly report and a detailed quarterly analysis on its financial and operating activities. These submissions are performed via an automated financial surveillance system, which permits constant evaluation and attempts to identify unusual trends and patterns within the firm.

Source: http://www.nyse.com/public/invprot/5a/5aix.htm. Reprinted by permission of the New York Stock Exchange.

Economic Analysis include conducting ongoing market surveillance to detect actual or possible manipulations. The Division of Trading and Markets oversees the compliance activities of the commodity exchanges and NFA. These duties include:

1. trade practice surveillance
2. financial and sales practice audits of selected registrants
3. review of exchange applications to trade new futures and option contracts

4   review of exchange and NFA rule submissions or amendments and oversight of ethics training of industry professionals

The Division of Enforcement investigates and prosecutes alleged violations of the Commodity Exchange Act and CFTC regulations. The Office of the General Counsel is the CFCT's legal advisor. The Office of the Executive Director handles the administrative functions of the CFTC.

2.5. REGULATION OF FINANCIAL INSTITUTIONS IN THE USA

The activities and operations of financial institutions are now typically regulated. In addition to mandated reserve requirements, capital requirements are also mandated for banks, insurance companies, and brokerage firms. Stock exchanges and the over-the-counter markets also face various regulations.

2.5.1. Banks

The US Federal Reserve System (USFRS), which was founded in 1913, is the **central bank** of the United States. Today the US Federal Reserve has four major duties:

1   to conduct US monetary policy with the twin goals of full employment and stable prices
2   to supervise and regulate banks to maintain their safety and soundness and to protect consumers
3   to guard against systemic risk that may arise in financial markets
4   to provide services to the US government, banks, and others, which includes playing a major role in operating the US payments system.

The USFRS comprises twelve regional US Federal Reserve banks operating under the oversight of the board of governors in Washington, DC. While the USFRS is part of the US government, its structure is designed to insulate it from short-term political pressure in two ways. The USFRS operates on its own earnings, rather than on government appropriations. The board of governors comprises seven members appointed for staggered 14-year terms. Hence, the current government has only a small amount of influence on US monetary policy. The President of the United States appoints members of the board, who must also be confirmed by the US Senate. The President of the United States, again with US Senate approval, designates one board member as the chairman and another as the vice-chairman.

The board of governors sets reserve requirements for depository institutions, approves discount rates, oversees the US Federal Reserve banks, and administers various regulations concerning such matters as the safety and soundness of the banking system, consumer protection, and bank mergers. The US Federal Reserve banks are the **lenders of last resort** for depository institutions. The US Federal Reserve Open Market Committee directs the most important instrument of monetary policy, the purchases and sales of securities in the financial markets, which expand and contract the US money supply.

Federal Reserve banks are important participants in the US payments system, facilitating the presentation of checks for payment by the banks upon which they are drawn. The US Federal Reserve's market share of check collections is about one-third, with the remainder being handled by banking organizations and private check processing firms. The Depository Institutions Deregulation and Monetary Control Act of 1980 authorized the Federal Reserve banks to service commercial banks, savings and loan associations, credit unions, and mutual savings banks.

The Department of the Treasury has two bureaus that are active in the regulation of US banks. The Office of the Comptroller of the Currency (OCC) charters and regulates national banks to insure a safe, sound, competitive banking system.[6] The OCC requires national banks to have good management practices and to comply with appropriate laws. According to the OCC mission statement, "The national interest requires that there be a safe and stable financial system that preserves public confidence and makes available a wide variety of financial services in a competitive marketplace." The Office of Thrift Supervision (OTS) was created by the Financial Institutions Reform, Recovery, and Enforcement Act of 1989 (FIRREA). OTS is the primary regulator of all federal and many state-chartered thrift institutions and supervises institutions under its jurisdiction to maintain their safety and soundness.

The USA has had a system of insurance of bank deposits since the 1930s. The system is administered through the Federal Deposit Insurance Corporation (FDIC). The FDIC guarantees each account at a bank or covered institution up to 100,000 USD in 1998. The FDIC supervises insured institutions to insure their safety and soundness. The FDIC may take over the operation of an insolvent bank and either liquidate it or sell it to another more financially sound financial institution. From the point of view of depositors, an insured deposit is safe, and there is no need to examine the credit-worthiness of a financial institution. Thus, deposit insurance removes market discipline in which banks maintain their soundness to attract customers. Further, if rates charged to financial institutions to obtain insurance do not reflect the riskiness of their capital structure, there may be an incentive for these institutions to over-invest in risky projects. The institution reaps most of the benefits if the projects succeed, but does not bear the full cost of failure.

In the USA, banks may be chartered by either the federal government or by state governments. Federally chartered banks are required to be members of the US Federal Reserve System, but state banks may elect not to join. The Depository Institutions Deregulation and Monetary Control Act of 1980 extended the reserve requirements of the US Federal Reserve to state-chartered banks. The deposits of state-chartered banks must be insured through the FDIC. This gives the federal authorities a means of supervising the safety and soundness of state-chartered banks.

2.5.2. Savings and loan associations

Savings and loan associations (S&Ls) are financial institutions whose primary mission historically was the provision of credit to the housing sector. S&Ls collected deposits and lent these to consumers to purchase housing, taking back a mortgage. The Garn–St Germain Depository Institutions Act removed many of the restrictions on S&L activities, and it has become increasingly difficult to distinguish S&Ls from banks. In 1989 regulation of S&Ls

was assigned to the Department of the Treasury's Office of Thrift Supervision. S&L deposits are insured though the FDIC.

2.5.3. Credit unions

A **credit union** is a not-for-profit financial institution created and owned by members who generally have a common link through their work or place of residence. Only members can use the credit union's services. The National Credit Union Administration (NCUA)[7] is an independent federal agency that supervises and insures more than 6,500 federal credit unions and insures more than 4,000 state-chartered credit unions. The National Credit Union Share Insurance Fund, administered by the NCUA, insures credit union deposits.

2.5.4. Insurance companies

Insurance companies bear risk in exchange for a fee called a **premium**. Life insurance companies write insurance covering loss due to the death of the insured. Property and casualty companies cover other types of losses, such as fire, theft, earthquake, and liability. In the United States, the McCarran–Ferguson Act authorizes state regulation of insurance companies. The National Association of Insurance Commissioners (NAIC)[8] is a voluntary organization, whose members comprise insurance commissioners from the various states. The NAIC develops model laws and regulations concerning insurance regulation, which it recommends to the states. It has developed a risk-based formula for determining the amount of capital that insurance companies need. These weights are applied to the firm's assets and liabilities according to a specified formula. This approach to capital determination is comparable to that for depository institutions developed by the Basil Committee described below.

2.5.5. Pension plans

The Employee Retirement Income Security Act of 1974 (ERISA) provides for the regulation of employer-sponsored pension plans by the Department of Labor. ERISA provides that plan fiduciaries, those with decision-making authority, have a duty to see that plan assets are diversified. This is the first legislation formally recognizing modern portfolio theory as a standard for investment managers. Moreover, in making investments for the fund, managers are to use the "care, skill, prudence, and diligence" of those who are knowledgeable in their field. This provision has been interpreted as strengthening the prudent man rule to require not just actions in line with what any business people might take, but actions conforming to those of professionals in the field. The legislation provides that the plans are to be administered for the exclusive benefit of the beneficiaries. This provision precludes not only practices that would obviously be contrary to the interests of participants, such as kickbacks, but has also been interpreted to cover excess expenses for items such as transaction costs, including brokerage commissions.

The Pension Benefit Guaranty Corporation (PBGC) was established by Title IV of the Employee Retirement Income Security Act in 1974. The PBGC protects the pensions of about 42 million US workers whose employers have defined benefit plans, by guaranteeing

143

pension payments in the event the employer defaults. A **defined benefit plan** provides a specified monthly benefit at retirement, often based on a formula combining salary and years of service. In contrast to defined benefit plans, **defined contribution plans** specify only the contribution to be made by the participant and the employer. Benefit levels are not guaranteed. PBGC is financed through premiums collected from companies that sponsor insured pension plans, investment returns on PBGC assets, and recoveries from employers responsible for underfunded terminated plans.

2.6. REGULATION OF FOREIGN PARTICIPANTS

In an **open economy** the government treats nondomestic firms and domestic firms identically. This type of economy is more of an ideal, and few if any countries meet this standard. Some governments practice **mutual recognition**, whereby they give nondomestic firms the same operating rights within their own jurisdiction that they would have in their home countries. Typically, mutual recognition requires substantial coordination among jurisdictions such as has been the case in the European Union. A policy of **reciprocity** grants nondomestic firms rights of access to local markets if the firm's home country grants similar rights to local firms. Reciprocity is often used as a foreign policy tool to try to gain access to others markets for local firms. Under the Second Banking Directive of the European Union, effective 1993, the European Union Commission is granted the power to "restrict the establishment of new banks coming from third countries, when such countries do not grant EC credit institutions national treatment" (Organization for Economic Cooperation and Development 1992, p. 70). But this approach may prevent a country's citizens from having access to more varied and less costly services. In some cases governments use reciprocity to determine access, but after determining access operate as an open economy.

If a government has a policy of discrimination, nondomestic firms face restrictions not faced by local firms, or they are prohibited from owning local firms. Many governments restrict portfolio investment by limiting the amount of domestic firm shares that can be owned by noncitizens. Direct investment may also be limited. Nondomestic firms may only be permitted to own minority interests in local firms. Local branches of nondomestic banks may not be permitted to participate fully in the local banking market. Both deposit seeking and lending may be restricted. Entry restrictions are common in financial services, both for most developing countries and even for a few developed countries such as Canada, Finland, Iceland, Norway, and Japan. Participation in industries that are considered essential for the national defense are often restricted or prohibited.

2.7. MULTINATIONAL REGULATION

2.7.1. Basil Committee

In 1974, after the collapse of the Herstatt Bank in Germany, the Group of Ten plus Switzerland and Luxembourg established the Standing Committee on Banking Regulations and Supervisory Practices known as the Basil Committee. Unlike central bankers, bank supervisory officials had previously been domestically focused. The Basil Committee provided these officials with an opportunity to meet, most for the first time. The Basil Committee on banking supervision focuses on two aspects of bank regulation: supervision and rules for internationally active banks. The goal is to insure that no bank goes unsupervised.

In 1975 the Basil Committee succeeded in reaching agreement on a concordat establishing the premise that the basic aim of international regulation is to insure that no bank escapes supervision. Further, it adopted the principle that banks' international business should be monitored on a consolidated basis, and that primary responsibility be allocated to the home country of the parent. In 1988 the Basil Committee proposed rules on capital adequacy that were subsequently implemented in member countries. These rules required banks to maintain shareholders' capital equal to 4 percent of risk-weighted assets (including off-balance sheet activities). Further, banks were also required to maintain a total capital ratio of 8 percent of an expanded list of assets and liabilities, including items such as loan loss reserves and subordinated debt. These standards have also contributed to making disclosure of financial information more uniform. Over time the Basil Committee succeeded in modifying members' secrecy laws to permit the exchange of information needed to insure adequate regulation of international banks.

2.7.2. *International Organization of Securities Commissions (IOSCO)*

The International Organization of Securities Commissions was established in 1974 by securities and futures regulators in states within the Americas and was expanded in 1983 to include regulators in all major developed and emerging markets.[9] The General Secretariat of IOSCO is in Montreal. Entities joining IOSCO must agree:

1 to cooperate together to promote high standards of regulation, in order to maintain just, efficient, and sound markets
2 to exchange information on their respective experiences, in order to promote the development of domestic markets
3 to unite their efforts to establish standards and an effective surveillance of international securities transactions
4 to provide mutual assistance to promote the integrity of the markets by a rigorous application of the standards and by effective enforcement against offenses

The objectives and principles of securities regulations are set forth in the document provided in box 5.2.

IOSCO has four regional committees that discuss regional problems, namely Africa/Middle East, Asia/Pacific, European, and Inter-American. In addition, there are two important standing committees. The Technical Committee reviews issues related to securities and derivative transactions and coordinates the response of members. The Technical Committee deals with

1 multinational disclosure and accounting
2 regulation of secondary markets
3 regulation of market intermediaries

BOX 5.2
Objectives and principles of securities regulations

This document[a] sets out 30 principles of securities regulation, which are based upon three objectives of securities regulation. The three objectives are:

1. The protection of investors;[b]
2. Insuring that markets are fair, efficient, and transparent;
3. The reduction of systemic risk.

The 30 principles need to be practically implemented under the relevant legal framework to achieve the objectives of regulation described above. The principles are grouped into eight categories.

A. Principles relating to the regulator

1. The responsibilities of the regulator should be clear and objectively stated.
2. The regulator should be operationally independent and accountable in the exercise of its functions and powers.
3. The regulator should have adequate powers, proper resources and the capacity to perform its functions and exercise its powers.
4. The regulator should adopt clear and consistent regulatory processes.
5. The staff of the regulator should observe the highest professional standards including appropriate standards of confidentiality.

B. Principles for self-regulation

6. The regulatory regime should make appropriate use of Self-Regulatory Organizations (SROs) that exercise some direct oversight responsibility for their respective areas of competence, to the extent appropriate to the size and complexity of the markets.
7. SROs should be subject to the oversight of the regulator and should observe standards of fairness and confidentiality when exercising powers and delegated responsibilities.

C. Principles for the enforcement of securities regulation

8. The regulator should have comprehensive inspection, investigation and surveillance powers.
9. The regulator should have comprehensive enforcement powers.
10. The regulatory system should ensure an effective and credible use of inspection, investigation, surveillance and enforcement powers and implementation of an effective compliance program.

D. Principles for cooperation in regulation

11. The regulator should have authority to share both public and nonpublic information with domestic and foreign counterparts.

Continued

12 Regulators should establish information sharing mechanisms that set out when and how they will share both public and nonpublic information with their domestic and foreign counterparts.

13 The regulatory system should allow for assistance to be provided to foreign regulators who need to make inquiries in the discharge of their functions and exercise of their powers.

E. Principles for issuers

14 There should be full, timely and accurate disclosure of financial results and other information that is material to investors' decisions.

15 Holders of securities in a company should be treated in a fair and equitable manner.

16 Accounting and auditing standards should be of a high and internationally acceptable quality.

F. Principles for collective investment schemes

17 The regulatory system should set standards for the licensing and the regulation of those who wish to market or operate a collective investment scheme.

18 The regulatory system should provide for rules governing the legal form and structure of collective investment schemes and the segregation and protection of client assets.

19 Regulation should require disclosure, as set forth under the principles for issuers, which is necessary to evaluate the suitability of a collective investment scheme for a particular investor and the value of the investor's interest in the scheme.

20 Regulation should ensure that there is a proper and disclosed basis for asset valuation and the pricing and the redemption of units in a collective investment scheme.

G. Principles for market intermediaries

21 Regulation should provide for minimum entry standards for market intermediaries.

22 There should be initial and ongoing capital and other prudential requirements for market intermediaries.

23 Market intermediaries should be required to comply with standards for internal organization and operational conduct that aim to protect the interests of clients and under which management of the intermediary accepts primary responsibility for these matters.

24 There should be procedures for dealing with the failure of a market intermediary in order to minimize damage and loss to investors and to contain systemic risk.

25 The establishment of trading systems including securities exchanges should be subject to regulatory authorization and oversight.

H. Principles for the secondary market

26 There should be ongoing regulatory supervision of exchanges and trading systems which should aim to ensure that the integrity of trading is maintained through fair and equitable rules that strike an appropriate balance between the demands of different market participants.

27 Regulation should promote transparency of trading.

Continued

> 28 Regulation should be designed to detect and deter manipulation and other unfair trading practices.
>
> 29 Regulation should aim to ensure the proper management of large exposures, default risk and market disruption.
>
> 30 The system for clearing and settlement of securities transactions should be subject to regulatory oversight, and designed to ensure that it is fair, effective and efficient and that it reduces systemic risk.
>
> [a]For convenience, the words "securities markets" are used, where the context permits, to refer compendiously to the various market sectors. In particular, where the context permits, they should be understood to include reference to the derivatives markets. The same applies to the use of the words "securities regulation". (See IOSCO By-Laws, Explanatory Memorandum.)
>
> [b]The term "investor" is intended to include customers or other consumers of financial services.
>
> *Source*: *Objectives and Principles of Securities Regulation*, Foreword and Executive Summary IOSCO Public Document: http://www.iosco.org/docs-public/1998-objectives.html

4 enforcement and the exchange of information

5 investment management

The Emerging Markets Committee's goal is to promote developing securities and derivatives markets by establishing standards and training programs and by promoting the exchange of information. Topics addressed by the committee include

1 Disclosure and accounting

2 Regulation of secondary markets

3 Regulation of market intermediaries

4 Enforcement and the exchange of information

5 Investment management

2.7.3. Other international efforts

There are also a number of ongoing international efforts that affect international securities markets and the ethical behavior of individuals who participate in those markets. The Organization for Economic Cooperation and Development (OECD)[10] is an organization comprising 29 members, who meet to develop and improve economic and social policy. On November 21, 1997, OECD member countries and five nonmember countries[11] adopted a Convention on Combating Bribery of Foreign Public Officials in International Business Transactions. This Convention deals with the offence committed by the person who promises or gives the bribe, in contrast with the person receiving the bribe. The convention will permit signatories to coordinate efforts to combat bribery of public officials.

Money laundering, the processing of criminal funds in order to disguise their illegal origin, is a crime in many countries. In 1988, the United Nations adopted the Convention Against Illicit Traffic in Narcotic Drugs and Psychotropic Substances (the Vienna Convention). The Vienna Convention obliges signatories to make money laundering a crime and also requires them to facilitate the identification, tracing, seizure, and forfeiture of the proceeds of narcotics trafficking and money laundering. The United Nations operates the International Money Laundering Information Network, an Internet-based network that assists governments in fighting money laundering.[12]

The Financial Action Task Force on Money Laundering (FATF)[13] was established as an intergovernmental body by the G-7 Summit in Paris in 1989 to examine measures to combat money laundering. In April 1990, the FATF issued 40 recommendations designed to provide a comprehensive blueprint for action against money laundering. These recommendation were modified in 1996. The goal is to prevent the use of these funds to facilitate further criminal activity and to prevent the funds from being used to affect legitimated commerce.

3. ETHICS

3.1. THE NEED FOR ETHICAL BEHAVIOR

Finance professionals deal with other people's money. Hence, they are often faced with temptation. There are opportunities to take advantage of clients, increasing one's own income and wealth at the client's expense. Further, the fact that the sums involved are typically large makes the temptation greater. These factors heighten the importance of integrity and ethics as an integral part of the finance profession. Investors often place their life savings in the hands of finance professionals. Integrity and ethical behavior are more important to customers than technical competence.[14] Investors can attempt to judge the ethical competence of a finance professional by examining their education and training (do they have a college degree? A graduate degree? Are their studies relevant? Do they have professional designations such as Chartered Financial Analyst described below?) But how does one judge whether their behavior is ethical? By their individual reputation or their firm's reputation?

Finance professionals may engage in many types of unethical behavior. These include frontrunning, failure to disclose conflicts of interest, favoring some clients over others without a proper basis, plagiarizing the work of others, churning, making recommendations that are unsuitable for the client, and trading on or communicating inside information. Frontrunning is the making of personal trades before client trades, and churning is excessive trading which benefits the broker by generating increased commissions without commensurate benefits for the client. Violations of fiduciary duties may also constitute ethical breaches. One such duty is that of **best execution**, which requires a broker to execute a trade in such a way that the client receives the best terms. The problem with achieving best execution, as described in detail by Macey and O'Hara (1997), is that what is best for the client may depend on the tradeoff between multiple factors such as price and speed.

For finance professionals ethical behavior must be an end for its own sake. Because the consequences of unethical behavior by finance professionals can be so devastating for investors, they quickly flee when unethical behavior is revealed. Moreover, unethical behavior by one individual or firm can reflect unfavorably on others. It may help to know that ethical behavior often is good economics, especially in the long run. Both individuals and organizations have reputational capital, which is a part of their human capital. Unethical behavior can seriously damage this reputational capital, reducing income and profits. Hence, there is an incentive for the finance profession to promote ethical behavior by its practitioners.

In August 1991 Salomon Brothers, a major US investment banking firm, disclosed that it had made illegal bids on US government securities. As a result of these activities, the firm was forced to pay fines of 122 million USD to the US Treasury and 68 million USD to the US Justice Department and to establish an indemnity fund of 100 million USD to pay claims from civil lawsuits arising out of the scandal, with any undistributed amount going to the US Treasury. But the cost of the scandal is more fully captured by the fall in Salomon's stock value during the week the scandal was announced, by about 1.5 billion USD (see box 5.3 for additional details). The value of firm reputation is underscored by the findings of Beatty, Bunsis, and Hand (1998), who report that underwriters who are subject to USSEC investigations "experience large declines in IPO market share" and the "stock prices of their clients decline significantly."

BOX 5.3
The Salomon case

The US Treasury regularly conducts auctions in which bonds are sold to the highest bidder, the next highest bidder, and so forth. When a price is reached that exhausts the available supply, each bidder at that price receives an allocation equal to the ratio of the quantity sought to the total quantity sought at that price.

In June 1990 and again in July 1990, Paul Mozer, the head of government bond trading for Salomon Brothers, submitted a bid for 4-year Treasury notes, that sought more than 100 percent of the available supply. The Treasury rejected the bid and instituted a limit on one buyer's bid of 35 percent of the available amount. To circumvent this restriction, in the December 1990 4-year bond auction, Mozer submitted two bids, one for 35 percent of the available issue for Salomon Brothers and another for 11 percent for a client, Warburg Asset Management. The order for the client was made without authorization. The same strategy was used in eight subsequent auctions.

In April 1991 the US Treasury sent a warning letter to Warburg. After obtaining a copy of the letter, Mozer informed Salomon management, including John Gutfreund, chairman; Thomas Strauss, president; John Meriwether, vice-chairman; and Donald Feuerstein, general counsel, that he had made bids that violated Treasury rules. Salomon management took no immediate action. In June the USSEC issued subpoenas to Salomon and several of its clients for information relating to the bids. Salomon began a review and disclosed its illegal bids in August.

As a result of these illegal bids, on August 18, 1991, the US Treasury prohibited Salomon from bidding for bonds for customer accounts. Subsequently, the Federal Reserve Bank of New York suspended trading with Salomon for 2 months, resulting in a loss of as much as 4 billion USD of trading volume. Salomon was forced to create reserves to recognize more than 385 million USD of potential liabilities and fines. Major customers, including the State of California and the International Bank for Reconstruction and Development (the World Bank), suspended trading with Salomon. Salomon's ranking as a stock underwriter dropped from fifth to tenth, resulting in millions of USD of lost income. Salomon was forced to bid aggressively for its remaining business, reducing its profit margins. Gutfreund, Strauss, Meriwether, and Feuerstein resigned, and Mozer was suspended.

(For additional information see Smith 1992.)

In 1996 Daiwa Bank was sentenced to pay a fine of 340 million USD for conspiring to conceal trading losses of 1.1 billion USD from the US government. (For additional information about this case see LeClair, Ferrell, and Fraedrich 1998.) The bank's top management learned of the losses in July 1995 and confirmed them through its own investigation in early August, but refrained from reporting them until the end of September, so that they could be reported along with the bank's regularly scheduled financial statements. The Japanese Ministry of Finance had advised the bank that the report could have significant negative impact on Japanese financial markets. In the time between their discovery and reporting them, the bank knowingly filed a number of false forms to conceal the losses. According to US sentencing guidelines for corporations, corporations can be held accountable for the transgressions of their employees. Firms that have made sincere and effective efforts to eliminate criminal activity may receive reduced penalties if the court believes that violations occurred despite their best efforts. The US attorney in this case told the court:

> It is virtually impossible for any financial institution to protect itself against every potential criminal act by its employees, particularly given the highly specialized nature and complexity of the securities now traded in the world's capital markets. It is precisely because of this complexity, however, that it is essential that corporations institute and insist upon a corporate culture of absolute compliance with the rules and regulations of the marketplace. One of the most important ways to do this is to establish and enforce a system of internal controls and checks and balances that are designed to protect against the criminal acts of corporate employees.

3.2. Approaches to Ethics

3.2.1. Fairness versus efficiency

Shefrin and Statman (1993) examine financial market regulation in terms of two goals: efficiency and fairness. In some cases it may be possible to increase fairness without affecting efficiency or to increase efficiency without affecting fairness. In other cases this may not be possible, so there is a tradeoff between efficiency and fairness. Shefrin and Statman (1993) argue that policymakers operate as if there is an efficiency/fairness frontier exhibiting a maximum level of fairness for a given level of efficiency or a maximum level of efficiency for a given level of fairness. Movements along the frontier represent reduced fairness to gain increased efficiency or reduced efficiency to gain increased fairness. Of course, the efficiency/fairness frontier may be multidimensional, in that there may also be tradeoffs among types of efficiency or categories of fairness.

These authors consider two types of efficiency. **Pareto efficiency** means that the *status quo* cannot be changed without making someone worse off. **Information efficiency** means that everyone has the same information and a common analysis of that information, so prices reflect that information.

Shefrin and Statman (1993) identify seven dimensions of fairness:

1 *Freedom to take or not take action without coercion*   To be fair, a transaction must be voluntary.

2 *Freedom from misrepresentation* Investors can rely on information that is provided by securities issuers and financial professionals in making their investment decisions. While this information may be incorrect, it is not intentionally so.

3 *Equal information* It is typically considered unfair for some investors to have information that others do not have. This is the basis of prohibiting insider trading.

4 *Equal information processing* Individuals who have fewer analytical skills are provided some protection. In a merit regulatory scheme certain types of transactions might be prohibited.

5 *Freedom from impulse* Some individuals make cognitive errors and exhibit lack of self-control. These observations may be used to justify the right to unwind certain transactions within a limited period.

6 *Efficient prices* Regulations might be imposed to prevent trading outside a prescribed price range, to prevent investors from being taken advantage of by temporary supply–demand imbalances.

7 *Equal bargaining power* Fixed rates or maximum rates might mitigate the negotiating power of some market participants and "level the playing field."

These dimensions of fairness may be conflicting. Protecting investors from their own impulses may reduce their freedom to take action.

3.2.2. *Virtue ethics*

According to MacIntyre (1984), "A virtue is an acquired human quality, the possession and exercise of which tends to enable us to achieve those goods which are internal" (quoted by Dobson 1997, p. 16). According to Dobson (1997) **virtue ethics** goes beyond mere avoidance of wrongdoing: "Moral behavior is not limited to adherence to a rule or guideline but rather involves the individual pursuing moral excellence as a goal in and of itself" (p. 16). In other words, the pursuit of ethical behavior is intrinsic to the meaning of being a finance professional. Profit maximization is no longer the objective. Instead, finance professionals pursue excellence, including moral excellence (Dobson 1993).

External goods include honor, fame, prestige, and material wealth. These are extrinsic to the practice of a profession. Excellence derives from the pursuit of intrinsic virtues. Such virtues include wisdom, fairness, integrity, and consistency. It is not possible to separate one's moral self from one's professional self. An ethical professional cannot substitute the values of the client or employer for their own. Virtue ethics distinguishes between a skill and a virtue. Both are needed to achieve professional excellence. According to Dobson (1997), "A critical difference between the two, however, is that exercising a virtue entails moral judgment whereas exercising a skill does not" (p. 20). A stockbroker may be skilled at "selling ice to Eskimos" – i.e., selling securities that are inappropriate for the customers. But no matter how successful, one cannot be virtuous in this activity, since the activity itself conflicts with fairness, wisdom, and integrity, which are the ultimate goals.

Having identified virtue as the goal, there are two aids that can be used to help attain the goal. The first is to develop an organization with a community of like-minded individuals. The shared vision must be the reason for the existence of the organization. According to Salomon (1992), "Corporations are real communities . . . and therefore the perfect place to start understanding the nature of the virtues" (quoted by Dobson 1997, p. 17). In addition to community, Dobson (1997) states: "The role of exemplars is critical for the application of virtue ethics, because these individuals disseminate the virtues throughout the profession" (p. 17). The performance of these moral exemplars can be observed both on the job and also as part of training sessions and workshops. This goes beyond the firm, as Jensen and Meckling's (1976) contractual nexus or Miller's (1986) wealth creating machine.

3.3. THE ASSOCIATION FOR INVESTMENT MANAGEMENT AND RESEARCH (AIMR)

3.3.1. Introduction to AIMR and the C.F.A.

The Association for Investment Management and Research (AIMR) is a global, nonprofit organization of more than 33,000 investment professionals from 77 countries. Its headquarters is in the USA, and there are more than 87 affiliated societies and chapters throughout the world. AIMR awards the designation Chartered Financial Analyst (C.F.A.), the most widely recognized and prestigious professional certification in finance. The C.F.A. is awarded after the candidate passes a series of three examinations. Since no more than one examination can be taken each year, the program takes a minimum of 3 years to complete. Major subject areas covered in these examinations include economics, accounting, finance, portfolio management, and ethics. As of 1996 there were about 23,000 C.F.A.s worldwide, and more than 40,000 industry professionals are enrolled to take the examinations.

3.3.2. The AIMR Code of Ethics

AIMR has a written Code of Ethics to which its members must adhere (see box 5.4). Notice that it encompasses both skills and virtues. Ethical analysts must both "act with integrity" and "maintain and improve their competence." To be an excellent analyst, neither excellent skills nor ethical behavior is sufficient. Both must be present. The code is amplified by the Standards of Professional Conduct.[15] These standards enumerate the fundamental responsibilities of a financial analyst and the minimum requirements that must be observed in the

---

BOX 5.4
The AIMR Code of Ethics

Members of the Association for Investment Management and Research shall:

- Act with integrity, competence, dignity, and in an ethical manner when dealing with the public, clients, prospects, employers, employees, and fellow members.
- Practice and encourage others to practice in a professional and ethical manner that will reflect credit on members and their profession.
- Strive to maintain and improve their competence and the competence of others in the profession.
- Use reasonable care and exercise independent professional judgment.

analyst's relationships with others in the profession, employers, clients and prospective clients, and the investing public.

AIMR's Code and Standards apply to members worldwide. The first standard requires that members "comply with all applicable laws, rules, and regulations (including AIMR's Code of Ethics and Standards of Professional Conduct) of any government, governmental agency, regulatory organization, licensing agency, or professional association governing the members' professional activities." In applying this standard, it is the most stringent laws and regulations that must be adhered to. If a member resides in a country with laws that are less strict than the Code and Standard, but does business in a country with laws and regulations more strict, the more strict laws and regulations must be followed. If a member resides in a country with laws and regulations more strict, but does business in a country with less strict laws, the more strict laws apply.

3.4. OTHER INTERNATIONAL EFFORTS TO FOSTER ETHICS

Transparency International is a Berlin-based organization with chapters in 15 countries that fight official corruption by promoting and strengthening international and national integrity. According to the organization:

> Corruption is one of the greatest challenges of the contemporary world. It undermines good government, fundamentally distorts public policy, leads to the misallocation of resources, harms the private sector and private sector development and particularly hurts the poor. Controlling it is only possible with the cooperation of a wide range of stakeholders in the integrity system, including most importantly the state, civil society, and the private sector. There is also a crucial role to be played by international institutions.[16]

In Hong Kong in 1995, the Independent Commission Against Corruption established the the Hong Kong Ethics Development Centre, comprising members from leading chambers of commerce in Hong Kong. More than 1,000 companies have used the resources of the centre.[17]

4. SUMMARY

Historically, financial markets have been largely self-regulated, and this practice continues through self-regulatory organizations such as stock exchanges. Government regulation of financial markets increased substantially during the first half of the twentieth century. Governments seek to prevent systemic risk, protect consumers of financial products, and achieve social objectives. Systemic risk occurs when the failure of one participant in the financial markets causes the failure of other participants, potentially leading to the collapse of the entire financial system.

Two alternative forms of regulation are merit regulation and disclosure regulation. Under merit regulation governments prohibit or require certain types of activities or pass judgment on the suitability of certain investments. Under disclosure regulation the government focuses on insuring that market participants fully disclose information so that investors can make knowledgeable decisions. Governments regulate the activities of financial markets and financial institutions and the access of nondomestic investors to domestic markets. In an open economy nondomestic and domestic individuals and firms are treated identically. Few, if any, economies meet this standard. If a country practices mutual recognition, nondomestic firms have the same operating rights within their own jurisdiction that they would have in their home countries. A policy of reciprocity grants nondomestic firms rights of access to local markets if the firm's home country grants similar rights to local firms.

The types of regulations needed may depend on the particulars of the financial system in a given country. If a stock market is the primary mechanism for risk sharing, there may be a need for widespread disclosure of information and for rules protecting those with limited self-control and analytical ability. If the primary mechanism for risk sharing is through banking institutions, as in a universal banking system, the need for these types of protection is reduced.

There have been several successful attempts to promote international regulation. The Basil Committee established by the Group of Ten promotes international cooperation among bank supervisory officials. The Committee has been successful in increasing the exchange of information among members and in developing uniform minimum capital requirements for internationally active banks. The International Organization of Securities Commissions (IOSCO) was established to promote high standards of regulation, in order to maintain just, efficient, and sound markets by increasing the exchange of information, developing common standards, and insuring the rigorous enforcement of the standards.

Bankruptcy is a legal process through which organizations restructure their finances. Bankruptcy codes can differ from country to country in areas such as who controls the firm following bankruptcy, whether there is an automatic stay, whether there are renegotiations of old liabilities and provision for new borrowings, and whether old equity holders retain any residual interests. In some countries the primary aim of bankruptcy is to liquidate the firm, while in others the goal is to maintain firms as going concerns. In addition to creditors and equity holders, bankruptcy laws must take the needs of employees, customers, and governments into account. Bankruptcy law affects the operations of solvent firms, because potential equity investors and creditors take these laws into account when making investment decisions.

The principal regulator of banks in the USA is the US Federal Reserve System, which was founded in 1913 and operates as the central bank of the United States. The board of governors sets reserve requirements for depository institutions, approves discount rates, oversees the Reserve banks, and administers various regulations concerning such matters as the safety and soundness of the banking system, consumer protection and bank mergers. The Federal Reserve directs purchases and sales of securities in the financial markets, to expand and contract the money supply. The Reserve banks are the lenders of last resort for depositary institutions and handle more than one-third of check collections.

Two bureaus of the Department of the Treasury are active in the regulation of US banks. The the Office of the Comptroller of the Currency charters and regulates national banks. And the Office of Thrift Supervision regulates other thrift institutions to maintain their safety and soundness.

Savings and loan associations (S&Ls) are financial institutions whose primary mission historically was the provision of credit for housing, but the removal of restrictions on the types of investments S&Ls can hold has made it increasingly difficult to distinguish them from banks. In 1989 regulation of S&Ls was given to the Department of the Treasury's Office of Thrift Supervision. A credit union is a financial institution created and owned by its members, who are the only ones allowed to use its services. The National Credit Union Administration, an agency of the US government, regulates credit unions. The USA has had a system of insurance of bank deposits since the 1930s. Bank and thrift deposits are insured through the Federal Deposit Insurance Corporation (FDIC), while the National Credit Union Share Insurance Fund insures credit unions. Insurance companies are regulated by individual states. The National Association of Insurance Commissioners develops model laws and regulations concerning insurance regulation, which it recommends to the states. In the USA pension plans are regulated by the Department of Labor, which enforces the Employee Retirement Income Security Act of 1974. ERISA requires that those running pension plans act with the "care, skill, prudence, and diligence" of those who are knowledgeable in their field and requires that the plan be managed for the exclusive benefit of the beneficiaries.

Historically there was little regulation of financial markets in the USA. Trustees investing others' money were restricted to a list of eligible securities. Dissatisfaction with this legal list approach in the 1930s led to the adoption of the prudent man rule, which states that trustees must "observe how men of prudence, discretion and intelligence manage their own affairs" and act accordingly. In 1911 the State of Kansas began regulating the issuance of securities within the state. These blue sky laws were of two types. Merit regulation attempted to judge the investment worth of a security and prohibited the sale of securities deemed too risky. Disclosure regulation concentrated on making the facts available, so that investors would have sufficient information to reach an informed decision.

In 1933 the US government began to regulate financial markets. The principal US federal regulator of financial markets is the Securities and Exchange Commission, an independent, nonpartisan, regulatory agency with responsibility for administering US securities laws. The Securities Act of 1933 requires the provision to investors of all significant information concerning securities that are offered for public sale and prohibits fraud and misrepresentation in the sale of securities. In the USA derivatives markets are regulated by the Commodity Futures Trading Commission. The CFTC reviews new contracts and conducts market surveillance.

The Association for Investment Management and Research (AIMR) is a global, nonprofit organization of more than 33,000 investment professionals from 77 countries. AIMR awards the designation Chartered Financial Analyst (C.F.A.) to individuals who successfully complete a series of three examinations covering topics such as economics, accounting, portfolio management, and ethics. AIMR has a written Code of Ethics and Standards of Professional Conduct, to which members must adhere. Analysts are expected both to act with integrity and to maintain their professional competence. Shefrin and Statman (1993) take the view that there is a tradeoff between efficiency and fairness, so that professionals are continually balancing the two. On the other hand, virtue ethics takes the view that ethical behavior is itself a goal, and that one cannot achieve professional excellence without ethical behavior. Having an organization with a community of individuals striving to achieve ethical behavior and having individuals who are ethical exemplars aid in the maintenance of an ethical organization.

Questions

1 Explain two reasons why regulation is needed for financial markets?
2 What is systemic risk in financial markets? Why is it important to avoid systemic risk?
3 What are the main advantages of self-regulation?
4 What is the main difficulty with governmental regulation?
5 What is merit regulation, and why do some governments use it?
6 What important dimensions of bankruptcy law differ from country to country?
7 What is the role of a receiver in UK bankruptcy?
8 What are the two main types of bankruptcy in the USA? Explain each.
9 Which agency is the main regulator of US securities markets, and what are its primary duties?
10 What are the major duties of the US Federal Reserve System?
11 How does a government with an open economy treat nondomestic firms?
12 Name two organizations that work for international regulators and describe their roles.
13 Why is ethical behavior important in the finance profession?
14 Why might there be a tradeoff between fairness and efficiency?
15 Explain the difference between internal and external goals.

■ Notes ■

1 Recall that a margin call is a request for additional collateral, i.e., margin.
2 The USSEC web site is http://www.sec.gov/.
3 The web site for the Financial Services Authority is http://www.sib.co.uk/sib.htm.
4 A directory of state securities regulators is provided at http://www.sec.gov/consumer/state.htm.
5 The web site for the National Futures Association is http://www.nfa.futures.org/about.html.
6 Some of the information in this chapter is based on web sites such as http://www.ustreas.gov/bureaus.html and similar US government web sites.
7 For additional information see http://www.ncua.gov/.
8 The NAIC web site is http://www.naic.org/.
9 The IOSCO web address is http://www.iosco.org/iosco.html.
10 The web site for the OECD is http://www.oecd.org/. This site provides additional information on the convention.
11 These were Argentina, Brazil, Bulgaria, Chile, and the Slovak Republic.
12 For more information about these efforts see https://www.imolin.org/.
13 The organization's web address is http://www.oecd.org/fatf/index.htm.
14 In 1980 the USSEC required all fund companies to have an ethical statement. The code of ethics of Fidelity Investments can be found at http://www451.fidelity.com:80/about/world/ethics_code.html.
15 The AIMR Standards are available at http://www.aimr.org/ethics/practice/standards.html#prof.
16 See http://www.transparency.de/mission.html.
17 Additional information can be found at the following web addresses: Independent Commission Against Corruption, http://www.cuhk.edu.hk/icac/index.htm; The Hong Kong Ethics Development Centre, http://www.cuhk.edu.hk/icac/edc.htm.

■ References ■

Beatty, Randolph P., Bunsis, Howard and Hand, John R. M. 1998: The indirect economic penalties in SEC investigations of underwriters. *Journal of Financial Economics* 50, 151–86.

Benston, George J. 1973: Required disclosure and the stock market: an evaluation of the Securities Exchange Act of 1934. *American Economic Review* 63, 132–55.

Beranek, William, Boehmer, Robert and Smith, Brooke 1996: Much ado about nothing: absolute priority deviations in Chapter 11. *Financial Management* 25, 102–9.

Dale, Richard 1993: *Risk and Regulation in Global Securities Markets*. New York: Wiley.

Dobson, John 1997a: Ethics in finance II. *Financial Analysts Journal* 53, 15–25.

—— 1997b: The role of ethics in finance. *Financial Analysts Journal* 49, 57–61.

Franks, Julian R., Nyborg, Kjell G. and Torous, Walter N. 1996: A comparison of US, UK, and German insolvency codes. *Financial Management* 25, 86–101.

Global Derivatives Study Group 1993: *Derivatives: practices and principles*. Washington: Group of Thirty.

Gorton, Gary and Schmid, Frank A. 1996: Universal banking and the performance of German firms. Working paper, University of Pennsylvania, Philadelphia.

Herring, Richard J. and Litan, Robert E. 1995: *Financial Regulation in the Global Economy*. Washington, DC: Brookings Institution.

Jensen, Michael C. and Meckling, William H. 1976: Theory of the firm: managerial behavior, agency costs and ownership structure. *Journal of Financial Economics* 3, 305–60.

Kaiser, Kevin M. J. 1996: European bankruptcy laws: implications for corporations facing financial distress. *Financial Management* 25, 67–85.

Kester, W. Carl 1994: Banks in the board room: the American versus Japanese and German experiences. *Global Finance Journal* 5, 181–204.

LeClair, Debbie Thorne, Ferrell, O. C. and Fraedrich, John P. 1998: *Integrity Management*. Tampa, FL: University of Tampa Press.

Longhofer, Stanley D. 1977: Absolute priority rule violations, credit rationing, and efficiency. *Journal of Financial Intermediation* 6, 249–67.

Longstreth, Bevis 1986: *Modern Investment Management and the Prudent Man Rule*. Oxford: Oxford University Press.

Lye, Charmaine and Lazar, Rosalind (eds) 1991: *The Regulation of Financial and Capital Markets*. Singapore: SNP Publishers for the Singapore Academy of Law.

Macey, Jonathan R. and Miller, Geoffrey P. 1991: Origin of the Blue Sky laws. *Texas Law Review* 70, 347–97.

Macey, Jonathan R. and O'Hara, Maureen 1997: The law and economics of best execution. *Journal of Financial Intermediation* 6, 188–223.

MacIntyre, Alasdair 1984: *After Virtue: a study in moral theory*, 2nd edn. Notre Dame, IN: University of Notre Dame Press.

Miller, Merton H. 1986: Behavioral rationality in finance: the case of dividends. *Journal of Business* 59, 451–68.

Organization for Economic Cooperation and Development 1992: *Banks Under Stress*. Paris: OECD.

Prowse, S. D. 1992: The structure of corporate ownership in Japan. *Journal of Finance* 42, 1121–40.

Shefrin, Hersh and Statman, Meir 1993: Ethics, fairness and efficiency in financial markets. *Financial Analysts Journal* 49, 21–9.

Smith, Clifford W., Jr. 1992: Economics and ethics: the case of Salomon Brothers. *Journal of Applied Corporate Finance* 5, 23–8.

Smith, Craig S. 1999: Bankruptcy in China proves maze to creditors. *Wall Street Journal*, A8, A9.

Salomon, Robert C. 1992: Corporate roles, personal virtues: an Aristotelian approach to business ethics. *Business Ethics Quarterly* 2, 317–39.

Tan, Boon Teik 1991: Regulation versus self-regulation in the securities industry. In Lye and Lazar (eds).

Van Hulle, Cynthis 1996: On the nature of European holding groups. Working paper, Katholieke Universiteit Leuven, Leuven.

Equities

■ Key terms ■

Capital plus warrants   warrants requiring an initial payment that is returned at expiration along with a stated percentage of the gain in a basket of securities.

Capped warrants   low exercise price warrants with the upside gain capped at a stated level.

Classified common stock   common stock that is divided into classes with different rights. Most commonly one class will have more votes per share than another class.

Closed-end investment company   a type of managed investment company that has a fixed number of shares outstanding and rarely raises new funds.

Convertible preferred   preferred stock that can be exchanged for another security, typically the common shares of the firm.

Country risk   risk due to the political and economic conditions in a particular country.

Covered warrant   a warrant for which the issuer is not the firm whose shares underlie the warrant.

Cumulative preferred   preferred stock for which the firm continues to have the obligation to pay any missed dividends.

Cumulative voting   a type of voting in which each share receives the same number of votes as there are directors, each share's votes can be voted for one or more directors, and the directors with the most votes win. If 2 directors are to be elected, it takes $1/2 + 1$ shares to elect one director.

Endowment warrants   a warrant that does not have a fixed exercise price, but instead can be exercised by payment of an outstanding amount that is computed from a fixed starting value that is reduced by any dividend payments and increased by an interest charge.

Floating rate preferred   preferred stock that has a dividend that is reset periodically.

Hedge fund   an investment organization whose management receives compensation in the form of performance incentives rather than based on the amount of assets held or the number of transactions made and that typically uses leverage in the execution of its investment strategies.

Index warrants   warrants with the payment at expiration linked to the value of an index such as the S&P 500 Index, the Nikkei Index, or the FT-SE 100 Index.

Installment warrants   a warrant that gives the owner the right to purchase shares held in trust by making periodic payments.

Intrinsic value of a warrant   the difference between the cost of acquiring an asset by exercising a warrant and the market value of the asset acquired.

Load   a commission charged at the time of the purchase of an open-end investment company.

Low exercise price warrants   warrants with a low exercise price such as 0.01 AUD.

Managed investment companies   corporations whose primary business is investing in other firms and in which investors purchase shares that represent an undivided interest in the firm's assets.

Mutual funds   an open-end investment company.

Net asset value   the value of the assets owned by an investment company less its liabilities.

No load   a type of open-end investment company that does not charge a commission at the time of purchase or sale.

Open-end investment company   a type of managed investment company that is continuously issuing new shares.

Participating preferred   preferred stock that has a dividend that is based at least in part on the firm's earnings.

Poison pill   a provision in a firm's bylaws or charter that provide protection if anyone acquires a significant ownership in the firm without the approval of the board of directors.

Preemptive rights   the right to participate in new equity offerings on a pro rata basis. Rather than one share one vote, some firms use a voting method called **cumulative voting**.

Premium   for warrants, the difference between the market price of a warrant and its intrinsic value.

Publicly traded investment companies   same as closed-end investment company.

Rear-end load   a commission charged at the time of the sale of an open-end investment company.

Right   a security distributed pro rata to existing equity owners that allows the purchase of additional equity at a specified subscription price prior to a specified expiration time.

Short sale   the sale of an asset in the hopes of buying it back later at a lower price.

Unit investment trusts   a fixed pool of securities in which each investor has an interest proportionate to their contribution.

Unit trusts   a type of managed investment company formed by a deed of trust between a trustee and an investment manager under which the investment manager will purchase securities for the beneficial interest of the unit holders who own a pro rata interest in the trust assets.

THIS CHAPTER describes the basic features of common and preferred stocks; then three types of equity issues that are important in international financial markets, but that are not typically discussed extensively in investments texts of this type, namely:

- depository receipts
- warrants
- rights offerings

We also discuss in detail a common way of managing investment portfolios, namely:

- pooled investment plans

In the final part of this chapter we consider problems faced by international investors, especially

- restrictions on foreign ownership

1. INTRODUCTION

The aggregate value of world equity markets is in the trillions of USDs. Table 6.1 shows the relative sizes of several of these markets, based on the number of listings, market value, and number of members. While number of members is straightforward, the other comparisons can be misleading. Both number of listings and market value of listings are often distorted because some exchanges allow trading in unlisted securities, while others do not. Also, cross holdings, the holding of stock in one listed company by another listed company, are common in some countries and rare in others. Cross holdings inflate the value of listings when measured in terms of market value of outstanding shares. Failure to account for cross holdings would overstate the value of equities on the Oslo Stock Exchange by 20 percent. Financial leverage and the aggregate return of the listed equities would also be significantly understated (see Bohren and Michalsen 1994). Nevertheless, clearly, equity exchanges are important economic institutions. Moreover, there has been extraordinary development of equity markets in the 1990s.

As a percentage of Gross Domestic Product (GDP), stock market capitalization in Chile, Hong Kong, Malaysia, and Singapore has been comparable to, or even exceeded, that of the USA and the UK. In many emerging markets, stock markets have played a more important role in raising capital for industry than in most industrialized countries. According to Robert Shakotko, manager of the emerging markets database at the International Financial Corporation, the World Bank's private finance vehicle, "With the advent of money that crosses national boundaries very quickly, it's become more important ... to have a functioning exchange and attract foreign money" (Vogel 1995, p. C1).

Table 6.1 Comparison of listings, market value, and membership for selected stock exchanges. The market value is for equities only and excludes bonds

Exchange	No. companies		Market value (billion USD)	No. members
Data for 1992	Domestic	Foreign		
Tokyo	1,651	119	2,321	124
New York	1,969	120	3,878	503
Toronto	1,049	70	243	79
UK	1,816	576	933	414
Germany	410	356	321	227
Paris	515	217	328	46
Zurich	180	240	195	25
Amsterdam	251	244	171	137
Milan	225	3	115	108
Australia	1,038	35	135	99
Hong Kong	386	27	172	620
Singapore	188	25	50	26
Taiwan	256	——	100	277
Korea	688	——	108	32
Data for 1997				
Tokyo	1,805	60	2,176	
New York	2,691	356	8,990	
London	2,465	526	2,072	
Frankfurt	450	1,011	796	
Paris	717	183	675	

Source: Tokyo Stock Exchange, 1994 and 1997. Reprinted by permission.

2. TYPES OF EQUITY

2.1. COMMON STOCK

Common stockholders are the owners of the firm, and the common stock is the evidence of their ownership. The common stockholders have the right to receive all the assets and earnings of the firm after the obligations of other equity and debt holders have been met. In the USA common stockholders usually have the exclusive right to elect the board of directors. In some countries, such as Germany, other stakeholders such as employees have a right to elect directors. In most cases each share of common stock has one vote, and a majority of the votes cast is required to elect all the directors. Shareholder votes are often required on major corporate decisions such as mergers. Companies have devised a number of ways to make it more difficult for stockholders to change the board of directors. The terms of the board members may be staggered so that only a few are elected each year. Stockholders would then have to wait for several years before a majority of the board could be elected.

162

There might be classified common stock with some classes having more votes than other classes. The class A shares might have one vote each and the class B shares ten votes each. Hence, an investor or group of investors might be able to maintain control of the firm without having enough resources to own a majority of the shares. Historically, the New York Stock Exchange has discouraged multiple classes of common stock, and this has contributed to its lack of popularity in the USA.

La Porta, Lopez-De-Silanes, and Shleifer (1999) examined the ownership structure of large corporations in 27 wealthy countries and found that very few of these firms were widely owned. Instead, they were mostly controlled by families or the government. Controlling shareholders typically had much more control than would be indicated simply by their claims on the cash flows of the firm. This power was accomplished by pyramid ownership structures in which there was a partial but controlling interest in one firm with a partial but controlling interest in another firm, and so forth. A second source of power is through participation in management. The exceptions are in the USA and other countries, particularly common law countries, with significant protection for minority shareholders. But even in the USA Holderness, Kroszner, and Sheehan (1999) have shown that for a group of publicly held companies managerial ownership increased from 13 percent in 1935 to 21 percent in 1995.

It has recently become popular for companies to have **poison pills**, provisions in their bylaws or charter that provide protection if anyone acquires a significant ownership in the firm without the approval of the board of directors. The pill might provide that all the existing shareholders other than the new holder have the right to purchase equity in the firm at a very cheap price. Such a provision makes it prohibitively expensive for outsiders to gain control of a firm. Historically, in the USA common stockholders have had **preemptive rights** – the right to participate in new equity offerings on a pro rata basis. This provision was designed to prevent the dilution of stockholders' ownership percentage. Now preemptive rights are typically eliminated in firms' charters.

Rather than one share one vote, some firms use a voting method called **cumulative voting**. In this method each shareholder can cast as many votes as they own shares times the number of candidates. Each shareholder's votes can be divided in any way, so that if n directors are being elected, a shareholder who owns $1/n$ of the shares can be assured of electing one director if all of that shareholder's votes are cast for a single director. Suppose that a firm has 100 shares outstanding and is electing five directors. The number of votes that can be cast is $(5 \times 100) = 500$, and it takes at least 100 votes to win a directorship. Hence, a shareholder that owns 20 shares could elect a director.

2.2. PREFERRED STOCK

Preferred stock is equity. Preferred stockholders often have a claim to a stated dividend and stated assets in the event of the liquidation of the firm. But the preferred stockholders cannot force the bankruptcy of the firm if the stated dividend obligations are not met. In some cases preferred stockholders gain extra rights such as the right to vote for directors or even to elect a majority of directors if the firm fails to meet its obligations to the preferred holders. The firm may be prohibited from paying dividends on common stock if its obligations to the preferred holders have not been met. The firm has an obligation to pay any missed dividends when its financial condition permits. **Participating preferred** does not have an entirely fixed dividend, but instead its dividend is based at least in part on the earning of the firm. **Convertible preferred** may be exchanged for another security, typically the common shares on the firm. **Floating rate preferred** has a dividend payment that is reset periodically. The reset rate may be based on some capital market rate such as LIBOR, or in some cases a Dutch auction is used to reset the rate.

Firms that have regulatory obligations to maintain certain levels of equity, such as banks and brokerage firms, may find preferred stock useful. Also, in the USA preferred stock has some tax advantages, in that corporate recipients of preferred stock dividends do not typically have to pay full US federal income tax on these dividends (dividends on common equity receive similar treatment).

2.3. OTHER TYPES OF EQUITY: DEPOSITORY RECEIPTS

The US banking firm J. P. Morgan created the American Depository Receipt (ADR) in 1927 to simplify investment in non-US companies by US investors. Sometimes the term Global Depository Receipt (GDR) is used, for marketing reasons or to indicate an issue that is being sold in several countries; but GDRs and ADRs sold in the USA are identical. Here we call both "depository receipts" (DR). Since a DR is considered to be a US security, it can be freely traded in the USA and is the same as other US securities for purposes of clearing and settlement. Therefore, DRs typically make it easier and cheaper to trade non-US securities in the USA. DRs are traded on the New York and American stock exchanges, on NASDAQ, and over-the-counter. In the USA there are more than 900 DR programs, with issuers from more than 40 countries. Figure 6.1 shows the percentage of capital raised and the number of depository receipt programs begun in the USA in 1994.[1] Karolyi (1998) provides an extensive discussion of why firms list their shares outside their home country.

Moreover, many countries throughout the world now have their own version of DRs. In September 1995 Unocal Corp. signed a depository agreement and became the first US Fortune 500 company to have its depository receipts listed on the Stock Exchange of Singapore. One interesting aspect of the agreement is that the DRs trade in USD rather than in SGD. This may account for the fact that the volume of trading is very low and that there was no trading at all on the listing day.

A DR is a negotiable certificate issued by a depository bank such as J. P. Morgan or the Bank of New York. DRs are created and destroyed at will. The depository bank arranges for a bank in the issuer's home country to serve as the local custodian. The bank may establish the DR program unilaterally or with the consent and support of the issuing firm. Figure 6.2 presents a schematic of the process by which the DRs are created and destroyed after the program has begun. Depository banks create DRs when shares are delivered to their custodial bank.

In the USA a non-US owner of the shares may deliver them to the custodial bank to have DRs created for sale in the US market. Or a US broker, acting for a US client, may purchase shares in the home market, through an affiliate or another brokerage firm, convert the USDs received from its client into the currency needed to pay for the shares, and deliver

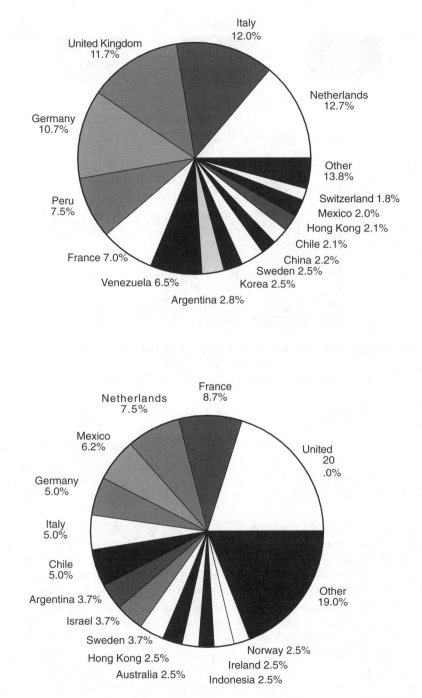

Figure 6.1 Percentage of public depository receipt offerings by country (1996), by capital raised (*above*); by number of programs (*below*). During 1996, 13,655 billion USD of new capital was raised through 80 public offerings from 28 countries; all offerings were for depository receipts. Reprinted by permission of the Bank of New York.

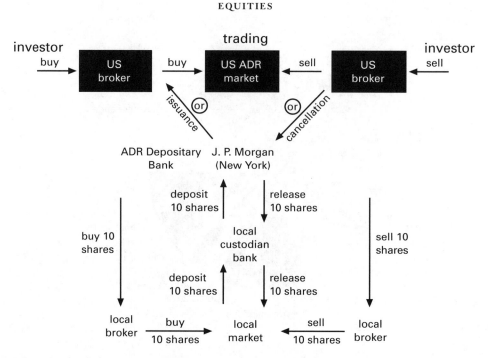

Figure 6.2 The ADR was created by J. P. Morgan in 1927 to facilitate US investment in non-US companies.
Source: by kind permission of J. P. Morgan.

the shares to the custodial bank. On the same day that the custodial bank receives the shares, the bank notifies the depository bank, which then issues the shares and delivers them to the broker for redelivery to their client. The DRs may be canceled through a process that reverses the previous steps, or a DR holder may simply take possession of the underlying shares.

There are four levels of DRs in the USA, differing primarily in the amount of information provided to investors and the consequent access granted to US capital markets. Unsponsored DRs are issued by depositories in response to market demand. In the past there was no issuer involvement, but today the issuer must sign certain documents. Sponsored Level-I DRs do not require compliance with US Generally Accepted Accounting Principles (GAAP) or disclosure beyond that required in the home country. Level-I DRs can be traded in the US over-the-counter market and on some non-US exchanges. Level-II DRs can be traded on a US exchange, but require financial statements conforming to US GAAP and disclosure following USSEC regulations. Level-III DRs require additional paperwork, but allow the issuance and sale of new shares to raise equity capital in the US market. In addition to the three levels of sponsored programs, companies can use US capital markets to raise funds through a sale of sponsored DRs to institutional buyers in a private placement. It usually costs less than 10,000 USD to establish a Level-I program and about 75,000 USD to establish a Level-II program.

From the point of view of the issuer, DRs can

1 increase the market for the issue,
2 enhance the image of the company in the international market,
3 provide a means for raising new equity capital and serve as a vehicle for acquisitions,
4 allow employees to invest in the parent company.

A number of active money managers prefer direct investment in the home market rather than the use of DRs. But for smaller institutions, cost, market access issues, and global custody problems may lead to a preference for DRs. Depending on the country in which the DR is issued and the particular arrangements, the advantages of DR programs to investors may include one or more of the following:

1 DRs are traded in the local market and the clearing and settlement process is the same as for local securities.
2 DRs are often quoted in local currency.
3 The depository bank arranges the conversion of dividends into local currency at competitive rates.
4 DRs overcome many obstacles to institutional investment outside the home country.
5 DRs sometimes reduce transfer taxes.
6 Whereas actual certificates may be in bearer form in some countries, in the USA DRs are registered certificates, providing a record of ownership in case of loss.
7 DRs may reduce legal problems from countries that claim jurisdiction over the estate of a deceased owner.
8 DRs may offer an efficacious way of attaining international exposure and diversification. Wahab and Khandwala (1993) report that adding as few as seven DRs to a portfolio comprising the US S&P's 500 substantially reduces the risk of the portfolio.

2.4. OTHER TYPES OF EQUITY: WARRANTS

A warrant is a security giving the owner a claim to an asset at a specified price before a specified time. Redmayne (n.d.) provides a detailed discussion of warrants. The specified price is the exercise price, and the specified time is the expiration date. Traditionally, warrants have given the right to purchase an equity interest in the issuer at the exercise price. If the warrant gives the right to purchase an asset, the **intrinsic value** of the warrant is the difference between the cost of acquiring the asset by exercising the warrant and the market value of the asset. The difference between the market price of a warrant and its intrinsic value is the **premium**.

Warrants have been issued in most financial markets, including those of Austria, Brazil, Germany, India, Italy, Japan, Korea, Malaysia, Mexico, Singapore, Switzerland, Thailand, the United Kingdom, and the United States. The large number of European warrants outstanding is testified to by the European Warrant Fund Inc., traded on the NYSE, which invests primarily in equity warrants, index warrants, covered warrants, and long-term options of European issuers. Historically, most warrants have been issued along with other securities. Most often, warrants are issued with (attached to) bonds. Typically, after the issue has been sold, the bonds and warrants trade separately. A firm might issue common stock and warrants together, or bonds and warrants together. In some cases, if the warrant is exercised, the bond could be used as payment, typically at face value.

Warrants are sometimes sold in combination with new issues of common stock. Such an offering may attract investors who are more speculatively minded. Since the common stock and warrants will usually trade separately, the company may attract demand both from equity investors and derivative investors. Further, if the firm is not able to raise all the capital it wants at one time, an appropriately priced warrant issue may give a reasonable prospect of obtaining more funds later. Hindalco Industries issued 4,473 million units, each comprising two shares and one warrant to purchase an additional share. The combination of a common stock and warrant offering is common for some types of financial firms in the international markets such as the UK.

There are many variations in the terms of warrants. The US investment company Tri-Continental Corporation has warrants outstanding that do not have an expiration date. In 1991 Eurotunnel issued a warrant permitting exercise when certain financial conditions were met. Danae Investment Trust warrants expire when the affairs of the trust are wound up, and the Hong Kong Investment Trust warrants expired 30 days after the 1995 annual report was issued. Occasionally, firms unilaterally extend the life of their warrants. This has posed a problem for investors in the USA who had developed strategies of shorting expiring warrants (recall that a **short sale** is the sale of an asset in the hopes of buying it back later at a lower price). In the USA some warrant issues have had provisions allowing the company to force exercise. Some warrants contain provisions that allow the firm to make adjustments to prevent the warrant from expiring worthless. The company may be able to convert an out-of-the-money warrant into a small amount of common stock or lower the exercise price so that the warrant's intrinsic value is positive.

The Australian Stock Exchange lists a number of warrants with unusual features. Most of these warrants can be exercised only at maturity. **Low exercise price warrants** are similar to equity warrants except that the exercise price is 0.01 AUD. **Capped warrants** are low exercise price warrants with the upside gain capped at a stated level. **Index warrants** link the payment at expiration to the value of an index such as the S&P 500 Index, the Nikkei Index, or the FT-SE 100 Index. **Installment warrants** give the owner the right to purchase shares held in trust by making periodic payments. In a typical example the owner pays the first installment and then, upon payment of the second installment at any time before expiration, receives the underlying shares. **Endowment warrants** do not have a fixed exercise price, but instead are exercisable by payment of an outstanding amount that is fixed initially and is then reduced by any dividend payments and increased by an interest charge. These warrants generally have a life of 10 years. At maturity the expiration price is the greater of zero or the outstanding amount. **Capital plus warrants** requires an initial payment, typically 1,000 AUD, and covers a basket of securities. The 1,000 AUD is returned at expiration, along with a stated percentage of the gain in the basket's value relative to its initial value.[2]

The issuance of warrants on a stand-alone basis without accompanying securities is less common. In a few cases warrants are issued alone, either as a way to raise equity capital or, more commonly, as a form of compensation. The UK firm Hanson used warrants as part of the payment in two takeovers. In the first instance, Hanson acquired Consolidated Gold Fields for a combination of cash and warrants. Then, Hanson offered identical warrants as part of the acquisition price of Beazer.

The International Finance Corporation issued 1,000,000 Asia Tiger 100™ Index Call Warrants through the investment banking firm of CIBC Oppenheimer. Upon expiration, the owner receives an amount based on the increase in value of the index over the initial value. These warrants are traded on the Chicago Board Options Exchange.[3]

While single company warrants most commonly allow for the purchase of an equity interest in the issuer, sometimes the warrant allows for the purchase of an equity interest in another firm. In 1983 Dart and Kraft Finance issued a warrant allowing the purchase of shares of Minnesota Mining and Manufacturing, a firm in which Dart and Kraft held an equity stake. Moreover, sometimes the exercise price of the warrant may change during the life of the warrant. Asahi Glass, a Japanese company, issued warrants that allowed the holder to purchase its common stock at a fixed price in USD. Therefore, this warrant changes value in response both to changes in the value of Asahi common stock and to changes in the USD/JPY exchange rate.

A growing phenomenon, especially in Europe, is the issuance of covered warrants The principal difference between a **covered warrant** and other warrants is that the issuer is not the firm whose securities underlie the warrant, or even another firm that acquired shares in the subject firm in the past. Instead, the issuer is an investment banker that acquires the shares for the express purpose of issuing the warrant. At first, the warrants were for shares of Japanese companies. Both Morgan Stanley and Baring Brothers have issued covered warrants on the shares of Fuji Fire and Marine. The success of the market for Japanese covered warrants has lead to growth in the number of issuers and the types of warrants issued. As of 1994, Swiss Bank Corporation had issued 94, Citicorp had issued 65, and Credit Lyonnais had issued 32. SG Warburg OTC issued a covered warrant with shares of the European firm Phillips as the underlying asset. Barclays de Zoete Wedd Warrants have the American Depository shares of the Mexican company Telmex as the underlying asset. Goldman Sachs has issued covered warrants on individual companies in a wide range of countries, including Belgium, Germany, Finland, France, Hong Kong, Russia, the Netherlands, Italy, Sweden, Spain, Switzerland, the UK, and the US.[4]

A distinctive feature of the covered warrant market is the many issues of basket covered warrants. These are warrants that allow the purchase or, sometimes, the sale of a basket of stocks at a fixed price until expiration. Some basket covered warrants are for particular countries, some for particular industries, and some for particular regions. Morgan Stanley's Argentine blue chip basket allows the purchase of shares in five firms (weights in parentheses): YPF ADR (32.80 percent); Telefonica ADR (32.20 percent); Galicia ADR (14.20 percent); Frances ADR (12.80 percent); and BAESA ADR (8.00 percent). Kidder Peabody International's US insurance basket comprised equal proportions of American Insurance, USF & G, Chubb, General Re Corp., and Marsh & McLennan. The warrants expired May 31, 1996, and were exercisable in USD. Four million warrants were issued, half in USD and half in CHF. Morgan Stanley's Eastern European exposure basket covered holdings in nine firms with weights ranging from 6.6 percent to 15.9 percent. Goldman Sachs has issued covered warrants covering baskets of stocks in various countries, including internet stocks in the USA.

2.5. OTHER TYPES OF EQUITY: RIGHTS OFFERINGS

The purpose of a rights offering is to raise new equity capital. We have previously explored several ways that firms can raise additional equity capital, including retained earnings, new

Table 6.2 Rights offerings in the USA and Japan, 1975–1991

| Year | Japanese firms | | | US firms | |
	Number	Proportion by number	Proportion by value	Number	Proportion by number
1975	166	0.582	0.770	10	0.11
1976	102	0.526	0.260	5	0.05
1977	120	0.296	0.315	3	0.05
1978	66	0.211	0.298	4	0.04
1979	54	0.166	0.274	4	0.05
1980	34	0.121	0.086	5	0.03
1981	67	0.199	0.256	3	0.02
1982	45	0.165	0.165		
1983	18	0.137	0.167		
1984	23	0.111	0.086		
1985	40	0.173	0.212		
1986	27	0.115	0.079		
1987	26	0.067	0.145		
1988	40	0.075	0.165		
1989	32	0.045	0.082		
1990	39	0.067	0.217		
1991	40	0.101	0.270		
1992	20	0.116	0.263		
1993	9	0.043	0.057		
1994	2	0.010	0.010		
1995	12	0.076	0.149		
1996	9	0.035	0.163		
1997	9	0.063	0.062		

The number of rights offerings and the proportion that these represent of the combined total of rights and public offerings is shown. For the Japanese data, the proportion of the funds raised through rights offerings is also shown. The Japanese data are taken from the PACAP database, and the US data, which are for American and New York Stock Exchange-listed firms, are derived from Eckbo and Masulis 1992. No rights offerings are reported for the US sample after 1981.
Source: Tokyo Stock Exchange, 1998. Reprinted by permission.

offerings of stock to the public (the first offering is called an "initial public offering," or IPO, and subsequent issues are called "secondary offerings"), and warrants. In recent years almost half of the equity in Canada has been raised through rights offers (see Eckbo and Varma 1994). It is also a popular method in many European countries such as the United Kingdom (see Marsh 1979; Loderer and Zimmerman 1988) and Japan. But while rights offerings were also used frequently in the USA until the 1970s, they are now rarely used.[5]

For each year, 1975–91, table 6.2 shows the number of rights offerings and the proportion of total offerings by number for US and Japanese firms. Unlike the US market, where the use of rights for NYSE- or AMEX-listed firms disappeared after 1981, Japanese firms

Table 6.3 Descriptive statistics for rights and public offerings by Japanese firms, 1975–1991

Characteristic	Type of offering		
	Rights	Public	t-statistic
Shares issued/total shares outstanding	0.233	0.088	35.76**
Amount offered	8,282	6,315	1.80*
Amount offered/market value of equity	0.056	0.083	−13.91**
Market value of equity	198,849	140,750	1.79*
Firm's total assets	256,934	201,300	1.46

The mean values for each sample are presented. The t-statistics are for a test of the difference in the means of the two samples.
*significant at the 0.10 level.
**significant at the 0.01 level.
Source: Ferris, Noronha, and McInish 1997. Copyright 1997, with permission from Elsevier Science.

continue to use rights offerings as a source of equity capital. Although the number of rights offerings by Japanese firms has varied widely, there is no evidence to suggest that a demise in their use is imminent. As shown in table 6.2, the percentage frequency of rights to public offers has declined from 1975 levels, but remains approximately 35 percent for the recent past. Table 6.2 also reports the proportion of new equity capital raised in Japan each year using rights. As with the relative frequency of rights offerings, there is significant variation in the annual percentage, which ranges from 19 percent to 96 percent. For the two most recent years for this sample, the rights method accounts for an average of 57 percent of all new equity raised by Japanese firms.

Descriptive characteristics for Japanese firms using rights and public offerings are presented in table 6.3. Several relationships are noteworthy. The first is the larger size of the rights issue in relation to a public offering. But, interestingly, the public offerings represent a significantly larger portion of the firm's total equity. This difference is statistically significant for both sub-periods and the sample period as a whole. Table 6.3 also shows that the rights-issuing firm is significantly larger than the corresponding public offering firm, despite the sub-period examined. This result holds whether market or book value is used to measure the firm.

2.5.1. How rights offerings work

Before exploring why firms use rights offerings, we explain how rights offerings work. A **right** is a security distributed pro rata to existing equity owners that allows the purchase of additional equity at a specified subscription price before a specified expiration time. The firm is free to set the subscription price at any level. If the subscription price is below the market price at the expiration date, holders of the rights must exercise them or the rights expire worthless, resulting in a loss of their value to the holder. Rights are distributed to the current holders of equity as a dividend, with the owner of each share receiving one or more rights. Typically, if the original owner of a right does not wish to exercise, the right can be sold to another investor before its expiration. The time between the issuance of the rights and their expiration is usually short and may amount to only a few weeks. Naturally, the stock price of the firm issuing the rights is likely to fluctuate during the period during which the rights are outstanding. The lower the subscription price is set compared with the current stock price, the more likely the stock price will be greater than the subscription price at expiration and that the rights will be exercised. Rights will be exercised only if the market price of the stock is above the exercise price, especially at the time of expiration. If the current market price of the shares is 10 USD, a subscription price of 5 USD is more likely to result in the right being exercised than a subscription price of 9.5 USD. In the latter case, the market price is more likely to decline below the subscription price. Since the purpose of a rights offering is to raise new equity, the firm desires that the rights be exercised.

Rights offerings do not change the value of the firm. Otherwise, firms could forget their operations and simply create value by issuing rights. This observation is an affirmation of Modigliani–Miller Proposition I (MM I), which says that "the market value of any firm is independent of its capital structure and is given by capitalizing its expected return at the rate . . . appropriate to its risk class" (Modigliani and Miller 1958, p. 268). *Ceteris paribus*, the value of the firm is increased by the amount of money raised in the rights offering.

Define the following terms:

n = the number of shares of a firm's stock outstanding before the rights offering
P_0 = the firm's stock price before the rights offering
z = the number of shares that can be purchased with one right
P_r = the rights subscription price (stated per share of stock purchased)

The value of each share after the rights offering and the theoretical value of a right can be computed on either a firm-wide or a portfolio basis.

Taking the firm-wide approach, if the rights offering is successful, there will be $n + zn$ shares outstanding. Given MM I, the value of the firm after the exercise will be

$$nP_0 + znP_r$$

so that the value of each share after the exercise is

$$(nP_0) + znP_r)/(n + zn)$$

and the value of a right is

$$[(nP_0) + znP_r)/(n + zn)] - P_r$$

Using the portfolio approach, a shareholder who owns 1 share of stock before the offering, worth P_0, will own $1 + z$ shares following the offering, worth $P_0 + zP_r$ together. The second term is the increase in the value of the portfolio, which is exactly the amount paid by the shareholder for the additional share. Each post-rights share is thus worth

$$[(P_0 + zP_r)/(1 + z)$$

and each right is worth

$$[(P_0 + zP_r/(1+z)] - P_r$$

It might be useful to consider a real example chosen because it is unusual and provides an interesting illustration. On May 21, 1986, Brock Hotel Corporation of Dallas, Texas, distributed 20 rights for each share of its common stock. Each right entitled the holder to purchase one share of common stock before expiration of the rights on June 6, 1986, at an exercise price of 0.15 USD. At the close of trading on May 20, 1986, Brock was trading at 20/32 (0.625) USD. Since the value of the stock was 0.625 USD just before the rights distribution, the projected value of the stock/rights portfolio, if the rights were exercised and the value of the stock did not change, is 0.625 USD + (20 × 0.15 USD) = 3.625. Therefore, the projected value of each post-rights share is 3.625 USD/21 = 0.1726 USD, and the projected value of a right is 0.1726 − 0.15 = 0.0226 USD. At the close of trading on May 22, 1986 (the first day of trading for the rights), the stock closed at 0.1875 USD, a slight increase over its projected value of 0.1726. Since the stock was worth more than projected, the right should also have been worth more. Specifically, the right should have been worth 0.1875 − 0.15 = 0.0375 USD. In fact, the right closed at 0.03125. Another way to look at this is that following the distribution of the rights the owner of one pre-rights share owned one share of stock and 20 rights for a total value of 0.1875 + (20 × 0.03125) = 0.8125, so the value of the stock/rights portfolio had increased slightly. In any event, the actual values of the stock and rights conform very well to their projected values, especially considering that due to the US convention of trading only in ticks of 1/64, 1/32, 1/16, 1/8, etc., not all theoretical values are attainable.

Since firms set the subscription price, naturally they set it at a level that is low enough to make the likelihood of success high. But a substantial price decline can result in an unsuccessful offering. Therefore, many firms using rights offerings arrange for a standby underwriting by an investment banker, who agrees to exercise any rights that are not exercised by the firm's stockholders. In this way, the success of the offering is guaranteed, but, of course, a fee must be paid to the underwriter. The potential usefulness of standby underwriting is illustrated by the case of the Cheung Kong Group, which announced a rights offering at a substantial discount to the market price just before the stock market crash of October 1987. Following the crash, the price of Cheung Kong Group stock fell well below the subscription price. The shareholders did not exercise their rights, forcing the underwriters to honor their commitment to buy a substantial number of shares at the exercise price (see box 6.1). In 1991 Time Warner announced that it would raise new equity using a rights offering. If all rights were exercised, the offering price was 105 USD, but the offering price was scaled down if only part of the rights were exercised. If only 60 percent were exercised, the price was 63 USD. On June 3, 1991, Time Warner stock sold for 119.125 USD, but following the announcement of the rights offering the price had fallen to below 10 USD per share. Stockholders were in the position of not knowing how much the shares would cost and, consequently, how much cash would be required to exercise. Time Warner was forced to abandon its variable-price rights offering. Subsequently, the firm completed a conventional rights offering (see Logue and Seward 1992).

In Norway seasoned equity issues on the Oslo Stock Exchange now take place almost exclusively through the use of underwritten rights offerings (Bohren, Eckbo, and Michalsen

> ## BOX 6.1
> ### Cheung Kong rights issues rejected by shareholders
>
> Shareholders have rejected almost completely four massive rights issues offered by Hong Kong financier Li Ka-shing's Cheung Kong Group, leaving underwriters to take up about half the shares.
>
> Cheung Kong (Holdings) Ltd., Hutchison Whampoa Ltd., Cavendish International Holdings Ltd. and Hong Kong Electric Holdings Ltd. offered the issues, which totaled 10.3 billion Hong Kong dollars ($1.32 billion), making them Hong Kong's biggest fund-raising exercise ever.
>
> The Cheung Kong group said the public subscribed to 0.10% of the Cheung Kong (Holdings) issue, 0.34% of the Hutchison issue, 0.11% of the Cavendish issue and 0.36% of the Hong Kong Electric issue.
>
> When the Cheung Kong group announced the rights issues in September, the offering prices were at a substantial discount to the market value of the companies' shares. But following last month's stock-market collapse, the market prices of the companies' shares fell well below the prices of the rights issues.
>
> Mr. Li and the companies themselves are committed to take up about half the shares in the rights offering, leaving the underwriters and sub-underwriters to absorb about 5.13 billion dollars of shares, said Stephen Clark, Citicorp International Ltd. director. Citicorp is one of the lead underwriters of the issue.
>
> Mr. Clark said the issues had been extensively sub-underwritten in Hong Kong and Europe. He said he didn't know which sub-underwriters were most exposed to the issues, but added that if sub-underwriting commitments triggered any failures, they would most likely be among Hong Kong investors and institutions.
>
> *Source*: *Wall Street Journal* 1987. Reprinted by permission.

1997). The market response to rights offerings that are not underwritten is significantly positive. Those that are underwritten elicit the least favorable response, probably because they are more expensive, and also because the expected takeup of shares by current shareholders is likely to be related to the profitability of the investments to be undertaken with the funds raised.

2.5.2. Factors influencing the choice of rights versus public offerings

The use of rights offerings avoids all or part of the substantial fees charged by investment bankers. On the other hand, rights offerings may have undesirable consequences, such as causing a decrease in the price of the firm's stock and requiring adverse changes in the terms of the firm's convertible securities. Several explanations have been proposed as to why some firms choose rights offerings and others do not. We explore some of these explanations:

(1)   Convertible wealth transfer hypothesis   If a firm's outstanding convertible securities contain an antidilution clause, then issuing rights at a discount can trigger an automatic reduction in conversion rates (see Eckbo and Masulis 1992). The value of the bonds is increased without any compensation for the firm, shifting wealth from equity holders. Thus, firms with convertible securities have an added incentive to avoid issuing rights with deep discounts.

Table 6.4 Percentage of capital raised using rights offerings by Japanese firms with and without outstanding convertible securities, by year, 1975–1991

Convertibles?	No	Yes
1975	0.962	0.839
1976	0.846	0.837
1977	0.777	0.292
1978	0.604	0.000
1979	0.588	0.675
1980	0.497	0.032
1981	0.589	0.072
1982	0.450	0.000
1983	0.528	0.163
1984	0.208	0.000
1985	0.543	0.000
1986	0.476	0.000
1987	0.731	0.000
1988	0.754	0.000
1989	0.415	0.011
1990	0.461	0.158
1991	0.766	0.462

Source: Ferris, Noronha, and McInish 1997. Copyright 1997, with permission from Elsevier Science.

Table 6.4 shows the results of a comparison of the equity-raising methods of Japanese firms with and without convertible securities in their capital structure. For each year only the firms that raise capital during that year are included in the sample. For the firms raising capital during a given year that have convertibles outstanding, column 2 shows the proportion that use rights offerings, and column 3 the proportion that do not. The t-statistic for the difference between the time series mean for these two sets of firms is 4.74, which is statistically significant at the 0.01 level. These findings suggest that incorporating antidilution clauses in convertible issues may influence the way firms raise additional equity capital.

(2) Information asymmetry At least two models have been developed that explain the choice of rights versus an underwritten offering based on information asymmetries. The first emphasizes the certification services provided by an underwriter. (Booth and Smith (1986) extend the work of Klein and Leffler (1981) on reputational signaling to develop this model.) Corporate insiders may know more about the prospects of the firm than outsiders do. These differences in knowledge are called "informational asymmetries." Insiders will be more inclined to issue new stock when they think the market price exceeds the stock's value. Recognizing this, investors will be suspicious of new stock issues. To allay their fears, firms may employ underwriters. Investors may then believe that the underwriters have assessed the firm's prospects and concluded that the stock price is reasonable.[6]

A second model based on information asymmetries emphasizes differences in firm quality (see Heinkel and Schwartz 1986). On this model lower-quality firms use a public offering and employ an uninformed underwriter. Higher-quality firms use rights offerings. Within the group of firms using rights offerings, the highest-quality firms signal their high quality by employing a standby underwriter; the remaining firms signal their quality by choosing an appropriate subscription price: the higher the price, the higher the quality of the firm.[7]

(3) Transaction costs hypothesis The transaction costs hypothesis contends that the choice of offer type depends on the relative cost of underwritten and rights offerings. This hypothesis was originally developed by Kraus and Stoll (1972) and was later examined by Hansen and Pinkerton (1982) and Hansen (1988). The price of existing shares falls significantly before the offering date of a rights offering (see Hansen 1988), but underwritten issues are not associated with any abnormal offering-period price behavior.[8] The price decline before a rights offering is viewed as compensation for transactions costs incurred by the buyers, including portfolio adjustment costs, commissions, taxes, and the like. If investors are to be induced to exercise rights rather than purchase shares outright, they must be compensated for any extra cost and effort involved. Hence the price of the firm's stock is expected to decline before the rights offering and then rebound, with the rebound providing the compensation.

An alternative view of the transactions cost hypothesis is presented by Kothare (1997), who finds that bid–ask spreads increase following rights offerings, but decline following public offerings. These findings are attributed to the fact that rights offerings lead to more concentrated ownership, whereas public offerings lead to more dispersed ownership. For actively traded shares the increased post-offering trading costs of rights offerings may offset their lower underwriting costs.

(4) Agency cost argument Another explanation of the choice between rights and underwritten offers involves agency conflicts that can be present in the modern corporation (see Smith 1977). The first is the possibility that managers and board members may receive benefits from the use of underwriters that do not accrue to the firm's general shareholders. The firm's board of directors may include an investment banker, or the investment banking firm may allocate oversubscribed issues to the managers. (Herman (1981) reports that 21 percent of the 200 largest nonfinancial and 27 percent of the 100 largest industrial firms include at least one investment banker on their board of directors.) Choice of issuing method also has implications for the monitoring of the firm's activities. The greater dispersion in share ownership resulting from a public offering may reduce the ability of shareholders to monitor the firm.

(5) Local institutional considerations Sometimes a firm may be constrained in setting the subscription price for a rights offering. In Japan it has been customary to set the offering price at the par value of the firm. This practice works if the stock price is just above the par value. Then the exercise price will be below the market price, and the rights will be exercised. But if the stock price is below the par value, a rights offering would not be possible, because the stock can be purchased more cheaply in the market than it can be obtained by exercising the rights. Also, if the price of the stock is substantially greater than the par value, a firm might be discouraged from using a rights offering. In Japan firms frequently base their dividends on par value. Therefore, an increase in outstanding shares leads to an increase in dividends. Suppose that a stock's par value is 10 JPY and its market price is 90 JPY. To raise 90 JPY requires the sale of one new share using a secondary offering and the sale of nine new shares using a rights offering. In the second case the firm's dividend is increased by nine times as much as in the first case. Therefore, a firm with a high stock price relative to par value might prefer a secondary offering.

3. EQUITY INVESTMENT VEHICLES

3.1. POOLED INVESTMENT PLANS

Plans, called by various names, such as "pooled investment plans" or "collective investment schemes", in which the funds of many individuals are combined and invested jointly are a very popular way for individuals to buy securities. These plans are available to investors in most countries. In the USA there are actually more pooled investment plans than there are operating firms trading on the New York Stock Exchange.

There are many differences throughout the world in the way investment funds are organized and operated. The corporate form of organization is predominant in the USA, but the trust form is predominant elsewhere.

3.1.1. Pooled investment plans in the USA

In the USA collective investment schemes are regulated under the Investment Company Act of 1940. As defined under the 1940 act, investment companies include any issuer that is engaged primarily in the business of investing or trading in securities or that holds securities with a value exceeding 40 percent of the issuer's assets. The 1940 act itself, or regulations issued by the US Securities and Exchange Commission, exempt a variety of companies including investment bankers and securities brokers, financial institutions, trust funds managed by banks, and companies engaged in operations through subsidiaries from the act's provisions. There are two main types of regulated investment companies: unit investment trusts and managed investment companies.

Unit investment trusts (UIT) own a fixed pool of securities, in which each investor has an interest proportionate to their contribution. (Note that UITs should not be confused with unit trusts described below.) The UIT is organized under a trust indenture or similar arrangement, does not have a board of directors, and issues only redeemable securities representing an undivided interest in the UIT's portfolio. The UIT is designed for investors who seek diversification but do not want active management. UITs most commonly hold fixed-income securities issued by the various states and their subdivisions (counties, cities, airport, sewer, school authorities, and the like). These fixed-income securities are known collectively as "municipal bonds."

Managed investment companies are by far the most popular in the USA. These are organized as corporations with a board of directors. Investors purchase shares in the corporation that represent an undivided interest in the firm's assets. **Net asset value** is the value of the assets owned by an investment company less its liabilities. Net asset value is often stated on a per share basis. There are two main types of managed investment companies: closed-end and open-end.

Closed-end investment companies have a fixed number of outstanding shares and only rarely raise new funds. Because they thought the name closed-end was confusing, these types of investment companies have switched to calling themselves **publicly traded investment companies**. Closed-end fund shares are traded on the secondary markets just like the shares of operating companies. Investors purchasing or selling these shares pay brokerage commissions and incur other costs just like those paid when trading other securities. There are many closed-end investment company shares traded on NASDAQ and listed on the NYSE. Since the value of closed-end fund shares is determined by supply and demand, the market price can be more or less than net asset value.

Open-end investment companies, which are also called **mutual funds**, are continually issuing new shares. The purchase and sale price (not including fees) is net asset value. Investors buy their shares directly from the fund through a distributor. Many distributors charge a **load**, or commission, at the time of the purchase. For stock funds this load was often as high as 8–9 percent of the purchase price, but with increased competition, loads of 4–5 percent are more common today.[9] While the load is typically charged at the time of the purchase, for a **rear-end load**, the fee is charged when the shares are redeemed. In the late 1940s investors in the USA were unfamiliar with mutual funds, so most funds hired sales forces that received a part of the load as compensation. Even today, many mutual funds are distributed through brokerage firms or distributors who charge a load. But as investors have increasingly become familiar with mutual funds, there has been substantial growth in **no load** mutual funds, funds that do not charge a commission. True no load funds do not have either a front- or a rear-end load.

3.1.2. Pooled investment plans outside the USA

The principal type of collective investment scheme in many countries is the contractual-type that is often referred to as **unit trusts**. A unit trust is an agreement, evidenced by a trust deed, between a trustee and an investment manager under which the investment manager will purchase securities (or sometimes other assets such as real estate or precious metals). The manager divides the beneficial interest in these assets into units for sale to investors. Each investor owns an interest in direct proportion to the funds contributed. The funds are invested by the fund manager acting for the investors in a portfolio of marketable securities.

Countries with significant assets invested in unit trusts include Australia, Hong Kong, and Korea. In Japan all collective investment schemes are contractual-type, and unit trusts also are well established in countries such as the United Kingdom and Singapore.[10]

In Japan, unit trusts can be either open-type, in that new funds are accepted for investment during the life of the fund, or closed-type, for which no new funds are accepted. Open-type funds typically allow redemptions at a price that represents a pro rata share of net asset value. Some closed-type funds permit redemptions during the life of the fund, and other have no distributions before the termination of the trust. Stock funds that invest in domestic and non-Japanese issues and index funds are typically of the open type. There are both unit-type and open-type funds that invest in stocks and bonds for income. Stock investment trusts can invest in both stocks and bonds, but bond investment trusts invest exclusively in fixed income securities.

Unit trusts available outside the USA typically charge a load. The US GROWTH FUND offered by DBS Asset Management Ltd. of Singapore is typical. The offer price includes a sales commission of 5 percent with discounts available for one-time purchases exceeding 100,000 SGD. Five Arrows Asian Enterprise Trust's (Five Arrows) prospectus provides for a "realization charge" of up to 2 percent at the time of the sale or the redemption of the units. According to the prospectus, the fee "shall be retained by the managers for their own benefit." This fee is similar to rear-end load. Dividends may be automatically reinvested in units of the trust, but unlike the practice in the USA, where these reinvestments are usually at net asset value, many non-US funds charge a load for reinvested dividends.

3.1.3. Fees of pooled investments

In addition to loads, which are paid directly by investors, there are typically other fees that are charged against the assets of pooled investments so that investors pay these charges indirectly. Management fees are the most important and common indirect expense. DBS Asset Management charges an annual fee of 1.25 percent of net asset value of its US GROWTH FUND, whereas Rothschild Asset Management charges 1.5 percent annually for managing Five Arrows. The trustee's fee for Five Arrows can be as much as 0.25 percent of net asset value annually. These fee levels are higher than the 0.5–1.0 percent typically in the USA. Naturally, pooled investment funds pay the costs of operating the fund, including taxes, brokerage commissions, legal and accounting fees, and the like. In some jurisdictions, such as Singapore, advertising costs associated with selling the fund can be charged to the fund. In the USA, section 12b-1 of the 1940 act permits the payment of an extra fee to the fund's management company out of fund assets to help defray marketing costs. In the USA more than 60 percent of all mutual funds assess a 12b-1 fee. These fees typically range from 0.25 percent to 1 percent of net asset value.

In the USA a few funds charge a transactions fee payable directly to the fund at the time of the purchase or sale of the fund. These fees are distinguished from loads, which are payments to the manager and distributor. These transactions fees are designed to help defray the costs of establishing and eliminating positions due to shareholder turnover. Transactions charges of this type are most common for funds investing in securities that are difficult or costly to purchase and sell, such as those in emerging markets.

3.2. INDEX FUNDS

There are several exchange-traded pooled investment funds. In May 1987, the Toronto Stock Exchange created a trust that holds baskets of the stocks in the Toronto 35 Index for investors wishing to own a diversified portfolio of senior Canadian corporations. Units representing an interest in the trust are traded on the Toronto Stock Exchange. Investors holding a prescribed number of units can redeem them for the underlying basket of stocks, and investors owning the underlying basket can submit them to the trust in exchange for units of the trust. The designated market maker on the floor of the exchange actively arbitrages the units and the underlying baskets.

In January 1993 the American Stock Exchange began trading shares of beneficial interest (Standard and Poor Depository Receipts, abbreviated SPDRs and pronounced "spiders") in a unit trust that holds a portfolio of all common stocks in the S&P 500 Index. The fund had one of the fastest fund launches in US history, growing to 700 USD by mid-1995. In 1996 trading began on the American Stock Exchange in another open-end fund, World Equity Benchmark Shares Foreign Fund, Inc. Units of the fund are called "WEBS" in an obvious play on the earlier spiders. The fund is managed as 17 separate portfolios, called "series," each designed to match the performance of the market in a particular country, namely Australia, Austria, Belgium, Canada, France, Germany, Hong Kong, Italy, Japan, Malaysia, Mexico, The Netherlands, Singapore, Spain, Sweden, Switzerland, and the United Kingdom. BZW Barclays Global Fund Advisors is responsible for the investment management of each series, and this management includes the use of portfolio optimization techniques. In 1996 six Singapore banks created an open-end mutual fund to invest in companies included in the Straits Times Regional Market Index. The DIAMONDS Trust, which began trading on the American Stock Exchange on January 20, 1998, is a unit investment trust designed to track the performance of the Dow Jones Industrial Average through its holdings of the stocks in that index.[11]

3.3. Hedge Funds

A **hedge fund** is an investment organization whose management receives compensation in the form of performance incentives rather than on the basis of the amount of assets held or the number of transactions made.[12] Typically, the managers are also substantial investors in the fund. In the USA hedge funds are structured as partnerships. By raising funds through a private placement, the hedge fund avoids registration under the Investment Company Act of 1940, which imposes substantial limitations on the types of investments that can be made. These US hedge funds cannot make a general solicitation. Funds can be raised in private offerings to an unlimited number of accredited investors, but non-accredited investors are limited to 35. An accredited investor is an established financial institution such as a bank, brokerage firm or insurance company, certain pension plans, and wealthy individuals. To avoid registration, the hedge fund is limited to no more than 100 beneficial owners. Naturally, hedge fund managers seek to raise as much as they can from this limited group, so that in practice minimum investments in US-based hedge funds are typically 250,000 USD or more.

Hedge funds are also organized outside the USA. Depending on the laws of the particular jurisdiction, these funds can be organized as either partnerships or corporations. As long as the investors in the fund come from outside the local jurisdiction, limitations on the raising of funds are typically not imposed. In the USA these hedge funds are referred to as offshore, and they are not open to US investors. Popular jurisdictions for hedge funds include Bermuda, the Cayman Islands, Curacao, the British Virgin Islands, the Bahamas, Luxembourg, Dublin (Ireland), Gibraltar, Liechtenstein, Switzerland, and Mauritius. Several European Community countries require registration, which has spurred the growth of Dublin as an offshore center, and a number of offshore funds are listed on the Dublin Stock Exchange.

The first hedge fund is attributed to Alfred Winslow Jones, who was born in Australia and moved to the USA with his family at the age of four. Jones established an investment partnership and measured market exposure using the following formula:

Market exposure = (long exposure − short exposure)/capital

Jones's idea was to judicially select equities that were expected to outperform the market and to finance the purchases of these equities by selling short the equities of securities that were not expected to outperform the market. This strategy is totally dependent on the manager's stock selection capability. Since, historically, equities have yielded positive returns, Jones did not seek to have zero market exposure. Jones's investment results were impressive, outperforming all mutual funds over a 10-year period. An article published in the US magazine *Fortune* in 1966 led to a spate of new hedge funds. In 1968, the USSEC found 140 partnerships functioning as hedge funds, most having been formed in that year.

Today hedge funds follow a variety of investment strategies. The most common are

1 Market neutral – this is an extreme version of the Jones approach, in which the manager seeks very low or zero market exposure.
2 Event-driven – the manager seeks arbitrage opportunities in bankruptcy securities and mergers.
3 Opportunistic – the manager takes advantage of opportunities wherever they are found, so that exposure to various markets and strategies changes. Global funds pay attention to economic developments around the world seeking investment opportunities. Some specialize in particular types of markets (e.g., emerging markets) or particular regions.
4 Derivatives – managers use all types of derivatives, including those covering foreign exchange. Most hedge funds use derivatives extensively, both because of the leverage they provide and because they can allow exposure to markets where cash instruments are either nonexistent or illiquid.

An example of an opportunity that attracted hedge funds with varied investment strategies arose in 1997. A number of closed-end investment companies in Taiwan were selling at discounts of about 20 percent from net asset value. Under Taiwanese law the shareholders of a fund that sell at a discount of more than 20 percent for more than 20 consecutive days can call a special shareholders' meeting and liquidate the fund. Seeing an opportunity, a number of hedge funds began buying the closed-end funds and offsetting the risk of these investments using derivatives.

---

4. PROBLEMS FACED BY INTERNATIONAL INVESTORS

This section describes two types of risk faced by international investors: risk of loss due to unfavorable political, economic, financial conditions in their home country and risk due to foreign share ownership restrictions. Investors also face risk due to currency fluctuations.

4.1. COUNTRY RISK

International investors face **country risk**, due the political and economic conditions in a particular country. Inflation, exchange controls, and tax regulations differ across countries.[13] Governments frequently change regulations to the disadvantage of nondomestic investors. In 1997, following a major drop in the value of Malaysian equities, the Malaysian government announced a series of measures, including the purchase of equities from domestic investors at above-market prices and restrictions on the transfer of securities. Although these regulations and policies were either short-lived or never implemented, they indicate the potential for such measures. *Institutional Investor*, a US magazine, publishes a country risk index for 112 countries every 6 months. The index is constructed from the results of a survey of 75–100 banks located outside the country being assessed. Political Risk Services publishes an International Country Risk Guide covering 130 countries. Political risks include 13 factors, such as racial and national tensions, military influence in politics, external conflict risk, and corruption in government. Financial risk factors include five factors, such as expropriation by government, repudiation of contracts by the government, and losses due to exchange controls. Economic risks include six factors, such as inflation and strength of the currency. International portfolios contain significant country risk (Ranjan and Freidman). In fact, according to Madura, Tucker, and Wiley (1997), "the most relevant factor explaining disparate returns across markets is country risk." Equity returns are higher for high credit risk countries, and volatility of returns is about the same as that for low credit risk countries (see Erb, Harvey, and Viskanta 1995).[14]

4.2. Foreign Ownership Restrictions

In many countries, the percentage of common stock that can be held by foreign investors is limited. Table 6.5 provides some historical examples. As shown in boxes 6.2 and 6.3 these restrictions can result in serious problems for international investors. Usually the foreign and domestic shares provide identical claims on the cash flows of the company. Limitations on foreign ownership may come about either through governmental laws and regulations, or they may originate with the firm through restrictions in its corporate charter or bylaws. The German Foreign Trade Act restricts foreign ownership of defense firms and airlines. Italy restricts ownership in banking, shipping, and airlines. US restrictions on the percentage of foreign ownership allowed for US commercial television stations led Australian Rupert Murdock to become a US citizen. Table 6.6 presents a list of companies on the Stock Exchange of Singapore that have foreign ownership restrictions. Firms in the commercial banking and newspaper publication business are subject to statutory restrictions. Most other firms, including finance companies, insurance companies, and the national airline and shipping companies – Singapore Airlines and Neptune Orient Lines, respectively – have self-imposed restrictions.

Countries also differ in the way these restrictions are administered. In Finland, before 1986, not only was the percentage of ownership of domestic Finnish companies restricted, but Finnish citizens were prohibited from owning equities of non-Finnish companies (see Hietala 1989). Eighty percent of the shares carried a stamp showing that their ownership was restricted to Finnish citizens. Thus, Finnish investors could buy either restricted or unrestricted shares, but non-Finnish investors could purchase only the restricted shares. Before 1983 foreign investors had little interest in Finnish shares. But then demand grew to the point that brokers had difficulty finding unrestricted shares to satisfy the foreign demand. There was only one price quotation on the exchange, but sellers were willing to sell only restricted shares at this price. Brokers were forced to form an unofficial market in unrestricted shares until 1984, when the exchange began to quote restricted and unrestricted shares separately.

Singapore has a system much like that in Finland. Foreign investors can buy shares from a domestic investor and register them as foreign-owned as long as the ownership restriction

Table 6.5 Examples of restrictions on foreign ownership

Country	Type of restrictions
Australia	10% in banks, 25% in uranium mining, 20% in broadcasting, and 50% in new mining ventures
Burma	Investment not allowed
Canada	20% in broadcasting and 25% in banks and insurance companies
Finland	20% limit
France	20% limit
India	40% limit
Indonesia	49% limit
Japan	25%–50% in a group of 11 major firms. Acquisition of over 10% of the shares of a single firm requires approval of the Ministry of Finance.
Malaysia	20% in banks, 30% in natural resources, and 70% in other firms
Mexico	49% limit
Netherlands	No restrictions for listed securities, special permission for unlisted securities
Norway	10% in banks, 20% in industrial and oil, 50% in shipping, 0% in pulp, paper, and mining
Spain	0% in defense and public information, 50% otherwise
South Korea	15% for major firms eligible for foreign investment
Sweden	20% of voting shares, 40% of total share capital
Switzerland	Firms can issue either bearer or registered shares; foreigners can hold only bearer shares

Source: Eun and Janakiramanan 1986. Reprinted by permission of the *Journal of Finance*.

level has not been reached. Once the restriction has been reached, foreign investors can be assured of being able to register their shares only if they purchase them from another foreign investor. Singaporeans are allowed to purchase foreign registered shares and retain the foreign registration. Once the foreign ownership restriction becomes binding, foreign and domestically registered shares are quoted separately.

Usually the shares owned by domestic investors and those owned by foreign investors are identical except for the identity of their owners. If the percentage of foreign ownership is below permitted levels, then the restrictions on foreign ownership have no practical effect. But when the restriction becomes binding, difficulties may arise. A binding restriction says, in effect, that the supply of foreign-registered stock is not sufficient to satisfy the demand of foreign investors who have a higher assessment of the value of the firm than local investors. The foreign-registered shares become more valuable, since these shares also carry the foreign registration. Figure 6.3 shows the prices of foreign shares compared with domestic shares for selected companies in Singapore, Malaysia, and the Philippines. In each case the foreign shares sell at a premium relative to the domestic shares.

BOX 6.2
Bank Bali's foreign shareholders hit by local investors seeking quick kill

PT Bank Bali's lofty standing among international investors has taken a sharp knock. Bank Bali is Indonesia's seventh largest commercial bank in terms of assets and has a market capitalization of more than US$400 million (S$559 million). Before the rights issue last month, the foreign shareholding in the bank was already at the limit.

A loophole in Indonesia's stock market rules, exploited by savvy local investors, has left many foreign shareholders badly bruised after a rights issue by the premier Indonesian bank, said banking executives. Indonesian laws limit foreign ownership in a listed company to 49 percent. Local shareholders can register new shares from a rights issue under the foreign category on a first-come-first-served-basis.

According to brokers, the 65.134 million new shares offered to existing shareholders under the rights issue were fully subscribed. Last week, many foreign shareholders found they could not exercise the rights because new shares held by local groups had been registered as foreign shares. The motive, say brokers, was simply to cash in on the significant premium the foreign shares of Bank Bali trade over the local portion. Foreign units of the stock are currently trading at 5,300 rupiah (S$3.18) apiece against 3,900 rupiah for the local shares. Assuming a full subscription rate, about 31 million of the new shares should be available for foreign shareholders. But broking sources say foreign shareholders with about 27 million rights certificates cannot convert their holdings to new shares.

"A whole lot of guys out there feel cheated . . . there is a negative sentiment and there is going to be some dumping," said a senior analyst who tracks the company. The affair has raised questions about loopholes in Indonesia's stock market rules, which often hurt foreign investors. A senior director of Bank Bali acknowledges the battering the bank's image has taken following the rights issue. But he added that what happened was legal and the first-come-first served rule was highlighted in the prospects of the rights issue. Indeed, the registration of local stock units in a rights issue as foreign shares is common practice in Jakarta. But in instances where the foreign shareholding is already at the limit, the "window" foreigners have can be quickly closed by local shareholders seeking a quick kill, analysts say.

The implications are far-reaching for foreign investors who cannot register their new shares. Besides having their stakes diluted in the bank's enlarged equity, they have to sell their rights certificates to local investors or keep their shares with nominees at the lower price commanded by non-foreign stock.

Bank Bali officials are talking with Bapepam to reach a solution.

Source: Lopez 1995. Reprinted by permission.

As figure 6.3 also shows, China presents a different case. Beginning in 1985 the government made all securities transferable, created a secondary market, and established new standards for common stocks. Banks and other financial institutions organized affiliated securities companies. The Shanghai Securities Exchange was founded in 1990, and the Shen Zhen Securities Exchange was founded in 1991.

Chinese firms issue shares in different categories, including A shares that are for locals only and B shares that are for foreign owners only. The B shares are limited to 25 percent of the outstanding shares. Because the local and foreign markets are segmented, arbitrage

---

BOX 6.3
Foreign holdings of Qantas shares may exceed government limits

Newly listed Qantas Airways said overseas investors may have bought more of its shares than the 49% allowed by the Australian government. Qantas said that foreign-ownership notices it received after Monday's trading debut suggest the level of shares held by overseas investors "may have exceeded 49%."

The government sold a 75% stake in Qantas through a July initial public offering that raised A$1.45 billion (US$1.07 billion). The remaining 25% of Qantas is held by British Airways. Public fears the airline could fall into foreign hands have made the level of Qantas's foreign ownership one of the most contentious issues of the float. In selling its interest in the domestic and international carrier, the government stipulated that the aggregate level of foreign ownership of Qantas can't exceed 49%, including a further restriction that no foreign airline can hold more than 35% of the stock.

More than 73 million Qantas shares exchanged hands on the Australian Stock Exchange during the airline's debut as a listed company. Qantas Chairman Gary Pemberton said that, until sales were settled, Qantas has no way of knowing the nationality of sellers among the 73 million shares traded Tuesday or if there had in fact been any breach of the limit. Qantas shares are trading initially on a deferred-settlement basis that allows investors to buy and sell shares without actually holding scrip, as the airline is still mailing shares to investors whom subscribed to the IPO. Accordingly, the company said it won't be in a position to know the new level of foreign ownership of its stock until around Aug. 18.

Mr. Pemberton said that under its articles of association and the Qantas Sale Act, the Qantas board was obliged to ensure that the maximum aggregate foreign-share-ownership limits were enforced. He said that in cases where such action became necessary it would be undertaken on a sequential basis.

[Author's comment: Subsequent to this article, it was decided that local shares sold to foreign investors could only be registered as foreign if all the original foreign investors did not exercise their rights.]

Source: *Asian Wall Street Journal* 1995. Reprinted by permission.

---

is limited or impossible. In this case the domestic shares sell at a premium relative to the foreign shares. This undoubtedly reflects, at least in part, the limited investment opportunities available in the domestic market.

Evidence has been offered supporting several explanations for differences in prices between foreign and domestic shares. One possibility is that foreign investors seek to create capitalization-weighted portfolios of shares for a particular country. If the desired investment level were to exceed the foreign shares available, these shares would sell at a premium relative to the local shares, and the premium would be greater for firms with more stringent foreign ownership restrictions. Consistent with this view, the premiums of foreign shares over domestic shares are greater for firms with tighter foreign ownership restrictions. Another reason why foreign shares are more valuable is that they are typically more liquid. Foreign investors, being less familiar with local firms, typically need more information to make their investment decisions. Also, firms with greater availability of information have a larger premium (see Bailey and Jagtiani 1994).

Table 6.6 Foreign ownership restrictions on the Stock Exchange of Singapore

Company	Limit	Status
ST Aerospace	15	Binding
Singapore Airlines	24.51	Binding
ST Automotive	25	Binding
ST Computer Systems	25	Binding
ST Electronic and Engineering	15	Binding
SNP	49	Not binding
Singapore Bus Service	20	Binding
Singapore Petroleum Company	49	Binding
Singapore Press Holdings	49	Binding
ST Shipbuilding and Engineering	15	Binding
STIC	49	Not binding
DBS	40	Binding
Focal Finance	20	Not binding
GK Goh Holdings	49	Not binding
Hong Leong Finance	20	Binding
ICB	40	Not binding
Kay Hian James Capel	49	Binding
Kappel Bank	40	Not binding
Kappel Finance	20	Not binding
Kim Eng Holdings	49	Not binding
NOL	49	Not binding
OCBC	40	Binding
OUB	40	Binding
OUT	20	Binding
Sing Investments	20	Binding
Singapore Finance	20	Not binding
Singapore Reinsurance	49	Not binding
Singapore Telecom	40	Not binding
Singapura Building Society	20	Not binding
Tat Lee Bank	40	Not binding
Tat Lee Finance	20	Not binding
UOB	40	Binding
UOF	20	Not binding
UOI	20	Not binding
Vickers Ballas	49	Not binding

Information concerning companies listed on the Stock Exchange of Singapore that have foreign ownership restrictions. "Binding" means that the foreign ownership limit has been reached, and "not binding" means that it is still possible for foreign investors to register shares purchased from local investors.
Source: Stock Exchange of Singapore.

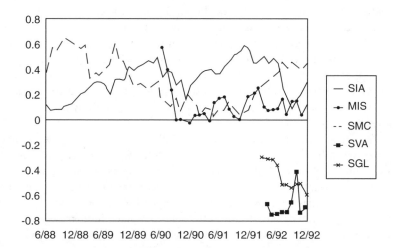

Figure 6.3 Premiums for foreign class stocks in other Asian markets. Price premiums and discounts for foreign class stocks in other Asian markets. Companies (markets) are Singapore International Airlines (Singapore), Malaysian International Shipping (Malaysia), San Miguel (Philippines), Shanghai Vacuum Electron (Shanghai, China), and China Southern Glass (Shenzen, China). Price premiums are computed as the log of the ratio of the price of the foreign class share to the price of the local class share. The Singapore and Malaysia markets parallel Thailand in creating a distinct market for foreign investors when the foreign ownership limit for a particular stock is reached. The Philippine market lists class B shares available to both locals and foreigners, and class A shares for locals only. The Chinese market lists class B shares for foreigners only and class A shares for locals only.
Source: Bailey and Jagtiani 1994. Copyright 1994. Reprinted from *Journal of Financial Economics* by permission of Elsevier Science.

5. SUMMARY

The common stockholders are the owners of the firm, and the common stock has the residual claim on the earnings and assets of the firm. Sometimes common stock is divided into classes, each with different rights, especially in voting. Preferred stock has a claim that is superior to that of common stock but inferior to that of the firm's debtors. (Superior claims are paid prior to inferior claims.) Usually firms can use preferred stock equity to meet any capital requirements imposed by regulators. Most preferred stock has a cumulative provision requiring that preferred stock obligations be met before any common stock dividends can be paid. There are a number of different types of preferred stock. Convertible preferred stock can be exchanged for another security, typically common stock in the issuer. Floating rate preferred stock has a dividend rate that is reset periodically.

In 1927, the US investment banking firm J. P. Morgan created the American Depository Receipt (ADR) to simplify investment in non-US companies by US investors. Many countries throughout the world now have their own version of DRs. In the USA there are over 900 DR programs with issuers from more than 40 countries, and DRs are traded on the New York and American Stock Exchanges, on NASDAQ, and over-the-counter. DRs are easier to trade, because they are traded in the local market, usually in local currency, and the depository arranges for the conversion of dividends into local currency.

A warrant is a security giving the owner a claim to an underlying interest at a specified price before a specified time. Warrants are both equities and derivatives. Warrants are used by firms to raise equity capital both at the time of issue and, if the warrant is exercised, at a latter time. Warrants have also been used in acquisitions. It is becoming more common for financial institutions to create covered warrants by purchasing underlying interests and then issuing warrants.

Rights offerings are used to raise equity capital. While the use of rights has declined in the USA, they are still used extensively in many countries, including Japan and the UK. Many explanations have been proposed about why some firms choose rights offerings and others do not. Antidilution clauses in convertible indentures may argue against the use of rights offering. Firms may employ underwriters to allay investors' fears that firms issue stock only when it is overpriced. Rights offerings may have hidden costs, in that price declines in the firm's stock value offset underwriting savings. Managers may choose underwritten offerings because they receive benefits from the underwriters.

Pooled investment plans are a common way for individuals and small institutions to invest. These plans are available to investors in most countries. In the USA there are more pooled investment plans than there are operating firms trading on the New York Stock Exchange. Unit investment trusts own a fixed pool of securities. By contrast, both open-end and closed-end investment companies manage their portfolios. Closed-end investment companies have a fixed number of shares outstanding, whereas open-end investment companies are continuously issuing new shares. The distributors of some closed-end investment companies (also called mutual funds) charge a commission or load when the shares are initially purchased, but no load mutual funds can be bought without a commission.

Outside the USA unit trusts are the most common type of pooled investment scheme. A unit trust is an agreement, evidenced by a trust deed, between a trustee and an investment manager under which the investment manager will purchase securities. The manager divides the beneficial interest in these assets into units for sale to investors. Each investor owns an interest in direct proportion to the funds contributed. The funds are invested by the fund manager acting for investors in a portfolio of marketable securities.

In many countries there are limits on the percentage of equity that nondomestic investors can hold. These restrictions often vary from industry to industry. When the percentage of shares owned by foreigners reaches its limit, it is common to trade the foreign-registered and domestically registered separately.

Questions

1 How can a depository receipt simplify trading in another country?
2 How do covered warrants differ from traditional warrants?
3 What are two possible explanations of why a firm would choose an underwritten offer rather than a rights offering?
4 Explain why rights offerings do not increase the value of the firm.
5 What is the difference between a load and a no-load mutual fund?

6 What is the difference between the way pooled investment schemes are organized in the USA and outside the USA?

7 How might restrictions on foreign ownership affect you as an investor?

8 How can restrictions on foreign ownership result in equities that have a claim on the same cash flow stream having different values?

9 What is the difference between a unit investment trust and a unit trust?

10 What are the advantages of depository receipts over owning the underlying security? Are there disadvantages?

■ Notes ■

1 ADR web sites include those of J. P. Morgan, http://www.adr.com/; the Bank of New York, http://www.bankofny.com/bus/Biisadr.htm; and Deutsche Morgan Grenfell, http://www.adr-dmg.com/deposit.htm.

2 For additional information see the Australian Stock Exchange web site, http://www.asx.com.au/derivatives/.

3 The Chicago Board of Trade also lists several other similar products, which can be reviewed at http://www.cboe.com/products/prodspec/txs-spec.htm.

4 For information about Goldman Sachs warrants see http://www.gs.com/warrants/main.ggi/english.

5 Gabelli Funds, Inc. provides a description of rights offerings and a discussion of its own rights offerings at http://www.gabelli.com/Gab_phtml/basics.html. Safeguard Scientifics, Inc. monitors US rights offerings and provides information at http://www.safeguard.com/ro.html.

6 In the USA, the certification services provided by an investment banker consist chiefly of meeting the due diligence requirement of section 11 of the Securities and Exchange Act of 1933. Included in this requirement is the expert certification of financial and legal information contained in the registration statement. Moreover, work by Beatty and Ritter (1986), Johnson and Miller (1988), and Carter and Manaster (1990) suggests that underwriter involvement in an equity issue can reduce the information asymmetry between the firm and investors. They further note that lower-quality firms tend to avoid the scrutiny of a public underwriter by using rights financing.

7 Bhagat (1983) presents the delay in the acquisition of equity funds and the uncertainty of offering success as costs associated with a rights issue. Heinkel and Schwartz (1986) recognize a distinction between an insured (standby) and an uninsured rights offering and introduce a standby agreement fee which serves as an additional cost. Heinkel and Schwartz also argue that the highest-quality firms incorporate a standby agreement in their rights offers that involves an exogenous fixed investigative cost to the underwriter. Intermediate-quality firms, however, simply use an uninsured rights offer.

8 Included among the studies that report no significant excess returns for underwritten offerings during either the pre- or post-offering period are Smith 1977, Mikkelson and Partch 1986, and Pettway and Radcliff 1985.

9 The two largest mutual fund groups in the USA are Fidelity Investments and Vanguard Group. You can obtain more information at web sites whose addresses are, respectively, http://www441.fidelity.com:80/ and http://www.vanguard.com/.

10 In the USA the Investment Company Institute provides a large amount of information about mutual funds in the USA, including statistics that show that the asset holdings of these funds total about 5,000 billion USD. The Institute's web address is http://www.ici.org/. AUTIF was formed in the UK in 1959 to act as a representative body for its members. It has more than 116 unit trust and investment fund managers as members, with nearly £100 billion funds under management, and represents more than 79 percent of the unit trust industry in the UK.

Its web address is http://preview.iii.co.uk/autif/. the AUTIF provides a glossary at http://preview.iii.co.uk/autif/gloss/. A site that provides free, daily comparative performance data and detailed information covering 600 UK investment trusts and closed-end offshore funds is http://www.trustnet.co.uk/. Web addresses of sites in other countries include Hong Kong Standard Tigernet, http://www.hkstandard.com/online/finance/007/mfunds/main.htm; Association of Unit Trusts and Investment Funds (UK), http://www.iii.co.uk/autif/about/; Investment Trust Association (Japan), http://www.highway.or.jp/toushin/index.htm.

11 Information on SPDRs, WEBS, and DIAMONDS can be obtained from the American Stock Exchange web address: http://www.amex.com/.

12 For information on Van Hedge Fund Advisors International, which tracks hedge funds, see http://www.vanhedge.com/indexes.html.

13 Country Risk Monitor ranks 80 countries for current and future business risk on the basis of the following criteria: (1) ability to pay foreign debt, (2) strength of trade performance, (3) government fiscal responsibility, (4) foreign indebtedness, (5) income per capita, (6) involvement in international trade. Their web address is http://www.bofa.com/econ_indicator/monitor.html. CMS's International Country Risk Guide covers 130 countries with country-by-country information on the comparative risk of lending or operating in each country. Their web address is http://www.textor.com/cms/dPRIC.html.

14 For a web site that deals with country risk and provides a comparison of various country risk services see http://stocks.miningco.com/library/weekly/aa081897.htm.

■ References ■

Asian Wall Street Journal 1995: Foreign holdings of Qantas shares may exceed government limits. Aug. 2, p. 18.

Bailey, Warren and Jagtiani, Julapa 1994: Foreign ownership restrictions and stock prices in the Thai capital market. *Journal of Financial Economics* 36, 57–87.

Beatty R. and Ritter, J. 1986: Investment banking, reputation and the underpricing of initial public offerings. *Journal of Financial Economics* 15, 213–32.

Bhagat, S. 1983: The effect of preemptive right amendments on shareholder wealth. *Journal of Financial Economics* 12, 287–310.

Bohren, Øyvind and Michalsen, Dag 1994: Corporate cross-ownership and market aggregates: Oslo Stock Exchange 1980–1990. *Journal of Banking and Finance* 18, 687–704.

Bohren, Øyvind, Eckbo, B. Espen and Michalsen, Dag 1997: Why underwrite rights offerings? Some new evidence. *Journal of Financial Economics* 46, 223–61.

Booth, J. R. and Smith, R. L. 1986: Capital raising, underwriting and the certification hypothesis. *Journal of Financial Economics* 15, 261–81.

Carter, R. and Manaster, S. 1990: Initial public offerings and underwriter reputation. *Journal of Finance* 45, 1045–67.

Eckbo, B. E. and Masulis, R. W. 1992: Adverse selection and the rights offer paradox. *Journal of Financial Economics* 32, 293–332.

Eckbo, B. E. and Varma, S. 1994: Managerial shareownership, voting power and cash dividend policy. *Journal of Corporate Finance* 1, 33–62.

Erb, Claude B., Harvey, Campbell R. and Viskanta, Tadas E. 1995: Country risk and global equity selection. *Journal of Portfolio Management* 21, 74–83.

Eun, Cheol S. and Janakiramanan, S. 1986: A model of international asset pricing with a constraint on the foreign equity ownership. *Journal of Finance* 41, 897–914.

Ferris, Stephen P., Noronha, Gregory and McInish, Thomas H. 1997: New equity offerings in Japan: an examination of theory and practice. *Journal of International Financial Markets, Institutions & Money* 7, 61–72.

Hansen, R. S. 1988: The demise of the rights issue. *Review of Financial Studies* 1, 289–309.

Hansen, R. S. and Pinkerton, J. M. 1982: Direct equity financing: a resolution of a paradox. *Journal of Finance* 37, 651–65.

Heinkel, R. and Schwartz, E. S. 1986: Rights versus underwritten offerings: an asymmetric information approach. *Journal of Finance* 41, 1–18.

Herman, E. S. 1981: *Corporate Control, Corporate Power*. New York: Cambridge University Press.

Hietala, Pekka T. 1989: Asset pricing in partially segmented markets: evidence from the Finnish market. *Journal of Finance* 44, 697–718.

Holderness, Clifford G., Kroszner, Randall S. and Sheehan, Dennis P. 1999: Were the good old days that good? Changes in managerial stock ownership since the great depression. *Journal of Finance* 44, 435–69.

Johnson, J. M. and Miller, R. E. 1988: Investment banker prestige and the underpricing of initial public offerings. *Financial Management* 17, 19–29.

Karolyi, Andrew 1998: Why do companies list shares abroad? A survey of the evidence and its managenal implications. *Financial Markets, Institutions and Instruments* 7, 1–60.

Klein, B. and Leffler, K. 1981: The role of market forces in assuring contractual performance. *Journal of Political Economy* 89, 615–41.

Kothare, Metta 1997: The effects of equity issues on ownership structure and stock liquidity: a comparison of rights and public offerings. *Journal of Financial Economics* 43, 131–48.

Kraus, A. and Stoll, H. R. 1972: Price impacts of block trading on the New York Stock Exchange. *Journal of Finance* 27, 569–88.

Lam Swee Sum 1995: Restrictions on foreign share ownership and its impact on market capitalisation [*sic*] and liquidity. *SES Journal* (Oct.), 4–11.

La Porta, Rafael, Lopez-De-Silanes, Florencio and Shleifer, Andrei 1999: Corporate ownership around the world. *Journal of Finance* 54, 471–517.

Loderer, C. and Zimmerman, H. 1988: Stock offerings in a different institutional setting: the Swiss case, 1973–1983. *Journal of Banking and Finance* 12, 353–78.

Logue, Dennis E. and Seward, James K. 1992: The time Warner rights offering: strategy, articulation and the destruction of shareholder value. *Financial Analysts Journal* 48, 37–45.

Lopez, Leslie 1995: Bank Bali's foreign shareholders hit by local investors seeking quick kill. *Asian Wall Street Journal*, July.

Madura, Jeff, Tucker, Alan L. and Wiley, Marilyn 1997: Factors affecting returns across stock markets. *Global Finance Journal* 8, 1–14.

Marsh, P. 1979: Equity rights issues and the efficiency of the UK stock market. *Journal of Finance* 34, 839–62.

Mikkelson, W. H. and Partch, M. M. 1986: Valuation effects of security offerings. *Journal of Financial Economics* 15, 31–60.

Modigliani, Franco and Miller, Merton H. 1958: The cost of capital, corporation finance and the theory of investment. *American Economic Review* 58, 261–97.

Pettway, R. H. and Radcliff, R. C. 1985: Impacts of new equity sales upon electric utility shares prices. *Financial Management* 14, 16–25.

Ranjan, Murli and Freidman, Joseph 1997: An examination or the impact of country risk on the international portfolio selection decision. *Global Finance Journal* 8, 55–70.

Redmayne, Julian n.d.: *Equity Warrants*. Nestor House, Playhouse Yard: Euromoney Books.

Smith, C. W. 1977: Alternative methods for raising capital: rights versus underwritten offerings. *Journal of Financial Economics* 5, 273–307.

Tokyo Stock Exchange 1994: *Fact Book*. Tokyo: TSE.

——1997: *Fact Book*. Tokyo: TSE.

——1998: *Fact Book*. Tokyo: TSE.

Vogel, Thomas T. Jr. 1995: Exchanges sprout in developing nations. *Wall Street Journal*, Nov. 14, pp. C1, C14.

Wahab, Mahmpud and Khandwala, Amit 1993: Why not diversify internationally with ADRs? *Journal of Portfolio Management* 19, 75–82.

Wall Street Journal 1987: Cheung Kong rights issues rejected by shareholders. Nov. 12.

CHAPTER SEVEN

Debt Securities

■ Key terms ■

Agency-type risk   risk that occurs when the value of a debt instrument diminishes due to the actions taken by an issuer.

Bankers' acceptance   a draft that orders a particular individual, business, or financial institution to pay a specified amount at a specified time that has been guaranteed (accepted) by a bank.

Basis point   0.01 percent of face value.

Bearer bonds   the identity of the owner is not recorded.

Book   the securities position owned by a firm.

Call money   loans that are repayable at the request of either party.

Commercial paper   a short-term unsecured promissory note issued by a corporation.

Conversion ratio   the number of shares received upon the conversion of a convertible bond.

Conversion value   the market value of the shares that would be received if the issue were converted immediately.

Convertible bonds   bonds that can be surrendered for equity in the issuer of the bonds.

Coupons   attachments to bearer bonds authorizing the payment of interest.

Debentures   unsecured corporate bonds.

Default risk   risk that the issuer will not pay the principal or interest when due or will fail to fulfill other terms of the indenture.

Discount   a bond selling below face value, or the sale of a non-interest-bearing instrument at less than face value.

Eurobonds   transnational bonds.

Exchangeable bonds   bonds that can be exchanged for the equity of a firm other than the issuer.

Face value   the principal payment due at the maturity of the bond issue, or, for bonds without a fixed maturity, their stated value.

Federal funds   deposits at the US Federal Reserve available for immediate transfer between financial institutions.

Fiscal agent   a financial institution that handles bond authentication and distribution and the duties of the paying agent.

Flat   a bond that does not trade plus accrued interest because the issuer has defaulted.

Foreign bonds   bonds issued in a country by nonresidents.

General obligation bonds   bonds backed by the "full faith and credit" of the issuer, so that the issuer, has promised to do whatever is necessary to repay the bonds.

Global offering   an initial offering of securities in more than one country at the same time.

Indenture   the agreement between the bondholders and the issuer of a bond.

Interest rate risk   risk due to fluctuations in the value of the instrument.

Islamic banking   banking practices that conform to the requirements of Islam.

Junk bonds   risky bonds with relatively low credit-worthiness.

Liquidity risk   risk that an issue cannot be sold readily at a price close to the current price.

Maturity value   the principal payment due at the maturity of the bond issue, or, for bonds without a fixed maturity, their stated value.

Par value   the principal payment due at the maturity of the bond issue, or, for bonds without a fixed maturity, their stated value.

Paying agent   a financial institution that receives the interest and principal payments from the issuer and pays them to the bondholders.

Plus accrued interest   the purchaser pays the seller the negotiated price plus interest from the last interest payment date to the settlement date.

Premium   a bond selling above face value.

Protective covenants   terms of a bond indenture that prohibit certain actions by the issuer.

Registered   the identity of the owner is known to the issuer.

Registrar   a firm, usually a financial institution, that maintains the ownership records of a securities issue.

Repurchase agreement (repos)   a contract in which one party sells securities to a counterparty in exchange for an immediate payment, with an agreement to repurchase the securities at a specified time and for a fixed price.

Revenue bonds   bonds whose interest and principal payments are contingent on having sufficient revenues from a specific revenue source.

Reverse repurchase agreement   a contract in which one party buys securities from a counterparty in exchange for an immediate payment, with an agreement to resell the securities at a specified time and for a fixed price.

Riba   interest.

Samurai **bonds**   bonds issued by non-Japanese in Japanese capital markets using Japanese investment bankers and denominated in JPY.

Security   an asset on which a particular creditor has a claim prior to the claims of other creditors.

Serial bonds   bond issues in which a portion of the bonds mature each year.

Shogun **bonds**   the market for USD-denominated bonds in Japan.

Sinking fund   a provision of a bond indenture calling for (1) the retirement of a portion of the bonds prior to maturity either by call or through open market purchases, or (2) the accumulation over the life of an issue of funds sufficient to retire the bonds at maturity.

Sovereign risk   risk that a country will not honor contractual obligations concerning its debt.

Straight-debt value of a convertible   the value of a convertible bond without the conversion feature.

Structured repo   the US term for repos with maturities longer than overnight.

Subordinated debentures   bonds having claims on a firm's assets and earnings that are inferior to those of other bonds.

Term bonds   a bond issue in which the entire principal must be repaid at a future date.

Term repo   the European term for repos with maturities longer than overnight.

Tri-party repo   a repo in which a third-party custodian effects the exchange of securities and cash on the purchase date and takes custody of the purchased securities.

Trustee   a representative of the bondholders who insures that the issuer fulfills its obligations.

Yankee bonds   domestic-currency-denominated nondomestic bonds.

Zero-coupon bonds   bonds that are initially sold at a discount and do not pay interest.

THIS CHAPTER is divided into three parts. In the first, we describe a number of issues related to debt securities, including:

- risks faced by debt investors
- the process of rating debt securities
- Islamic banking

Then, we describe the most common types of money market instruments, namely:

- government issues such as treasury bills
- negotiable certificates of deposit
- commercial paper
- repurchase agreements
- call money
- US federal funds
- bankers' acceptances

Next, we describe bond markets, including:

- bond characteristics
- convertible and exchangeable bonds
- how bonds are traded in secondary markets
- call features
- US municipal bonds
- global bond markets
- the use of auctions in connections with debt securities.

1. INTRODUCTION

It is common to classify debt securities as either money market instruments or capital market instruments. Money market instruments have a maturity of less than one year, whereas capital market instruments have longer maturities. The principal capital market debt instrument is the bond, a security issued by firms and governments evidencing debt and requiring that the issuer make one or more payments to the owner.[1]

2. ISSUES CONCERNING DEBT INSTRUMENTS

2.1. RISKS FACED BY DEBT INVESTORS

Investors in debt instruments face many types of risk:

The value of debt instruments varies inversely with interest rates. In other words, an increase in interest rates decreases the value of debt, while a decrease in interest rates increases the value of debt. **Interest rate risk** is the risk of capital loss due to fluctuations in interest rates.

Default risk is the risk that the issuer will not pay the principal or interest when due, or will fail to fulfill other terms of the indenture. Default risk is often highest at the maturity of an issue, because an issuer can make small interest payments but cannot make a large principal payment.

Liquidity risk is risk that an issue cannot be sold readily at a price close to the current price.

Agency-type risk is the risk that occurs when the value of a debt instrument diminishes due to the actions taken by an issuer. Issuers may undertake mergers that substantially change the industries in which a firm operates, increasing operating risk. In addition, the higher debt/equity ratios often associated with acquisitions may increase financial risk. Investors typically try to anticipate agency risks. To the extent that they are successful, investors can either write contracts that limit the actions of issuers to reduce agency risks or demand extra interest to compensate for these risks. Nevertheless, issuers sometimes take unforeseen actions, so that investors sustain a loss which they had not anticipated and for which they were not compensated. Box 7.1 describes an actual case in which agency risk led to capital losses for bondholders.

Sovereign risk is the risk that a country will not honor contractual obligations concerning its debt. Sovereign risk is unique, because there is generally no mechanism to force countries to fulfill their promises.

2.2. RATINGS

There are many debt issuers in the major capital markets, so most individual and institutional investors are not easily able to assess the quality of each issue. Because of this problem, there are a number of firms that specialize in helping investors assess the safety of debt

---

BOX 7.1
The Marriott Corporation

In 1993 the Marriott Corporation, which operated a variety of businesses related to the hotel industry, reorganized into two companies. Marriott International's businesses were involved in lodging and facilities management, food services, senior living services, and distribution. It had revenues of about 7.4 billion USD, operating profits of 314 million USD, and net income of 145 million USD. Host Marriott owned hotels and other real estate. It had revenues of 1.7 billion USD, operating profits of 148 million USD, and a net loss of 66 million USD. Management proposed spinning off Marriott International, which represented almost 80 percent of the value of the pre-spin-off firm, with Marriott Corporation retaining most of its debt. The projected interest coverage of Marriott Corporation would have declined from 2.6 times prior to the spin-off to 1.3 times after the spin-off. On the day that the spin-off was announced, Moody's downgraded the rating on the firm's senior debt.

Subsequently, the value of Marriott Corporation's common stock increased by 80.6 million USD, and the value of Marriott Corporation's debt declined by 194.6 million USD. Hence, the spin-off destroyed value overall, but there was a wealth transfer from the bondholders to the stockholders. Despite the fact that the bond indenture provided no protection against this type of reorganization, the bondholders filed a number of suits designed to stop the proposed spin-off. The bondholders were eventually successful in forcing Marriott to revise the terms of the proposed spin-off in a number of ways, including swapping the old bonds for new bonds with longer maturities and higher interest payments.

Source: Parrino 1997.

---

issues by assigning ratings.[2] The USSEC has designated four nationally recognized statistical rating organizations for rating all US corporate bond issues: Moody's, S&P, Fitch IBCA, and Duff & Phelps. Moody's began rating bonds in 1909, and S&P began in 1916. Both Moody's and S&P rate all taxable publicly issued bonds in the USA, whereas Fitch and Duff & Phelps provide ratings only when they are hired by the issuer. Several rating agencies specialize in particular industries. Thomson Bankwatch rates issues of financial institutions, and A. M. Best rates insurance companies. IBCA also specialized in the issues of financial institutions prior to its merger with Fitch to form Fitch ICBA.

In 1996 there were three rating agencies in Japan: Nippon Investors Services, Inc., Japan Credit Rating Agency, and Japan Bond Research Institute. The rating agencies provide a simple and easily understood symbol to show an issue's relative credit quality. Rating agencies may rate negotiable certificates of deposit and commercial paper as well as bonds. Debt issuers typically must pay to obtain a Japanese rating.

S&P rates bonds as AAA, AA, A, BBB, BB, B, CCC, and C with additional ratings grades for bonds with special characteristics. Rating categories A–CCC are further divided into categories 1–3. Table 7.1 lists Moody's and S&P's rating categories (Cantor and Packer 1996a). The first four categories are called "investment grade," and the three remaining categories are "speculative." These terms do not show whether these are good investments, since that judgment depends on factors such as the risk preferences of the investor and differences in expected returns from one instrument to another. An investment grade rating indicates that S&P has no reason to believe that payments will not be timely. The analysis considers the

Table 7.1 Rating symbols for long-term debt

Interpretation	Moody's	Standard and Poor's
INVESTMENT-GRADE RATINGS		
Highest quality	Aaa	AAA
High quality	Aa1	AA+
	Aa2	AA
	Aa3	AA–
Strong payment capacity	A1	A+
	A2	A
	A3	A–
Adequate payment capacity	Baa1	BBB+
	Baa2	BBB
	Baa3	BBB–
SPECULATIVE-GRADE RATINGS		
Likely to fulfill obligations, ongoing uncertainty	Ba1	BB+
	Ba2	BB
	Ba3	BB–
High-risk obligations	B1	B+
	B2	B
	B3	B–
Issues are in poor standing and may be in default	Caa1	CCC+
	Caa2	CCC
	Caa3	CCC–
Have extremely poor prospects	C1	CC
	C2	C
	C3	

Source: Compiled from http://www.moodys.com/ratings/ratdefs.htm#lttaxable and http://www.standardandpoors.com/ratings/corporates/index.htm

operating and financial risk of the firm, security provisions such as subordination of other debt or the pledging of collateral, and the rules of bankruptcy. In 1989 S&P began to rate bonds as to their protection from event risk. An example of event risk is the 1992 restructuring of Marriott Corporation, a firm owning a variety of businesses, including hotels and restaurants, into two separate entities. One held the business with the most favorable prospects. The second held the remaining businesses and was obligated for most of the firm's debt. Naturally, the bond's price declined as a result of the reorganization, resulting in an uncompensated transfer of wealth from the bondholders to the equity holders.

Bonds that have a speculative rating are called either "junk bonds" or, because of their high coupon rates or high current yields, "high yield bonds." Historically in the USA these bonds represented "fallen angels," bonds initially issued with a higher rating, but which had been downgraded because of poor performance. In 1976 Drexel Burnham Lambert, an investment bank, began to seek out firms to raise new funds using low-rated debt. At the same time Drexel began to develop a secondary market for these bonds. Initially, companies that offered new issues of junk bonds were companies that had previously used bank term loans and other similar sources of financing. By 1983 junk bonds were beginning to become an important source of financing for acquisitions. In the early 1990s there were many defaults of junk bonds, but the market subsequently recovered and remains a major sector of the US corporate bond market.

Hickman (1958) studied the efficacy of ratings in the USA in predicting subsequent default over the period 1900–43 and concluded that the record was remarkably good. Since the early 1970s interest rates have been more volatile, making it more difficult for many issuers to sustain their credit quality.

Rating agencies also rate countries or sovereign credits (see Cantor and Packer 1996b). These sovereign ratings are important, because countries are the largest issuers in the international capital markets. Moreover, rating agencies rarely assign a credit rating to a governmental entity or private company located in a country that is higher than the rating received by the country on its own debt.[3] As of September 1995 both Moody's and S&P's rated 49 countries. In a general sense these ratings measure the same thing as ratings of other issuers: safety of principal and interest payments. The agency examines the country's willingness and ability to honor its external obligations. In dealing with countries, willingness is especially important, because it is generally not possible for a citizen of one country to enforce a claim against another country. Economic self-interest is one of the most important factors in encouraging countries to pay their debts. Countries that have a history of paying their debts generally have low borrowing costs and easier access to credit markets. A stable government with a history of smooth transfer of power is desirable. Relations with other nations and with the country's own citizens are also important. Important economic factors include trends in economic growth, diversification of the economy, the current level of external debt, and liquidity, including balance-of-payments considerations.

2.3. ISLAMIC BANKING

Many practices in modern banking violate commandments of the Shari'ah, Islamic law. The holy book of Islam, the Qur'an, forbids the charging of **riba**, or interest. The predominant view among Islamic scholars is that the prohibition against riba bans not just usury, but also the charging of any fixed or predetermined payment beyond the principal. There is a growing movement to develop alternative banking practices that conform to the requirements of the Shari'ah. Banking practices that conform to the requirements of Islam are known as **Islamic banking**. The actual implementation and practices allowed differ from country to country, but share many elements. Lenders must share in the risks as well as the rewards of activities financed by loans. Hence, depositors are not promised fixed returns, but share in the profits and losses of the bank. The banks, in turn, do not make loans requiring the payment of fixed interest. Instead they enter into various types of partnerships and joint ventures with their clients.[4] According to Bilal (1999), Islamic "instruments give more importance to the valuation of anticipated profits than to collateral." Dow Jones sponsors the Dow Jones Islamic Market Index, which includes 600 companies from 30 countries (including the USA). Companies included in the index do not provide goods and services that violate Shari'ah law. These forbidden products include alcoholic beverages, pork, and tobacco, and forbidden services include those provided by defense companies, hotels, casinos, and non-Islamic financial concerns. The index also excludes companies with high debt ratios. Not all countries or Islamic investors eschew all these goods and services. Cigarette companies trade on the Jakarta Stock Exchange, and casino stocks trade on the Kuala Lumpur Stock Exchange.

3. MONEY MARKETS

All modern financial centers have money markets that allow financial and nonfinancial institutions to obtain funds to meet short-term liquidity needs and to invest surplus funds on a short-term basis. In the countries with the largest financial centers, such as the USA and Japan, the money markets include instruments denominated both in local currency and also in other major currencies.

3.1. DOMESTIC MONEY MARKET INSTRUMENTS

There are many types of money market instruments traded in financial markets throughout the world. Similar types of instruments are traded in major financial centers, but the particular instruments that are most actively traded depend largely on government policies, regulations, and taxes, or on historical developments within each country. There have been active money markets in the USA for many years. In the USA the principle wholesale interbank market is the Federal funds market, in part because there are no reserve requirements for Federal funds. While there has been a small money market in Japan for many years, its size and diversity have grown rapidly since 1985, when the Bank of Japan began to establish new markets, such as the market for commercial paper, and to relax requirements concerning denominations, maturities, and market participation. The principle interbank market for JPY in Japan is the call market. In Australia a change in Australian reserve requirements in 1988 resulted in an increase in the usage of negotiable certificates of deposit as the primary money market instrument and a corresponding reduction in bankers' acceptances.

Many countries have active markets for short-term debt instruments. More than 500 billion USD of US Treasury bills are outstanding. These bills have a maturity of 1 year when they are issued and are sold on a 360-day discount price without a coupon. The minimum purchase amount is 10,000 USD, with multiples of 5,000 USD thereafter.

There is a large over-the-counter secondary market in US Treasury bills (see Fleming and Remolona 1997). In the USA there are about 1,700 registered US government securities broker-dealers, including 250 depository institutions and 1,450 securities firms, but most trading volume is accounted for by 13 primary dealers. Brokers handle much of the trading even between dealers. Brokers act only as agents and allow the dealers to trade with each other anonymously. Brokers provide dealers with screens for disseminating quotes and trading information. Dealer spreads for the most active 5-year notes are less than two basis points. Broker commissions are negotiable but may range from 12.50 USD per 1 million USD of 3-month treasury notes to about 40 USD per 1 million USD for notes and bonds.

The dealers trade 22–3 hours each day, 5 days a week, but 95 percent of the trading takes place during New York trading hours.

There are also active markets in Tokyo and London. The trading day begins in Tokyo at about 7:00 a.m. Tokyo time. Many institutions holding inventories of US Treasury bills pass their **book**, the record of and responsibility for securities positions, to London at about 16:00 Tokyo time. These positions are then managed in London until near the end of the trading day, say 13:00 London time (8:00 a.m. New York time), when the book is passed to New York. At the end of the trading day in New York, the book is passed back to Japan, and the cycle starts again.

The Japanese Treasury bill market was established in 1986, when bills of 6 months' maturity were issued. Primary issues are in minimum denominations of 10 million JPY, and purchase of these issues is restricted to financial institutions, insurance companies, and securities companies. In addition, corporations, but not individuals, can participate in the secondary market.

3.1.1. Negotiable certificates of deposit

Negotiable certificates of deposit (CD) are instruments issued by commercial banks evidencing time deposits. CDs are traded domestically within many countries and in international markets. The instruments first began trading in 1961, when the First National City Bank of New York announced that it would begin issuing negotiable certificates of deposit in large denominations and that a major US government securities dealer had agreed to make a market in these instruments. Other large US banks quickly followed City Bank's lead. Banks use this market to purchase funds to finance loan and investment demand. An active secondary market quickly developed and flourishes today. This market allows corporations and others with large amounts of short-term funds to buy these negotiable certificates of deposit and resell them after a short holding period.

Interest rates increased in the first part of the 1960s, so US banks could no longer issue CDs, because market interest rates rose above the rates that depository institutions were permitted to offer at that time.[5] To avoid these ceilings, US banks began issuing CDs in London in 1966. These instruments allow banks to purchase deposits that can be used to fund lending to customers. They proved so popular that banks in other countries began issuing their own CDs. In Japan any bank that is eligible to accept deposits can issue certificates of deposit. Maturities range from 2 weeks to 2 years. British banks began issuing GBP CDs in 1968, and Singapore and Hong Kong followed with local currency CDs in 1975 and 1977, respectively.

3.1.2. Commercial paper

Commercial paper is a short-term unsecured promissory note issued by a corporation. Commercial paper sold at a discount through dealers makes it possible for nonfinancial corporations to raise funds directly from investors without going through banks. Firms with the highest credit ratings issue most commercial paper, so no security is required. **Security** refers to assets on which a particular creditor has a claim prior to the claims of other creditors. Firms that do not have high credit ratings themselves may be able to transfer sufficient assets to a subsidiary to give it a high credit rating. The subsidiary can then issue commercial paper. Most commercial paper is sold through dealers, who purchase the paper from

201

the issuer and resell it to investors. Dealer fees amount to about 10 basis points per year, or about 1 basis point for 36 days. The largest commercial paper dealers are investment banking firms such as Merrill Lynch and Goldman Sachs and investment banking subsidiaries of commercial banks such as Citicorp and Bankers Trust, a US bank specializing in derivatives. Large banks obtain funds at rates comparable to the commercial paper rate. To obtain a profit, the banks must recover their cost of funds plus operating expenses and profits. The growth of the commercial paper market demonstrates that many firms can obtain funds more cheaply by directly accessing the money markets than through the banking system.

Only very large firms issue commercial paper directly without going through dealers. In the USA, finance subsidiaries of major durable goods manufacturers use commercial paper to raise funds to finance the promissory notes received from their customers when they buy new automobiles and other company products. The three largest issuers of commercial paper in the USA are General Motors Acceptance Corporation, General Electric Capital, and Ford Motor Credit. There are about 125 direct issuers of commercial paper. Distribution costs, including agent fees, rating fees, backup credit fees, and the like, might amount to only 15 basis points for larger commercial paper issuers. At the time it is initially placed, commercial paper normally carries maturities of from 30 to 270 days. Maturities of longer than 270 days must be registered with the USSEC, which makes it too costly and cumbersome for issuing firms. Settlement for commercial paper transactions is on the same day as the transaction, and more than 40 percent of the commercial paper issued in the USA is in book-entry form.

Borrowers frequently issue new paper to pay off their maturing issues. Credit lines from banks may be required to insure that there will be sufficient liquidity if the firm cannot refinance maturing paper by selling new commercial paper. This occurred in 1970 when the default of Penn Central Railroad on 82 million USD of commercial paper temporarily disputed the market. The bank lines that firms use to insure liquidity do not guarantee the credit-worthiness of the issuer, and these letters of credit generally have "material adverse conditions" clauses which allow them to be withdrawn if the issuer's financial condition changes materially. When Mercury Finance was accused of falsifying its books and defaulted on 19 million USD of commercial paper, its banks withdrew lines of credit of more than 500 million USD (*Wall Street Journal Interactive Edition* 1997).

In the USA companies without the highest credit ratings have been able to issue commercial paper using several methods to provide credit enhancements. The issuer can pay a fee to a bank to obtain a letter of credit that cannot be withdrawn. Lenders then focus on the credit-worthiness of the bank. Since most US banks do not have a sufficiently high credit rating to issue these letters of credit, most are issued by non-US banks. Insurance firms also issue indemnity bonds that permit the issuance of letters of credit.

The US commercial paper market is also open at least to some extent to non-US firms. In mid-1998, Bank America arranged a $200 million USD commercial paper program for a wholly owned subsidiary of China National Metals & Minerals Import & Export Corporation, China's main company for importing and exporting metals and minerals for the last 48 years. Bank of America issued a letter of credit to support the commercial paper program.[6]

While the US commercial paper market is the largest, there are also active commercial paper markets in other countries. There is an active commercial paper market in Japan.[7] The minimum denomination is 100 million JPY, and maturities range from 2 weeks to 9 months. To be eligible for issuing commercial paper, companies must meet strict financial requirements related to net worth and liquidity ratios. More than 500 firms are eligible to issue commercial paper, but fewer than half of these have done so.

Some US firms issue commercial paper in the USA and at the same time issue USD-denominated commercial paper in the Euro commercial paper market. Most Euro commercial paper is denominated in USD, though there are also significant amounts denominated in other currencies, such as the ECU and JPY. Maturities in the Euro market are typically longer than in the USA, say 60–180 days, and because of the longer maturities there is a more active secondary market. The credit quality of the Euro market has been lower than that of the US market, and this has been reflected in a higher level of defaults.

3.1.3. Repurchase agreements

In a **repurchase agreement** (repo) one party sells securities to a counterparty in exchange for an immediate payment, with an agreement to repurchase the securities at a specified time and for a fixed price. A **reverse repurchase agreement** involves an initial purchase with an agreement for a subsequent sale. The economic effect of a repurchase agreement is the same as that of a collateralized loan, but there may be important legal differences, if, say, one party files for bankruptcy protection. In evaluating repos, it is important to look at both the quality of the securities that are the subject of the repo and the credit standing of the counterparty. Due to regulatory and legal factors that encourage repos, the French repo market was the second largest (after the USA) in 1996. French repos use a floating rate index, which is a weighted average of overnight interbank rates published daily by the bank of France. There is also an active market in transforming floating rates into fixed rates, and vice versa. For many years the Japanese government bond market was inefficient due to lack of an active repo market. But, beginning in 1995, the government has encouraged the development of a repo market. There is an active repo market in Japan (called *gensaki*) which is open to corporations, but not individuals. The minimum transaction size is 10 million JPY, but the typical transaction size is 100 million JPY. In Germany securities lending and repo transactions are made in all DEN-denominated government securities, Euros, bank bonds, and government bonds of OECD countries. Contracts are most often for 1 week to 3 months.

Historically, most repos have been overnight. If a trader buys an option and hedges it by buying the underlying bond, a repo can be used to finance the bond purchase. The advantage of a repo over straight borrowing is that the repo is collateralized, providing protection from counterparty credit risk. More recently, an active market for longer-maturity repos, called **structured** (in the USA) or **term** (in Europe) **repos**, has emerged. Because of the longer-term risk exposure, the structured repo market is limited to firms rated double A or above.

A growing sector of the repo market is the **tri-party repo**, in which a third-party custodian effects the exchange of securities and cash on the purchase date and takes custody of the purchased securities. The custodian transfers securities that have been agreed to as acceptable to the buyer into a segregated account with title vested in the buyer. The custodian provides services such as daily mark-to-market, cross-currency valuations, and determinations as to whether margins are in excess of deficit. The custodian unwinds the transaction on the repurchase date. A tri-party repo addresses an important issue of risk, in that in standard or "hold in custody" repos, the buyer relies on the seller to protect its interest in the collateral. Tri-party repos relieve the seller of clerical and custodial duties.

3.1.4. Call money

Call money refers to loans that are repayable at the request of either party. There is an active call market for short-term financing in Japan. All transactions must be handled by one of the nine companies licensed to do so by the Ministry of Finance. Both secured and unsecured transactions are possible. Secured transactions require collateral securities that are eligible for pledging with the Bank of Japan. These securities include government bonds, financing bills, government guaranteed bonds, and bank debentures. The maturities for the secured transactions range from overnight up to 6 days. Unsecured transactions were first permitted in 1985, and the value of unsecured transactions now exceeds that of the secured transactions. In the USA, brokers' call money loans were the chief money market instruments of interest to banks. In this type of loan the broker-dealer retains title to the securities but transfers them to the lender or the lender's agent as collateral for a loan. Most such loans are payable on demand. In the USA call money provides an important source of funding for brokerage firms supplying money to their customers for margin purchases. Margin customers sign an agreement allowing the brokerage firms to pledge the customers' securities as collateral for these loans. Rates on call money are reported each day in the *Wall Street Journal*.

3.1.5. Federal funds

In the USA, the Monetary Control Act of 1980 requires banks and a number of other depository institutions that are insured by the US government to maintain reserves representing specified percentages of their deposit liabilities. These reserves may be held in cash, but are most commonly held as deposits in a Federal Reserve bank. These deposits at the Federal Reserve, called **Federal funds**, are available for immediate transfer between financial institutions. Deposits in Federal Reserve banks earn no interest, so banks have an incentive to maintain only the required deposit level. Banks can also borrow Federal funds from other banks that have excess funds. Loans of Federal funds between financial institutions are most commonly for 1 day – i.e., overnight – and can be made either directly from one institution to another or through brokers. No reserve requirements apply to these loans. In some cases the loans are secured using US government securities.

3.1.6. Bankers' acceptances

A bankers' acceptance is a bill of exchange, a draft that orders a particular individual, business, or financial institution to pay a specified amount at a specified time. When the drawee, the person required to make the payment, acknowledges the obligation by writing "Accepted" with appropriate signatures on the front, the draft becomes an acceptance. Typically, banks accept drafts on behalf of their customers, after which the instrument is called a **bankers' acceptance**. Bankers' acceptances usually arise from letters of credit in foreign trade. An importer in New York might arrange for the delivery of goods from an exporter in Brazil. After satisfying a US bank of its credit-worthiness, the importer obtains a letter of credit from the US bank in favor of the exporter, authorizing the exporter to draw a draft upon the US bank in payment for the goods. The draft may call for payment, say, 90 days after arrival of the goods in New York. The importer sends this letter of credit to the exporter. After shipping the goods, the exporter can **discount** the draft with its local bank and receive immediate payment. The exporter's bank will send the draft along with the shipping documents to its correspondent bank in the USA, and the correspondent bank will present the draft for acceptance. Once accepted, the shipping documents are released, and the importer can claim the shipment. The exporter's bank may instruct the correspondent bank to hold the acceptance for it as an investment or to sell the acceptance in the secondary market and credit its account. In any event, the ultimate owner of the instrument is the party financing the transaction.

3.2. NONDOMESTIC MONEY MARKETS

The Eurocurrency market comprises all bank deposits and loans in any nondomestic currency (see Melnik and Plaut 1991). Two large parts of the market are bank deposits in USD held outside the USA and bank deposits in JPY held outside Japan. The terminology derives from the origins of these markets in Europe, though these markets are now worldwide. About two-thirds of Eurocurrency activity is in USD. Eurocurrency deposits are actively traded mostly through brokers. Eurodollar certificates of deposit are commonly available in maturities of 30 days to 1 year, although shorter or longer maturities can also be negotiated. USD funds clear through CHIPS, whereas communications are typically through SWIFT.

4. BONDS

4.1. BOND CHARACTERISTICS

4.1.1. How bonds work

A bond is a security in which an issuer contractually agrees to make one or more payments to an investor. The agreement between the bondholder and the issuer is called the **indenture**. Some countries allow **bearer bonds**, in which the identity of the owner is not recorded. About 3 percent of Japanese government bonds are in bearer form. The remaining 97 percent are **registered** – i.e., the identify of the owner is known. The institution maintaining the ownership records is called the **registrar**. In Japan the Bank of Japan acts as registrar. Some countries allow the principal to be registered, while the interest is paid using bearer coupons. Historically, in the USA bonds of states and subdivisions of states issued bonds in bearer form, but now all new issues must be in registered form. If a bond is registered, the issuer can pay interest and principal payments directly to the owner, though both the issuer and the owner are likely to act through agents such as banks and brokerage firms. If a bond is held in bearer form, **coupons** are attached to the bond. These are detached and submitted by the owner for payment when due.

Because bondholders are dispersed and do not typically know each other's identity, a **trustee** is appointed to represent the bondholders. It is the duty of the trustee to enforce the term of the indenture. Besides specifying the rate and dates of interest payments and the timing of principal repayment, bonds often have **protective covenants** that prohibit certain actions by the issuer. The issuer may be prohibited from issuing additional debt, especially debt that has a superior claim, or from paying dividends unless specified financial conditions are met.

We use the terms **face value**, **par value**, and **maturity value** interchangeably to mean the principal payment due at the maturity of the bond issue. In rare cases bonds do not have fixed maturities, in which case the face value is the stated value of the bond. The individual bonds within a given issue may all have the same face value, or they may have different face values. Further, the typical amount of face value differs from bond type to bond type and from country to country. Therefore, for convenience, we take the face value of each bond to be 1,000 units of local currency. Prices for bonds are usually stated in percent of face value, so a price of 94 is 94 percent of the face value of the bond. Interest rates are also often stated in percent of face value at an annualized rate. A 5 percent bond pays 5 percent of face value each year, even though actual payments might occur semiannually or quarterly. A **basis point** is 0.01 percent of face value. If a bond market yield increases by 50 basis points from 5 percent, the new yield is 5.5 percent. A bond selling at a discount is selling below face value, while a bond selling at a **premium** is selling above face value.

Most bonds are **term bonds**, in which the entire principal must be repaid at a future date. Typical maturities of bonds vary substantially from country to country. In the USA, both the US government and corporations commonly issue bonds with short maturities of 1 or more years and with longer maturities of 30 years or more. Issues with maturities of 100 years were common in the USA in the nineteenth century, and firms such as International Business Machines and Walt Disney issued 100-year bonds in the early 1990s. But in Japan bonds with a maturity of 20 years are called "super long-term coupon bonds" (Yamamoto 1993).

4.1.2. Interest payments

Most bonds pay interest either annually or semiannually. Typically, German government bonds pay interest on the same day each year (see Urich 1991), on either the 1st or 20th of the month (or the next business day if it is a holiday). In the USA, bonds typically pay interest every 6 months, but the dates on which interest is paid vary from issue to issue. Corporate bonds often have a **paying agent**, a bank that has the responsibility of receiving interest and principal payments from the issuer and disbursing them to the bond owners. Most commonly, the interest payments on bonds are set at the time of issue. Floating rate bonds with interest payments determined subsequent to the issue are becoming more common. In the early 1990s the German government issued three floating rate bonds with quarterly coupon payments of 3-month LIBOR or 3-month DMG minus 20 basis points. LIBOR is the London Interbank Offer Rate, the rate at which funds are exchanged between banks in London. **Zero-coupon bonds** are sold initially at a discount and do not pay interest. Zero-coupon bonds may present a problem for US taxpayers, because the US government taxes part of the discount each year, even though it is not received until maturity.

4.1.3. Call features

There are two distinct types of bond calls. One involves the call of an entire issue, whereas the other involves a call of only selected bonds. Commonly an entire issue cannot be called until several years after issuance. The call price may be par, but if the issue has not been outstanding too long, it is likely to be greater than par. The floating rate bonds issued by the German government were callable in one case 2 years after issuance and in another 5 years after issuance. No other German government bonds have call features. Issuers prefer callable bonds, because they can refinance if interest rates decline. Investors take the opposite view. Sometimes bonds are callable under certain circumstances but not under others. An issue might be callable in case of a merger, but not simply to take advantage of lower interest rates. Also, calls of an entire issue, which we are discussing here, are typically different from calls for sinking fund purposes described below.

A second type of call involving only a part of an issue is designed to prevent "crisis at maturity." If at maturity there happens to be a recession or crisis, such as a war, it might be difficult to refinance the issue. Bond professionals have developed several ways of dealing with the potential for a crisis at maturity. One approach is to have a **sinking fund** provision. Historically, in the USA, issuers would simply buy US government bonds or similar instruments each year, so that by the time the bonds matured, the bond portfolio would be of sufficient size to retire the debt. Now the typical procedure is for the issuer to repurchase a portion of the issue each year. If the bonds are selling at a discount, the issuer simply buys the bonds in the open market. Otherwise the bonds can usually be called at face value. The specific bonds called are determined by lot, so that an investor holding a portfolio of the bonds could expect to have a number of bonds called each year equal to a pro rata portion of each year's call.

4.2. BEYOND PLAIN VANILLA BONDS

4.2.1. Convertible and exchangeable bonds

Some bonds can be surrendered to the issuer in return for equity. **Exchangeable bonds** can be exchanged for the equity of a firm other than the issuer. Dart & Kraft has an issue that can be exchanged for shares of Minnesota Mining and Manufacturing. General Cinema has an issue that can be exchanged for shares of both R. J. Reynolds and Sea–Land Corporation. **Convertible bonds** can be surrendered for equity in the issuer of the bonds. Alaska Air Group has an issue maturing in 2014 with 6.875 percent coupons convertible into 29.762 shares of common stock for each 1,000 USD of face value. 29.762 is the **conversion ratio**, which is the number of shares received upon conversion. The conversion price is 1,000/29.762 = 33.60 USD per share. Suppose that the market price of the underlying shares is 15.875 USD. The **conversion value** is the market value of the shares that would be received if the issue were immediately converted, i.e., in this case 29.762 × 15.875 = 472.50. Stated as a percent of face value the conversion value is 47.25. The bond's

straight-debt value of a convertible is its value were it not convertible. In determining the straight value, factors such as the credit rating of the issuer and the amount of debt senior to this issue must be taken into account. One way to determine the straight value is to examine the value of comparable nonconvertible bonds. We obtained a straight value of 78 for this bond from the Value Line Convertibles Survey.

The minimum value of a convertible bond is the greater of its (1) conversion value or (2) straight value. Thus, since 78 is greater than 47.25, the minimum value of this Alaska Air bond is 78. The actual market price of this bond was 85.

4.2.2. Secured bonds and debentures

Another way of classifying corporate bonds is by the type of collateral offered. In the USA, mortgage bonds have a claim on specific assets of the firm, with first mortgage bonds having a superior claim to second mortgage bonds, and so forth. Unsecured corporate bonds are called **debentures**. Debentures can also be issued with varying degrees of seniority. **Subordinated debentures** have an inferior claim to interest and principal payments. In Japan, mortgage bonds are issued under the Secured Bond Trust Law, and there are 19 valid types of mortgages, including mortgages on real estate and on the general assets of the firm. General mortgage bonds have been issued by utilities such as Nippon Telegraph and Telephone Company. Both nonfinancial and financial corporations are allowed to issue debentures in Japan.

4.2.3. Index bonds

In 1997, the US government auctioned its first issue of inflation-adjusted bonds. The issue comprised 7 billion USD of 10-year notes. The securities carry a stated rate of interest that does not change over the life of the issue. The principal value is adjusted semiannually for inflation by multiplying the initial face value by an index ratio. The index used is the US City Average All Items Consumer Price Index for All Urban Consumers published by the US Department of Labor (CPI). The ratio is calculated by dividing the CPI on the original issue date by its value on a given valuation date. The inflation adjustment to the principal is not payable until maturity, at which time the holder will receive the greater of the inflation-adjusted principal or the initial par value. Semiannual interest payments are a fixed percentage of the adjusted principal, so the interest payment changes to reflect inflation.

4.2.4. US municipal bonds

In the USA, issues of any state or any entity created by a state (such as cities, counties, school districts, water districts, airport authorities, etc.) are called municipal bonds. Interest payments on municipal bonds are generally exempt from US federal income tax. **General obligation bonds** are backed by the "full faith and credit" of the issuer. In other words, the issuer agrees to do what is necessary to repay the bonds. States, cities, counties, and the like must continue to operate even if they cannot pay their debts. So remedies in the case of default may be painful for the debt holders.

In addition to general obligation bonds, municipalities issue **revenue bonds**, whose interest and principal payments are contingent on having sufficient revenues from a specific revenue source. These bonds are used to finance many kinds of facilities, including roads,

---

BOX 7.2
Washington Public Power Supply System

The Washington Public Power Supply System, known as Woops, initiated work on five nuclear power plants with an initial projected cost of about 8 billion USD. Each plant was financed separately, and the financing for plants 1, 2, and 3 was guaranteed by a US government agency. The first three plants were almost complete when Woops announced that its funds were insufficient to complete the projects. Moreover, Woops decided to abandon plants 4 and 5, which had already cost more than 2 billion USD, because they had become uneconomic. The bondholders for plants 4 and 5 expected to receive payment from 88 utilities that had entered into contracts with Woops to pay for the plants, whether or not they received any electricity. But Washington State's highest court ruled that these contracts were unenforceable, because the utilities lacked the authority to enter into the contracts. As a result of this decision, Woops defaulted, becoming the largest municipal default in US history.

(For additional information see Seligman 1989 and Sitzer, Noe, and Perko 1994.)

---

bridges, tunnels, airports, and utilities such as sewers, electric distribution, water, etc. In some cases specific tax revenues are pledged to pay off the issue. The State of Alabama pledged its sales tax revenue to pay some of its bond issues. These bonds were given a high rating, because the safety of the revenue was high, and the size of the revenue in relation to the issue size was also high.

In the USA, municipal bonds deal with the potential for crisis at maturity in another way. Municipal bonds are generally not term bonds. Instead they issue **serial bonds**, in which a portion of the bonds mature each year. In other words, if an issue of 20 million USD is sold in say 2000, some of the issue will mature in 2001, some in 2002, and so forth. Investors can purchase bonds with a maturity that matches their investment horizon. Banks typically purchase the shorter maturities, whereas individuals or other investors who are fully taxed for income tax purposes purchase the longer maturity. Box 7.2 describes the largest default of municipal bonds in US history.

4.2.5. Catastrophe bonds

Property insurance companies may face unacceptably large losses from the occurrence of a major disaster. Historically, they have turned to reinsurance companies to underwrite the portion of the risk that they do not wish to bear. Lack of adequate capital within the reinsurance industry has led to efforts to develop alternative sources of risk protection relying on the capital markets. There have been several issues of short-term (5–11 months) catastrophe-linked bonds in the USA, but the market is growing, and market participants forecast that as much as 2 billion USD of catastrophe bonds will be sold in 1998. USAA issued 50 million USD of bonds through Merrill Lynch.[8] The bonds had a maturity of 6 months and paid interest of 300 basis points over LIBOR. The bondholders risked loss of principal if USAA experienced losses of over 1 billion USD from August 1996 through July 1997. Goldman Sachs and Co. is underwriting a Tokio Marine & Fire Insurance Co. issue of 10-year bonds whose interest payments are tied to whether and to what extent an earthquake damages Tokyo. Bondholders receive premiums collected by Tokio Marine, which could provide a yield of 400–500 basis points over LIBOR. If an earthquake occurs, the bondholders could lose their principal.[9]

4.3. BOND MARKETS

4.3.1. Trading bonds

Most secondary market trading of bonds is in the over-the-counter market. In the USA, there is almost no trading of either government or corporate bonds on exchanges. Seventy-five percent of *Bundesobligationen*, 5-year notes issued by the Federal Republic of Germany, are traded over-the-counter. About 95 percent of secondary market trading in Japanese government bonds takes place over-the-counter.

There are different ways of handling interest when trading bonds. Most often bonds trade **plus accrued interest**. The buyer pays the agreed-upon price plus accrued interest from the last interest payment to the trade settlement date. Then the buyer receives interest from the last interest payment date to the current interest payment date from the issuer. Netting the interest paid from the interest received leaves the bondholder with the correct amount of interest. There are exceptions to this way of trading. German government bonds trade this way most of the time, but the method of trading changes near interest payment dates. Near a coupon payment date, an ex-coupon date is established. A bond that trades and settles in the ex-coupon period trades with negative accrued interest. In other words, the seller retains the coupon and receives the purchase price less interest from the settlement date to the next interest payment date. Trades made before the ex-date that settle after the ex-date can be made with either positive or negative accrued interest. Most international investors prefer to settle this latter type of trade on a negative interest basis, to avoid risk due to failure of the seller to remit the interest payment when received. Defaulted bonds are another exception to the practice of trading bonds plus accrued interest. Bonds that are in default may be traded **flat**, so that only the agreed-upon price is exchanged. All interest payments paid by the issuer after the settlement date, including any back interest, are the property of the buyer.

4.3.2. Global markets

It is now common for issuers to raise funds in multiple countries. Historically, a company headquartered in one country might sell bonds in another. A more recent trend has been for a firm to offer its bonds in more than one country simultaneously. These are called **global offerings** (Karmin and Zuckerman 1998; Gowland 1990). Another recent innovation has been the issuance of bonds with the principle payable in one currency and the interest in another.

Bonds issued in a country by nonresidents are called **foreign bonds**. One part of this market is for domestic-currency-denominated nondomestic bonds. Countries often make a distinction between domestic and nondomestic bond issues in terms of factors such as regulatory requirements and taxes. There may be differences in who can purchase the bonds, in the sizes of the issues that are allowed, and in information-reporting requirements. After World War II many nonresidents issued bonds in the USA. These bonds are called **Yankee bonds**. In recent years the market share of these USD-denominated bonds has declined.

The largest market for foreign bonds is Switzerland. This does not mean that the Swiss are the largest holders of these bonds, but simply that more of these bonds are denominated in SWF than in other currencies. Since the SWF is a stable currency, issuers and investors might prefer to issue bonds in SWF rather than in their own currency. Nonresidents issue bonds in the Japanese capital markets using Japanese investment bankers and denominating the bonds in JPY. These bonds are called *samurai* **bonds** (Packer and Reynolds 1997). The Asian Development Bank issued the first samurai bonds in 1970.[10] The International Bank for Reconstruction and Development (i.e., the World Bank) issued *samurai* bonds in 1971,[11] and Australia followed in 1972. The first corporation to issue these bonds was Sears in 1979. There are also important markets for nondomestic bonds denominated in local currency in the UK, Germany, and the Netherlands.

Another type of foreign bond is the bond issued in a country by nonresidents, but in a nonlocal currency. The market for USD-denominated bonds in Japan (*shogun* bonds) began in 1985 with an issue by the World Bank. The first private issuer of *shogun* bonds was Southern California Edison Company in 1985. An easing of Japanese government regulations for larger issuers helped the growth of the market. The US government also allowed US corporations to issue bonds outside the USA in bearer form.

Eurobonds are transnational issues typically underwritten by an international investment banking syndicate. Most Eurobonds are in bearer form, with interest paid annually. Eurobonds are generally free of withholding tax, but if tax is withheld, the issuer has to increase the interest payment to offset the tax. Some Eurobond issues have a paying agent and a trustee. The paying agent receives the interest and principal payments from the issuer and pays them to the bondholders. The trustee represents the bondholders and makes sure that the issuer fulfills its obligations. Other issues have only a **fiscal agent**, who handles bond authentication and distribution and the duties of the paying agent. The fiscal agent is a representative of the issuer. Even though Eurobonds may be issued entirely outside the country in whose currency the bonds are denominated, the country in whose currency the bonds are denominated can still exercise control over the issues in a number of ways. One is by restricting access to its markets for other issues of uncooperative investment bankers. Since most currency transactions are settled in the domestic market for that currency, a government can effectively block Eurobond issues through currency regulations.

4.3.3. Auctions

Auctions are used in a variety of ways in connection with debt instruments. Probably the most common use is in the issuance of securities. In the USA, as well as in other countries, Treasury bills are typically issued through an auction procedure. Auctions have also been used in the repurchase of securities. Box 7.3 provides details concerning auctions.

5. SUMMARY

The market for fixed-income securities is very important and includes the markets for both private and governmental debt. The market is much larger than the market for equities. The two major segments of the market are the money market, which encompasses debt instruments with maturities of less than 1 year, and the capital market, which includes debt instru-

BOX 7.3
Auctions

Cassady (1967) defines an auction as a system of allocating property "based on price making by competition of buyers for the right to purchase." Auctions may be useful in a variety of circumstances and often offer more speedy sales than alternates. Sometimes the purchaser has a more accurate assessment of the value of an item than the seller, especially for unique items such as antiques, art, and rare coins, books, stamps, and wine. The use of an auction may also solve agency problems, by making it more difficult for the seller's agent to collude with the buyer.

For simplicity, Rasmusen (1989) categorizes auctions as either private-value or common-value. In private-value auctions each participant knows his or her own valuation with certainty, but may not know the valuations of other participants. Such a circumstance may come about when individuals are buying for their own consumption or pleasure and not for resale. In its strict form, if the auction is private-value, individuals do not change their assessment of value given knowledge of others' proposed bids, though they may change their bidding strategy. By contrast, for common-value auctions, each participant uses their own private information to estimate a true price. Knowledge of others' assessments would be useful in assessing and validating one's private information. In this type of auction one's assessment is based on the asset's resale value rather than one's own internal assessment. Auctions for US Treasury bills are common-value auctions, since after the auction everyone agrees that the market price is the true value. Rasmusen (1989) further considers three common types of auctions:

1 *English (also called first-price open-outcry) auction* After the beginning of the auction one participant initiates the bidding, and subsequent bidders are then free to respond with higher bids. Participants are free to revise their bids at any time, though there may be requirements that new bids exceed the current high bid by some minimum amount, and only bids at certain values may be allowed. When no bidder wishes to make a higher bid, the item is sold to the high bidder at the bid price. Many agricultural commodities are sold at auction in the USA in this way.

2 *First-price sealed bid* Each bidder submits a bid without knowing the bids of other participants. The highest bidder pays the amount of their bid and receives title to the object. Auctions of this type are common for treasury bills. The Monetary Authority of Singapore (MAS) sends letters to financial institutions inviting bids for a fixed amount of treasury bills. Each tender is for at least 250,000 SGD and must be submitted before a fixed time. The MAS ranks the bids by price from highest to lowest. The MAS goes down the bid schedule to identify the bid that exhausts the offer amount. All higher bids are filled first, and the remaining supply is allocated pro rata to bids at the lowest successful price. The USA follows a similar procedure, except that all purchasers pay the price of the lowest successful bidder. Both Singapore and the USA allow small orders that are not part of the bidding process.

3 *Dutch or descending auction* The auctioneer announces a bid that he continuously lowers until someone takes the object at that price. US firms sometimes use a version of this procedure to repurchase their shares (Bagwell 1992; Gay, Kale, and Noe 1996). A firm will announce the number of shares to be repurchased (this is a USSEC regulation) and a price range. Individual stockholders will indicate the number of shares they are willing to sell at a given price. The firm will pay all shareholders the lowest price necessary to acquire the number of shares sought. All shareholders receive the same price (this is also an USSEC rule). Shareholders bidding the lowest successful price receive a pro rata number of shares based on the ratio of their quantity offered to the aggregate quantity offered at that price.

ments with maturities of more than 1 year. Domestic markets are confined to a single country, whereas the Eurocurrency market comprises all bank deposits and loans in any nondomestic currency.

Investors owning debt instruments face many types of risk. Some of the most important are interest rate risk, the risk of capital losses due to increased interest rates; default risk, the risk that the issuer will not fulfill the terms of the bond contract; liquidity risk, the risk of being locked into an investment that cannot be readily sold; agency risk, the risk that the issuer will take actions that reduce the value of the investment; and sovereign risk, the risk that a governmental borrower will not fulfill its obligations. To help investors evaluate these risks, a number of firms critically examine debt issues and issue an opinion in the form of a rating.

The most common types of money market instruments are government issues such as treasury bills; negotiable certificates of deposit (CD) issued by commercial banks evidencing time deposits; commercial paper, a short-term unsecured promissory note issued by a corporation; repurchase agreements, in which one party sells securities to a counterparty in exchange for an immediate payment, with an agreement to repurchase the securities at a specified time and for a fixed price; reverse repurchase agreements, in which there is an initial purchase with an agreement for a subsequent sale; call money, loans that are repayable at the request of either party; federal funds, deposits with the US Federal Reserve system; and bankers' acceptances, drafts that order a particular party to pay a specified amount at a specified time that has been acknowledged by the person required to make the payment and guaranteed by a bank.

Bonds are securities in which an issuer contractually agrees to make one or more payments to an investor. Bonds share similar features worldwide. The agreement between the bondholder and the issuer is called the indenture. The indenture sets out the rights and obligations of the issuer and of the owners of the bonds, including the interest amounts and the various agents in the issue. Some bonds can be exchanged or converted into other securities of the issuer or of another firm. Global bond markets, which are growing in importance, comprise two different types of issues. Foreign bonds include bonds issued in a country by nonresidents, in either the domestic currency or in a nondomestic currency. Eurobonds are transnational bond issues typically underwritten by an international investment banking syndicate.

Questions

1 What are the risks faced by debt investors?
2 How do you define agency-type risk faced by debt investors?
3 What are the differences between default risk and liquidity risk of holding debt investments?
4 What is the use of rating agencies to evaluate bond issues? What kind of firm-related factors do they consider in assessing the quality of debt issues?
5 What is the main difference between money markets and capital markets?
6 What kind of unsecured short-term debt instruments can be used by corporations to raise funds? Which firms can use these instruments?
7 What kinds of overnight investments do US banks use most commonly?
8 Describe a banker's acceptance and explain how it can be used to finance trade.
9 What are the characteristics of exchangeable and convertible bonds?
10 What is crisis at maturity, and how can it be reduced?

◼ Notes ◼

1 For a information on debt securities see http://www.e-analytics.com/bonds/bonddir.htm and http://www.bondmarkets.com/research/historcl.shtml.

2 Many of the rating services have web sites: Moody's, http://www.moodys.com/moodys/mdyindex.htm; S&P's, http://www.standardandpoors.com/ratings/corporates/index.htm; Fitch IBCA, http://www.fitchibca.com/home/frame.html; Duff & Phelps, http://www.dcrco.com/; Thomson Bankwatch, http://www.bankwatch.com/bankw.htm; and A.M. Best, http://www.ambest.com/other.html. The A.M. Best rating system is described at http://www.ambest.com/ratings/preface/pc/contents.htm.

3 Moody's sovereign ceilings for foreign currency ratings can be found at http://www.moodys.com/repldata/ratings/ratsov.htm.

4 A bibliography on topics related to Islamic banking and links to financial institutions following Islamic practices is at this web address: http://islamic-finance.net/. Chapter 4 of the book *Interest-free Commercial Banking* by A. L. M. Gafoor can be found at http://www.noord.bart.nl/~abdul/chap4.html.

5 A deposit is a loan from the depositor. Banks induce customers to make these loans in the form of deposits by offering interest and/or by facilitating payments.

6 For additional information see http://www.bankamerica.com/news/news422.html.

7 For an announcement by Merrill Lynch of a commercial paper program in Japan see http://www.ml.com/woml/press_release/19980302-1.htm.

8 The web site of USAA's real estate subsidiary provides information concerning the parent: http://realco.usaa.com/main/rc_parent.asp.

9 According to the Nov. 28, 1997, issue of *Euroweek*, "Institutional investors eager for a new asset class snapped up the first securitization of Japanese earthquake risk, issued by Tokio Marine and Fire Insurance Co. Tokio Marine issued $100 million of 10-year floating rate notes in a global 144A private placement." Obtained from http://www.gs.com/about/media/articles-97.html.

10 The web site for the Asian Development Bank is http://www.adb.org/. For additional information on Japanese, bond markets, see Takagi 1993; Tatewaki 1991; Urich 1991.

11 For a discussion of the global bond issues of the World Bank see http://www.worldbank.org/foddr/global.htm.

◼ References ◼

Bagwell, Laurie Simon 1992: Dutch auction repurchases: an analysis of shareholder heterogeneity. *Journal of Finance* 47, 71.

Bilal, Gohar 1999: Islamic finance: alternatives to the Western model. *The Fletcher forum of world affairs* 23, 145.

Cantor, Richard and Packer, Frank 1996a: Determinants and impact of sovereign credit ratings. *Federal Reserve Bank of New York*, Research Paper no. 9608 (Apr.).

——1996b: Multiple ratings and credit standards: differences of opinion in the credit rating industry. *Federal Reserve Bank of New York*, Staff Reports no. 12 (Apr.).

Cassady, Ralph 1967: *Auctions*. Berkeley: University of California Press.

Fleming, Michael J. and Remolona, Eli M. 1997: Price formation and liquidity in the U.S. treasury market: evidence from intraday patterns around announcements. *Federal Reserve Bank of New York*, Staff Reports no. 27 (July).

Gay, Gerald D., Kale, Jayant R. and Noe, Thomas H. 1996: (Dutch) auction share repurchases. *Economica* 63, 249–57.

Gowland, D. H. 1990: *International Bond Markets*. London: Routledge.

Hickman, W. Braddock 1958: *Corporate Bond Quality and Investor Experience*. New York: National Bureau of Economic Research.

Karmin, Craig and Zuckerman, Gregory 1998: U.S. firms step up volume of "global" bond offerings. *Wall Street Journal*, Sept. 2, p. C1.

Melnik, Arie L. and Plaut, Steven E. 1991: *The Short-term Eurocredit Market*, Monograph Series in Finance and Economics. New York: New York University Salomon Center.

Packer, Frank and Reynolds, Elizabeth 1997: The Samurai bond market. *Current Issues in Economics and Finance, Federal Reserve Bank of New York* 3.

Pamrio, Robert 1997: Spinoffs and wealth transfers: the Marriott case. *Journal of Financial Economics* 43, 241–74.

Rasmusen, Eric 1989: *Games and Information: an introduction to game theory*. New York: Blackwell.

Seligman, Joel 1989: The Washington Public Power Supply System debacle. *Journal of Corporation Law* 14, 889.

Sitzer, Howard D., Noe, Cyrus and Perko, James D. 1994: The Washington Public Power Supply System: then and now. *Municipal Finance Journal* 14, 59.

Takagi, Shinji 1993: *Japanese Capital Markets*. Oxford: Blackwell.

Tatewaki, Kazuo 1991: *Banking and Finance in Japan*. London: Routledge.

Urich, Thomas J. 1991: *U.K., German and Japanese Government Bond Markets*, Monograph Series in Finance and Economics. New York: New York University Salomon Center.

Wall Street Journal Interactive Edition 1997: Mercury Finance's chief resigns amid serious financial squeeze. Feb. 3.

Yamamoto, Shigeru 1993: The Japanese bond market. In Shinji Takagi (ed.), *Japanese Capital Markets*, Oxford, Blackwell, 217.

CHAPTER EIGHT

Debt Securities:
Theoretical Considerations

■ **Key terms** ■

Annuity a series of payments of the same amount.

Broad expectations hypothesis the view that investors expect the return for any investment horizon to be the same, regardless of the maturity of the default-free instruments selected.

Current yield the annual coupon rate divided by the market price of the bond.

Duration a measure of the rate of change in an asset's price relative to the rate of change in interest rates originally developed by Macaulay; hence often called **Macaulay's duration**.

Forward interest rate the interest rate for a period beginning at $t > 0$.

Immunized a portfolio whose value does not change with changes in interest rates.

Liquidity hypothesis the view that because risk-averse investors prefer to invest in short-term instruments to avoid interest rate risk, issuers of long-term bonds have to pay a liquidity premium.

Local expectations hypothesis a version of the expectations hypothesis that states that over a specific short holding period the holding period return is the same regardless of the maturity of the default-free bonds held.

Macaulay's duration the measure of duration developed by Macaulay, which expresses the rate of change in the value of an asset in relation to the rate of change in interest rates.

Market segmentation hypothesis the hypothesis that because borrowers and lenders have different horizons a risk premium is needed to attract speculators to bridge supply and demand differences.

Modified duration Macaulay's duration divided by $-(1 + y)$, where y is the yield-to-maturity or required return. This measure shows that for a given yield change there is an inverse relationship between modified duration and the percentage change in price.

Preferred habitat hypothesis the hypothesis that because investors and borrowers have a preference for particular maturities along the term structure, risk premiums are needed to induce investors and borrowers to shift from one part of the yield curve to another.

Pure expectations hypothesis forward interest rates are determined exclusively by expectations concerning future interest rates.

Return-to-maturity expectations hypothesis   the view that over a given horizon the returns earned by an investor will be the same whether an investor purchases a zero-coupon bond or rolls over a series of shorter-horizon bonds.

Spot interest rate   the interest rate for a period beginning at t = 0.

Term structure of interest rates   a graph reflecting data for a group of bonds that shows the term to maturity on the horizontal axis and the interest rate on the vertical axis.

Total realized compound yield   the expected annual yield of an investment over a stated horizon, given an indicated reinvestment rate.

Yield-to-maturity   the discount rate that equates the future cash flows of a bond with the market price.

Yield-to-maturity expectations hypothesis   the view that over a given horizon the yields earned by an investor will be the same whether an investor purchases a zero-coupon bond or rolls over a series of shorter-horizon bonds.

THIS CHAPTER is divided into two parts. In the first, we describe

- ■ procedures for calculating bond yields
- ■ a method for comparing one bond with another in making an investment decision
- ■ the importance, construction, and meaning of bond yield curves

Then, we define a measure of average bond life called duration and illustrate its uses.

---

1. INTRODUCTION

In addition to understanding the characteristics of debt securities and their markets, it is also important to understand some fundamental techniques used to analyze these instruments. This chapter presents three techniques – yield-to-maturity, total realized compound yield, and duration – that should be familiar to all students of finance. In each case both the calculation of the measure and illustrations of how the measure is used are provided.

2. BOND YIELDS

2.1. CURRENT YIELD AND YIELD-TO-MATURITY

Unlike common stocks, most bonds promise a fixed stream of future cash flows. It is common practice to calculate measures that summarize this cash flow stream. The **current yield** is the annual coupon rate divided by the market price of the bond. The **yield-to-maturity** is the rate of return that equates the fixed payment stream to the bond's market price. In other words, the yield-to-maturity is the rate of return that makes the net present value of the bond zero. This is the same as the internal rate of return of the bond.

217

The market price of the bond (P) is:

$$P = C/(1+y)^1 + C/(1+y)^2 + C/(1+y)^3 + \ldots + C/(1+y)^n + M/(1+y)^n$$

where C = the periodic coupon payment on the bond, F = the payment on the bond at maturity, and y = the bond's yield-to-maturity. If C is paid semiannually, y is one-half of the annual yield-to-maturity. If P, C, and F are known, then y can be calculated. The yield-to-maturity cannot be found analytically, but only by trial and error. The trial and error process can be facilitated by recognizing that if market interest rates equal the coupon rate of a given bond, the market price of the bond will be 100, which is its face value expressed in percent, and by the use of various bond factor tables. Box 8.1 explains how to use the interest-rate-factor or time-value-of-money tables. Box 8.2 illustrates the estimation of yield-to-maturity. Alternately, a calculator may be used.

BOX 8.1
Time value of money tables

Four interest-rate-factor or time-value-of-money tables are commonly provided. The construction of the tables depends on three variables: the number of periods, the interest rate per period, and the number of payments. Period n begins at time n − 1 and ends at time n. In other words, the first period (period 1) begins at time 0 and ends at time 1. Payments are assumed to occur at the end of a period.

Present value of a single payment

The first table commonly provides factors for the present value of a single payment at the end of n periods hence. In other words, a discount factor is provided, which, for an indicated interest rate, r, gives the equivalent at time t of a payment t + n periods in the future. The formula for the present value factor is $1/(1 + r)^n$. Table 8.1.1 is an example of a present value table.

Table 8.1.1 Present value at time t of 1 unit payable at time t + n at interest rate r

n	4%	5%	6%	7%	8%
1	0.9615	0.9524	0.9434	0.9346	0.9259
2	0.9246	0.9070	0.8900	0.8734	0.8573
3	0.8890	0.8638	0.8396	0.8163	0.7938
4	0.8548	0.8227	0.7921	0.7629	0.7350
5	0.8219	0.7835	0.7473	0.7130	0.6806
6	0.7903	0.7462	0.7050	0.6663	0.6302
7	0.7599	0.7107	0.6651	0.6627	0.5835
8	0.7307	0.6768	0.6274	0.5820	0.5403
9	0.7026	0.6446	0.5919	0.5439	0.5002
10	0.6756	0.6139	0.5584	0.5083	0.4632

Interest rates are typically expressed as a rate per year. If the market interest rate is 6 percent, then 1 USD paid at the end of 4 years is worth 0.7921 USD at the beginning of the first period (obtained by looking across the row for n = 4 and down the column for r = 6%).

If the compounding period is less than 1 year, before using the present value table, it is necessary to divide the interest rate by the number of compounding periods. In other words, if the market interest rate is 8 percent compounded semiannually, 1 USD paid at the end of 4 years is worth 0.7307 USD at the beginning of the first period. The appropriate factor is obtained by dividing the interest rate in half (because of the semiannual compounding) and then looking under the appropriate number of periods, which in this case is 8 (4 years × 2 compounding periods).

Future value of a single payment

Alternatively, a future value table, comprising future value factors for a single payment n periods hence, may be provided. For a given interest rate, r, these factors reflect the value at time t + n of one unit payable at time t, which has the formula $(1 + r)^n$. The future value interest factor is the reciprocal of the present value interest factor. Selected future value interest factors are presented here:

Table 8.1.2 Future value at time t + n of 1 unit payable at time t at interest rate r.

n	4%	5%	6%	7%	8%
1	1.0400	1.0500	1.0600	1.0700	1.0800
2	1.0816	1.1025	1.1236	1.1449	1.1664
3	1.1249	1.1576	1.1910	1.2250	1.2597
4	1.1699	1.2155	1.2625	1.3108	1.3605
5	1.2167	1.2763	1.3382	1.4026	1.4693
6	1.2653	1.3401	1.4185	1.5007	1.5869
7	1.3159	1.4071	1.5036	1.6058	1.7138
8	1.3686	1.4775	1.5938	1.7182	1.8509
9	1.4233	1.5513	1.6895	1.8385	1.9990
10	1.4802	1.6289	1.7908	1.9672	2.1589

Again, if the interest rate is quoted as an annual rate, and the actual compounding period is more frequent, the interest rate must be divided by n, the number of compounding periods, and the appropriate number of periods must be used when obtaining the future value factor from the table.

Present value of an annuity

The present value and future value tables are for use in evaluating single payments. Frequently, one needs to obtain the present value or future value of an **annuity**, a series of payments of the same amount. Tables giving present value and future value annuity factors are also commonly provided. The formula for the present value annuity factor is $(1 - (1/(1 + r)^n)/r$. Note that the present value annuity factors can be constructed from the

Continued

present value factors. For period 1 the present value annuity factor and the present value factor are the same. For period 2, the present value annuity factor is the sum of the present value factor for periods 1 and 2. For period 3, the present value annuity factor is the sum of the present value factors for period 1, 2, and 3. A table of present value annuity factors is presented here:

Table 8.1.3 Present value annuity factors. Each factor represents the present value of 1 unit payable at the end of each of n periods at the interest rate r

n	4%	5%	6%	7%	8%
1	0.9615	0.9524	0.9494	0.9346	0.9529
2	1.8861	1.8594	1.8334	1.8080	1.7833
3	2.7751	2.7323	2.6730	2.6243	2.5771
4	3.6299	3.5460	3.4651	3.3872	3.3121
5	4.4518	4.3295	4.2124	4.1002	3.9927
6	5.2421	5.0757	4.9173	4.7665	4.6229
7	6.0021	5.7864	5.5824	5.3893	5.2064
8	6.7327	6.4632	6.2098	5.9713	5.7466
9	7.4353	7.1078	6.8017	6.5152	6.2469
10	8.1109	7.7217	7.3601	7.0236	6.7101

If the market interest rate is 6%, the present value at time t of 1 USD paid at the end of periods 1–4 is 3.4651 USD (obtained by looking across row 4 and down the column for r = 6%). If semiannual compounding is used, the annual interest rate must be divided by 2, and the appropriate number of periods must be used.

Future value of an annuity

A table is also commonly presented for the future value of an annuity. The formula for future value annuity factors is $((1 + r)^n - 1)/ r$. Table 8.1.4 is a typical future value annuity table.

Table 8.1.4 Future value annuity factors. Each factor represents the present value of 1 unit payable at the end of each of n periods at the interest rate r

n	4%	5%	6%	7%	8%
1	1.0000	1.0000	1.0000	1.0000	1.0000
2	2.0400	2.0500	2.0600	2.0700	2.0800
3	3.1216	3.1525	3.1836	3.2149	3.2464
4	4.2465	4.3101	4.3746	4.4399	4.5061
5	5.4163	5.5256	5.6371	5.7507	5.8686
6	6.6330	6.8019	6.9753	7.1533	7.3359
7	7.8983	8.1420	8.3938	8.6540	8.9228
8	9.2142	9.5491	9.8975	10.260	10.637
9	10.583	11.027	11.491	11.978	12.488
10	12.006	12.578	13.181	13.816	14.487

The table for future value annuity factors can also be constructed from the table for future value factors, but the procedure is somewhat different than for the present value case. For the future value annuity table, the entries for period 1 are all 1.0000, regardless of the interest rate. The remaining entries in the future value annuity table can be constructed from the future value table as follows:

> entry in future value annuity = the sum of (a) 1 and (b) the sum of the entry in
> table for period n   future value table for period 1 through oeriod n − 1

Consider the entry for a 4 percent interest rate for n = 3. Examining the future value table for periods 1–3 we see: period 1, 1.0400; period 2, 1.0816; and period 3, 1.1249. The entry for period 3 in the future value annuity table is the sum of the first two entries in the future value table (1.0400 + 1.0816 = 2.1216) plus 1, which gives 3.1216.

Procedures similar to those for the other tables apply when the compounding period is more frequent than annual.

BOX 8.2
Calculating yield-to-maturity

Suppose that we wish to calculate the yield-to-maturity for a bond with a coupon rate of 6 percent, a maturity value of 1,000 USD, and a current market price of 982 USD. We know that if market interest rate were 6 percent, the market value of the bond would be 100 (stated as a percent of face value) or 1,000 USD. Moreover, since bond prices fall when interest rates rise and the market value of the bond is less than 1,000 USD, we know that the yield-to-maturity is higher than 6 percent. Finding yield-to-maturity is a trial and error process. Let us begin by calculating the market value of the bond if market interest rates were 8 percent, which is:

$$30(0.9615 = 0.9246 + 0.8890 + 0.8548) + (0.8548 \times 1030) = 963.70$$

Note that, following custom, we discount both the coupon payments and the final payment at maturity, using the semiannual rate. Given our result of 963.70, which is less than 982, we know that the yield-to-maturity is between 6 percent and 8 percent. We can obtain a more exact yield-to-maturity by testing additional values, by using a calculator that will solve a yield-to-maturity problem, or by linear interpolation. We will illustrate the latter approach.

We know that 6 percent and 8 percent discount rates produce market values of 1,000 and 963.70, respectively. We wish to know the yield-to-maturity associated with a market price of 982. Define the following:

$$A = 1,000 - 982 = 18,$$

$$B = 1,000 - 963.70 = 36.3,$$

$$C = 6\% - ?\%, \text{ and}$$

$$D = 6\% - 8\% = -2\%$$

Continued

221

6%	?%	8%
1,000	982	963.70

Then, A/B = C/D, so that

$$(A/B)D = C.$$

Substituting values gives

$$(-2\%)\,(18/36.3) = 6\% - ?\%.$$

Rearranging terms and simplifying gives

$$?\% = 6.99.$$

Hence, the estimated yield-to-maturity is 6.99%.

Hawawini and Vora (1982) describe over 400 years of efforts to approximate the yield-to-maturity. These authors present a variety of formulas, all of which are more accurate than the popular formula presented here. Why has a less accurate formula proved to be the most popular? I cannot speak for others, but I find this formula easier to remember because it is intuitive. The numerator comprises the annual coupon payment plus the annual appreciation if the bond sells at a discount or minus the annual depreciation if the bond sells at a premium. The denominator is the average investment, which is the average of the bond's initial value and the bond's terminal value. This formula is:

$$(C + ((F - P)/n))/((P + F)/2) \qquad\qquad 7.1$$

where C is the annual coupon payment, P is the current market value of the bond, and F is the maturity value of the bond, normally 100. Hawawini and Vora (1982) recommend an alternative formula developed by Henderson in 1907. Before presenting this alternative formula, it will be useful to define several new variables and to use these variables to redefine formula 7.1. Let $g = C/P$ and $k = -((F - P)/P)$. Dividing both the numerator and denominator of 7.1 by P, substituting g and k, and simplifying gives:

$$(g - (k/n))/((1 + 0.5k)) \qquad\qquad 7.2$$

Henderson's formula is identical to formula 7.2 except that 0.6 is substituted for 0.5, as follows:

$$(g - (k/n))/((1 + 0.6k)) \qquad\qquad 7.3$$

2.2. TOTAL REALIZED COMPOUND YIELD

As we have already noted, the yield-to-maturity is the internal rate of return for a bond. It is well known in capital budgeting that the internal rate of return has a number of limita-

222

tions, especially in comparisons of one investment with another. These limitations also apply to comparisons of one bond with another. The two most important limitations in bond comparisons are the reinvestment rate problem and the horizon problem. Suppose that an investor wants to compare the relative merits of two bonds with the same maturity, but different coupon rates, over a stated horizon, say three years. Suppose, further, that each bond has an identical yield-to-maturity. On the basis of yield-to-maturity the two bonds are equally attractive. The problem with this conclusion is that the reinvestment rate of the cash flows may differ from the yield-to-maturity. If these cash flows can be reinvested at a rate higher than the yield-to-maturity, then the bond with the higher coupons is more attractive, since these intermediate cash flows can be invested more favorably. If the comparison were made using yield-to-maturity, this feature of the two investments would be entirely missed.

A related problem in making comparisons based on yield-to-maturity is called the "horizon problem." In this case consider two bonds with the same coupon rate and yield-to-maturity, but with differing maturities. Here again the yield-to-maturity fails to capture the possibility that the proceeds from the bond with the earlier maturity may be invested at either a higher or a lower rate than the yield-to-maturity. If expected market interest rates are higher (lower) than the yield-to-maturity, the shortest (longest)-lived bond is probably the best alternative.

In comparing two bonds, the appropriate approach is to calculate the expected future value of each investment over the investor's investment horizon using a projected reinvestment rate. This future value can then be annualized over the investment horizon to produce the total realized compound yield. If the investment horizon is n years, then the **total realized compound yield** is (future value/initial value)^n − 1. If the compounding period is semiannual, then n is the number of semiannual periods, and the result must be multiplied by 2 to obtain an annual rate. Note that the investor's investment horizon can be longer or shorter than the maturity of any given investment. If a bond is used that has a shorter maturity than the investor's investment horizon, then the future value must include the return from investing the proceeds of the bond at maturity, along with the return from investing the intermediate cash flows. If a bond with a longer maturity than the investment horizon is used, then the market value of the bond at the end of the investment horizon must be calculated based on the expected reinvestment rate. Box 8.3 illustrates the way in which total realized compound yield is calculated when the investment horizon and the bond maturity are the same and when the investment horizon is longer than the bond maturity.

3. THE TERM STRUCTURE OF INTEREST RATES

3.1. Introduction

For a group of bonds that are similar except for maturity, the term structure of interest rates is a graph that shows the term to maturity on the horizontal axis and the interest rate on the vertical axis. The term structure of interest rates can take on a variety of shapes. Graphs of the term structure for US Treasury bonds for selected years are presented in figure 8.1. In 1982 the term structure was upward-sloping, while in 1981 it was downward-

---

BOX 8.3
Calculating total realized compound yield

1. Calculate the total realized compound yield given the following information:

Bond maturity:	3 years
Bond coupon rate (semiannual payments):	6%
Bond face value:	1,000
Bond price (% of face value):	79
Reinvestment rate:	8%
Investment horizon:	3 years

Step 1: Calculate the future value:

$$(6.6330 \times 30) + 1{,}000 = 1198.99$$

Step 2: Calculate the total realized compound yield:

$$[(1198.99/790)^{1/6} - 1] \times 2 = 0.072 \times 2 = 0.1440 \text{ or } 14.4\%$$

2. Calculate the total realized compound yield given the following information:

Bond maturity:	3 years
Bond coupon rate (semiannual payments):	6%
Bond face value:	1,000
Bond price (% of face value):	79
Reinvestment rate:	8%
Investment horizon:	5 years

Step 1: Calculate the future value

$$((6.6330 \times 30) + 1{,}000) \times 1.1699 = 1402.69$$

Step 2: Calculate the total realized compound yield

$$[(1402.69/790)^{1/10} - 1] \times 2 = 0.0591 \times 2 = 0.1182 \text{ or } 11.825\%$$

---

sloping.[1] Care must be taken in constructing the term structure, since the yield on particular bonds can reflect more than just the time value of money. Other factors that might affect the computed yield-to-maturity include default risk and whether a bond is callable. As a result, yield curves are most commonly calculated for government issues where default risk is low and other features of the bonds tend to be similar.

3.2. THEORIES OF THE TERM STRUCTURE OF INTEREST RATES

3.2.1. Introduction

There are three major hypotheses concerning the determinants of the term structure: the expectations hypothesis, the liquidity premium hypothesis, and the market segmentation hypothesis.

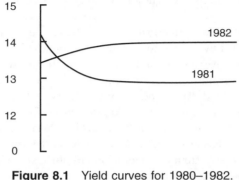

Figure 8.1 Yield curves for 1980–1982.
Source: *Federal Reserve Bulletin*.

3.2.2. Expectations hypothesis

Spot interest rates are interest rates that begin at time t = 0. An interest rate that begins at time t > 0 is called a **forward interest rate**. According to the **pure expectations hypothesis**, forward interest rates are determined exclusively by expectations concerning future interest rates. An upward-sloping term structure indicates that in the future interest rates are expected to increase, and a downward-sloping term structure indicates that in the future interest rates are expected to decrease. Current forward rates are unbiased expectations of future spot rates. Suppose that investors have a choice at time 0 of either purchasing a bond that matures at time t or purchasing a series of 1-year bonds and rolling over each bond at maturity. Let $_tr_{t+n}$ be the interest rate, with spot rates indicated by t = 0 and forward rates by t > 0. Then, if the pure expectations hypothesis holds, we expect that

$$(1 + {_0}r_n)^n = (1 + {_0}r_1)(1 + {_1}r_2)(1 + {_2}r_3)\ldots(1 + {_{n-1}}r_n)$$

For n = 5 we would have

$$(1 + {_0}r_5)^5 = (1 + {_0}r_1)(1 + {_1}r_2)(1 + {_2}r_3)(1 + {_3}r_4)(1 + {_4}r_5).$$

There are several versions of the expectations hypothesis. In its most comprehensive form, the **broad expectations hypothesis**, investors expect the return for any investment horizon to be the same, regardless of the maturity of the default-free instruments selected. To invest for 5 years, an investor can use a series of 1-year bonds, a 5-year bond, or a bond with maturity beyond 5 years, which will be sold at the end of the investment horizon. Critics of this hypothesis say that there is substantial price risk associated with longer-maturity bonds, so the returns from the three different investment strategies should differ in significant ways. Cox, Ingersoll, and Ross (1981) demonstrate mathematically that this form of the expectations hypothesis cannot be true.

A more restricted version of the expectations hypothesis, the **local expectations hypothesis**, postulates that the holding period return is the same regardless of the maturity of the default-free bonds held only over a specific short holding period. An investor with a 3-month investment horizon can achieve the same return using a 5-year, 10-year, or 15-year bond. This version of the expectations hypothesis solves the problems associated

225

with the broader version of the expectations hypothesis identified by Cox, Ingersoll and Ross (1981).

The **return-to-maturity expectations hypothesis** postulates that over a given horizon the returns earned by an investor will be the same whether an investor purchases a zero-coupon bond or rolls over a series of shorter-horizon bonds. If an investor buys a zero-coupon bond with a 5-year horizon, the total return is the payment at maturity divided by the initial purchase price of the investment minus 1. This version of the hypothesis states that, beginning with the same initial purchase price, investors expect to end up with the same outcome by investing in bonds with maturities shorter than the 5-year horizon and rolling over the proceeds at the maturity of each short-term bond. A closely related hypothesis is the **yield-to-maturity expectations hypothesis**, which postulates that the expected yield from holding a zero-coupon bond over a given horizon is the same as the expected yield from rolling over a series of short-term bonds. If compounding is in continuous time, the yield-to-maturity expectations hypothesis is the same as the unbiased expectations hypothesis.

Most early tests, beginning with Macaulay (1938), find no empirical support for the expectations hypothesis. In fact, much of the time changes in interest rates have been the opposite of what is predicted by the expectations hypothesis. More recent evidence has been mixed. Meiselman (1962) finds empirical support for the pure expectations hypothesis. Santomero (1975) also finds support for the expectations hypothesis, but with substantial liquidity premiums. Nelson (1972) and McCulloch (1975) do not find support for the expectations hypothesis. Froot (1989) reports that while the expectations hypothesis does not hold for short rates, it does hold for long rates. Despite the mixed evidence, most scholars and practitioners who study interest rates believe that the yield curve incorporates the market's expectations concerning future interest rates.

Forward rates are not particularly accurate predictors of future spot rates (see Culbertson 1957; Fama 1976). Fama (1976) concludes that a simple prediction that the future spot rate will be the same as the current spot rate is a better prediction than that the future spot rate will equal the current implied forward rate. Culbertson (1957) reaches a similar conclusion. Nevertheless, investors may find the information obtained by examining forward rates useful. Investors are often faced with the alternative of locking into a particular rate over a given horizon or of investing in a series of shorter-term instruments over the same horizon. Which alternative an investor prefers depends on the investor's view of future interest rates relative to those of the market as reflected in the term structure.

3.2.3. Liquidity hypothesis

Hicks (1939) was an early proponent of the **liquidity hypothesis**, the view that risk-averse investors prefer to invest in short-term instruments, because long-term bonds have greater interest rate risk than short-term bonds. Issuers of long-term bonds would have to pay a liquidity premium to induce investors to hold these more risky instruments. Hence, if the liquidity premium hypothesis holds, expected forward rates are an upwardly biased expectation of future spot rates. This implies that the expected return from holding a series of 1-year bonds is less that the expected return from holding a single bond over the same time horizon.

3.2.4. *Market segmentation and preferred habitat hypotheses*

Culbertson (1957) developed the **market segmentation hypothesis**, which argues that individuals and institutions prefer to lend short-term because this increases their flexibility to meet unexpected contingencies. Borrowers, on the other hand, prefer long maturities to decrease refinancing risk. Neither investors or borrowers are willing to shift their horizon. Hence, speculators are needed to offset differences between long and short demand by borrowing short and lending long, but these speculators will need to be compensated for the risk they incur by receiving risk premiums on the bonds they purchase.

Modigliani and Sutch (1966) developed the **preferred habitat hypothesis**, which asserts that investors and borrowers have a preference for particular maturities. Some borrowers, such as manufacturers, may be financing long-lived projects, which may be more suited to financing with long-lived bonds rather than, say, by using commercial paper. Insurance companies and pension funds may have obligations with long maturities. Other borrowers such as banks have short-lived liabilities and, therefore, may prefer assets with shorter maturities. Thus, different groups of borrowers and lenders have different preferences concerning the preferred maturities of the instruments they desire. Along some portions of the yield curve, supply is likely to be high relative to demand, resulting in lower interest rates; while for other maturities the demand is likely to be high relative to the supply, resulting in relatively high interest rates. The relatively higher interest rates needed to equate supply and demand when there is an excess of demand can be viewed as a positive risk premium. The relatively lower interest rates needed to equate supply and demand when there is an excess of supply can be viewed as negative risk premiums. Hence, according to this hypothesis, the shape of the yield curve is determined at least in part by positive or negative risk premiums needed to induce investors and borrowers to switch out of their preferred habitats. In the preferred habitat hypothesis, borrowers and lenders themselves are induced to shift their supply and demand to take advantage of differences in relative risk premiums. Cox, Ingersoll, and Ross (1981) argue that the liquidity hypothesis can be considered a special case of the preferred habitat hypothesis. These two hypotheses, along with the market segmentation hypothesis, support the idea that the term structure reflects both the time value of money and risk premiums. Fama (1976) provides evidence of the existence of risk premium in interest rates.

3.3. CONSTRUCTING FORWARD RATES FROM THE TERM STRUCTURE

If we ignore premiums, forward rates can be estimated empirically from the term structure. Let us make two assumptions concerning our empirical term structure: (1) We have a bond that matures at each point on the term structure (which may be each 6 months or each year), and (2) the first bond in the term structure is a bond with a single payment at the end of the first period, i.e., a zero-coupon bond. Then we can use the information in our empirical term structure to construct spot rates. Define $_t r_{t+n}$ as the spot rate at time t for a zero-coupon bond maturing at $t + n$. For each bond we know its current market price, P, its coupon rate, C, and its maturity value, F. For the bond maturing in 6 months we have:

$$P = (C + F)/(1 + {_0}r_1).$$

Since P, C, and F are known, we can solve for $_0r_1$.

For a bond maturing in one year, we have:

$$P = (C+F)/(1+_0r_1) + (C+F)/(1+_0r_1)(1+_1r_2).$$

Since P, C, F, and $_0r_1$ are known, we can solve for $_1r_2$. Proceeding in this way, we can calculate the current spot rate for the first period and one-period forward rates, $_0r_1, _1r_2, \ldots,$ $_tr_{t+n}$, for subsequent periods.

Suppose that investors believe that future interest rates will be higher than the current spot rate. This expectation will be incorporated into the price of a long-term bond, and an investor purchasing that bond will be locking into those interest rates. If a particular investor believes that future interest rates will be even higher than the market forecast, that investor would prefer to purchase a series of individual shorter-term bonds rather than one bond than spans the entire horizon. If the term structure is upward-sloping, then future interest rates are expected to increase. To see this, consider two bonds, one maturing in 1 year and the second maturing in 2 years. We know by the assumption that the yield curve is upward-sloping that

$$\left(1+_0r_2\right)^2 > \left(1+_0r_1\right)^2 \qquad 7.4$$

But if the term structure reflects expectations,

$$\left(1+_0r_2\right)^2 = (1+_0r_1)(1+_1r_2) \qquad 7.5$$

Substituting the right-hand side of 7.5 into the left-hand side of 7.4 gives

$$(1+_0r_1)(1+_1r_2) > \left(1+_0r_1\right)^2$$

or

$$_1r_2 > _0r_1$$

Hence, the forward rate for period 2 is higher than the spot rate for period 1. Likewise, if investors expect future interest rates to decline, forward rates will be lower than the current spot rate.

3.4. CALCULATING SPOT RATES FROM FORWARD RATES

Suppose that, instead of a term structure of yields-to-maturity, we wanted to have a term structure of spot rates. These spot rates can be calculated from the forward rates $_0r_1$, $_1r_2, \ldots, _tr_{t+n}$. The spot rate $_0r_n$ is

$$\left(1+_0r_n\right)^n = (1+_0r_1)(1+_1r_2) \ldots (1+_{n-1}r_n)$$

Hence, even though the yield curve is constructed from coupon-bearing bonds, it may be possible to use the information in the term structure to construct an equivalent term structure for zero-coupon bonds.

4. DURATION

We have seen that the term structure of interest rates can be upward-sloping or downward-sloping, depending on expectations for future spot interest rates. Suppose we wish to know how a uniform change in the term structure affects the price of a bond. Consider a bond that pays interest semiannually for n years and that has a coupon payment of C and a maturity value of F. Let y be the required yield. If interest rates are expressed on a per year basis and the bond has semiannual payments, y is one-half the annual rate, and the periods are semiannual periods. If the bond payments are on an annual basis, y is the annual interest rate, and the periods are annual periods. As we saw above, if y is the required yield, the market price of the bond (P) must be:

$$P = C/(1+y)^1 + C/(1+y)^2 + C/(1+y)^3 + \ldots + C/(1+y)^n + M/(1+y)^n$$

To determine the change in price for a small change in y, we take the first derivative and rearrange terms to obtain

$$dP/dy = -(1/(1+y))\left[\left(c/(1+y)^1\right) + \left(2c/(1+y)^2\right) + \ldots + \left(nC/(1+y)^n\right) + \left(nM/(1+y)^n\right)\right]$$

Multiplying both sides by $1/P$ gives

$$dP/dy(1/P) = -(1/(1+y))\left[\left(c/(1+y)^1\right) + \left(2c/(1+y)^2\right) + \ldots\right.$$
$$\left. + \left(nC/(1+y)^n\right) + \left(nM/(1+y)^n\right)\right](1/P) \qquad 7.6$$

The quantity in brackets multiplied by $(1/P)$ is known as **Macaulay's duration**.

From equation 7.6 we can see that Macaulay's duration is

$$-dP/dy(1/P)(1+y)$$

Dividing Macaulay's duration by $(1 + y)$ gives a measure known as **modified duration**.

Duration provides a summary measure that is useful in comparing individual bond issues and bond portfolios. Broadly speaking, duration can be viewed as the average life of a bond. Macaulay's duration contemplates a uniform shift in the yield curve. For small movements in the yield curve, bonds with the same duration will experience the same change in price. This characteristic gives duration a role in investment management and in the management of financial institutions. Banks, insurance companies, and other financial institutions have both assets and liabilities whose values fluctuate with changing interest rates. It may be desirable to attempt to see that interest rate-induced changes in liabilities are matched by comparable interest rate-induced change in the value of assets. Otherwise, if changes in interest rates cause the value of liabilities to increase, while the value of assets does not increase by a corresponding amount (or even decreases), the firm may face insolvency or bankruptcy. A portfolio or balance sheet whose overall position is not affected by interest rate changes is called **immunized**. Some financial institutions may find it more difficult to immunize their asset/liability positions by the judicious choice of investments. This is especially true if the assets or liabilities that need to be immunized have particularly short or long horizons. Banks have substantial liabilities in the form of demand deposits, most of which have a duration of zero. Assets with similarly short maturities include federal funds.

There are some regularities concerning duration that it is worthwhile to know:

1 The duration of a zero-coupon bond equals the maturity of the bond.
2 The duration of a portfolio is the weighted average of the durations of the individual bonds in the portfolio, where the weights are the proportion of current market value invested in each bond.
3 Except for certain deep-discount bonds, holding other factors constant, the duration of a bond increases with its maturity.
4 Holding other factors constant, the duration of a bond decreases with an increase in its interest rate.
5 The duration of a perpetual annuity is $(1 + y)/y$.
6 If T is the number of payments, the duration of an annuity is

$$[(1+y)/y]-[T/((1+y)T-1)],$$

7 The modified duration of a zero-coupon bond is shorter than the maturity of the bond.

Box 8.4 presenty a sample duration calculation, provides an illustration of how duration affects bond price changes, and shows how duration is used in bank asset/liability management.

BOX 8.4
Illustration of how duration affecty bond values

1. Calculation of duration Calculate the duration of the following bond given the information provided:

Market rate of interest: 10%

Bond characteristics
Payment period: Semiannual
Coupon rate: 8%
Maturity: 3 years

Semiannual periods	Cash flow	Present value of cash flow at 5%	Weight		Weight X number of periods
1	40	38.10	0.0400		0.0400
2	40	36.28	0.0382		0.0764
3	40	34.55	0.0364		0.1092
4	40	32.91	0.0347		0.1388
5	40	31.34	0.0330		0.1650
6	40	776.06	0.8177		4.9062
		949.24		Duration in half-years:	5.4356

The duration of this bond is 5.4356 half-years or 2.718 years.

2. Illustration of duration and its effect on interest rate changes   Suppose we have two zero-coupon bonds with identical market prices of 907.03. One of the bonds matures in 1 year and the other in 2 years. We know that the duration of the first bond is 1 year and that the duration of the second bond is 2 years. What is the duration of a portfolio that holds one of each of the bonds? The duration can be calculated as follows:

Semiannual periods	Cash flow	Present value of cash flow at 5%	Weight		Weight X number of periods
1					
2	1,000.00	907.03	0.5		1
3					
4	1,102.50	907.03	0.5		2
		1,814.06		Duration in half-years:	3

If an investor holds a portfolio comprising these two bonds, the duration of the portfolio is 3 half-years or (3/2 =) 1.5 years. At the end of 1.5 years the portfolio will be worth $(1,000 \times 1.05) + (1,102.5/1.05) = 2,100$. The first term is the maturity value of the first bond plus interest for 6 months. The second term is the market value of the second bond at the end of 1.5 years. Suppose that an investor wishes to invest to meet an obligation of 2,100 due in 1.5 years. The investor can purchase a zero-coupon bond with a maturity value of 2,100 and be sure of having the funds to pay the obligation regardless of changes in interest rates.

Alternatively, the investor can purchase the two-bond portfolio with a duration of 1.5 years. This portfolio will also yield 2,100 at the end of 1.5 years regardless of interest rate fluctuations. The reason is that over the duration horizon the two aspects of valuation affected by interest rate changes – the reinvestment rate and the capital loss – are exactly counterbalanced. To see this, consider the effects of an increase in the interest rate from 5 percent to 5.1 percent. At the end of 1.5 years the 1,000 payment received at the end of period 2 will be worth 1,050.10, rather than 1,050, an increase of 0.10. But the market value of the bond maturing at the end of period 4 will be worth only 1,040.90, rather than 1,050, a decrease of 0.10. Hence, the increase and decrease offset each other, and the value of the portfolio is unchanged. Given our assumptions that shifts in the yield curve are uniform, any bond or portfolio with the same duration will be equally suitable to protect against interest rate changes over the duration horizon.

3. Illustration of a bank asset/liability management problem   Suppose that a bank has 1,000 USD of assets with a duration of 7 years and liabilities of 1,000 USD with a duration of 7 years. Current interest rates are 10 percent. How much equity does a bank need to be able to absorb a 1 percent change in interest rates and still have equity of 50 USD?

We know that

$$\Delta P = -(1/(1+y)) \text{ Macaulay duration} \times \Delta y$$

Therefore, the change in value of the liability portfolio is $1000[(1/(1.1)) \times 0.01] = -9.09$ USD, and the decline in value of the asset portfolio is $1000[(7/(1.1)) \times 0.01] = -63.64$ USD. The net change in shareholders' equity is -63.64 USD $- (-9.09$ USD$)$, or -54.55 USD. Hence, to insure that stockholders' equity is at least 50 USD if interest rates increase 1 percent, the bank must have initial equity of 50 USD + 54.55 USD = 104.55 USD.

5. SUMMARY

Most debt securities make one or more fixed payments prior to maturity. Investors are interested in determining their return on holding these instruments. The current yield is the coupon rate divided by the market price of the bond. The yield-to-maturity is the rate of return that equates the fixed payment stream to the bond's market price. The yield-to-maturity cannot be calculated analytically, but must be determined through trial and error. Yield-to-maturity is equivalent to internal rate of return. It is well known that there are problems in using the internal rate of return to compare investments. A particularly important problem in comparing bonds is that the reinvestment rate may differ from the yield-to-maturity. To overcome these problems, bonds can be compared using total realized compound yield.

For a set of bonds that are similar except in their maturity, the **term structure of interest rates** is the graph showing the yield-to-maturity of each bond on the vertical axis and the maturity of each bond on the horizontal axis. Historically, actual term structures have taken on a variety of shapes, including upward-sloping and downward-sloping. A spot interest rate is the interest rate from time 0 to time t > 0. A zero-coupon bond is a bond with a single future payment. If the first bond in the term structure is a zero-coupon bond maturing at the end of period 1, its yield is the spot rate for period 1. A forward rate is an interest rate for a period beginning and ending at t > 0. If the second bond in the term structure matures at the end of period 2 and the spot rate for period 1 is known, the forward interest rates from the beginning to the end of period 2 can be derived. Proceeding in a similar way, forward rates for each future period can be derived.

There are three major hypotheses concerning the determinants of the term structure: the expectations hypothesis, the liquidity premium hypothesis, and the preferred habitat/market segmentation hypothesis. The pure expectations hypothesis asserts that the shape of the term structure depends on investors' expectations concerning future interest rates. According to the liquidity hypothesis, investors prefer to invest in short-term instruments to avoid interest rate risk, whereas many borrowers prefer to borrow using long-term bonds because of the horizon of their investments. Hence, borrowers have to pay a liquidity premium to induce investors to lend long-term. The market segmentation hypothesis postulates that there is a mismatch in the supply and demand for funds, because borrowers prefer to lend long-term to avoid refinancing risk, and lenders prefer to lend short-term to maintain flexibility. Hence, a risk premium is needed to induce speculators to arbitrage between long and short rates. The preferred habitat hypothesis asserts that some investors and some borrowers have a short horizon, whereas others have a long horizon. Risk premiums are needed to induce investors and borrowers to shift from one part of the yield curve to another.

Macaulay's duration is a measure of the average life of a bond developed by Macaulay. If a bond promises only one future payment at the maturity of the bond, the duration of the bond is the same as its maturity. But if a bond makes a number of payments before making the final payment at maturity, the duration of the bond is less than the maturity of the bond. Consider two bonds with differing payment patterns and maturities, but with the same initial market value and with the same duration. If interest rates change, the two bonds experience the same change in value. Hence, duration can be a useful tool in managing financial assets. Suppose that a financial institution is borrowing money in order to make investments. Both the assets and the liabilities of the institution are subject to interest rate risk. If the liabilities have more risk than the assets, the firm runs the risk that an increase in interest rates will result in financial ruin. The financial institution can limit or eliminate this risk by its choice of the duration of the asset and liability portfolios. If each portfolio has the same duration, the combined asset/liability portfolio is protected from changes in value due to interest rate changes – i.e., immunized. Investors and borrowers with especially long- or short-lived assets/liabilities will find it more difficult to immunize their portfolios.

Questions

1 What is the definition of yield-to-maturity?
2 What limitations make yield-to-maturity inappropriate for comparing the relative merits of investing in two bonds.
3 When comparing two bonds in making an investment decision, what measure would be more useful than yield-to-maturity?
4 What are the main hypotheses that have been advanced to explain the term structure?
5 Are forward rates derived from the yield curve unbiased expectations of future spot rates?
6 If investors expect future interest rates to be the same as current interest rates, what would be the shape of the term structure?
7 Why are financial institutions concerned with the durations of their assets and liabilities?
8 Why is duration a more appropriate indicator of interest rate risk than maturity?
9 How is a bond's coupon rate related to its duration?
10 If a zero-coupon bond and a bond with a maturity longer than that of the zero-coupon bond have the same duration, why do they have the same sensitivity to interest rate risk?

▪ Note ▪

1 Bloomberg provides online yield curves for the US, Japan, and several other countries at its web site: http://www.bloomberg.com/markets/iyc.html.

▪ References ▪

Cox, John C., Ingersoll, Jonathan E. Jr. and Ross, Stephen A. 1981: A reexamination of traditional hypotheses about the term structure of interest rates. *Journal of Finance* 36, 769–99.

Culbertson, J. W. 1957: The term structure of interest rates. *Quarterly Journal of Economics* 71(Nov.), 485–517.

Fama, Eugene F. 1976: Forward rates as predictors of future spot rates. *Journal of Financial Economics* 3, 361–77.

Froot, Kenneth A. 1989: New hope for the expectations hypothesis of the term structure of interest rates. *Journal of Finance* 44, 283–305.

Hawawini, Gabriel A. and Vora, Ashok 1982: Yield approximations: a historical perspective. *Journal of Finance* 37, 145–56.

Hicks, J. 1939: *Value and Capital*. London: Oxford University Press.

Macaulay, Frederick 1938: *Some Theoretical Problems Suggested by the Movement of Interest Rates, Bond Yields, and Stock Prices in the U.S. since 1956*. New York: National Bureau of Economic Research.

McCulloch, J. Houston 1975: An estimation of the liquidity premium. *Journal of Political Economy* 83, 95–119.

Meiselman, David I. 1962: *The Term Structure of Interest Rates*. Englewood Cliffs, NJ: Prentice-Hall.

Modigliani, Franco and Sutch, Richard 1966: Innovations in interest rate policy. *American Economic Review* 56, no. 2, 178–97.

Nelson, Charles 1972: Estimation of term premiums from average yield differential in the term structure of interest rates. *Econometrica* 40, 277–88.

Santomero, Anthony M. 1975: The error-learning hypothesis and the term structure of interest rates in Eurodollars. *Journal of Finance* 30, 773–83.

CHAPTER NINE

International Parity Relationships

■ Key terms ■

Absolute purchasing power parity adjusted for exchange rates, the prices of goods and services are the same from country to country, so that the law of one price holds for these items.

Arbitrage the ability of market participants to buy in one market and sell in another, to take advantage of price differentials.

Covered interest rate arbitrage a series of transactions in which (1) a currency is borrowed and converted into a second currency, (2) the second currency is (a) immediately invested at interest and (b) sold forward to lock in its conversion rate into the first currency, so that (3) at maturity, the proceeds of the loan of the second currency can be delivered on the forward contract, obtaining enough of the first currency to repay the loan with interest.

Covered interest rate parity two investment approaches give the same terminal wealth: (a) at time t, buy risk-free bonds denominated in currency a and enter into a forward contract to exchange the end-of-period proceeds for currency b, or (b) exchange currency a for currency b at time t and buy risk-free bonds denominated in currency b.

Currency board a note-issuing authority that announces an exchange rate against some nondomestic currency and carries out trades of domestic currency at that rate.

Fixed exchange rate system an exchange rate system in which the value of each currency in terms of other currencies is fixed by reference to a standard common value such as gold or the USD.

Floating exchange rate system a system in which exchange rates are determined by supply and demand.

Gold standard an exchange rate system in which countries fix the value of their currency in terms of gold and are willing to buy and sell at that price.

Home bias the propensity of investors to prefer to invest in their home country even when superior returns or diversification benefits are available in another country.

Interest rate parity the rate of return from holding risk-free financial assets is the same regardless of the currency in which the assets are denominated.

International Fisher effect exchange rate changes are in an equal and opposite direction to interest rate differences between countries.

Law of one price   the price of an item expressed in different currencies is the same.

Nominal effective exchange rate   a composite exchange rate in which each trading partner's nominal exchange rate is weighted by its share of international trade.

Purchasing power parity   the prices of an item expressed in different currencies is the same, taking exchange rates into account.

Real effective exchange rate   a composite exchange rate in which each trading partner's real exchange rate is weighted by its share of international trade.

Real exchange rate   the exchange rate between two countries after taking changes in prices in the two countries into account.

Relative purchasing power parity   exchange rate changes reflect differences in the rate of change in price indexes from country to country.

Special drawing rights   reserve assets created by the International Monetary Fund.

Unbiased expectations hypothesis   current forward rates are unbiased predictors of future spot rates.

Uncovered interest rate parity   two investment approaches give the same terminal wealth: (a) buy risk-free bonds denominated in currency a at time t and exchange the proceeds for currency b at time t + 1, or (b) exchange currency a for currency b at time t and buy risk-free bonds denominated in currency b.

IN THIS CHAPTER we

- describe exchange rate systems
- explain purchasing power parity and interest rate parity
- show the relationship between interest rates and forward rates
- explain why there might be deviations from parity relationships

---

1. INTRODUCTION

There are two principal types of exchange rate systems: fixed rates and floating rates. Both types exist today, but the leading international trading countries, such as Japan and the USA, have floating rates. International organizations such as the International Monetary Fund have been established to facilitate the operations of foreign exchange markets.

There are two important parity conditions in international finance: purchasing power parity and interest rate parity, along with a number of important related concepts. **Purchasing power parity** (PPP) states that the price of an item expressed in different currencies must be the same. **Interest rate parity** states that the rate of return from holding risk-free financial assets must be the same, regardless of the currency in which the assets are denominated. These two parity conditions rely on **arbitrage**, the ability of market participants to buy in one market and sell in another, to take advantage of price differentials. For purposes of our initial discussion, we assume that arbitrage works. Later we will explore reasons why arbitrage might not work.

In this book we use the following convention in quoting currencies. Recall that JPY is the Japanese yen and USD is the US dollar. In a currency pair, the first currency mentioned is the one that is going to be bought or sold. Hence, USD/JPY means that we are buying USD using JPY or selling USD and receiving JPY.[1] In this chapter we consider spot market transactions in which the exchange typically takes place in 1 or 2 days and forward transactions in which the exchange is, at least part, beyond the spot settlement period. In forward transactions the exchange rate used at a future date is specified at the time of the contract. We consider the spot and forward market trading more fully in the next chapter.

2. EXCHANGE RATE SYSTEMS

Table 9.1 shows the International Monetary Fund's (IMF) classification of exchange rate arrangements for its members (see box 9.1 for a description of the IMF). There are two basic types of exchange rates, floating and fixed, with variations on each. A country with **floating exchange rates** allows its currency's value in terms of other currencies to be determined by supply and demand. This is the predominant type of exchange rate system today and is used by countries such as Japan and the USA. Closely related are managed floating systems in which a country allows supply and demand to play a part in the

Table 9.1 Exchange rate arrangements

Panel A: PEGGED

Country or countries	*Pegged to*
Angola, Antigua & Barbuda, Argentina, The Bahamas, Barbados, Belize, Djibouti, Dominica, Grenada, Iraq, Lithuania, Marshall Islands, Fed. States of Micronesia, Oman, Palau, Panama, St. Kitts & Nevis, St. Lucia, St. Vincent and the Grenadines, Syrian Arab Rep.	USD
Benin, Burkina Faso, Cameroon, C. African Rep., Chad, Comoros, Rep. of Congo, Côte d'Ivories, Equatorial Guinea, Gabon, Guinea-Bissau, Mali, Niger, Senegal, Togo	FRF
Jordan, Latvia, Libya, Myanmar	SDR
Bosnia and Herzegovina, Bulgaria, Estonia	DEM
Lesotho, Namibia, Swaziland	ZAR
Bhutan, Nepal	INR
Brunei Darussalam	SGD
Cape Verde	PTE
Kiribati	AUD
San Marino	ITL
Bangladesh, Botswana, Burundi, Cyprus, Fiji, Iceland, Kuwait, Malta, Morocco, Samoa, Seychelles, Slovak Republic, Tonga, Vanuatu	Other composite

Table 9.1 *Continued*

Panel B: FLEXIBILITY LIMITED IN TERMS OF A SINGLE CURRENCY OR GROUP OF CURRENCIES

Country or countries	Type of limit
Bahrain, Qatar, Saudi Arabia, United Arab Emirates	Single currency
Austria, Belgium, Denmark, Finland, France, Germany, Greece, Ireland, Italy, Luxembourg, Netherlands, Portugal, Spain	Cooperative arrangements

Panel C: MORE FLEXIBLE

Country or countries	Type of flexibility
Algeria, Belarus, Bolivia, Brazil, Cambodia, Chile, People's Republic of China, Colombia, Costa Rica, Croatia, Czech Republic, Dominican Rep., Ecuador, Egypt, El Salvador, Ethiopia, Georgia, Honduras, Hungary, Islamic Republic of Iran, Israel, Kazakhstan, Kenya, Kyrgyz Rep., Lao P.D. Rep., Former Yugoslav Republic of Macedonia, Malawi, Malaysia, Maldives, Mauritania, Mauritius, Nicaragua, Nigeria, Norway, Pakistan, Poland, Romania, Russia, Singapore, Slovenia, Solomon Islands, Sri Lanka, Sudan, Suriname, Rep. of Tajikistan, Tunisia, Turkey, Turkmenistan, Ukraine, Uruguay, Uzbekistan, Venezuela, Vietnam	Other managed floating
Islamic State of Afghanistan, Albania, Armenia, Australia, Azerbaijan, Canada, Dem. Rep. Congo, Eritrea, The Gambia, Ghana, Guatemala, Guinea, Guyana, Haiti, India, Indonesia, Jamaica, Japan, Korea, Lebanon, Liberia, Madagascar, Mexico, Moldova, Mongolia, Mozambique, New Zealand, Papua New Guinea, Paraguay, Peru, Philippines, Rwanda, São Tomé and Príncipe, Sierra Leone, Somalia, South Africa, Sweden, Switzerland, Tanzania, Thailand, Trinidad and Tobago, Uganda, United Kingdom, United States, Republic of Yemen, Zambia, Zimbabwe	Independently floating

These are the exchange rate arrangements as classified by the IMF as of Mar. 31, 1998.
Source: International Monetary Fund, Oct. 1998.

BOX 9.1
The international monetary fund

The International Monetary Fund (IMF) is an international organization that was established by 44 nations at Bretton Woods, New Hampshire, USA, in July 1944. The IMF became operational in 1946 and now has more than 180 members. The purpose of the IMF is to promote a stable system of trading currencies, so that international payments can take place smoothly. Each member contributes financial resources called a "quota" to the IMF, based on the size of its economy. The USA has the largest quota, which was about 35 billion USD in 1998 and represented about 18 percent of the total quotas. Each country pays 75 percent of its quota in its own currency and the remainder in gold or a convertible currency. The IMF uses this fund to make loans to members who are experiencing payments difficulties. Each member has the right to borrow several times the amount of its quota subscription under one of several programs operated by the IMF. Since the IMF expects repayment, these loans may be accompanied by strict requirements for addressing the problems that have led to the payments difficulties. Examples of IMF lending include 18 billion USD to Mexico in 1995 and 35 billion USD to Indonesia, Korea, and Thailand in the first 7 months of 1998.

Special drawing rights (SDR) are a reserve asset created by the IMF. The value of the SDR is tied to a composite basket of currencies for the five countries having the largest exports of goods and services: namely, the USD, DEM, FRF, JPY, and GBP. The relative weighting of each currency reflects the country's relative importance in international trade and in reserve assets. As of January 1, 1996, the weightings were: USD, 39 percent; DEM, 21 percent; JPY, 18 percent; FRF, 11 percent; and GBP, 11 percent. SDRs constitute only about 2 percent of the world's reserve assets.

Ultimate authority for the IMF is vested in a board of governors. Each member appoints a governor and alternate to the board. Policies of the board of governors are implemented by 24 executive directors who meet several times a week as an executive board. A managing director who chairs the executive board and a staff of about 2,600 carry out day-to-day operations of the IMF. The principal offices of the IMF are located in Washington, D.C., USA.

Source: http://www.imf.int/external/index.htm

---

determination of its currency's value, but also attempts to manage the value of its currency through central bank purchases and sales. Singapore attempts to keep its currency's value in line with a basket of the currencies of its trading partners, but the exact weighting of each is not disclosed. Countries belonging to the European Monetary Union (EMU) are committed to maintaining a fixed exchange rate between their national currency and the euro, but the euro's value floats (see box 9.2 for a discussion of the euro and box 9.3 for a discussion of the effects of exchange rate fluctuations).

In contrast to floating exchange rates, in a **fixed exchange rate system**, the value of a country's currency is established at a fixed rate. Historically, the fixed rate might have been in terms of gold or silver. In the early years of the twentieth century, except for the years surrounding World War I, most countries were on the gold standard. The **gold standard** is a fixed exchange rate system in which countries define the value of their currency in terms of gold. Many countries left the gold standard during the depression beginning in 1929.

The Bretton Woods agreement of 1944 established a fixed exchange rate system in which the USA undertook to buy and sell gold at 35 USD per ounce, and other countries defined

BOX 9.2
The euro

One of the most significant developments in forex markets during the 1990s was the implementation of the three-stage plan for committing the European Union (EU) governments to monetary union (European Monetary Union, or EMU). This plan was initially negotiated in 1989 and was confirmed in the Treaty on European Union agreed to at Maastricht in February 1992. Stage 1 concentrated on the removal of capital and trade barriers and the creation and implementation of a single financial area working out of the European Exchange Rate Mechanism. Stage 2 established which countries would join the single currency initially. These countries are 11 of the 15 member states of the EU: Austria, Belgium, Finland, France, Germany, Ireland, Italy, Luxembourg, Netherlands, Portugal, and Spain. Denmark, Greece, Sweden, and the United Kingdom did not join the monetary union on January 1, 1999. Bilateral exchange rates between the individual currencies and the euro were established at stage 2, and a number of new institutions, including the European Central Bank (ECB), which officially began operation on July 1, 1998, were established. Stage 3 began on January 1, 1999, which marked the beginning of EMU. The euro became a currency, replacing the European currency unit, and forex operations denominated in euros began after the holiday weekend. Also, the European Central Bank began monetary and forex operations denominated in euros. During a 3-year transition period, national currencies and the euro may coexist. The latest date for the introduction of euro notes and coins and the elimination of national currencies is January 2002. National debt must be converted to the euro by that date, but thousands of treasury and corporate bonds were redenominated during January 1999, and many thousands more during the subsequent few months.

Source: This discussion is based in part on information obtained from the Reuters web site (http://www.reuters.com/).

BOX 9.3
Personal reflections (1)

Two bridges connect the Malaysian mainland with the island on which Singapore is located. During the Asian currency crisis of 1997 merchants had trouble adjusting their prices to the falling value of the MYR relative to other currencies, including the SGD. As a result many Singaporians crossed into Malaysia to buy groceries and other items. Parking lots of Malaysian shopping centers were filled with cars with Singapore plates. I was able to purchase books at one store at half their prices in Singapore. Apparently the merchant updated prices only when a new shipment of books arrived. Because petrol prices are lower in Malaysia than in Singapore, the Singapore government prohibits Singaporians from entering Malaysia if their petrol tanks are less than three-quarters full. These examples reflect deviations from PPP in the very short run.

the value of their currencies in terms of the USD. Each country agreed to maintain the value of its currency within 1 percent of its stated value. An economic shock such as the development of a new technology that changes the supply and demand for a product can lead to changes in the real equilibrium value of currencies. In a fixed exchange rate system these shocks are reflected first in the accumulation or depletion of reserve assets such as gold and the USD. If disequilibrium persists, a change in the stated exchange rate is needed. Countries with overvalued currencies experiencing losses of reserve assets are typically forced to devalue or lower the stated value of their currency. A lower value of the domestic currency vis-à-vis other currencies makes repayment of debts denominated in other currencies more expensive, often forcing a restructuring of both public and private sector debts. A deficiency of a fixed rate system is that there is not much pressure on countries with undervalued currencies to correct problems causing the undervaluation. This puts most of the burden of correcting system problems on countries experiencing overvaluation.

Table 9.1 shows that a number of countries peg the value of their currency to the USD, the French franc (FRF), or the South African rand (ZAR). Other countries peg their currency to that of an important trading partner or neighbor, such as Nepal with India and Brunei with Singapore. Brunei notes are accepted in Singapore on a one-for-one basis with Singapore currency. A few countries peg their exchange rates to an official basket of currencies such as the SDR or to a basket of the currencies of their trading partners. We have already mentioned that Singapore attempts to keep its currency in line with that of undisclosed weighting of its major trading partners. All the countries which have a fixed exchange rate vis-à-vis the USD have a fixed exchange rate with each other. But since the USD is floating relative to other currencies, the values of these currencies also float along with the USD. Similar statements can be made about countries pegging their currency to other individual currencies or to baskets.

One way of enforcing a fixed exchange rate system is through a currency board. A **currency board** is a note-issuing authority that announces an exchange rate against some nondomestic currency and carries out trades of domestic currency at that rate. The currency board is prohibited from owning any domestic assets, so its notes are backed entirely by holdings of nondomestic monetary assets. Currency boards are not typically central banks. Montagu-Pollock (1998) indicates that there have been 77 historically recorded currency boards. Argentina and Hong Kong operate currency boards. Argentina requires that the currency board hold reserves equivalent in value to 100 percent of the value of notes issued. The currency board of Hong Kong, the Hong Kong Monetary Authority, has foreign exchange reserves of more than seven times the cash in circulation and more than three times cash and demand deposits. The currency board system has the advantage of removing monetary policy from the hands of politicians. A difficulty of the system is that equilibrium is achieved through asset price changes rather than exchange rate changes, making the system prone to banking system collapse. (See Moffet and Torres 1988 for a discussion of the currency board in Argentina and suggestions for forming a monetary union between Argentina and Brazil.)

3. PRICE PARITY RELATIONSHIPS

3.1. THE LAW OF ONE PRICE

The **law of one price** states that the price of identical items must be the same, regardless of where they are traded. We begin with a simplistic example. Suppose that the US government announced that it would either buy or sell postage stamps at its official price, and that the price in New York for a given stamp was 1 USD, whereas the price in Philadelphia for the same stamp was 2 USD. No one would buy stamps in Philadelphia. In fact, many people would buy stamps in New York and sell them in Philadelphia. The US government would lose so much on the transactions that it would probably be forced to abandon this differential pricing very quickly. Then, the US government will sell stamps for the same price in both cities. We cannot tell whether the new price will be 1 USD, 2 USD, or something in between. Likewise, suppose that investors could borrow or lend money in New York at 5 percent or in Dallas for 6 percent. Many investors would borrow in New York and lend in Dallas, so eventually the interest rates in the two cities would be forced together. But again we do not know whether the equilibrium rate will be 5 percent, 6 percent, or between 5 percent and 6 percent.

The law of one price also applies to prices and interest rates in an international setting. The only complication is that we must take exchange rates into account. Suppose that for a given exchange rate the price of an item is higher in Tokyo than in Mexico City. Then arbitrage will force these two prices together. But we do not know whether the price in Tokyo will fall, the price in Mexico City will increase, or whether the prices will stay the same and the exchange rate will change. Any one or any combination of these outcomes is possible. Suppose that an identical hat sells for 10 USD in New York and 2000 JPY in Tokyo, and that in the foreign exchange markets 1 USD costs 400 JPY. Assume that there are no transportation costs, taxes, or other barriers to trade. Individuals could buy hats in Tokyo for 2000 JPY and sell them in New York, receiving 10 USD. The 10 USD could be exchanged for 4000 JPY, resulting in a profit of 2000 JPY per hat. If the price of hats in New York fell to 5 USD, then the profit opportunity would be eliminated. An increase in the price of hats in Tokyo to 4000 JPY or a change in the exchange rate to 1 USD for 200 JPY would also eliminate profit opportunities.

Despite its being called a "law", there are conditions that might prevent the law of one price from holding, such as transaction costs, transportation costs, and taxes.

3.2. Purchasing Power Parity: Absolute

Absolute purchasing power parity claims that price parity holds for the price levels of two countries. Suppose that we compute the price level of country 1 and country 2 as follows:

$$L_1 = \Sigma w_{1,i} p_{1,i}$$

$$L_2 = \Sigma w_{2,i} p_{2,i}$$

where p indicates the price level and w indicates the relative weights of item i in the index. Thus, $p_{1,i}$ and $p_{2,i}$ are the prices in countries 1 and 2, respectively, of item i. The index comprises the basket of goods that we wish to compare. If there are two items, say a and b, in each index, then

$$L_1 = w_{1,a} p_{1,a} + w_{1,b} p_{1,b}$$

$$L_2 = w_{2,a} p_{2,a} + w_{2,b} p_{2,b}$$

Even if the law of one price holds, absolute PPP may not hold, since this would require the weights to be the same for each country. If PPP holds, a trader can either purchase the basket of goods represented by L_1 or take the same amount of money, exchange it for the currency of country 2, and purchase the basket of goods represented by L_2.

Case 1: PPP at time t

Let $S_{USD,XYZ,t}$ be the spot USD/XYZ exchange rate at time t (which, when the meaning is clear, we denote simply as S_t). If the exchange rate is USD/XYZ 0.2500, then $S_t = 0.2500$, so that in value terms (USD) $S_t \equiv (XYZ)$, which shows that 1 USD equals 0.2500 XYZ. XYZ is the currency for country XYZ. P_{US} and P_{XYZ} are prices in the US and XYZ, respectively. For a homogeneous product, X, if there are no transaction costs, the following condition must hold to prevent profitable arbitrage:

$$P_{X,USD,t}S_t = P_{X,XYZ,t} \qquad\qquad 9.1$$

where $P_{X,USD,t}$ is the price of basket X in USD at time t, $P_{X,XYZ,t}$ is the price of basket X in XYZ at time t, and S_t is the exchange rate of USD for XYZ. If an economy starts from scratch, the choice of P and S is arbitrary. A choice for P dictates S, or a choice of S dictates P. There are three unknowns in equation 9.1. Many different values for $P_{X,USD,t}$, S_t, and $P_{X,XYZ,t}$ would be consistent with the equality expressed in the equation, but once two of the values are specified, the third is determined.

Suppose that the price of gold in the USA is 300 USD per ounce, and that USD/XYZ 0.25. Hence, substituting these values in equation 9.1, it is clear that the price of gold in XYZ must be 75, assuming that there are no obstacles to shipping gold from one country to another. With an exchange rate of USD/XYZ 0.25, the price of 300 USD and 75 XYZ are equivalent, so there is no arbitrage opportunity. But with the same exchange rate, if one of the prices changed and the other did not, there would be an arbitrage opportunity. Speculators could buy in one country and ship to the other, earning unlimited profits. While it might take time, we expect that arbitrage would eventually force the prices to be equivalent again.

3.3. PURCHASING POWER PARITY (PPP): RELATIVE

If absolute PPP holds, not only must the prices at time t be equivalent, taking exchange rates into account, i.e.,

$$P_{X,USD,t}S_t = P_{X,XYZ,t} \qquad\qquad 9.2$$

but we must expect that the prices at t + 1 will also be equivalent:

$$P_{X,USD,t+1}S_{t+1} = P_{X,XYZ,t+1} \qquad\qquad 9.3$$

Dividing the left-hand side of equation 9.3 by the left-hand side of equation 9.2, and the right-hand side of equation 9.3 by the right-hand side of equation 9.3, and rearranging terms, we obtain:

Table 9.2 Interest rates, exchange rates, and consumer prices for Brazil, the United Kingdom, and the United States

	1994	1995	1996	1997
	Interest rates			
Brazil	Not available	49.93	25.73	24.79
United Kingdom	5.15	6.33	5.77	6.48
United States	4.27	5.51	5.04	5.07
	Exchange rates (year-end values)			
USD/BRL	0.846	0.973	1.039	1.116
USD/GBP	0.6400	0.6452	0.5889	0.6047
GBP/BRL	1.3219	1.5081	1.7642	1.8458
	Consumer price index (1990 = 100)			
Brazil	24,724	41,044	47,512	50,803
United Kingdom	114.3	118.2	121.1	124.9
United States	113.4	116.6	120.0	122.9

Source: International Monetary Fund, *International Financial Statistics*, Oct. 1998.

$$(P_{X,XYZ,t+1}/P_{X,XYZ,t}) = (P_{X,USD,t+1})/(P_{X,USD,t})(S_{t+1}/S_t) \qquad 9.4$$

Note that P_{t+1}/P_t is the price relative, which is a measure of inflation. Note also that the prices at t and t + 1 are for the same basket of goods. Equation 9.4 is called **relative purchasing power parity**, which states that exchange rate changes reflect differences in the rate of change in price indexes from country to country. The price indexes used in measuring relative PPP usually comprise baskets of good. There are numerous difficulties in developing baskets that are meaningful in many countries.

Example

Using the data in table 9.2, to see whether PPP holds between the United Kingdom and Brazil, we can restate equation 9.4 as:

$$(P_{X,BRL,t+1}/P_{X,BRL,t}) = (P_{X,GBP,t+1})/(P_{X,GBP,t})(S_{t+1}/S_t)$$

Substituting the values from table 9.2 gives:

$$(50,803/47,512) = (124.9/121.1)(1.8458/1.7642)$$

which simplifies to

$$1.0693 \neq (1.0314)(1.0463)$$

or

$$1.0693 \neq 1.0791$$

We can see that exchange rate changes and changes in consumer prices are in the same direction. But the equality does not hold exactly. Of course, it would be unusual to obtain an exact equality, due to measurement problems, transaction costs (such as bid–ask spreads), and the like. Whether this constitutes evidence for or against PPP depends on one's view of how close is close enough.

Case 2: PPP at time t and t + 1 with inflation

Suppose that inflation in goods prices is expected in the USA and in XYZ, but that the rates differ. The rate in the USA is λ_{US}, and the rate in XYZ is λ_{XYZ}. We know that

$$P_{X,USD,t+1}/P_{X,USD,t} = 1 + \lambda_{US} \tag{9.5}$$

and

$$P_{X,XYZ,t+1}/P_{X,XYZ,t} = 1 + \lambda_{XYZ} \tag{9.6}$$

Substituting equation 9.5 and equation 9.6 in equation 9.4 gives

$$(1 + \lambda_{XYZ})/(1 + \lambda_{US}) = (S_{t+1}/S_t) \tag{9.7}$$

In other words, relative changes in exchange rates reflect the different rates of inflation in each country. Supply and demand conditions for basket X can change during period t, but these changes are reflected in the prices in both countries, so the parity relationship is maintained.

3.4. Real Exchange Rates

The **real exchange rate** is the exchange rate between two countries after taking relative prices into account. If we start at a point where PPP roughly prevailed, examination of real exchange rates over time provides a measure of how exchange rates are deviating from PPP. Considering absolute price levels, we know from equation 9.1 that

$$P_{X,USD,t}S_t = P_{X,XYZ,t}$$

We can define the real exchange rate as

$$R_t = (P_{X,USD,t}S_t)/P_{X,XYZ,t} \tag{9.8}$$

In practice, the real exchange rate can be regarded as an index. Based on equation 9.4, we can define the real exchange rate as

$$R_t = (P_{X,XYZ,t+1}/P_{X,XYZ,t})/((P_{X,USD,t+1})/(P_{X,USD,t})(S_{t+1}/S_t)) \qquad 9.9$$

If we began at parity and relative PPP holds, then, over time, R_t in equation 9.9 will equal 1.0.

Exchange rates are constantly changing. If bilateral prices also change so as to offset exchange rates, there is no change in the real exchange rate. But if PPP does not hold, then real exchange rates change.

So far we have been discussing bilateral exchange rate measures. Sometimes it may be desirable to construct a multilateral index for a country. An index can be constructed for country A by weighting the bilateral indexes for each trading partner by its share of country A's total international trade. If the exchange rates that are weighted are nominal exchange rates, then a **nominal effective exchange rate** is obtained. If the exchange rates that are weighted are real exchange rates, then a **real effective exchange rate** is obtained. The International Monetary Fund publishes tables of these exchange rates by country by year and by parts of years.

4. INTEREST RATE PARITY

4.1. INTRODUCTION

At time t, an investor can hold either $(USD)_t$ or $(XYZ)_t$. The risk-free interest rate during the coming period is r_{US} and r_{XYZ} for the USA and XYZ, respectively. Hence, at the end of period 1 the investor will have either $(USD)_t(1 + r_{US})$ or $(XYZ)_t(1 + r_{XYZ})$. Interest rate parity states that the relationship between the current and forward exchange rates for two currencies and the respective interest rates for those two currencies must be such that the rate of return is equivalent no matter which currency is held.

At time t, a given amount of USD can be exchanged for $(USD)_t S_t$ of $(XYZ)_t$, so that

$$(USD)_t S_t = (XYZ)_t$$

If an investor retains USDs and invests them, at t + 1 the investor will have

$$(USD)_t(1 + r_{US})$$

Alternatively, if an investor exchanges USD for XYZ, then at t + 1 the investor will have

$$(USD)_t S_t(1 + r_{XYZ})$$

units of XYZ. These two outcomes can be exchanged for each other using the exchange rate prevailing at t + 1, S_{t+1}. Since the two sums are equivalent at t, if investors are free to choose, they will select the alternative that produces the most profitable outcome. Hence, arbitrage will tend to make the following relationship hold

$$(USD)_t(1 + r_{US})S_{t+1} = (USD)_tS_t(1 + r_{XYZ}).$$ 9.10

Rearranging terms gives

$$(1 + r_{US})/(1 + r_{XYZ}) = S_t/S_{t+1}.$$ 9.11

Equation 9.11 expresses **uncovered interest rate parity**, which states that changes in exchange rates reflect differences in interest rates.

Example

We can use the data in table 9.2 to investigate whether uncovered interest parity holds for 1997 between the USA and Brazil. Equation 9.11 can be restated as

$$(1 + r_{US})/(1 + r_{BRL}) = S_t/S_{t+1}$$

Substituting from table 9.2 gives

$$(1.0507/1.2479) \neq (1.039/1.116)$$

which simplifies to

$$0.8420 \neq 0.9310$$

Again, whether this is sufficiently close to conclude that uncovered interest rate parity holds depends on how close is close enough.

Covered interest rate parity asserts that two investment approaches give the same terminal wealth:

1 Buy risk-free bonds denominated in currency a and enter into a contract to exchange the end-of-period proceeds for currency b.
2 Exchange currency a for currency b at the beginning of the period and buy risk-free bonds denominated in currency b.

At t, the conversion rate for the cash inflow of $(USD)_t(1 + r_{US})$ at $t + 1$ can be locked in at the rate $F_{t,t+1}$.[2] On the other hand, the sum of USD_t can be exchanged for $S_t\ USD_t$ units of XYZ at t and invested, yielding $(USD)_tS_t(1 + r_{XYZ})$ at $t + 1$. If covered interest rate parity holds, these two alternatives produce an equivalent end-of-period wealth, namely

$$(1\ USD)_t(1 + r_{US})F_{t,t+1} = (USD)_tS_t(1 + r_{XYZ}).$$

Rearranging terms shows that the forward rate reflects differences in interest rates in each country, so that

$$S_t/F_{t,t+1} = (1 + r_{US})/(1 + r_{XYZ}).$$ 9.12

247

Example

The author found a copy of the *Financial Times* (London) for August 25, 1994, in a drawer and wondered whether covered interest parity prevailed on that date. The GBP/CHF spot rate was 2.0253 and the 1-year forward rate was 1.9881. The 1-year interest rates in GBP and CHF, respectively, were 6 13/16 percent and 4 9/16 percent. These rates are all quote midpoints and do not take bid–ask spread into account. Restating equation 9.12 gives

$$S_t / F_{t,t+1} = (1 + r_{GB}) / (1 + r_{SW})$$

Substituting the values from the *Financial Times* gives

$$2.0253 / 1.9881 \approx 1.06887 / 1.04625$$

or

$$1.018711 \approx 1.02162$$

Dividing 1.02162 by 1.01871 gives 1.0028556, so the difference between the two sides of the expression is less than one-third of one percentage point. It is likely that transaction costs would prevent arbitrage from forcing rates together more closely.

4.2. COVERED INTEREST ARBITRAGE AND THE TRADING OF DEPOSITS

Currency deposits are traded in over-the-counter markets just like foreign exchange. These deposits are traded directly among banks and through brokers. A wide range of maturities, such as overnight, spot settlement, 1 week, and 1–12 months, may be traded. The bid price is the rate that will be paid for deposits, and the ask price is the rate that will be charged for loans. One of the best-known quotations is the London Interbank Offer Rate, LIBOR, which is the offer rate for London deposits. The bid rate would be lower. As in all interest rates, quotes are stated in terms of a rate per year. Most markets use a 360-day year convention in making quotes, so a quote of 7 percent for a 30-day deposit means that one will receive $(1 + 0.07(30/360)) = 1.0058333$ at the end of the month. Two important exceptions to the 360-day convention are Great Britain and Australia, which use 365-day years. It is important that one ascertain what a particular interest rate quote means before actually entering into a contract.

If interest rate parity does not hold, then **covered interest rate arbitrage** will be profitable. Covered interest arbitrage is one mechanism that will tend to make interest rate parity hold. In covered interest rate arbitrage,

1. A currency is borrowed and converted into a second currency.
2. The second currency is
   a. immediately invested at interest and, at the same time,
   b. sold forward to lock its conversion rate into the first currency.
3. Hence, at maturity, the proceeds of the loan of the second currency can be delivered on the forward contract to obtain enough of the first currency to repay the loan with interest and show a profit.

4.3. THE UNBIASED EXPECTATIONS HYPOTHESIS AND UNCOVERED INTEREST PARITY

Two closely related concepts are the unbiased expectations hypothesis and uncovered interest parity. Let $E(S_{t+1})$ be the exchange rate at $t + 1$ expected at t, and S_t be the exchange rate at t. Let F_t be the forward rate at time t for period $t + 1$. Exchange rates and forward rates are expressed as units of the currency for XYZ per USD. Finally, let $1 + r_{US}$ and $1 + r_{XYZ}$ be the interest rate for the next period in the USA and in XYZ. The **unbiased expectations hypothesis** implies that the actual distribution of future spot rates is centered on the current forward rate, so the current forward rate does not systematically overestimate or underestimate the future spot rate. Hence,

$$E(S_{t+1}) = F_t \qquad\qquad 9.13$$

In some cases this is restated as

$$E(S_{t+1})/S_t = F_t/S_t \qquad\qquad 9.14$$

Using terminology based on McCallum (1994), we can refer to these as the forward rate and discount rate versions of the relation.

In our terminology, covered interest parity is

$$(1 + r_{XYZ})/(1 + r_{US}) = F_t/S_t \qquad\qquad 9.15$$

In other words, changes in exchange rates reflect changes in relative interest rates. Note that all the terms in equation 9.15 are as of time t. Hence, there is a strong theoretical presumption that covered interest arbitrage will hold. This brings us to uncovered interest parity, which states that actual exchange rates at two points in time will reflect relative interest rates over the period, namely:

$$(1 + r_{XYZ})/(1 + r_{US}) = S_{t+1}/S_t \qquad\qquad 9.16$$

Equating the right-hand sides of equation 9.15 and equation 9.14 gives

$$S_{t+1}/S_t = F_t/S_t \qquad\qquad 9.17$$

which is similar to equation 9.15. This is why the unbiased expectations hypothesis and uncovered interest parity are often considered together.

4.4. INTERNATIONAL FISHER EFFECT

The **international Fisher effect** states that exchange rates change in an equal and opposite direction to interest rate differences between countries. Continuing our notation from the previous section, if the international Fisher effect holds,

249

$$(E(S_{t+1}) - S_t)/(S_t) = ((1 + r_{XYZ})/(1 + r_{US})) - 1 \qquad 9.18$$

At some future date let the exchange rate be USD/XYZ 100, the US interest rate be 10 percent, and the XYZ interest rate be 20 percent. Substituting gives

$$(E(S_{t+1}) - 100)/(100) = ((1 + 0.2)/(1 + 0.1)) - 1$$

which simplifies to

$$E(S_{t+1}) = 109$$

The exchange rate expected to prevail in the future time is the current exchange rate adjusted for interest rate differentials for the two currencies.

Some authors relate the international Fisher effect to inflation. Suppose that interest rates comprise a real component, λ, which is the same everywhere, and an inflation component, τ, so that

$$r_{US} = (1 + \lambda_{US})(1 + \tau_{US}) \qquad 9.19$$

and

$$r_{XYZ} = (1 + \lambda_{XYZ})(1 + \tau_{XYZ}) \qquad 9.20$$

Substituting equation 9.19 and equation 9.20 into equation 9.18 gives

$$(E(S_{t+1}) - S_t)/(S_t) = (((1 + \lambda_{XYZ})(1 + \tau_{XYZ}))/((1 + \lambda_{US})(1 + \tau_{US}))) - 1$$

which, given that $\lambda_{XYZ} = \lambda_{US}$, simplifies to

$$E(S_{t+1}) = ((1 + \tau_{XYZ})/(1 + \tau_{US}))(S_t) \qquad 9.21$$

Hence, the expected change in the spot rate reflects differences in inflation. If the rate of inflation is uncertain, τ represents expected inflation.

Example

Suppose we wish to determine the expected GBP/BRL exchange rate in 1 year. Restating equation 9.21 gives

$$E(S_{t+1}) = ((1 + \tau_{BRL})/(1 + \tau_{GBP}))(S_t)$$

Substituting the information for 1997 from table 9.2 gives

$$E(S_{t+1}) = ((1.069)/(1.0314))(1.7642)$$

Simplifying gives

$$E(S_{t+1}) = 1.8290$$

This result is relatively close to the actual exchange rate at the end of 1997, which was 1.8458. Again, because of measurement problems, transaction costs and possibly other factors, we would not expect the relation to hold exactly.

4.5. DEVIATIONS FROM PARITY RELATIONSHIPS

In this section we discuss reasons why parity relationships might not hold. We begin with reasons that apply to all types of parity relationships. Then we discuss specific reasons why PPP might be violated.

4.5.1. General explanations for failure of parity relationships

Measurement problems   Numerous data and measurement problems are encountered in testing parity relationships.

1   Prices may be measured at different times. Interest rates, commodity prices, or exchange rates may be stale due to thin trading. In testing PPP, the prices for the components of a price index may not be synchronous. One country may measure prices on the 15th of the month while another uses the end of the month. If the prices are collected at different times, they could not have been available for use by arbitrageurs in making their decisions.
2   Prices obtained from one vendor or geographic location may reflect peculiarities of the costs or supply/demand conditions and may not reflect the market as a whole.
3   If government statistics are used, the methods of collection and the type of products covered may differ from country to country.

Lack of market efficiency   Our assumption that arbitrage will force prices together is based on the idea that markets are efficient. There are a number reasons why markets might not be efficient.

1   If speculators do not recognize price differentials or for some reason are not willing or able to take advantage of them, deviations from parity can persist.
2   Institutions such as banks and telecommunications and transportation firms may not exist or may not be reliable.
3   Restrictions on short selling may prevent investors who believe that valuations of assets are excessive from trading on their view.
4   **Home bias** refers to the propensity of investors to prefer to invest in their home country even when superior returns or diversification benefits are available in another country. Tesar and Werner (1995) document that investors have a strong bias toward the securities of their home country. Even when investors do diversify internationally, they tend to select investments that are relatively close geographically, such as in a neighboring country.

251

5   Investors may favor certain types of investments and avoid others even if they are mis-priced. Kang and Stulz (1997) report that non-Japanese holdings of Japanese stocks reflect a strong bias against small firms, and disproportionately more shares in manufacturing firms, firms with good accounting performance, and firms with low unsystematic risk and low leverage.

Costs of arbitrage   Even for items traded internationally, such as gold, there may be a number of costs that must be taken into account by arbitrageurs. These types of difficulties place significant barriers on the operation of arbitrage. In fact, the opportunities for profits would probably have to be significant to cover these costs. Once the startup costs have been paid and an arbitrage program has been established, continuing arbitrage can be sustained with much lower profit expectations. Examples of these costs include:

1   Transaction costs including transportation, insurance, taxes and tariffs, and export restrictions may pose problems. If wheat prices are different in Kansas and Chicago, it is hardly surprising that they are different in Kansas and Russia, which for a number of years imported grain from the USA. In fact, if trade is to take place, the price in Russia must be sufficiently higher than the price in Kansas to warrant paying for the cost of shipping the grain to Russia.
2   Logistical problems such as communication (due to technology or language) may present formidable obstacles to arbitrage. A trader living in Tokyo and trading in New York must be up during the middle of the night.
3   Information costs are often higher for traders dealing outside their home markets. Potential arbitrageurs may be unfamiliar with local business people, have difficulty deciding who is reliable and who is not, not be able to read the local language, face unfamiliar government regulations and different social and business practices, including accounting standards.

Risk   Our analysis so far has not considered how risk affects parity relationships.

1   If traders and investors are averse to risk, they may incorporate a risk premium into future prices for commodities, interest rates, and foreign exchange. These premiums may make arbitrage difficult and limit parity relationships.
2   Because the future is uncertain, risk may make it desirable to favor decisions that allow flexibility and to avoid becoming locked into a particular course of action. Hence, risk can considerably slow trade and investment adjustments that restore parity relationships. Suppose that the JPY appreciates relative to the USD, so that it becomes unprofitable for Japanese manufacturers to export to the USA. Should Japanese manufacturers abandon the US market? The answer depends in part on expectations for USD/JPY exchange rates. If the exchange rate is likely to remain unfavorable, so that these exports will never be profitable, then the US market should be abandoned. But suppose that there is a likelihood that the USD will appreciate against the JPY. If distribution facilities in the USA are abandoned, it may be costly and difficult or impossible to reestablish them. Under these circumstances, Japanese manufacturers might be willing to sustain losses for long periods in the hope that eventually their exports to the USA will be profitable. In fact, the US operations can be considered an option on the USD/JPY exchange rate.
3   The risk that arises from having to trade and invest in individual countries is sovereign risk. Differences in risk from country to country can also affect parity relationships.

Holding even the risk-free bonds of some countries may be risky. When speaking of risk-free bonds, we typically mean free of default risk. But other risks, such as political risk, are present. Investors demand compensation for bearing these risks, and this compensation leads to interest rate differentials across countries.

4.5.2. Specific explanations of why PPP might fail to hold

Specific reasons why tests of PPP might fail include the following

Non-traded goods Some goods are traded internationally, and others are not. See box 9.4 for a personal reflection concerning nontraded goods. The costs of these nontraded goods may be a significant component of the costs of traded goods, since manufacturers and shippers use local services. Differences in the rates of inflation between traded and nontraded goods can result in the failure of PPP tests.

It is easy to imagine goods that must be consumed locally and are not amenable to being shipped from one country to another. Hotel rooms in Buenos Aires must be consumed on the spot. Differences in room prices from one city to another reflect differences in building costs, land costs, and the like. But even after taking cost differences into account, exchange rates can make the room rates in a city excessively high or low from the point of view of those using a nondomestic currency. Since surplus rooms cannot be shipped to another city experiencing a shortage, there is no direct way for arbitrage to force the price of rooms in Buenos Aires vis-à-vis other cities to reflect just cost difference rather than exchange rate differences.

Of course, this is overstating the case somewhat, since there is an indirect mechanism through which arbitrage can work. Travelers often choose their destinations based on costs. If hotel rooms become relatively cheaper in one location, tourists will tend to switch to that location, and this will influence exchange rates, tending to force the elimination of price differences that do not reflect costs. Also, companies compare costs when deciding where to locate plants and offices. This indirect mechanism is likely to be incomplete and slower to work than direct arbitrage.

BOX 9.4
Personal reflections (2)

During the late 1990s I traveled to Poland to present a paper at the University of Warsaw. I visited the flat of a Polish academic and admired his collection of Polish paintings. I was told that these paintings could not be taken out of the country. The goal of this regulation is, apparently, to prevent Poland from losing it cultural heritage. But I wonder if the indirect consequences have been fully considered. Lower demand for older Polish paintings, which are the likely target of these types of regulations, will result in lower prices. Lower prices for older paintings will no doubt result in lower prices for new paintings, since these are to some extent substitutes. Lower prices for new paintings will reduce the supply, so that, from the perspective of 100–200 years hence, the cultural heritage of Poland may be diminished rather than enhanced by restrictions on exports of paintings.

Differences in tastes   If consumers in one country value a particular good more highly than consumers in another, changes in price of the good have different impacts on the living standards in the two countries. Hence, the speed of response to price changes may differ, affecting PPP.

5. EMPIRICAL EVIDENCE

5.1. THE LAW OF ONE PRICE AND PPP

There is considerable empirical support for the law of one price and PPP (Cheung et al. 1995; Lothian 1997). Froot, Kim, and Rogoff (1995) examined nominal exchange rates for barley, butter, cheese, eggs, oats, peas, silver, and wheat, going back as far as 1273. These authors report that deviations from the law of one price today do not differ dramatically in volatility or persistence from those in the Middle Ages. MacDonald (1993) found that there is "a long-run relationship between a number of bilateral USD exchange rates and their corresponding relative prices." Crownover, Pippenger, and Steigerwald (1996) examined absolute purchasing power parity using annual prices over 66 years for a basket of 221 goods and services weighted according to the consumption pattern of a four-person household in the Federal Republic of Germany. The authors report that deviations from PPP do not persist, suggesting "that absolute PPP should be treated as a serious empirical relation." Wei and Parsley (1995) studied PPP using data for 12 tradable sectors in 91 OECD countries. Since 1973 there is strong evidence of mean reversion toward PPP with an estimated half-life of 4–5 years. (The half-life is the amount of time that it takes to correct one-half of the deviation from PPP.) Abuaf and Jorion (1990) report that deviations from PPP are substantial in the short run, but have a half-life of about 3 years. Using black market rates, rather than official rates, Phylaktis and Kassimatis (1994) found that long-run movements in real exchange rates for eight Pacific Basin countries were consistent with PPP. Further, the half-life of deviations from PPP was about 1 year. Box 9.5 provides some of the author's personal reflections related to PPP.

MacDonald (1993) cites a number of studies which report that long-run PPP does not hold; but many argue that studies that fail to support PPP are flawed, because they do not allow for deviations from PPP due to transaction costs, nontraded goods, risk, measurement problems, and real economic shocks. Reasons often cited for deviations from PPP include:

BOX 9.5
Personal reflections (3)

When I was about 10 years old, I can remember my family driving from our home in Birmingham, Alabama, USA, to the Florida Gulf Coast about 6 hours' drive away. When we arrived in south Alabama, there were fields of watermelons, which I regarded as a great treat, selling at four or five for 1 USD, a fraction of their price in Birmingham. Is this a violation of the law of one price?

---

1 *Transaction costs*   Michael, Nobay, and Peel (1994) examined PPP using USD prices of wheat traded contemporaneously in the USA, Japan, and the Netherlands. While short-run deviations from PPP are found, these do not produce profitable arbitrage opportunities. Wei and Parsley (1995) found that deviations from PPP are positively related to transportation costs.

2 *Nontraded goods*   Dutton and Strauss (1997) found that an increase in the domestic price of nontraded goods relative to traded goods was associated with an appreciation in the real exchange rate. Hence, the authors concluded that relative price movements of traded and nontraded goods are an important determinant of real exchange rate behavior.

3 *Risk*   Bhatti and Moosa (1994) developed and tested a model in which risk plays an important role in PPP. These authors argue that one reason for the failure of standard tests of PPP is their failure to take uncertainty into account. Wei and Parsley (1995) found that deviations from PPP are positively related to exchange rate volatility.

4 *Measurement problems*   Apte, Kane, and Sercu (1994) tested for relative PPP and reported that previous rejections of PPP are probably due to measurement problems such as delays in reporting goods prices relative to the reporting of exchange rates. Sjaastad (1998) demonstrated that Swiss real exchange rates contain significant measurement error.

5 *Real economic shocks*   Real economic shocks can permanently change the structure of the financial and trading relationships between two countries. Kim and Enders (1991) argue that these real economic shocks can induce permanent deviations from PPP. Dibooglu (1996) reports that PPP is affected by "real shocks that alter equilibrium prices between tradables and nontradables."

5.2. COVERED INTEREST RATE PARITY

Tests have shown deviations from covered interest parity, but that these deviations are eventually eliminated. Levi (1977) showed that different forms of taxation across countries may lead to profitable covered interest arbitrage. Fletcher and Taylor (1994) found profit opportunities in excess of transaction costs for covered interest arbitrage. These opportunities are not short-lived, but "diminish over time, and eventually disappear." Using JPY/USD, DEM/USD, GBP/USD, CAD/USD exchange rates, Abeysekera and Turtle (1995) also found strong evidence that covered interest rate parity does not hold. These authors indicate that their findings may be due, at least in part, to transaction costs, settlement procedures, risk premia, and regulatory and capital constraints. Blenman (1995) and Committeri, Rossi, and Santorelli (1993) showed that measurement problems may affect tests of covered interest parity.

5.3. THE UNBIASED EXPECTATIONS HYPOTHESIS AND UNCOVERED INTEREST PARITY

The empirical evidence overwhelmingly rejects the hypothesis that forward rates are unbiased predictors of future spot rates. (Forward rates reflect expectations, whereas spot rates reflect the unfolding of economic events. Hence, if uncovered interest rate parity holds, it holds on average over multiple periods, rather than for any specific period.) Hodrick (1987, p. 4) states that "A major conclusion . . . is that very strong evidence exists against the hypothesis that forward exchange rates . . . are unbiased predictors of future spot rates." MacDonald (1988, p. 1970) indicates that previous research suggests the "overwhelming rejection" of the unbiasedness hypothesis "as applied to the forward market for foreign exchange." Fama (1984) found that this failure is because forward rates contain time varying premiums. McCallum (1994) suggests that the failure of the unbiasedness hypothesis may result from efforts of the monetary authorities to manage exchange rates so as to inhibit rapid changes in interest rates.

As noted by Bhatti and Moosa (1995), a general conclusion that has emerged from both direct and indirect tests of the uncovered interest rate hypothesis is that it does not hold. Nevertheless, these authors develop an alternative approach to testing uncovered interest parity and conclude that the "tests are strongly supportive of UIP in all cases." Ayuso and Restoy (1996) also conclude that "the standard UIP relation between exchange rates and interest rates is a reasonable approximation" within Europe. These authors attribute this finding to low risk premiums. Frachot (1996) develops a model in which standard versions of uncovered interest rate parity do not hold if volatilities are stochastic. Term premiums are shown to be present if variances are not deterministic. Under these conditions, the author concludes "that rejection of the standard UIP hypothesis is not surprising."

5.4. INTERNATIONAL FISHER EFFECT

Theoretical models developed by Fama and Farber (1979), Solnik (1973), Stulz (1981), and others indicate that real interest rates should vary across countries and through time. Empirical studies by Cumby and Obstfeld (1981) and Merrick and Saunders (1986) report that real interest rates differ across countries. Hence, the evidence does not support the international Fisher effect.

6. SUMMARY

In this chapter we began by describing the two most important types of exchange rate systems: floating exchange rates and fixed exchange rates. In floating exchange rate systems, such as the USA, Japan, and the European Monetary Union, a currency's value vis-à-vis other currencies is determined by supply and demand, with little or no central bank intervention. Other countries fixed the exchange rate between their currency and the USD, FRF, or other individual currencies or baskets of currencies. The International Monetary Fund is an international organization formed in 1944 to facilitate the smooth operations of the foreign exchange markets. The IMF, which now has more than 180 members, lends funds to members experiencing payment difficulties.

We also described two important parity relationships in international markets: purchasing power parity (PPP) and interest rate parity. Purchasing power parity asserts that the law of one price holds for all types of goods and services. The law of one price states that for a given set of exchange rates the price of an item from country to country must be the same. When PPP applies to price levels, it is called "absolute purchasing power parity," and when it is applied to indexes, it is called "relative purchasing power parity." There is strong evidence that PPP holds at least in the long run.

Interest rate parity states that the rate of return from holding risk-free financial assets must be the same, regardless of the currency in which the assets are denominated. Suppose that for a given exchange rate an investor has equivalent amounts of two currencies. Uncovered interest rate parity states that the expected terminal wealth from these two investments is the same given the exchange rate expected to prevail when the investments mature. Alternatively, covered interest rate parity states that the expected terminal wealth is the same whether one invests funds and contracts for the exchange of the proceeds or exchanges the funds now and invests the proceeds.

In covered interest rate arbitrage an investor borrows in one currency, exchanges the borrowings for a second currency, invests the proceeds, and at the maturity of the investment exchanges the proceeds for the original currency and pays off the loan. If interest rate parity does not hold, then uncovered interest rate arbitrage will be profitable. There is also strong evidence that covered interest rate parity does not hold, even though capital and foreign exchange markets are integrated.

The parity conditions described here depend on the presence of arbitrage, the ability of market participants to buy in one market and sell in another, to take advantage of price differentials. If interest rate parity holds, it seems reasonable to postulate that the current forward rate is an unbiased predictor of the future exchange rate. This unbiased expectations hypothesis implies that the actual distribution of future spot rates is centered on the current forward rate, so that the current forward rate does not systematically overestimate or underestimate the future spot rate. The empirical evidence overwhelmingly rejects the unbiased expectations hypothesis. Possible explanations for this rejection include the possibility that forward rates contain time-varying risk premiums or that the efforts of monetary authorities to manage exchange rates prevent rapid equilibrium adjustments. The international Fisher effect states that exchange rates change in an equal and opposite direction to interest rate differences between countries. Both theoretical models and the empirical evidence show that real interest rates are not the same across countries. Hence, the international Fisher effect is unlikely to hold.

If investors are not able to arbitrage effectively, then parity relations may not hold. Three possible reasons why arbitrage may not work applicable to both PPP and interest rate parity are lack of efficient markets and transaction costs. Regulatory barriers, lack of knowledge, lack of needed institutions, and similar possibilities may prevent investors from taking advantage of arbitrage opportunities. Costs of transportation, commissions, costs of obtaining information, and so forth may prevent profitable arbitrage. The presence of risk may prevent parity. If investors view exchange rate changes as temporary, they may not make changes in trade flows that would otherwise be expected. In this case PPP relationships may become distorted. There is also evidence that deviations from PPP are related to exchange rate volatility. If exchange rates include risk premiums, then interest rate parity may not hold.

There are several additional explanations for deviations from PPP. Many goods and services do not lend themselves to international trade. Services provided by accounting and legal firms, hair stylists, and restaurants are not frequently traded. Some goods may be too perishable to be traded, while others may not be traded due to government regulations. Empirical evidence shows that changes in the relative price of traded and nontraded goods affects PPP. Differences in tastes affect relative PPP directly, because they cause the consumption basket to differ from country to country. Hence, changes in the price of an item do not affect the standard of living to the same extent in each country.

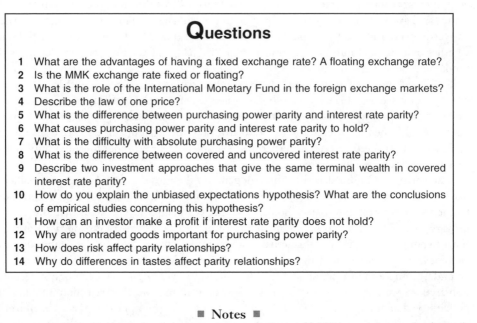

Questions

1 What are the advantages of having a fixed exchange rate? A floating exchange rate?
2 Is the MMK exchange rate fixed or floating?
3 What is the role of the International Monetary Fund in the foreign exchange markets?
4 Describe the law of one price?
5 What is the difference between purchasing power parity and interest rate parity?
6 What causes purchasing power parity and interest rate parity to hold?
7 What is the difficulty with absolute purchasing power parity?
8 What is the difference between covered and uncovered interest rate parity?
9 Describe two investment approaches that give the same terminal wealth in covered interest rate parity?
10 How do you explain the unbiased expectations hypothesis? What are the conclusions of empirical studies concerning this hypothesis?
11 How can an investor make a profit if interest rate parity does not hold?
12 Why are nontraded goods important for purchasing power parity?
13 How does risk affect parity relationships?
14 Why do differences in tastes affect parity relationships?

▪ Notes ▪

1 This is a standard foreign exchange trading convention (DeRosa 1996). But it is not one that is always used by those dealing with end users, such as nonfinancial firms, or by textbook writers. In fact, one can easily find examples in which the second currency is the one being bought and sold. Readers need to be careful to ascertain which convention is being used.
2 We denote the locked in rate by "F," because a contract for exchanging currency at time t > 0 at a rate that is fixed at t = 0 is a forward contract.

▪ References ▪

Abeysekera, Sarath P. and Turtle, Harry J. 1995: Long run relations in exchange markets: a test of covered interest parity. *Journal of Financial Research* 18, 431–47.

Abuaf, Niso and Jorion, Philippe 1990: Purchasing power parity in the long run. *Journal of Finance* 45, 157–74.

Apte, Prakash, Kane, Marian and Sercu, Piet 1994: Relative PPP in the medium run. *Journal of International Money and Finance* 13, 602–22.

Ayuso, Juan and Restoy, Fernando 1996: Interest rate parity and foreign exchange risk premia in the ERM. *Journal of International Money and Finance* 15, 369–82.

Bhatti, Razzaque H. and Moosa, Imad A. 1994: A new approach to testing ex ante purchasing power parity. *Applied Economics Letters* 1, 148–51.

——1995: An alternative approach to testing uncovered interest parity. *Applied Economics Letters* 2, 478–81.

Blenman, Lloyd P. 1995: Tests of covered interest parity: a comment. *Applied Economics Letters* 2, 49–50.

Cheung, Yin-Wong, Fung, Hung-Gay, Lai, Kon S. and Lo, Wai-Chung 1995: Purchasing power parity under the European Monetary System. *Journal of International Money and Finance* 14, 179–89.

Committeri, M., Rossi, S. and Santorelli, A. 1993: Tests of covered interest parity on the Euromarket with high-quality data. *Applied Financial Economics* 3, 89–93.

Crownover, Collin, Pippenger, John and Steigerwald, Douglas G. 1996: Testing for absolute purchasing power parity. *Journal of International Money and Finance* 15, 783–96.

Cumby, Robert E. and Obstfeld, Maurice 1981: A note on exchange-rate expectations and nominal interest differentials: a test of the Fisher hypothesis. *Journal of Finance* 36, 697–703.

DeRosa, David F. 1996: *Managing Foreign Exchange Risk*. Chicago: Irwin.

Dibooglu, Selahattin 1996: Real disturbances, relative prices and purchasing power parity. *Journal of Microeconomics* 18, 69–87.

Dutton, Mailyn and Strauss, Jack 1997: Cointegration tests of purchasing power parity: the impact of non-traded goods. *Journal of International Money and Finance* 16, 433–44.

Fama, Eugene F. 1984: Forward and spot exchange rates. *Journal of Monetary Economics* 14, 319–38.

Fama, Eugene and Farber, A. 1979: Money, bonds and foreign exchange. *American Economic Review* 69, 639–49.

Fletcher, Donna J. and Taylor, Larry W. 1994: A non-parametric analysis of covered interest parity in long-date capital markets. *Journal of International Money and Finance* 13, 459–75.

Frachot, Antoine 1996: A reexamination of the uncovered interest rate parity hypothesis. *Journal of International Money and Finance* 15, 419–37.

Froot, Kenneth A., Kim, Michael and Rogoff, Kenneth 1995: The law of one price over 700 years. Working Paper, Cambridge, MA: Harvard Business School.

Hodrick, R. J. 1987: *The Empirical Evidence on the Efficiency of Forward and Futures Foreign Exchange Markets*. Newark, NJ: Harwood Academic Publishers.

International Monetary Fund 1998: *International Financial Statistics*. Oct.

Kang, Jun-Koo and Stulz, Rene M. 1997: Why is there a home bias? An analysis of foreign portfolio equity ownership in Japan. *Journal of Financial Economics* 46, 3–28.

Kim, J. O. and Enders, Walter 1991: Real and monetary causes of real exchange rate movements in the Pacific Rim. *Southern Economic Journal* 57, 1061–70.

Levi, Maurice 1977: Taxation and abnormal international capital flows. *Journal of Political Economy* 85, 635–46.

Lothian, James R. 1997: Multi-country evidence on the behavior of purchasing power parity under the current float. *Journal of International Money and Finance* 16, 19–35.

MacDonald, Ronald 1988: *Floating Exchange Rates: theories and evidence*. London: Unwin Hyman.

—— 1993: Long run purchasing power parity: is it for real? *Review of Economics and Statistics* 75, 690–5.

McCallum, Bennett T. 1994: A reconsideration of the uncovered interest parity relationship. *Journal of Monetary Economics* 33, 105–32.

Merrick, J. and Saunders, Anthony 1986: International expected real interest rates: new tests of the parity hypothesis and U.S. fiscal policy effects. *Journal of Monetary Economics* 18, 3131–322.

Michael, Panos, Nobay, A. Robert and Peel, David 1994: Purchasing power parity yet again: evidence from spatially separated commodity markets. *Journal of International Money and Finance* 13, 637–57.

Moffet, Matt and Torres, Craig 1998: Brazil and Argentina, long rivals, move closer. *Wall Street Journal*, Nov. 12, pp. A25, A26.

Montagu-Pollock, Matthew 1998: Not yet ready to peg out. *Asiamoney* 9, 17–21, 25, 30.

Phylaktis, Kate and Kassimatis, Yiannis 1994: Does the real exchange rate follow a random walk? The Pacific Basin perspective. *Journal of International Money and Finance* 13, 476–95.

Sjaastad, L. A. 1998: On exchange rates, nominal and real. *Journal of International Money and Finance* 17, 407–39.

Solnik, Bruno 1973: *European Capital Markets: toward a general theory of international investment*. Lexington, MA: Lexington Books.

Stulz, Rene 1981: A model of international asset pricing. *Journal of Financial Economics* 9, 383–406.

Tesar, Linda L. and Werner, Ingrid M. 1995: Home bias and high turnover. *Journal of International Money and Finance* 14, 467–92.

Wei, Shang-Jim and Parsley, David 1995: Purchasing power disparity during the floating rate period: exchange rate volatility, trade barriers and other culprits. National Bureau of Economic Research, Working Paper 5032.

CHAPTER TEN

Foreign Exchange

■ **Key terms** ■

American terms   a currency quotation for which the unit of account – i.e., the currency measured in 1 unit – is not the USD.

Big figure   the number that must be added to the quoted shorthand price to complete the quote.

Big number   see **Big figure**.

Counterpurchases   a type of countertrade in which the goods to be exchanged are not identified precisely in advance, and the actual exchanges are separated in time.

Countertrade   the exchange of goods for goods in international trade, so that no money changes hands between the buyer and the seller.

Cross-rate   an exchange rate between two currencies, neither of which is the USD.

Currency swap   exchange of two currencies at a stated exchange rate, with an agreement to reverse the transaction at a stated future date.

Direct quotation   the price of one unit of a nondomestic currency in terms of the domestic currency.

Discount   if the exchange rate for future delivery is different from the current spot rate, the currency that is worth less in the future sells at a discount.

European terms   a currency quotation for which the USD is the unit of account, so that the quote is so many units of currency per 1 USD.

Foreign exchange swaps   the standard type of forward trade in the interbank market, in which two currencies are exchanged now, with a subsequent exchange in the reverse direction at an agreed date.

Forward   foreign exchange transactions, including foreign exchange swaps and outright forwards, for settlement beyond the normal settlement date.

Forward points   same as **Swap points**.

Hard currency   a currency that is freely and readily convertible into another currency.

Indirect quotation   the price of one unit of a domestic currency in terms of a nondomestic currency.

Offset arrangements   a type of countertrade in which the goods to be exchanged are identified in advance, but the actual exchanges are separated in time.

Outright forward   a forward position that requires a single exchange of two currencies at a future date beyond the normal settlement date.

Pip   the last unit of measurement in a foreign exchange quotation.

Point   see **Pip**.

Premium   if the exchange rate for future delivery is different from the current spot rate, the currency that is worth more in the future is at a premium.

Reciprocal quotation   a quotation that is the reciprocal of the quotation normally used.

Spot   the market for immediate delivery, according to established settlement times.

Swap points   the bid and ask prices in a swap and the values used to determine the bids and asks for outright forwards.

IN THIS CHAPTER we

- provide an overview of trading in foreign exchange
- explain how foreign exchange is traded and quoted for immediate delivery (the spot market)
- describe the currency transactions that involve exchanges beyond the standard settlement date (forward markets)
- describe alternatives to dealing in foreign exchange

---

1. INTRODUCTION

The foreign exchange market is the market in which currencies are traded. This market is huge, with the daily value of trading exceeding 1 trillion USD.[1] More than 50 percent of foreign exchange transactions are cross-border transactions, and more than 60 percent are interbank transactions. The typical trade size is 10 million USD or more. This interbank trading, which is the focus of this chapter, provides enormous liquidity to the market. There are also a number of others who trade in the foreign exchange markets. The interbank trades are the wholesale market, and the remaining trades are the retail market. The participants in the retail market include firms needing foreign exchange as part of their business, investors and speculators who have a view about expected exchange rate changes or expected interest rate changes, and individuals who need foreign exchange as tourists. Most of these commercial transactions are between banks and the banks' nonbank customers. Central banks sometimes buy or sell currencies to influence the exchange rate.

2. FOREIGN EXCHANGE MARKETS

2.1. OVERVIEW

There are two basic types of foreign exchange trades: spot and forward. The **spot** market is the market for immediate delivery, according to established settlement times. Agreements for trades beyond the normal settlement times are **forward** transactions. There are two types of forward trades: foreign exchange swaps and outright forwards. These forward transactions are mostly **foreign exchange swaps** in which two currencies are exchanged now, with a subsequent exchange in the reverse direction at an agreed date. According to the Bank for International Settlements (1998), 40 percent of foreign exchange transactions are in the spot market, with the remainder in the forward market. A number of authors provide useful introductions to foreign exchange markets (Bishop 1992; Carew and Slatyer 1994; Luca 1995; Manuell 1986; Walmsley 1992).

2.2. ORGANIZATION OF THE FOREIGN EXCHANGE MARKET

The foreign exchange market is an over-the-counter market. It does not take place on an organized exchange or in a centralized location. There are more than 200 major banks throughout the world that quote rates for buying and selling a given currency.[2] These banks trade directly with each other, using telephones and electronic communications systems. Prior to trading with each other, the banks enter into an agreement such as the International Foreign Exchange Master Agreement, which can be found at the Federal Reserve Bank of New York web site.[3] This agreement spells out the relationship between the parties, including details concerning delivery and netting. Since foreign exchange trading gives rise to claims against the bank's trading partners that may amount to as much as the aggregate value of the trades consummated, each bank also establishes a credit limit for each of the other banks with which it will deal in the interbank market. This limit is based on the creditworthiness of the customer bank and the financial condition and size of the bank extending the credit.

Several characteristics of the direct interbank market may affect the desirability of trading there. Quotes in the interbank market are always two-sided, comprising both a bid and an ask. Hence, a bank that wants to establish a long position may find itself selling rather than buying. Also, the identity of the counterparty is known. This creates an obligation for reciprocity. Banks that call and initiate trades expect to be called when their trading partners have trades to initiate. Ordinarily, this would be beneficial, but in some cases, a bank might wish to trade without creating reciprocity expectations. If the currency is not one regularly dealt in, it may be difficult for the bank to meet the reciprocity expectations of its counterparties.

Because of the disadvantages of direct dealing, banks also commonly use foreign exchange brokers. Large speculators can also deal with either banks or brokers. These brokers do not take positions themselves but, instead, intermediate the trading of others. Foreign exchange brokers such as Tullet & Tokyo Forex, Inc. have offices in major foreign exchange centers, where they often maintain 100 or more telephone lines open to other banks. Thus, the foreign exchange brokers are able to provide quick and broad coverage of the market, which enhances both the trader's feel for the market and the trader's ability to trade with multiple counterparties simultaneously. Trading through brokers is anonymous, which can prevent the identity of the bank initiating a trade from influencing the direction of the market and also avoids creating reciprocity expectations. This type of information leakage is common in floor-based equity markets. Also, banks can offer one-sided quotes through brokers. The bank is, in effect, placing a limit order through the broker and becoming a supplier rather than a demander of liquidity. This strategy may allow the bank to obtain a better price. At the same time, a bank that uses a broker rather than offering a two-sided quote to the market can be sure that it will only buy when it wants to buy and will only sell when it wants to sell.

Both direct dealing and dealing through brokers are common. A Bank for International Settlements survey published in April 1992 showed that the market share of brokers exceeded 30 percent in the United States, United Kingdom, France, and Canada. According to the Bank for International Settlements, Japan was the only major country in which the market share of dealing systems was greater than that of brokers. In Japan the market share of dealing systems was more than 40 percent, while that of brokers was about 25 percent.

There are also several direct, trade-matching systems for foreign exchange similar to proprietary trading systems for equities such as Instinet, Posit, and Tradepoint. The oldest system is the Reuters Dealing 2000–2™ which allows the posting and hitting of orders electronically. This systems allows dealers to communicate with trading partners without the need to use telephone lines.[4] Another is the Electronic Broking Service (EBS) established in 1990 by a group of banks to provide interbank brokerage services. According to its web site, EBS "is the world's leading electronic foreign exchange broker with 800 banks using some 2,500 workstations to transact average daily volumes in excess of $90 billion." Dow Jones/Telerate and a group of Japanese banks established a similar system called MINEX™. In 1995 trades on the MINEX system were very frequent, to the point of being almost continuous at times, but typically in small sizes of 1 million USD. MINEX was purchased by EBS.

Some banks make markets in many currencies, while others specialize in only one or a small number of currencies. Banks use services provided by firms such as Telerate, Knight Ridder, and Reuters to transmit indicative quotes. These spot and forward quotes for each currency can be advertised on individual pages provided for each bank.

The BIS (1998) ranked countries in the following order in term of their percentage share of foreign exchange trading: United Kingdom, 32 percent; United States, 18 percent; Japan, 8 percent; Singapore, 7 percent; Germany, 5 percent; France, 4 percent; Australia, Canada, and the Netherlands, 2 percent each. All other countries had a 1 percent share or less.

In an earlier study, which is still relevant, Goodhart and Demos (1991) ranked cities as international financial centers. The three major currencies traded in foreign exchange markets after the USD are the JPY, GBP, and the euro. The first step toward developing the ranking is to identify cities with dealers who regularly quote all three currencies. Then, the centers quoting all three currencies can be ranked, based on the number of Reuters entries entered from each city. While there is some bias in this measure, because the market share of Reuters differs from city to city, this approach nevertheless provides another objective way of determining relative importance of financial centers. Using this approach, these authors identified five major international financial centers (in alphabetical order): Hong Kong, London, New York, Singapore, and Tokyo. Next, there are three middle-sized centers: Sydney, Toronto, and Zurich. Small centers quoting exchange rates for all three major currencies are Chicago, Los Angeles, Melbourne, Oslo, San Francisco, and Wellington, and a group from the Middle East, Abu Dhabi, Bahrain, Dubai, Jeddah, and Kuwait.

2.3. SOME SOURCES OF POSSIBLE CONFUSION

All foreign exchange transactions involve two currencies. While this may seem straightforward, in reality, it can be quite confusing. Hopefully, recognizing several potential sources of confusion will help avoid them. When dealing with, say, wheat, we might speak of buying or selling wheat for USD. It would be very unusual to speak of buying and selling USD for wheat. But in the foreign exchange market one might just as easily speak about buying or selling CHF for USD or buying and selling USD for CHF. What makes this potentially confusing is that buying CHF using USD is exactly the same as selling USD for CHF. Further, neither currency might be a domestic currency for the trader.

Also, for every trade there is both a buyer and a seller. In order to understand the motivation and actions of the participants in the foreign exchange market, it is important to keep in mind which firms are doing the buying and selling. The two parties to most trades are the market maker and the nonmarket maker. The market maker sells at the ask and buys at the bid, whereas the nonmarket maker sells at the bid and buys at the ask. Examples can be constructed from either point of view.

Another source of confusion is the use of the terms "swap" and "forward." As already defined, a forward is a trade with a settlement date beyond the standard spot settlement date, and a swap combines a spot and forward trade in a single transaction. In this chapter the term "swap" always refers to a foreign exchange swap, which is the only type of forward trading done in the interbank foreign exchange market. By contrast, a **currency swap** involves the exchange of long-dated borrowing denominated in different currencies. Another potential source of confusion is that the term "forward" may be used to mean either a foreign exchange swap or an outright forward, which is a combination of a swap and a spot trade. We explain outright forwards more fully later. In this text we are careful to distinguish between foreign exchange swaps and outright forwards.

Some authors use the terms "direct" and "indirect" to describe quotations. We find this terminology potentially confusing and therefore do not use it here. For further discussion see box 10.1.

3. DEALING IN FOREIGN EXCHANGE

Ninety percent of foreign exchange trading is conducted vis-à-vis the USD. In other words, the exchange rates are quoted in terms of each currency and the USD. This is done to facilitate trading. For a set of n currencies, there are potentially n^2 combinations. Eliminating the n combinations of each currency with itself and dividing the difference by 2 to eliminate reciprocal quotations gives a potential $(n^2 - n)/2$ quotations between different currencies. Using only the USD quotations reduces this number to $n - 1$.

BOX 10.1
Confusion over direct and indirect quotations

There is some potential confusion over the use of the term "direct quotation." One author defines a direct quotation as "Exchange rate quotations representing the value measured by number of dollars per unit" (Madura 1995, p. 706). Using this definition, the direct quotation for 1 AUD would be, say, 0.8830 USD. On the other hand, for a direct quotation, "the exchange rate is expressed in terms of the domestic currency (e.g., for Australia, USD1/AUD1.1325)" (Allan et al. 1990, p. 217). Clearly, these definitions are not the same.

The first definition takes the viewpoint of a particular country, in this case the USA, and ignores other countries. But a definition that changes depending on where one is can be very confusing. In this book we take a global perspective. Hence, to avoid confusion, we do not use the terms "direct" and "indirect quotation." But if one must, we suggest the following definitions: A **direct quotation** expresses the price of one unit of a nondomestic currency in terms of the domestic currency. An **indirect quotation** expresses the price of one unit of a domestic currency in terms of a nondomestic currency. Thus, a quotation of AUD1/0.8830USD would be a direct quotation in the USA but an indirect quotation in Australia. And a quotation of USD1/AUD1.1325 is indirect in the USA and direct in Australia.

3.1. SPOT DEALING IN FOREIGN EXCHANGE

3.1.1. Quoting American and European terms (ignoring spreads)

There are two ways of quoting foreign exchange: **American terms** and **European terms**. (The quotations in this section ignore spreads.) American terms refers to the way that all prices are quoted in the USA, the USD price of one unit of the item. In other words, the price of corn in the USA is, say, 1.90 USD per bushel. Using this same approach, the price of one JPY is 0.0750 USD, and the price of one CHF is 0.60 USD.[5]

For the European method the unit of trade is 1 USD. The quotation then indicates the number of units of the local currency that have the same value as 1 USD. Prices for European quotations are the reciprocal of the American quotations. The European method is used throughout the world for all currencies except the British pound, the Irish punt, the Australian and New Zealand dollars, and the South African rand. The use of American quotes for these currencies is a holdover from the days when the GBP was not a decimal currency. A **reciprocal quotation** is a quotation that is the reciprocal of the quotation normally used. In other words, for the GBP a reciprocal quotation would be in European terms.

3.1.2. Two-sided spot quotes using American or European terms

Of course, dealers do not typically quote one price. Instead, they quote a price at which they are willing to sell, the ask, and a price at which they are willing to buy, the bid. Naturally, the bid is lower than the ask. If one bank called another bank and asked for a CHF quote, the response might be 1.6557/1.6568 or 1.6557/68 or even 57/68. This quotation is a USD/CHF exchange rate. Recall that we have chosen to indicate the currency that is expressed as a unit of 1 on the left-hand side of the "/." Some authors use a different convention, reporting a European quote as 1.6557 CHF/USD. Obviously, this does not affect our analysis in any way. The quotation of 57/68 omits the **big figure** or the **big number**, which is the number that must be added to the quoted shorthand price to complete the quote. In this case the big number is 1.65. This shorthand convention is used to save time, because the markets are very active. Since everyone is supposed to know where the market is trading and what the big number is, there is no need to announce it. The last unit of measurement in the quotation is called either a **pip** or a **point**. In this case it is the fourth decimal place.

Consider further the quotation of USD/CHF 1.6557/68. The first amount is the bid, and the second is the ask. But bid and ask for what? The answer is that the bid indicates how many CHF will be paid for 1 USD, and the ask indicates how many CHF it will take to buy 1 USD. Hence, if a dealer could buy at the bid and sell at the ask, there would be a gain of $1.6568 - 1.6557 = 0.0011$ CHF. For the AUD the quotation might be AUD/USD 0.6963/70. In this case the dealer is offering to buy 1 AUD for 0.6963 USD or sell 1 AUD for 0.6970 USD. For each AUD traded at the bid and ask, the dealer will have a gain of $0.6970 - 0.6963 = 0.0007$ USD. The reason that the bid and the ask mean different things for the USD/CHF quote and the AUD/USD quote is that the Swiss frank is quoted in European terms and the Australian dollar is quoted in American terms.

3.1.3. Cross-rates (ignoring spreads)

A **cross-rate** is an exchange rate between two currencies, neither of which is the USD. There are active cross-markets for some currencies, including the euro with the GBP, CHF, and JPY. For currencies without an active cross-market, cross-rates are calculated from the standard USD quotes.[6]

3.1.3.1. CROSS-RATES BETWEEN AN AMERICAN-QUOTED AND A EUROPEAN-QUOTED CURRENCY (IGNORING SPREADS)   This section examines cross-rates for currencies quoted in different terms, i.e., American and European. Consider the following quotes:

| USD/CAD 1.3500 and GBP/USD 1.6500

We seek to compute CAD/GBP and GBP/CAD. First note that

$$\text{(a)} \quad 1.3500\,\text{CAD} = 1\,\text{USD}$$

Multiplying both sides of (a) by 1.6500 gives

$$\text{(a1)} \quad 1.6500\,(1.3500)\,\text{CAD} = 1.6500\,\text{USD}$$

We know that

$$\text{(b)} \quad \text{GBP} = 1.6500\,\text{USD}$$

Setting the left-hand side of (b) equal to the left-hand side of (a1) gives

$$GBP = 1.6500 \, (1.3500) \, CAD$$

so that GBP/CAD 2.2275. The reciprocal rate is CAD/GBP 0.4489. In general:

> *For two currencies, one quoted in European terms and the other in American terms, to calculate the cross-rate with the American-quoted currency as the unit of account, multiply the two spot rates.*

3.1.3.2. CROSS-RATES FOR TWO CURRENCIES QUOTED IN EUROPEAN TERMS (IGNORING SPREADS) In this section, we use the spot rates to calculate the cross-rate for two currencies quoted using European terms. Suppose the following rates prevail:

$$USD/CAD \, 1.35 \text{ and } USD/CHF \, 1.65$$

Our goal is to calculate CAD/CHF and CHF/CAD. We begin by noting that

$$\text{(a)} \quad 1.35 \, CAD = USD$$

$$\text{(b)} \quad 1.65 \, CHF = USD$$

To obtain CAD/CHF, first set the left-hand side of (b) equal to the left-hand side of (a) to obtain:

$$1.65 \, CHF = 1.35 \, CAD$$

Then, divide through by 1.65 to obtain:

$$CHF/CAD \, 0.818.$$

Alternatively, suppose one wants to know the exchange rate between Singapore dollars (SGD) and Philippine pesos (PHP). This is, of course, a cross-rate. One would first obtain the USD/SGD and USD/PHP exchange rates. In this case, to obtain the cross-rate, one simply converts the rate of the currency that is to be the unit of account to an American quote and multiplies the two quotes:

$$USD/SGD \times 1(USD/PHP)$$
$$= USD/SGD \times PHP/USD$$
$$= PHP/SGD.$$

From these results, we can deduce the following rule:

> *To calculate the cross-rate from the spot rates for two currencies quoted in European terms, convert the quote of the currency that is to have unit value to an American quote and multiply the two spot quotes.*

3.1.3.3. CROSS-RATES FOR TWO CURRENCIES QUOTED IN AMERICAN TERMS (IGNORING SPREADS) Consider an example with two currencies, both quoted in American terms.

Suppose that the following spot rates prevail: AUD/USD 1.4300 and GBP/USD 1.6500. Our goal is to obtain a quote in terms of either AUD/GBP or GBP/AUD. Then, to obtain AUD/GBP, convert the GBP/USD quote to European and multiply the two spot rates:

$$AUD/USD\,1.4300 \times 1/(GBP/USD\,1.6500) = AUD/GBP\,0.8667.$$

And to obtain GBP/AUD convert AUD/USD to European and multiply the two spot rates:

$$1/(AUD/USD\,1.4300) \times GBP/USD\,1.6500 = GBP/AUD\,1.1538.$$

From these results, we can deduce the following rule:

> *To calculate the cross-rate from the spot rates from two currencies quoted in American terms, convert the quote of the currency that is not to be the unit of account to European terms, and multiply the two spot rates.*

3.1.4. Cross-rates taking spreads into account

Thus far in our discussion of cross-rates we have ignored all transactions costs, including spreads. We now consider how to calculate two-sided cross-rates from two spot rates quoted in any combination of American and European terms. But note that the spreads for crosses calculated from the spot rates are larger than the actual market spreads for the active cross-markets.

3.1.4.1. CROSS-RATES WITH TWO-SIDED QUOTES WHEN ONE CURRENCY IS QUOTED IN EURO-PEAN TERMS, THE OTHER IN AMERICAN TERMS Merchants might be interested in the NZD/CHF exchange rate. Some might want to use CHF to buy NZD, and others might want to use NZD to buy CHF. We can calculate both rates beginning with the first.

Assume the following quotes: USD/CHF 1.6545/50 and NZD/USD 0.6195/0.6200.

Using CHF to Buy NZD:
Step 1   Use CHF to buy 1 USD. It takes 1.6550 CHF to buy 1 USD.

Step 2   Use the 1 USD to buy NZD. Traders can buy 0.6200 NZD for 1 USD (which is the same as selling 1 USD for 0.6200 NZD). Selling a USD is the same as buying a NZD. The 1 USD obtained in step 1 can buy 1.6129 NZD, which is obtained from solving (1/0.6200).

Step 3   Calculate the offer rate in CHF for NZD. 1.6550 CHF buys 1.6129 NZD, so that 1.6129 NZD/1.6550 CHF. Dividing by 1.6129 and rearranging gives NZD/CHF 1.0261.

Sell NZD for CHF:
Step 1a   Sell 1 NZD for USD. 1 NZD sells for 0.6195 USD.

Step 2a   Use 1 USD to buy CHF. 1 USD buys 1.6545 CHF. Stated differently, we can sell 1 USD for 1.6545 CHF.

Step 3a   Calculate the CHF amount received for 1 NZD. Since 1 USD buys 1.6545 CHF, 0.6195 USD buys 0.6195 × 1.6545 CHF, or about 1.0250 CHF. Therefore, the bid price in CHF for 1 NZD is 1.0250. Combining the results of steps 3 and 3a gives NZD/CHF

1.025/61 as the cross-rate quote. Given the USD/CHF and NZD/USD quotes, if the cross-quote differed from this, there would be arbitrage opportunities. In other words, there would be an opportunity to make a profit by buying one currency at its direct rate, exchanging it for the other currency at the cross-rate, and then selling this second currency at its direct rate.

Obviously, this was a rather tedious way of obtaining the cross-rates. Instead, the following rule can be used:

> *For two currencies, one quoted in European terms and the other in American terms, the cross-rate bid is the product of the two spot bids, and the cross-rate ask is the product of the two spot asks, with the American-quoted currency as the unit of account.*

In this case multiplying the two bids 1.6545×0.6195 gives 1.0250, and multiplying the two asks 1.6550×0.6200 gives 1.0261, which, of course, is the same answer as we obtained before.

3.1.4.2. CROSS-RATES WITH TWO-SIDED QUOTES WHEN BOTH CURRENCIES ARE QUOTED EUROPEAN   To calculate the cross-rate for two-sided quotes when both currencies are quoted in European terms:

> *Divide by the spot rate of the currency that is to have unit value,[7] remembering to divide bid by offer or offer by bid, but never bid by bid or offer by offer.*

To see how this works, suppose that we have the following two quotes: USD/CHF 1.6545/50 and USD/JPY 115.05/07. We wish to calculate the CHF/JPY exchange rate. We calculate $115.05/1.6550 = 69.51$ and $115.07/1.6545 = 69.55$. Thus, CHF/JPY 69.51/59.

An alternative approach would be to convert the quote of the currency that is to be the unit of account to American terms and multiply bid by bid and ask by ask. Suppose we want to calculate CHF/JPY given the above quotes. First, we convert USD/CHF 1.6545/50 to CHF/USD 0.6042/44. $0.6042 \times 115.05 = 69.51$, and $0.6044 \times 115.07 = 69.55$, so that the CHF/JPY quote is 69.51/55.

3.1.4.3. CROSS-RATES WITH TWO-SIDED QUOTES WHEN BOTH CURRENCIES ARE QUOTED IN AMERICAN TERMS   To calculate the cross-rate from the spot rates from two currencies quoted in American terms:

> *Divide by the spot rate of the currency that is not to be the unit of account, remembering to divide bid by offer or offer by bid, but never bid by bid or offer by offer.*

Suppose that the following quotes prevail: AUD/USD 0.7040/60 and NZD/USD 0.5520/30. Suppose that we want to know the value in AUD of 1 NZD. Then, the NZD is the unit of account, and following our rule, we divide by the spot rate for the AUD. $0.5530/0.7040 = 0.7855$, and $0.5520/0.7060 = 0.7819$, giving NZD/AUD 0.7819/55.

Alternatively, one can convert the quote of the currency that is not to be the unit of account to European terms and then multiply the spot rate bids and asks. To calculate AUD/NZD, convert NZD/USD 0.5520/30 to USD/NZD 1.8083/1.8115. Noting that $1.8083 \times 0.7040 = 1.2730$ and $1.8115 \times 0.7060 = 1.2789$, we have AUD/NZD 1.2730/89.

It might be useful at this point to repeat that the bid and offer rates calculated in the way just described should be viewed as the worst bid and offer. A cross-dealer should not offer worst prices because, as we have seen, these rates can be obtained by a series of transactions in USD. But in active currency crosses, such as the CHF/JPY and GBP/JPY, it may be possible to obtain more favorable prices from a cross-dealer rather than dealing in each individual currency.

3.2. FORWARD TRANSACTIONS

In this section we consider two common transactions involving the future delivery of currencies: foreign exchange swaps and outright forwards. Forward contracts involve an agreement today on the delivery of currency at a time beyond the normal settlement period. Forward maturities of 1 week, 2 weeks, and 1–12 months are common, although other maturities can be negotiated. Forward rates are quoted with respect to spot rates.

3.2.1. Foreign exchange swaps

Almost all the forward interbank dealing is in the form of foreign exchange swaps, the exchange of two currencies at a stated exchange rate, with an agreement to reverse the transaction at a stated future date. Suppose that we have a spot quote of USD/CHF 1.6557/68. A 1-month foreign exchange swap might be quoted in terms of **swap points** or **forward points**. Such a quote might be 25/15. The left-hand side is the rate at which a bank will buy CHF now for resale in 1 month, the right-hand side is the rate at which the bank will sell CHF now for repurchase in 1 month. If the bank did a buy/sell with one customer and a sell/buy with another, there would be a profit of $25 - 15 = 10$. Conversely, if a customer did these two transactions, the cost would be 10 (or 0.0010 CHF).

The actual prices at which the swap is transacted make almost no difference to the cash flows of the transaction (see Luca 1995). It is the swap points that matter. To see this, it may be helpful to review the cash flows associated with various swap positions. To get a complete picture, we will examine two swaps, a sell/buy and a buy/sell. On a round-trip basis (i.e., both a buy and a sell) the market maker bank should earn the spread, of 10 pips.

First, consider a customer who wants to buy USD and sell CHF now and sell USD and buy CHF 1 month from now. The cash flows will be:

Timing of cash flows	Calling bank (customer)	Responding bank*
Now	−X CHF	+X CHF
	+1 USD	−1 USD
1 month	+(X − 0.0025) CHF	−(X − 0.0025) CHF
	−1 USD	+1 USD
Net cash flow	−0.0025 CHF	+0.0025 CHF

*Quoting spot: USD/CHF 1.6557/68, swap points: 25/15. X stands for an exchange rate agreed to by the parties.

Next, consider a customer who wants to sell USD and buy CHF now and buy USD and sell CHF 1 month from now. The cash flows will be (note that a minus sign indicates an outflow and a plus sign an inflow):

Timing of cash flows	Calling bank (customer)	Responding bank*
Now	+X CHF −1 US	−X CHF +1 USD
1 month	−(X − 0.0015) CHF +1 USD	+(X − 0.0015) CHF −1 USD
Net cash flow	+0.0015 CHF	−0.0015 CHF

*Quoting spot: 1.6557/68 USD/CHF, swap points: 25/15. X stands for an exchange rate agreed to by the parties.

Combining the two transactions gives:

Timing of cash flows	Calling bank 1 (customer)	Calling bank 2 (customer)	Responding bank*
Now	−X CHF +1 USD	+X CHF −1 USD	0 CHF 0 USD
1 month	+(X − 0.0025) CHF −1 USD	−(X − 0.0015) CHF +1 USD	+0.0010 CHF 0 USD
Net cash flow	−0.0025 CHF	+0.0015 CHF	+0.0010 CHF

*Quoting spot: 1.6557/68 USD/CHF, swap points: 25/15. X stands for an exchange rate agreed to by the parties.

Thus, as predicted, these two transactions have cost customers 0.0010 CHF, which is the bank's profit. Naturally, for purposes of this illustration, we have assumed that the forward points remain unchanged.

It is evident that the value of X makes little difference, because the current payment or receipt of X is offset by an equal and opposite payment 1 month from now. If the value of X used as the base price to compute the swap were different by, say Δ, the cash flows would differ by 1 month's interest on Δ. Also, if different base rates are used on the buy/sell and sell/buy swaps, so that one used X and the other Y, there would be an amount X − Y to either invest or fund over the life of the swap.

3.2.2. Outright forwards

An **outright forward** is a forward contract that requires the exchange of two currencies at a future date beyond the normal settlement date. Only one exchange of currency is involved. Outright forward contracts are typically between a bank and its commercial or retail customers. Importers or exporters who have payments maturing or coming due in the future can enter into outright forward contracts with banks to lock in the purchase or sale price of the payment currency.

In addition to showing the spread at which foreign exchange swaps can be carried out, swap or forward points are also used to calculate the outright forward price. Ascertaining the sign when the first number is subtracted from the second does this. If the sign is negative, each swap point is subtracted from its associated spot quote. If it is positive, they are added. In each case the swap point on the left of the "/" is added to or subtracted from the spot bid, and the swap point on the right of the "/" is added to or subtracted from the spot offer. Hence, if USD/CHF 1.6557/68 is the current spot quote, and the swap points are 25/15, the outright forwards are $(57 - 25)/(68 - 15)$, which gives the result 1.6532/53. The swap points are subtracted, because the swap points are in descending order. The spot spread is 11 $(68 - 57)$, the swap spread is 10 $(25 - 15)$, and the outright forward spread is 21 $(53 - 32$, or, alternatively, $11 + 10)$.

Another way to determine whether the forward points should be added or subtracted is to know that the spread is never smaller in the forward market than in the spot market. If by rare chance the two swap points are equal, then the points should be added, and the spread is the same in the spot and forward markets.

Outright forwards are not traded in the interbank market. But there is a close relationship between foreign exchange swaps and outright forwards. In fact, an outright forward can be created from a combination of a foreign exchange swap and a spot trade. To understand how banks create outright forwards, when only foreign exchange swaps are traded in the interbank market, we will continue the previous examples: spot, USD/CHF 1.6557/68; swap points, 25/15. Consider the cash flows from the previous swap positions, but with an additional spot trade to eliminate the current currency inventory. In the first case, the spot trade is at the bid of 1.6557. This creates an outright forward position in which CHF is delivered in 1 month. In the second case, the spot transaction is at 1.6568, and the CHF are purchased in 1 month.

Timing of cash flows	Calling bank (customer) Case 1	Calling bank (customer) Case 2	Responding bank*
Now	+1.6557 CHF −X CHF +1 USD	−1.6568 CHF +X CHF −1 USD	+0.0011 CHF
1 month	+(X − 0.0025) CHF −1 USD	−(X − 0.0015) CHF +1 USD	+0.0010 CHF
Net cash flow	+1.6532 CHF	−1.6553 CHF	+0.0021 CHF

*Quoting spot: USD/CHF 1.6557/68, outright forward: 1.6532/53, swap points: 25/15.

Hence the cost of creating the two outright forward contracts is the spot spread plus the swap spread.

If the exchange rate for future delivery is different from the current spot rate, the currency that is worth more in the future sells at a **premium**, and the currency that is worth less in the future sells as a **discount**. In this case the CHF is at a premium and the USD at a discount.

> *For currencies quoted in European terms, if the forward points are in descending order, the non-US currency is at a premium; otherwise the USD is at a premium. For currencies quoted in American terms, if the forward points are in descending order, the USD is at a premium; otherwise the non-US currency is at a premium.*

4. ANOTHER LOOK AT INTEREST RATE PARITY

4.1. INTEREST RATE PARITY WITHOUT SPREADS

According to interest rate parity, the forward exchange rate reflects differences in interest rates available on two currencies. First, ignoring spreads, suppose that at a future date the USD/CHF spot rate is 1.38, and that the interest rate for 30-day USD deposits is 5 percent and that the interest rate for 30-day CHF deposits is 2 percent. At the end of 30 days, 1.38 CHF plus interest grows to $(1 + 0.02(30/360)) \times 1.38 = 1.3823$, and a USD deposit plus interest is worth $(1 + 0.05(30/360)) = 1.00417$. Interest rate parity states that it must be true that the current USD/CHF exchange rate for delivery in 30 days (i.e., the forward rate) is 1.00417 USD/CHF 1.3823. Of course, this is not a conventional way of quoting an exchange rate. But dividing both sides by 1.00417 gives the conventional quote of USD/CHF 1.3766.

In other words, if one starts with amounts of two different currencies that are equivalent given the current spot exchange rate, then the current forward exchange rate must be the ratio of the future values of the investment outcome from holding each currency. Forward rates reflect the current spot exchange rate and the interest available on each currency.

Let $currency_1$ be the currency that is the unit of account, r_1 be the annual interest rate for the currency that is the unit of account, r_2 be the annual interest rate for a second currency, S_t be the spot exchange rate for $currency_1/currency_2$, M be the maturity of the foreign exchange contract, and $F_{t,M}$ be the forward exchange rate at time t for maturity M. We assume that interest rates for both currencies are quoted on a 360-day year. Then, if the rate of return is the same regardless of the currency in which the investment is made, the following relation must hold:

$$1 + (r_1(M/360)) = S_t(1 + (r_2(M/360)))$$

Hence,

$$F_{t,M} = [S_t(1 + (r_2(M/360)))]/[1 + (r_1(M/360))].$$

If interest rate parity were violated, no one would be willing to hold the overvalued currency. Continuing the example at the beginning of this section, suppose that a bank indicated that it was willing to buy or sell CHF for USD at the rate of 1.3800 for delivery in 30 days. Under these circumstances no one would want to hold USDs. Suppose that a trader held 1.38 CHF at the beginning of the month, and the above spot exchange rate prevailed. We have already seen that at the end of the month the trader would have 1.3915 CHF. The trader could exchange the 1.3915 CHF with the bank for 1.3915/1.38 = 1.008333 USD. Thus, it pays anyone holding USD at the beginning of the month to use them to buy CHF and at the same time enter into an agreement with the bank to sell the CHF plus interest to the bank at the end of the month. Then USD investors would have 1.008333 versus the alternative of investing the USD directly and ending the month with 1.00667. In such a case, investors will quickly overwhelm the bank, so that it can no longer offer a rate that deviates from interest rate parity.

4.2. Interest Rate Parity with Bid–Ask Spreads

In reality, both the spot foreign exchange market and the deposit market have bid–ask spreads. Nevertheless, if markets are efficient, interest rate parity still holds after taking these spreads into account.

Case 1 Suppose that at some future date a trader is faced with the following market conditions: spot, USD/CHF 2.2533/84; USD 1-month interest rate, $10^{11}/_{16}$–$10^{13}/_{16}$ percent; CHF 1-month interest rate, $5^7/_8$–6 percent. At the end of the month, an investor who borrowed 1 million USD for 1 month owes $1,000,000 (1 + (10^{13}/_{16} (30/360))) = 1,009,010$. The investor can take the 1 million USD of borrowing and buy CHF in the spot market. Buying CHF is the same as selling USD, so the proceeds of the sale of the USD are 2,253,300. Lending the CHF proceeds at $5^7/_8$ yields 2,264,332 CHF at the end of the month. To break even, the investor needs to buy USD at a rate that provides an amount sufficient to pay off the loan. Hence the sale price needs to be $2,264,332/1,009,010 = 2.2441$. This is the outright forward price that the investor is willing to bid (i.e., the bid price) in a fully competitive market without transaction costs other than the spread.

Case 2 Alternatively, continuing to use the same market interest and exchange rates, the investor can borrow 2,258,400 CHF which, at the interest rate of 6 percent, results in a loan balance of 2,269,692 CHF. The loan proceeds can be sold for 1 million USD, which, when invested at the interest rate of $10^{11}/_{16}$ percent, yields 1,008,906 USD at the end of the month. In order to pay off the CHF loan with the USD investment, an exchange rate of 2.2497 is required. This is the ask price that is required on an outright forward. Comparing the spot quote of 2.2533/84 with the required forward quote of 2.2441/97 shows that the forward points must be 92/87.

Case 3 Suppose that at some time in the future a trader is faced with the following quotes: USD/JPY 88.40/50; 2-month USD interest rate, 8–8.125 percent; 2-month JPY interest rate, 10–10.125 percent; 2-month forward points, 40/50. Consider the following transactions:

1 The trader borrows 885 million JPY at 10.125 percent, so that at the end of 2 months the amount due is $885,000,000 (1 + (60/360) 0.10125) = 899,934,375$ JPY.
2 The trader enters into a swap in the interbank market in which (a) 885 million JPY are used to purchase USD at 88.50 to obtain 10 million USD, (b) the second leg of the swap calls for the sale of the USD for JPY at 88.90 (88.50 + 40).
3 The 10 million USD are invested for 2 months at 8 percent, so that at maturity the value of the investment is $10,000,000 \times (1 + (60/360) (0.08)) = 10,133,333$ USD.

4 The investment matures, yielding 10,133,333 USD, which is exchanged for 10,133,333 × 88.90 = 900,853,304 JPY, which, less the loan repayment of 899,934,375 JPY, produces a profit for the trader of 918,929 JPY. Profits of this magnitude are rare or nonexistent. Modern communications and active participation in these markets by banks, hedge funds, and other traders and speculators help to keep profit opportunities in check.

Covered interest rate arbitrage transactions keep the spot, forward, and interest rate quotes from getting out of line with each other. If traders can borrow one currency, exchange it for another, invest the proceeds, and make a profit when the process is reversed at a later date, they will continue to undertake this covered interest arbitrage until either exchange rates or interest rates change to make this trading unprofitable.

5. THE TIME PATTERN OF TRADING IN JPY

The foreign exchange market is virtually a 24-hour-a-day market for 6 days a week. Figure 10.1 reports the time pattern of activity in JPY in Tokyo, London, and New York for the year beginning October 1, 1992. The figure shows that there are patterns of activity by half-hour of the day based on Greenwich Mean Time. Some of these patterns are described in Goodhart and Demos (1991). Examination of the daily ebb and flow of trading can provide additional understanding of the foreign exchange markets.

In Tokyo there are two distinct periods of trading, with little trading during the Tokyo lunch hour from half-hour 7–9. Goodhart and Demos (1991) report that the patterns for Singapore, Hong Kong, and Australia are each similar to the Tokyo pattern. The fact that Singapore and Australia also follow this pattern, despite differing local times, demonstrates the domination of Tokyo in this market.

The London profile is also bimodal, with two periods of high activity. But the lull in the middle of the day is much less pronounced than in Asia. This may reflect different lunch times for countries in different time zones and the lack of a single dominant market center.

By contrast, New York traders do not appear to take a lunch break. Goodhart and Demos (1991) quote one source as suggesting, probably in jest, that "the market perception is the New Yorkers go to lunch and do not come back." In any event, it's not just New Yorkers, since Goodhart and Demos report a similar pattern in Toronto. Actually, the practice of not returning after lunch may have a sound motivation. It is well known that traders do not like to carry positions overnight and especially over the weekend. Note that Asian traders who have not closed out their positions at the end of the Asian day can stay late (or leave orders with their branches in Europe) and offset their positions in Europe, where trading has begun before the end of the Asian day. Similarly, European traders who have not closed out their positions at the end of the European day can offset their positions in New York, where trading is still strong. But because days begin first in the middle of the Pacific and then in Asia and Europe, there is almost no trading in Asia or Europe from the 36th half-hour to the 45th half-hour of the trading day. This problem is especially serious for New Yorkers at weekends, when trading will not resume until the following Monday morning in Japan. Consequently, New Yorkers are forced to complete their transactions relatively early in the day, especially on Fridays.

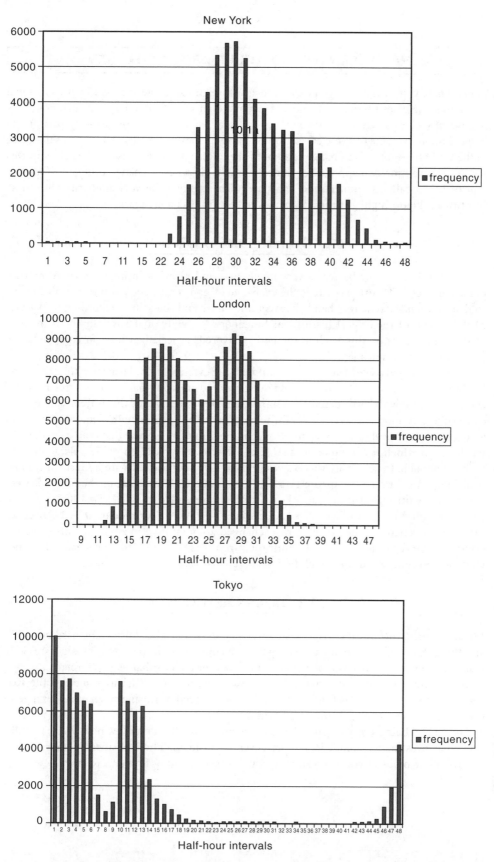

Figure 10.1 The time pattern of yen trading in New York, London, and Tokyo.

6. ALTERNATIVES TO CURRENCY EXCHANGES

Unfortunately, it is not always possible to use foreign exchange markets in international trade. In some cases there may be no active markets in which to exchange a currency. This is especially likely in developing countries and some states that were formerly part of the Soviet Union. In some of these cases, trading partners may index their non–USD sales price to the USD (or another) exchange rate. But other alternatives may also be available. In this section we examine two approaches to dealing with currency exchange problems. One is a type of barter called "countertrade," and the other is to be creative. Familiarity with these substitutes should highlight the advantages of foreign exchange markets.

6.1. BARTER (COUNTERTRADE)

Countertrade, a type of barter, is very much alive and growing in importance in international commerce. **Countertrade** is the exchange of goods for goods in international trade, so that no money exchanges hands between the buyer and the seller. According to Ng Wei Min, Director of the Export Institute of Singapore, "In spite of the availability of modern financial instruments, this trading method is favored, especially where foreign exchange problems are common-place."[8]

AT&T arranged a sale of switching equipment to Sevtelecom, the local telephone company for Murmansk, Russia. Due to exchange restrictions, only one-half of the purchase price could be paid for with hard currency.[9] A **hard currency** is a currency that is freely and readily convertible into another currency. For the remainder, AT&T negotiated a countertrade deal in which the firm agreed to accept apatite concentrate, a rock phosphate that is an ingredient in fertilizer, for which it had no direct use. (Countertraders typically provide only goods that they are not able to sell easily themselves.) AT&T then contracted with a German trading firm, Helm A.G., to sell the apatite. After subtracting Helm's fee, some of the proceeds were paid to the apatite manufacturer, and the remainder were paid to AT&T. Brian Fluck, assistant treasurer with AT&T, also describes several variations of countertrade used by his firm. In **offset arrangements** the goods to be exchanged are identified in advance, but the actual exchanges are separated in time. In **counterpurchases** the goods to be exchanged are not identified precisely in advance, and the actual exchanges are separated in time.

6.2. BEING CREATIVE[11]

Fluck says that "even if a currency is convertible in theory, the shortage of hard currency and the lack of effective markets may make it inconvertible in practice. This is especially true in countries with balance-of-payment problems or deficits that use up foreign currency reserves." But there may be alternatives to exchange markets. Charities such as the Red Cross often receive USD as funding, but need local currency. Business can often arrange to exchange local currency for these USD funds.

Of course, being creative can take many forms. Box 10.2 describes how Pepsi pursues profitable investments outside its regular beverage business. These businesses contribute to the overall firm objectives by creating goodwill and generating foreign exchange.

BOX 10.2
Not exactly countertrade

The following reports an interview with Christoph Adamski, Vice-president, World Trade, Pepsi-Cola International:

In countertrade, you specifically take an existing product off the shelf and you try to find a market. You wait for an offer from your business partner, who typically goes into a back room and looks around to see what he can sell. . . . trades where someone else takes title, and we just engineer the transaction are unsatisfactory. You can do this once successfully, but after you introduce the partners, the chances that you can do it again are fairly remote. We take a different approach. We look at the country's competitive advantages . . . and then build long-term businesses around those strengths.

If you go to ethnic markets, you may find basmati rice under the brand name Seasons Harvest. That's a Pepsi brand we developed in India under our own label. We market it . . . [worldwide] to discharge our export obligations to the Indian government. This enabled us to get into the Indian market three or four years ahead of Coca-Cola, which in our little world is quite a feat. And, in China we gained access to the Szechwan province, where we're building two Pepsi plants, one in Chengdu and one in Chonquing.

Why did we get this business? Because we agreed to open a silk dying and printing factory in Chengdu, which is a multinational joint venture combining Italian technology with Korean management expertise. We're there as a promoter of the business, and we also have our Chinese market. That's a business that we're setting up as a profit center to run independently. We'll have access to the foreign exchange generated in this venture so that we can feed our operations. Plus, we have the added benefit of transferring a technology that is in high demand to China, and in doing so, reaping the political benefits that have helped us get a license.

Source: *Financial Executive* 1994. Reprinted with permission from Financial Executives Institute, 10 Madison Ave, P.O. Box 1938, Morristown, NJ 07962-1938.

7. SUMMARY

The foreign exchange market is an over-the-counter market which involves the exchange of one currency for another and which handles a daily volume of more than 1 trillion USD. The major participants in foreign exchange markets are banks, brokers, commercial firms, and central banks. There are two types of foreign exchange trades: spot trades and forward trades. In the spot market, delivery is normally within 1 or 2 business days, depending on the currencies involved. Agreements for delivery beyond the normal spot settlement times are forward transactions.

There are two types of forward transactions: foreign exchange swaps and outright forwards. Most forward transactions in the interbank market are foreign exchange swaps, whereas outright forwards predominate in bank dealings with commercial customers. In a foreign exchange swap two currencies are exchanged now, with a subsequent exchange in the reverse direction at an agreed date. An outright forward is an agreement to exchange currencies at a settlement date beyond the spot settlement date. Combining a foreign exchange swap and a spot trade can create outright forwards.

The standard practice is to quote all exchange rates against the USD. If the quote is in the form of 1 USD against an amount of another currency, the quote is in European terms. If the quote is in the form of the number of USDs for 1 unit of another currency, the quote is in American terms. European terms are used in the interbank market for most currencies. An exchange rate between two currencies, neither of which is the USD, called a cross-rate, can then be calculated from the separate USD quotes on the two currencies. For some very active currency pairs, cross-rates may be quoted and traded directly.

Questions

1 Distinguish between spot and forward transactions.
2 What are some advantages and disadvantages of reciprocity expectations?
3 Consider the following quote: CHF/USD 1.22/1.2241.
   a. Is this quote American or European?
   b. Interpret the bid. Interpret the ask.
   c. If a dealer completes two trades, one at the bid and one at the ask, what is the dealer's gain?
4 Suppose a currency increases in volatility. What is likely to happen to the bid–ask spread? Why?
5 How are nonactive currencies quoted? Why?
6 Consider the following quotes: CHF/USD 0.80, USD/CHF 1.25. Which is in American terms, and which is in European terms? How can you tell?
7 In a swap do prices matter, or only swap points?
8 What are the differences between foreign exchange swaps and outright forwards? When would each be used?

■ Notes ■

1 Recall that all currencies are identified by their ISO codes. A list of the ISO codes used in this book is provided on p. ii.
2 According to its web site, "Bank of America provides 24-hour trading capabilities in all major currencies, as well as cross-currency rates and most 'exotic' or minor currencies." The bank's web address is http://www.bofa.com/capmarkets_trade/fx.html.
3 This agreement is technical and may not be of interest to nonprofessional readers. The text of the Agreement can be found at: http://www.ny.frb.org/fmlg/ifema.pdf.
4 Reuters transaction products are described at the Reuters web site at http://www.reuters.com/products/tran001.htm. The web address for the Electronic Broking Service is http://www.ebsp.com/.
5 For spot quotes for a wide range of currencies see http://quotes.reuters.com/, http://www.oanda.com/converter/classic, or http://www.citibank.com/us/investments/market/.
6 For cross-rates see http://quotes.reuters.com/.
7 A currency has unit value of one if the currency is expressed in terms of x units of another currency.
8 *Business Times* (Singapore), July 27, 1995.
9 This paragraph is based on *Financial Executive* 1994.
10 This section is based on *Financial Executive* 1994.

■ References ■

Allan, Richard, Elstone, Rob, Lock, Geoff and Valentine, Tom 1990: *Foreign Exchange Management.* Sydney: Allen and Unwin.

Bank for International Settlements 1998: *Central Bank Survey of Foreign Exchange and Derivatives Market Activity in April 1998: preliminary global data.* Basel: Bank for International Settlements.

Bishop, Paul 1992: *Foreign Exchange Handbook.* New York: McGraw-Hill.

Carew, Edna and Slatyer, Will 1994: *FOREX: the techniques of foreign exchange.* Singapore: Heinemann Asia.

Financial Executive 1994: How to stay in the money, internationally. 10 (May/June), 16–22.

Goodhart, Charles and Demos, Antonis 1991: Reuters screen images of the foreign exchange markets: the yen/dollar and the sterling/dollar spot market. *Journal of International Securities Markets*, 28, 35–64.

Luca, Cornelius 1995: *Trading in the Global Currency Markets.* Englewood Cliffs, NJ: Prentice-Hall.

Madura, Jeff 1995: *International Financial Management*, 4th edn. New York: West.

Manuell, Guy 1986: *Floating Down Under: foreign exchange in Australia.* North Ryde, Australia: The Law Book Company.

Walmsley, Julian 1992: *The Foreign Exchange and Money Markets Guide.* New York: Wiley.

Markowitz and the Capital Asset Pricing Model

■ Key terms ■

Active investment management   the selection of securities for inclusion in a portfolio based on economic criteria.

Beta   the ratio of the systematic risk of an asset to the systematic risk of the market, or an empirical estimate of that ratio.

Capital Market Line   in the graph with return on the vertical axis and risk on the horizontal axis, the line through the points $(0, R_f)$ and (σ_m, R_m) (where R_f = the risk-free rate, R_m = the return on the market portfolio, and σ_m = the risk of the market) that shows the relationship between risk and return for all efficient portfolios.

Differencing interval   the interval over which a return is calculated.

Dominates   (a portfolio that) has more return for a given level of risk or less risk for a given level of return.

Efficient   (a portfolio that has) the most return for a given level of risk and the least risk for a given level of return.

Efficient frontier   the set of efficient portfolios.

Hedge fund   an investment fund characterized by the use of leverage, short selling, and management fees based on performance.

Holding period return   the ratio of (1) the change in price from the beginning to the end of a period plus any dividends paid to (2) the beginning price.

Homogeneous expectations   the assumption in the Capital Asset Pricing Model that all investors see the same risk-return profile for assets.

Index fund   a portfolio with predetermined holdings comprising all the assets in the market or some identified subset of the market such as a particular stock index.

Intrinsic value   the value of an asset based on an analysis of its business, assets, and cash flows.

Log price relative   the log of the price of an asset at the end of a period minus the log of that asset at the beginning of a period, adjusted for dividends.

Market portfolio   the portfolio comprising all assets in proportion to their aggregate values.

Passive investment management   the strategy of owning a portfolio that comprises the securities in an index in the same proportions in which they are included in the index or in owning a subset of these securities designed to mimic the performance of the index.

Portfolio   one or more assets owned by an investor.

Price relative   the ratio of the price at the end of a period to the price at the beginning of a period.

Risk-averse   an investor who requires more return to undertake more risky investments.

Risk-neutral   an investor who evaluates investments in terms of the expected outcome or mean of the possible outcomes.

Risk-seeking   an investor who requires less risk to undertake a more risky investment.

Security Market Line   in a graph with risk on the vertical axis and return on the horizontal axis, the line through the points $(0, R_f)$ and (β_m, R_m) (where R_f = the risk-free rate, R_m = the return on the market, and β_m = the beta of the market) that shows the relationship between risk and return for all portfolios, both efficient and inefficient.

Systematic risk   the risk that an asset shares with the market.

Unsystematic risk   the risk that is unique to an asset.

THIS CHAPTER provides an introduction to Modern Portfolio Theory (MPT)

- by describing assumptions of MPT and the reasons for the results of MPT
- by presenting and discussing the meaning of the major insights of MPT into portfolio construction

Then, the most important extension of MPT, the Capital Asset Pricing Model (CAPM) is introduced. We describe

- the reasoning which Sharpe, Lintner and Mossin used to derive the CAPM from MPT
- the major results of the CAPM
- several important applications of the CAPM

---

1. INTRODUCTION

In the late 1950s Harry Markowitz's work (1959) revolutionized the practice of investment management. Before describing Markowitz's contribution, it may be useful to briefly describe the pre-Markowitz approach. Box 11.1 presents excerpts from a standard investment management book by the well-known authors Graham and Dodd (1940). Notice the emphasis on individual issues in this excerpt. The central idea of the traditional approach is to build a portfolio by analyzing each asset and deciding whether it should be part of the portfolio. One way to do this is to determine the stock's **intrinsic value**, its value based on an analysis of its business, assets, and cash flows. If the market price of the asset is less than

---

BOX 11.1
Traditional portfolio building: Graham and Dodd

"The functions of security analysis may be described under three headings: descriptive, selective, and critical. In its more obvious form, descriptive analysis consists of marshalling the important facts relating to an issue and presenting them in a coherent, readily intelligible manner. This function is adequately performed for the entire range of marketable securities by the various manuals. . . . A more penetrating type of description seeks to reveal the strong and weak points in the position of an issue, compare its exhibit with that of others of similar character, and appraise the factors which are likely to influence its future performance. Analysis of this kind is applicable to almost every corporate issue. . . . In its selective function, security analysis goes further and expresses specific judgements of its own. It seeks to determine whether a given issue should be bought, sold, retained, or exchanged for some other."

Source: Graham and Dodd 1940.

---

its intrinsic value, it should be added to the portfolio. In this way a portfolio of the most undervalued assets would be built up. Of course, it has long been recognized that investors should not just put all available funds in the most undervalued asset, but instead should diversify by holding a variety of undervalued assets. In fact, most investors hold many assets. Markowitz showed that the traditional approach focusing on individual assets was meaningless for answering questions when multiple assets are held.

An **index fund** is a portfolio with predetermined holdings comprising all the assets in the market or some identified subset of the market such as a particular stock index. Index funds do not try to improve performance by selecting particular assets for their portfolio. In an interview, Merton Miller, 1990 winner of the Nobel Prize in economic science, was asked: "Based on your experience, how do you think people should invest for the future . . . Should they buy index funds?" Miller replied, "Absolutely" (Tanous 1997). The theoretical reasoning for this answer is based on the Capital Asset Pricing Model presented here.

2. MODERN (MARKOWITZ) PORTFOLIO THEORY

2.1. THE MEANING OF RISK IN A PORTFOLIO

Markowitz's key idea is this:

| *The risk of an asset has no meaning except with reference to the portfolio in which the asset is held.*

In this context, we define a **portfolio** as one or more assets owned by an investor. Many writers prefer to define a portfolio as two or more assets owned by an investor. Why do we say one asset instead of two? Simply to emphasize that *everything that we say about portfolios in this chapter applies to both single-asset and multi-asset portfolios.*

How risky is it to own stock in Microsoft? No matter how much one knows about Microsoft, including projected sales, its assets and liabilities, and its cash flows, one does not have enough information to answer this question. Why? Because holding Microsoft in a two-asset portfolio with Royal Dutch Shell is completely different from holding it in a two-asset portfolio with International Business Machines or in a two-asset portfolio with US Treasury bills. The major focus of the remainder of this section is to demonstrate why this is so.

Suppose that we wish to describe the distribution of possible returns for a financial asset over the coming period, where the period may be of any length, including a minute, day, week, or year. To simplify the analysis we assume that:

1 there are no taxes or transactions costs,
2 financial markets are competitive, so that each investor owns only a small portion of the economy's wealth and is not able to influence asset prices,
3 asset returns are normally distributed so that the distribution can be completely characterized by its mean and variance (σ^2).

Hereafter, following standard practice, we refer to the mean of this distribution as its "expected value," denoted as $E(R)$. For those who need it, a brief introduction to the mathematics used here is provided in appendix 1.

The expected value of a portfolio (i.e., the mean of the distribution of the possible portfolio returns) over a coming period is:

$$\sum_{v=1}^{n} X_v R_v \qquad \text{11.1}$$

where X_v is the proportion of funds invested in security v, and $E(R_v)$ is the expected return on asset v. In other words, the expected return on a portfolio is the weighted average of the expected returns of each of the securities in the portfolio, where the weights are the proportions of funds invested in each asset. This statement is not as complicated as it might seem. Simply put, if one-half of a portfolio is invested in one asset and the other one-half in a second asset, the expected return of the portfolio is simply one-half of the expected return of the first asset plus one-half of the expected return of the second asset. And if one-third of a portfolio's assets are invested in one security and two-thirds in a second, the expected return of this portfolio is one-third of the expected return of the first asset plus two-thirds of the expected return of the second.

The risk of a portfolio, as measured by the variance of possible returns over the coming period, is:

$$\sum_{a=1}^{n} \sum_{b=1}^{n} X_a X_b \sigma_{a,b} \qquad \text{11.2}$$

where the Xs are the proportions of funds invested in each asset, $\sigma_{a,b}$ is the covariance of asset a with asset b, and n is the number of assets in the portfolio. Recall that the covariance of an asset's returns with itself is the variance of returns of that asset. For each portfolio, there are n^2 terms in this risk expression, n of which are variances, and the remaining $n^2 - n$ of which are covariances. Further, since $\sigma_{a,b} = \sigma_{b,a}$, the covariances come in pairs, so there are only $(n^2 - n)/2$ different covariance terms. Note that if only one asset is held, equations 11.1 and 11.2 become the mean and variance of that asset.

What are the implications of these results for the construction of portfolios? The return of a portfolio is simply a linear combination of the returns of the individual assets in the portfolio. But the risk of a portfolio is not a linear combination of the risks of the individual assets in the portfolio. Instead, the risk of a portfolio involves the covariance of the returns for each combination of assets in the portfolio. To make this concrete, consider a two-asset portfolio (n = 2). The expected return for this portfolio is

$$E(R_p) = X_1 E(R_1) + X_2 E(R_2) \qquad 11.3$$

where X is the proportion of the portfolio invested in the indicated asset, and E(R) is the expected return of the indicated asset.

The variance of the return for this two-asset portfolio is:

$$\sigma_p^2 = X_1^2 \sigma_1^2 + X_2^2 \sigma_2^2 + 2X_1 X_2 \sigma_{1,2} \qquad 11.4$$

Suppose that the first asset in this two-asset portfolio is Microsoft. Then, the risk of the portfolio depends not only on the risk of Microsoft (σ_1) and the risk of the second security (σ_2), but also on the way the returns of Microsoft and the second security move together, i.e., the correlation between asset 1 and 2, $\sigma_{1,2}$.

In equation 11.4, the third term on the right-hand side can be restated as: $X_1 X_2 \rho_{1,2} \sigma_1 \sigma_2$, where $\rho_{1,2}$ is the coefficient of correlation between assets 1 and 2. The coefficient of correlation, ρ, has a range of +1 to −1.

If the prices of asset 1 and 2 move together, the correlation is positive, but if the price of one goes up when the price of the other goes down, the correlation is negative. If the prices of the two assets are perfectly correlated, the correlation is either +1 or −1. If the movements of the assets' prices are random with respect to each other, the correlation is zero.

If the risk of holding Microsoft in a portfolio depends on what other security is in the portfolio, what sense does it make to talk about the risk of Microsoft without reference to the portfolio in which it is held? According to Markowitz, it makes no sense. Further, it should be clear that:

| *The risk of a portfolio can be less than the risk of any of the assets in the portfolio.*

This is possible for two reasons. The X's representing the proportion of funds invested in each asset are squared, so that for a two-asset portfolio with equal amounts invested in each, $X_1^2 = 0.25$ and $X_2^2 = 0.25$. Squaring these makes them smaller. Also, the coefficient of correlation typically does not equal +1, reducing the contribution of the correlation to the portfolio risk calculation. The smaller the coefficient of correlation between two assets, the greater the diversification benefits, but it is not necessary that two assets have a zero or negative correlation for a portfolio to have lower risk for the same level of returns. The only requirement is that the correlation between the assets is less than 1. But the lower the return on a given asset, the more likely it is that adding that asset to a portfolio will not only lower

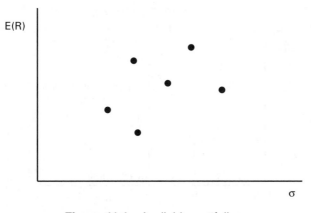

Figure 11.1 Available portfolios.

risk, but also will lower return. Whether the decreased risk is sufficient to offset the reduced return depends on factors such as the investor's attitude toward risk.

2.2. EFFICIENT PORTFOLIOS AND THE EFFICIENT FRONTIER

A portfolio is **efficient** if it has the highest return for a given level of risk and the lowest risk for a given level of return. One portfolio **dominates** another if it has more return for a given level of risk or less risk for a given level of return. We seek to graph the **efficient frontier**, the set of efficient portfolios, in risk-return space. Given a set of available portfolios, such as are shown in figure 11.1, what can we say about the shape of the efficient frontier? As can be seen by examining the two assets plotted in figure 11.2, the expected return of the portfolio comprising positive amounts of these two assets always lies on the line connecting the two portfolios. If 100 percent of the portfolio is invested in asset 1, the portfolio will plot at $(\sigma_1, E(R_1))$. If 100 percent of the portfolio is invested in asset 2, the portfolio will plot at $(\sigma_2, E(R_2))$. If the portfolio funds are divided between the two assets, the return will plot along the line connecting the two assets, and the risk will fall between the two vertical dotted lines. As we have stated, the coefficient of correlation, ρ, has a range of +1 to −1. Substituting $\rho_{1,2}\sigma_1\sigma_2$ for $\sigma_{1,2}$ in equation 11.4 and letting $\rho_{1,2} = +1$ gives

$$\sigma_p^2 = X_1^2\sigma_1^2 + X_2^2\sigma_2^2 + X_1X_2\sigma_1\sigma_2 \qquad 11.5$$

Taking the square root of both sides gives:

$$\sigma_p = X_1\sigma_1 + X_2\sigma_2 \qquad 11.6$$

Evaluating all the solutions to equation 11.6 from $(X_1 = 1, X_2 = 0)$ to $(X_1 = 0, X_2 = 1)$ and plotting these gives the dotted line shown in figure 11.2. When $\rho = +1$, the possible levels of risk that can be attained are a linear combination of the risks of the individual assets.

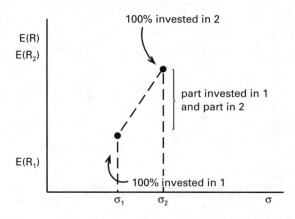
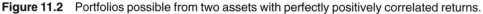

Figure 11.2 Portfolios possible from two assets with perfectly positively correlated returns.

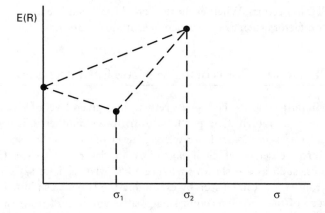

Figure 11.3 Portfolios possible from two assets with perfectly negatively correlated returns.

When $\rho = -1$, then equation 11.4 becomes

$$\sigma_p^2 = X_1^2\sigma_1^2 + X_2^2\sigma_2^2 - X_1X_2\sigma_1\sigma_2 \qquad 11.7$$

Taking the square root of both sides gives:

$$\sigma_p = X_1\sigma_1 - X_2\sigma_2 \qquad 11.8$$

The dotted lines in figure 11.3 show the levels of risk resulting from various combinations of investments in assets 1 and 2 when $\rho = -1$.

If ρ is between $+1$ and -1, the graph lies between the graphs for these extremes. In this case the graph will be curved as shown in figure 11.4. Recall that we assume that there are no taxes or transactions costs and that financial markets are competitive, so that each investor

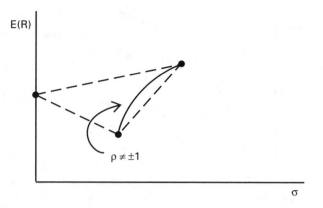

Figure 11.4 Possible portfolios when two assets are not perfectly correlated.

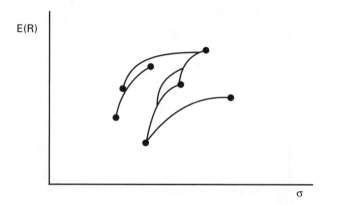

Figure 11.5 Some possible portfolio combinations with available portfolios.

owns only a small portion of the economy's wealth and is not able to influence asset prices. Given the available portfolios, conceptually, the efficient frontier can be built up from the various possible combinations of these portfolios, as shown in figure 11.5. The resulting efficient frontier is shown in figure 11.6. Notice that all the assets on this efficient frontier are risky. Hence, we will refer to this as the risky asset efficient frontier.[1]

2.3. INVESTORS' CHOICES ALONG THE EFFICIENT FRONTIER

Interestingly, the only assumptions needed to derive the efficient frontier are those concerning transactions costs and competitive markets and those stating that the only relevant dimensions of the distribution of possible security returns over the coming period are the expected return (i.e., the mean) and the variance. To go further, we need to say something about investors' attitudes toward risk.

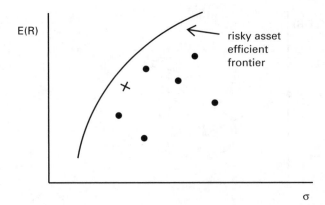

Figure 11.6   Risky asset efficient frontier.

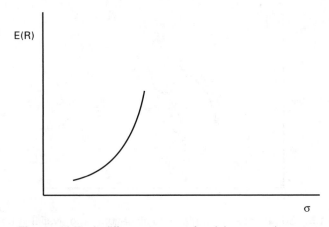

Figure 11.7   Indifference curve for risk-averse investor.

An investor who requires more return to undertake more risky investments is called **risk-averse**. An investor who requires less return to undertake a more risky investment is called **risk-seeking**. And an investor who evaluates investments in terms of their expected outcomes (i.e., the means of their outcomes) is **risk-neutral**. We add a fourth assumption: investors are risk-averse. Figure 11.7 shows the indifference curve of a risk-adverse investor in risk-return space.

Following the typical analysis from economics, the choice along the efficient frontier with only risky assets is determined by the tangency of the investor's indifference curve with the efficient frontier, as seen in figure 11.8.

2.4. ADDING A RISK-FREE ASSET

An early extension of the Markowitz analysis involved adding a fifth assumption: that there is a risk-free asset that can be freely lent and borrowed. Denoting the risk-free asset as secu-

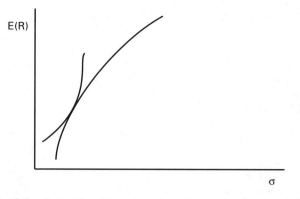

Figure 11.8 Portfolio choice for risk-averse investor and risky asset efficient frontier.

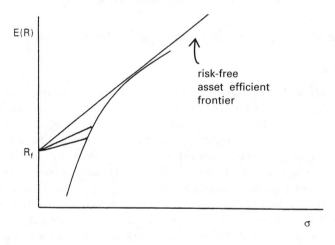

Figure 11.9 Risk-free asset efficient frontier.

rity 1, by definition, $\sigma_1 = 0$. Letting asset 2 be any other risky asset, $\rho_{1,2} = 0$. Thus, the combination of the risk-free asset and any risky portfolio has the level of return indicated in equation 11.3, but the following level of risk:

$$\sigma = X_2 \sigma_2 \qquad\qquad 11.9$$

In other words, all of the risk comes from the risky asset, and the possible risk levels that can be attained lie on the line that begins at $(\sigma_1, E(R_1))$ and runs through $(\sigma_2, E(R_2))$. The highest of these lines runs from $(\sigma_1, E(R_1))$ and is just tangent to the efficient frontier. In fact, this line dominates all the other lines with a lower slope. This line also dominates all the points below it on the efficient frontier with only risky assets. We call this line the risk-free asset efficient frontier (see figure 11.9).

291

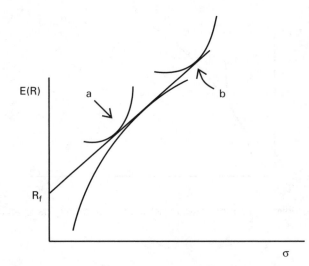

Figure 11.10 Investor choices along the risk-free asset efficient frontier.

It is very important to understand that each point along the risk-free asset efficient frontier is a particular combination of investment in the risk-free asset and the risky tangency portfolio. Figure 11.10 shows two possible indifference curves for an investor. If the investor's indifference curve is tangent to the risk-free asset efficient frontier at point a, the investor chooses a portfolio that comprises 60 percent of the risky tangency portfolio and 40 percent of the risk-free asset. If the investor's indifference curve is tangent at point b, the investor chooses a portfolio comprising 120 percent of the risky tangency portfolio and borrows 20 percent at the risk-free rate. Note than in either case the investor chooses the same risky portfolio. The only difference between the two positions is the amount of the risk-free asset held or borrowed. The part of the risk-free asset efficient frontier to the left of the tangency point is called the "lending line," because it includes only portfolios with a positive holding of the risk-free asset (such as a US government bond – buying a bond is the same as lending to the government). The part of the risk-free asset efficient frontier to the right of the tangency point is called the "borrowing line," because it involves borrowing at the risk-free rate.

2.5. THE BENEFITS OF DIVERSIFICATION

Theoretical developments in financial economics beginning with Markowitz have resulted in a substantial amount of work concerning the benefits of diversification. Suppose that one selected stocks for a portfolio randomly: say, by throwing darts at the stock page in the local newspaper. If a number of portfolios were selected in this way, each would comprise a randomly selected subset of the market, so the expected return of each of these portfolios is the market return. What would happen to the risk of the portfolio as the number of stocks included in each portfolio increased? We investigate this question using actual data for a

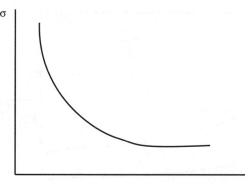

Figure 11.11 Risk of randomly selected portfolios of various sizes.

Table 11.1 Correlation matrix for selected stock markets, based on daily returns for October 20, 1987, through December 20, 1989

	AU	BE	FR	GE	HK	JA	NE	SW	UK
Australia (AU)	−0.11								
Belgium (BE)	0.08	0.33							
France (FR)	0.10	0.36	0.55						
Germany (GE)	0.14	0.34	0.46	0.58					
Hong Kong (HK)	0.04	0.27	0.26	0.29	0.32				
Japan (JA)	0.16	0.30	0.43	0.41	0.43	0.26			
Netherlands (NE)	0.22	0.23	0.40	0.54	0.65	0.31	0.36		
Switzerland (SW)	0.25	0.20	0.44	0.51	0.55	0.25	0.33	0.59	
United Kingdom (UK)	0.47	0.06	0.23	0.26	0.44	0.17	0.26	0.49	0.41

Source: Lau and McInish 1993. Reprinted by permission JAI Press Inc., Greenwich, Connecticut, and London, England.

sample of US common stocks. We calculate the standard deviation of returns for each one-stock portfolio and then average these across stocks. Next, we calculate the standard deviation of each possible two-stock portfolio and average across these, the standard deviation of every possible three-stock portfolio and average across these, and so forth. We present the results in figure 11.11. The unsystematic risk of the portfolios diminishes rapidly as the portfolio size increases, so most of the risk is diversified away with a portfolio of only 10–20 securities. This reduction in unsystematic risk arises from the fact that the returns of individual stocks are not perfectly correlated.

We have examined the benefits of diversification for a portfolio of US stocks. Would it be possible to gain even more diversification benefits from an internationally diversified portfolio? Table 11.1 presents the correlation of returns for the stock markets of various pairs of countries. Most of these correlation coefficients are less than 0.6, and many are less than 0.3. This gives some indication that there might be benefits to diversifying interna-

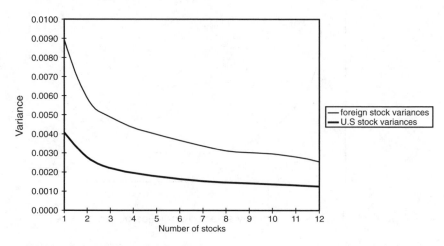

Figure 11.12 Comparison of risk of randomly selected portfolios comprising US stocks only with similar portfolios comprising both US and non-US stocks.

tionally. Figure 11.12 also compares the risk of portfolios of various sizes that comprise US stocks with portfolios that comprise both US and non-US stocks. For every portfolio size the internationally diversified portfolio has lower risk than the US-only portfolio.

The benefits of international diversification arise from the diversity of economic conditions in different countries and also from differing distributions of industries in each country. Australia has an above-average concentration in natural resources, while Singapore relies on technology, financial services, tourism, and transportation (Griffin and Icarolyi 1998). The benefits of international diversification are attenuated somewhat, because there is a tendency for volatility to be transmitted across markets, so that high volatility in one market results in high volatility in other markets (Solnik, Boucrelle, and Fur 1996). Of course, this diminishes the value of international diversification. Brush (1997) presents evidence that long/short portfolios such as those used by **hedge funds** have risk–return characteristics that improve the efficient frontier.

Statman (1987) challenged the view that the benefits of diversification are exhausted with portfolios of only 10–20 stocks. Instead, he argued that diversification benefits are not exhausted until the cost of achieving these benefits is more than the value of the benefits. To determine the cost–benefit tradeoff, Statman compared the risk and return profile of portfolios of various sizes with the return for a diversified portfolio that is levered to produce comparable risk. To better understand Statman's approach, assume that an investor's alternative to owning a portfolio of only a few stocks is to own shares in the Standard & Poor 500 Index, a broad-based index of US common stocks. Also, assume that the investor can borrow at the risk-free rate plus 100 basis points. To determine whether it would be better to hold the levered mutual fund portfolio or an undiversified portfolio, an investor simply plots the undiversified portfolio on the Capital Market Line. If the undiversified portfolio plots above the CML, there are additional benefits to be gained from diversification, but these must be weighed against the added costs of having a larger portfolio. One possibility would be to buy shares in the Vanguard Index Trust, a US mutual fund holding a portfolio designed to replicate the S&P 500.[2] The result of substituting the Vanguard Trust for the S&P 500 is to shift the CML downward by the amount of the expenses incurred by the trust. This, of course, reduces the advantage of owning a broadly diversified portfolio. But if there are costs associated with maintaining a non-fully-diversified portfolio, these costs would reduce the advantages of such a portfolio relative to the S&P 500 portfolio. Statman (1987) concludes that a well-diversified portfolio must include at least 30 stocks for a borrowing investor and 40 stocks for a lending investor.

Tesar and Werner (1995) examined long-term international investment patterns. They report international investment holdings as a percentage of domestic bond and equity market capitalization in 1990 as follows: Canada, 4.2 percent; Germany, 10.2 percent; Japan, 10.7 percent; and the United States, 2.7 percent. In 1990 US stock market capitalization was more than 12 times that of Canada. Hence, if Canadian investors diversified using the market portfolio approach, they would hold 12 times more US securities than Canadian securities. By contrast, holdings of US equities by Canadians constitute only 4.7 percent of the value of the domestic Canadian market. This tendency of investors to invest locally is called home bias. Moreover, when investors do invest outside their own country, they tend to invest in nearby countries. The empirical evidence shows that, despite the results of Markowitz, investors do not hold well-diversified portfolios.

As we have seen, international diversification can bring the same benefits as domestic diversification. (For additional information on international diversification see Aggarwal and Schirm 1995 and Sinquefield 1996.) Various indexes are available that can be used as benchmarks in international investing. Morgan Stanley Capital International reports daily performance for over 3,000 indexes covering 4,300 companies, 51 countries, 24 regions, and 38 industries. The indexes have a market capitalization of more than 1.5 trillion USD. Each index uses the same base date, and the same methodology is used to select securities for inclusion and to adjust for changes in capitalization and dividends. The indexes have a variety of uses, including performance measurement and asset allocation. Dow Jones publishes a number of indexes for the world, parts of the world, and sectors. These global indexes track data for more than 2,800 companies in 34 countries, representing more than 80 percent of market capitalization worldwide. More than 120 industries are represented. Each index is invisible, meaning that the constituent stocks are sufficiently thick for investors to be able to reasonably purchase them for their portfolios.[3]

3. THE CAPITAL ASSET PRICING MODEL

Markowitz's work had a direct impact on the practice of portfolio management, and it also led to further basic research in financial economics. One of the principal developments of this research was the Capital Asset Pricing Model (CAPM) developed by Sharpe (1964), Lintner (1965), and Mossin (1966). Sharpe and Markowitz shared a Nobel Prize in economics for their work in investments. The CAPM extends the Markowitz framework to explain the relationship between risk and return for assets. Heretofore, we have assumed:

1 There are no taxes or transactions costs.
2 Financial markets are competitive, so that each investor owns only a small portion of the economy's wealth and is not able to influence asset prices.
3 The distribution of asset returns is normal, so it can be fully described by its expected return and variance.
4 Investors are risk-averse.
5 There is a risk-free asset that can be freely lent and borrowed.

Now we add an other assumption, namely:

6 All investors evaluate securities over the same one-period horizon and have identical estimates of asset return distributions; i.e., investors have **homogeneous expectations**.

Assumption 6 leads immediately to the result that all investors face the same risk-free efficient frontier. Each investor has a different indifference curve. But in every case this curve is tangential to the same efficient frontier. Recall that every portfolio along the risk-free efficient frontier comprises a combination of the risk-free asset and the risky portfolio, possibly with zero weights (i.e., we allow for 100 percent investment in either the risk-free asset or the risky portfolio). Thus, this assumption leads to the first implication of the CAPM:

I *All investors hold the same portfolio of risky assets.*

At first, this implication of the CAPM may seem strange, especially since we know that, in fact, real investors do not hold well-diversified portfolios. But, as it turns out, the implication nevertheless has importance for portfolio management. To see why, recognize that someone must own every asset with a positive price. Assets that have value are not allowed to go unclaimed. Since all risky assets must be part of some portfolio, and there is only one risky portfolio held by investors, the CAPM implies that all assets must be part of this risky portfolio. Moreover, each asset must be held in proportion to its value in the market. Otherwise, there would be assets that were not in any portfolio. Because of the importance of the tangency portfolio in the CAPM, it is given a special name: the **market portfolio**. And with these additional assumptions, the risk-free efficient frontier becomes the **Capital Market Line** (CML) (see figure 11.13). Because it is an efficient frontier, the Capital Market Line comprises only efficient portfolios. And all efficient portfolios plot on the capital market line. Thus, one of the major results of the CAPM is that:

I *For efficient portfolios, there is a linear relationship between risk and return as expressed by the Capital Market Line (CML).*

The equation for the CML is:

$$E(R_k) = R_f + \frac{E(R_m) - R_f}{\sigma_m} \sigma_k$$

11.10

We explain how this equation is obtained in appendix 2.

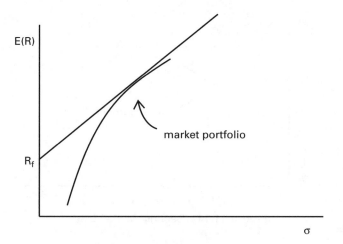

Figure 11.13 Capital Market Line.

The CML captures the relationship between risk and return for efficient portfolios. What is the relationship between risk and return for all portfolios, including inefficient portfolios? To answer this question, note that $\rho = +1$ for efficient portfolios. All efficient portfolios are perfectly correlated with the market portfolio, because the only risky component of these portfolios is the market portfolio. Hence, we can rewrite the equation for the CML[4] as

$$E(R_k) = R_f + \frac{E(R_m) - R_f}{\sigma_m} \rho_k \sigma_k \qquad 11.11$$

When $\rho = +1$, we have the CML. When $\rho < +1$, we have an expression for the relationship between risk and return for inefficient portfolios.[5]

But equation 11.11 is not the usual way of expressing this relationship. Instead, following custom, we define a new variable, **beta**:

$$\beta_k = \frac{\rho_k \sigma_k}{\sigma_m} \qquad 11.12$$

Variance or standard deviation captures the total risk of an asset. **Systematic risk** is risk that an asset shares with the market, and **unsystematic risk** is risk that is unique to the asset. Efficient portfolios, including the market portfolio, have only systematic risk. ρ can be viewed as the proportion of an asset's total risk that is systematic. Thus, the numerator of the right-hand side of expression 11.12 is the amount of systematic risk for asset k, and the denominator is the amount of systematic risk for the market portfolio. Hence, beta is a measure of systematic risk, and, in fact, is the ratio of an asset's systematic risk to the systematic risk of the market. Substituting expression 11.12 into equation 11.11 gives:

$$E(R_k) = R_f + \beta_k (E(R_m) - R_f) \qquad 11.13$$

297

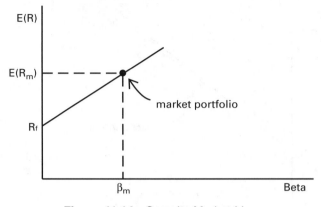

Figure 11.14 Security Market Line.

Equation 11.13 shows the relationship between risk and return for all assets and portfolios, both efficient and inefficient, and is called the **Security Market Line** (SML). According to the CAPM, there is a linear relationship between risk and return, expressed by the SML, so that the expected return of an asset equals the risk-free rate plus a risk premium depending on the amount of systematic risk the asset has relative to the market portfolio. Figure 11.14 shows a graph of the SML.

In the CAPM only systematic risk is relevant. Why? There are several ways one can think about this. In a Markowitz context, risk depends on the portfolio in which an asset is held. In the CAPM, the only risky portfolio held is the market portfolio. Hence, the risk of an asset must be judged in relation to the market portfolio, which means in relation to its systematic risk. Alternatively, investors can hold the market portfolio, which has only systematic risk. Holding a portfolio perfectly correlated with the market portfolio can eliminate unsystematic risk. Since there is no need to hold portfolios with unsystematic risk, the market does not compensate investors for the unsystematic risk in their portfolios.

Another question addressed by the CAPM is: What is the appropriate measure of risk? The answer is that the appropriate measure of risk is systematic risk as expressed by beta. Beta has become a pervasive measure of risk. The Value Line Investment Survey and the Value Line Mutual Funds Survey, which provide investment information for individual investors in the USA, publish betas for all stocks and equity-based mutual funds covered. Further, the CAPM provides a way of unifying corporate finance and investments and also provides important tools for performance evaluation.

We have seen previously that the risk of a portfolio, as measured by its variance or standard deviation of returns, is not a linear combination of the risk of the assets comprising the portfolio. But if risk is measured by beta, the risk of the portfolio is a weighted average of the risk of the assets in the portfolios. That is:

The beta of a portfolio is a weighted average of the betas of the assets in the portfolio, where the weights are the proportion of funds invested in each asset.

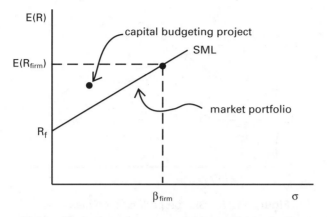

Figure 11.15 Illustration of an acceptable capital budgeting project.

3.1. THE CAPM IN CAPITAL BUDGETING

The SML indicates the relationship between risk and return for all assets. In other words, given an asset's level of risk, as measured by beta, the expected return can be obtained from the SML. The return obtained in this way is the required rate of return for projects with this beta – i.e., in this risk class. For a capital budgeting project to be acceptable, it must plot on or above the SML. If a firm undertakes a capital budgeting project that plots above the SML, investors will bid up the firm's stock price until the expected return on the stock again plots on the SML. Hence, the market value of the project will be greater than its book value, which is the cost of undertaking the project. If a project plots above the SML, it is acceptable, regardless of the risk class of the firm's other projects.

Figure 11.15 shows the risk class for an all-equity firm and a potential capital budgeting project for this firm. This project is acceptable for this firm, despite the fact that the return on the project is less than the required return on the firm as a whole. Acceptance of this project will reduce the overall rate of return of the firm, but it will also reduce the overall risk, or beta, of the firm. The reduction in risk more than offsets the reduction in return, so that undertaking the project increases the firm's value. Extension of these examples to other cases such as the levered firm is beyond the scope of this book.

3.2. PORTFOLIO PERFORMANCE EVALUATION

A fundamental problem in applying the CAPM is that the CAPM is an *ex ante* model, describing a future period and, therefore, is not strictly applicable to historical periods. We solve this problem by a simple expedient: we assume that the CAPM also holds *ex post*. Given this assumption, the CAPM becomes the basis for a number of practical applications, including portfolio performance evaluation and estimation of beta.

A number of measures based on the CAPM have been developed for evaluating the *ex post* performance of portfolios. *The greatest contribution of these measures is that they focus on*

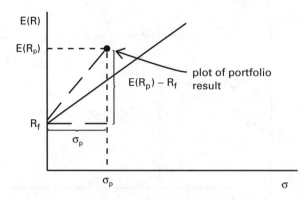

Figure 11.16 Sharpe performance measure.

both risk and return. We have learned from Markowitz that investors are interested in both. Yet it is surprising how many times in real-life situations only one of these is considered and the other is ignored.

Sharpe suggested a performance measure based on the CML, namely:

$$\frac{R_p - R_f}{\sigma_p} \qquad 11.14$$

To obtain Sharpe's measure, plot the actual portfolio performance in risk–return (σ, R) space. Sharpe's measure is the slope of the line through $(0, R_f)$ and (σ_p, R_p), as shown in figure 11.16.[6]

Treynor developed a measure based on the SML:

$$\frac{R_p - R_f}{\beta_p} \qquad 11.15$$

To obtain Treynor's measure, plot the actual portfolio performance in risk–return (β, R) space. Treynor's measure is the slope of the line through $(0, R_f)$ and (β_p, R_p), as shown in figure 11.17.

Jensen developed a third measure. Jensen noted that the expected return on a portfolio is

$$[R_f + \beta_p (R_m - R_f)] \qquad 11.16$$

If the expression in equation 11.16 is subtracted from the actual performance, R_p, the resulting difference, called "alpha," provides an assessment of risk-adjusted performance:

$$R_p - [R_f + \beta_p (R_m - R_f)] = \alpha_p \qquad 11.17$$

Graphically, the Jensen measure is the vertical distance from the SML to the point (β_p, R_p), as shown in figure 11.18.

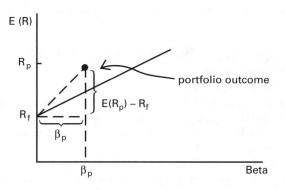

Figure 11.17 Treynor performance measure.

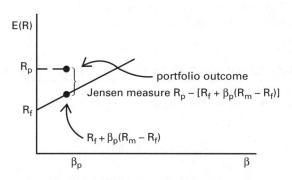

Figure 11.18 Jensen performance measure.

The Sharpe (1966) measure is based on the CML, whereas the Treynor (1965) and Jensen (1968) measures are based on the SML. The Sharpe and Treynor measure is the slope of the line through the point of the vertical axis representing the risk-free rate and a given return in risk-return space. A higher slope indicates better performance. Portfolios with the same slope have the same performance. The Jensen measure gives all portfolios that are on a line parallel to the SML equal performance rankings. All three of these measures have been used extensively.[7] Selecting a suitable performance measure is a matter of judgment and depends on the specific attributes that are being evaluated. There are also a number of potential problems, including the selection of an appropriate benchmark and evaluating market timers. Market timers may always have portfolios that plot on the SML but achieve superior returns by holding low-risk assets when equity returns are negative and high-risk assets when equity returns are high.

Numerous additional performance measures have been designed by financial service providers to aid investors in making investment decisions. One of the best known of these is Morningstar, which rates mutual funds based on their historical performance and assigns ratings of 1–5 stars.[8] To illustrate the calculation of the star rating over a 3-year historical period, we indicate variables for a particular fund, for a group of similar funds, and for treasury bills by the subscripts f, g, and t, respectively. Then, the steps in the Morningstar procedure are:

1 Calculate a return score as $\text{RETSCORE}_f = (\text{RET}_f - \text{RET}_t)/(\text{RET}_g - \text{RET}_t)$, where RET is the 3-year annualized return.
2 Next, calculate a RISKSCORE.
   a. The first step is to calculate the shortfall of return relative to treasury bills. For each month during the 3-year period, considering only months for which $\text{RET}_f < \text{RET}_t$, $\text{SHORT}_f = \Sigma(\text{RET}_f - \text{RET}_t)$, and considering months for which $\text{RET}_g < \text{RET}_t$, $\text{SHORT}_g = \Sigma(\text{RET}_g - \text{RET}_t)$.
   b. The risk measure is $\text{RISKSCORE}_f = \text{SHORT}_f/\text{SHORT}_g$.
3 Next, a performance measure (SCORE) is calculated as $\text{SCORE} = \text{RETSCORE}_f - \text{RISKSCORE}_f$.
4 Finally, the funds in each rating group are ranked by SCORE, from highest to lowest. The top 10 percent of funds receive five stars, the next 22.5 percent receive four stars, the middle 35 percent receive three stars, the next 22.5 percent receive two stars, and the bottom 10 percent receive a single star.

3.3. ESTIMATING BETA FROM HISTORICAL DATA

Next, we explain how to estimate beta using historical data. Rearranging equation 11.13 in *ex post* form gives:

$$R_k = R_f(1 - \beta_k) + \beta_k R_m \qquad 11.18$$

We estimate equation 11.18 using the following linear regression model:

$$R_k = b_0 + b_1 R_m + \varepsilon_k \qquad 11.19$$

where b_0 is a constant term, b_1 is the coefficient of the return on the market, and ε_k is a random error term. The estimation of equation 11.18 requires returns on the asset and on the market. Typically these are calculated using the **holding period return**:

$$R_t = \frac{P_t - P_{t-1} + D_t}{P_{t-1}} \qquad 11.20$$

which simplifies to:

$$R_t = \frac{P_t + D_t}{P_{t-1}} - 1 \qquad 11.21$$

The **price relative** is the ratio of the price at the end of a period to the price at the beginning of a period. Sometimes the **log price relative** is used:

$$\ln\frac{P_t}{P_{t-1}} = \ln(P_t) - \ln(P_{t-1}) \qquad 11.22$$

The prices must be adjusted for dividends prior to taking logs. The log price relative version is often easier computationally, because multiple period returns can be calculated from single period returns simply by adding the log price relatives for the appropriate periods. The return on the market can be calculated by using the value for an index such as the Standard & Poor 500, the New York Stock Exchange Composite Index, or Morgan Stanley's Europe, Australia, and Far East (EAFE) Index, depending on the assets being evaluated.

The length of time over which returns are calculated for use in estimating beta is called the **differencing interval**. Any differencing interval can be used, but it is important in comparing betas that all are estimated in the same way, including the use of the same differencing interval and the same market index. For the same asset, if the true beta is greater (less) than 1.0, betas estimated using shorter differencing intervals tend to be lower (higher) than those estimated using longer differencing intervals.

3.4. Passive versus Active Investing

In the last 25 years there has been a significant movement toward passive investment management. **Passive investment management** is the strategy of owning a portfolio that comprises the securities in an index in the same proportions in which they are included in the index or in owning a subset of these securities designed to mimic the performance of the index. The alternative to passive investment management is **active investment management**, which is the selection of securities for inclusion in a portfolio based on economic criteria, such as past earnings or stock price performance. The theoretical underpinning for this movement is the conclusion of the CAPM that investors should hold the market portfolio. Another important justification is the finding of most efficient markets studies that, historically, mutual fund managers have not outperformed benchmark market indexes.

Pensions & Investments reported that at the end of 1996 assets invested in US and international stock markets and in bond index funds amounted to 600 billion USD. Holding a market index provides diversification benefits and also reduces costs. L. Robert Frazier, assistant treasurer for asset management at Kimberly–Clark Corp., estimates that the company's pension plan should save about 100 million USD in fees over the next decade through indexing. Ninety percent of Kimberly–Clark's 2 billion USD pension fund is indexed (Laderman 1996).

4. SUMMARY

The development of Modern Portfolio Theory, begun in the early 1950s by Harry Markowitz, has revolutionized the practice of investment management. Since Markowitz's findings apply to all assets and portfolios, for simplicity, we define a portfolio to include both single-asset and multi-asset portfolios. Using only a few assumptions concerning the nature of financial markets, such as that asset returns are normally distributed so that the distribution of these returns can be characterized by its mean E(R) and variance (σ), Markowitz derived several important results.

Markowitz's most important finding is that *the risk of an asset has no meaning except with reference to the portfolio in which the asset is held*. Markowitz also demonstrated that *the contribution of an asset to the risk of a portfolio depends on the way the returns of the asset move in relation to the returns of the other assets in the portfolio*.

An efficient asset is an asset that has more return for a given level of risk or less risk for a given level of return. An efficient frontier is the set of efficient portfolios. When there are only risky assets, the efficient frontier is curved. But if there is a risk-free asset, the efficient frontier is the line through the point $(0, R_f)$ tangential to the risky asset efficient frontier.

The Capital Asset Pricing Model is a major extension of the work of Markowitz. If all investors see the same efficient frontier, it can be shown that all investors will hold the same risky portfolio, which therefore must comprise all the assets in the market. This portfolio is called the "market portfolio." The risk that a security shares with the market portfolio is called "systematic risk," and the remaining risk is called "unsystematic risk." The Capital Market Line (CML) runs through the points $(0, R_f)$ and $(\sigma_m, E(R_m))$.

There is a linear relationship between risk and return for all portfolios. This relationship, the Security Market Line (SML), runs through the points $(0, R_f)$ and (β_m, R_m) and expresses the relationship between risk and return for all assets. The risk of an asset depends on the risk-free rate and a risk premium. The risk premium depends on how much systematic risk an asset has relative to the market and the excess of the market return over the risk-free rate.

The CAPM has proved useful in a variety of contexts, including estimating the cost of capital, estimating risk for portfolios, and developing measures for *ex post* portfolio performance evaluation. Three portfolio performance measures are particularly well known. In mean-variance space, the Sharpe measure is the slope of the line from the risk-free asset to the point where the portfolio plots. In mean-beta space, the Treynor measure is the slope of the line from the risk-free asset to the point where the portfolio plots. In mean-beta space, the Jensen measure is the distance from the SML to the point where the portfolio plots. The CAPM has also given rise to a significant movement to passively invest in portfolios designed to mimic indexes rather than trying to beat the market.

Questions

1 Can two assets that are positively correlated form a portfolio with less risk than either of the assets in the portfolio?
2 Why is it impossible to quantify an asset's risk without knowing the portfolio in which it will be held?
3 Why does the market portfolio have only systematic risk?
4 In equilibrium, can an asset traded in a competitive market plot above the SML?
5 How many assets should there be in a diversified portfolio?
6 What do the Sharpe, Treynor, and Jensen performance measures have in common?
7 Name at least two factors that must be the same to make it appropriate to compare two assets' estimated betas.
8 What does it mean for an investor to be risk-averse?
9 What are the advantages of passive management over active management?
10 What does beta measure, and how is beta useful in portfolio management?

APPENDIX 1

An introduction to the mathematics of Modern Portfolio Theory

1. Introduction

This appendix provides the basic mathematical tools needed to understand Markowitz portfolio theory. First we explain how single and double summation signs work. Then we show how to calculate the mean and variance of the returns for a discrete distribution (i.e., one that has a finite number of specific values). Similar results could be obtained for a continuous distribution using calculus, but additional complication would not yield any important insights. In all our calculations, we require that

$$\sum_{q=1}^{n} p_q = 1 \qquad\qquad A1$$

where p_q is the probability that outcome q will occur.

2. Single and double summation signs

In the following expression

$$\sum_{i=1}^{n} r_i \qquad\qquad A2$$

the upper-case Greek letter sigma denotes addition, $i = 1$ is the index of summation, and n is the upper limit of summation. To evaluate this expression, begin at the starting point indicated by the index of summation and continue until the limit of summation is reached. In this case if $n = 4$, expression A2 is equivalent to: $r_1 + r_2 + r_3 + r_4$.

To evaluate the following expression

$$\sum_{i=1}^{n} \sum_{j=1}^{n} r_{i,j} \qquad\qquad A3$$

one begins by setting the first index of summation to its initial value and then pairing it with each possible value for the second summation, beginning with the initial value and continuing until the upper limit of the summation is reached. Then the second value for the first summation is paired, in turn, with each possible value of the second summation. This process is repeated until the final observation pairs the upper limit of summation for each of the summations.

If $i = 2$ and $j = 3$, expression A3 becomes: $r_{11} + r_{12} + r_{13} + r_{21} + r_{22} + r_{23}$.

3. Calculating the mean and variance for individual asset returns

Suppose that there are a finite number, n, of possible returns on asset j over the coming period. Then the mean or expected return for this distribution is:

$$E(R_j) = \sum_{q=1}^{n} p_q R_{j,q} \qquad\qquad A4$$

where $R_{j,q}$ is a possible return on asset j, p_q is the probability that $R_{j,q}$ will occur, and n is the number of possible returns.

The variance is

$$\sigma_j^2 = \sum_{q=1}^{n} p_q [R_{j,q} - E(R_j)]^2 \qquad\qquad A5$$

where $E(R_j)$ is the expected return on asset j (calculated using equation A4), $R_{j,q}$ is a possible return on assets j, p_q is the probability that $R_{j,q}$ will occur, and n is the number of possible outcomes.

4. Covariances of pairs of asset returns

The covariance of the returns for two assets measures how the returns move in relation to each other. If the asset prices go up and down together, the covariance is positive, and if one asset's price goes up (down) when the other goes down (up), the covariance is negative. If the covariance is zero, the prices of the two assets are independent. The covariance is calculated as:

$$\sigma_{k,j} = \sum_{q=1}^{n} p_q [R_{k,q} - E(R_k)][R_{j,q} - E(R_j)] \qquad \text{A6}$$

where $E(R_k)$ and $E(R_j)$ are the expected returns on assets k and j respectively, $R_{k,q}$ and $R_{j,q}$ are possible returns on security k or j respectively, p_q is the probability that $R_{k,q}$ and $R_{j,q}$ will occur at the same time, and n is the number of possible outcomes. The probability that $R_{k,q}$ and $R_{j,q}$ occur together is the joint probability and is the same as the probability of a particular n occurring.

5. Correlation coefficients for pairs of asset returns

Like the covariance, the coefficient of correlation is always calculated for pairs of securities. What constitutes a large covariance? Few investors could say. Since the coefficient of correlation has a range of +1 to −1, it is much easier to tell whether a particular coefficient of correlation is large. The coefficient of correlation for two assets is the ratio of their covariance to the product of their standard deviations:

$$\rho_{k,j} = \frac{\sigma_{k,j}}{\sigma_k \sigma_j} \qquad \text{A7}$$

where $\rho_{k,j}$ is the coefficient of correlation between asset k and asset j.

As we stated,

$$-1 \geq \rho \geq 1 \qquad \text{A8}$$

Also, we note that

$$\sigma_{j,j} = \sigma_j^2 \qquad \text{A9}$$

and

$$\sigma_{k,j} = \sigma_{j,k} \qquad \text{A10}$$

6. Calculating the mean and variance of returns for portfolios

Let n = the number of securities in a portfolio (note that here n is defined differently from above). The expected return – i.e., the mean of the distribution of possible returns over the coming period – is:

$$E(R_p) = \sum_{v=1}^{n} X_v (ER_v) \qquad \text{A11}$$

where X_v is the proportion of funds invested in each asset v, and $E(R_v)$ is the expected return on security v.

The variance of returns is:

$$\sigma_p^2 = \sum_{v=1}^{n} \sum_{g=1}^{n} X_v X_g \sigma_{k,g} \qquad \text{A12}$$

where $\sigma_{k,g}$ is the covariance of the returns for security v with those of security g.

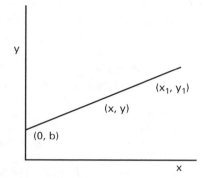

Figure 11A2.1 A line with three points.

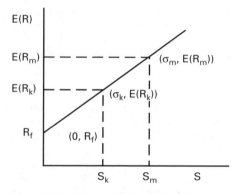

Figure 11A2.2 The Capital Market Line.

APPENDIX 2

The geometry of the Capital Market Line

In geometry texts, a line is typically defined in terms of two points, say $(0, b)$ and (x, y). The point slope formula for the line is

$$y = mx + b$$

where m, the slope, is

$$m = (y - b)/(x - 0)$$

But we know that the slope of a line is the same everywhere. Hence, we can define the slope in terms of $(0, b)$ and any other point, say (x_1, y_1) (see figure A2.1). Figure A2.2 shows a graph of the Capital Market Line with three points marked in risk-return space. The intercept $(0, R_f)$ is the risk-free asset,

$$E(R_k) = R_f + \frac{E(R_m - R_f)}{\sigma_m}\sigma_k$$

$(\sigma_m, E(R_m))$ is the market portfolio, and $(\sigma_k, E(R_k))$ any other efficient portfolio. Substituting $(0, R_f)$ for $(0, b)$, $(\sigma_m, E(R_m))$ for (x, y), and $(\sigma_k, E(R_k))$ for (x_1, y_1) in equations A1 and A2 gives the equation for the Capital Market Line:

■ Notes ■

1   For another look at and efficient frontier and the benefits of diversification see http://www.adr-dmg.com/intro.htm.
2   During 1998 the fund incurred expenses of 0.18 percent of net asset value, but was still able to match the performance of the S&P 500.
3   The web address for Dow Jones indexes is http://www.dowjones.com/indexes/home.html, and the web address for Morgan Stanley Dean Witter is http://www.ms.com/.
4   Note that this substitution is not mathematically allowable. Hence, we call this an "intuitive derivation."
5   Note this is not a derivation of the CML, but an intuitive explanation of how it comes about.
6   An update and extension of Sharpe's original work can be found in Sharpe 1994.
7   For an application of the Jensen measure in assessing mutual fund performance see Cumby and Glen 1990.
8   The Morningstar web address is http://www.morningstar.net/.

■ References ■

Aggarwal, Raj and Schirm, David C. 1995: *Global Portfolio Diversification: risk management, market microstructure, and implementation issues.* New York: Academic Press.

Brush, John S. 1997: Comparisons and combinations of long and long/short strategies, *Financial Analysts Journal* 53, 81–9.

Cumby, Robert E. and Glen, Jack D. 1990: Evaluating the performance of international mutual funds. *Journal of Finance* 45, 497–521.

Graham, Benjamin and Dodd, David L. 1940: *Security Analysis: principles and technique.* New York: McGraw-Hill.

Griffin, John M. and Karolyi, Andrew G. 1998: Another look at the role of the industrial structure of markets for international diversification strategies. *Journal of Financial Economics* 50, 351.

Jensen, Michael C. 1968: The performance of mutual funds in the period 1945–1964. *Journal of Finance* 23, 389–416.

Laderman, Jeffrey M. 1996: The stampede to index funds. The McGraw-Hill Companies Inc. web site at http://www.businessweek.com/1996/14/b346989.htm.

Lau, Sie Ting and Mclnish, T. H. 1993: Comovements of international equity returns: a comparison of the pre- and post-October 19, 1987, periods. *Global Finance Journal* 4, 1–19.

Lintner, John 1965: The valuation of risk assets and the selection of risky investments in stock portfolios and capital budgets. *Review of Economics and Statistics* 20, 13–37.

Markowitz, Harry M. 1959: *Portfolio Selection.* New Haven, CT: Yale University Press.

Mossin, J. 1966: Equilibrium in a capital market. *Econometrica* 40, 768–83.

Sharpe, William F. 1964: Capital asset prices: a theory of market equilibrium under conditions of risk. *Journal of Finance* 19, 425–42.

——1966: Mutual fund performance. *Journal of Business* 39, 119–38.

——1994: The Sharpe ratio. *Journal of Portfolio Management* 21, 49–59.

Sinquefield, Rex 1996: Where are the gains from international diversification? *Financial Analysts Journal* 52, 8–14.

Solnik, Bruno, Boucrelle, Cyril and Fur, Yann Le 1996: International market correlation and volatility. *Financial Analysts Journal* 52, 17–34.

Statman, Meir 1987: How many stocks make a diversified portfolio? *Journal of Financial and Quantitative Analysis* 22, 353–63.

Tanous, Peter J. 1997: *Investment Gurus*. New York: New York Institute of Finance.

Tesar, Linda, and Werner, Ingrid M. 1995: Home bias and high turnover. *Journal of International Money and Finance* 14, 467–92.

Treynor, Jack L. 1965: How to rate management investment funds. *Harvard Business Review* 43, 63–75.

CHAPTER TWELVE

Futures

■ **Key terms** ■

Accrued interest   interest earned, but not paid, since the last interest payment date.

Backwardation   spot prices exceed futures prices, or nearby futures prices exceed more distant futures prices.

Basis   the difference between the cash price of an asset and its futures price.

Basis risk   the possibility of incurring losses due to changes in basis.

Cash (also called **Spot**)   the market for more or less immediate delivery of an asset.

Cheapest to deliver   the concept that a futures contract price is determined by the price of the instrument whose cash market price and conversion factor make it the most economical to deliver.

Clearinghouse   an organization affiliated with a futures exchange that is the intermediary for all futures contracts and guarantees performance on all of the contracts.

Close out   to acquire an offsetting position.

Contango   authors disagree on the definition. According to some, a market is in contango when the futures price is higher than the current spot price, which is the opposite of backwardation. Others state that a market is in contango when the current futures price is higher than the expected futures price, which is the opposite of normal backwardation.

Convenience yield   a return or benefit obtained from holding a physical asset.

Conversion factor   the relationship between the price of the contract grade specified as the benchmark grade for a futures contract and other deliverable grades.

Cost of carry   financing, storage, insurance, and other costs of storing an asset for delivery in the future.

Cost of carry market   a market in which futures prices exceed spot prices by the cost of carry.

Delivery   the exchange of ownership of an asset under the terms established by the market on which the contract is traded.

First Position Day   the first day that a short is allowed to give an official notice of intent to deliver.

Initial margin   for a futures contract, the amount of cash or acceptable securities deposited at the initiation of the contract.

Long   the party that has bought a futures contract without acquiring an offsetting position and is obligated to take delivery of the underlying asset at maturity.

Maintenance margin   for futures contracts, the amount below which the margin in the account cannot decline without a margin call.

Margin call   a request for more margin.

Market-on-close   an order to be executed at the closing price or as near to the closing price as possible.

Maturity   the period within which delivery of the underlying asset can be made to satisfy the futures contract.

Net hedging hypothesis   the view that futures prices tend to rise (fall) over the life of a contract if hedgers are net short (long).

Normal backwardation   the view that the current futures price is lower than the expected futures price, so that futures prices tend to rise over the life of the contract.

Notional   a fictional amount used to represent the face value of the assets underlying the derivative contract.

Open interest   the total number of long (or short) contracts that exist at any given time.

Pit   the location on the floor of a futures exchange where treading occurs.

Position day   the day on which the short first notifies the exchange of an intention to deliver, but not the first such day, which is called **First position day**.

Quality option   the right to select what will be delivered on a futures contract.

Settlement price   the price established by an exchange for official use, including the determination of the allowable trading range on the next trading day and the gains and losses to be posted to each account in the daily marking to market.

Short   the party that has sold a futures contract without acquiring an offsetting position and who is obligated to deliver the underlying asset at maturity.

Spot   see cash.

Spread (futures)   simultaneously shorting one futures contract and going long on another.

Timing option   the right to decide when to make delivery on a futures contract.

To arrive   a type of deferred delivery in which the price is based on delivery at a specified point, and the seller pays the freight.

Variation margin call   a margin call in which the margin must be deposited within the same day and often within the hour.

Wild card option   for the CBOT Treasury bond futures contract, the right to announce an intention to deliver until 8 p.m., even though the settlement price, which is the 2 p.m. price, is fixed.

THIS CHAPTER explains how futures contracts work and provides additional information about the trading of these contracts. Specifically we

- describe the origin of futures trading
- analyze each element of the definition of a futures contract to clarify its meaning
- describe the institutional arrangements involved in trading futures, including aspects of clearing and settlement such as clearinghouses, margin, marking-to-market, and settlement prices.

Then we discuss a number of features of futures market trading, including

- the profile of possible outcomes for futures contracts
- the relationship between cash and futures prices
- additional topics related to the economics of futures contracts such as the risks of speculative positions
- uses of futures contracts
- trading of futures contracts on stock indexes and individual stocks.

1. INTRODUCTION

Futures markets are used by hedgers, who seek to reduce or eliminate the risk they face from holding inventories, and by speculators, who assume the risk transferred from the hedgers. The primary economic role of futures trading is to allow those engaged in various lines of commerce to manage the risk they face due to fluctuations in the price of their inventory. These inventories comprise many disparate types of assets, including agricultural commodities, various precious metals, financial products of all types, and currencies. Inventory prices can fluctuate widely, and many businesses do not have sufficient capital to survive if the price changes are particularly severe. Historically, producers, consumers, and middlemen dealing in agricultural and mineral products have used futures. But today, futures on financial instruments dominate the market, and their growth is still continuing at a high rate.

Since the first introduction of contracts on financial instruments, volume has soared. In 1976, 128,568 futures and options contracts on financial instruments were traded on the CBOT, while 18,766,588 contracts were traded on agricultural products and metals. By contrast, 120,268,387 financial instrument contracts were traded in 1996, compared with 50,806,091 agricultural product and metals contracts.

2. HOW FUTURES CONTRACTS WORK

2.1. A BRIEF HISTORY OF FUTURES MARKETS

From very early times, traders have entered into forward contracts for future delivery. Trading in **to arrive** contracts, a type of deferred delivery in which the price is based on delivery at a specified point and the seller pays the freight, began in Antwerp, Amsterdam, Bremen, Le Havre, Alexandria, and Osaka from the seventeenth to the mid-nineteenth centuries. The first commodity exchange opened in Osaka, Japan, in about 1640 to trade actual rice. But the precursor of modern futures markets began with the trading of to arrive contracts in Chicago in the 1830s, before the development of railroads. In 1848 a group of 82 men founded the Chicago Board of Trade (CBOT), where both actual commodities and forward contracts were consummated. Gradually, the contracts became standardized with respect to the delivery period and grade, with allowances for price adjustments when the delivered grade differed. These developments caused more merchants to use the exchange and also led to the entry of speculators. Increases in the volume of trading led to decreases in the cost of trading, which, in turn, led to further increase in the volume of trading. Over time, the contracting process became more and more impersonal and more standardized.

But there were many instances in which members went bankrupt. In 1877 D. H. Lincoln, president of the Board of Trade (now the Chicago Board of Trade), was suspended, and his accounts were settled for one-fourth of the amount due. In 1888 another president of the Board of Trade, Mr. Dow, failed and paid off his accounts at 45–50 percent of the amount due.

The records of the CBOT were destroyed by fire in 1871, but out-of-town newspaper reports show that trading in modern futures contracts was already taking place in the 1860s. The introduction of the clearinghouse completed the process of developing modern futures contracts. The clearinghouse rigorously enforced margin requirements and spread the risk of loss due to failure over the whole membership, rather than just specific counterparties. Now, futures trading is conducted on exchanges around the world, including in Osaka, where the earlier contracts became the basis for futures trading. Today the Osaka Grain Exchange trades contracts in red beans and imported soybeans.[1]

The usefulness of futures trading is evident from its contribution to the economic development of Chicago. Grains from the US Midwest were sent to Chicago for use by that city and for transshipment to the eastern USA and throughout the world. A return flow of manufactured goods also went through Chicago. In the nineteenth century the transportation system was poor. Roads were unpaved, so that rains often made them impassable, and there was a shortage of warehouse and dock facilities. Prices of agricultural commodities fluctuated widely, often being very high just before harvest and very low just after harvest. The availability of futures trading contributed to the development of storage and transportation facilities, because business executives could build storage facilities and purchase grain with much less risk by locking in the sales price of the grain through the use of futures contracts.

In the 1970s, with the abandonment of fixed exchange rates under the Bretton Woods system, exchange rates began to fluctuate more widely. Interest rates also began to exhibit more volatility. These developments led to the introduction in Chicago of the first futures contracts on currencies and fixed-income instruments.

2.2. The Futures Contract in Detail

Futures contracts are traded on exchanges. Trades for nonmembers are made by **futures commission merchants**. Futures are standardized contracts in which one party agrees to sell (or in some cases to pay the liquidating value of the contract) to another party a spec-

Table 12.1 Contract highlights for the CME US Treasury bond futures and the Simex JPY futures contract

	CME US Treasury bond contract	SIMEX JPY contract
Contract size	One US Treasury bond with a face value of 100,000 USD	12,500,000 JPY
Deliverable grade	US Treasury bonds that have at least 15 years until the earliest of maturity or first call date.	
Contract months	March, June, September, and December	March, June, September, December, and spot month
Price quotation	Whole and fractional points. One full point equals 1,000 USD.	1 point = 0.000001 USD per JPY
Tick size	1/32 of one point	1 point
Daily price limits	Generally, 3 points above or below the previous day's settlement price, but can be expanded to 4.5 points. There are no limits beginning the second business day preceding the first day of the delivery month.	None
Position limits	None	1,000 contracts net long or net short in all contract months combined.
Last trading day	Seventh business day preceding the last business day of the delivery month.	Second business day immediately before the third Wednesday of the contract month.
Delivery method	Federal Reserve book-entry wire transfer	Physical delivery
Last delivery day	Last business day of the delivery month.	There is only one delivery day: the third Wednesday of the contract month.
Trading hours	Monday through Friday 7:20 a.m. to 2:00 p.m. Sunday through Thursday there is an evening session from 5:00 to 8:30 p.m. in winter and 1 hour later in summer. All times are Chicago time. On the last trading day of the contract, trading ends at noon.	08:15–17:05 Singapore time.

ified amount of a product of a standardized quality at a specified future date at an agreed-upon price. It is necessary to understand each element of this definition to understand futures. In the process of describing futures, it may be useful to consider specific contracts. In table 12.1 we describe the basic characteristics of two futures contracts: the US

Treasury bond contract traded on the CBOT and the JPY contract traded on the Singapore International Monetary Exchange (SIMEX). A virtually identical JPY contract is traded on the Chicago Mercantile Exchange (CME).

We consider each of the elements of the definition of a futures contract, in turn.

2.2.1. Standardized contracts in which one party agrees to sell to another party

All aspects of a futures contract are set in advance except one: the price. The price is determined on the floor of the exchange or, for computer-based exchanges, in the exchange's computer.

There are two parties to a futures contract. The party that agrees to make delivery is called the **short**, and the party that agrees to take delivery is called the **long**. **Delivery** is the exchange of ownership of an asset under the terms established by the market on which the contract is traded. Delivery takes place in a predetermined and fixed sequence of events established by the exchange on which the contract is traded. It is common to use the terms **cash** or **spot** when referring to the market for immediate (within the normal settlement terms) delivery of an asset. Thus, when dealing with US Treasury bond contracts, a reference to cash would be a reference to a US Treasury bond available for delivery using normal spot settlement procedures. When dealing with currencies, cash trades are typically for 1- or 2-day delivery, in contrast to futures contracts, which initially call for delivery months in the future.

2.2.2. A specified amount of a product of a standardized quality

Each contract is for a specified amount of the asset covered by the contract. For an agricultural commodity such as wheat, the contract might call for the making and taking of delivery of 5,000 bushels. The CBOT US Treasury bond contract is for bonds with a face value of 100,000 USD, while the SIMEX contract is for 12.5 million JPY. In some contexts, especially in connection with interest rate swaps, the face value or market value of the assets underlying the derivative is called the **notional** value.

The reference to quality derives from the fact that futures contracts originated for agricultural commodities. An agricultural contract might cover a particular grade of wheat. But the rules allow different grades to be delivered, and the futures exchange specifies how the price for one grade can be converted into the price for another grade. Thus, a conversion formula, or **conversion factor**, indicates how to convert a price for the grade specified as the benchmark grade for a futures contract into a price for other deliverable grades.

For the US Treasury bond contract, quality has a closely related, but slightly different, meaning from that for agricultural contracts. The CBOT trades US Treasury bond contracts with a face value of 100,000 USD. In May, contracts for Treasury bonds trading on the CBOT had maturities in June, September, December, March of the next year, and beyond. Hypothetically, Treasury bond contracts could specify the exact bond that could be delivered on the March contract, on the June contract, and so forth. In other words, all the contracts might call for the delivery of a US Treasury bond with a coupon rate of 7.25 percent and maturing May 15, 2016. This approach has the advantage of simplicity. But there might be problems if the face value of the bonds contracted for through the futures

---

BOX 12.1
Shanghai woes

In this discussion we examine how Chinese Treasury futures contracts, which were the most actively traded contracts on the Shanghai Securities Exchange in 1995, came to be indefinitely suspended from trading in May of that year.

During 1995 Chinese Treasury bonds commanded a premium over the bank deposit rate, because of the government's practice of paying additional interest at maturity to compensate for inflation. In July 1992 the government raised the bank deposit rate from 8.28 percent to 12.24 percent. Just before the bank deposit rate increase, bond 327 was issued with a coupon rate of 9.5 percent. The Shanghai Securities Exchange traded a futures contract with this bond as the underlying asset. Margin of about 1 percent of the value of the underlying interest was required.

Since bond 327 was the last issue before the rate increase, there was a possibility that the government might unilaterally increase the yield on this issue by making a one-time payment at maturity. Shanghai International Securities Company (Sisco), China's largest brokerage firm, did not believe that the government would make this adjustment. China Economic Development Trust and Investment Corp., China's fifth largest brokerage firm, and a group of other brokerage firms did believe that the adjustment would be made. These divergent beliefs set the stage for a trading war.

On February 23, 1995, the day the contract matured, trading exploded. During the last 8 minutes of trading, contracts changed hands with a value based on the underlying interest of more than 38 billion USD, which represented more than three times the amount of Chinese government bonds issued during 1994. For the day, contracts with a value of the underlying interest of more 105 billion USD were traded. In the process Sisco exceeded the 300,000-contract limit for members. Nonmember institutions were limited to 30,000 contracts, and individuals were limited to 10,000 contracts. Despite these trading limits, Sisco had placed one individual order to sell several million contracts, but the exchange's computer did not detect this violation of the trading rules.

Just after the close of trading, the general manager of the Shanghai Securities Exchange and the head of the Shanghai Securities Administration required the head of Sisco to come to the exchange. Several hours later they announced that all trades during the last 8 minutes of trading were canceled, but that other trades would settle on schedule. Following the close of trading, the government announced an additional coupon payment of 5.5 percent, which left Sisco with a substantial loss. But the loss was smaller than it would have been had the exchange not canceled millions of contracts. Sisco was suspended, and an investigation was begun.

According to *Asiamoney*, "The exchange's announcement caused an uproar the following morning. Police lined the entrance to the exchange as a crowd of investors threatened to storm the trading floor," and the president of the exchange spent the next 3 days arbitrating disputes on settlement price.

(For additional information see *Shanghai Shanghaied* 1995.)

---

markets was large in relation to the value of these bonds outstanding. Instead, a variety of bonds can be delivered on the contracts. Box 12.1 describes a related problem encountered in futures trading in Shanghai.

An alternative approach is to define what can be delivered in such a way that more than one US Treasury bond could be delivered. But this leads to a problem. Table 12.2 provides a list of US Treasury bonds that were eligible for delivery on the CBOT T-bond contract as of October 1997. The long and the short have agreed to exchange the bonds at a specified price. If the two bonds are not of equal value, then only the less valuable bond would ever be delivered, which would defeat the purpose of having more than one bond eligible for delivery. To minimize this problem, the exchange has a procedure for adjusting the contract price to a value commensurate with the value of the bond actually delivered. In the case of US Treasury bonds on the CBOT, the standard is that the bond cannot be callable or mature for at least 15 years, and the delivered bond is priced to yield 8 percent. The CBOT publishes conversion factors for each bond, showing how the price agreed to by the long and the short will be adjusted, depending on which bond was delivered. These conversion factors as of October 1997 are provided in table 12.2.

Since only one thing can be delivered on the JPY futures contract, namely spot JPY, quality is not an issue for this contract.

2.2.3. At a specified future date at an agreed upon price

Maturity is the period within which delivery of the underlying asset can be made under the terms of the futures contract. Some futures contracts are liquidated by a cash payment at maturity, so that there is no delivery. Also, some futures contracts have a single delivery day. But for most futures contracts, the short can initiate the delivery process at any time within a prescribed period. The delivery process can be better understood by examining a particular contract such as the CBOT contract for US Treasury bonds.

The delivery process on the US Treasury bond contract is a 3-day sequence. The short can initiate this sequence at any time beginning 2 business days prior to the first business day of the delivery month and ending 2 business days before the last business day of the delivery month. While deliveries continue through the last business day of the delivery month, trading for this contract stops on the seventh business day preceding the last business day of the delivery month. As long as trading continues, the parties to a contract can close out the position by taking an opposite position. But once trading ends, the parties must make or take delivery.

There are a number of decisions in the hands of the short on a CBOT Treasury bond futures contract that may lead to profit opportunities. As we have indicated, the short side of a CBOT Treasury bond contract can choose from a variety of bonds to deliver. This right to select what will be delivered is called a **quality option**. Moreover, within limits, the short can decide when to deliver, which is called a **timing option**. For the CBOT Treasury bond futures contract, the short may announce an intention to deliver until 8 p.m., even though the settlement price, which is the 2 p.m. price, is fixed. This **wild card option** gives the short the possibility of making an additional profit if the price of a deliverable bond falls. Finally, after trading on the contract has ceased in the delivery month, the short can still pick one of several days as the delivery date. If the daily accrual of interest on the deliverable bonds is greater than the daily cost of carry, the short will choose to hold off on delivery as long as possible. Otherwise, the short will deliver as soon as possible.

The clearinghouse coordinates the delivery process and guarantees performance on the contracts, but does not actually make the deliveries, which are done by the parties themselves. The day on which the short first notifies the exchange of an intention to deliver is called the **position day**. The **first position day** is the first day that a short is allowed to give an official notice of intent to deliver. For the US Treasury bond contract the first posi-

Table 12.2 Bonds that can be delivered on the Chicago Board of Trade 10-year US Treasury note futures contract as of October 1997

	Coupon	Issue date	Maturity date	Cusip number	Issue amount ($ billions)	Conversion factors					
						Dec. 1997	Mar. 1998	Jun. 1998	Sep. 1998	Dec. 1998	Mar. 1999
1.	$5^{5}/_{8}$	02/15/96	02/15/06	91282W81	14.01	0.8616	0.8646	0.8680	0.8711	0.8746	0.8778
2.	$5^{7}/_{8}$	11/15/95	11/15/05	912827V82	13.51	0.8769	0.8819	0.8846	0.8878	0.8907	0.8939
3.	$6^{1}/_{8}$	08/15/97	08/15/07	9128273E0	12.00	0.8789	0.8789	0.8813	0.8835	0.8859	0.8882
4.	$6^{1}/_{4}$	02/18/97	02/15/07	912827 2J0	13.10	0.8892	0.8912	0.8938	0.8958	0.8980	0.9002
5.	$6^{1}/_{2}$	05/15/95	05/15/05	912827T85	12.50	0.9185	0.9208	0.9228	0.9251	—	—
6.	$6^{1}/_{2}$	08/15/95	08/15/05	912827U83	13.00	0.9166	0.9185	0.9208	0.9228	0.9251	—
7.	$6^{1}/_{2}$	10/15/96	10/15/06	912827Z62	10.00	0.9067	0.9088	0.9105	0.9126	0.9144	0.9166
8.	$6^{5}/_{8}$	05/15/97	05/15/07	9128272U5	13.95	0.9112	0.9130	0.9145	0.9164	0.9179	0.9199
9.	$6^{7}/_{8}$	05/15/96	05/15/06	912827X80	14.00	0.9328	0.9345	0.9358	0.9375	0.9388	0.9406
10.	7	07/15/96	07/15/06	912827Y55	10.01	0.9392	0.9403	0.9417	0.9429	0.9444	0.9456
11.	7	08/15/96	07/15/06	912827Y55	10.00	0.9392	0.9403	0.9417	0.9429	0.9444	0.9456
12.	$7^{1}/_{4}$	08/15/94	08/15/04	912827Q86	12.07	0.9626	—	—	—	—	—
13.	$7^{1}/_{2}$	02/15/95	02/15/05	912827S86	12.05	0.9736	0.9741	0.9750	—	—	—
14.	$7^{7}/_{8}$	11/15/94	11/15/04	912827R87	12.05	0.9934	0.9938	—	—	—	—
Total amount eligible for delivery:					$172.25	$172.25	$160.18	$148.13	$136.08	$123.58	$110.58

This table contains conversion factors for all long-term US Treasury notes eligible for delivery as of October 30, 1997.
Source: Chicago Board of Trade. Reprinted by permission.

tion day is 2 business days prior to the first business day of the delivery month, and this is the day the longs and shorts notify the clearinghouse of their open positions. On position day the short notifies the clearinghouse that he or she intends to deliver, which initiates the delivery process. Once a delivery notice is filed with the clearinghouse, delivery cannot be canceled. On the next day, called the "notice of intention day," the clearinghouse matches the oldest long with the delivering short, and the short invoices the long for the amount due for the sale. On the third day, the delivery day, the financial instrument is delivered to the long in exchange for the invoice amount. This completes the delivery process. There is no delivery of actual bond certificates. Instead, since US Treasury bonds are held in book-entry form only, they are transferred electronically.

The delivery process for the JPY contract on the SIMEX is less complicated, because there is only one delivery day and one financial instrument, JPY deposits, that can be delivered. Recall that for currencies, delivery is in the country of the currency being delivered at a bank designated by the clearinghouse, so in this case delivery is in Japan.

2.3. ADDITIONAL FEATURES OF FUTURES TRADING

2.3.1. Open interest

The number of contracts held long must equal the number of contracts held short at all times. In fact, the long and the short are just two sides of the same contract. The number of long contracts (or the number of short contracts) is called the **open interest**, so

number of contracts long = number of contracts short = open interest

The open interest is the number of contracts actually in existence at any particular time. When trading in a particular maturity begins, there is no open interest. As market participants begin to place orders and trade with each other, the open interest grows. At any given time, exchanges trade a number of contracts that are identical except for their maturity date. The contract nearest to maturity typically has the largest open interest and the highest trading volume.

2.3.2. The clearinghouse

While the number of long and short contracts is equal in the aggregate, the individual contracts are not matched with each other until the maturity of the contract. In other words, the counterparty to a specific long contract is not a specific short, and the counterparty to a specific short contract is not a specific long. Instead, all longs and shorts are obligated to an intermediary, the **clearinghouse**. The clearinghouse guarantees performance on the contract among the clearing members, so the credit risk of the counterparties is reduced. After a trade on a futures exchange is cleared, the clearinghouse interposes itself between all clearing members. In the case of default, protection is provided by the customer's margin, by the equity of the futures commission merchant and clearing member, and finally by the reserve fund of the clearinghouse. In 1986 a large customer of Volume Investors, a clearing member of the COMEX, defaulted on a margin call. The clearinghouse seized all of Volume

Investors' margin. Traders with accounts at Volume Investors lost all their posted margin.

Because all contracts are standardized, it is possible to offset positions prior to maturity. If a long sells a contract (goes short), then the long and short positions are offset, and the clearinghouse cancels both positions, reducing the open interest by one contract. Shorts can also **close out** their position by acquiring an offsetting contract (i.e., by going long).

Very few futures contracts for financial instruments are actually settled by delivery. Less than 1 percent of financial futures contracts on the CBOT result in delivery. Reasons for the infrequency of deliveries include:

1   The cost of closing out a position is small, because commissions on futures contracts are typically round-trip commissions, so all of the commission is paid when the position is initiated, and there is no additional commission for acquiring an offsetting position.

2   Exactly what can be delivered on a futures contract is specified in the contract and by the rules of the exchange on which the contract is traded. For many contracts, more than one item can be delivered. When the delivery is made (within the limits set by the exchange) is at the option of the party making the delivery – i.e., the short. Longs who have specific needs have an incentive to close out the position rather than accept delivery. In some cases the long on a US Treasury bond futures contract may need bonds with a specific maturity or coupon rate. In this case the long would not want to take delivery, since the short might deliver a bond that would not meet the long's needs.

3   Location is not an issue in the delivery of financial assets. For nonfinancial contracts there may be multiple delivery locations, in which case the short selects the delivery location. For these contracts, there is the risk that the delivery location selected by the short will not meet the needs of the long.

4   For many futures contracts, the short can choose one of several days on which to make delivery. If a long wishes to purchase the securities on a specific day, then the position must be closed out and the purchase made in the cash market.

2.3.3. Open outcry and settlement price

Trading for futures contracts on many exchanges is through the open outcry system. In Chicago trading takes place in the **pit**, a many-sided, staired depression where traders can stand to view and trade with each other. For active contracts, because of the large numbers of members who may be in the pit where the contract is traded, the open outcry method produces so much noise that it is difficult to hear the bids and offers of potential counterparties. So the exchanges have devised a system of hand signals that are used along with the vocalizations. Some of these hand signals are illustrated in figure 12.1.

Because of the open outcry method of trading, it is possible for trading to take place at different prices at the same time. One member may make an offer to sell at one price, and a second trader may make an offer to sell at a slightly higher price. A third trader may then simultaneously buy the contracts from both traders. This is, in part, the reason why futures exchanges do not publish closing prices like the stock exchanges. On stock exchanges the closing price is the last trade of the day. But futures exchanges determine a **settlement price** at the end of trading. This settlement price has a variety of official uses. It is the price that is used in determining the invoice price for delivery purposes at the maturity of the contract. An additional use of the settlement price is in determining the daily transfer of cash between longs and shorts, described below.

Quantity

Buy four contracts

Sell twenty financial futures

Price

Grain futures: 1/4 cent
Grain options: 2/8 or 1/4 cent
Treasury bond & note futures:
7, 17, & 27/32 of a point

Grain futures: 1/2 cent
Grain options: 4/8 or 1/2 cent
Treasury bond & note futures:
9, 19, & 29/32 of a point

Figure 12.1 CBOT hand signals indicating quantities and prices. Hand signals adjust to the tick size, which varies for each contract.
Source: Chicago Board of Trade, *Commodity Trading Manual*. Reprinted by permission of the Chicago Board of Trade © 1994.

2.3.4. Margin

To protect itself, the clearinghouse requires that each party to the contract deposit cash or acceptable securities such as US Treasury bills. This deposit is called **initial margin**. The economic function of margin for futures contracts differs from that for stock. For stock, margin is a form of down payment, but for futures, margin is a performance guarantee. Initial margin must usually be posted no later than the beginning of trading on the day after the trade day.

The amount of margin is typically based on the volatility of the asset that underlies the futures contract. The greater the volatility of the asset's price, the greater the amount of margin that is required. In some cases, because the risk for hedgers is lower than that for

321

speculators, the amount of margin is higher for speculators than it is for hedgers. Also, margin may be smaller for positions that involve a short position in one contract and a long position in another contract – i.e., a spread – if it is likely that there will be gains on one contract when there are losses on the other. An example is the SIMEX margin on the JPY contract when traded in combination with the SIMEX GBP contract.

Typically, the most difficult aspect of futures contracts to understand for people who have not dealt with them before is that the price negotiated does not change hands immediately. In fact, it is possible in theory, though extremely unlikely in practice, that no money will change hands between the long and the short prior to the maturity of the contract and the actual exchange of cash and assets. Futures contracts are marked to market daily. That is, each day the amount lost on losing contracts is transferred to the accounts holding contracts that have gains. The amount of gain or loss is determined by subtracting the settlement price for the previous trading day from today's settlement price and multiplying the difference by the number of units of the asset covered by the contract. This is different from most other markets, in which at least some cash changes hands among the counterparties shortly after the transaction is consummated. No money passes between the long and the short if the settlement price does not change from one day to the next.

At some point, if losses persist, the margin in the account will fall below the **maintenance margin** requirement, and the brokerage firm will ask the account owner to deposit more margin. The request for additional margin is called a **margin call**. Like the initial margin, the maintenance margin must usually be posted by the beginning of trading on the next day. If prices change substantially during the trading day, a clearinghouse may issue a **variation margin call**, a call for additional margin that must be posted within a short time, possibly within the hour.

With the growth of futures contracts on stocks and bonds, regulators have worried about coordinating the margin requirements for futures contracts and for the underlying assets. In the USA these concerns have led to a ban on futures contracts on individual stocks.

2.3.5. Daily price and position limits

Many futures contracts have daily price limits that prevent trading at a price that is higher or lower than a prescribed amount relative to the previous day's settlement price. If the equilibrium price moves outside this limit, then trading ceases and cannot resume as long as the equilibrium price remains outside the limit. On the next trading day the new settlement price is the same as the previous day's price limit. Suppose that the US Treasury bond contract settlement price was 94 yesterday. Then, trading today cannot take place at prices outside the range 91–7. Suppose the equilibrium price moves to 99 and remains there for the remainder of the trading day. Then trading cannot take place. But the settlement price today will be 97, which is up the limit. Tomorrow the permissible price range will be 94–100, and if the equilibrium price is within this range, trading can resume.

There have been instances when the futures prices for agricultural contracts have been up or down the limit on a number of consecutive days. Therefore, no trading can take place. The exchange sometimes increases the limit to a level that allows trading to commence if it believes that this would be in the best interest of the market. The price limits prevent those in the market from experiencing margin calls that are too great on one day.

In some cases exchanges limit the number of contracts that are permitted to be held net long or net short. The purpose of these restrictions is to prevent one person or one firm from dominating the futures market or from being able to require the delivery of more of a particular asset than is readily available for delivery. These restrictions are more common on agricultural contracts than on financial contracts. The supplies of the latter are typically larger and somewhat expandable. Banks can create foreign exchange deposits, and there are active markets for lending stocks and bonds. But the supplies of agricultural products cannot be increased until the next harvest.

2.3.6. Accrued interest and invoice amount

In the USA bonds pay interest semiannually. A bond with a coupon rate of 6.5 percent and a face value of 100,000 USD pays 3,250 USD of interest every 6 months. When title to a bond changes hands between interest payment dates, the parties exchange the agreed-upon price plus interest accumulated for the number of days from the last interest payment date. This interest amount is called **accrued interest**. Interest accrues at the daily rate of (1/-number of days in half-year). The number of days in a half-year varies from 181 to 184, depending on the particular date and on whether the year is a leap year.

The conversion factor and the settlement price are used to determine the contract invoice amount at delivery as follows:

invoice amount = (contract size × settlement price × conversion factor) + accrued interest

The reason why the settlement price is used rather than the original contract price is that price changes between the original contract price and the current settlement price have already been compensated for through the daily mark to market.

3. THE ECONOMICS OF FUTURES CONTRACTS

3.1. FUTURES OUTCOME PROFILES

Figure 12.2 shows the profiles of possible outcomes at maturity for futures contracts. (a) shows the long futures outcomes, (b) illustrates the short futures outcomes, and (c) presents both the long and the short positions on one graph. The value of the underlying asset is presented on the horizontal axis, and the monetary outcome is presented on the vertical axis. Short futures have the possibility of unlimited losses from a price increase. Even though prices are limited to falling to zero, such a decline will produce gains on a short futures contract so great that they are effectively unlimited. Therefore, we will sometimes refer to the gains as being unlimited, even though we know that this is not strictly true. Likewise, long futures positions can realize potentially unlimited gains from a price increase in the underlying asset, but losses are limited to the value of the contract at the initiation of the position. Because these potential losses are so large, we often view them as unlimited from a practical viewpoint, especially in relation to the initial margin.

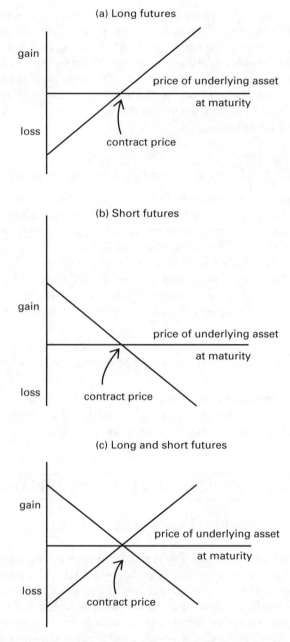

Figure 12.2 Profiles of futures contract outcomes at maturity.

3.2. THE RELATIONSHIP BETWEEN CASH AND FUTURES PRICES

3.2.1. The concept of cheapest to deliver

The short can deliver any asset that meets the terms established by the market on which the contract is traded. The traders in the market realize that the short will deliver the asset that is the **cheapest to deliver**, and the futures price reflects this fact. Consider three hypothetical bonds deliverable on the US Treasury bond contract that have the following conversion factors (CF) and cash market prices (CP):

Bond	CF	CP
#1	1.3620	1.3870
#2	1.1360	1.1360
#3	0.9760	0.9890

We ignore accrued interest. The implied cash price (ICP) is the price that is realized if an asset is delivered on a futures contract. For any given bond, its implied cash price (ICP) is

$$ICP = CF \times FP$$

where FP is the futures contract price. Assume that the futures price is 1.0000 so that the invoice price for each bond per 1 USD of face value equals its conversion factor. The conversion factor, implied cash price, and cash price for each of these three bonds is:

Bond	CF	ICP	CP
#1	1.3620	1.3620	1.3870
#2	1.1360	1.1360	1.1360
#3	0.9760	0.9760	0.9890

Bond #1 will not be delivered, because its invoice price will be based on 1.3620, but its actual market value is 1.3870. Hence, it would be better to sell this bond rather than deliver it on this contract. Likewise, bond #3 will not be delivered, because its cash market price is higher than the price that would be received by delivering it. But bond #2 will be delivered, because its cash market price exactly equals the price that will be received from its delivery.

The futures price is 1.0000 precisely because the implied cash price of bond #2 is 1.1360. To see this, suppose that the implied cash price of bond #2 increased slightly to 1.1370. At maturity the short must deliver one of these three bonds. Suppose that a trader can go long this futures contract at 1.0000. Then, when bond #2 is delivered, the invoice price will be based on the conversion factor of 1.1360, but the trader can immediately sell this bond in the cash market, and the proceeds will be based on 1.1370. Thus, going long this futures contract and selling this bond produces an immediate risk-free profit. Note that if we were not at maturity and could not immediately buy the bond and deliver it on the contract, the arbitrage profit must take into account the carrying costs of the bond and the interest costs of the daily marking to market between the time of purchase and the delivery date. But, in either event, if an arbitrage opportunity exists, traders will buy futures contracts and/or sell bond #2 in the cash market until the opportunity for a risk-free profit is eliminated.

Consider another way of looking at the concept of cheapest to deliver. Suppose that the US government repurchased all of bond #2, so that it was not available for delivery. Then one of the two remaining bonds would have to be delivered. One possibility is that the futures price will increase to 1.013, which produces the following relationships:

Bond	CF	ICP	CP
#1	1.3620	1.3800	1.3870
#3	0.9760	0.9890	0.9890

In other words, the price of the futures contract has been bid up to 0.9890 ((0.9760 × 1.0130) = 0.9890), so that the implied cash price equals the actual cash price, and bond #3 is the cheapest to deliver. Due to arbitrage, this is the probable outcome. Alternatively, if the cash price of bond #3 falls to 0.9760 instead, it is also economically feasible to deliver it on this contract when the futures price is 1.0000. Of course, it is possible for bond #3 to become deliverable through a combination of an increase in the price of the futures contract and a decline in the price of bond #3.

3.3.2. Cost of carry, contango and backwardation

Many assets that underlie futures contracts, including financial assets, can be bought and stored for future delivery. Costs associated with this storage include costs of the warehouse space, transportation costs, spoilage, insurance costs, and interest. Hence, if an underlying asset can be stored, the market would reflect **cost of carry**, and a **cost of carry market** is a market in which prices reflect the carrying costs. Because these costs accumulate over time, if future supply depends on the current rate of storage, then futures prices will be higher than current spot prices, reflecting the cost of carrying these items. In this case, the following relationship will hold

$$F_{0,T} = S_0(1+r)$$

where $F_{0,T}$ is the price at time 0 for a futures contract maturing at time T, S_0 is the spot price of a commodity at time 0, and r is the cost of carrying the item from 0 to T expressed as a percentage of the value of S. In a full cost of carry market the futures price equals the spot price times the quantity one plus the cost of carry. Otherwise, it will pay merchants to buy the product and store it for future delivery. Some define a market in which futures prices are higher than current spot prices as **contango**. In March 1996 the prices of gold on the New York Mercantile Exchange for April, June, and August delivery were 399.60, 402.50, and 401.50 respectively. Figure 12.3 shows the time path of a commodity that reflects full cost of carry.

The concept of cost of carry applies to agricultural products, metals, and financial instruments. If the production of an agricultural commodity is seasonal, and the stock of the commodity is small relative to its rate of production, it is unlikely to be economical to store the commodity beyond a certain point. Suppose that a particular crop is harvested in May of each year. Within limits, the amount produced can be adjusted by adding more acreage

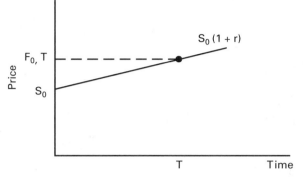

Figure 12.3   Full cost of carry.

BOX 12.2
Cost of carry for the Value Line futures contract

On July 14, 1999, the cash Value Line Index (VLA) closed at 1059.4. Contracts on this index are traded on the Kansas City (US) Board of Trade (KCBT). Trading volume on these contracts is low, and only the September contract traded on this day. Its settlement price was 1070.85. What are the cost of carry values for this contract and the December and March contracts?

Rates for September, December, and March are, respectively, 4.62 percent, 4.79 percent, and 4.73 percent. The estimated yield on the Value Line Index is 1.8 percent. The number of days to maturity for each contact is: September, 64; and December, 155, and March, 246. The cost of carry formula is:

VLA * [1% + (T – bill rate – Value Line Investment Survey estimated median yield)] *
(calendar days until futures expiration/360)

Substituting the September values gives :

$$1059.4 * [1 + (4.62 - 1.8)] * (64/360) = 719 \text{ basis points.}$$

The cost of carry for the December contract is 1820 basis points, and for the March contract is 2845 basis points. Note that the cost of carry values are increasing over time, reflecting a positive cost of carry. (The information in this box was obtained from the KCBT and from the KCBT's web site at http://www.kcbt.com/.)

---

to production, cultivating more intensively, and the like. In this case it would not make sense to incur storage costs to hold the product beyond the next harvest. But the stocks of commodities such as gold and silver and of financial assets are large relative to the current consumption, so these are always being held in inventories. Box 12.2 shows the cost of carry calculation for the Value Line futures contract traded on the Kansas City Board of Trade.

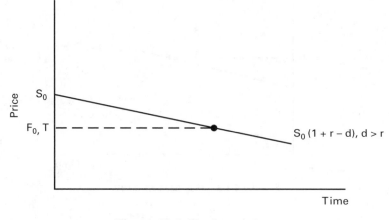

Figure 12.4 Backwardation.

The cost of carry, r, may not reflect full market rates for storage, interest, and other costs if some firms have cost advantages in these areas. Moreover, the cost of carry may be reduced. In some cases holding inventories provides firms with advantages, because they can use these in the manufacturing processes. It is possible that certain products are in short supply for current delivery, and that although the supply can be increased in the intermediate term, it cannot be increased immediately. Oil or grains may be in cargo ships headed toward our ports, but until the ships arrive, there may be a shortage. In this case the physical asset is said to have a **convenience yield**, which may partially or completely offset the cost of carry. Moreover, any dividends or interest that can be earned must reduce the cost of carrying the financial instruments. Hence, the cost of carry model must be restated as follows:

$$F_{0,T} = S_0(1+r-d)$$

where d is the convenience, dividend, or interest rate yield. If $d > r$, figure 12.3 becomes figure 12.4, and the market is said to be in **backwardation**. In March 1996 prices for live cattle on the Chicago Mercantile Exchange for delivery in April, June, and August were 64.55, 64.20, and 63.00 respectively. Hence, this market is in backwardation.

3.3.3. Basis

Basis is the difference between the cash price of an asset and its futures price. For agricultural commodities, basis can change because of changes in ability to deliver the underlying commodity at the designated delivery point. A farmer growing wheat in Iowa may contract to sell that wheat in Chicago through a futures contract. But a shortage of transportation may cause prices to rise in Chicago and fall in Iowa. If the farmer cannot get his crop to Chicago, he will have to cover his short futures position at a loss and will also have to sell his crop in the cash market in Iowa for less. The possibility of incurring losses due to changes in basis is referred to as **basis risk**.

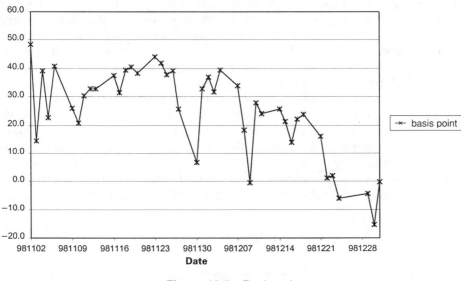

Figure 12.5 Basis point.

At the maturity of a futures contract the cash price at the delivery point and the futures price must be equal. Figure 12.5 shows an example of the convergence of the cash and futures prices to each other and of the basis to zero. As the graph shows, prior to maturity, basis may change daily even for contracts on financial instruments, although the causes are not always as obvious. Since financial instruments are delivered through the banking system, delivery costs are typically not an issue. But changes in interest rates can cause changes in the cost of carrying the securities, resulting in a change in basis. Changes in the instrument that is cheapest to deliver, can also affect basis. Consider 24 bonds deliverable on the June 1990 US Treasury bond contract. Suppose that an investor held the bond that was cheapest to deliver. Naturally, the futures prices reflect the cash price of this cheapest-to-deliver bond. Next, suppose that one of the 23 other bonds becomes cheapest to deliver, so that the futures price now reflects the cash price of this bond. In this case, there has been a change in the basis for the cash bond that was originally cheapest to deliver.

3.4. SPREADS

A **spread** involves simultaneously shorting one futures contract and going long another. This is done to take advantage of expected differential movements in the prices of the underlying assets. Futures spreads can involve two contracts for the same underlying asset on the same exchange but with different contract months, contracts for the same underlying asset but on different exchanges, or contracts for different underlying assets.

Suppose that a speculator believes that the British pound will weaken relative to the Japanese yen. Then the speculator can short a contract on GBP and go long a contract on

JPY. If the expectation turns out to be correct, then both positions can be closed out, and the speculator will realize a profit if transaction costs are not too high. If a speculator expects the relationship between long and short interest rates to change, then a speculator can take opposite positions in a short- and long-maturity interest rate contract. Which contract is shorted and which is bought depends on the direction of the expected change in interest rates and which rate is expected to change the most.

A spread is typically less risky than taking an outright position. This is because in most cases the prices of the underlying assets tend to move together. If interest rates rise, then both long and short rates tend to rise. The margin required on spreads is also typically less than on straight positions. But, of course, there are commissions on two contracts instead of one. In addition, the speculator must be concerned that both legs of the spread are put on simultaneously. On some exchanges it is possible to enter both orders together and to specify the differential price that one requires if the order is to be filled.

3.5. Commissions

Brokers charge a commission for executing a futures trade for a customer. This commission covers not only execution services, but also accounting and other services related to a futures position. The commission may also cover costs of providing advice on trading strategies. Commissions may be fixed or, as in the USA, negotiable. Only large customers have sufficient clout to actually negotiate commissions. When commissions are negotiable, there may be considerable variation in commission charges from firm to firm. Commissions may vary from contract to contract and may be lower for spreads than for long or short positions. Because positions that are not held overnight require less accounting and interactions with the clearinghouse, commissions for these trades may be lower.

In any event, the commission charges on futures contracts as a percentage of the value of the underlying asset covered by the contract are typically small. Their low cost, of course, encourages the use of futures in a variety of trading strategies.

3.5.1. A comparison of futures contracts and forward contracts

At this point it may be useful to itemize some of the differences between forward and futures contracts.

1　Unlike forward contracts, the terms of futures contracts are standardized. Futures contracts are traded for specific delivery dates and amounts, and no deviations are possible. Forward contracts also have standard trading sizes and amounts, but it is possible to arrange customized terms.

2　The standardized feature of futures contracts, along with the use of the clearinghouse as the counterparty to every contract, makes it possible to close out futures contracts prior to maturity without the knowledge or cooperation of a specific counterparty. The counterparty to a forward contract may not agree to close out the contract prior to maturity. In this case, instead of closing out the position, it is usually possible to arrange a second forward contract taking an opposite position with another counterparty. While this eliminates economic risk due to price fluctuations, credit risk is doubled, since there are now two contracts instead of one. Further, it will be necessary to make or take delivery on two contracts instead of one.

3   Futures contracts are marked to market daily, while there may be no transfers of funds between the counterparties to a forward contract until maturity. The marking-to-market feature of futures contracts reduces credit risk, but may make it more difficult to use futures contracts in the hedging transactions. Also, the marking-to-market feature of futures contracts causes the cash flow streams of futures and forward contracts to be different.

4   Many futures contracts have daily price limits, but there are no limits on the price movements of forward contracts.

Because of the differences between futures and forward contracts, especially the daily cash flows on futures contracts, the price for delivery on a futures contract will be different from the price for delivery on a forward contract if interest rates are stochastic – i.e., if interest rates changes are uncertain over time. Since we know that interest rates are stochastic, we expect futures and forward prices to differ.

3.6. RISKS OF SPECULATIVE POSITIONS IN FUTURES

There are a number of ways of thinking about the hazard of taking speculative risks in futures contracts. It is widely believed that most futures traders (some say more than 90 percent) lose money. If we accept this 90 percent figure, then, since futures are a zero–sum game, the gain for the remaining 10 percent of traders equals the loss of the other traders less transactions costs.

What is the probability of losing all one's money in the futures market? Examination of the gambler's ruin problem may provide some insights. Suppose that there are two players, the first with an initial stake of 100 USD, the second with a stake of 1000 USD. The players agree to toss a fair coin, with the first player paying the second 1 USD if the coin lands on side one, the second player paying the first 1 USD otherwise. The game will continue until one player is bankrupt. What are the odds that each player will be the one that goes bankrupt?

The probability of ruin for the first player is

$$1-(100/-1100)=0.909$$

and the probability of ruin for the second player is

$$1-(1000/-1100)=0.091.$$

Most small players who continue the game indefinitely are going to be wiped out. But this seems reasonable, since the rare small player who does not get wiped out is likely to be a big winner.

In assessing the risk of a futures position, one cannot look simply at the probability distribution of terminal futures prices. The reason for this is that any futures price that occurs prior to the maturity of the futures contract that is sufficient to exhaust the speculator's

331

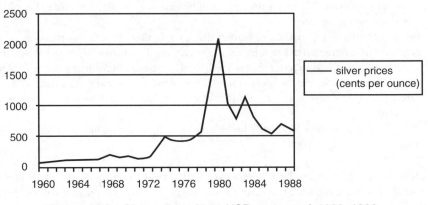

Figure 12.6 Silver prices (0.01 USD per ounce) 1960–1988.

resources will bankrupt the speculator, so the position is closed out. In the case of a premature termination of the position, the ultimate futures price is immaterial.

From another perspective, in most markets all speculators are small relative to the market as a whole. Hence, large speculators may eventually go bankrupt even if they consistently take on only relatively small positions. And, of course, large speculators often take on large positions. Evidence for this viewpoint is seen in the occasional bankruptcy of large speculators. In 1979 and 1980 three brothers who were members of a wealthy Texas oil family accumulated very large positions in silver in both the cash and the futures markets. As a result of their buying, the price of silver went from about 5 USD per ounce in 1978 to a price of almost 22 USD per ounce at the end of 1979. Silver reached a month-end high of more than 44 USD during 1980, but ended the year at about 16 USD per ounce (see figure 12.6, which shows the year-end closing prices). At one point the Hunts' profits were billions of USD. These large increases in prices greatly expanded the supply of silver as firms cut back on their use of the metal and reduced their inventories and as individuals melted family heirlooms to take advantage of the unprecedented prices. As a result, the price of silver began to fall. Eventually, the Hunts were faced with a margin call that they were unable to meet, which forced the liquidation of their futures positions. The Hunts lost not only their profits gained in the run-up in prices, but also lost most of their initial wealth.

3.7. FUTURES PRICES AND EXPECTED SPOT PRICES

We have not yet considered the question: Is the current futures price an unbiased estimate of the future spot price? Obviously, for any particular futures contract, the futures price at any given time is unlikely to be the spot price actually realized. But over a large number of contracts futures prices could accurately forecast future spot prices on average.

The answer depends on at least two further questions: Are speculators risk-averse? Are futures contracts risky? We stated earlier that there are two reasons for taking positions in futures contracts: hedging and speculating. Hedgers are seeking to eliminate risk, while speculators are taking on the risk that the hedgers do not want. Why do speculators take on

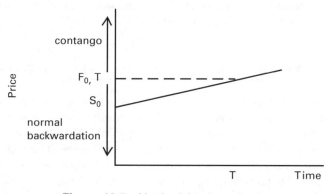

Figure 12.7   Net hedging hypothesis.

risk? If speculators are risk-averse, then they take on risk because the hedgers are compensating them for doing so. This is referred to as the **net hedging hypothesis**. In this case, if speculators are net long, then if they are to make a profit, the price of the futures contract must rise over the life of the contract. The theory that futures prices will rise over the life of the contract is called **normal backwardation**. If speculators are net short, futures prices are expected to fall over time, which is the opposite of normal backwardation. Some authors define this as contango, so that contango is the opposite of normal backwardation rather than the opposite of backwardation.[2] Figure 12.7 shows futures prices that represent normal backwardation and contango.

But if speculators were risk-neutral, they would not demand any compensation for bearing the risk that hedgers transfer to them. In this case we would expect futures prices to be unbiased forecasts of future spot prices. Or if speculators are risk-seeking on average, they might actually be willing to pay hedgers for providing the opportunity to take risks, just like the customers of a casino. Hieronymus (1978) and Gray (1963) argue that speculators are not risk-averse and that, consequently, futures markets provide hedging services at zero cost.

Even if speculators are risk-averse, futures prices might be unbiased estimates of future spot prices if futures contracts are not risky. At first this might seem unlikely. But speculators, like all investors, should evaluate risk in terms of all their holdings. It is possible that futures contracts do not add to the risk of a portfolio, so that futures prices are an unbiased estimate of future spot prices.

4. USES OF FUTURES CONTRACTS

4.1. THE USE OF FUTURES CONTRACTS IN HEDGES

The principal use of futures contracts is hedging, and hedging activities provide the primary justification for the existence of futures markets. Futures contracts are not gambling, but instead permit increased production of goods and services by providing a way for producers, wholesalers, and retailers to manage their risk.

4.2. FUTURES CONTRACTS AS INVESTMENT VEHICLES

Individuals and institutions can use futures contracts to expose their portfolios to fluctuations in the value of the underlying assets without actually owning those assets. They can provide an alternative to actually owning gold, silver, fixed-income securities, or stocks. We discuss futures on portfolios of stocks (stock index futures) below. The S&P 500 is a value-weighted index comprising 500 stocks, each in proportion to their total or aggregate market value. It would probably take some time to purchase each of the 500 stocks in the index. Further, a portfolio replicating the index might require many odd-lot positions or even fractional shares, which, of course, are not possible, not to mention bookkeeping and similar problems. A futures contract on the S&P 500 may provide the desired exposure while eliminating or minimizing many of these problems.

Some investors favor a strategy of holding a futures contract and at the same time holding a low-risk security such as a US Treasury bill with a face value equal to the value of the assets underlying the futures contract. In some cases, this strategy may provide a low-cost alternative to owning the underlying asset.

4.3. USING FUTURES TO MANAGE THE INVESTMENT HORIZON

It is possible to use longer-term financial instruments and short futures positions to invest short-term or to use short-term financial instruments and long futures positions to invest long-term. Consider an investor in March who wishes to invest funds until June. There are myriad alternatives. One simple solution would be to buy a suitable government instrument such as a US Treasury bill with the appropriate maturity. Another alternative would be to buy a US government bond with a maturity of more than 15 years and to simultaneously short a US Treasury bond contract on the CBOT with a June maturity. The bond can be delivered on the contract in June. Thus, the investor has purchased a bond at a known price and has also locked in the sales price of the bond. Hence, the rate of return on this transaction can be computed (except for interest on the daily marking-to-market of the futures contract) and compared with other alternatives for making short-term investments. At times the futures/spot strategy has produced higher returns than simply buying short-term instruments.

As indicated, it is also possible to invest long-term using a combined futures spot strategy. Suppose that one wanted to invest for more than 15 years. One possibility would be simply to purchase a bond with the desired maturity immediately. An alternative would be to go long a US Treasury bond contract with, say, a June maturity. In this case the futures contract will lock in the purchase price of the bond that will be purchased in June. Then, one invests the funds from March until June using a short-term instrument. Of course, for this particular futures contract, one must worry about exactly what will be delivered. This may or may not be of primary importance, depending on one's investment needs.

Table 12.3 CME Standard & Poor's 500 stock index contract

Contract size	USD 500 × the S&P 500 stock index.
Contract months	March, June, September, December
Price quotation	Index points and decimal fractions of index points in increments of 0.05.
Tick value	0.05 index point = 25 USD
Daily price limits	Coordinated with trading halts of the underlying stocks
Position limits	5,000 contracts net long or net short in all contract months combined
Last trading day	The business day immediately before the day of the determination of the final settlement price
Delivery	There is no delivery. Instead, all open positions at the close of the final trading day are settled in cash. The cash payment is determined by the quotations of the S&P 500 at the opening on the expiration Friday. If a stock does not trade on Friday, its most recent sales price is used.
Trading hours	08.30–15.15

5. STOCK INDEX FUTURES, FUTURES ON INDIVIDUAL STOCKS, AND VOLATILITY FUTURES

5.1. STOCK INDEX FUTURES

There are a number of futures contracts traded on stock indexes. The S&P 500 Index traded on the CME is typical; table 12.3 shows the basic features of this contract. At maturity the value of the contract is 500 USD times the S&P Index value. There is no delivery of the underlying stocks, but instead the contract is settled in cash. The final settlement price is determined in a somewhat unusual way. Settlement prices are usually determined from prices at the end of the trading day. But by placing large **market-on-close** orders (orders to be executed at the closing price), large institutions can move prices temporarily and affect the closing S&P 500 Index value. On the NYSE, where most of the S&P 500 stocks are traded, it is more difficult to manipulate the opening price than the closing price. The opening is a batch trade, and the volume of trading at the opening price is typically the largest volume of the day. Moreover, if there is an imbalance of orders, the specialist can delay the opening and broadcast indicated opening prices in an effort to generate orders on the opposite side of the market. For these reasons, the CME switched from using the closing S&P Index value to the opening value in determining final settlement at contract maturity.

Specifically, for the S&P 500 Index contract, trading stops on a Thursday, normally the Thursday prior to the third Friday of the contract month. Then the settlement price for the expiration Friday is determined by the opening prices of the S&P Index stocks. If a particular stock does not trade on the expiration Friday, then its most recent trade price is

Table 12.4 Highlights of OM individual stock futures contract

Contract size	Usually 100 shares
Example underlying stocks	Electrolux B, Ericsson B, Astra A, Volvo B, and Nordstrom
Contract months	Cycle 1: January, April, July, and October; cycle 2: February, May, August, November; cycle 3: March, June, September, and December.
Price quotation	Per share
Tick size	SEK 0.01
Daily price limits	None
Position limits	None
Settlement	Physical delivery and payment takes place on the third Swedish bank day following expiration.
Trading hours	10.00–16.00 Monday through Friday

used. This contract, like those of other index futures, is settled in cash, based on the closing value of the index, and there is no actual delivery of stock. Asian-style derivatives base the terminal settlement on an average of prices over a period of time. An example is the federal funds contract traded on the CBOT, which settles on the basis of the average daily federal funds rate during the expiration month (Chance and Rich 1996).

5.2. FUTURES ON INDIVIDUAL STOCKS

The Saão Paulo Stock Exchange and the Rio de Janeiro Stock Exchange traded forward contracts on individual shares beginning in the early 1970s. Subsequently, trading was begun in the 1970s in futures contracts on individual stocks (Braga 1996). Trading of futures on individual stocks began on the Swedish Futures and Options Exchange, OM Stockholm, and is now conducted there and on its sister exchange OMLX, the London Securities and Derivatives Exchange, and on the Sydney Futures Exchange. The basic features for one of these contracts are described in table 12.4. The OM Exchange is a computer-based exchange. Both options and futures are traded on more than 20 underlying shares. The contracts typically cover 100 shares and are in one of three maturity cycles. A new 6-month contract is listed every 3 months on the first trading day following the expiration of the near contract. Hence, there are always two futures contracts trading on each underlying security. The exchange has developed its own computer software for determining margin.

5.3. VOLATILITY OF FUTURES

OMLX, the London Securities and Derivatives Exchange, trades a number of futures contracts which fluctuate in value based on changes in the volatility of an underlying asset. The underlying assets whose volatility is tracked include the German DAX stock index, the Swedish OMX Index, and the British FTSE 100. There are no position limits on these contracts.[3]

6. SUMMARY

To arrive contracts were traded before the 1900s in Antwerp, Amsterdam, Bremen, Chicago, Le Havre, Alexandria, and Osaka. Modern futures contracts evolved in Chicago during the late 1800s. The two most important developments were standardization and impersonalization. Standardization simplifies trading, since only the price must be negotiated. Impersonalization makes it possible to close out contract positions prior to maturity by reversing the initial trade. Impersonalization also eliminates the need to assess the credit of a particular counterparty by substituting a clearinghouse as the counterparty for all contracts. The clearinghouse guarantees performance among the clearing members on all contracts and manages a system of margins, or performance payments. Most people are used to thinking about spot or cash markets, where prices for the more or less immediate delivery of assets are negotiated. In futures markets, the prices negotiated are not for immediate delivery but, instead, are for delivery at a date that may be months in the future.

There are two parties to a futures contract, the long, who agrees to take delivery, and the short, who agrees to make delivery. The value of the contracts is marked-to-market daily. The exchange posts a settlement or official price that is used in determining gains and losses and for other purposes. If the losses mount, they will eventually cause the account to fall below the maintenance margin requirement, and a margin call requesting additional margin is issued. For some contracts, only prices that are within a specified range around the previous day's settlement price are permitted. The number of contracts that an individual or group acting together can own may also be limited.

Some futures contracts permit more than one asset to be delivered, and some also permit delivery over a number of days at the end of the contract. The choice of what is delivered and when it is delivered is the prerogative of the short. Because shorts deliver the asset that is most economical, based on a comparison of futures and cash prices, the futures price is determined by the price of the asset that is cheapest to deliver. Some traders and speculators undertake positions known as spreads by simultaneously going long one contract and shorting another contract to take advantage of expected changes in the relative prices of the two contracts.

When futures prices are above current cash prices, the market is in contango, and when futures prices are below current cash prices, the market is in normal backwardation. Contango can result from a market that primarily reflects storage costs, while normal backwardation may reflect high current demand when supplies cannot be increased in the short term. If speculators are risk-adverse, contango and normal backwardation can reflect the need to attract long or short speculators to bear the risk transferred from hedgers.

The difference between the cash price for an asset and the futures price is called "basis." Basis, which can change from trade to trade, affects the cash flows of the contract and also the effectiveness of the contract in hedging.

337

Questions

1 What is the definition of a futures contract?
2 What is the meaning of the term "notional"?
3 How does a conversion factor plan a role in a futures contract?
4 What is the role of the clearinghouse?
5 How does initial margin differ from maintenance margin?
6 How does margin for futures differ from margin for equities?
7 Explain the concept of "cheapest to deliver."
8 What is the difference between contango and normal backwardation?
9 What are the similarities and differences between forward and futures contracts?
10 What is the principal use of futures contracts?

■ Notes ■

1 Links to derivative-related web sites, including exchanges throughout the world, can be found at http://www.slu.edu/departments/finance/638links.html.
2 According to Campbell R. Harvey's hypertextual finance glossary located at http://www.duke.edu/~charvey/Classes/wpg/glossary.htm, contango is "a market condition in which futures prices are higher in the distant delivery months," and backwardation is "the opposite of contango." Stoll and Whaley (1993) defines normal backwardation as "A market in which futures prices tend upward," and contango as "A market in which futures prices tend downward" (p. 64). Also see http://www.contingencyanalysis.com/glossarybackwardation.htm.
3 Additional information is available at http://www.crbindex.com/conspecs/omlx/index.htm.

■ References ■

Braga, Bruno Saturnino 1996: Derivatives markets in Brazil: an overview. *Journal of Derivatives* 4, 63–78.

Chance, Don M. and Rich, Don R. 1996: Asset swaps with Asian-style payoffs. *Journal of Derivatives* 3, 64–77.

Gray, Roger 1963: Onions revisited. *Journal of Farm Economics* 45; repr. in *Selected Writings on Futures Markets*, vol. 2, ed. A. E. Deck (Chicago: Chicago Board of Trade, 1997), 325–8.

Hieronymus, Thomas A. 1978: *Economics of Futures Trading*. New York: Commodity Research Bureau.

Shanghai Shanghaied 1995: *Asiamoney* 6 (Oct.), 15–20.

Stoll, Hans R. and Whaley, Robert E. 1993: *Futures and Options: theory and applications*. Cincinnati, OH: South-Western.

CHAPTER THIRTEEN

Options

■ **Key terms** ■

American option an option that can be exercised at any time prior to expiration.

At the money the price of the underlying asset equals the striking price.

Bear spread a spread that is profitable when the price of the underlying asset decreases.

Bull spread a spread that is profitable when the price of the underlying asset increases.

Calendar spread the purchase of one option and the sale of another, both with the same striking price, but with different expiration dates.

Call an option that gives the owner the right, but not the obligation, to buy an underlying asset at a fixed price at or until the expiration of the contract, or in some cases to receive the liquidating value in cash.

Covered writing an option while owning an offsetting position in the underlying asset or its equivalent.

Delta the change in the price of an option in response to a change in the value of the underlying asset.

European option an option that can be exercised only at expiration.

Excess premium the difference between the premium of an option and its minimum value.

Exercise the process whereby the owner of an option requires the exchange of assets for cash, or in some cases the payment of a terminal value.

Exercise price see **Striking price**.

Expiration date the date on which the option contract terminates.

Gamma the change in an option's delta in response to a change in the price of the underlying asset.

Implied volatility an estimate of an asset's volatility that is obtained from the options market.

In the money for a call, the price of the underlying asset is greater than the striking price; for a put, the price of the underlying asset is less than the striking price.

Intrinsic value of an option   same as **Minimum value of an option**.

Knock-in   an option that can be exercised only subsequent to the price of the underlying asset trading at a specified price.

Leg   one of the two transactions of a spread or straddle.

Minimum value of an option   ignoring interest, the greater of (1) the amount the option is in the money or (2) zero.

Naked   writing an option position without owning an offsetting position in the underlying asset or its equivalent.

Neutral spread   a spread that is profitable when the price of the underlying asset is unchanged.

Open interest   the number of contracts that are currently in existence: i.e., the sum of the number of contracts owned and the number of contracts written divided by 2.

Out of the money   for a call, the price of the underlying asset is less than the striking price; for a put, the price of underlying asset is higher than the striking price.

Owner   the party to an option contract who has the legal right to force exercise of the contract.

Premium   the price of an option contract.

Price spread   the purchase of one option and the sale of another, both with the same maturity, but with different striking prices.

Put   an option that gives the owner the right, but not the obligation, to sell an underlying asset at a fixed price at or until the expiration of the contract, or in some cases to receive the liquidating value in cash.

Put–call parity   for European options, the sum of the put premium and the price of the underlying asset must equal the sum of the call premium and the value today of the discounted exercise price.

Rho   the rate of change of the value of the option with respect to interest rates.

Spread   the simultaneous purchase of one option contract and the sale of another.

Straddle   the purchase or sale of both a put and a call on the same stock.

Striking price   the price at which the exchange of the underlying asset, or its equivalent in cash, will take place.

Theta   the rate of change in the value of an option related to the change in the length of time until its expiration.

Time spread   see **Calendar spread**.

Uncovered   see **Naked**.

Vega   the change in an option's value with respect to a change in the volatility of the underlying asset.

Volatility spread   see **Straddle**.

Writer   the party that has sold an option contract other than in a closing transaction.

> **THIS CHAPTER** describes options contracts. Specifically, we
>
> - introduce a number of basic terms used in options markets
> - describe trading in over-the-counter and exchange-traded options
> - discuss option premiums and related concepts
> - describe the process of exercising options
>
> Then, we
>
> - review reasons for entering into options positions
> - explain the risks of option contracts
> - introduce several option trading strategies
> - provide detailed information concerning actual options on individual stocks, futures contracts, and indexes

1. INTRODUCTION

Historically, options were traded over-the-counter. In 1973 the Chicago Board Options Exchange (CBOE) began exchange trading of option contracts. These contracts are standardized so that only the price paid by the buyer to induce the seller to enter into the contract is determined on the floor of the exchange. Trading in options has grown steadily, and during the year ended July 1999 more than 221 million option contracts were traded on the CBOE. Options are now traded on three additional exchanges in the USA and on many exchanges throughout the world. Initially, exchange-traded options were contracts for the purchase or sale of common stock of particular companies. The types of financial assets covered by exchanged traded options have been broadened to include indexes and futures contracts. Stock indexes were the first to be covered by option contracts, but options now cover a diverse array of financial products, including indexes measuring losses from natural catastrophes such as earthquakes.

This chapter describes option contracts. In section 2, we present basic terms that are needed to understand option markets. Then we describe the way trading in option contracts is done both over-the-counter and on exchanges. Next, we explore the pricing of option contracts. Then we describe the process of exercising options and the circumstances under which they are likely to be exercised.

In the second part of this chapter, we describe why investors buy and sell options and the risks of trading options. We also explain several common options trading strategies used by investors and describe representative options on individual equities, futures contracts, and indexes.

2. HOW OPTIONS WORK

2.1. OPTION TERMINOLOGY

Earlier we defined an option as a contract in which one party gives another party the right, but not the obligation, to buy or sell an underlying asset (which is sometimes called an "underlying interest"), or its value in monetary terms, at a stated price prior to a stated expiration. The party that grants the right is called the **writer**, and the party that receives the right is called the **owner**. The price at which the owner of the contract and the writer exchange the underlying asset is called the **striking price** or the **exercise price**. If the option is a **put** option, upon exercise the owner delivers the underlying asset to the writer. If the option is a **call** option, upon exercise the writer delivers the underlying interest to the owner. The owner has the legal right to **exercise** the option, which entails either the exchange of assets for cash or the payment of a terminal value.

If the option can be exercised only at expiration, it is a **European option**. If the option can be exercised at any time during its life, it is an **American option**. The origin of the terms "European" and "American" in referring to options is not known. Both types of options are traded in the USA and Europe, as well as around the world. For European options, the **expiration date** is the day on which the option can be exercised, while for American options it is the last day the option can be exercised. Because the right to exercise at more times has value, an American option is typically slightly more valuable than a European option.

For European options with the same maturity and striking price, there is a special relationship between put and call prices called **put–call parity**. Let R_p = the put premium, R_c = the call premium, X = the exercise price, X_p = the present value of the exercise price of the option payable at expiration when discounted at the risk-free rate, and P_a = the price of one unit of the underlying asset. Then

$$R_p + P_a = R_c + X_p. \qquad 13.1$$

The put–call parity relationship can be used to change the form of a transaction, which may be advantageous if laws recognize form over substance.

Suppose that A is a businessperson who needs 400 USD to finance inventory. B is willing to lend the money, but wants to charge 200 USD interest for the year, a rate that is prohibited as usury. Instead of consummating a loan, the parties enter into the following transactions:

1　A sells B an asset for 400 USD and also writes B a put on the asset.
2　B writes A a call on the asset.

Both the put and the call are European and have a strike price of 600 USD.

At the beginning of the transaction there is one cash flow: B pays and A receives 400 USD. At expiration, if the asset is worth more than 600 USD, A exercises the call, paying B 600 USD. If the asset is worth less than 600 USD at expiration, B exercises the put, receiving 600 USD from A. In either case there is only one cash flow at expiration: A pays B 600 USD. This outcome can also be shown by rearranging equation 13.1 to give:

$$X_p = R_p + P_a - R_c \qquad 13.2$$

Equation 13.2 shows that owning an asset and a put on that asset and writing a call on the asset, assuming that the strike price for the put and the call is the same, is equivalent to owning a risk-free bond with a face value equal to the striking price (Knoll 1994).[1]

A call is **in the money** if the price of the underlying asset is greater than the striking price, and a put is in the money if the price of the underlying asset is less than the striking price. A call is **out of the money** if the price of the underlying asset is less than the striking price, and a put is out of the money if the price of the underlying asset is higher than the striking price. When the price of the underlying asset equals the striking price, both puts and calls are **at the money**. At maturity, if the call is in the money, the call will have the value $P_a - X$, and the put will have no value. At maturity, if the put is in the money, the call will have no value, and the put will have the value $X - P_a$. If the option is at the money at maturity, $X = P_a$, which is the definition of at the money, and both the put and the call will have no value.

The margin on the purchase of an option contract is usually 100 percent; i.e., the entire purchase price (premium) must be paid on settlement day. If the writer of a call option owns the underlying asset, the writer is **covered**; if the writer of a put has a short position in the underlying asset, the writer is covered. If the writer of an option does not have an offsetting position in the underlying asset, then the position is **naked** or **uncovered**. There may be no margin required for covered writing, and the writer may even be able to spend the premium. The margin required for naked writing is generally a percentage of the value of the underlying asset. If the equity in an option writer's account falls below the maintenance margin requirement, the writer receives a margin call, a request for additional margin. Because of the short settlement time and the volatility of option values, many firms will not allow customers to buy options unless the money is already in the customer's account.

2.2. OVER-THE-COUNTER OPTIONS

For many years, and continuing today, options have been traded in the over-the-counter market. In this market, those seeking to enter into option contracts approach an option dealer, possibly through a regular brokerage firm. The terms of the contract are negotiated, and the deal is struck. When the deal is consummated, the owner pays a fee to the writer. Because it is the inducement for the writer to enter into the risky contract, the fee is called the **premium**, just like the payment that a policyholder makes to an insurance company in compensation for issuing a policy. Over-the-counter options provide more flexibility than exchange-traded options. One example of the type of flexibility that can be achieved is a **knock-in** option. This provision specifies that the option can be exercised only subsequent to the price of the underlying asset trading at a specified price. Box 13.1 describes a real-life example of a knock-in option.

The dealer may take the other side of the contract for its own risk or may find a counterparty willing to take the risk. Today many banks have sophisticated departments that are willing to write options of various kinds. But these are typically available only in large sizes. These banks do not attempt to manage their risk resulting from being the counterparty to all these contracts on a contract-by-contract basis. Instead, they manage the risk of their entire derivative portfolio.

The Chicago Board Options Exchange (CBOE) is attempting to compete with the over-the-counter options market by allowing for more flexibility in exchange-traded options. In 1993 the Chicago Board Options Exchange began trading FLexible EXchange (FLEX) options, which permit institutional trades to negotiate strike prices over a wide range, rather

> ## BOX 13.1
> ### Knock-in options and the short squeeze
>
> In November 1994 Venezuelan par bonds were selling at about 45. About 6.7 billion USD of the bonds were outstanding. LM International purchased put options covering 500 million USD of the Venezuelan par bonds. The unusual aspect of this case is that the put options had a knock-in feature. Like other puts, LM International had the right, but not the obligation, to sell designated Venezuelan bonds until the expiration of the contract in December 1994 at a price of 45. The knock-in feature specified that the put option could not be exercised unless the bonds first traded at 51. Because of their lower likelihood of being exercised, knock-in options have a lower premium than do otherwise comparable options without the knock-in feature. LM International purchased the put options from a group of banks and investment bankers, including Merrill Lynch, Morgan Stanley, Bankers Trust, Chase Manhattan Bank, and Banque Paribas. Merrill Lynch sold the puts to LM International acting as a dealer and hence was counterparty to the transaction. Some of the bankers may also have been acting as dealers.
>
> Following purchase of the options, LM International bought bonds and call options on the bonds in an attempt to force the price of the bond up to 51 so that the put could be exercised if the price subsequently fell. The call purchases added to demand for the bonds, because the writers of the calls covered their positions by buying bonds in the market. Also, 150 million USD of bonds had been sold short by speculators. LM International was hoping that purchasing enough bonds to move the price up quickly would force the shorts to cover their positions, further adding to demand.
>
> On December 9, 1994, the price of the bonds soared from 45 to almost 51. Merrill Lynch, seeing that the knock-in provision was about to be activated, sought to hedge its position by offering to sell an unlimited amount of bonds at $50^{7}/_{8}$. A battle between LM International and Merrill Lynch ensued, with LM International buying and Merrill Lynch selling large quantities of bonds. As much as 1.5 billion USD of the bonds changed hands on December 9, and LM International acquired from 800 to 1,000 million USD of the bonds. But LM International failed to move the price to 51 and activate its put option. This proved costly, because several days later Mexico devalued its peso, which caused the value of financial assets to plummet throughout South America. By January 10, 1995, the value of the bonds had fallen to 39.
>
> (For additional information see *Wall Street Journal*, 1995.)

than simply trading the exchange's pre-specified contracts. During 1998 the exchange doubled the number of FLEX options trading on individual stocks, and volume increased to 498,893 contracts. Volume also increased on FLEX index options to 569,073 contracts, mostly on the exchange's SPX contract.

2.3. Exchange-traded Options

In the early 1970s, exchanges began developing and trading options contracts. Some older established exchanges such as the Philadelphia Stock Exchange began to trade options, and in some cases separate exchanges such as the Chicago Board Options Exchange have been established to trade options.

Exchange-traded options are made possible by the standardization of contracts. Each contract specifies the (1) underlying interest, (2) striking price, and (3) expiration date. The only thing negotiated on the exchange is the premium. Unlike over-the-counter options, exchange-traded options are depersonalized, in that the writer and the owner are not paired until the owner decides to exercise. Instead, all contracts are with an intermediary. In the USA this intermediary is the Option Clearing Corporation, an entity organized by the exchanges for the purpose of serving as the counterparty for all options contracts. Since a specific individual or firm is not a counterparty, traders do not have to worry about the ability of the counterparty to perform on the contract. Because all contracts are identical, it is possible to enter into an option contract and, subsequently, close out the position prior to expiration by acquiring an offsetting position. To close out a position, a writer buys a contract, and an owner sells a contract. The number of options written is equal to the number of options owned. The **open interest** is the number of contracts that are currently in existence: i.e., number of contracts owned = number of contracts written = open interest.

Options are traded on exchanges in much the same way as stocks. Orders must be placed with a member of the exchange. In general, the same types of orders can be placed for options as for stocks, including market orders, limit orders, and stop orders. Because of the wide spreads and thin markets, many investors place only limit orders when trading options on individual stocks. When dealing with actively traded contracts, such as those on many of the indexes, a market order may be appropriate. There are typically no price limits on exchange-traded options. A number of options exchanges have specialists or comparable officials to make markets, maintain the limit order book, and the like. Exchanges with designated market makers include the Chicago Board Options Exchange and the European Options Exchange (EOE) in Amsterdam.

Just as electronic exchanges have been developed for equities, futures, and foreign exchange trading, so electronic exchanges are also being developed for trading options. A low-cost electronic exchange for trading options is scheduled to open in January 2000. To meet this competition, the Philadelphia, Pacific, and American stock exchanges reduced their options transactions fees (Sears 1999).

2.4. THE OPTION PREMIUM AND RELATED CONCEPTS

2.4.1. The minimum value of an option

Because of the possibility of arbitrage, assuming a zero interest rate, the **minimum value of an option** is the greater of (1) the amount the option is in the money or (2) zero. This is also the value of the option at expiration. The minimum value is sometimes called the **intrinsic value**. Box 13.2 provides the formula for the minimum value of puts and calls, taking positive interest rates into account. Figure 13.1 presents profiles of gain and loss outcomes (payoffs) at maturity for various options positions, assuming that the options always trade at their minimum value (i.e., denoting the premium as R, for calls, $R = \max(P_a - X, 0)$, and for puts, $R = \max(X - P_a, 0)$). For the long call, the value of the option increases as the price of the underlying asset (P_a) increases beyond the exercise price (X), while for the long put, the value of the option increases as the price of the underlying assets falls below the exercise price. Since each short is the counterparty to a long, the value of the short position is decreasing when the value of its corresponding long is increasing.

BOX 13.2
The minimum value of puts and calls

For an American put, the minimum value is max (0, X − S), where X is the striking price, and S is the price of the underlying stock. X − S is the amount that the option is in the money.

A European put cannot be exercised immediately. Therefore, to lock in a price, the put and the underlying stock must be held until expiration. To lock in a value for a European put, a trader can buy both the put and the underlying stock. To prevent arbitrage profits at expiration, this position must be worth:

$$X - (S + R_p)e^{r(T-t)}$$

where R_p is the price of the put, r is the risk-free rate, and T − t is the time until expiration. The present value of this equation can be found by multiplying both sides by $e^{-r(T-t)}$ to obtain, after rearranging terms,

$$Xe^{-r(T-t)} - S = R_p$$

Hence, the minimum value is max (0, X $e^{-r(T-t)}$ − S).

Similar reasoning can be used to show that for European calls and American calls on nondividend-paying stocks, the minimum value is

$$Max(0, S - Xe^{-r(T-t)})$$

An American call on a dividend-paying stock can always be exercised to capture X − S, if that is appropriate. If the firm decides to declare a dividend of sufficient size, the owner of the American call may be forced to exercise. This is equivalent to shortening the maturity of the option. Hence, the owner of an American call cannot count on the gain from paying the exercise price at the stated expiration of the option. Therefore, the minimum value of an American call on a dividend-paying stock is

$$Max(0, S - X)$$

Several aspects of the profiles in figure 13.1 are worth noting. If the option premium equals the minimum value of the option, then the cost of initiating an options position when the option is at the money, which is the point of inflection in figure 13.1 (a)–(d), is zero. Secondly, figure 13.2 shows that the combination of a long put and a short call produces the same profile as that of short futures contracts. The combination of a long call and a short put produces the same payoff profile as that of a long futures position.

Figure 13.3 illustrates outcomes at maturity, assuming that R > 0. For option owners, this means that the option premium must be subtracted from the outcome due to the change in price of the underlying asset. For option writers, changes in the value of the underlying asset offset the premium revenue partially, wholly, or enough to produce a loss.

2.4.2. Premiums and excess premiums

Options do not typically sell for either zero or the amount the option is in the money, even ignoring interest, except at maturity. To understand why, suppose that there is a stock that sells for 10 USD at the beginning of period 1, and that at the end of period 1 it will sell for

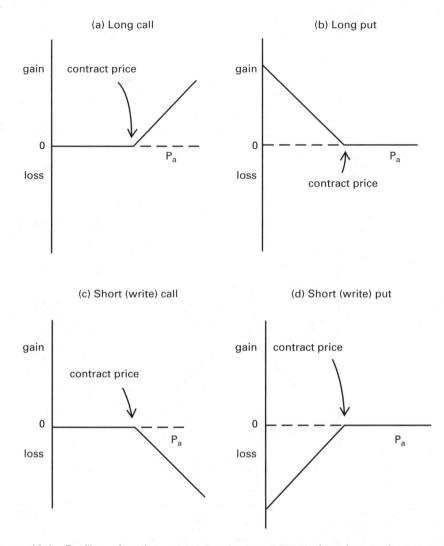

Figure 13.1 Profiles of option contract outcomes at maturity when options premiums equal the minimum value of the option. Let X = the exercise price, P_a = the price of the underlying asset, and R = the premium. At contract initiation, X = P_a; for calls, R = max(P_a − X, 0); and for puts, R = max(X − P_a, 0).

either 7 USD or 12 USD. Consider two alternatives. One is to buy 100 shares of stock, and the other is to buy an option on the stock with a striking price of 10 USD. If the premium on the option is zero, which would be the preferable alternative: buying the stock or buying the option contract?

Clearly, the answer is that the option is better. If the stock is purchased, either there will be a gain of 200 USD or a loss of 300 USD (we ignore commissions in these examples). But if the option is purchased and the stock increases in value to 12 USD, the option will

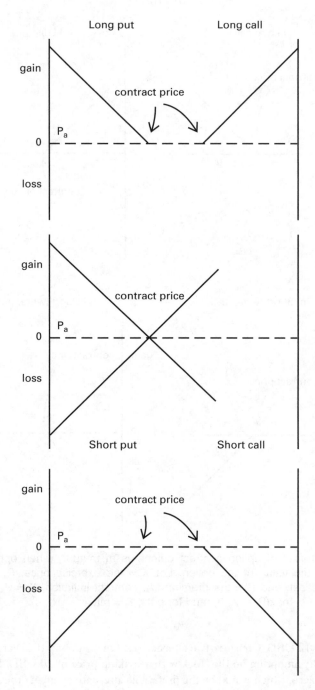

Figure 13.2 Comparison of outcome profiles for positions comparable to futures outcomes. Let X = the exercise price, P_a = the price of the underlying asset, and R = the premium. At contract initiation, X = P_a; for calls, R = max(P_a − X, 0); and for puts, R = max(X − P_a, 0).

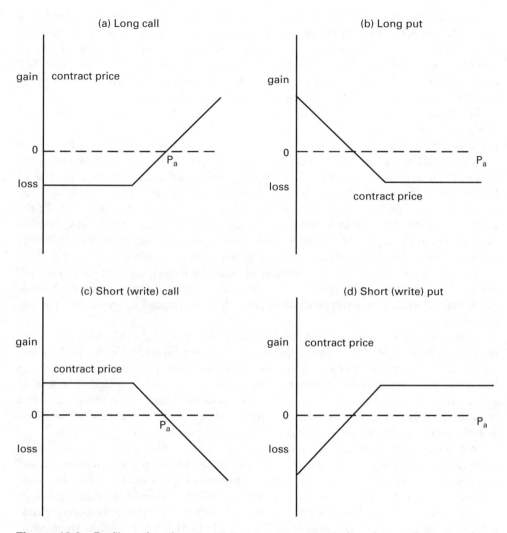

Figure 13.3 Profiles of option contract outcomes at maturity when options premiums exceed the minimum value of the option. Let X = the exercise price, P_a = the price of the underlying asset, and R = the premium. At contract initiation, X = P_a; for calls, R > max(P_a – X, 0); and for puts, R > max(X – P_a, 0).

be exercised, and the profit will be 200 USD ((12–10) × 100). On the other hand, if the stock declines in value, the option will simply expire. So, if the stock increases in price, owning the option will produce the same profit as owning the stock, but if the stock falls in price, the option will have zero profit compared to a loss from owning the stock. Undoubtedly, if the premium is zero, the option is preferred. And because owning the option potentially has value, since it is almost always possible that the price of the underlying asset will change so that the option will be in the money at maturity, the option premium will not be zero. This explains why options typically sell for more than their minimum value.

For warrants, the excess of the price of the warrant over its minimum value is the premium. The price of a warrant and the premium of an option are economically the same thing. But there is no term for the excess of the premium on an option compared with its minimum value. This is because option terminology developed before there was a secondary market for these contracts. For lack of an alternative, we will call the difference between the premium for an option and its minimum value the **excess premium**.[2]

The amount of an option's premium depends on whether the option is in the money and also on its excess premium. The excess premium is affected by many factors. One of these is the likelihood that an out-of-the-money option will become in the money by a given amount or that an in-the-money option will become more in the money. A second is the time until maturity of the contract. The longer the time until expiration, the more chance for the underlying asset to increase in value. A third is the riskiness of the underlying asset, usually measured by its volatility or standard deviation of returns. The more volatile the price of an asset, the more an option on that asset is worth. To understand why, contemplate an option that is out of the money and whose underlying security is so safe that its price will not change before expiration. Clearly, this option is worthless.

A fourth factor affecting option values is whether the underlying asset pays cash dividends. If a firm retains all its earnings, its value will be higher (by the amount of the dividends and subsequent earnings on the dividends) than the value of a comparable firm that pays dividends.

A fifth factor is interest rates. Interest rates affect the value of the deferred payment for the underlying asset. For call owners, this is offset to some extent by the loss in the interest on the premium. Of course, call writers receive not only the premium, but they can invest this premium to receive additional interest during the contact period. The level of interest rates also affects whether it is better to exercise an American put option early. If a put is in the money and the premium is approximately equal to the amount that the option is in the money, it may be advantageous to exercise the put and invest the proceeds.

In general, as shown in figure 13.4, the excess premium is greatest when the price of the underlying asset equals the striking price of the option. As an option becomes more and more in the money, *ceteris paribus*, its premium becomes larger and larger. But the excess premium typically becomes smaller and smaller. We will illustrate why the excess premium typically declines as the option becomes more and more in the money. We begin by considering an option with a striking price of 12 (see table 13.1). We will consider three possible prices at which the option might be initiated: 12, 15, and 18. And we assume that the only possible outcomes are that the price will increase by one-third or decrease by one-third at maturity. Finally, we assume that the excess premium is 2, so that the option premium is the amount that the option is in the money plus 2. It is this last assumption that we wish to show is unrealistic.

Table 13.1 shows the returns on the option premium if the option is purchased when the price of the underlying asset is 12, 15, or 18. In each case there is a 100 percent loss if the stock price declines. But, if the stock price increases, the return differs in each case. Given that the gain and loss in each case are equally likely, the expected or average return decreases as the option becomes more and more in the money. Yet the risk due to price movements in the underlying security is the same. To equalize the returns, if the underlying asset sells for 15, the excess premium would have to be 1. Then the premium on the option at the beginning of the period would be 4, and the return in the favorable outcome

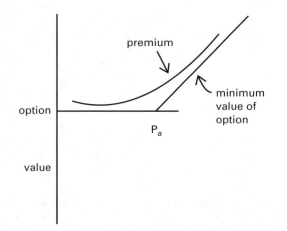

Figure 13.4 Profile of typical option premium for given exercise price (X) as price of underlying security changes.

Table 13.1 Illustration of possible outcomes for option positions acquired at three different prices for the underlying asset

A. Price of the underlying security	12	12	15	15	18	18
B. Amount the option is in the money (by definition, A 12)	0	0	3	3	6	6
C. Excess premium (by assumption, 1)	2	2	2	2	2	2
D. Purchase price of the option (by definition, B + C)	2	2	5	5	8	8
E. Price of underlying security at maturity (A ± $\frac{1}{3}$)	8	16	10	20	12	24
F. Amount option is in the money at maturity	0	4	0	8	0	12
average % return ($\frac{1}{2}$ of up and down return)	−100	−200	−100	−160	−100	−150
average % return ($\frac{1}{2}$ of up and down return)	50		30		25	

For each initiation price, there are two equally likely outcomes, one in which the price of the underlying security falls by one-third and one in which the price of the underlying security increases by one-third. We assume that (1) the striking price is 12, (2) the option is held to maturity, and (3) the excess premium is 2. The results show that as the option becomes more and more in the money, its return declines. This demonstrates that these options cannot have the same excess premium, but that the excess premium must decline as the option becomes more and more in the money. Similar considerations apply when an option becomes more and more out of the money.

would be 200 percent. When the price of the underlying asset is 18, the excess premium would have to be 0 to equalize the returns. The beginning-of-period option premium would be 6, and the return would be 200 percent if the stock price increases. Thus, as the option becomes more and more in the money, the excess premium declines. The excess premium

BOX 13.3
Estimating Black–Scholes option values

Price of underlying asset	Option premium	Intrinsic value = minimum value	Excess or premium over intrinsic value
120	21.21	19.83	1.38
110	12.17	9.92	2.25
100	5.20	0	5.20
90	1.36	0	1.36
80	0.24	0	0.24

We used the program found at the following web site: http://www.ggw.org/donorware/options/ to calculate the Black–Scholes option values for a European call option with a strike price of 100, a 2-month life, (T – t) = 0.166, a standard deviation of 0.3, and an interest rate or 0.05. The option premiums calculated for each of the values of the underlying asset are shown in the table.

also declines as the option becomes more and more out of the money, but this is typically easier to understand, so we will not illustrate this case.

In box 13.3 we use another set of option values to illustrate figure 13.4.

2.5. Option Pricing Models

There are a number of models that have been developed for pricing options, and these are widely used by option professionals. We discuss two of the most popular, the binomial model and the Black–Scholes model. These two models are based on the idea that arbitrage causes assets that have the same payoffs at time t + 1 to have the same value at time t. We limit our discussion to European options that do not pay dividends. American options are subject to early call, which makes the determination of their value more complicated. Likewise, options that pay dividends are more difficult to evaluate, since, among other things, the payment of a large dividend may force early exercise for American options.

2.5.1. The binomial option pricing model

Let B represent bonds earning the risk-free rate, r. Consider the case where we have an asset selling for P_0 at t = 0 that has only two possible values at t + 1. Either it will be worth uP_0, or it will be worth dP_0. Then, at t + 1, a call option on one unit of the asset with a striking price of P_0 will have a value at t + 1 of either $C_u = (uP_0 - P_0)$ or $C_d = 0$. Our goal is to form a portfolio that replicates the outcome from owning a call by borrowing at the risk-free rate and buying n units of the risky asset. In other words, if the price of the risky asset increases, we have

$$C_u = nuP_0 - B(1+r) \qquad 13.3$$

And, if the price of the risky asset decreases, we have

$$C_d = ndP_0 - B(1+r) \qquad\qquad 13.4$$

Obviously, n, P_0, and $B(1 + r)$ must have the same values in equations 13.3 and 13.4. Hence, we can use these equations to obtain B, the amount we need to borrow, and n, the number of shares of the risk assets we need to buy, to replicate the call:

$$n = C_u - C_d / (u - d) P_0$$
$$B = (dC_u - uC_d) / ((u - d)(1 + r))$$

We can illustrate these results. Let $P_0 = 55$, $r = 0.08$, $u = 1.15$, $d = 0.9$. We can compute $C_u = 63.25$ and $C_d = 49.50$. Substituting gives

$$n = (8.25 - 0) / ((1.15 - 0.9)55) = 0.6$$
$$B = 0.9(8.25) / ((1.15 - 0.9)(1.08)) = 27.50$$

Hence, the value of the call must be

$$nP_0 - B = 0.6(55) - 27.50 = 5.50$$

The accuracy of the binomial model can be improved by increasing the number of potential outcomes considered, so that the model become multiperiod. Dividing the period into smaller and smaller time intervals does this. In the two-period case, there are four outcomes to be analyzed. These are uu, ud, du, and dd, where the first item of the pair is the outcome at time $t + 1$ and the second item is the outcome at time $t + 2$. With the addition of more periods, the number of potential outcomes becomes very large. In general there are 2^n possible outcomes, where n is the number of periods. The computational difficulty can be reduced, because a number of the paths lead to the same terminal outcomes if $u = 1/d$. In the two-period case the outcomes ud and du produce the same terminal stock and option values, so there are only three outcomes to be evaluated.

If we assume that stock returns are lognormally distributed with mean μ and standard deviation σ over time interval beginning at t and ending at T, then for large n

$$u = e^{\sigma\sqrt{(T-t)}/n} \qquad\qquad 13.5$$

$$d = 1/u \qquad\qquad 13.6$$

Further, the probability of an increase in the value of the stock at the end of any period is

$$\pi_u = \left((1+r)^{(T-t)/n} - d\right) / (u - d) \qquad\qquad 13.7$$

where $T - t$ is the expressed as a proportion of a year, and n is the number of periods. $\pi_d = 1 - \pi_u$. The assumption that the outcomes are determined by σ makes the outcome profile symmetric. The input values for the binomial model can be estimated using historical stock returns.

Box 13.4 presents the paths, outcomes, and outcome probabilities for a European call option with a strike price of 100 when the price of the underlying asset is 100. Note the effect of dividing the interval T into two periods rather than one. When T is considered as only one period, there are only two possible outcomes: u, which produces a terminal value of 116.18 with probability of 0.5427, and d, which produces a terminal value of 86.07 with probability 0.4573. Dividing the interval T into two periods changes the values of u and d and increases the number of paths to uu, ud, du, and dd. Of course, ud and du produce the same terminal outcome. The increase in the number of paths and terminal outcomes considered leads to a more accurate estimate of the call's value. The process can be continued until a desired level of accuracy in comparison with the Black–Scholes model is achieved. Algorithms for calculating multiperiod option values using computers have been developed.

2.5.2. Black–Scholes model

Fischer Black and Myron Scholes derived the following expression for the value of a European style call option (c):

$$c_t = S_t N(d_1) - Xe^{-r(T-t)}N(d_2)$$

where $d_1 = (\ln(S_t/X) + r + 0.5\sigma^2)(T - t))/(\sigma(T - t)^{0.5})$
$d_2 = d_1 - \sigma(T - t)^{0.5}$

$N(.)$ = the cumulative normal distribution function, S_t is the current market price of the asset, X is the striking price of the option, σ is the standard deviation of the asset's return, r is the risk-free rate, t is the time the option is being valued, T is the time of expiration. See box 13.5 for some examples of Black–Scholes option values.

If a current market price of an option, c, is known along with the remaining variables in the Black–Scholes model except for σ, an estimated value for σ can be obtained using the Black–Scholes formula. An estimate of an asset's volatility obtained from the options market is called **implied volatility**. In 1993 the Chicago Board of Trade introduced the CBOT volatility index, which has the ticker symbol VIX, as a new index of implied volatility for the US equity market. The index is calculated in real time using implied volatilities for eight OEX calls and puts chosen to have an average time to maturity of 30 days. The VIX index changes frequently and by significant amounts. (For a discussion of the VIX index see Fleming, Ostdiek, and Whaley 1994 and Bittman 1998.)

There has been a great deal of work to extend the Black–Scholes model to remedy its limitations. Merton (1976a,b) demonstrated how the model could be adjusted to account for dividends that were paid continuously. MacBeth and Merville (1979) found that the model systematically underpriced in the money options and overpriced out of the money options. Moreover, these biases tended to be greater, the longer the life of the option.

2.5.3. Option Greeks

Option Greeks are very important to investment professionals.[3] They express how option value changes when one of the inputs into the Black–Scholes option pricing model changes,

BOX 13.4
The binomial tree

The binomial model can be used to achieve a closer and closer approximation to the Black–Scholes results by increasing the number of periods during a fixed time interval that are used to derive the binomial results. We will illustrate this concept using equations 13.5–13.7 from the text.

Consider a European call option with a strike price of 100 and a life of 0.25 years when the price of the underlying asset is also 100. Assume that the annual interest rate is 10 percent (0.10) and that the annual standard deviation is 0.3. The Black–Scholes value of the option is 10.89. We wish to calculate the value of the call and graph a binomial tree using the binomial model.

	$n = 1$	$n = 2$
Value	12.73	9.93
u	$e^{0.3\sqrt{0.25}} = 1.1618$	$e^{0.3\sqrt{0.25/2}} = 1.1119$
d	$e^{-0.3\sqrt{0.25}} = 0.8607$	$e^{-0.3\sqrt{0.25}} = 0.8994$
π_u	$((1 + 0.1)^{0.25} - 0.8607)/$ $(1.1618 - 0.8607) = 0.5427$	$\pi_u = ((1 + 0.1)^{0.25/2} - 0.8994)/$ $(1.1119 - 0.8994) = 0.5299.$
$1 - \pi_u$	0.4573.	0.4701

Path	Outcome		
	Per unit	Total	Probability
u	1.1618	116.18	0.5427
d	0.8607	86.07	0.4573
			1.0000
uu	1.2363	123.63	0.2808
ud, du	1.00	100.00	0.5018
dd	0.8089	80.89	0.2210
			1.0000

0	t + 1	t + 2
	Time	T

> ## BOX 13.5
> ### Calculating Black–Scholes option values
>
> A number of programs are available for calculating Black–Scholes option values. At the time this book was written one was available at http://www.ggw.org/donorware/options/ (see also http://www.numa.com/derivs/ref/calculat/option/calc-opa.htm). To calculate the Black–Scholes option, we need the equity price, the striking price, the volatility, the rate per year, and the term in years. In the example here we will assume that in each case the rate per year is 0.05 and the volatility is 0.3.
>
> 1 Suppose that a stock is selling for 50 USD and has a bid of 49.75 USD. The bid is good for 15 minutes. If we view this bid as a free option offered to the market, what is the option's value? The equity price is 50 USD, the striking price is 49.75 USD, and the term is 0.0000004. Entering these values into the program gives an option value of 0.25 USD.
> 2 Suppose that a stock's price is 60 USD. If an option has a striking price of 60 USD and a life of 1 month, what is the option's value? Answer: 2.28.
> 3 Try calculating option values for the information given in (2), but varying each element of the calculation one at a time. First change the striking price to 70 USD and to 40 USD. Then vary the time to maturity, the interest rate, the volatility, and the interest rate, in turn.

holding the other inputs constant. The formulas for the Greeks are obtained using calculus and differ for puts and calls. We consider only calls on nondividend-paying assets.

Delta is the rate of change in the price of an option in response to a change in the value of the underlying asset. The delta for a call is $\partial c / \partial P = N(d_1)$.[4] The delta of a call option is positive, because an increase in the price of the underlying asset increases the value of the option. Call options that are deep in the money have deltas that are close to 1.0, because the value of the option increases by almost exactly the same amount as the value of the underlying stock. Call options that are deep out of the money have deltas that are positive, but small. Put option deltas are negative, because a decrease in the value of the underlying asset reduces the value of the option. The delta is close to −1 for deep in the money put options and close to 0 for deep out of the money put options. When an option is deep out of the money, a large change in the value of the stock produces a small absolute change in the value of the option, giving a small delta. The delta for a long and short position in an underlying asset is +1 and −1, respectively.

Gamma is the only Greek that does not measure option premium sensitivity to a change in one of the Black–Scholes inputs. Rather, gamma measures the rate of change in an option's delta in response to a change in the price of the underlying asset. An option's gamma is largest when the option is at the money. Both puts and calls have positive gammas. For a given gamma, an increase in a stock's price produces a larger profit than a decrease in a stock's price of the same size.

Theta is the rate of change in the value of an option related to the change in the length of time until its expiration. A negative theta indicates that the value of an option position is declining through time. As an option becomes more in the money or out of the money, theta tends toward zero. For an at the money option, theta declines gradually when maturity is distant, but declines more and more rapidly as maturity gets closer and closer.

Table 13.2 The option value and Greeks for a put and a call

	Call	Put
Value of option	4.941	3.464
Delta	0.598	−0.402
Gamma	0.0365	0.0365
Theta	−5.601	−2.689
Vega	13.679	13.679
Rho	12.473	−11.788

This table presents the Black–Scholes option value and the Greeks for a European call and put with a life of 1 half-year. Each option has a striking price of 50. The price of the underlying asset is also 50, the interest rate is 6 percent (0.06), and the standard deviation is 30 percent (0.30). The underlying assets does not pay a dividend.

Vega is the rate of change of the value of an option with respect to the volatility of the underlying asset. Puts and calls have the same vega, which is always positive. Long positions benefit from an increase in volatility. Vega is a major determinant of an option's value, and a change in vega can significantly change the option premium.

Rho is the rate of change of the value of the option with respect to interest rates. Rho is always positive for calls and always negative for puts. Large changes in interest rates do not have much effect on option values.

The Greeks are useful in constructing portfolios that have a desired exposure to particular determinants of an option's value. Consider a European call option on a nondividend-paying stock with a striking price of 50 when the price of the underlying asset is 50. Assume that the interest rate is 6 percent, volatility is 30 percent per year, and the maturity of the option is 6 months. The value of a call, the value of a put, and the Greeks for each of these options are presented in table 13.2. Using these data, suppose that a trader wishes to construct a portfolio comprising calls and stock such that the delta of the portfolio is 0. Letting asset 1 be the call and asset 2 be the stock, the delta of this two-asset portfolio is

$$n_1 \delta_1 + n_2 \delta_2 = 0 \qquad\qquad 13.8$$

where n_1 is the number of calls, each covering 100 shares, and n_2 is the number of shares purchased, in hundreds. If an option is written or shares of a stock are shorted, n is negative. Letting $n_1 = -1$ and solving equation 13.8 we obtain 0.598. For each call written, 59.8 shares of stock should be shorted. Of course, options do not typically cover 59.8 shares, so a larger number of calls and shares of stock will be required to actually construct a zero-delta portfolio. For small changes in the value of the stock, the value of the option stock portfolio will not change.

Next consider zero-delta portfolios constructed using calls and puts.

Portfolio 1 We begin with a portfolio that involves buying calls and puts. Letting $n_1 = 1$ in equation 13.8 and substituting gives

$$0.598 + n_2(-0.402) = 0$$

Solving for n_2 gives $n_2 = 1.49$.

Portfolio 2 Traders can also construct a zero-delta portfolio by writing calls and puts. Letting $n_1 = -1$ and substituting into equation 13.5 gives

$$-n_1\delta_1 + n_2\delta_2 = -0.598 + n_2(-0.402) = 0$$

Solving for $n_2 = -1.49$.

Next, consider the vega of portfolios 1 and 2. The vega of a two-asset portfolio is $n_1v_1 + n_2v_2$, which simplifies to $v_1(n_1 + n_2)$, since $v_1 = v_2$ for puts and calls with otherwise identical terms. Hence, the vega of portfolio 1 is

$$(1 + 1.49)\,13.679 = 34.06$$

and the vega of portfolio 2 is

$$(-1 - 1.49)\,13.679 = -34.06.$$

Even though the two portfolios have a zero delta, they do not have a zero vega. In fact, the vegas of the two portfolios are dramatically different. If a trader expected volatility to increase, portfolio 1 would be preferred, and if a trader expected volatility to decrease, portfolio 2 would be preferred.

2.6. EXERCISING OPTIONS

2.6.1. Exercising options versus closing out positions

At the maturity of an option contract, the excess premium is zero, and the option is worth the amount it is in the money. Also, ignoring commissions, the amount received when an option is exercised is the amount the option is in the money. To see this, consider a call option with a striking price of 10 whose underlying security is selling for 12. Upon exercise, assuming that the option requires delivery rather than cash settlement, the owner receives the underlying security, which has a value of 12, but pays a price of 10. When the underlying security is sold for 12, the purchase price is recouped plus an additional 2. This, of course, is equal to the amount the option is in the money, which is 12 minus 10.

In most cases there is an incentive for both the writer and the owner of an exchange-traded option to close out the position at expiration rather than exercise the option. Upon exercise, the owner of a call pays the striking price plus commission and receives the underlying asset. If the owner does not wish to own the asset, then it must be sold, realizing its market price less commission. Thus, in exercising an option, an owner may pay two commissions on the underlying interest: one at the striking price and one at the market price. Typically, it is more economical to just sell the option.

The writer has similar motives for closing out the position rather than waiting for it to be exercised. If the call writer is covered, then the stock is sold to the option owner at the striking price less commission and must be replaced at the current market price plus commission. If the writer is uncovered, the asset must be purchased for delivery at the market price plus commission and delivered at the striking price less commission. In either case, the writer incurs two commissions. Therefore, for the writer too, it is typically more economical to close out the position rather than exercise.

2.6.2. *Exercising exchange-traded options*

Owners and writers of exchange-traded options can simply close their positions by entering into an offsetting position on the exchange. Because most options have positive excess premiums, American exchange-traded options are rarely exercised prior to maturity. Upon exercise, the owner gains the amount that an option is in the money, but if the option trades at more than this amount, the excess premium is lost upon exercise. Hence, as long as there is a positive excess premium, it will generally make sense to close out the position rather than exercise the option. But there are some circumstances when early exercise makes sense.

Suppose that an investor owns an American exchange-traded call option. If a large dividend is declared on the underlying security, it may make sense to exercise, because dividends go to the owner of the security on the record date. Consider a call option on 100 shares of stock selling for 25 with a strike price of 20 and with an excess premium of 1. In this case, the premium is 6, the sum of the amount the option is in the money and the excess premium. Suppose that the company announces a dividend on this stock of 2. Thus, when this stock goes *ex* dividend, *ceteris paribus*, the stock will be worth 23, and the option will be worth the amount that it is in the money, 3, plus the excess premium. If the excess premium does not fall, the post-dividend option premium will be 4. But if the option is exercised prior to the dividend, the owner will receive the amount that the option is in the money, 5. Hence, it is better to exercise than to hold the option and forgo the dividend.

Some readers may ask, why not just sell the option for 6? The answer is that once the firm announces the forthcoming dividend, the option will no longer be worth 6, but rather its price will decline to 5. Thus, the owner of the option at the time the dividend is announced realizes the loss. Typically, this is only a problem for dividend-paying stocks if the amount of the dividend is large.

For American exchange-traded put options, if the earnings from investing the amount realized upon exercise is greater than the expected profit from continuing to hold the option, the excess premium may disappear, and it may make sense to exercise. From a legal perspective, whether or not an option is exercised is at the discretion of the owner of the contract. But from an economic perspective, either the writer or the owner can decide. To understand this concept, consider a call option that is expiring in the money. Suppose that an investor has written this contract. If the investor does not close out this contract prior to maturity, what is the probability that the contract will be exercised and that the investor will be required to sell the stock? If the probability is not 1, it must surely be close to 1. If the owner of the contract exercises the option, the amount that the option is in the money, less commissions, will be obtained. But if the option expires, it is worthless. Hence, from an economic viewpoint, the owner has no choice but to exercise an option at maturity if the option is in the money, as long as commissions are not too great. Naturally, any particular

> ## BOX 13.6
> ### Should this put be exercised or closed out?
>
> The author was involved in the management of a small investment portfolio that purchased 3,000 shares of common stock in a firm we will call ABC Industries at 30 (including commission). The stock advanced to 36. Believing that the stock would go higher, we placed a limit order to sell (write) 10 put options with a striking price of 35 at a premium of 0.75. Each option covered 100 shares of ABC. The broker was instructed to sell the options one at a time or in any increments of 1 (some traders prefer to limit their trades to a certain number of contracts or more, but we decided not to do this). At the end of the day one contract had been sold. The proceeds were 0.75 per share less commission of 0.35 per share. Thus, the aggregate net proceeds were only $((0.75 - 0.35) \times 100) = 40$ USD. The failure to sell all the contracts combined with the high commission on just one contract made this transaction unexpectedly poor from the first day. But things got worse. Instead of rising, the price of ABC fell to 34 on expiration day. Now we were faced with the choice of (1) repurchasing the put contract or (2) doing nothing and waiting until the owner of the contract exercised, in which case we would acquire 100 shares of ABC at 35 USD each plus commission. What would you do?
>
> Answer: There is no right or wrong answer. Some managers might exercise, and some might not. We decided not to close out the position, which forced the owner to exercise.
>
> 1   If the option-writing strategy is chosen, the manager has incurred a loss of 40 USD, an inconsequential amount of money. But the transaction will probably be enumerated separately, distracting from an otherwise excellent performance.
> 2   If the option is allowed to expire in the money, the option will be exercised, and 100 shares of the underlying stock will be purchased for the account. How will the account look then? The cost of the 100 shares is 3,500 plus a commission of, say, 25. Now the fund owns 3,100 shares with a cost of 30.17 and a market value of 34. No loss is ever realized to detract attention from the overall profit on this trade.

owner can sell their contract. But if an option is in the money at expiration, and if a writer does not close out a position, some owner will be forced to exercise it. Of course, owners who do not wish to exercise an option can sell to other owners, but eventually someone will be stuck with exercising it. There is a natural tendency to sell the options that must be exercised to market participants whose costs of exercising are relatively low.

There might be a number of reasons why either an owner or a writer desires to exercise. Perhaps the owner of an in the money call or the writer of an in the money put simply desires to own the underlying asset. Other considerations may also apply. For an actual case see box 13.6.

2.6.3. Exercising over-the-counter options

Suppose the owner of an over-the-counter call option expects a short-lived downturn in the market and wishes to protect the position temporarily. Since there is probably no secondary market for the option, one possibility is to exercise the option. Of course, this is only feasible if the option is in the money. Further, exercise sacrifices the excess premium. Another approach is to hedge by buying a put or writing a call on an exchange.

We have already seen circumstances, such as when a large dividend is declared when the value of a put makes it more valuable dead than alive, in which the owner of an exchange traded option would exercise early. In general, the owner of an over-the-counter option would exercise under these same circumstances as long as the terms of the two options were comparable. Historically, the striking price for an over-the-counter option was reduced by the amount of a dividend on the *ex* dividend date. Such a contract term would affect the desirability of exercising prior to a dividend.

3. OPTION STRATEGIES

3.1. REASONS FOR OWNING AND WRITING OPTIONS

There are three primary reasons for owning options:

1 Many firms and individuals use options to speculate because of the leverage they provide. For a premium that is typically small in relation to the value of the underlying interest, an investor profits from the change in price of 100 shares of the underlying security. The example in table 13.1 shows a case for which there is a return of 200 percent on the option's premium when the price of the underlying asset increases by only one-third.
2 A second reason for using options rather than other types of financial instruments is that the loss is limited to the initial payment, the premium. At first it might seem strange that only being able to lose the entire investment is an advantage. But with some other types of financial instruments, such as futures and buying stock on margin, an investor can lose more than the initial investment. While the loss is also limited for stocks and bonds, these instruments require a much larger initial outlay to generate the same profit potential.
3 Options are useful in meeting many of the needs of hedgers.

There are also three primary reasons for writing options:

1 Option writing can be used to speculate on a price decrease in the underlying asset. Suppose that an investor expects the price of JPY to fall relative to the USD. One alternative is to short a futures contract on JPY. Another is to enter into a forward contract to sell JPY. A third alternative is to write a call on JPY. If no offsetting position is held in the underlying asset or in an equivalent such as a convertible security, the writer is naked, or uncovered. If the price of JPY falls relative to the USD, then the premium on the contract should also fall. In fact, if there is a positive excess premium, then the premium must fall over time unless the price of the underlying asset increases. By contrast, if a put option is purchased, the price of the underlying asset typically must fall for the owner to have a gain.
2 Like owning options, writing options can be used in hedging strategies.
3 A third reason for writing options is because of the income that they provide. In most cases this strategy would be used in combination with a position in the underlying asset. This is known as covered writing. Suppose that an investor owns 100 shares of the US firm International Business Machines (IBM) which are selling at 56, and that a call option

on IBM with an expiration in 2 months and a striking price of 55 has a premium of 2.5. By selling this call, the investor receives 250 less commission. It is usually possible to get a clear picture of what could happen by assuming that the option is held to maturity, and then considering the results of only a few outcomes. In this case four possible outcomes are of interest (we ignore commissions in these examples):

a. The option is out of the money. The investor's loss on the long position in the underlying stock will be 56 minus the stock's price. If the loss on the stock is greater than the 2.5 received as the premium, the overall outcome will be a loss.

b. The option is at the money. The investor will have a loss of 1 on the underlying stock. This loss will only partially offset the option premium, so that the overall result is a 1.5 gain.

c. The price of the underlying asset does not change. The writer can buy back the option for 1. Or the writer can wait for the owner to exercise and sell the stock, which is currently worth 56, for the striking price of 55. Since we are ignoring commissions, these two actions are equivalent. In either case the writer incurs a loss of 1 that will offset part of the premium received initially, so that the overall outcome is a gain of 1.5.

d. The value of the underlying security increases. The investor will have a gain on the stock position but a loss on the option position. Suppose that the stock increases in value to 60. There will be a $(60 - 56) = 4$ gain from the ownership position in the stock. But the option will be 5 in the money at expiration, so that the option position produces a loss of $(5 - 2.50) = 2.5$. Hence, the overall outcome is a gain of 1.5.

In general, the writer of a covered option earns the entire excess premium if the option closes either at or in the money. But if the option closes out of the money, the writer earns the entire premium less any loss on the underlying security. Thus, in this case, if the option is at or in the money at maturity, there will be a gain of 1.5, but if the option is out of the money, the outcome will be: (price of underlying asset $- 56) = + 2.5$.

3.2. RISKS OF OWNING AND WRITING OPTIONS

The most important risk of owning an option is the possibility of losing one's entire premium in a very short period of time. The author once met a broker who decided to purchase an option for his own account. The broker walked from his desk to the firm's clerk and handed in the order for transmission to the firm's trading desk. Before the broker had time to return to his desk, there was an announcement that reduced the value of the option to almost zero. Clearly, the time needed for an investor to lose his or her entire investment can be very short in the options market.

Uncovered writers face the possibility of essentially unlimited loss from an unfavorable move in the price of the underlying asset. Covered writers face the risk of losing their entire investment in the underlying asset.

Writers can be assigned unwanted exercise notices, and trading in either the underlying asset or the option itself may be halted by the exchanges. There are other risks, but these mostly have to do with potential problems in the operations of the options markets.

3.3. OPTION SPREADS AND STRADDLES

3.3.1. Spreads

It is common on an exchange to have a number of different options trading on the same underlying asset at any given time. These options differ in either striking price or expiration date. Some traders enter into strategies involving a **spread**, the simultaneous purchase of one option contract and the sale of another. A **bull spread** is profitable if the price of the underlying asset increases, and a **bear spread** is profitable if the price of the underlying asset declines. If the spread is profitable when the price does not change, it is a **neutral spread**.

If the two options involved in a spread have different expiration dates, the spread is a **time** or **calendar spread**. If the longer-lived option is purchased and the shorter-lived option is sold, the spreader hopes that the time value of the shorter-lived option will fall faster than that of the longer option. This is most likely to happen if the price of the underlying stock either does not change or falls. There will probably be no margin required on this strategy because the short position is fully covered by the long position. Also, the premium on the longer-lived asset will be larger than the premium on the shorter-lived asset, so that the spreader will have to pay the difference when the spread is initiated.

If the two options involved are of the same maturity, but differ in striking price, the spread is a **price spread**. For calls, if the option with the lower striking price is bought and the option with the higher striking price is sold, the spreader will profit from an increase in the price of the underlying asset above the lower striking price until the higher striking price is reached. This is a bull spread. Since the long option position provides protection for the short position, there will probably be no margin on this transaction. But the spreader will have to pay the difference in the two premiums when the spread is initiated.

It is difficult to make profits on spreads, for several reasons. One is that the transaction costs are high. There are two commissions at the outset and two more commissions unless the options expire out of the money. Also, there are bid–ask spreads that are incurred on both assets. An additional difficulty is that the spreader must be careful that both **legs** of the spread (the purchase and sale at the initiation of the spread are the two legs) are put on at the same time. Otherwise the spreader will have an exposed side.

3.3.2. Straddles

The change in an option's value with respect to a change in the volatility of the underlying asset is known as the option's vega. A **straddle** or **volatility spread** involves the purchase of both a put and a call on the same stock or the sale of both a put and a call on the same stock. If the put and the call are purchased, the spread is long volatility. In other words, an increase in the riskiness of the underlying asset will increase the value of both options. If both the put and the call are written, the position is short volatility, so an increase in the riskiness of the underlying asset will decrease the value of both options.

4. OPTIONS ON INDIVIDUAL STOCKS, FUTURES, AND INDEXES

The underlying interests for options are varied. The most common option types are on individual stocks, futures contracts, and indexes. We will examine specific examples of each of these types of options.

4.1. EQUITY OPTIONS ON INDIVIDUAL STOCKS

Options on individual stocks are traded on many exchanges, including the Chicago Board Options Exchange. The CBOE options are American options that cover 100 shares, unless an adjustment for a stock split or stock dividend has been required. Both puts and calls are traded. For each stock, options are traded on the nearest 2 months and on quarterly cycles. Each underlying stock is assigned to one of three cycles: (1) January, April, July, October; (2) February, May, August, November; or (3) March, June, September, December. The last trading day is the third Friday of the expiration month, and the options expire the next day. Based on the trading price of the underlying stock, the increments of striking prices used are 2.50 USD for prices of 25 USD or less, 5 USD for prices up to 200, and 10 USD for prices over 200 USD. Settlement is by delivery of the underlying stock. Initially, the striking prices straddle the price of the underlying stock. As the price of the stock changes, new striking prices are added, so there is at least one option with a striking price above and one with a striking price below the current price of the underlying asset. Of course, the options that had previously begun trading continue to trade.

4.2. OPTIONS ON FUTURES

Put and call options on the JPY futures contract described in the last chapter are traded on the SIMEX. Upon exercise of a call, the owner receives a long position in the futures contract; upon exercise of a put, the owner receives a short position in the futures contract. Contracts are traded with expirations in March, June, September, and December, and in several additional months. There is a position limit of 1,000 contracts in the option and the underlying futures contract combined. The minimum price fluctuation is 0.000001 USD per JPY, or 12.50 USD per contract. Quotations are in USD, so a quoted option price of 0.005 translates into a contract price of 625 USD. To determine whether an option on a futures contract is in the money, the striking price of the option contract must be compared with the price of the futures contract, not the asset underlying the futures contract.

4.3. INDEX OPTIONS

The European Options Exchange lists European puts and calls on an index of Dutch stocks. The contracts have an initial life of 3 months, and each month a new contract is added.

Contracts are also traded with initial lives of 6, 9, and 12 months on a January, April, July, and October cycle and with initial lives of 2 and 3 years on a November cycle. The contract size is 100 times the index value. Quotations are 1 NLG per index unit, so the aggregate premium is 100 times the quotation. Trading ends on the third Friday of the expiration month if it is a business day, or the day before if it is not. There is no physical delivery; the contract is settled in cash.

4.4. CATASTROPHE-LINKED OPTIONS

Insurance companies face a problem in providing coverage for low-frequency, high-severity losses. Facing the possibility of a catastrophic loss, insurance companies can purchase reinsurance from other companies or maintain large amounts of capital. The occurrence of two major natural catastrophes in the USA, Hurricane Andrew in 1992 and the Northridge earthquake in 1994, severely diminished the availability of reinsurance. To address this shortage, a number of new innovative products have been developed. We discussed catastrophe-linked bonds in the chapter on fixed-income securities. In this chapter we turn our attention to options.

In the traditional reinsurance market, one insurance company can examine the specific risks of another insurance company and assess the nature and extent of the risks faced. This makes the issuance of a reinsurance policy covering this specific risk possible. Because it would be difficult for investors to evaluate the potential losses from the policies of an individual firm, derivatives based on the policies of an individual company are not likely to be viable. An alternative is to use an index that reflects industry-wide loss experience.

Illustrating this approach, the Chicago Board of Trade developed several European option contracts on indexes of catastrophe losses, which Property Claim Services (PCS) computes (Litzenberger, Beaglehole, and Reynolds 1996).[5] The indexes are based on PCS's survey of a wide range of insurance companies and on its own independent data. PCS computes an index for each state within the USA, and these are aggregated into regional indexes and a national index. Option contracts are traded on three individual state indexes (California, Florida, and Texas), on indexes for each of the six regions of the USA, and on the national index. Because the primary risk in the Western USA is from earthquakes, which do not have a seasonal pattern, only one contract expiration, December, is used for the Western index contract and the California index contract. The Texas index, Florida index, and remaining regional index contracts, where the risk is primarily from hurricanes, are traded with quarterly expirations. The contracts are settled in cash.

Both hedgers and speculators are needed to make these contracts successful. Insurance companies and reinsurance companies could trade these contracts among themselves, providing a price-discovery benefit. But without speculators, new capital is not attracted to the market. One difficulty in attracting speculators to the market is that the Black–Scholes option pricing model cannot be used to value catastrophe options, because the underlying interest is not a traded asset (Canter, Cole, and Sandor 1996).

5. SUMMARY

There are two parties to each options contract: the owner and the writer. For calls, the owner has the right, if he or she chooses, to purchase an underlying interest from the writer at a stated price, the striking price. For puts, the owner has the right, if he or she chooses, to sell an underlying interest to the writer at the striking price. Options terminate on the expiration date. If the option is American, it can be exercised at any time, but if it is European, it can be exercised only at maturity. Some contracts provide for a settlement in cash rather than physical delivery. Writers are covered if they have an offsetting position in the underlying security or its equivalent. Otherwise they are naked.

Option positions can be taken in either the over-the-counter or the listed markets. Exchange-traded options are standardized. All contracts are with an intermediary, such as the Option Clearing Corporation in the USA. Individual writers and owners are matched only upon exercise. Only the price of the option, the premium, is negotiated on the exchange. The types of orders that can be placed and the way in which option trades are executed on exchanges is essentially the same as for stocks. The Chicago Board Options Exchange and the European Option Exchange both have designated market makers and central limit order books.

The minimum value of an option, ignoring interest, is the amount that the option is in the money, but cannot be negative. The premium for an option is the sum of an option's minimum value and its excess premium. The value of the excess premium is affected by a number of factors, including (1) the riskiness of the underlying security, (2) the life of the option, (3) the extent to which the option is in or out of the money, (4) the cost of carrying the underlying interest, (5) potential gains from exercise, and (6) the level of interest rates.

The margin on the purchase of an option contract is usually 100 percent. Covered writers typically do not post margin, while the level of margin required for naked writers is usually based on the value of the underlying interest.

The change in the price of an option in response to a change in the value of the underlying asset is called the option's "delta." The delta of a call option is positive. Gamma is the change in an option's delta in response to a change in the price of the underlying asset. An option's gamma is largest when the option is at the money.

Upon exercise, the economic value of the owner's position is the amount the option is in the money, less commissions. Because most options have a positive excess premium, American options are usually exercised near expiration, if at all. It is usually more economical for both the owner and the writer of an option to close out the position rather than exercise.

Ownership of options is attractive to many investors, because of the leverage they provide, and because the loss is limited to the amount of the premium. Writers can speculate on price changes in the underlying asset or seek to earn premium income. Both owners and writers use options for hedging.

The owner of an option risks losing the entire premium in a short period of time. The writer of an option faces the prospect of loss due to an unfavorable price movement in the underlying asset.

Some investors enter into a spread, the simultaneous purchase of one option contract and sale of another. If the two options involved in a spread have different expiration dates, the spread is a calendar spread. If the two options involved have the same maturity, but differ in striking price, the spread is a price spread.

Questions

1 What is the difference between a call option and a put option? For the put and call, which party has an obligation to make delivery if the option is exercised?
2 For options with the same basic features, explain whether an American option is more valuable than a European option.
3 Define each of the option Greeks.
4 Define open interest.
5 Why does the author recommend the use of limit orders rather than market orders when initiating new positions in individual options?
6 When is a put option in the money, out of the money, and at the money?
7 Why is an uncovered option position riskier than a covered position?
8 What determines the amount of the option premium?
9 What are the main reasons for owning options? writing options?
10 What is the difference between a time and a price spread?

▪ Notes ▪

1 The sale of assets combined with the use of option contracts was used in the Middle Ages in Europe to avoid prohibitions against the charging of interest.
2 Some authors refer to this as "time value," but the excess premium also reflects volatility and other aspects of the option's value.
3 The following web sites provide programs for calculating option Greeks: http://www.axone.ch/Calculators/MultiOptionCalc.htm, http://www.intrepid.com/~robertl/option-pricer1/option-pricer.cgi.
4 The formulas for the other Greeks considered here are quite complicated, and we do not present them. They can be found in standard options texts such as Kolb 1997.
5 Property Services Group is a division of American Insurance Services Group, whose web address is http://www.aisg.org/index.html.

▪ References ▪

Bittman, James B. 1998: *Trading Index Options*. New York: McGraw-Hill.
Canter, Michael S., Cole, Joseph B. and Sandor, Richard L. 1996: Insurance derivatives: a new asset class for the capital markets and a new hedging tool for the insurance industry. *Journal of Derivatives* 4, 89–104.
Fleming, Jeff, Ostdiek, Barbara and Whaley, Robert E. 1994: Predicting stock market volatility: a new measure. Working paper, Duke University, Durham, NC.
Knoll, Michael S. 1994: Put–call parity and the law. Working paper, Los Angeles: University of Southern California.
Kolb, Robert W. 1997: *Futures, Options and Swaps*. Oxford: Blackwell.
Litzenberger, Robert H., Beaglehole, David R. and Reynolds, Craig E. 1996: Assessing catastrophe reinsurance-linked securities as a new asset class. *Journal of Portfolio Management*, special issue, 76–86.
MacBeth, James D. and Merville, Larry J. 1979: An empirical examination of the Black–Scholes call option pricing model. *Journal of Finance* 34, 1173–86.
Merton, Robert C. 1976a: The impact on option pricing of specification error in the underlying stock price returns. *Journal of Finance* 31, 333–50.
——1976b: Option pricing when underlying stock returns are discontinuous. *Journal of Financial Economics* 3, 125–44.
Sears, Steven M. 1999: Philadelphia exchange to reduce fees for options transactions. *Wall Street Journal*, Feb. 8.
Wall Street Journal 1995: Funds, Merrill battle over Venezuela bonds. Feb. 15, pp. C1, C14.

CHAPTER FOURTEEN

Swaps

■ Key terms ■

Accreting swap a swap for which the notional principal increases at one or more times during the tenor of the swap.

Actuals any assets that are exchanged at the effective date.

All-in cost the total cost of a financial transaction, including underwriting fees, interest expenses, and servicing costs.

Amortizing swap a swap for which the notional principal decreases at one or more points during the tenor of the contract.

Basis swap a floating rate based on one index is exchanged for a different floating rate based on a different index.

Bond equivalent yield differential an adjustment used to standardize interest rates on instruments ordinarily quoted on a bank discount basis.

Bucketing the practice in which a firm assumes the counterparty risk vis-à-vis a customer rather than executing the order on an established market.

Buckets a period used to aggregate cash flows for assessing swaps.

Bucket shops firms that regularly bucket customer orders.

Buy down a swap with an initial fixed-rate coupon below the market rate, requiring a payment by the fixed-rate payer.

Buy up a swap with an initial fixed-rate coupon above the market rate, requiring a payment by the floating rate counterparty.

Cap a pre-specified maximum rate that will be paid on a swap.

Collar a swap with both a floor and a cap.

Counterparty the parties to a swap.

Delayed-rate-setting swap a swap that commences immediately, but for which the coupon rate is set later, according to a procedure specified in the swap agreement.

Effective date the date on which a swap commences (same as **Value date**).

Fixed-for-floating   one counterparty pays a fixed rate, and the other pays a variable rate.

Flat   in options terminology, a rate is a market rate.

Floating rate   a variable rate used to calculate periodic payments on a swap.

Floor   a limit on the minimum rate that will be paid.

Law of comparative advantage   producers should specialize in the items for which they have the lowest opportunity cost.

Macrohedge   hedging using a portfolio approach rather than swap by swap.

Maturity date   the date on which a swap ends (same as **Termination date**).

Money market equivalent yield differential   a method of quoting LIBOR rates based on actual days/360 days.

Notional assets   fictional amounts used to calculate the value of payments required during the life of a swap.

Off-market swap   swap with a nonzero initial net present value.

Par swap   a swap for which the fixed and floating legs have about the same present value, so that the net present value of the contract is zero.

Participating forward   a swap with either a fixed cap and a flexible floor or a fixed floor and a flexible cap.

Payment dates   the date on which swap payments occur.

Plain vanilla   the basic form of a swap.

Range forward   a swap combining a long cap with a short floor.

Reference rate   a cash market rate used to calculate the floating rate payments for a swap.

Reset dates   the date on which a reference rate is observed.

Reversible swap   a swap in which the counterparties switch roles as the fixed and floating receiver.

Roller coaster swap   a swap that allows for both increases and decreases in notional principal.

Seasonal swap   a swap designed to de-season a firm's cash flows.

Swap   a contract evidenced by a single document in which two parties agree to exchange periodic payments.

Swap book   the portfolio of swaps.

Swap coupon   the fixed rate used to calculate periodic payments on a swap.

Swaptions   an option on a swap, giving the holder the right to enter into a swap at a later date.

Tenor   the life of a swap.

Termination clauses   provisions of a swap contract detailing how losses are determined in the event of default.

Termination date   the date on which a swap ends (same as **Maturity date**).

Value date   the date on which a swap commences (same as **Effective date**).

Yield curve swap   a floating-for-floating swap in which each leg of the swap is tied to a different point on the yield curve.

Zero-coupon swaps   a swap with a fixed rate swap coupon that is zero.

THIS CHAPTER has two main objectives. First, we explain how swaps work. Specifically, we explore

- basic interest rate, currency, and commodity swaps
- variations on these swap types
- options on swaps
- the economics and valuation of swaps

Next, we discuss the reasons for the development of the swaps market and the creation and management of swaps. Specifically, we describe

- the way swaps are used
- the role of swap dealers
- the management of swap risk

1. INTRODUCTION

Swaps are the most recent innovation in derivatives. Since their development in the 1980s, the notional value of swaps has grown rapidly. Today swaps are well established and have become standard tools used by commercial firms, institutional investors, and banks. Swaps are used in such varied applications as restructuring a firm's balance sheet, changing an investor's asset allocation, and protecting a producer from inventory price risk. The two most common types of swaps are interest rate swaps and currency swaps. As of June 30, 1997, the notional value of these swaps outstanding was 22.115 trillion USD and 1.585 trillion USD, respectively.[1] Tables 14.1 and 14.2 give breakdowns of interest rate swaps and currency swaps respectively, outstanding as of June 30, 1997, for each major currency. There were also 5.033 trillion USD of options related to swaps outstanding at the end of June 30, 1997. Clearly a market this large demands the attention of students of finance.

2. TYPES OF SWAPS

A **swap** is a contract evidenced by a single document in which two parties agree to exchange periodic payments. (Brown 1989; Marshall and Kapner 1990, 1993; McCord 1993; and Saber 1994 provide useful introductions to the swap market.) In some cases, assets are also exchanged at the beginning and end of the swap. The contract commences on its **effective date**, or **value date**, and ends on its **maturity date**, or **termination date**. The two parties to a swap are called **counterparties**. **Actuals** are assets that are exchanged at the effective date. If no assets are exchanged at the effective date, then fictional amounts, called **notional assets**, or notional principal, are used to calculate the value of payments required during the life, or **tenor**, of the swap agreement. A notional asset is not really an asset. Instead, it is an amount used to calculate swap payments.

There are three major categories of swaps: interest rate, currency, and commodity. Each of these has a basic form, often referred to as **plain vanilla**, and an almost limitless number of variations.

Table 14.1 Notional value of interest rate swaps outstanding, by currency[a]

Currency	As of Dec. 31, 1996	As of June 30, 1997	Change (%)	% of total, June 30, 1997
Deutschmark (DEM)	2,486,242	2,863,516	15.2	12.9
French franc (FRF)	1,560,924	2,068,368	32.5	9.4
British sterling (GBP)	1,367,070	1,677,758	22.7	7.6
Japanese yen (JPY)	4,441,799	4,944,313	11.3	22.4
US dollar (USD)	5,827,482	6,449,395	10.7	29.1
Other currencies (OTH)	3,487,392	4,112,138	17.9	18.6
Total	$19,170,909	$22,115,488	15.4	100.00

[a] Totals have been adjusted for both sides of currency swaps. Amounts are in million USD. Reprinted by permission of the International Swap Dealers' Association.

Table 14.2 Notional value of currency swaps outstanding, by currency[a]

Currency	As of Dec. 31, 1996	As of June 30, 1997	Change (%)	% of total, June 30, 1997
Deutschmark (DEM)	121,503	123,472	1.6	7.8
French franc (FRF)	56,501	63,655	12.7	4.0
British sterling (GBP)	68,565	69,816	1.8	4.4
Japanese yen (JPY)	269,798	281,136	4.2	17.7
US dollar (USD)	559,289	604,305	8.0	38.1
Other currencies (OTH)	483,980	442,391	−8.6	27.9
Total	$1,559,636	$1,584,775	1.6	100.00

[a] Totals have been adjusted for both sides of currency sways. Amounts are in million USD. Reprinted by permission of the International Swap Dealers' Association.

2.1. PLAIN VANILLA SWAPS

2.1.1. Interest rate swaps

In a plain vanilla interest rate swap, one party pays, and the other receives, periodic payments of the net of:

(1) a fixed rate of interest, the **swap coupon**, on a stated amount of debt
less
(2) a variable or **floating rate** of interest on the same given amount of debt.

This is called a **fixed-for-floating** swap. Since the amount of debt covered by the fixed and floating rates is the same, there is no need to exchange the actual debt at either the

371

effective date or at maturity. In other words, the debt is a notional amount, used simply to determine the periodic interest payments. Note that (1) minus (2) can be either positive or negative, so that either party may actually be required to make the payment. Likewise, either party may actually receive the payment. The counterparties can agree to make these payments monthly, semiannually, yearly, or at other times.

The floating rate is based on a specific cash market rate, the **reference rate**, which is observed on specific dates, the **reset dates**. Payments occur on the **payment dates**. Floating rates such as LIBOR plus a stated percentage (e.g., LIBOR + 2.5 percent) or the yield on a US Treasury note of comparable tenor plus a stated percentage are common. **All-in cost** is the total cost of a swap transaction, including underwriting fees, interest expenses, and servicing costs. The all-in cost is often stated as an annual percentage rate, payable semi-annually. The all-in cost is typically quoted against LIBOR flat. **Flat** means that the LIBOR rate is a market interest rate.

2.1.2. Currency swaps

A currency swap typically involves an initial exchange of currencies by the counterparties, with an exchange in the opposite direction at the end of the swap. The counterparties might initially exchange JPY for USD, with one paying JPY and receiving USD, while the other pays USD and receives JPY. At the maturity of the swap, the counterparties exchange currencies in the opposite direction. In other words, the party that received USD at the initiation of the swap pays USD at the maturity of the swap. Each party's interim payments are based on the prevailing rates for the currency that it receives. So the swap coupon for the party that receives USD at the initiation of the swap is based on USD interest rates (because the USDs that are received could have been invested at these rates). Likewise, the swap coupon for the party that receives JPY is based on JPY interest rates.

To make currency swaps more concrete, suppose that firm A, which is located in Germany, would like to borrow USD to finance an investment in the USA. The firm is well known in Germany, but not in the United States. It can borrow DEM for 1 year at a fixed rate of 9 percent in Germany, but must pay 12 percent for USD in the USA. Firm B would like to borrow DEM to finance an investment in Germany. This firm, which is well known in the USA, but hardly known at all in Germany, can borrow USD at 10 percent in the USA and DEM at 13 percent in Germany. Both these firms can reduce their cost of borrowing by executing a fixed-for-fixed currency swap. At the effective date of the swap, firm A borrows 10 million DEM in Germany, and firm B borrows 5 million USD in the USA. The two firms then exchange currencies. At the maturity of the swap, firm A pays firm B 5.5 million USD, and firm B pays firm A 10.9 million DEM. Each counterparty then has enough funds to pay off its loan. The cash flow for the combined swap and borrowings are as illustrated in table 14.3. It might be worthwhile to note at this point that replacing each firm's direct borrowing with a swap exposes each firm to additional risks, such as counterparty credit risk. Also, it is common to allow termination of a loan through early repayment, but swap agreements do not typically have provisions for voluntary early termination.

In the case just illustrated, each firm has a comparative advantage in its home market. According to the **law of comparative advantage**, each party should specialize in producing the goods for which it has the lowest opportunity cost. It might be easier to under-

Table 14.3 Illustration of the cash flows from a fixed-for-fixed currency swap

Timing	Firm A		Firm B	
	Action	Cash flow	Action	Cash flow
At the effective date of the swap	Borrows DEM	+10 million DEM	Borrows USD	+5 million USD
	Exchanges DEM	−10 million DEM +5 million USD	Exchanges USD	−5 million USD +10 million DEM
At maturity	Exchanges USD	−5.5 million USD +10.9 million DEM	Exchanges DEM	+5.5 million USD −10.9 million DEM
	Repays bank	−10.9 million DEM	Repays bank	−5.5 million USD
Net cash flow		−0.5 million USD		−0.9 million USD
Cost of funds	0.5/5 = 10%		0.9/10 = 9%	

stand the concept of comparative advantage by first examining product markets. Assume that the following conditions hold:

1 Country A can produce boxes of pencils using resources that cost 1 USD each and pens at a cost of 1.5 USD each.[2]
2 Country B, on the other hand, produces boxes of pencils at a cost of 1.50 USD each and pens at a cost of 3 USD each.
3 Each country has 6 USD of resources.
4 Country A can produce 6 boxes of pencils or 4 pens, but given the preferences of its consumers, it now produces 3 boxes of pencils and 2 pens.
5 Country B can produce 4 boxes of pencils or 2 pens, but given the preferences of its consumers, it now produces 2 boxes of pencils and 1 pen.

Hence, considering both countries together, currently there is production and consumption of 5 boxes of pencils and 3 pens using 12 units of resources. In country A, in terms of resources, it costs (6/4) 1.5 boxes of pencils to produce a pen. In country B it costs (4/2) 2 boxes of pencils to produce one pen. In terms of boxes of pencils, the cost of pens is higher in country B than in country A. Hence, country A has a comparative advantage in producing pens, and country B has a comparative advantage in producing boxes of pencils.

If all the consumers in both countries purchase the 3 pens they currently consume from country A at a resource cost of 4.5, country A can also produce 1.5 boxes of pencils. Country B can then produce 4 boxes of pencils. Then aggregate production and consumption would be 3 pens and (1.5 + 4) 5.5 boxes of pencils, which is 0.5 boxes of pencils larger than current consumption. When each country concentrates on producing the items for which it has a comparative advantage, aggregate production can be higher.

2.1.3. Commodity and equity swaps

The Chase Manhattan Bank introduced commodity swaps in 1986, and these swaps rapidly became a standard product offered by many firms. One firm pays a fixed price to receive a floating price, and the other firm pays a floating price to receive a fixed price. The floating reference price is often an average over some period, rather than the price at a point in time. In a standard commodity swap, counterparties make payments based on the following formula:

$$\text{Payment amount} = (\text{Fixed price} \times \text{no. of units of commodity Y})$$
$$- (\text{floating price} \times \text{no. of units of commodity Z})$$

If the payment amount is positive, the firm agreeing to pay fixed makes the payment. Otherwise, the firm agreeing to pay floating makes the payment.

If Y and Z are the same commodity, as is usually the case, this formula becomes:

$$\text{Payment amount} = (\text{Fixed price} - \text{floating price}) \times \text{number of units of commodity}$$

Consider an oil producer who wants to fix the price received for its oil over the next 5 years. When the oil is produced and sold on the spot market, the firm receives the current spot price. Hence, the goal of the firm is to swap the floating spot price received for a fixed price. The firm can accomplish its goal by entering into a swap in which it receives a payment if the floating price is less than a fixed price and makes a payment if the floating price is greater than a fixed price. If payments are received, they supplement the funds received from cash market sales. If payments are made, they offset funds received from cash market sales. These swap payments and receipts stabilize the cash flow.

In 1989, Banker's Trust developed equity swaps as an extension of commodity swaps. In an equity swap, one counterparty agrees to pay, and the other agrees to receive the difference between a fixed rate and a floating rate. The primary difference between an equity swap and a commodity swap is that for the equity swap the floating rate is based on the total return (capital gain or loss plus dividends) on an index of equities. The index might be the Financial Times Index (London), the S&P 500, the Nikkei Index, or an index for a specific industry. A portfolio manager might use an equity swap to gain rapid exposure to the equity markets of a particular country or region.

There are many possibilities. The floating leg of the swap might provide for the payment of the return on the S&P 500 or the Nikkei Index, whichever was greater. Of course, since the floating leg has a higher present value, a higher swap coupon is required to maintain the zero net present value of the swap at its initiation. A portfolio manager who owns US stocks might swap the return on the S&P 500 for the return on the Nikkei Index, effectively converting an equity portfolio of one country into an equity portfolio of another. Further, the floating leg of a swap might call for payment based on a weighted average of the performance of a variety of indexes.

2.2. BEYOND PLAIN VANILLA SWAPS

2.2.1. Variations in swap terms

Plain vanilla swaps can be tailored to meet the needs of a wide variety of clients. The possibilities are almost endless, but it may be useful to review a few examples to stimulate the reader's imagination. Several common variations involve changes in the amount of the notional principal over the life of the swap. **Amortizing swaps** provide for a decrease in the notional principal at one or more points during the tenor of the contract. For a special type of amortizing swap, the notional principal decreases in a manner consistent with the repayment of mortgages. **Accreting swaps** provide for an increase in the notional principal at one or more points during the tenor of the swap. **A roller coaster swap** allows for both increases and decreases in notional principal, following some pre-specified formula. In one formulation, payments by the floating ratepayer are added to, and receipts by the floating ratepayer are subtracted from, the notional amount.

Another common variation involves alternative specifications of the reset date. An average rate over a period is often used rather than a rate at a particular time. A bank relying on the overnight repo market to finance a project would probably encounter a different borrowing cost every day. A swap contract could be tied to the average of these rates.

A **par swap** is one for which the fixed and floating legs have about the same present value, so the net present value of the contract is zero. Occasionally, a swap counterparty requires a swap coupon that is different from the current market price. Such a need might arise from a desire to match a specific cash market obligation. In this case the periodic swap could have a positive or negative initial net present value. Swaps with a nonzero initial net present value are called **off-market swaps**. An initial payment to bring the overall contract net present value to zero is then required. Of course, the net present value of a swap changes quickly after its creation, as interest rates, currency exchange rates, and other factors that affect the obligations of the counterparties change.

In a **basis swap** a floating rate is exchanged for another floating rate, with each leg tied to a different index. The **yield curve swap** is also a floating-for-floating swap, but in this case each leg of the swap is tied to a different point on the yield curve. Floating-for-floating swaps are also typically available for currencies. As we have discussed in a previous chapter, there are LIBOR (London Interbank Offer Rates) quotes available for a number of currencies, including GBP, USD, and DEM. One or both legs of the swap could be tied to one of these rates. In another type of currency swap, there is no initial exchange of funds. Instead, the swap might call for one party to pay a fixed amount plus a fixed rate in DEM, while the counterparty pays a fixed amount plus a floating USD LIBOR rate. This type of swap provides the DEM party with protection against changes in the USD exchange rate.

Zero-coupon swaps have a fixed rate swap coupon that is zero. Hence, no payments are made on the fixed leg of the contract until maturity, when a single large payment is required. **Seasonal swaps** are designed to de-season a firm's cash flows. This can be accomplished in a variety of ways. One is to use a fixed-for-fixed swap with mismatched payment dates. Swaps that commence immediately, but for which the coupon rate is set later according to a procedure specified in the swap agreement, are called **delayed-rate-setting swaps**. **Reversible swaps** call for the counterparties to switch roles as the fixed and floating receiver.

2.2.2. Swaptions, caps, and floors

Swaptions are options on swaps. The holder of a swaption has the right to enter into a swap at a later date. Swaptions are useful if a firm may need a swap at a future date but the need is not certain. The firm may have given a customer the option of purchasing its

Table 14.4 Hypothetical USD LIBOR interest rate cap premiums

Cap tenor	Premium[a]	
	4% cap	5% cap
2 years	0.71%	0.27%
3 years	1.87%	0.92%
5 years	4.98%	3.03%

[a] as a % of the notional principal.

floating-rate debt at the end of 6 months. If the customer exercises its option, then the firm may want to convert the floating rate into a fixed rate using a swap. If the customer does not exercise the option, the firm will do nothing.

Floating rate obligations under a swap agreement can also be limited by the purchase of a cap or a floor. A **cap** pre-specifies the maximum rate that will be paid, and a **floor** places a limit on the minimum rate that will be paid. If the actual market rate is above the cap rate or below the floor rate, the holder of the cap or the floor, respectively, receives a payment. Hence, a cap is similar to a multiperiod call option, and a floor is similar to a multiperiod put option. On each reset date one option expires and the next begins. If the expiring option is in the money, the holder receives a payment. Otherwise, there is no payment on the cap or floor for that period. Caps and floors can be incorporated directly into swaps or purchased separately from a cap dealer. Table 14.4 illustrates hypothetical cap premiums for USD LIBOR interest rates and table 14.5 illustrates hypothetical collar premiums.

A **collar**, or **range forward**, combines a long cap and a short floor. If, on a given reset date, the floating rate index rises above the cap level, the cap seller pays the cap buyer. If the index rate falls below the floor level, the floor seller pays the floor buyer. If the index level is equal to or between the cap and the floor, no payment is made. For example, a firm might enter into a range forward swap on the price of gold with a cap of 310 USD and a floor of 250 USD. In this case, there would be no payments as long as the price of gold was in the range of 250–310 USD. But if the price exceeded 310 USD, then one counterparty, say A, would be required to pay the other counterparty, say B. If the price fell below 250 USD, then counterparty B would pay counterparty A. Notice that whether a cap or a floor decreases or increases risk depends on which side of the agreement one is on. This is equivalent to options where the writer has unlimited risk (or nearly so) and the purchaser has limited risk. Through an appropriate selection of the cap and floor prices, a range forward swap can be initiated without the need for up-front payments.

Participating forwards provide either a fixed cap and a flexible floor (which would be useful for a commodity user) or a fixed floor and a flexible cap (which would be useful for a commodity producer). In other words, one of the prices involved in the swap is fixed. For the fixed cap and flexible floor, the commodity user is compensated if the price of the commodity rises above the cap price. On the other hand, if the price falls below the cap price, the commodity user must pay an agreed-upon percentage of the difference between the cap

Table 14.5 Hypothetical cap and floor available when current interest rates are 6%

| Tenor | Premium[a] | |
	5% floor	6% floor
2 years	3.25%	3.14%
3 years	3.63%	3.42%
4 years	3.98%	3.65%

[a] as a % of the notional principal.

price and the market price to its counterparty. As with range forwards, if a suitable cap or floor rate is selected, participating forwards can be initiated without the need for any up-front payments.

---

3. THE ECONOMICS OF SWAPS

Given that there are already numerous financial products available to firms, why has the market for swaps grown so rapidly? One reason is that financial objectives can often be accomplished more quickly, easily, and cheaply using swaps. Another reason for the widespread use of swaps is their usefulness in solving a wide variety of problems.

3.1. ADVANTAGES OF SWAPS

Many capital market participants find swaps useful because, compared with alternatives, swaps are implemented more quickly and cheaply.

(1)   Firms that are active participants in the swaps market can implement swaps almost immediately. The most important terms, such as the tenor of the swap, the price, and the reference rates, can be negotiated, with the remaining details left for later. If both parties agree, the party on the side of the swap that is out of the money can make a payment to the in the money party to terminate the swap. Even if a swap counterparty will not agree to terminate a swap, another swap with offsetting obligations can often be initiated.

Case   A company intended to finance a major acquisition using debt. As the negotiations proceeded, interest rates began to increase rapidly. When the acquisition agreement was signed, the purchaser entered into a swap to lock in the current interest rate. The rapidity with which swaps can be implemented was a critical factor in the choice of this strategy.

(2)   Swaps often have cost advantages over other strategies. The costs incurred in a swap may be less than the marketing and distribution costs, legal fees, rating agency fees, and similar costs of alternatives, especially if the alternatives involve the distribution or purchase of securities from the public. Taxes associated with the actual transfer of assets may be avoided. Further, swaps may provide an attractive vehicle for exploiting market inefficiencies.

3.2. USES OF SWAPS

Swaps can be used in a variety of ways, as these examples show.

(1) Swaps may provide a way to overcome lack of information about how particular markets operate, lack of experience in dealing in other markets, and other barriers. It is well known that investors have a home country bias. In other words, investors prefer to invest in their home markets, often even when the returns in nondomestic markets are higher. There are many obstacles to investing outside one's home country. A partial listing includes lack of information about investment opportunities, lack of information about how the markets work and who can be trusted in these markets, and currency risks. If two firms can borrow more cheaply in their own countries than in each other's country, this inefficiency can be exploited so that each can potentially have lower borrowing costs.

Case In 1981, the World Bank, an international organization formally known as the International Bank for Reconstruction and Development, needed SFR and DEM to finance its operations in Switzerland and Germany. Salomon Brothers arranged a swap between the World Bank and International Business Machines in which the World Bank assumed SFR obligations of IBM and IBM assumed USD obligations of the World Bank. This swap allowed the World Bank to obtain the funds it needed without directly tapping German or Swiss capital markets. The fact that two major institutions found it advantageous to use a swap to achieve their objectives provided early validity of the use of this strategy (Brown and Smith 1995, p. 1).

(2) Firms that do not have credit ratings may find it difficult and costly to borrow.

Case The subsidiaries of a major firm had difficulty borrowing at an acceptable fixed rate because of their lack of an independent credit rating. However, the subsidiaries found that they could borrow short-term at acceptable rates. Of course, because the borrowings were short-term, the borrower paid a variable or floating interest rate. To convert these floating rate borrowings to a fixed rate, the parent entered into a swap agreement with an outside counterparty. The agreement was downstreamed to the subsidiary using a second swap between the parent and subsidiary. The firm felt that the combination of short-term debt with 100 percent backup through a revolving credit agreement combined with a swap was the equivalent of a fixed rate debt (Einzig and Lange 1990, p. 56).

(3) Swaps may provide a way of dealing with regulatory barriers. Many countries restrict portfolio investments by nondomestic investors. Swaps may provide a vehicle for gaining exposure to these markets. In addition, many countries place restrictions on the ownership of various types of assets. Firms may be able to gain exposure to the markets more easily using swaps than using actual assets. In other cases, swaps can be used to accomplish strategies that cannot be accomplished directly due to regulatory obstacles.

Case An insurance broker collected premiums through agents. Government regulations required the collected funds (which typically amounted to $100 million) to be invested in federal funds until they were received by the insurance broker. The broker wished to invest in longer-maturity instruments. A floating-for-fixed interest rate swap was an effective way of accomplishing this objective (Einzig and Lange 1990, p. 56).

(4) Investors may also face delays and high costs in altering their asset allocation. Swaps may allow asset allocations to be changed more quickly.

Case An Australian pension fund holds a portfolio of US stocks that proxies the S&P 500. The firm would like to convert its equity exposure to a fixed rate exposure in AUD for a 6-month period. This can be accomplished with a series of swaps. First, the fund swaps it equity return for a fixed USD swap coupon. Finally the fund enters a fixed-for-fixed interest rate swap, which completes the conversion of the fund's equity exposure into a fixed AUD exposure.

(5) Firms that wish to make changes in their capital structure may find that selling or repurchasing equities and bonds cannot be accomplished quickly or cheaply. Swaps may provide a way of keeping the debt/equity ratio at a desired level between security issuance dates. Swaps can also be useful in managing individual debt and equity issues.

Case Firms commonly issue fixed-income debt that is noncallable for an initial period. Suppose that interest rates decline substantially during the call protection period. A firm might want to lock in these lower rates, but the existing debt must be dealt with first. One possibility is to repurchase the debt in the open market, but there is no guarantee that all the debt can be repurchased and that the cost of repurchasing the debt will not wipe out the firm's gain from the fall in interest rates. Futures contracts with suitable length or timing of maturities are unlikely to be available. Swaps represent a practical alternative. In this case it is the flexibility of the swap contract that gives it an advantage. Here the firm can enter into a swap with a delayed starting date, which corresponds to the date on which the bonds can be called (Goodman 1990, p. 46; Brown and Smith 1990, p. 60).

(6) Swaps allow firms to accomplish changes in their inventories (including inventories of financial assets) without actually acquiring or disposing of the assets. Hence, long-established relationships with suppliers and customers that might be disrupted by other approaches are avoided through the use of swaps. The Phibro swaps described in box 14.1 are typical. Since all the swaps are settled in cash rather than through delivery, the client and vendor relationships of the swap counterparties are not affected. This approach might also avoid taxes that are triggered by an actual asset sale.

4. VALUATION OF SWAPS

At the initiation of a swap the net present value of the contract is zero. This is most often accomplished by setting both the fixed rate payment and the floating rate payment at market rates. If nonmarket rates are used, then sufficient payment(s) must be made at some point during the life of the contract to restore the initial net present value to zero. Of course, after the commencement of the swap, changes in market interest rates may well cause the swap to become an asset for one party and a liability for the other.

For most swaps semiannual payments are required. If the swap does not call for semiannual payments, market rates that are quoted on a semiannual basis must be adjusted. The general formula for converting payments compounded at one frequency per year into equivalent payments compounded at another frequency is

$$r_q = q\left((1 + r_z/z)^{z/q} - 1\right)$$

where q and z indicate the number of compounding periods per year.

BOX 14.1
Illustrative strategies available to producers and users of fuel oil

Crude oil and related products are essential to the operations of many firms, and, consequently, there are also many firms involved in their development and production. Phibro, Inc. is a trader of energy-related commodities and a provider of energy risk management. The following are four strategies Phibro suggests as being potentially useful to companies.

Strategy 1: Operating hedge

An oil producer wishes to lock in a budget forecast for crude oil production for the next 12 months. The producer has budgeted 19 USD per barrel, a level at which the firm can conformably service its debt and earn an adequate profit margin. However, the firm wishes to achieve this objective while retaining some upside potential and avoiding premium payments. An average price range forward collar with a 12-month tenor may accomplish these objectives. The contract is based on the second nearby NYMEX light sweet crude oil contract. Settlement is in cash versus the average semiannual NYMEX close. The floor is 19 USD, the ceiling is 22 USD, and the premium is zero.

Using this swap, the producer can lock in a price range of 19–22 USD per barrel for a designated amount of its production. Average semiannual second nearby NYMEX West Texas Intermediate (WTI) prices below the floor result in cash payments of the differential from Phibro to the producer, whereas average prices above the ceiling result in cash payments from the producer to Phibro. The producer has protected its budgeted oil price without up-front premium and has retained 3 USD per barrel of upside potential above the floor level. Because the hedge contract is for cash settlement, the producer sells its oil as it normally would on the spot market.

Strategy 2: Strategic hedge

The producer wishes to develop marginal producing properties but is hesitant to do so because of price uncertainty. Prices below 16 USD a barrel make the economics of the project unattractive, and therefore the producer seeks floor protection at that price. To fully subsidize the purchase of this floor for the 5-year expected producing life of the reserves, the producer is willing to forgo prices above a certain level. A long-dated average price range forward with a tenor of 5 years may accomplish the producer's objectives. The basis is the second nearby NYMEX light sweet crude oil contract along with a floor of 16 USD and a cap of 23 USD. Settlement is in cash, versus the average semiannual NYMEX close. The premium is zero.

Over each semiannual period, average second nearby NYMEX WTI prices below 16 USD result in cash settlements of the differential times the semiannual volume from Phibro to the producer. Average prices above 23 USD result in cash settlements from the producer to Phibro. Average prices within the range require no cash settlements. The producer has locked in the minimum return on marginal properties, while retaining an additional 7 USD per barrel upside potential, and paying no up-front premium. The development of such reserves could improve the firm's balance sheet with no threat to margins. Moreover, the bank, which usually lends 50 percent of the NPV of such reserves at a base case price, may wish to increase its credit because of the reduced price uncertainty.

Strategy 3: Fixed prices crack spread

An oil refiner is contemplating a refinery expansion to meet rising demand for refined products. The refiner will need to finance the expansion largely with bank debt, and in an effort to secure attractive terms, the producer may want to lock in its crack spread on a portion of the refinery's capacity of 50,000 barrels per day. The crack spread certainty will allow the security in servicing the debt needed for the refinery expansion. The tenor of the swap is 4 years. The contract is based on the semiannual average Platt's mean US Gulf Coast unleaded gasoline price minus the semiannual average NYMEX WTI first nearby contract price. Settlement is in cash. The premium is 0. Crack spreads below 3.50 USD per barrel require cash settlements of the differential from Phibro to the refiner, whereas spreads above 3.50 require cash settlements of the differential from the refiner to Phibro.

Strategy 4: Long hedge

A forest products company burns 1mm barrels a year of residual fuel oil to run it mills. Its profits have been eroded recently by the sharp upward move in oil prices. Fearing higher future prices and an inability to fully pass these additional costs on to its customers, the firm would like protection for its exposure to cost changes in US Gulf Coast 1 percent residual fuel oil prices. The firm can consider an oil price swap at a price of 19 USD with a tenor of 5 years. The basis of the swap is Platt's mean assessment USGC 1 percent residual fuel oil (waterborne). The swap calls for semiannual cash settlement versus average Platt's mean close. The premium is 0. At the end of each semiannual period, average Platt's mean quotations are compared to 19 USD. Prices above 19 USD require cash settlement of the differential times the semiannual volume from Phibro to the company, whereas prices below 19 USD necessitate cash settlements of the differential from the company to Phibro. The company continues to procure its physical fuel through normal channels. The cash settlements offset higher or lower prices, locking the user in at the swap level.

Source: Phibro, Inc. Reprinted by permission.

In order to aid in understanding swaps it may be useful at this point to consider the valuation of several swap contracts.

Case 1   A firm has issued 10 million USD of bonds with 5 years to maturity with a fixed coupon of 8.65 percent. The firm approaches a dealer and seeks a quote for paying floating rather than fixed. The dealer looks at the 5-year US Treasury yield and offers to pay that rate plus 46 basis points, or 8.42 percent, in return for LIBOR. To calculate the firm's cost, first note that the swap requires the following payments:

Payment on current debt	8.65 percent
Receipt from swap dealer	−8.42 percent
Payment to swap dealer	LIBOR

It appears that the firm's cost is LIBOR plus (8.65 percent − 8.42 percent) = 0.23 percent. But there are two additional features of bond and swap quotations that must be taken into account. The fixed payment for a swap and the payments on bonds are calculated using **bond equivalent yield differential**, based on either actual days/365 days or 30 days/360 days. LIBOR is quoted using **money market equivalent yield differential** based on actual days/360 days. The following formula equates money market yield differences (M) and bond equivalent yield differences:

$$M = (360/365)B$$

For this example, B = 0.23 percent, so that

$$M = (360/365)B = (360/365)\,0.23 \text{ percent} = 0.227 \text{ percent}$$

Hence, the firm's cost is LIBOR + 0.227 percent.

Case 2 A dealer is quoting interest rate swaps at 9.63 percent semiannual versus LIBOR flat for a 5-year swap with a 10,000,000 notional value. A client would like to pay 9.5 percent fixed. This is an off-market rate. What adjustments in the cash flows are required?
A. One approach is to adjust the LIBOR payments as well. First, convert the fixed reduction of (9.63 percent − 9.50 percent) to money market basis as follows:

$$M = (360/365)B = (360/365)(-0.13 \text{ percent}) = -0.128 \text{ percent}.$$

Hence, the required floating rate is LIBOR − 0.128 percent.
B. Another approach is to calculate the lump sum payment required to compensate for the reduced fixed rate payments. The formula is

$$PV = P\left(\left(1 - (1 + r/m)^{-nm}\right)\big/(r/m)\right)$$

where PV is the present value, P is the annuity, r is the yield, m is the number of periods per year, and n is the number of years or tenor. For this case, the reduced payments are (0.0013(10,000,000 USD))/2 = 6,500 USD semiannually, r = 8.42 percent, m = 2, and n = 5.

$$PV = 6,500 \text{ USD}\left(\left(1 - (1 + (0.0842/2))^{-10}\right)\big/(0.0842/2)\right) = 52,174 \text{ USD}.$$

This is the payment by the fixed rate payer that is required at the initiation of the contract. If the initial swap coupon has an off-market rate that is lower than the market rate, as in this case, the payment is called a **buy down**. If the initial swap coupon is above the market rate, the floating rate payer will make a payment, and this is called a **buy up**.

Case 3 Continuing case 2B, what payment is required, if any, to terminate this swap at the first reset date if dealers are quoting fixed 9.87 percent versus LIBOR flat. Note that interest rates have increased, so that the fixed rate payer now has a valuable contract. Assume that the first floating rate coupon is 8.65 percent.

Obligation of the fixed rate payer		USD
Present value of semiannual payment	$475,000 \times ((1 - (1 + 9.87/200)^{-9})/(9.87/200)) =$	3,386,009
Present value of terminal payment	$(1 - (1 + 9.87/200)^{-9}) =$	6,482,115
Present value of fixed interest payment at first reset date		475,000
Total obligation		10,343,124

Obligation of the floating rate payer		USD
Present value of interest and terminal payment at LIBOR flat		10,000,000
Present value of semiannual payment at first reset date	$(8.65/200)10{,}000{,}000 =$	432,500
Value of buy down	$6{,}500\,((1-(1+9.87/200)^{-9})/(9.87/200)) =$	46,332
Total obligation		10,478,832

Net payment from floating rate payer to fixed rate payer		135,708

If the termination is between reset dates, then the cash flows outlined here must be discounted to the termination date. In addition, if the LIBOR flat rate has changed, the first floating interest payment will be different, and the difference between this rate and the original rate for the period from the termination date to the reset date must be taken into account.

5. THE CREATION AND TRADING OF SWAPS

When the swap market was in its infancy, each swap dealer wrote his or her own contract. The initial agreement to enter into the swap was consummated over the telephone by agreement on a few key points, such as the tenor of the agreement, the swap coupon rate, the floating rate index and premium, and similar matters. These were confirmed in writing on a confirmation. But the actual agreement might be signed some time later and dealt with a wide variety of issues, which were of less immediate concern, but which might also be important. These included issues such as the definition of default and the terminal value of the swap in the event of default, the identification of the jurisdiction in which disputes would be resolved, and the like. Legal review of each swap contract resulted in substantial costs. As the market developed, it became clear that standardization was needed. In 1985 the International Swap Dealers' Association published its first code, *The Code of Standard Wording, Assumptions and Provisions for Swaps, 1985 Edition*. The British Bankers' Association also developed its own documentation, the *British Bankers' Association Interest Rate Swaps*. The availability of these standard documents greatly facilitated the development of the swaps market.

As we have seen, after their initial development, the market for swaps grew rapidly. But in 1987 the trading of swaps in the USA stopped for several years due to regulatory uncertainty. To understand why, it is necessary to understand some of the history of the regulation of futures trading in the USA. When trading in futures contracts began in Chicago, the contracts were for the actual delivery of agricultural commodities, and the right to demand and make delivery was incorporated in every contract. This right could be terminated only by the agreement of both parties, which necessitated their entering into offsetting transactions on the floor of the exchange.

Eventually, a number of unscrupulous individuals set up firms that took orders from the public, but did not execute the orders on the exchange. Instead, the firms, which did not have adequate capital, assumed the counterparty risk themselves, typically without informing the customer. This practice is called **bucketing**, and hence the firms were called **bucket shops**. The firms happily collected money from their customers for the initial margins plus any gains due to the firm as a result of marking the contracts to market daily. Small gains due to customers were also happily paid. If customers held contracts giving them substantial gains, the firm would simply fold up their operations and declare bankruptcy. The same individuals would then reopen under a new name in a new location. These bucket shops were legal as long as the firms intended to perform on the contracts, but it was difficult to prove that a firm did not intend to deliver until it was too late for the customers to recover their money. To combat these practices, individual states passed laws outlawing bucket shops as a form of gambling.

Subsequently, some investors attacked the legality of futures exchanges using the bucket shop laws. In *Board of Trade* v. *Christie*, the Supreme Court of the USA ruled that the futures contracts were legal because of the intent to deliver rather than make cash settlement. This ruling placed the right to deliver at the center of the determination of whether a contract was legal or illegal.

In 1933 the US Congress passed the Commodities Exchange Act giving the newly established Commodity Exchange Authority jurisdiction to regulate "transactions involving sale of a commodity for future delivery." In 1974 Congress changed the name of the regulatory authority to the Commodity Futures Trading Commission and expanded its jurisdiction. Trading of futures contracts off an exchange was declared illegal.

The development of the swaps market in the early 1980s raised a number of legal issues. Were swap dealers illegal bucket shops under state laws, since the swaps were typically settled in cash? Alternatively, were swaps illegal off-exchange futures contracts? In 1987, the CFTC stated that swaps were futures and, therefore, illegal. The market for swaps in the USA was effectively closed down. After these actions created a firestorm, the CFTC backed down and decided to exempt swaps from its jurisdiction. Here, two problems were encountered. The first problem involved regulatory jurisdiction. Critics complained that the CFTC did not have the authority to exempt swaps from its jurisdiction because the CFTC did not have the authority to regulate swaps. Since most swaps do not contemplate delivery, they do not meet the definition of "transactions involving sale . . . for future delivery." Further, equities, debt instruments, loans, and foreign exchange are not commodities, as stated in the legislation. Moreover, even if swaps were futures contracts involving commodities, trading off an exchange was never contemplated. The second problem was that if swaps were not under its jurisdiction, the CFTC did not have the authority to make regulations preempting state bucket shop laws.

The US Congress remedied this situation in 1991 when it gave the CFTC explicit authority to exempt swaps from its regulation if they met the following criteria:

1 Exemption is in the public interest.
2 The counterparties are institutions.
3 The credit-worthiness of the counterparties is a material consideration.
4 The agreements are not standardized and are not traded through a centralized facility.

The requirement that credit-worthiness be a material consideration prevents the use of clearinghouses for swaps. The requirements that the contracts not be standardized hampers the creation of an over-the-counter secondary market in swaps.

6. SWAP RISKS

Parties to a swap face credit risk due to the possible default of their counterparty. Of course, at the initiation of the swap, when the swap is typically at the money, there is no credit risk. Further, credit risk is minimized by the fact that either no principal is exchanged or, as in the case of currency swaps, the principal exchanged is of comparable value. As we have seen, in the USA there are requirements that counterparty risk be a significant factor in the swap. These requirements are designed to limit the competition of swaps with exchange-traded futures and to limit the use of swaps to more credit-worthy firms. Users of swaps can minimize counterparty risk by limiting the value of swaps with a single dealer.

Dealers can establish limits on the exposure that they can have with each client, establish policies concerning acceptable counterparties (such as only companies rated single A), and have agreements to assign excess exposure to a particular client to a third party. Unlike futures contracts, swaps do not typically provide for a system of margining. The lack of a margining system tends to limit the use of swaps to entities with good credit ratings. In some cases, less credit-worthy firms can enter into swaps if their lower credit standing is factored into the rate.

Swap dealers face sovereign risk, in that changes in laws and regulations in a particular country may affect the ability of counterparties in that country to fulfill their swap obligations. Swap dealers may limit their exposure to swaps in a particular country.

Swap dealers face clearing and settlement risks (see table 14.6). One way of minimizing these risks is by the use of a master agreement, which provides for the offsetting of amounts due and amounts owed to a counterparty in the event of default.

All swap agreements include **termination clauses** that provide for the calculation of losses should a counterparty default. The termination clause may be activated not only by a failure to make required payments under the swap, but also by such events as the downgrading of a counterparty's credit rating. The most widely used method of terminating a swap is the agreement value approach. The nondefaulting counterparty obtains quotes from swap dealers concerning the replacement cost of the swap. The party that holds the out of the money side of the swap then makes a payment to the party that is in the money.

Unlike typical swap users, swap dealers hold many swaps. The changes in the value of these swaps are not offset by changes in the value of the dealer's inventory of commodities and financial instruments. Hence, management of the risk of this swap portfolio requires special attention. The portfolio of swaps is called the **swap book**. When the market for swaps was just getting started, swap banks matched clients with offsetting needs. The necessity of identifying two counterparties with opposite needs was an obstacle to the growth of the swap market. As the market grew and the dealers became more sophisticated, swap dealers began to manage their swaps as a portfolio rather than individually. Hence, the

Table 14.6 Examples of potential operating risks from swap dealings. The cause of the risk is identified in the first column. Then the effect on the firm's market risk and credit program are delineated

Operational risk	Market risk impact	Credit risk impact
Incorrect data entry	Incorrect gaps, positions	Incorrect counterparty exposure
Unverified market data	Incorrect valuations, risks	Incorrect potential exposure, collateral
Careless limit monitoring	Limits exceeded, unauthorized trading	Limits exceeded, insufficient line
Incorrect confirmations	Inappropriate hedges	Incorrect counterparty exposure, netting
Faulty event monitoring	Missed exercise, increased risk exposures	Missed payments, increased exposure
Late reports	Trading blind	Unauthorized payments

Source: *Brewer* 1997, p. 47. Reprinted by permission of Derivatives Strategy.

dealer attempts to assess the exposure of the entire portfolio to risks such as those from interest rate changes, yield curve shifts, exchange rate changes, basis changes (between LIBOR and US Treasury bills, between commercial paper and Federal funds, and the like).

The portfolio approach to hedging is called a **macrohedge**. In one such approach, to hedge the fixed side of the swap book, the swap dealer determines the cash flows that are due during coming periods. The length of these periods, which are called **buckets**, is arbitrary. The dealer then derives a zero–coupon yield curve for the swaps portfolio and for a US Treasury note. These two yield curves are used to calculate the amount of the Treasury note needed to hedge the dealer's swap exposure. (This method is described fully in Bansal, Ellis, and Marshall 1993 and in Kapner and Ellis 1992.)

7. SUMMARY

A swap is a contract evidenced by a single document in which two counterparties agree to exchange periodic payments. The contract commences on its effective date and ends on its maturity date. The basic version of a swap is referred to as "plain vanilla." In a plain vanilla interest rate swap, one counterparty agrees to make payments based on a floating rate, and the other makes payments at a fixed coupon rate. The payments are typically calculated with reference to a notional amount, since actual principal is not usually exchanged at the beginning or end of the contract. At each payment date the floating rate payment and the fixed payment are compared, and the party owing the largest payment pays the difference to the counterparty. The required floating rate payment is determined at each reset date.

In a plain vanilla currency swap, the counterparties swap exchange currencies at the effective date and at maturity. The rates used to calculate both legs of the intermediate payments may be fixed. In a plain vanilla commodity swap, one counterparty pays a fixed price to receive a floating price, and the other counterparty pays a floating price to receive a fixed price. The floating reference price is often an average over some period rather than the price at a particular point in time. Commodity swaps have been extended to include swaps with floating or coupon rates based on the prices of financial products such as the S&P 500.

The possibilities for modifying plain vanilla swaps are endless. One modification that is now common affects the way the floating rate is calculated. Other modifications affect variables, such as the way the notional principal is calculated and the timing of payments.

Options on swaps are called "swaptions." The holder of a swaption has the right to enter into a swap at a later date. A cap can be used to establish a maximum rate to be paid on the floating rate of a swap, and a floor can be used to establish the minimum rate that can be paid on a floating rate. A collar combines a long cap with a short call.

Swaps have been highly successful for the following reasons:

1   They can be implemented speedily.
2   They permit cost savings due to avoidance of marketing, legal, and distribution costs. Taxes may also be avoided.
3   They provide a way to make investments that would otherwise not be possible due to regulatory limitations.

Also contributing to the popularity of swaps is the variety of situations in which they are useful. These include:

1   providing a way for commercial enterprises to alter the capital structure as needed and for investment managers to alter their asset allocation
2   providing protection against losses due to fluctuations in inventory prices, including inventories of physical products and of financial assets

A swap dealer is a counterparty to most swaps. The largest swap dealers are commercial banks. Swap dealers hold swaps in their investment portfolio. Swap dealers manage the risk of their swap book in a number of ways. Use of master agreements limits risk of default affecting just contracts on which the defaulting party has losses. Firms may also limit their dealing with individual counterparties based on the credit-worthiness of the counterparty. It is now common practice to manage the swap book using a macrohedge or portfolio approach. Methodologies have been developed to help swap counterparties evaluate the risk they face given various changes in asset prices and market rates for interest, foreign exchange, and the like.

Swap valuation is based on the net present value of the fixed and floating leg of the swap. At the initiation of the swap, the net present value is zero. Subsequent movements of market interest rates may result in the counterparty having an asset with a positive value, which represents a liability for the other counterparty.

Questions

1 Define the following: swap, actuals, notional assets, and value date.
2 What are the major categories of swaps? Explain briefly.
3 Give an example of a plain vanilla interest rate swap.
4 What is the main advantage of using currency swaps?
5 Is a swaption the same as a swap? Explain.
6 What kinds of variations are available on swap terms?
7 Explain the advantages of swaps.
8 The word bucket has two different meaning in this chapter. Explain each.
9 Explain the risks faced by swap participants.
10 How can a dealer hedge against swap exposure?

▧ Notes ▧

1 The notional value is a nominal amount used to determine payments to each counterparty and does not represent an actual amount owed. Because of offsetting obligations of the counterparties, the actual amount at risk is only about 1–2 percent of the notional principal. These figures were obtained from the International Swap Dealers Association. Up-to-date information may be obtained from their web site: http://www.isda.org.

2 If you prefer not to have fractional units of production, you can assume that all monetary values and units of production are in millions.

▧ References ▧

Bansal, V. K., Ellis, M. E. and Marshall, J. F. 1993: The spot swap yield curve: duration and use. *Advances in Futures and Options Research* 6, 279–90.

Brewer, Wendy 1997: Minimizing operations risk. *Derivatives Strategy Magazine*, July–Aug., p. 47.

Brown, Brendan 1989: *The Economics of the Swap Market*. London: Routledge.

Brown, Keith C. and Smith, Donald J. 1990: Forward swaps, swap options, and the management of callable debt. *Journal of Applied Corporate Finance* 2, 59–71.

——1995: *Interest Rate and Currency Swaps: a tutorial*. Charlottesville, Virginia: The Research Foundation of the Institute of Chartered Financial Analysts.

Einzig, Robert and Lange, Bruce 1990: Swaps at Transamerica: analysis and applications. *Journal of Applied Corporate Finance* 2, 48–58.

Goodman, Laurie S. 1990: The uses of interest rate swaps in managing corporate liabilities. *Journal of Applied Corporate Finance* 2, 35–47.

Kapner, K. R. and Ellis, M. E. 1992: Swap yield curves: par, spot, and forward and the pricing of short-dated swaps. In *The Swaps Handbook: 1991–92 Supplement*, ed. J. F. Marshall and K. R. Kapner.

Marshall, John F. and Kapner, Kenneth R. 1990: *Understanding Swap Finance*. Cincinnati, OH: Southwestern Publishing.

——1993: *Understanding Swaps*. New York: Wiley.

McCord, James H. and Martin, Allan C. 1993: Derivatives – power tools for pension funds. *Financial Executive*, Nov./Dec. 1993.

Saber, Nasser 1994: *Interest Rate Swaps: valuation, trading and processing*. New York: Irwin.

CHAPTER FIFTEEN

Hedging

■ Key terms ■

Basis   the difference between the cash price of an asset and its futures price.

Cross-hedge   the use of a futures contract on one asset to hedge price movements in another asset.

Currency overlay manager   a firm employed to actively and independently manage a portfolio's foreign exchange exposure with a view to reducing risk from this source.

Economic approach to hedge determination   a method of determining whether a short or a long hedge is required by examining the gains and losses from the cash asset and the derivative position.

Gap management   the selection of assets and liabilities according to their duration to achieve a target hedge.

Hedge   an asset position whose payoffs are acquired to offset risk due to price fluctuations of other assets.

Hedge fund   an investment fund that (1) charges a management fee based on its overall performance, (2) increases exposure to unsystematic risk by the use of leverage, and (3) minimizes exposure to systematic risk through the use of short selling.

Hedge ratio   the number of derivative contracts that are needed to hedge a given natural position.

Hedging   the practice of taking positions in financial products to reduce or eliminate risk.

Long hedge   a position in a financial instrument that benefits from an increase in the price of an asset.

Natural long   a cash position that suffers a loss from a decrease in the price of an asset.

Natural short   a cash position that suffers a loss from an increase in the price of an asset.

One-sided natural position   an ownership interest that benefits from price movements in one direction but is not affected by movements in the opposite direction.

Perfect hedge   a hedge position that completely eliminates risk due to fluctuations in the price of the hedged asset.

Short hedge   a position in a financial instrument that benefits from a decline in the price of an asset.

Speculation   the taking of positions in financial assets that are especially risky or short-term in nature, or entering into derivative contracts with the intention of profiting from price changes rather than using the gains to offset losses on other assets.

Speculator   a type of investor who engages in speculation.

Stress test   evaluating the value of a portfolio of derivatives by changing assumptions concerning future levels of various economic and financial variables such as interest rates.

Substitute action approach to hedge determination   a method of determining whether a short or long hedge is required by examining the definitions of a long and a short hedge.

Two-sided natural position   an ownership interest that benefits from price movements in one direction, but loses from price movements in the opposite direction.

Value at risk   the monetary amount of the decline in value that a derivatives portfolio can be expected to sustain during a specified percentage of time periods.

We have seen in previous chapters that there has been an explosion of trading in derivative financial instruments during the last 25 years. This growth is due to the usefulness of these instruments in hedging and speculation. IN THIS CHAPTER, we explore the concept of hedging and explain its economic role and the economic basis of hedging. We also explore how derivatives can be used to hedge.

This chapter is divided into two main sections. In the first section, we provide the background necessary to understand hedging. Specifically, we

- define hedging and identify its economic purpose
- discuss types of inventory positions and how each can be hedged
- discuss how to ascertain what type of hedge is needed

Then, in the next section, we provide a detailed graphical and quantitative discussion of natural and derivative outcomes. We use these graphs to explain the various considerations in hedging. Further, we consider hedging strategies for each of these natural positions, using the following potential derivative positions:

- long futures, short futures, buying calls, buying puts, writing calls, and writing puts.

---

1. INTRODUCTION

Investors start business to earn a return by supplying needed products and services. Risk is inherent in all business activities, and the expected earnings from a business must be sufficient to compensate investors for bearing these risks. Nevertheless, there may be some specific risks that investors in a given business do not wish to bear. This is especially true if there is a small but real risk that a particular occurrence could have serious consequences and possibly even lead to the bankruptcy of the organization. Consider a firm that has a single manufacturing facility. If the plant were destroyed by fire, earthquake, or by other causes the firm might be ruined. Consequently, businesses often purchase casualty insurance, to allow the plant to be rebuilt, and business interruption insurance, to compensate for lost profits during the period the firm is out of business. If the likelihood of loss is very high, the insurance premium will be prohibitive. If the likelihood of loss is very small, insurance may not be necessary.

Another type of risk faced by many firms is that loss due to fluctuations in the value of their inventories will seriously affect the financial viability of the firm. This type of risk cannot typically be transferred to others by purchasing insurance. Instead, modern economies have developed alternative ways of transferring risk due to inventory fluctuation from one party to another. The process of transferring inventory risk is called "hedging." Hedging promotes economic development by enabling investors to undertake projects that they would find too risky if hedging were not available. Derivative instruments have been developed to satisfy hedging needs. We have considered futures, options, and swaps. Specialized markets for trading derivatives both on exchanges and over-the-counter have been developed.

2. BACKGROUND AND FRAMEWORK FOR UNDERSTANDING HEDGING

2.1. HEDGING DEFINED

Hedging is the practice of taking positions in financial products to reduce or eliminate risk. Failure to clearly understand the purpose of hedging can lead to large financial losses and in a number of cases has bankrupted firms. A key to understanding the meaning of hedging is to understand what hedging is not. Hedging is not speculation; hedging is the opposite of speculation. In this book, we define **speculation** as the taking of positions in financial assets that are especially risky or short-term in nature, or entering into derivative contracts with the intention of profiting from price changes, without owning an asset with offsetting price fluctuations. Thus, while the goal of a hedger is to eliminate risk, the goal of a speculator is to make a profit by taking risk. A **speculator** is a type of investor.

Derivative instruments are the tools typically used in hedging. But as the definition of speculation makes clear, speculators can use the same instruments for speculating that hedgers use. Indeed, the only way to distinguish a hedging transaction from a speculative transaction is to ascertain the motive of the initiator of the transaction. Hedging and speculation are often opposite sides of the same coin.

2.2. ECONOMIC PURPOSE

Hedging serves real economic purposes and, in fact, can considerably reduce the costs of production. Hedging can lower the risk faced by investment bankers in underwriting securities, lowering the cost of capital. It can decrease the risk faced by producers in holding inventories as part of their production process, lowering the cost of producing many types of products. Hedging can help financial institutions manage the risk profiles of their assets so that their level of risk is tailored to specific requirements. Because hedging is so useful, managers and investors need an understanding of this tool.

391

It is impossible to have hedging without speculation. Without speculators, the hedging markets will not work. Therefore, it follows logically that speculation also serves real economic purposes and contributes to reducing the costs of production. Individuals who attack speculation as an evil may lack an understanding of how risk management works. We return to these topics later in the chapter, but first we must explore hedging.

Businesses of all kinds, including manufacturers, retailers, farmers, and financial services, are there to make a profit by selling a product or service for more than its cost of production. Often, fluctuations in the prices of inventories of various types are large enough to threaten the financial viability of the firm. If firms hold large inventories or are committed to making purchases at a fixed price, they may suffer from a fall in price. Or if a firm is committed to delivering products at a fixed price and these products are not held in inventory, the firm may suffer a loss if the price of the product increases. The competitors of these firms may be new entrants or established firms without inventories. In either case they will not have suffered inventory losses. Hence, a firm that does have inventories will not be able to pass these losses on to its customers. Therefore, firms frequently seek to protect themselves from changes in the prices of inventories. This protection is called a **hedge**. A **perfect hedge** completely eliminates risk due to fluctuations in the price of the hedged asset.

Why would anyone want a perfect hedge? Hedgers give up potential gains from their positions in assets to protect themselves from losses. Some individuals and firms seek to profit from inventory price fluctuations. In other words, they speculate. But we think it best to view speculation as a separate activity from a firm's normal business. Why would an oil company drill for oil and build refineries and distribution networks if its goal was to speculate on the price of oil? It would be far simpler for the oil firm to speculate using financial instruments and derivatives. Then all the firm needs is a trader, capital, and a telephone to call brokers. Why would a farmer labor in the hot sun all day in order to speculate on the price of agricultural products? Of course, he or she would not. The goal of producers is to sell their products at a price that covers the costs of their inputs and leaves a profit. In the case of the farmer, these costs include seeds, fertilizer, land and buildings, equipment, farm labor, taxes, and interest. If the farmer can make money by predicting price movements, there would be no need to own a farm. The farmer could make much more money much more easily simply by becoming a speculator. Hence, in our view, firms do not operate businesses to make money from speculation. In other words, businesses want to make money from their operations, not from inventory profits.

Hedging is not free. There are transaction costs. Moreover, if speculators demand compensation for absorbing the net supply of hedgers, the speculators will earn this compensation from the hedgers on the side of the market most in demand. The risks faced by a business due to inventory fluctuations must be significant for it to be worthwhile to incur hedging costs. If fluctuations in inventory prices could lead to financial distress, resulting in, say, the downgrading of a firm's credit rating or even bankruptcy, hedging is probably justified. A stable earnings stream may attract better employees and protect managers' jobs. If the firm's stockholders hold undiversified portfolios, it may be more cost-effective for the firm to hedge than for the stockholders to hedge.

The essence of investing is risk taking. Clearly, investors may find hedging useful for making temporary alterations in their portfolios. Whether other types of hedging make sense for investors is an open question. International investors face both investment risk and exchange rate risk. Moreover, the exchange rate risk is typically greater, resulting in more return variability, than the investment risk. Some argue that this risk should be hedged, and others argue that it should not be hedged. We explore the reasons for the contradictory views later.

2.3. NATURAL LONGS AND SHORTS

2.3.1. Natural longs

Many individuals and firms own raw materials that they are holding for use in the production process. Refineries own inventoris of crude oil. This oil may be in tanks on site, or it may be in large ocean-going tankers in transit from distant oil fields. Manufacturers of food products hold large inventories of agricultural commodities, such as wheat, soybeans, and corn. Meat packers own cattle and hogs. Industrial metals such as copper used in manufacturing electronic goods may be held in inventory. Jewelry and photography film manufacturers, among others, hold inventories of precious metals such as gold and silver. All these manufacturers are natural longs. A **natural long** suffers a loss from a decrease in the price of an item used in the course of their business. A natural long may, but does not necessarily, benefit from an increase in the price of the item.

Not all natural longs are involved in manufacturing. Banks hold large positions in fixed income and equity securities. If the prices of these financial instruments go up, then the banks are better off. But if the prices decline, the banks incur losses. Thus, banks are natural longs with respect to this part of their portfolio. Pension plans, insurance companies, and individual investors also own large positions in fixed-income securities and in stocks. They too are natural longs.

Of course, natural longs are happy to benefit from price increases. The problem is that, while there may be profits if prices increase, there may be losses if prices decline. If these losses are sufficiently large, they can lead to the bankruptcy of a business. Probably the best example of the problems that can be encountered by natural longs is the widespread bankruptcies of savings and loan associations in the USA. It is well known that increases in interest rates cause prices of fixed-income securities to fall, and that decreases in interest rates cause prices of fixed-income securities to rise. In general, the longer the maturity of the instrument, the greater its price change in response to a given interest rate movement.

Savings and loans borrowed funds in the form of deposits from their customers. These deposits, which represented liabilities of the savings and loan, were typically repayable in full at face value on demand, usually over a short horizon. For many years, the rates which US savings and loans could pay depositors were fixed by US government regulation. In the early 1980s interest rates increased dramatically. The difference between what savings and loans were allowed to pay depositors and market interest rates became so great that investors began to make enormous withdrawals from savings and loans. To prevent these outflows, the government was forced to remove restrictions on the interest rates that these institutions could pay depositors. Since the deposits were essentially cash equivalents, these liabilities did not fluctuate in value with changes in market interest rates. So the increase in interest rates did not affect the value of the liabilities of savings and loans, but did increase their costs of funds.

The savings and loans used their deposits to invest primarily in mortgages on residential and commercial real estate. Mortgages are long-term financial instruments. When deposit interest rates were fixed, the rates that savings and loans earned on the mortgages were higher than the rate paid to depositors, so that after expenses most savings and loans earned a profit. With respect to their holdings of mortgages, the savings and loans were natural longs. When interest rates increased, the value of the mortgages declined. In many cases, the value of the assets fell below the obligations owed to depositors, and the savings and loan became insolvent. The US government insured most of these institutions through the Federal Savings and Loan Insurance Corporation. Hence, the US government came to own a large part of the savings and loan industry, which required a number of years to liquidate.

2.3.2. Natural shorts

Just as there are businesses that are natural longs, there are also businesses that are natural shorts. A **natural short** gains from a decrease in the price of an item used in the course of its business. A natural short may, but does not necessarily, suffer losses from an increase in the price of the item. For manufacturers, being a natural short means that the business has a negative inventory. In other words, the business has agreed to sell its products at a fixed price, but does not own the materials needed to manufacture these goods or does not have the item in stock. These products may incorporate large amounts of raw materials that the firm does not own. Hence, in effect, the firm has negative inventory. An insurance company may have sold an insurance contract, which calls for the policyholder to pay a premium of 50,000 USD in 6 months. If the insurance company has guaranteed a fixed rate of interest to the policyholder and interest rates fall, the policyholder will be better off, but the insurance company will be worse off. Note that the fall in interest rates results in an increase in the value of the policy. Thus, the insurance company is a natural short.

2.4. Two-sided versus One-sided Positions

Both **two-sided** and **one-sided natural positions** can arise from a firm's inventory positions. Two-sided natural longs benefit from an increase in the price of an item used in the course of their business, but also suffer losses from a decrease in the price of the item. Likewise, a two-sided natural short benefits from a decrease in the price of an inventory item, but suffers losses from an increase in the price of the item. By contrast, a one-sided natural long or short faces risk if the price moves against them, but does not benefit from a favorable price move. The definitions of long and short used here allow for both one-sided and two-sided outcomes by ignoring price changes that are favorable. Protection is needed only for the unfavorable outcomes. One-sided natural positions most commonly arise out of contractual relationships such as those between firms and their suppliers or customers.

An investor who owns a portfolio of common stocks has a two-sided natural long position. The investor benefits from an increase in the price of the stocks and suffers from a decline in the price of the stocks.

An oil exploration and production company may have agreed to deliver oil to a refinery under a firm contract at a fixed price over the next 5 years. If the price of oil increases, the production company is worse off, but if the price of oil declines, the producer is better off. The producer is a two-sided natural short, and the refinery is a two-sided natural long.

A farmer often has a one-sided natural long position. Consider a Florida farmer with orchards of orange trees. A decrease in the price of oranges harms the farmer. If prices increase, the farmer may or may not benefit. The outcome depends on the reason why prices increase. Suppose that a freeze destroys the orange crop in Brazil. Then, the farmer will benefit from the higher prices. But suppose that instead the price increase is due to a freeze in Florida. Then, the farmer's crop may be destroyed. In this case the farmer will not benefit from the price increase. Thus, the farmer has a one-sided rather than a two-sided position. It is also important to specify which side requires the hedge. In the farmer's case, a one-sided hedge with downside protection is needed.

Suppose that a grain elevator firm enters into a contract to buy a farmer's entire crop of wheat at a fixed price. If the farmer has a small crop due to a drought in the region, the price might be high, but the farmer's output will be small. Hence, the grain elevator will not benefit much from a price increase. But if good weather results in a very large harvest, the price will probably be low, and the elevator will experience a large loss on its purchases at the higher contract price. Hence, the grain elevator has a one-side natural short position.

2.5. LONG AND SHORT HEDGES

There are two types of hedges: long hedges and short hedges. To understand hedging, one must understand each type and be able to recognize when each is appropriate. We have seen that there are natural longs and natural shorts. The position that is required to hedge a natural long is called a "short hedge." The position that is required to hedge a natural short is called a "long hedge." Knowing that short hedges go with natural long positions and that long hedges go with natural short positions will minimize potential confusion resulting from terminology.

A **long hedge** is a position in a financial instrument that benefits from an increase in the price of an asset. Likewise, a **short hedge** is a position in a financial instrument that benefits from a decline in the price of an asset. A natural long incurs losses from a price decline. Since a position in a financial instrument that benefits from a price decline provides protection against this loss, it is a suitable hedge. A natural short experiences losses from a price increase. Therefore, a position that benefits from a price increase provides a suitable hedge.

2.6. DETERMINING THE TYPE OF HEDGE NEEDED

There are two basic ways of determining whether a short hedge or a long hedge is needed in a particular circumstance. We consider each.

2.6.1. The economic approach to hedge determination

One way is to look at the gain and loss profile of the natural position and to take a derivative position that provides protection from risk of loss. We call this the **economic approach**

to hedge determination. Assume that the goal of the hedger is to completely eliminate risk due to price fluctuations in the natural position. Then, to provide a hedge, a derivative must provide a gain when the natural position has a loss. If the goal of a hedger is to completely eliminate risk, the monetary value of losses in the hedge position must exactly match the monetary value of gains from the natural position. If the natural position is two-sided, then it may be cheaper to allow losses on the hedge position to offset gains on the natural position. In these cases the hedger gives up the potential for gains in return for the protection afforded by the hedge. The hedger may be willing to give up these potential gains to save money on the cost of obtaining the protection of the hedge and because the firm is not in the business of speculating on price changes on inventory assets.

2.6.2. The substitute action approach to hedge determination

Alternatively, one can use the **substitute action approach to hedge determination** by deciding what action with respect to the natural position is required to eliminate the price risk. In other words, a firm with a natural long position in an inventory item can eliminate its price risk by selling the inventory. If selling the actual inventory is not desirable or practical, the sale can be replicated using a derivative instrument. Thus, a financial position that locks in a sale price provides a short hedge. Similarly, if a natural short purchased an offsetting position in the asset, price risk would be eliminated. Again, replicating the purchase with a derivative instrument provides a hedge. We call this the "substitute action approach."

The substitute action approach applies primarily to futures, but it also provides an indication of which options contracts are likely to provide the most effective hedge. The following definitions from the CBOT specify the substitute action approach for futures:

> The short hedge is, in essence, the sale of a futures contract as a substitute for the sale of the actual commodity.

> The long hedge is, in essence, the purchase of a futures contract as a substitute for the purchase of the actual commodity (Chicago Board of Trade, n.d.).

These definitions are too narrow, in that they do not allow for the use of other types of derivatives. But once the appropriate type of hedge has been determined, a decision can be made on whether to use futures or options.

Risk of price changes from a natural long position in an asset can be eliminated by buying or selling the asset (depending on whether one is a natural long or short) or by a long or short hedge. In other words, selling a futures contract as a substitute for selling the actual asset can eliminate the risk. Why not just sell the underlying interest? Often it is not available for sale. A farmer's crops are still growing in the field and cannot yet be harvested. Oil in transit has not yet arrived at the refinery. Premiums to be invested may not have arrived from the policyholders. A building to be financed with permanent funds may not have been fully built. Until the actual investment can be made, a futures contract can be used to lock in the pruchase price of that asset. Similar considerations apply to long hedges.

For identifying hedge types when futures contracts are to be used, the CBOT definitions are often easier to apply than the economic outcome approach. When applied to options, the CBOT definitions provide some indication of which option positions are likely to provide the most effective hedges. Since a put locks in a sales price, it is likely to provide the best hedge for a natural long position. And since a call locks in a purchase price, the call is likely to provide the best hedge for a natural short position. In some cases the economic approach is easier to use with futures hedges too. Naturally, when used correctly, these two approaches give the same answer concerning the required hedge.

2.6.3. Problems with obtaining a perfect hedge using futures

We assume that in most cases the goal of a hedger should be to obtain a perfect hedge. When deviating from this goal, the hedger becomes a speculator subject to all the associated risks. If the goal of a hedger is to completely eliminate risk, the monetary value of losses in the hedge position must exactly match the monetary value of gains from the natural position.

There are a number of potential obstacles that may prevent a perfect hedge from being achieved. We defined "basis" as the difference between a cash price and a futures price or between two futures prices. We also indicated some reasons why basis might change over the life of a futures contract, such as changes in the availability of transportation. Changes in basis affect the efficacy of futures in hedging. We examine additional problems in obtaining a perfect hedge in the remainder of this section.

Maturity mismatch   An importer may need to buy JPY in 6 weeks to make a payment for purchases, but the futures contracts available for hedging may have maturities of 4 weeks or 8 weeks. The investor faces a risk that the forward prices of JPY for 4, 6, or 8 weeks would move differentially.

Contract size mismatch   On the other hand, the importer mentioned previously might be able to find a futures contract with the needed maturity, but the amount of currency covered by the contract is unlikely to exactly match the importer's needs.

Cross-hedge   A **cross-hedge** is the use of a futures contract on one asset to hedge price movements in another asset. An investor might use the CBOT US Treasury bond contract to hedge a cash long position in corporate bonds, since there are no futures contracts on individual corporate bonds. In general, interest rate movements will cause the price of the corporate bonds and the US Treasury bonds to move together. But there might be differences. For example, changes in the rate of taxation of corporate bonds relative to government bonds would cause differential price changes in the two types of bonds.

2.7. POTENTIAL PROBLEMS WITH HEDGING PROGRAMS

The purpose of hedging programs is to reduce risk. But managers need to be careful about how hedging programs are implemented. There are numerous examples of programs that started out hedging, but later individuals implementing the program begin to speculate rather than hedge.

Problems with hedging programs are not limited to rogue employees. One of the largest derivative losses of all time came about through an apparent failure of senior management to understand the nature of the hedging program. MG Refining and Marketing (MGRM) was the US subsidiary of the German firm Metallgesellschaft AG (MAG), a conglomerate with more than 250 subsidiaries in the fields of trade, engineering, and financial services. MGRM operated a hedging program that began to require substantial cash flow to cover margin losses on the futures positions used to hedge the firm's natural long position. Reacting to the increasing cash flow requirements, senior management installed a new management for MGRM. The new management liquidated the hedge, which eventually resulted in a loss of 1.3 billion USD on the exposed natural position. Additional details are provided in box 15.1.

2.8. RISK OF HEDGING PROGRAMS

There have been many cases in which hedging programs have not worked out as expected. We have discussed the operational problems encountered by MGRM and possible problems due to changes in basis. These risks must be taken into account before the hedge is established. Managers need to **stress test** their hedges by examining the outcomes if the assumptions made in initiating the hedge prove to be incorrect. Moreover, managers need to consider both usual and worst case departures from expectations. Failure to adequately consider these worst case scenarios is one of the main reasons that hedging programs fail.

3. HEDGING WITH FUTURES AND OPTIONS CONTRACTS

In this section we deal with hedging using futures contracts and options contracts, but not swaps or forward contracts, which are over-the-counter alternatives to futures. The concepts presented here for futures also apply generally to all derivatives. It may be possible to initiate the options strategies examined here using either exchange-traded or over-the-counter options.

3.1. HEDGING WITH FUTURES

Figure 15.1 repeats the profiles of possible outcomes at maturity for futures contracts. (a) shows the long futures outcomes, and (b) the short futures outcomes. The value of the underlying asset is presented on the horizontal axis, and the monetary outcome on the vertical axis. Short futures have the possibility of unlimited losses from a price increase. Even though prices are limited to falling to zero, such a decline may produce gains on a short futures contract so great that they might as well be unlimited. Therefore, we sometimes refer to the gains as being unlimited, even though we know that this in not strictly true. Likewise, long futures positions can realize potentially unlimited gains from a price increase in the underlying asset, but losses are limited to the value of the contract at the initiation of the position. Because these potential gains are so large, we view them as unlimited from a practical viewpoint.

BOX 15.1
Metallgesellschaft AG

The experience of Metallgesellschaft AG (MAG) during the early 1990s illustrates the risks of hedging programs. MAG was a German conglomerate whose major stockholders included several German banks and the Kuwait Investment Authority. One of MAG's subsidiaries, the US firm MG Refining and Marketing (MGRM) sold and stored petroleum products. In connection with its sales activities, MGRM entered into 5-year fixed price contracts with its customers on heating oil, gasoline, and diesel fuel. Customers were allowed to terminate their contracts if market prices increased significantly above the MGRM contract price. MGRM wanted to profit from its marketing and storage expertise, but did not want to speculate on oil price fluctuations.

MGRM's natural position was short, so to hedge, the firm entered into long crude oil contracts traded on the New York Mercantile Exchange. Because of their liquidity, the firm mostly used contracts with a 1-month maturity, rolling over the contracts as they matured. MGRM went long sufficient contracts to offset its entire natural short position. (For a discussion of using short-term futures contracts to hedge longer-term cash positions see Culp and Miller 1994, 1995.) Futures prices equal the current spot price plus the basis. If the basis is positive, the market is in contango, and if the basis is negative, the market is in backwardation.

For a physical commodity, basis reflects physical storage costs (warehouse space) and interest costs, less any benefit (convenience yield) from having inventory on hand to prevent stock outs. Futures markets for most physical commodities are typically in contango, but when MGRM initiated its hedging program, and continuing for several years thereafter, the crude oil futures market was in backwardation. Consequently, each time the futures contracts expired, there was a gain. In 1993 crude oil prices fell dramatically, causing losses on the futures leg of MGRM's hedge. Moreover, the market moved to contango. MGRM experienced a gain on its natural position that more than offset its loss on its futures position, but there was a cash flow problem, because the futures contract was market-to-market daily, requiring significant additional margin, while the futures position was not market-to-market until delivery. MGRM quickly exhausted a 500 million USD line of credit. Moreover, the New York Mercantile Exchange asked for additional margin above that normally required. At first MGRM's parent met its needs for funds to meet its margin requirements, but as the demand for funds grew, the parent became alarmed and brought in new management for the subsidiary. The new management team liquidated the hedging program. Termination of the hedging program left MGRM unhedged, and subsequent oil price increases resulted in losses of 1.3 billion USD. Culp and Miller (1995) characterize this as evidence of operational risk, in that it reflects a failure of the parent's board to understand that MGRM was hedging, not speculating.

Combining the two–sided natural long position shown in figure 15.2 with the short futures position shown in figure 15.1 and combining the two–sided natural short position shown in figure 15.2 with the long futures position shown in figure 15.1 produce the outcome shown in figure 15.3 (a). Regardless of fluctuations in the price of the underlying asset, the outcome on the hedged position is unchanged. Hence, a two–sided natural long can be hedged using a short futures position, and a two–sided natural short can be hedged using a two–sided long futures position.

If the natural position is not two–sided, the use of a futures contract can produce a loss. Figure 15.3 (b) shows the outcome profile from combining a one-sided natural long

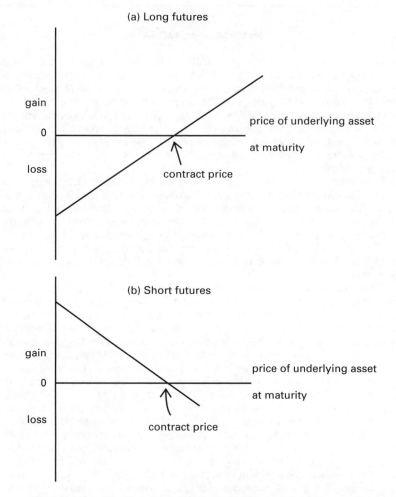

Figure 15.1 Profiles for futures contract outcomes at maturity.

position with a two-sided futures position, and figure 15.3 (c) shows the outcome profile from combining a one-sided natural short position with a long futures position. In both cases unlimited losses remain possible with the hedged positions. Hence, futures contracts are not typically used in hedging one-sided natural positions. We illustrated this earlier in this chapter using the case of a Florida orange producer.

3.2. HEDGING WITH OPTIONS

In this section we begin an analysis of options as hedges. To simplify the analysis, at first we make two assumptions about the options examined: (1) the premium is zero, and (2) the price of the underlying interest equals the striking price of the option. We eliminate these assumptions later.

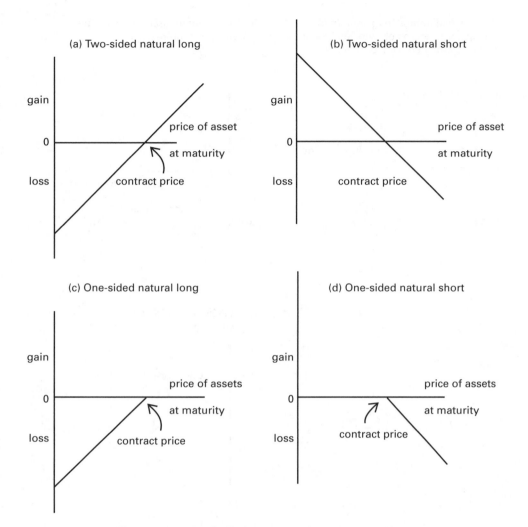

Figure 15.2 Profiles of outcomes for natural positions.

3.2.1. Case 1: Assuming premiums are zero and the hedge is initiated when the contract is at the money

Given our two assumptions, figure 15.4 shows the profile of outcomes at maturity from owning calls, writing calls, owning puts, and writing puts. In hedging, the goal is to eliminate risk of loss due to a price change. Note that when premiums are zero, short positions can produce only losses. Hence, under these circumstances, these short options positions cannot be useful in hedging. But the long put and long call positions can be very useful in hedging. Figure 15.5 shows the outcome profiles for four cases: combining a long put with a two-sided natural long position, combining a long call with a two-sided natural short position, combining a long put with a one-sided natural long position, and

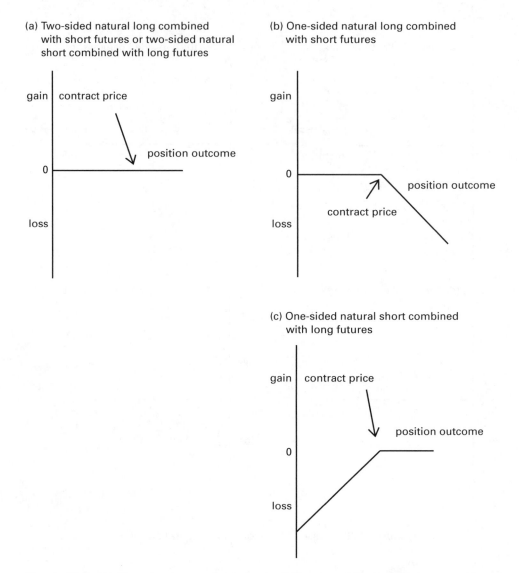

(a) Two-sided natural long combined with short futures or two-sided natural short combined with long futures

gain | contract price

position outcome

0

loss

(b) One-sided natural long combined with short futures

gain

0

contract price

position outcome

loss

(c) One-sided natural short combined with long futures

gain | contract price

position outcome

0

loss

Figure 15.3 Profiles of outcomes for natural positions combined with futures positions.

combining a long call with a one-sided natural short position. We can see that in these cases the options provide an effective hedge, since none of the potential outcomes produce a loss.

Notice that, in the absence of premiums, a long put and a short call together have exactly the same gain/loss profile as a short futures position. And, again in the absence of premiums, a long call and a short put have the same gain/loss profile as a long futures position.

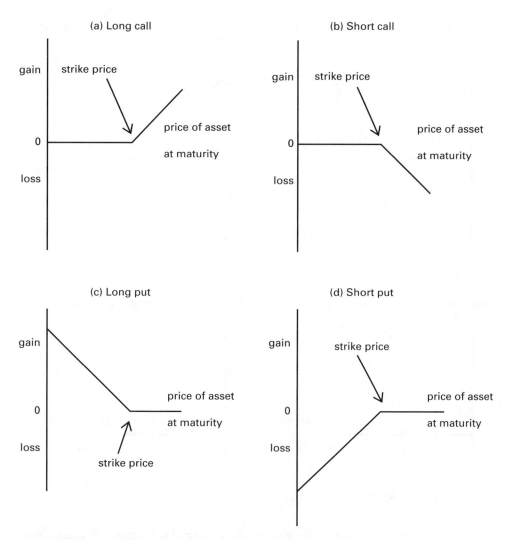

Figure 15.4 Outcome profiles from option positions. Premium = 0, asset price = strike price at start.

3.2.2. Case 2: Hedging with options when premiums are positive

Next, we drop the assumption that the premium is zero, but retain the assumption that the price of the underlying security equals the striking price when the hedge is initiated. The presence of a positive premium results in a displacement of the option outcome profile by the amount of the premium. The results for long and short positions can be seen in figure 15.6. For long positions, the potential gain is reduced by the premium, and there is now also the possibility of the loss of the entire premium. This displacement affects the usefulness of the option positions in hedging. A long call can still be used to hedge a natural short position,

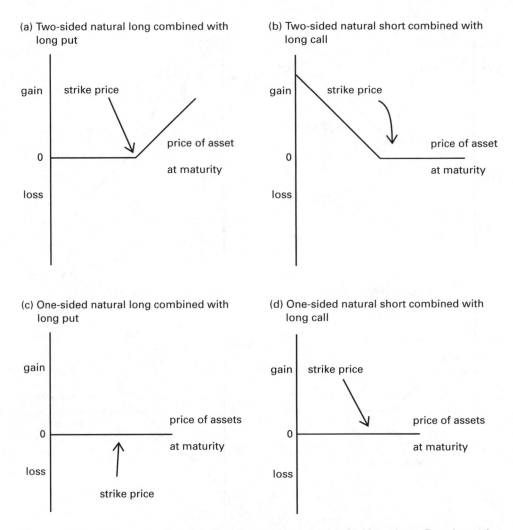

Figure 15.5 Outcome profiles from natural positions hedged with options. Premium price = 0, asset price = strike price at start.

and a long put can still be used to hedge a natural long position. But the gain from the hedge is reduced by the amount of the premium. For these two long positions, the premium can be viewed as a fee paid by the owners of these contracts to obtain the protection afforded by the contracts. Given the assumption that the price of the underlying asset equals the striking price at the initiation of the hedge, the premium is entirely an excess premium. If the option closes out of the money, the cost of the hedge is the option premium. If the option closes in the money, the cost of the hedge is also the option premium, but there may also be a gain on the option that will partially offset the cost. A hedger with a natural two–sided position may prefer to use options rather than sacrifice the potential gains from a favorable move in the price of the underlying asset by using futures or forward contracts.

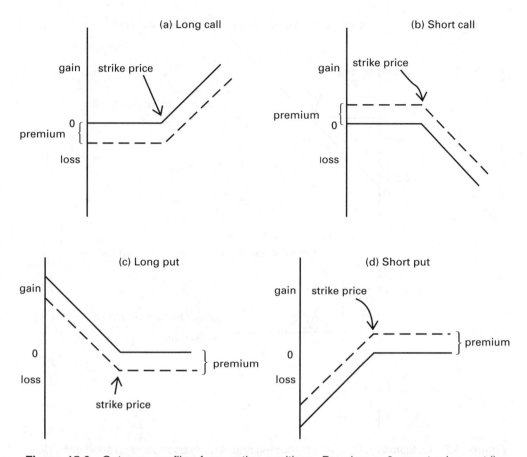

Figure 15.6 Outcome profiles from option positions. Premium > 0, asset price = strike price at start. Solid line: premium = 0, which replicates figure 15.4; dashed line: premium > 0.

But the most important difference in potential hedging strategies for case 2 is that the short put and the short call positions now can produce gains. Potential losses on natural positions can be partially or fully offset by the premium, so that it is also possible to have an overall gain equal to the amount of the premium. The entire premium will be gained if the option is out of the money at expiration. The gains on these short options can be used to offset losses on natural positions. A hedger who seeks protection only against small price changes in the underlying asset may write options rather than buy options. If the price of the underlying asset does not change between the initiation of the contract and the contract's maturity, then the hedger will earn the excess premium.

Suppose that an investor has a long position in the stock of IBM. This is a two-sided natural long position. This position can be hedged by buying a put. If the price of IBM falls, the put will provide protection, but the protection will be reduced by the amount of the premium. If the price of IBM remains the same, the entire premium will be lost. If the

405

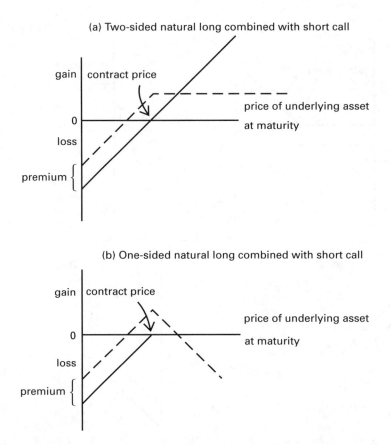

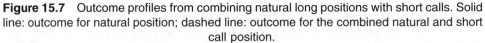

Figure 15.7 Outcome profiles from combining natural long positions with short calls. Solid line: outcome for natural position; dashed line: outcome for the combined natural and short call position.

price of IBM increases, all the increase in value less the option premium will be retained by the owner of the put.

Alternatively, an investor who holds IBM long can hedge by writing a call. In this case, a fall in the price of IBM will be hedged up to the amount of the premium. If the price of IBM increases, losses on the option position will offset gains on the natural position fully, except that the option premium will be earned. If the price of IBM does not change, the premium will be earned. Thus, investors who expect little or no change in the price of the underlying asset might prefer to hedge a long position by writing a call rather than by buying a put. But there is a risk that the prediction is wrong and the price of the underlying assets will change substantially. The outcome profile for a two-sided natural long combined with a short call is illustrated in figure 15.7 (a) and for a one-sided natural long combined with a short call in figure 15.7 (b).

If the investor had a short position in IBM, then the position could be hedged by buying a call or by writing a put. If the alternative of writing a put is chosen, then the amount of protection afforded is limited to the premium received. However, the investor also gives up the potential for gain if the price of the stock declines below the strike price.

3.2.3. Case 3: Hedging with in the money and out of the money options

Heretofore, we have assumed that only at the money options were used for hedging. Now we drop that assumption and briefly consider the use of out of the money and in the money options for hedging. If a hedge is obtained by writing options, the protection is provided by the premium. Hence, options that are out of the money provide less protection than in the money options. On the other hand, options that are in the money have more risk than out of the money options. If the hedge is held until the expiration of the option, the writer must pay the amount that the option is in the money. If an out-of-the-money call has been written, the price of the underlying asset can increase up to the strike price before any money will be due at maturity. Every increase in the price at maturity of an in the money call that has been written requires an additional payment. Writing puts as hedges works similarly. The hedger must evaluate the tradeoff between added protection and added risk.

In the money or out of the money options may also be purchased as hedges. For simplicity, we assume that the hedges are held until the expiration of the options. An out of the money option can be purchased for a lower premium, so less money is at risk. On the other hand, an out of the money option does not provide any hedge protection for the difference between the price of the underlying asset when the hedge is initiated and the strike price of the option. Purchase of in the money options puts more premium at risk. On the other hand, the delta of an in the money option is higher, so it provides more protection. Again, the hedger must evaluate the tradeoff between added protection and added risk.

3.2.4. Case 4: Overall results

For completeness, we can drop all our assumptions and allow a positive premium, a positive excess premium, and the option to be either in the money or out of the money at the initiation of the hedge. In this case the option would generally have a positive excess premium, and, when the option is in the money, it would also have a positive contribution to the premium from that source. The hedging considerations are very similar to those considered above. When the option is in the money, the option premiums do not change dollar for dollar with changes in the price of the underlying asset. The reason for this is that changes in the options premium due to changes in the price of the underlying stock are partially offset by changes in the excess premium.

When out of the money options are used at the initiation of a hedge, the premiums are greater than zero, but less than they would be if the option were at the money. Buying an out of the money put or call will provide hedging protection, but the amount of protection is not as great as it would be if the option were at the money. On the other hand, the cost of the out of the money call and put are lower than that for an at the money option. The hedger must decide whether the higher premium cost is worth the added protection. If out of the money options are written to initiate hedges, again the premium is less than if the options were at the money. Hence, writing these options provides less protection, since the

407

protection comes from the premium. On the other hand, the potential losses on the option position are also reduced. Again, the hedger's tradeoff between the reduced premium and the reduced possibility of loss on the option position must be assessed.

Under some circumstances a natural long could be hedged by shorting a put, and a natural short could be hedged by buying a call. If the options are out of the money when the hedge is initiated, then the options could expire worthless and thus produce a gain. This gain would offset any loss on the underlying position up to the amount of the premium. While it is unlikely that use of these option positions would be desirable in hedging, we present them for the sake of completeness.

3.3. HEDGING WITH SECURITIES

Consider the US savings and loans discussed earlier. As mentioned, these savings and loans are natural longs with respect to their portfolios of mortgages. Therefore, a short hedge is required. The deposits of the savings and loans do not serve as a hedge, because the value of these deposits generally does not fluctuate. Above, we examined the use of derivatives in establishing a hedge for the savings and loans. It is also possible to hedge using other types of securities. Of course, the savings and loan would be hedged if it simply sold its mortgages and held short-term instruments such as commercial paper with a 1-day maturity. Based on the substitute action approach, it is clear that if the sale of the mortgages would eliminate price risk, a suitable hedge must provide the same type of protection. In the previous sections we explored the use of derivatives to achieve this goal. Another approach would be for the savings and loan to raise funds by issuing long-term bonds or long-term certificates of deposit. These securities could provide an effective hedge, since their prices fluctuate in the appropriate direction when interest rates change.

Banks are major dealers in derivatives markets. In the course of their operations, they may find themselves with natural short positions in fixed-income obligations. One approach is to hedge these price risks with additional derivative contracts. But the bank might also be able to hedge by buying fixed-income securities.

3.4. HEDGE RATIOS

There are at least two approaches used to determine the appropriate **hedge ratio**, the number of contracts that are needed to hedge a given natural position. One is the historical approach, in which a historical relationship between the price changes of the futures contract prices and the price changes of the cash market are used to estimate a hedge ratio. Another uses theoretical models to derive hedge ratios.

3.4.1. Historical data approach

In the historical approach, past price relationships are estimated and used to calculate hedge ratios. Suppose that we wish to use a futures contract on a cash commodity to hedge a natural position. We can derive the formula for the minimum risk hedge ratio. Let σ_F be the variance of the futures price, σ_s be the variance of the spot price, σ_{Fs} be the covariance of the prices of the futures and spot contracts, and ρ_{sF} be the coefficient of correlation between the cash price and the futures price. We know that the variance of a portfolio (p) of one unit of the cash asset (s) and X units of the futures contract (F) is:

$$\sigma_p^2 = \sigma_s^2 + X^2\sigma_F^2 + 2X\rho_{sF}\sigma_s\sigma_F$$

Taking the derivative of portfolio risk with respect to X gives the following hedge ratio:

$$\text{Hedge ratio} = (\rho_{sF}\sigma_s\sigma_F)/\sigma_F^2 = \sigma_{sF}/\sigma_F^2 \text{ or } (\rho_{sF}\sigma_s)/\sigma_F$$

One way to estimate this hedge ratio is to regress the historical spot price holding period returns (R_s) on the historical futures holding period returns (R_f):

$$R_s = \alpha + \beta R_f + \varepsilon$$

where α and β are parameters to be estimated and ε is a random error term. The estimate of β is the risk-minimizing hedge.

In some cases we may have more than one spot price to deal with. Suppose that a bakery uses flour to produce bread. We are concerned about two commodity prices, the price of flour and the price of bread, and the price of the futures contract. Assume that both the flour and the bread are quoted in one unit, which we can define in any way we wish as long as we use the appropriate corresponding prices. Using historical data, we can regress the holding period returns for flour (R_{fl}) against the holding period returns for the futures contract (R_f), denoting the coefficient of the change in the price of the futures contract for flour by β_{fl}:

$$R_s = \alpha + \beta_{fl}R_f + \varepsilon$$

We can also regress the change in the price of bread against the change in the price of the futures contract, denoting the coefficient of the futures contract in this regression as β_b:

$$R_s = \alpha + \beta_b R_f + \varepsilon$$

These results produce an estimated hedge ratio of

$$\text{Hedge ratio} = \beta_b - \beta_{fl}.$$

If β_b is 0.92, and β_{fl} is 0.62, the estimated hedge is 0.30. In other words, for every unit of bread that the bakery produces, a futures contract covering only 0.30 units of flour is needed. In estimating these hedge ratios, issues arise concerning the appropriate interval over which to measure price changes (daily, weekly, or monthly), nonsynchroneity in the various price series, and possible day-of-the-week, time-of-the-year biases.

3.4.2. Theoretical approach

There are many instances in which it is also possible to determine a hedge ratio using a theoretical model. One of the most common examples is the use of duration by financial institutions in constructing hedges. Recall that duration is the time-weighted maturity of an asset. Financial institutions hold a portfolio of long and short positions in financial assets, many of which have a promised cash flow stream that is known in advance. Efforts by financial institutions to match, at least to some extent, the duration of their assets and liabilities is called **gap management**. Some financial institutions attempt to match the duration of their assets and liabilities exactly so that they are immunized from risk due to fluctuations in interest rates. Others may have objectives such as limiting potential losses due to interest rate fluctuations to a stated amount.

Financial institutions can use both securities and derivatives to accomplish their hedging goals. Spot and futures prices converge at maturity, so it might well make sense to hedge a portfolio of bonds using futures contracts covering a portfolio of underlying assets with similar maturities.

3.5. Summary of Section 3

A natural long position can be hedged by shorting a futures contract, buying a put, or writing a call. A natural short position can be hedged by going long a futures contract, buying a call, or writing a put. Under some circumstances a natural long can be hedged by shorting a put, and a natural short by shorting a call. If the natural position is two-sided, the futures position offsets both gains and losses on the natural position. A hedger may prefer to buy an option, risking the loss of the premium in exchange for the possibility of gain on the underlying asset. The hedger may also prefer to write an option, risking the possibility of loss on the underlying asset in exchange for the possibility of gaining the option premium. In this case the protection afforded by the hedge is limited to the amount of the option premium. Hence, the amount of protection provided by writing a call or put depends on whether and to what extent the option is in the money and the amount of the excess premium. By writing options, the hedger also potentially sacrifices at least a portion of the potential gain from the underlying asset. If the natural position is one-sided, the futures would generally not provide a suitable hedge. Instead, a long or short options position would be more appropriate. If the option-writing approach is used, again, it must be remembered that the protection is limited to the amount of the premium. Further, when the natural position is one-sided, there is potential for substantial loss on short option positions that will not be offset by a gain on the underlying asset.

4. ADDITIONAL HEDGING TOPICS

4.1. Hedge Funds

In 1949 Alfred Windslow Jones developed the concept of the **hedge fund**, which had three unusual characteristics: namely, the use of leverage, short selling, and performance fees (see Lederman and Klein 1995 for a description of hedge funds). Jones's goal was to emphasize asset selection ability rather than market timing. In an extreme case, the monetary amount of assets held long and short would be equal, and the short position would be chosen to hedge the systematic risk of the long positions. If the hedge is successful, the portfolio has exposure only to the unsystematic risk of the long securities. Of course, if the fund manager can also select assets likely to experience unfavorable unsystematic events, the fund could benefit from superior asset selection in the short positions as well. Because the combined long and short positions are presumably less risky, the fund manager can increase the risk level of the fund through the use of leverage. The third innovation is the use of a performance fee in which the fund manager receives, say, 20 percent of the profits of the fund rather than a fee based on the amount of assets the fund holds.

An example might help. Suppose that a fund started with 100 USD. The fund might borrow another 40 USD and buy stocks with an aggregate value of 140 USD. To offset part of the risk, the fund might short stocks with an aggregate value of 60 USD, so that if the hedge is effective, the net exposure to the systematic risk of the market is $140 - 60 = 80$ USD, or 80 percent of the initial value of the portfolio. The fund pays interest on 40 USD of borrowing but earns interest on the proceeds of the short sale, although at a lower rate.

Jones's fund was highly successful, but obscure, until the publication of an article by Carol Loomis (1966). This article publicized Jones's outstanding results. Over the previous 10 years, the Dreyfus fund had the best performance among mutual funds. Jones's results bested Dreyfus's performance by 87 percentage points even after taking fees into account. The publication of this article began a period of rapid growth of the hedge fund industry. By the mid-1990s the value of the equity held by hedge funds had grown to 70 billion USD.

4.2. Value at Risk

The Group of Thirty's Global Derivatives Study Group (1993) made 20 recommendations for derivatives dealers and end-users and four recommendations for regulators and governments.[1] From our perspective the most important recommendations were:

1 "Dealers should mark their derivatives positions to market, on at least a daily basis, for risk management purposes."
2 "Dealers should use a consistent measure to calculate daily the market risk of their derivatives positions and compare it to market risk limits."
   a. "Market risk is best measured as 'value at risk' using probability analysis based upon a common confidence interval (e.g., two standard deviations) and time horizon (e.g., one-day exposure)."
   b. "Components of market risk that should be considered across the term structure include: absolute price or rate change (delta); convexity (gamma), volatility (vega), time decay (theta); basis or correlation; and discount rate (rho)."
3 "Dealers should regularly perform simulations to determine how their portfolios would perform under stress conditions."

Value at risk is the monetary amount of the decline in value that a derivatives portfolio can be expected to sustain during a specified percentage of time periods.[2] The specified percentage is typically either 1 percent or 5 percent, and the time period can be daily, weekly, monthly, or any other period. Daily periods are commonly used. Assume a 5 percent probability and a daily time period. If value at risk is 50,000 USD, then this portfolio can expect to sustain a decline in value of 50,000 USD or more on 5 days out of 100 days. This number can be presented to the board of directors, investors, and regulators to indicate the exposure of the firm.

There are a number of ways to calculate value at risk (for a more detailed discussion see Linsmeier and Pearson 1996). We will describe a popular method used to calculate daily value at risk. Assume that we are calculating daily value at risk using a 5 percent probability. The first step is to identify the variables that determine the value of each derivative in the portfolio. For interest rate derivatives this might involve exchange rates for each currency and interest rates for each currency. Typically, interest rates for multiple points along the yield curve are required. Other types of derivatives might require stock and commodity prices, inflation rates, and the like. Once these factors are identified, data is collected for the last 101 days. Then, beginning at day −100 the percentage change in each variable is calculated for each day, to yield 100 changes. For each variable, the oldest change is applied to yesterday's value to create a hypothetical value for today. Then the next oldest change is applied to the first hypothetical value to create a hypothetical value for tomorrow. This process continues until 100 projected values have been calculated for each variable.

In the next step the projected values for each day are used to value each derivative, and an aggregate portfolio value is obtained for each day. These portfolio values are sorted from highest to lowest, and the portfolio value with the fifth largest loss is the value at risk.

The value at risk measure has a number of obvious limitations. If too much historical data is used, the measure may not reflect current market conditions. If too little data is used, the measure may not be estimated accurately. Moreover, the measure will not indicate what would happen to the portfolio if the determinants of the derivatives' values took on a worst case or very extreme outcome. These might be more important than more common but less drastic outcomes. This is undoubtedly the reason why the Group of Thirty recommends stress testing of the portfolio. This allows for the consideration of more extreme outcomes than are likely to be found using the value at risk approach.

4.3. HEDGING FOREIGN EXCHANGE RISK

Firms are increasingly operating globally. Hence, they may have revenues and expenses in many different currencies. Companies have developed sophisticated strategies for managing their foreign exchange and minimizing risk due to currency fluctuations. Companies such as Coca-Cola use hedging to protect their profits (see box 15.2). There has also been a marked increase in cross-border portfolio investment in recent years. This trend has led to interest in whether investors should hedge their foreign exchange exposure. The answer for individuals and portfolio managers may not be the same as the answer for companies. We have argued that risk is inherent in investments. The question is whether hedging risk due to currency fluctuations reduces risk sufficiently to justify its cost. There has been no definitive answer to this question, but a number of factors that are useful in making a decision have been identified.

Some argue that currency risk should be fully hedged all the time, some that currency risk should be partially hedged, and some that there is no need for hedging.

BOX 15.2
Coca-Cola tells analysts that currency hedging protects profits

According to its president, M. Douglas Ivester, Coca-Cola uses hedges mostly to protect itself from currency fluctuations. The firm benefits from a portfolio effect because of its dealings in almost 200 currencies. Firms dealing in fewer currencies would not realize this portfolio effect to the same extent. The purpose of Coke's hedging program is to eliminate risk to earnings due to currency fluctuations, according to Ivester. To increase this protection, Coke extended its hedging horizon, which had been 3 months, to 3 years.

(For additional details see *Wall Street Journal* 1996.)

Fully hedging currency risk In our discussion of futures, we indicated that the net hedging hypothesis argued that speculators must be compensated for taking risk from hedgers. Using similar reasoning, Perold and Schulman (1988) conclude that "to assume one will receive a premium for holding foreign currency is to assume the other side of the transaction will pay a premium for U.S. dollars, that 'they need our currency more than we need theirs.'" While there may be periods of time when one can earn a premium for holding a particular currency, there is no reason to believe that these premiums will be consistently positive or negative. Moreover, these authors present evidence that there is substantial risk reduction from hedging currency risk.

Partial hedging Black (1990) developed a model that leads to the proposition that there is an optimal hedge ratio that applies to every investor who holds nondomestic securities. "When average risk tolerance is the same across countries, every investor will hold the same mix . . . of exchange risk (in a diversified basket of foreign currencies)."

No hedging According to Delaney (1997), "many investment experts don't believe in hedging to begin with. They argue that it's nearly impossible to predict currency swings, the ascents and declines cancel each other out over the long term anyway, and hedging mechanisms are just an added expense for shareholders." Froot (1993) argues that the benefits from currency hedging are short-term, and that over the long term the costs of hedging outweigh the benefits. According to Mark Riepe, a vice-president of Ibbotson Associates,[3] "Those who choose to hedge their foreign currency raise the correlation with U.S. stock, and so the diversification benefit won't be nearly as great" (Clements 1997).

Additional factors are also related to whether a portfolio should be hedged.

Concentration of investments in a particular country An international portfolio manager may like the prospects for the companies in a particular country. These companies may come from different industries and provide diversification benefits. In the process of making decisions about which companies to buy, an international portfolio manager is also making decisions about the currency exposure of the portfolio. While the underlying investments may be desirable, the concentration of currency exposure in particular countries may not be. In this case the fund managers may seek to hedge this currency exposure.

413

Diversification benefits from holding a portfolio of currencies   We have argued previously that there are risk-reduction benefits from holding a diversified portfolio. The view that an international investor who buys a portfolio of international stocks should hedge all currency risk so that only the domestic currency is held is contrary to this prescription. Hedging typically concentrates the portfolio in a single currency. In some cases this would be beneficial, but in many cases it would be harmful. Suppose that a Russian investor held an internationally diversified portfolio, but, in an effort to reduce currency risk, hedged 100 percent back into the Russian ruble. When the ruble lost most of its value vis-à-vis other currencies in the late 1990s, the investor would be significantly worse off. In late 1997 the value of the Indonesian rupia declined from just over 2,000 to 1 USD at mid-year to more than 15,000 to 1 USD less than 6 months later. Indonesians who hedged their international holdings back into their domestic currency certainly suffered significant losses.

If it is agreed that a portfolio's currency exposure should be hedged, then who should do the hedging? Traditional equity and fixed income managers may not be equipped to manage currencies. There is a growing practice of employing a **currency overlay manager** to actively and independently manage foreign exchange exposure. The overlay manager begins with the existing exposure of the portfolio and attempts to reduce risk through the net sale of nondomestic currencies. Note that the overlay manager is hedging, as defined in this chapter. The goal is to reduce risk. Hence, Layard-Liesching (1997) argues that "the currency overlay manager is not permitted to increase preexisting currency exposure by the net purchase of foreign currency." Manning (1996) reports on the status of currency overlay management in a number of countries. The largest overlay market is in the USA. Outside the USA, the largest markets are in the Netherlands and Australia. Though the potential markets in Japan and the UK are large, the market for overlay management has been slower to develop than in the USA, where the currency overlay management business grew from almost nothing at the beginning of the 1990s to have more than 40 billion USD under management by the mid-1990s.

Some investment professionals view currencies as a separate asset class that should be managed in the same way as any other assets. Arnott and Pham (1993) argue that currency markets are not efficient, because two of the largest participants do not have a profit motive. Central banks attempt to limit exchange rate volatility, and corporations seek to hedge their inventory positions and cash flows. Levich and Thomas (1993) take a similar view, stating that "A more aggressive active currency overlay strategy earned the highest returns . . . of any strategy we examined, yet was less risky than not hedging at all" (p. 69). According to Day (1997), "active management of currencies . . . can enhance portfolio returns" (p. 39).

5. SUMMARY

Hedging is the practice of taking positions in financial products to reduce or eliminate risk. To the extent that an individual or firm is pursuing another goal, they are not hedging. A perfect hedge completely eliminates risk due to fluctuations in the price of the hedged asset. Producers, financial institutions, individuals, and others often face risk from fluctuations in the price of assets owned or contracted for. Natural longs face risk of loss due to price decreases in an asset, and natural shorts face risk due to price increases in an asset. One-sided natural longs and shorts do not have the potential for gain from a favorable movement in the price of the asset, whereas two-sided natural longs and shorts do have a prospect of such a gain. Natural longs require short hedges, and natural shorts require long hedges.

Hedging fulfills the economic function of allowing the transfer of risk due to price fluctations in these assets to others. Speculators take positions in derivatives contracts with the intention of profiting from price changes. Since it is unlikely that the desired positions of long and short hedgers match exactly, speculators are necessary for the functioning of hedging markets. But hedging and speculation are clearly different activities.

One approach to determining the needed hedge position is to compare the economic outcome from carrying the underlying asset with the economic outcome from the contemplated derivative position. Gains on the derivative position should offset losses on the underlying asset. This is the economic outcome approach. Alternatively, the substitute action approach identifies hedge positions by examining whether a purchase or sale of the cash asset would eliminate risk due to fluctuation in the asset's price. Then, a substitute action involving, say, the purchase or sale of a futures contract, is undertaken instead. There are a number of reasons why a futures position might not provide a perfect hedge, including basis risk, changes in the relationship between the cash price of an asset and its futures price, maturity mismatch, contract size mismatch, and the use of cross-hedges by hedging one asset using a derivative on another asset.

Historically, many firms, especially financial institutions, have hedged using securities, but derivative instruments have become increasingly popular for hedging. These derivative instruments include long and short positions in futures and forward contracts and the purchase and writing of puts and calls. For two-sided natural positions, common hedging strategies are long and short futures positions, and the purchase of puts and calls. Hedgers purchasing options give up the premium paid in return for the protection afforded by the option. On the other hand, hedging using options may preserve potential for gain from price movements in the underlying asset. Hedgers who use futures typically give up the potential for gains if the price movement in the underlying asset is favorable for the protection afforded when the price movement in the underlying asset is unfavorable. Hedging with futures avoids the necessity of paying the option premium. It is also possible to hedge by writing options, but these hedging strategies generally provide less protection from unfavorable price movements in the underlying asset. On the other hand, depending on the actual movements in the price of the underlying asset, the financial outcome may be superior to the other alternatives.

The concept of the hedge fund was developed by Alfred Windslow Jones. A hedge fund uses leverage, short selling, and performance fees. Short selling is used to create portfolios in which short positions hedge long positions, reducing the exposure of the portfolio to market forces. Leverage is used to increase the risk level of the fund and performance fees that compensate managers for favorable performance. There has been rapid growth of the funds being managed by hedge funds.

The Group of Thirty recommended that firms holding portfolios of derivatives calculate the risk of the portfolio on a daily basis. This measure, commonly called "value at risk," measures the monetary amount of the decline in value that a derivatives portfolio can be expected to sustain during a specified percentage of time periods. A statement that the daily value at risk is 42,300 USD at the 5 percent probability level means that this derivatives portfolio can be expected to sustain a loss of 42,300 USD or more on 5 of the next 100 days.

Questions

1 Define hedging.
2 What is the difference between a hedger and a speculator?
3 Why are both hedgers and speculators needed in a market?
4 Define natural long and natural short and give examples of each.
5 Define two-sided and one-sided hedges and give examples of each.
6 What kind of hedge completely eliminates the risk due to changes in the price of the hedged asset? Can you give an example?
7 If you are a producer of a raw material, are you in a natural long or a natural short position? How can you hedge against the decrease in price of the raw material?
8 Why were the savings and loans faced with bankruptcy? How should they have hedged themselves to avoid bankruptcy?
9 How does an option premium affect the outcome of a hedge using options?
10 How are a long and a short hedge affected by an increase in the price of a hedged asset?
11 Define the economic approach to hedge determination and the substitute action approach.
12 What are the main problems with obtaining a perfect hedge using futures?

■ Notes ■

1 The Group of Thirty's web address is http://www.group30.org/.
2 J. P. Morgan developed a popular value at risk program called RiskMetrics®. It has announced that it is spinning off its risk metrics group. The J. P. Morgan web address is http://www.jpmorgan.com/.
3 Ibbotson provides consulting services and data. The firm's web address is http.//www.ibbotson.com/.

■ References ■

Arnott, Robert D. and Pham, Tan K. 1993: Tactical currency allocation. *Financial Analysts Journal* 49, 47–52.

Black, Fischer 1990: Equilibrium exchange rate hedging. *Journal of Finance* 45, 899–907.

Chicago Board of Trade, n.d.: *A Guide to Financial Futures at the Chicago Board of Trade*. Chicago: CBOT.

Clements, Jonathan 1997: International investing raises questions on allocation, diversification, hedging. *Wall Street Journal*, July 29, p. C1.

Culp, Christopher L. and Miller, Merton H. 1994: Hedging a flow of commodity deliveries with futures: lessons from Metallgesellschaft. *Derivatives Quarterly* 1, 7–15.

——1995: Metallgesellschaft and the economics of synthetic storage. *Journal of Applied Corporate Finance* 7, 62–76.

Day, Paul 1997: Active currency management to enhance returns. In *Managing Currency Risk*, Charlottesville, VA: Association for Investment Management and Research, 39–49.

Delaney, Kevin J. 1997: Funds generally don't hedge Asian bets. *Wall Street Journal*, Dec. 22, p. C27.

Froot, Kenneth A. 1993: Currency hedging over long horizons, Working paper no. 4355. Washington, D.C.: National Bureau of Economic Research.

Global Derivatives Study Group 1993: *Derivatives: practices and principles*. Washington, D.C.: Group of Thirty.

Layard-Liesching, Ronald 1997: The role of currency overlay managers. In *Managing Currency Risk*, Charlottesville, VA: Association for Investment Management and Research, 50–7.

Lederman, Jess and Klein, Robert A. (eds) 1995: *Hedge Funds*. Chicago: Irwin.

Levich, Richard M. and Thomas, Lee R. 1993: The merits of active currency risk management: evidence from international bond portfolios. *Financial Analysts Journal* 49, 63–70.

Linsmeier, Thomas J. and Pearson, Neil D. 1996: Risk measurement: an introduction to value at risk. Working paper, Urbana–Champaign, IL: University of Illinois.

Loomis, Carol J. 1966: The Jones nobody keeps up with. *Fortune*, Apr., 237–47.

Manning, Mike 1996: Currency risk management – recent developments. *emfa (European Derivative Investment and Funds Association) Newsletter*, Sept., 14–16.

Perold, Andre F. and Schulman, Evan C. 1988: The free lunch in currency hedging: implications for investment policy and performance standards. *Financial Analysts Journal* 44 (May/June), 45–52.

Wall Street Journal 1996: Coca-Cola tells analysts that currency hedging protects profits. May 7.

Index of Names

Index of Subjects